Fodor's 5th Edition

# Israel

D1384193

Fodor's Travel Publications • New York, Toronto, London, Sydney, Auckland
www.fodors.com

# CONTENTS

# MAPS

Circled letters in text correspond to letters on the photographs. For more information on the sights pictured, turn to the indicated page number (A) on each photograph.

# DESTINATION
# ISRAEL

Israel packs an abundance of riches into its small perimeter. This amazing amalgam of cherished religious sites, plentiful archaeological treasures, and incomparable natural wonders has a history so long and dense that at every turn you feel the past in the present. Holy Land to Jews, Christians, and Muslims, Israel emits a powerful spiritual aura: biblical place names—— Galilee, the Judean Desert, Jerusalem—suddenly demythologize and come vibrantly alive. In Israel, too, you can tread white-sand Mediterranean beaches, explore wildflower valleys and haunting deserts, float on the Dead Sea, and dive along brilliant coral reefs. In the quiet of its holy shrines or on its sun-drenched hiking trails, Israel is a place to renew the spirit.

To most visitors Jerusalem means the Old City, its ancient walls embracing sites deeply sacred to three of the world's great religions: Judaism, Christianity, and Islam. Even non-believers can't help but feel a palpable spiritual presence here, where history, faiths, and cultures commingle as perhaps nowhere else. No Jewish shrine is holier than the Ⓑ**Western Wall,** the remains of the Second Temple, whose stones vibrate with prayers

Ⓑ 36
Ⓒ 52

uttered by centuries' worth of pilgrims. Nearby, on the Temple Mount, also known as the Haram Esh-Sharif, stands the Ⓐ**Dome of the Rock,** a dazzling gold-topped sanctuary. It was built over a site Muslims venerate, the rock from which the prophet Muhammad is said to have ascended to heaven. Northwest of the Temple Mount, the Muslim Quarter merges into the Christian at the Ⓒ**Via Dolorosa,** the route Jesus walked to Calvary carrying his heavy cross, a journey often reenacted by the devout. At the end of the route stands the the most hallowed site in Christianity, the Ⓓ**Church of the Holy Sepulcher.**

Ⓓ 46

# JERUSALEM

Whether you're inside the walls of the Old City or outside them in the "New City," Jerusalem ricochets you back and forth, from the archaic and religion-bound to the modern and worldly. Right near the city center, for example, is Ⓕ**Me'a She'arim,** an ultra-Orthodox Jewish enclave with the feel of an Eastern European Jewish quarter. Dressed according to sect, residents here live as if nothing has changed in centuries. Yet not far away you're jolted back into the present by the teeming, thoroughly secular pedestrian mall of Ⓖ**Ben Yehuda Street,** lined with souvenir shops and sidewalk cafés, where you can sit back and take in the night scene. It's sure to include packs of young Israeli soldiers and the occasional street performer. In contrast, the Ⓙ**Old City** takes you back in time again, with its ancient stone alleyways and arches. When you enter the Muslim Quarter through the Damascus Gate, be prepared to leave any notion of personal space behind. Streets here are narrow and crowded with travelers, pilgrims, and vendors of everything from fresh produce to Bedouin caftans and videocassettes. This is the *souq,* with its sometimes overwhelming sensory stimulation: the thunder of a wheelbarrow careening along pavement; the intense colors and smells of turmeric and fenugreek; the strong scent of fresh mint, wafted by women hoping to entice a sale; the blare of Arabic music; the Babel of languages. As an antidote to this brilliance and tumult, visit the serene synagogue of the Ⓔ**Hadassah Hospital** and watch the light stream through its 12 stained-glass windows by Marc Chagall. Or wander among the exhibits of the Ⓗ**Israel Museum,** which houses an extensive Judaica collection and some of the region's richest archaeological finds. More sobering is the Ⓘ**Yad Vashem Memorial,** which commemorates the victims of one of the most horrific events of all-too-recent history, the Holocaust. This is Jerusalem: a heady mix of profound sensations both worldly and emotional to which no one can remain indifferent.

Ⓘ 74

# AROUND
# JERUSALEM

Ⓐ 114

A few miles east of Jerusalem is the Ⓐ**Judean Desert,** a bleak landscape of dramatically sculpted cliffs. In Qumran, the first Dead Sea Scrolls were found in 1947, in one of the caves that dot the craggy hills. It's easy to envision hermits seeking refuge here in biblical times. The road that continues along the Dead Sea cuts through an incredible geography: high mountains overlooking a vast salt lake, all far below sea level. To experience the ⒹⒺ**Dead Sea**, take a float on the salty water, far too buoyant for swimming—and while you're at it, slather yourself with some of its famously cu-

Ⓑ 123

Ⓒ 133

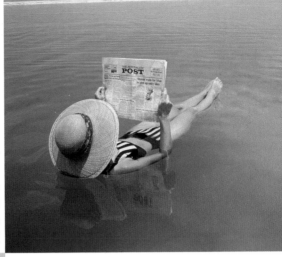

rative black mud. Don't miss the greenery and waterfalls of the nearby Nahal David nature reserve. A bit farther south looms Ⓑ**Masada.** Atop this mountain plateau are the remains of the Roman king Herod's 40 BC palace-fortress. The site has spectacular views of the surrounding landscape and is famous for its sad history as the place where nearly 1,000 Jews committed mass suicide in their revolt against the Romans around

Ⓔ▷113

AD 70. A shorter side trip (when politics allow), only five miles south of Jerusalem, is Ⓒ**Bethlehem,** Jesus' birthplace. In the town's center stands the Church of the Nativity, built over what's thought to be the grotto where he was born. And about 30 miles southwest of the capital is Ⓕ**Tel Maresha,** fascinating for its network of underground caves carved out some 2,000 years ago. These include the Columbarium, where it's hypothesized that pigeons were kept for food, fertilizer, and sacrifice. Any of these excursions brings a welcome diversion from the intensity of Jerusalem.

Ⓕ▷131

(A) 149

Representing the country's fast-moving present and future, ©**Tel Aviv** is Israel's economic and cultural nerve-center. Hugging the Mediterranean are the beautiful ⒺⒻ**Tel Aviv beaches** and a long seaside promenade. Hayorkan Street is vibrant with clubs and cafés, and people-watching is a major pastime. The city's energy buzzes at the outdoor Ⓐ**Carmel Market** where crowds jostle in search of knickknacks and fresh produce; it's a great place to see savvy Tel Avivians shop. Nightlife? If, like the locals, you want to party till the wee hours, nap in late afternoon to

# TEL AVIV

(B) 155
(C) 144

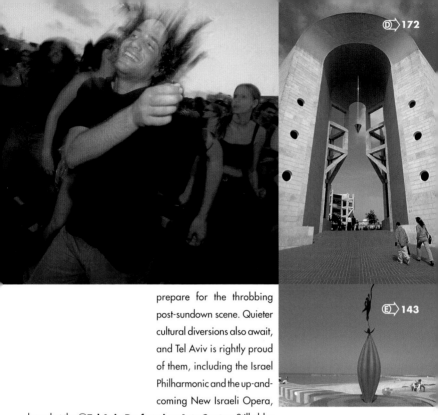

D 172

E 143

prepare for the throbbing post-sundown scene. Quieter cultural diversions also await, and Tel Aviv is rightly proud of them, including the Israel Philharmonic and the up-and-coming New Israeli Opera, based at the Ⓓ**Tel Aviv Performing Arts Center.** Still older venues call; visitors and natives alike are inescapably drawn to Jaffa. This ancient port city, now annexed to Tel Aviv, dates from at least biblical times. Among its charms are the 1906 clock tower, the El-Mahmoudiye Mosque, and a bustling flea market. A walk through the hilltop section of restored Ⓑ**Old Jaffa,** with its galleries and cafés set amid reconstructed ruins, is a must; come in the evening for a waterside dinner and sweeping views of Tel Aviv.

F 173

Wending your way up the Mediterranean coast, you're never too far from a sandy beach, a comfortable hotel, or a delicious meal of fresh fish. But the coast offers more than pampering: it has layers of history to uncover and rugged Mt. Carmel to explore. In Haifa, Israel's third largest city, the golden dome of the ⒟**Baha'i Shrine** dominates the skyline. The shrine is

# NORTHERN COAST
# AND WESTERN GALILEE

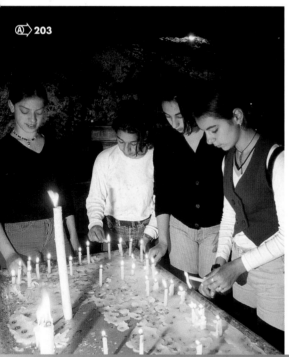

Ⓐ 203

the world center for the Baha'i faith and its lush gardens offer a tranquil resting spot with panoramic vistas. In nearby Ⓐ**Elijah's Cave,** according to tradition, the prophet hid from the wrathful King Ahab in the 9th century BC. Farther south in Ⓒ**Caesarea,** Herod built a seaport between 22 and 10 BC, creating an artificial harbor in an amazing feat of ancient engineering. The vast remains of the prosperous Roman city include a huge amphitheater, today a spectacular venue for star-lit concerts overlooking the sea. Caesarea later became an important Byzantine Christian city and Crusader outpost.

Ⓑ 220

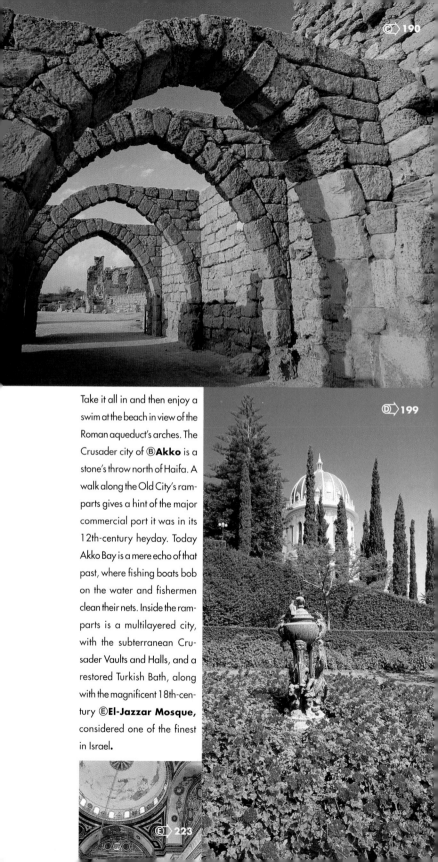

© 190

Take it all in and then enjoy a swim at the beach in view of the Roman aqueduct's arches. The Crusader city of ⑧**Akko** is a stone's throw north of Haifa. A walk along the Old City's ramparts gives a hint of the major commercial port it was in its 12th-century heyday. Today Akko Bay is a mere echo of that past, where fishing boats bob on the water and fishermen clean their nets. Inside the ramparts is a multilayered city, with the subterranean Crusader Vaults and Halls, and a restored Turkish Bath, along with the magnificent 18th-century ⑤**El-Jazzar Mosque,** considered one of the finest in Israel.

Ⓓ 199

Ⓔ 223

# LOWER GALILEE

Ⓐ 244

Galilee's verdant valleys, rolling hills, and lyrically lovely Sea of Galilee are wonderful counterparts to its historical riches. In early spring, you can join the urbanites from Haifa who flock to this countryside to drink in the beauty of the wildflowers that carpet its fields and slopes; to hike the trail along Ⓐ**Mt. Gilboa** with its far-reaching views; and to swim at Gan Hashelosha National Park. For Christians, Galilee is the place where their faith was born and took root; it encompasses

Ⓑ 250

Ⓒ 250

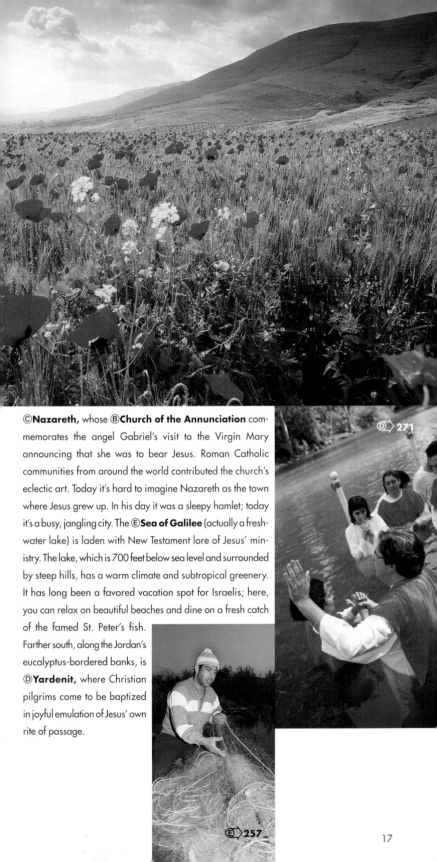

ⒸNazareth, whose ⒷChurch of the Annunciation commemorates the angel Gabriel's visit to the Virgin Mary announcing that she was to bear Jesus. Roman Catholic communities from around the world contributed the church's eclectic art. Today it's hard to imagine Nazareth as the town where Jesus grew up. In his day it was a sleepy hamlet; today it's a busy, jangling city. The ⒺSea of Galilee (actually a freshwater lake) is laden with New Testament lore of Jesus' ministry. The lake, which is 700 feet below sea level and surrounded by steep hills, has a warm climate and subtropical greenery. It has long been a favored vacation spot for Israelis; here, you can relax on beautiful beaches and dine on a fresh catch of the famed St. Peter's fish.

Farther south, along the Jordan's eucalyptus-bordered banks, is ⒹYardenit, where Christian pilgrims come to be baptized in joyful emulation of Jesus' own rite of passage.

Ⓓ 271

Ⓔ 257

# LOWER GALILEE

Lower Galilee is an archaeology maven's dream. In ⒡**Zippori,** excavations have brought to light a Roman-era city with exquisite mosaics and a sophisticated aqueduct system. Another jewel is ⒢⒣**Bet She'an,** once the

⒡ 253

Roman-Byzantine city of Scythopolis, with the best-preserved Roman theater in Israel. According to the gospel of Matthew, it was in Tabgha, farther north, that Jesus performed the miracle of feeding a crowd of thousands with five loaves of bread and two fish. Here, in the ⒥**Church of the Multiplication,** excavations have revealed a beautifully preserved Byzantine

⒢ 247

⒣ 247

mosaic floor with lively depictions of local wildlife and a graceful image of the fish and bread. In nearby ①**Capernaum,** the once-prosperous town where Jesus called many of his disciples, stand the ruins of a synagogue built of imported white limestone that dates between the 2nd and 5th century AD. Its columns and marble steps perch on the site of an even earlier synagogue, perhaps the one where Jesus taught. Ⓚ**Megiddo** (Armageddon) was one of history's greatest battlegrounds thanks to its strategic location between Egypt and Mesopotamia. Modern digs have uncovered layers of civilization from as long ago as 4000 BC, including a palace from King Solomon's time, remains of 5,000-year-old temples, and Canaanite-period gate.

Ⓚ 243

# UPPER GALILEE
# AND THE GOLAN

Ⓐ 304

Ⓑ 281

Skiing, kayaking, wine making—in Israel? Yes, indeed.
Blessed with abundant water
and fertile soil, the agricul-
turally vital Upper Galilee and
Golan include some of the
country's loveliest scenery,
spanning green valleys and
majestic peaks. History a-
bounds here, too. The holy
hilltop city of Ⓑ**Zfat** (Safed)
became a haven for Sephardic
Jews fleeing the Inquisition. In
the 16th century, Zfat was a
thriving commercial and intellectual center where rabbinical scholars developed the
Kabbala, a mystical interpretation of Hebrew scripture.
Along the winding cobble-
stone streets of the charming
Old City you'll find historic synagogues, the Crusader fortress, and a large
Orthodox community. Summertime, the streets are alive with music festivals and
arts events. Nearby Mt. Meron has an ancient Jewish holy site, the tomb of Rabbi

Shimon Bar Yochai, and hiking
trails with spectacular vistas. To
the north there is excellent hiking amid the gushing springs,
greenery, and waterfalls of
the Upper Hula Valley and its
multitude of nature reserves.
Bordering on the Golan, the
Ⓕ**Tel Dan Nature Reserve**
is the site of the Jordan's headwaters, and the remains of the

Ⓒ 280

settlement that marked the northernmost outpost of the ancient Israelites' territory. This is the region for rafting or kayaking along the ©**Upper Jordan,** and for visiting or staying at one of the many historic and comfortable *kibbutzim* or *moshavim* (communal settlements) that dot the landscape. Ⓐ©**Mt. Hermon,** at the northern reaches of the Golan and some 9,000 feet above sea level, is the site of the country's only ski resort. Skiing in the Middle East is a great novelty, though Mt. Hermon becomes even more glorious in summer, when it's abloom with flowers and herbs. If you've had enough of outdoor exertion, head south to modern, suburban Katzrin, where an ancient Jewish olive-oil producing village is being excavated. Relax at Katzrin's ⓓ**Golan Heights Winery** and treat yourself to a tasting of its world-class wines; then head out again for some birdwatching at the Gamla Nature Reserve.

# EILAT AND THE NEGEV

A marvelous combination of cultural interest and pure geological fascination is the big draw of this desert region, not to mention the luxurious spas. In the north, the vibrant bedouin market comes alive in Ⓐ**Beersheva** on Thursday. A keen eye will

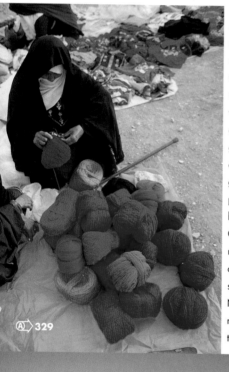

lead you to wonderful handmade textiles, beaded bags and jewelry, copperware, and other treasures. Farther east toward the Dead Sea, the spa town of Ⓓ**Ein Bokek** beckons with its curative hot springs and black mud. But most beguiling is the Ⓑ**Negev** itself, a landscape of craters, valleys, gorges, and craggy mountains painted in gorgeous reds, browns, yellows, and greens. One of the best ways to experience it is to sign on for a camel trek tracing the fabled spice trade routes of the ancient Nabateans. Don't miss the phenomenal Makhtesh Ramon, the world's largest natural

Ⓐ▷ 329

Ⓑ▷ 319

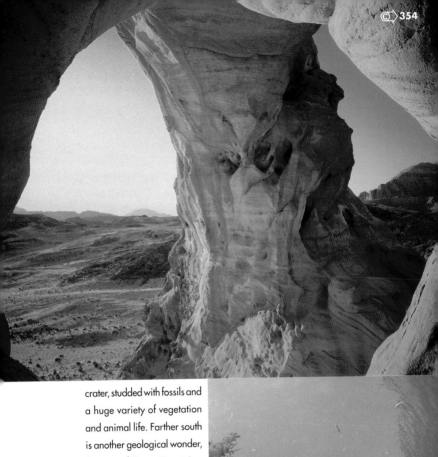

crater, studded with fossils and a huge variety of vegetation and animal life. Farther south is another geological wonder, the rugged Timna Mountains, where King Solomon and his predecessors mined copper. Thanks to erosion over the millennia, ©**Timna Valley Park** has fantastic rock formations, including the mighty red piers known as Solomon's Pillars. Here, too, are the remains of a 14th-century BC shrine to the Egyptian goddess Hathor. Still farther south is the Red Sea, with its coral reefs and dazzling marine life. You can take in all of this from the resort city of ©**Eilat,** a terrific base for snorkeling and diving.

Ⓓ 334

Ⓔ 339

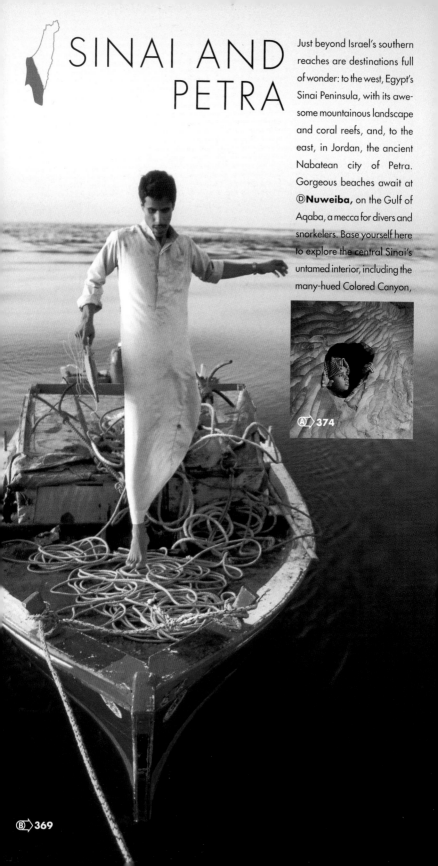

# SINAI AND PETRA

Just beyond Israel's southern reaches are destinations full of wonder: to the west, Egypt's Sinai Peninsula, with its awesome mountainous landscape and coral reefs, and, to the east, in Jordan, the ancient Nabatean city of Petra. Gorgeous beaches await at Ⓓ**Nuweiba,** on the Gulf of Aqaba, a mecca for divers and snorkelers. Base yourself here to explore the central Sinai's untamed interior, including the many-hued Colored Canyon,

Ⓐ 374

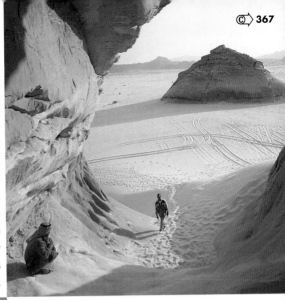
©⟩ 367

the Tih desert, or the remote ©**El Makhrom** mountains. To the south is Mt. Sinai, where it's said Moses received the Ten Commandments; you'll be amply rewarded for the strenuous climb to the top by glorious panoramas. Hugging the mountain's lower slopes is the fortresslike St. Catherine's Monastery, dating back to the second century AD. At the peninsula's southern tip, near ®**Sharm el Sheikh,** is Ras Muhammad National Park,

Ⓓ⟩ 367

arguably the finest dive site in the world. The eastbound excursion out of Israel, to Jordan's mysterious canyon city of Ⓐ**Petra,** should not be missed. Its temples, tombs, monuments, and palaces, carved in the first century AD out of solid sandstone cliffs, are famed for their elaborate facades, which change color dramatically—peach to rose to red—as the daylight waxes and wanes. The largest of these structures is the monument at the summit of Ⓔ**Jabal a-Deir.** Though it requires an arduous climb, the edifice is magnificent, as are the sweeping views of the surrounding mountain landscape.

Ⓔ⟩ 380

# GREAT ITINERARIES

## Highlights of Israel
**10 to 12 days**

Holy sites and turbulent politics are common preconceptions about Israel. Both have their place, of course, but a tour around the country reveals its surprises: an astonishing diversity of landscape and people, good food and wine, and a unique blending of modern culture and ancient civilization. After two or three days exploring the extraordinary city of Jerusalem, head for the Dead Sea.

### DEAD SEA
**1 day.** East of Jerusalem is a world of visual extremes. After a drive through the bleak Judean Desert, follow the shores of the Dead Sea, with the sheer baked-brown cliffs soaring above. Farther south, steep trails, or a cable car, lead up to Ⓐ Masada, where ancient Jewish rebels met their tragic end. A float in the briny Ⓒ Dead Sea, a black-mud face mask, and a hike in the green Ein Gedi round out this vigorous day. Heading back to Jerusalem, stop at Jericho (political climate permitting), the world's oldest city, and mix archaeology with baklava and orange juice.
☞ *Dead Sea Region in Chapter 2*

### GALILEE
**3 days.** Both mountainous and fertile, Galilee has rich historic sites and rustic getaways galore. Drive up the Jordan Valley or skirt around the West Bank (depending on political conditions) to the archaeological dig of Ⓑ Bet She'an and the evocative ruined Crusader castle of Belvoir. At the subtropical Hammat Gader hot springs, soak in the remains of Roman baths. Next day, meander along the rushing streams of the Tel Dan

or Banias nature reserves; then head south again to poke around the old synagogues and art galleries of Zfat. On day three, Nazareth's great Basilica of the Annunciation beckons, with its international artwork. The fine mosaics of Zippori are nearby. After lunching on some Arab *meze* (salads), head to the coast and the sea grottos of Rosh Hanikra.
☞ *Chapters 4, 5, and 6*

### MEDITERRANEAN COAST AND TEL AVIV
**2 or 3 days.** Ease down the coast, beginning with Akko—with its Crusader halls, picturesque harbor, and Turkish sea-walls. The port city of Haifa offers a panoramic view from the top of Mt. Carmel and the magnificent gardens of the Bahai'i Shrine. Snack and swim, farther south, in Roman Caesarea, and head for Tel Aviv. In the cosmopolitan hub you can take in a museum, go shopping, walk the beach promenade, or just kick back on the sand. Tel Aviv nightlife sparkles with jazz clubs, the Philharmonic, and fine dining on the Med.
☞ *Chapters 3 and 4*

### EILAT
**2 days.** Fly down to sun-drenched Eilat. For the aquatically inclined, Eilat has snorkeling and scuba diving on the coral reef, cruises on the Red Sea, and a spectacular underwater observatory. Take a side trip to Timna and its eerie landscapes, natural red rock pillars, and ancient copper mines. Sunbathe, eat very well, and return home refreshed.
☞ *Eilat and Environs in Chapter 7*

## Active Israel
**13 to 17 days**

This is the Israel you didn't know existed, a land of the outdoors; of underground and underwater; of desert canyons and mountain streams. The only limits are your energy and the heat: be sure to watch out for the sun.

### JERUSALEM
**2 days.** The holy city offers up a surprising number of activities that mix history and a good workout. The steep hike along the ramparts gives an eagle-eye view of the Old City. As you head underground and wade thigh-deep through Hezekiah's ancient water tunnel, your candles will reveal the chisel marks of ancient diggers. Cap off your day with a guided moonlit jeep-ride deep into the Judean Desert. Next day, drive west, with Archaeological Seminars, and join a dig at Bet Guvrin or Maresha, completing the experience with a guided crawl through a nearby network of caves.
☞ *Chapter 1 and West of Jerusalem in Chapter 2*

### DEAD SEA REGION
**2 days.** After passing through the stark Judean desert, the Ein Gedi preserve delights with its sparkling water and greenery. Hike the full trail, over its reeds and waterfall, to the lofty Lover's Cave. In the afternoon, the salty Dead Sea is a perfect soak for stiff muscles. Luxuriate overnight at an Ein Bokek spa and, the following morning, climb Masada's Snake Path before dawn to catch the sunrise across the water.
After exploring Herod's great palace-fortress, go west to the Negev.
☞ *Dead Sea Region in Chapter 2*

Ⓐ 123

## NEGEV DESERT

**2 days.** With Sde Boker College as your base, venture on a jeep trip into the Wilderness of Zin to uncover its hidden oases. A trail with stone steps and ladders leads up the magnificent white-chalk canyon of Ein Avdat. End your day with a camel-ride to a bedouin encampment for a traditional feast. Overnight in Mitzpe Ramon, and, next day, tour the immense, water-eroded Ramon Crater before driving south to Eilat.
☞ *The Heart of the Negev in Chapter 7*

## EILAT AND ENVIRONS

**3 to 7 days.** The lunar red-rock canyons in the hills behind Eilat make for an eerie day of exploration, by camel or jeep. Next, take to the water: snorkeling over the tropical reef and parasailing off the beach. If scuba is your thing, consider a 2-day cruise (or longer) working your way down the Red Sea dive sites off the Sinai. On an overnight jaunt to St. Catherine's Monastery in the Egyptian Sinai Desert, you can climb Mt. Sinai at daybreak and greet the sun where Moses, many believe, stood. Fly back to Tel Aviv.
☞ *Eilat and Environs in Chapter 7 and The Sinai in Chapter 8*

Rosh Hanikra

Tel Dan
Mt. Hermon
Banias   DISENGAGEMENT
91 km   Kfar Blum   ZONE
Ayelet   Sde Nechemia
Hashachar   Gadot
90   GOLAN
HEIGHTS
Zfat   Rosh Pina
85   Vered Haglil
Akko   GALILEE
66 km   Sea of
Galilee   Gamla
Haifa
4   79
Zippori   Tiberias   27 km
70   Nazareth   Hammat Gader
2   Belvoir
Caesarea   65   20 km   Bet She'an
71
Netanya   90
4
145 km   Jordan River
2   WEST
BANK
Jerico
Tel Aviv   1
Jerusalem
38   90
30 km   Bet Guvrin
Maresha   Hebron   Dead
Sea
GAZA STRIP   84 km   Ein Gedi
Masada
Ein Bokek
115 km   25
204
10 km   Sde Boker
Ein Avdat   Hatzeva
25 km   Mitzpe
Ramon
135 km
40

### KEY

| | |
|---|---|
| — — — | Air Travel |
| —————— | Ground Travel |
| ·········· | Alternate route in times of political unrest |

Timna
90
20 km
TO ST. CATHERINE'S
MONASTERY   Eilat

GOLAN
HEIGHTS

JORDAN

27

LEBANON

Mt. Hermon
Kfar Blum
Sde Nechemia
Hula Nature Reserve
Ayelet Hashachar — Gadot — DISENGAGEMENT ZONE
**Rosh Pina**
GOLAN HEIGHTS
Vered Haglil
Tabgha — Mt. of Beatitudes — Capernaum
**Akko** 57 km 85
Ginosar
4
Gamla
**Haifa** GALILEE **Tiberias** *Sea of Galilee*
4 30 km Cana
**Nazareth** Yardenit
70 Mt. Tabor
40 km Megiddo Afula Belvoir
2 71
**Caesarea** 65
**Bet She'an**
Netanya Jenin
30 km 20 km
4
2 90
WEST BANK *Jordan River*
**Tel Aviv** 100 km
Jericho
1 **Jerusalem** 48 km
1
38 Qumran
30 km **Bethlehem** 90
Bet Guvrin *Dead Sea*
Maresha Hebron 100 km
GAZA STRIP Ein Gedi
**Masada**
15 km
**Ein Bokek**
115 km 25
204
**Sde Boker**
10 km Ein Avdat Hatzeva
25 km
**Mitzpe Ramon**
135 km
40
90
TO ST. CATHERINE'S MONASTERY **Eilat**

SYR

295

**MEDITERRANEAN COAST**
**1 day.** A day on the blue, blue Med means more waterside play. From the Tel Aviv marina, take a windsurfer or a sailboat out beyond the waves. Spend a few hours hang-gliding off a sea-cliff near Netanya. At Caesarea, scuba-dives explore underwater remains of the ancient port and relics of Roman wrecks.
☞ *The Northern Coast in Chapter 4*

**UPPER GALILEE AND GOLAN HEIGHTS**
**3 days.** The mountainous and agricultural Galilee is soothing after the brilliant desert and beaches down south, but it still offers plenty of action. Base yourself in a Hula Valley town, such as Rosh Pina. If it's late spring or summer, Jordan River kayaking (from Kfar Blum) or tubing (from Sde Nechemia) both make for a tranquil morning. In early spring, you can white-water raft the Jordan south of Gadot. Waterskiing the subtropical Sea of Galilee off Tiberias can fill an afternoon. In winter, skiers can try the novelty of the Middle Eastern slopes of Mt. Hermon. On day 2, get up early to go bird-watching: Gamla is home to eagles and vultures, and the wetlands of the Ⓓ Hula Nature Reserve are a popular stop for migratory birds. The same day,

bounce through pine forests along mountain trails in a jeep, from nearby Baba Yona's Ranch or from the Ayelet Hashachar Kibbutz at Tel Hatzor. Finally, a day-long or overnight horseback trip from Vered Hagalil, near Zfat, takes you down to the shores of the Sea of Galilee. Plan to be there between February and April, when wildflowers carpet the landscape.
☞ *Upper Galilee and the Golan in Chapter 6*

**KEY**
– – – Air Travel
——— Ground Travel
········· Alternate route in times of political unrest

JORDAN

# Christian Highlights

**6 days**

Visit the Holy Land, they say, and you'll never read the Bible the same way. For believer and nonbeliever alike, the shrines and biblical landscapes make a profound impact. While some sites connected to scripture have been hallowed by tradition, others are demonstrably genuine.

## JERUSALEM AND BETHLEHEM

**2 days.** Begin your tour retracing the climax of Christ's story, in Jerusalem. The walk down Palm Sunday road leads to the ancient olive trees of the Garden of Gethsemane, where you can contemplate Jesus' Passion and arrest. Following the Via Dolorosa, walk the ⒻStations of the Cross to the ⒺChurch of the Holy Sepulcher. The Garden Tomb, the site of Calvary for many Protestants, offers a spot of tranquillity. In the afternoon, you can catch a glimpse of the Dead Sea Scrolls at the Israel Museum. The next day, explore the dig at the Ophel: Jesus almost certainly climbed the steps exposed here. A visit to the Room of the Last Supper on Mt. Zion and the scale-model of ancient Jerusalem at the Holyland Hotel can fill a morning, before a drive to Jesus' birthplace in Bethlehem (political climate permitting).
☞ *Chapter 1 and Bethlehem in Chapter 2*

## ON THE WAY TO GALILEE

**1 day.** Plunge east through the barren Judean Desert and visit Qumran, where the Dead Sea Scrolls were written and found. Head up the Jordan Valley or drive west and around the West Bank (depending on political conditions) to ancient Bet She'an and the impregnable Crusader stronghold of Belvoir. Farther north, at Yardenit, pilgrims come to be baptized in the Jordan River. Overnight in Tiberias.
☞ *Dead Sea Region in Chapter 2 and Jezreel and Jordan Valleys in Chapter 5*

Ⓔ 45

## SEA OF GALILEE

**1 day.** In this tranquil region, Jesus' ministry unfolded. The ancient wooden boat at Ginosar vividly evokes Gospel descriptions of life on the lake. After meditating on Jesus' famous sermon in the gardens of the Mount of Beatitudes, descend to Tabgha and the beautiful mosaics of the Church of the Multiplication. From a lakeshore perch at the nearby Primacy you can marvel at how scripture (John 21) and landscape blend before your eyes. Farther east, ancient Capernaum was the center of Jesus' local ministry. End your day with a sunset cruise across the Sea of Galilee.
☞ *Tiberias and the Sea of Galilee in Chapter 5*

## THE GALILEE HILLS AND THE JEZREEL VALLEY

**1 day.** Head for the hills, stopping briefly in Cana, site of "the first miracle," on your way up to Nazareth. In Jesus' childhood town, the massive, modern Church of the Annunciation houses eclectic artwork. A drive through the lush Jezreel Valley—the New Testament "Armageddon"—takes you to the many-layered excavations in the ancient

city of Megiddo. Finish your day at the fine church and scenic view on Mount Tabor, "Mount of Transfiguration." Overnight on the Mediterranean coast.
☞ *Chapter 5*

## MEDITERRANEAN COAST

**1 day.** While the Jews in antiquity preferred the inland hills, the coast was the gateway for Greeks, Romans, and the European Crusaders. The Old City of Akko was the main port and one-time capital of the medieval Crusader kingdom. In Haifa, the Stella Maris monastery atop Mt. Carmel marks the grotto where the Carmelite order was founded. Continuing down the coast to Caesarea, finish your day exploring Herod's great cosmopolitan city, where Peter converted Cornelius and Paul defended his faith.
☞ *Chapter 4*

Ⓔ 44

FODOR'S
CHOICE

*Even with so many special places in Israel, Fodor's writers and editors have their favorites. Here are a few that stand out.*

## QUINTESSENTIAL ISRAEL

Ⓙ **Bar mitzvahs at the Western Wall, Jerusalem.** On Monday and Thursday mornings, 13-year-old boys are welcomed into the adult Jewish community. ☞ p. 53

**Machaneh Yehuda, Jerusalem.** In the pre-Shabbat shopping frenzy all kinds of Jerusalemites rub shoulders among stalls piled with produce. ☞ p. 81

**Nahalat Binyamin, Tel Aviv.** Install yourself in a café, here or on Sheinkin Street, and enjoy music and local color. ☞ p. 150

**Sunset on the Gulf of Eilat.** Sip a drink on the Promenade and watch the distant Red Sea go crimson. ☞ p. 314

## BIBLICAL HIGHLIGHTS AND HOLY PLACES

Ⓓ **Western Wall, Jerusalem.** The most important Jewish shrine in the world, this stone wall was part of the retaining wall of the ancient Temple Mount. ☞ p. 53

**Calvary, Jerusalem.** Different theories claim either the Church of the Holy Sepulcher or the Garden Tomb to be the site of Jesus' Crucifixion. ☞ p. 67

**Dome of the Rock, Jerusalem.** Muslim tradition identifies this site and the El-Aqsa Mosque with Muhammad's ascent to heaven to receive the teachings of Islam. ☞ p. 47

**Hezekiah's Tunnel, Jerusalem.** This underground aqueduct once saved the precious water supply of the ancient City of David. ☞ p. 62

Ⓔ **Via Dolorosa, Jerusalem.** The 14 Stations of the Cross on the Way of Sorrow mark the path Jesus is believed to have walked to his Crucifixion. ☞ p. 52

**Church of the Nativity, Bethlehem.** This ancient church encompasses the cave in which Jesus is believed to have been born. ☞ p. 135

Ⓖ **Baha'i Shrine, Haifa.** Topped by a golden dome, the mausoleum of Baha'i founder Mirza Husayn Ali sits amid the shrine's magnificent gardens. ☞ p. 199

**Mount of Beatitudes, Galilee.** The site of the Sermon on the Mount has a tranquil garden and a fine view of the Sea of Galilee. ☞ p. 264

**Tel Beer Sheva, the Negev.** Some consider this well atop the hill of biblical Beersheva to be Abraham's Well. ☞ p. 332

## ARCHAEOLOGICAL GEMS

**Israel Museum, Jerusalem.** Artifacts from the past illuminate the area's long and colorful history. ☞ p. 78

**Herodian Quarter, Jerusalem.** Learn ancient interior design from the remains of mansions from the Second Temple period. ☞ p. 55

Ⓑ **Herod's Palace/Masada.** This monument to King Herod's taste for opulence is also the site of the Jews' last stand against the Romans. ☞ p. 123

**Maresha/Bet Guvrin, near Jerusalem.** Wander through the man-made caves that served as storerooms, cisterns, and quarries during the Hellenistic period. ☞ p. 131

**Crusader city, Akko.** A stroll through this area—both above- and belowground—gives a sense of Akko's past glory. ☞ p. 223

**Crusader city, Caesarea.** Look down to see Byzantine mosaic floors—several in a glorious bathhouse—along the seashore. ☞ p. 192

**Zippori, Galilee.** Recently excavated mosaic floors and elaborate water systems recall Jewish life in the Roman period. ☞ p. 253

**Bet She'an, Galilee.** Explore the impressive remains of the great Roman-Byzantine city of Scythopolis. ☞ p. 247

**Avdat, the Negev.** Ancient ruins of this hilltop city were left by the Nabateans, Romans, and Byzantines. ☞ p. 324

## DINING

**Auberge Shulamit, Rosh Pina.** Home-smoked meats and sophisticated fish dishes draw crowds to this charming inn. $$$$ ☞ p. 294

Ⓕ **Mul-Yam, Tel Aviv.** Dine on imported oysters and seafood in a lovely setting at the old port. $$$$ ☞ p. 165

Ⓒ **Picciotto, Zichron Ya'akov.** Sample the seasonal produce and such fowl as quail, alongside wines from nearby wineries. $$$$ ☞ p. 215

**Uri Buri, Akko.** Near the lighthouse in old Akko, this restaurant is famed for Uri's creative ways with seafood and fish. $$$$ ☞ p. 226

**Last Refuge, Eilat.** Enjoy fresh seafood on a wooden balcony overlooking the mountains of Jordan. $$$ ☞ p. 343

**Le Tsriff, Jerusalem.** Locals flock to this backstreet gem for meat, seafood, and vegetable pies in perfect crusts. $$$ ☞ p. 89

## LODGING

Ⓘ **American Colony, Jerusalem.** Rooms are modest, but this 19th-century limestone oasis draws travelers for its ambience and service. $$$$ ☞ p. 93

Ⓐ **Carmel Forest Spa Resort, near Haifa.** Pine trees are the setting; health and tranquility the themes; indulge in sybaritic delights. $$$$ ☞ p. 208

**Herod's, Eilat.** The most opulent hotel in all of Israel has a waterfall that cascades into the spa's huge whirlpool. $$$$ ☞ p. 345

Ⓗ **Sheraton Tel Aviv Hotel and Towers.** Comfortable rooms and a well-designed lobby make the Sheraton a haven. $$$$ ☞ p. 168

**Ramat Rachel, Jerusalem.** Great views and superb facilities give this rustic kibbutz hotel a resort feel. $$$ ☞ p. 96

**Church of Scotland Centre, Tiberias.** Stone buildings with porches, a serene wild garden, and a private beach are the draws here. $$ ☞ p. 261

# 1   JERUSALEM

Revered by three of the world's great religions—Judaism, Christianity, and Islam—Jerusalem has drawn pilgrims and plenipotentiaries to its splendid mountain isolation for thousands of years. Yet the city's domes, spires, and ancient walls share the skyline with modern office towers, and its archaeological treasures vie for attention with rich museums, quirky shops, and fine restaurants.

By Mike Rogoff

**T**HE WORD "UNIQUE" IS EASY to throw around, but Jerusalem has a real claim on it. A mountainous walled city with a 5,000-year history of almost continuous occupation, Jerusalem is sacred to more than one-third of the world's population.

For Jews, Jerusalem has always been the focal point of devotion and spiritual yearnings and, for many, the psychic center of their nationhood. "The world is like a human eye," wrote a Jewish sage in the 1st century AD: "the white is the ocean that girds the earth, the iris is the earth upon which we dwell, the pupil is Jerusalem, and the image therein is the Temple of the Lord."

For 2,000 years Christians have also venerated Jerusalem as the place where their faith was shaped—the site of the death, burial, and resurrection of Jesus of Nazareth. A famous Renaissance map shows the continents of Asia, Africa, and Europe as the leaves of a clover meeting in the holy city, a reality at once spiritual, historical, and (almost) geographically accurate.

Islamic tradition identifies Jerusalem as the *masjad el aqsa,* the "farthermost place" from which Muhammad ascended to Heaven for his portentous meeting with God, making it the third-holiest city for Muslims, after Mecca and Medina. A Muslim tradition claims that the great rock of Jerusalem's Mt. Moriah, site of the onetime Jewish Temple and present Dome of the Rock, is made of stones from the Garden of Eden, and that on the Day of Judgement, "the holy Kaaba stone of Mecca will come to Jerusalem to be joined with it."

The first known mention of Jerusalem is in Egyptian "hate texts" of the 20th century BC, although recent archaeological evidence gives the city a founding date of up to 1,000 years earlier. Many scholars identify Jerusalem with the Salem of Abraham's time (about 18th century BC). Joshua defeated the Amorite king of Jerusalem in the mid-13th century BC, but the Israelites were unable to retain possession of the city. It was only King David, in 1000 BC, who took it again, made it his capital, and thus propelled it onto the center stage of history. His son Solomon built the Temple of the Lord, now known as the First Temple, giving the city a preeminence it enjoyed until its destruction by the Babylonians in 586 BC.

Returning exiles at the end of the 6th century BC rebuilt the Temple—which would become known as the Second Temple—and began the slow process of revival. By the 2nd century BC, Jerusalem was again a vibrant Jewish capital, albeit one with a good dose of Hellenistic cultural influence. Herod the Great (who reigned 37 BC–4 BC) renovated the Second Temple on a magnificent scale and expanded the city into a cosmopolis of world renown. This was the Jerusalem Jesus knew, a city of monumental architecture, teeming—especially during the Jewish pilgrim festivals—with tens of thousands of visitors from elsewhere in the country and from abroad. It was here that the Romans crucified Jesus (circa AD 29) and here, too, that the Great Jewish Revolt against the Roman overlords erupted, ending in AD 70 with the total destruction (once again) of the city and the Temple.

The Roman emperor Hadrian redesigned Jerusalem as the pagan polis of Aelia Capitolina (AD 135), an urban plan that became the basis for the Old City of today. The Byzantines made it a Christian center, with a massive wave of church building (4th–6th centuries AD), until the Arab conquest of AD 638 brought the holy city under Muslim sway. Except during the golden age of the Ummayad dynasty, in the late 7th and early

8th centuries, Jerusalem was no more than a provincial town under the Muslim regimes of the early Middle Ages, until the Crusaders stormed it in 1099 and made it the capital of their Latin Kingdom. With the reconquest of Jerusalem by the Muslims, the city again lapsed into a languid provincialism for 700 years under the Mamluk and Ottoman empires. The British conquest in 1917 thrust the city back into the world limelight as rising rival nationalisms vied to possess it.

Jerusalem was divided by the 1948 war: the much larger Jewish western sector became the capital of the State of Israel, and Jordan annexed the smaller, predominantly Arab eastern sector (including the Old City). The Six-Day War of 1967 reunited the city under Israeli rule, but the concept of an Arab "East" Jerusalem and a Jewish "West" Jerusalem still remains, even though new Jewish neighborhoods in the northeastern and southeastern sections have rendered the distinction somewhat oversimplified.

The focal point of any visit to Jerusalem is the walled Old City, a square kilometer of exotic sights, sounds, and smells, its air thick with chants and charcoal smoke, the *souk* (Arab bazaar; pronounced "shook") redolent with the tang of tamarind and alive with the tinkle of trinkets. Its 40,000 inhabitants—Jewish, Christian, and Muslim—jostle in the cobblestone lanes with an air of ownership, at best merely tolerating the "intruders" from other quarters. Devout Jews in black and white scurry from their neighborhoods north and west of the Old City, through the Damascus Gate and the Muslim Quarter, toward the Western (or Wailing) Wall. Arab women with baskets of fresh produce on their heads flow across the Western Wall plaza to the Dung Gate and the village of Silwan beyond it. It is not unusual to stand at the Western Wall, surrounded by the burble of devotions, and hear the piercing call to prayer of the Muslim *muezzin* above you, with the more distant bells of the Christian Quarter providing a counterpoint.

Step outside the Old City and you'll see a vibrant modern city of 650,000—not as cosmopolitan as Tel Aviv, to be sure, but with a variety of good restaurants, concert halls, markets, and high-quality stores, as well as quaint neighborhoods that embody an earlier simplicity. In a city that prides itself on its sense of historical continuity, a municipal by-law makes it mandatory to face even high-rise commercial buildings with the golden "Jerusalem stone," the local limestone that has served Jerusalem's builders from time immemorial. The result is an unusual sense of historical significance, even in the most modern quarters.

No matter how oblivious they are to the burden of the city's past or the various grand designs for its future, contemporary Jerusalemites are not untouched by the subtle spirit that infuses the place. Even the irreverent Mark Twain, who visited Jerusalem in 1867, was moved to write, "The thoughts Jerusalem suggests are full of poetry, sublimity, and, more than all, dignity." He may have gotten a bit carried away, but to see these limestone buildings glow golden in the sunset is to understand the mystical hold Jerusalem has had on so many minds and hearts for so many thousands of years.

# Pleasures and Pastimes

## Antiquities
If you thrill to the thought of standing where the ancients once stood, you'll be in your element in this city of memories. From Old Testament walls and water systems to Second Temple streets and stones, the past calls to the attentive soul like a siren to a sailor. Scale models and out-

standing local museums, such as the Israel Museum and the Bible Lands Museum, help give depth and perspective to the intense experience of exploring Jerusalem's past.

### Arts and Crafts

Handicrafts in Israel are worth seeking out, with jewelry and Judaica exceptional standouts in design and workmanship. Jerusalem offers good selections of these, as well as fine works in other specialties: paper cutting, ceramics, weaving, and harp making.

### Dining

Although dining out is less an institution in Jerusalem than in the more cosmopolitan Tel Aviv, you still can eat very well in the holy city, and its timeworn stone and unique ambience create some magical corners in which to do so. Jerusalem's culinary horizons have expanded beyond recognition in recent years, with fine French establishments, fish specialists, some Asian eateries, and funky, eclectic bar-restaurants competing with the perennially popular Middle Eastern and Italian-style offerings. Less popular is seafood, though there are some outstanding exceptions. There's a reason for this trend: the high percentage of religious Jews who live in or visit Jerusalem (in contrast, again, with epicurean Tel Aviv) has resulted in a considerable number of kosher restaurants. Drop your preconceptions: "kosher" does not mean Grandma's traditional Eastern European delicacies (though you'll find these, too). It implies a set of culinary restrictions, rather than a specific cuisine: no pork or shrimp, for example; no mixing of meat and milk products; no cooking on the Sabbath. These requirements account for the popularity of meatless restaurants and those cuisines, like Middle Eastern, that don't use a lot of dairy products anyway. But the quality of meals need not suffer; some of Jerusalem's finest dining rooms are kosher (and, incidentally, closed for Friday dinner and Saturday lunch in observance of the Jewish Sabbath). Having said that, several *non*kosher restaurants—not all of them pricey—help to keep the flag of haute cuisine flying.

### Holy Places

Central to two faiths and holy to a third, Jerusalem is an almost bewildering collage of religious traditions and the shrines that have sanctified them. Pilgrims of one faith still tend to make time to view the shrines of the others. Sites such as the Western Wall, Calvary, Gethsemane, and the Haram esh-Sharif bring the thrill of recognition to ancient history. The devout cannot fail to be moved by the holy city, and its special, if sometimes dissonant, moods and modes of devotion tend to fascinate the nonbeliever as well.

### Scenic Views

Jerusalem is a city of hills—hard going for cyclists, but marvelous for the photographer and the romantic. Quite different views of the Old City unfold from Mt. Scopus and the Mount of Olives (you're facing west, so it's best to go in the morning) and the Haas Promenade, to the south. Mt. Scopus also looks east, to the Judean Desert and the Dead Sea; Mt. Herzl looks west; and Nebi Samwil, in the northwest, gives a commanding view in all directions.

# EXPLORING JERUSALEM

Jerusalem is built on a series of hills, part of the Judea-Samaria range, and straddles the "watershed," the mountain divide that runs north–south through much of the country. The city's eastern edge is marked by the high ridge of Mt. Scopus–Mount of Olives, beyond which the arid Judean Desert tumbles down to the Dead Sea. To the west are the

Judean Hills, or the Mountains of Judah, many capped by modern farming villages and draped in the new pine forests that have transformed and softened their rugged landscape. North and south of the city—Samaria and Judea, respectively—is what is known as the West Bank, since 1967 a contested area administered mostly by Israel, apart from those cities and areas now under autonomous Palestinian control. The West Bank is part of the same highlands, geographically and historically, as Jerusalem itself.

The city has two centers of gravity: the downtown area of West Jerusalem (the "New City"), with its central triangle of Jaffa Road, King George Street, and Ben Yehuda Street; and the Old City, farther east. Most of the restaurants and many of the hotels we recommend are in or near the downtown area. Most of the others are farther west, where the modern Jewish neighborhoods share the hills with the city's best museums. The walled, squarish Old City is divided into four major residential quarters—Jewish, Christian, Muslim, and Armenian—and entered through seven gates, of which the Jaffa, Zion, and Dung gates are the most frequently used by tourists.

Recent Arab nationalist unrest has made parts of East Jerusalem a less-welcoming place than it was once. When all is said and done, however, most of the city is safe, as Israeli cities are in general. Jerusalem is a great city to see on foot, and most of its outlying sights are reasonably accessible by public transportation. In many parts of Jerusalem, a rental car is sometimes more a bother than a boon; you can spend the same money more productively on cabs.

Of the key areas described, our Old City walking tour plunges you in at the deep end, taking you from the Western (Wailing) Wall and the El-Aqsa Mosque to the Church of the Holy Sepulcher, with a heady whirl of ancient ruins and the all-important shrines of the three religions that call this city holy. The Jewish Quarter walk explores that attractively restored quadrant of the Old City, with its intriguing potpourri of archaeological sites unearthed in the 1970s. The Tower of David and Mt. Zion tour begins and ends with a museum, as it skirts (or climbs) the Old City walls en route to David's Tomb and the site of Jesus's Last Supper. The City of David tour concentrates on Old Testament Jerusalem, exploring a geographically tiny area below and outside the Dung Gate. Mainly Christian landmarks are explored under the title Mount of Olives and East Jerusalem, with highlights including the Mount of Olives itself and its spectacular view; the Garden of Gethsemane; and the Garden Tomb. Also included are the Rockefeller Museum of Archaeology, Damascus Gate, and the option of a walk along the Old City ramparts. Swing across town to West Jerusalem to visit Yad Vashem, Israel's most prominent Holocaust memorial and museum complex; Marc Chagall's famous stained-glass windows at the Hadassah Hospital; the village of Ein Kerem; and a large-scale model of Second Temple–period Jerusalem. Take time off to walk the Center City and visit the magnificent Israel Museum, where the Dead Sea Scrolls (and much else) are on display. Nearby are the Knesset (Israel's parliament) and the Bible Lands Museum.

## Great Itineraries
Most travelers spend only a few days in Jerusalem, but if you have more time or your interest ranges beyond the classic sights, a combination of the following suggestions can easily fill your days.

IF YOU HAVE 1 DAY: A GENERAL ORIENTATION
Catch the morning view from the top of the Mount of Olives or the view anytime from the Haas Promenade. Enter the Old City through

# Exploring Jerusalem *(Boxes Refer to Detail Maps)*

← TO TEL AVIV

West Jerusalem

ROMEMA

Central Bus Station

Jaffa Rd.

Weizmann Blvd.

Yerushalayim

Sha'arei

Rte. 1

Yirmiyahu

Malchei Yisra'el

MACHANEH YEHUDA

Jaffa Rd.

Agrippas

Bezalel

Herzl Blvd.

GIVAT RAM

BET HAKEREM

Ben-Zvi Blvd.

King

Hebrew University

Begin Blvd.

Ruppin Rd.

Knesset

Ruppin Rd.

Haim Hazaz Blvd.

Ramban

REHAVIA

GIVAT RAM

Azza

Shmuel Bait

Israel Museum

Sha'arei Zedek Hospital

Harav Uziel

TO YAD VASHEM

NAYOT

BAYIT VEGAN

Bezalel Bazak

Herzog Blvd.

Tchernichovsky

Hapalmach

GONEN (KATAMON)

Shahal

Shai-Agnon

Ben Zakkai

Eliyahu Golomb

Sharett

Eliyahu Golomb

Pat

East Jerusalem

AMMUNITION HILL

Eshkol Blvd.

Road #1

Hadassah Hospital

MT. SCOPUS

Hebrew University

Wadi Joz

Shemu'el Hanavi

St. George

Nablus Rd.

Saladin St.

Augusta Victoria Hospital

Strauss

Me'a She'arim

ME A SHE ARIM

Hanevi'im

Ha-rav Kook

Horkonas

Old City

MOUNT OF OLIVES

Zion ehuda Sq.

Shivtei Yisra'el

Damascus Gate

Sultan Suleiman St.

Herod s Gate

MUSLIM QUARTER

Jericho Rd.

Lions (St. Stephen s) Gate

Jaffa Rd.

New Gate

Church of the Holy Sepulcher

Via Dolorosa

TEMPLE MOUNT

Hillel

Solomon

Mamilla

CHRISTIAN QUARTER

Suq Khan e Zeit

Dome of the Rock

Independence Park

Agron

King David St.

Jaffa Gate

David St.

Jewish Quarter Rd.

Western Wall

Keren

Hayesod

JEWISH QUARTER

El-Aqsa Mosque

Kidron Valley

Jericho Rd.

Jewish Cemetery

abotinsky

ARMENIAN QUARTER

Dung Gate

King David Rd.

Sultan s Pool

Hebron Rd.

MT. ZION

Zion Gate

CITY OF DAVID

SILWAN

GERMAN COLONY

Emek Refa'im

Yehuda

Derech Bethlehem

Hebron Rd.

Haas Promenade

N

**KEY**
Rail Lines

0    500 yards

0    500 meters

the Dung Gate to visit the Western Wall, El-Aqsa Mosque, and Dome of the Rock. Return via the Western Wall plaza and ascend to the Jewish Quarter to explore its fascinating archaeological treasures. Visit the Church of the Holy Sepulcher en route to the Jaffa Gate. Take a cab or bus over to West Jerusalem (the New City) to visit the Israel Museum (Dead Sea Scrolls, archaeology, Judaica, and art) or Yad Vashem (a museum and memorial to the Holocaust).

### IF YOU HAVE 1 DAY: A CHRISTIAN ORIENTATION

Begin with the view from the Mount of Olives, and then walk or drive down to the Garden of Gethsemane, with its ancient olive trees. Enter the Old City through the Dung Gate to visit the Western Wall (the holiest Jewish site) and the Muslim shrines, the El-Aqsa Mosque and Dome of the Rock. Join the Via Dolorosa near the serene courtyard of St. Anne's Church and the Pools of Bethesda (site of the healing of the lame man) and follow the Stations of the Cross to the Church of the Holy Sepulcher. If you're Catholic, you may want to join the Franciscans' Friday-afternoon walk of the stations. If you're Protestant—particularly, Evangelical—be certain to include the Garden Tomb (check times) in addition to or instead of the Holy Sepulcher. After this, you have four options. Option one: visit the Room of the Last Supper on Mt. Zion after lunch, and go on to the Church of the Nativity, in Bethlehem (a 15-minute drive; ☞ Bethlehem *in* Chapter 2). Option two: have lunch in and explore the archaeological finds of the Jewish Quarter, ending at the Room of the Last Supper. Option three: have lunch near the Jaffa Gate, and visit the Tower of David Museum on the history of Jerusalem, also ending the day (time permitting) at the Room of the Last Supper. Option four: have lunch on the way to the Room of the Last Supper, and then go to the Israel Museum to see the Dead Sea Scrolls. Check the sites' opening hours when planning your day.

### IF YOU HAVE 2–3 DAYS: A GENERAL ORIENTATION

Begin with the view from the Mount of Olives; then explore the City of David. Cab around to the Jaffa Gate to visit the Tower of David Museum, which covers the action-packed history of Jerusalem (try to catch the 11 AM tour). Eat lunch inside Jaffa Gate and follow the Ramparts Walk to Mt. Zion. Explore the Jewish Quarter. On the second day, plunge back into the Old City through the Dung Gate and visit the Western Wall and the Muslim shrines on the Temple Mount. Stroll through the souk to the Church of the Holy Sepulcher and end at the Jaffa Gate. Have lunch in the Israel Museum (note hours). If you're a museum person, this will fill your afternoon; if not, see the Dead Sea Scrolls, and then head over to downtown Ben Yehuda Street for coffee and serious people-watching. Begin the third day at Yad Vashem, the Holocaust museum and memorial. Visit the stained-glass Chagall windows at Hadassah Hospital. Have a leisurely lunch in picturesque Ein Kerem; then take in the Church of the Visitation. Take the rest of the afternoon off for a well-earned break at your hotel pool or in the shops.

### IF YOU HAVE 2–3 DAYS: A CHRISTIAN ORIENTATION

On the first day, see the Western Wall, El-Aqsa Mosque, and Dome of the Rock, the Pools of Bethesda and St. Anne's Church, the Ecce Homo Convent (site of the fortress where Jesus was tried), the Via Dolorosa, and the Church of the Holy Sepulcher. In the afternoon, visit Bethlehem (☞ Bethlehem *in* Chapter 2). On the second day, start with the view from the Mount of Olives (Catholics should add the Pater Noster Convent on the Mount of Olives—with the Lord's Prayer in more than 70 languages on ceramic tiles—and Dominus Flevit, halfway down the slope), and then walk or drive down to the Garden of Gethsemane. Visit the Room of the Last Supper on Mt. Zion (Catholics should add the Dormition Abbey, where, tradition says, Mary fell into eternal sleep) and enter the Jewish Quarter through Zion Gate. If biblical archaeology speaks to you, consider a walking tour with Archaeological Seminars (☞ Contacts and Resources *in* Jerusalem A to Z, *below*). In the afternoon, visit the Israel Museum or Yad Vashem. Spend the third day on the west side of town (the New City), picking up whichever of the two museums you didn't manage the day before. Visit the biblically inspired Chagall windows at Hadassah Hospital; and the Holyland Hotel's scale model of Jerusalem in the days of Jesus, built to a 50th of the city's actual size. Protestants should use this day to visit the Garden Tomb, in East Jerusalem. Catholics will want to visit the Church of St. John the Baptist and the Church of the Visitation, in Ein Kerem, on the western edge of town.

*Numbers in the text correspond to numbers in the margin and on the Exploring the Old City, Exploring East Jerusalem, and Exploring West Jerusalem and Center City maps.*

## Old City: The Classic Sights

Drink in the very essence of Jerusalem as you explore the city's primary religious sites and touch the different cultures that share it. All of these holy places demand modest dress: no shorts and no sleeveless shirts.

### A Good Walk

You can begin at the Dung Gate (literally, "Refuse Gate" in Hebrew), named apparently because of the accumulation of organic waste from the donkeys that worshipers had parked here in ancient times. Just inside the gate is the **Ophel Archaeological Garden** ①, often called the Western and Southern Wall Excavations. The most impressive and evocative remains here are those of King Herod the Great's grand structures, ones that Jesus knew well.

It's a few steps to the entrance of the **Western (Wailing) Wall** ② plaza. (Expect a routine check of your bags by security personnel at the plaza's entrance.) This is the most important Jewish shrine today, not because the structure itself is historically sacred but because it's close to the onetime Jewish Temple and is the last remnant of the enclosure of that temple.

Between the Western Wall and the Ophel Archaeological Garden, a ramp ascends to the vast plaza covering the summit of the biblical Mt. Moriah, called the **Temple Mount** by Jews and Christians, **Haram esh-Sharif** (the Noble Enclosure) by Muslims. The ancient Jewish Temple once stood here, both the "First" of King Solomon, and the "Second." Today the Temple Mount is administered by the Waqf, the Muslim religious council. In times of political unrest, seek local advice about the advisability of visiting the Temple Mount. Tall cypress trees create shady retreats from the glare of the whitish limestone pavements. Immediately in front of you as you enter the area is the large, black-domed **El-Aqsa Mosque** ③, the third-holiest mosque in the Muslim world. Two hundred yards to the left is the brilliantly golden **Dome of the Rock** ④, with its wondrously decorated interior.

As you exit the Temple Mount at its northeastern corner, through the al-Asbat Gate, the Lions' (also known as St. Stephen's) Gate is on your right. Stay within the city walls and turn left. Twenty yards on, an unobtrusive dark wooden door on your right opens onto the tranquil courtyard-garden of the **Pools of Bethesda and St. Anne's Church** ⑤. The Pools of Bethesda are the authentic site of the healing described in the New Testament

MOUNT OF OLIVES

Tomb of Jehosafat

Absalom's Pillar

Tomb of St. James

Zechariah's Tomb

Tomb of the Virgin

Gethsemane

Lions' (St. Stephen's) Gate

Golden Gate

Temple Mount/ Haram esh-Sharif

El-Aqsa Mosque

Bab al-Asbat

Dome of the Rock

Jericho Rd.

El-Omariya Rd.

Rockefeller Museum

Sultan Suleiman Rd.

St. Anne's Church

Pools of Bethesda

Bab Hutta Rd.

Bab el-Silsila

Monastery of the Flagellation

Bab al-Qattanin

Bab al-Ghawanmeh

Herod's Gate

Aqabat Shaddad

Aqabat el-Bustami

Aqabat el-Rahbar

Al-Mujahideen Rd.

School Antonia

Saladin St.

Ibn Al Jarrah Rd.

Aqabat e l Mawlawiya

**MUSLIM QUARTER**

Via Dolorosa

Aqabat esh Sheikh Rihan

Aqabat el-Saraya

ElWad Rd.

ElWad Rd.

El-Hakkari

Aqabat el-Takiyet (Khaki Sultan)

Aqabat el-Khalideh

Damascus Gate

Suq Khan e-Zeit

Via Dolorosa

Suq el'Attarin

Suq el Lahhamin

Deir el Habes

Nablus Rd.

Hatzanhonim St.

**CHRISTIAN QUARTER**

St. Francis Rd.

Greek Orthodox Patriarchate

Greek Orthodox Patriarchate Rd.

Christian

Christian Q. Rd.

Rd. 1

Custodia di Terra Santa

Casa Nova Rd.

Notre Dame de France

New Gate

Hospital St. Louis

**OPHEL**

Kidron Valley

Gihon Spring — **24**

**23**

**22**

**CITY OF DAVID**

Pool of Siloam

Robinson's Arch — **1**

Western (Wailing) Wall Plaza

Steps to Western Wall

Dung Gate

St. Peter in Gallicantu

Melchizedek Rd.

Deutscher Platz — **13**

**14**

Misgav Ladach St.

**JEWISH QUARTER**

Ma'aleh Hashalom

**12**

**11**

Jewish Quarter Rd.

Bab es-Silsilah St. (Rd.)

Habad St.

**10**

**MT. ZION**

Ararat St.

Cathedral of St. James

**ARMENIAN QUARTER**

Zion Gate

**21**

**18**

**19** **20**

Christ Church

St. James St.

Armenian Orthodox Monastery

Armenian Orthodox Patriarchate Rd.

Muristan

Quarter Rd.

David St.

Pool of Hezekiah

**16**

Citadel

**17**

Hativat Etzioni

Hativat Yerushalayim

Casa Nova Hospice

**17** **i** **15**

Jaffa Gate

Sultan's Pool

Jaffa Rd.

Mamilla Rd.

Hutzot Hayotzer

Mishkenot Sha'anannim

100 yards

100 meters

0

0

(John 5), and the Romanesque St. Anne's Church has amazing acoustics, which visiting groups often sample by singing hymns.

NEED A
BREAK?
As you leave St. Anne's Church, turn right. About 100 yards up the road, a little **café** serves freshly squeezed orange juice, Turkish coffee, and mint tea. It's on the corner of a lane on your left. There are public toilets across the street.

About 300 yards up the road, look for a ramp on your left leading to the blue metal door of a school. On Friday afternoon at 3, the brown-robed Franciscans begin their procession of the **Via Dolorosa** ⑥ (Way of the Cross) in the school courtyard. Chapels along the way are open at that time. (In summer, the procession starts at 4; contact the Christian Information Center for specifics; ☞ Visitor Information *in* Jerusalem A to Z, *below*.)

Just beyond the start of the Via Dolorosa, an arch crosses the street. Before the arch, on the street corner on the right, is the entrance to the **Ecce Homo Convent of the Sisters of Zion** ⑦, with a basement of ancient pavements and cisterns. Just beyond the arch, steps on your right bring you into a small vestibule, separated from the convent's chapel by a glass panel; from here there's a view back onto a second span of the same arch.

The Via Dolorosa runs down into El-Wad Road, one of the Old City's most important thoroughfares. To the right, the street climbs toward the Damascus Gate; to the left, it passes through the heart of the Muslim Quarter and reaches the Western Wall. It's a sensory experience to sit at a café here sipping cardamom-flavor Turkish coffee and watch the passing parade. Arab matrons in bright embroidered dresses rub shoulders with black-hatted Hasidic Jews in beards and side curls; and local Muslim kids in the universal uniform of T-shirt, jeans, and sneakers dodge around groups of pious Christian pilgrims almost oblivious to the tumult.

As you turn left onto El-Wad Road, Station III of the **Stations of the Cross** is immediately on your left. A few steps beyond it, also on the left, is Station IV and, on the next corner, Station V. The Via Dolorosa turns right and begins its ascent toward Calvary. Halfway up the street, a brown wooden door on your left marks Station VI. At the top of the stepped street is a brown metal door: Station VII. The little chapel contains one of the columns of the Byzantine Cardo, the main street of 6th-century Jerusalem, which ran from the Damascus Gate (off to your right) to today's Jewish Quarter, some 300 yards to your left. Step to the left, and then walk 30 yards up the street facing you—you are now at Station VIII, marked by nothing more than an inscribed stone in the wall. Return to the main street (Suq Khan e-Zeit) and turn right (left as you reach Station VII from VI). The street is almost impossibly crowded on Saturday, when Arab Jerusalem does its shopping—beware of pickpockets in these quarters. One hundred yards from Station VII, a ramp parallel to the street ascends to your right; take the ramp and the small lane above it to its end. A column in the Wall represents Station IX.

Step through the open door on your left into the courtyard of the **Ethiopian Monastery** ⑧, also known as Deir es-Sultan, an esoteric enclave of this poor but colorful sect. From the monastery's upper chapel, descend through a lower one and out a small wooden door to the court of the **Church of the Holy Sepulcher** ⑨ (☞ site map, *below*). (If you continue along Suq Khan e-Zeit without going up to the Ethiopian Monastery, a right turn brings you more quickly to the Holy Sepulcher.) Many Christians venerate this site as that of the death, burial, and resurrection of Jesus; you'll find Stations X, XI, XII, XIII, and XIV here. (Many Protestants believe these events occurred at Skull Hill and the Garden Tomb, north of the Damascus Gate; ☞ Mount of Olives and East Jerusalem, *below*.) The present vast structure is 12th-century Crusader, with a plethora of interior structures and decorations added since then. The property is shared by four different denominations, an unusual arrangement that lends the church much of its color.

To get to the Jaffa Gate from the church courtyard, ascend to the right as you leave the church, turn left at the main street (Christian Quarter Road), go as far as David Street, and turn right again. You can reach the Jewish Quarter (☞ *below*) by turning left from the courtyard, making an immediate right past the high white-stone Lutheran Church of the Redeemer and continuing as far as David Street, then turning left and taking any of the next three lanes to the right.

TIMING

You'll need 3–3½ hours for this walk, more if you like to linger. The Via Dolorosa takes no more than 30 minutes, but the full pilgrim procession takes an hour. Add 30–45 minutes to visit the Ophel Archaeological Garden; you can easily pass up this site if you're short on time or on interest in antiquities. Several sites close for a few hours over lunch. Afternoons are less crowded, but pay attention to the short opening hours of the Temple Mount (Haram esh-Sharif). Note that some Christian sites are closed on Sunday, the entire Temple Mount is closed on Friday, and photography is forbidden at the Western (Wailing) Wall on Saturday.

## Sights to See

★ ❾ **Church of the Holy Sepulcher.** Most Christians believe this is the site where Jesus was crucified by the Romans, was buried, and rose from the dead. Belief in the transcendent significance of those events, both personal and universal, is the basis of the Christian faith. The first church was built here circa AD 326 by Helena, mother of the Byzantine emperor Constantine the Great, and destroyed by Persian invaders in 614. It was rebuilt almost immediately, destroyed again by the Egyptian caliph El-Hakim in 1009, and once more restored, on a reduced scale, apparently as a cluster of shrines not under one roof. In the 12th century the Crusaders unified the shrines into the present vast structure (which is only two-thirds the length of its Byzantine predecessor). Many claim that the very antiquity of the tradition argues in favor of its authenticity; the early Christian community, fiercely committed to the point of martyrdom, would likely have preserved the memory of the site where events on which their entire faith hinged had taken place. The church is outside the city walls of Jesus's day—an important point, for no executions or burials took place within Jerusalem's sacred precincts.

Note the fine stone carving above the Gothic entrance (☞ site plan, *above*). As you enter the church's dim interior, steep steps to the right take you up to **Golgotha** (the word comes from Aramaic, through Greek), otherwise known as Calvary (through Latin), meaning "the place of the skull" (Mark 15). The chapel on the right is Roman Catholic and contains **Station X** (where Jesus was stripped of his garments) and **Station XI** (at the front—note the mosaic—where Jesus was nailed to the cross). On the right wall is a mosaic depicting the Old Testament story of Abraham's binding of Isaac—the sacrifice of the son by the father, seen by some Christians as a symbolic parallel to the death of Jesus himself.

The central chapel—all candlelight, oil lamps, and icons—is Greek Orthodox. Under the altar, and capping the rocky hillock on which you

# Church of the Holy Sepulcher

Calvary/Golgotha Upper level detail

stand, is a bronze disc with a hole, purportedly the place where the cross actually stood and thus **Station XII**, where Jesus died on the cross. (You can reach through the hole to touch the rock.) The Franciscans indicate the spot between XI and XII, at the icon of Mary, as **Station XIII**, where Jesus's body was taken down. At ground level opposite the entrance is a rectangular, pink stone slab called the **Stone of Unction**, where it is said that the body of Jesus was cleansed and prepared for burial. Greek pilgrims can often be seen rubbing crosses and clothing on the stone in order to take home a trace of the site's sanctity. The tomb itself (**Station XIV**) is in the cavernous rotunda to the left of the entrance, encased in a small, pink marble edifice.

Some 50 ft above the tomb is the great dome that is the landmark of the Christian Quarter. Though repaired in the early 1980s as part of critical structural renovations to the church, the dome remained unfinished for another decade, a symbol (and a victim) of the denominational rivalry that has beset Holy Land sites, and the Holy Sepulcher in particular, for centuries. An agreement in 1995 between the Greeks, "Latins" (Roman Catholics), and Armenians on the great dome's interior decoration was hailed as an almost miraculous breakthrough in ecumenical relations, and the dome was dedicated in December 1996 in an unprecedented interdenominational service. (Both the artist and the philanthropist who resolved the stalemate were American Catholics.) The Status Quo Agreements—a list of possessions and privileges that was frozen in the 19th century—apply to this church; so, for example, in late afternoon, each of the church's four "shareholders" in turn—Greek Orthodox, Latins, Armenians, and Copts (Egyptians)—exercises its right to a procession from Calvary to the tomb, with fully frocked chanting clergy and censers streaming pungent smoke.

Enter the tomb between the sentinels of giant brass candleholders. The only hint of what it must have been like 2,000 years ago is the ledge in the inner chamber (now covered with marble) on which Jesus's body would have been laid. This detail resembles hundreds of Jewish tombs from the Second Temple period (the time of Jesus), discovered both in Jerusalem and elsewhere. You can see more pristine examples of such ancient tombs in the Chapel of St. Nicodemus, a dark chamber opposite the Coptic chapel in the back of the sepulcher.

The Holy Fire ceremony takes place here on the Greek Orthodox Easter. The church is typically packed with candle-carrying pilgrims tense with excitement; the patriarch enters the tomb, a flash of fire appears through its portholes, a messenger emerges with a flaming torch, congregants light their candles from those of their neighbors, and within moments the whole church seems to be ablaze.

Among the church's many chapels, the most interesting is the **Chapel of St. Helena.** From the corridor at the eastern end of the church, steps lead down to a crypt adorned with a fine Armenian mosaic floor and an even deeper grotto where, tradition has it, Helena, mother of Constantine the Great, found the True Cross of Christ (circa AD 326). ☒ *Between Suq Khan e-Zeit and Christian Quarter Rd.,* ☎ *02/627–3314.* ☒ *Free.* ☼ *Apr.–Sept., daily 5 AM–8 PM; Oct.–Mar., daily 5 AM–7 PM.*

★ **❹ Dome of the Rock.** This splendid octagonal building is the original one completed in AD 691 over the great rock—the summit of Mt. Moriah—from which the prophet Muhammad is said to have risen to heaven, where he received from God the teachings of the Islamic faith. Considering the original builders were immediate heirs of Byzantine artistic traditions, it's hardly surprising that the shrine's layout resembles those of its contemporaries, like the Byzantine Church of San Vitale in Ravenna, Italy. The exterior glazed ceramic tiles, in shades of blue, were repaired during renovations in the 1950s and '60s, but the marvelous gold dome was restored in the 1990s, with 176 pounds of 24-carat gold electroplated on copper.

The shrine's interior is wondrous. Granite columns support arches, some bearing the original green-and-gold mosaics set in arabesque motifs—in observance of Islamic religious tradition, no human or animal forms appear in the artwork. The mosaics were restored in 1027, preserving much of the original work. Some of the Arabic inscriptions in the mosaics are quotations from the Koran; others are dedications. One of the latter originally lauded Abd el-Malik, caliph of the Damascus-based Ummayad dynasty, who built the shrine; some 140 years later, the caliph of a rival dynasty removed el-Malik's name and replaced it with his own, but he neglected to change the date! Notice the outstanding marble slabs that adorn the walls. Without the benefit of power tools, medieval stonemasons were able to expose the natural grain of the marble, creating impressive symmetries.

The huge **rock** around which the shrine is built is considered by more than one faith to be the center of the world. In addition, Jewish tradition identifies it as the place where Abraham bound and almost sacrificed his son Isaac (Genesis 22). With King David's conquest of Jerusalem in 1000 BC, however, the rock became part of (relatively) indisputable history. Against the warning of his counselors—who said it was arrogant to count the people of Israel, as they were like "the sands of the sea and the stars of the sky"—the triumphant king undertook a national census, thus inviting divine retribution in the form of a plague (II Samuel 24). At the last minute, God stayed the hand of the Angel of Death, as he was about to smite Jerusalem. It was on the rock—"the threshing floor of Araunah [or Ornan] the Jebusite"—that David saw the angel and here that he erected an altar and burned a repentance offering to the Lord. In the absence of other convincing candidates, modern scholars identify the rock with that threshing floor.

One generation later, David's son Solomon built his temple here. Did the rock become the innermost chamber, the Holy of Holies, of the Temple (meaning the sanctuary would have stood where the Dome of the Rock stands today)? Or did it become the altar in the Court of the Israelites (with the sanctuary a bit to the west)? Judaism grapples with the question to this day.

At the southwestern corner of the rock, an ornamented canister is said to contain several hairs of the prophet Muhammad's beard. The reliquary is opened for faithful Muslims one day a year, during the holy month of Ramadan. A small opening in the marble facade below it allows you to put your hand in and feel the indentation in the rock; the faithful believe it was created by the prophet's foot as he ascended to heaven. A few steps to the right bring you to a staircase leading down to a small grotto, perhaps once a cistern or a grain store in the pre-Davidic days. Legend calls it the Well of Souls, the entrance to the netherworld and the place where the dead pray. An Islamic tradition relates that as Muhammad rose to heaven, the rock tried to follow him and had already left a void (the cave) when the archangel Gabriel intervened to hold it down. For times and entrance fees, *see* Temple Mount, *below*.

❼ **Ecce Homo Convent of the Sisters of Zion.** The arch that crosses the Via Dolorosa outside the convent and continues into the present-day Ecce Homo Church was once thought to have been the gate of Herod's Antonia Fortress and thus the spot where the Roman governor Pontius Pilate presented Jesus to the crowd with the words *"Ecce homo!"*

("Behold, the man!"). Recent scholarship, however, has established that the structure was a triumphal arch built by the Roman emperor Hadrian in the 2nd century AD.

The basement of the convent has two points of interest. The first is an impressive arched reservoir with a barrel-vault roof, apparently built by Hadrian in the moat of Herod's older Antonia Fortress. The second is the famous *lithostratos,* or stone pavement, etched with games played by bored Roman legionnaires. One such diversion—the notorious Game of the King—called for the execution of a mock king, a sequence tantalizingly reminiscent of the New Testament description of the treatment of Jesus by the Roman soldiers. Contrary to tradition, however, the pavement of large, foot-worn brown flagstones is not from Jesus's day but was laid down a century later. ⊠ *Via Dolorosa,* ☎ 02/627-7292. ☜ NIS 6 ($1.50) ☉ *At press time, Mon.–Sat. 8:30–5, Sun. 9–4. Site may return to closing Sun. and Mon.–Sat. 12:30–2.*

★ ❸ **El-Aqsa Mosque.** The name of the mosque—"the Farthermost Place"—comes from the Koranic story of Muhammad ascending to heaven from the nearby rock (☞ Temple Mount, *below*) to meet with God. At the far (southern) end of this cavernous building, under the landmark copper dome, is the *mihrab,* the niche indicating the direction of prayer toward Mecca. This wall is believed to be the only remnant of the original building created by the Ummayad dynasty in the early 8th century AD. Since then the mosque has been destroyed several times by earthquake and rebuilt. The rows of square stone columns on the right (west) as you enter date from the 14th century; the round marble ones in the center and on the left are the products of renovations in the 1920s and '30s. Persian rugs are interspersed with modern runners, on which individual prayer mats have been patterned. The mosque's finest feature is the wonderfully complex set of stained-glass windows beneath the dome.

In the 12th century, the Templars, one of the Crusader monastic orders, made its headquarters here, taking its name from the ancient site itself; but this spot has been the setting for more-recent dramas, too. In 1951, King Abdullah of Jordan (the late King Hussein's grandfather) was assassinated in the mosque; and in 1969, a demented arsonist set fire to a priceless wooden *minbar,* or pulpit, in an attempt to destroy the building. West of the mosque is the **Islamic Museum,** displaying some fine stone-relief work and carved wood from El-Aqsa's earlier incarnations. For times and entrance fees, *see* Temple Mount, *below.*

❽ **Ethiopian Monastery.** Standing in the monastery's courtyard beneath the medieval bulge of the Church of the Holy Sepulcher, you are surrounded by those churches of Christendom that revere this site. An Egyptian Coptic monastery lies close by, next to the Ninth Station of the Cross; and around you the skyline is broken by a Russian Orthodox gable, a Lutheran bell tower, and the crosses of Greek Orthodox, Armenian, and Roman Catholic churches.

The robed Ethiopian monks, tall and slender, gentle and shy, live in tiny cells in the rooftop monastery. Their small, dark church is adorned with modern paintings, one of which depicts the visit of the Queen of Sheba to King Solomon. Ethiopian tradition holds that more passed between the two than is related in the Bible (I Kings 10) and that their supposed union produced an heir to the Ethiopian royal house. The script in the paintings is Gehz, the ecclesiastical language of the Ethiopian church. ⊠ *Roof of the Church of the Holy Sepulcher, access from Suq Khan e-Zeit.* ☜ *Free.* ☉ *Daily during daylight.*

❶ **Ophel Archaeological Garden.** Often known as the Western and Southern Wall Excavations, this site was extensively excavated in the 1970s, under the direction of archaeologist Benjamin Mazar. He unearthed very little of Old Testament Jerusalem but a great deal from the Herodian, Byzantine, and Arab periods. Have a look at the artist's reconstruction of the area on display at the entrance (you can buy your own copy from the attendant), and walk down to the corner of the massive wall facing you. (For purposes of orientation, this is the southwest corner of the Temple Mount.)

King Solomon's First Temple on Mt. Moriah was destroyed by the Babylonians in 586 BC. Fifty years later, Jews returning from the Babylonian Exile began building the Second Temple on the same site (where the Dome of the Rock now stands). In the 1st century BC, when King Herod the Great rebuilt the Second Temple, he expanded the enclosure around it by constructing a massive retaining wall on the slopes of Mt. Moriah and filling the inside with thousands of tons of rubble, thus producing the huge plaza still known today as the Temple Mount. The great stones near the corner—their well-cut borders characteristic of the Herodian period—are not held together with mortar; their sheer weight gives the structure its stability.

Now exposed and accessible to the left of the corner is the pavement of a street from the Second Temple period. Two thousand years ago, the retaining wall would have been some 50% higher above the street than it is today, and its foundations, plumbed by British army engineer Charles Warren in 1867, extend as deep below you as the present height of the wall rises above you. Left of the corner and far above your head is the protrusion known as **Robinson's Arch** (named for the 19th-century American explorer Edward Robinson), which is the beginning of a bridge to the Temple Mount, once reached by a staircase from the commercial area where you now stand. On the street is a pile of square-cut building stones from the top of the original wall, lying where they were discovered, dramatic evidence of the destruction the Romans wrought here in AD 70.

A staircase takes you back to the higher level. Turn left (east). Fifty yards on, a small, modern spiral staircase on your left descends below present ground level to an intriguing, partially reconstructed labyrinth of Byzantine dwellings, mosaics and all; from here you reemerge outside the present city walls. Alternately, go straight, passing through the city wall by a small arched gate. The wide staircase to your left, a good part of it original, once brought hordes of pilgrims through the now-blocked gates of the southern wall of the Temple Mount and into the sacred temple precincts. The rock-hewn *mikva'ot* (plural of *mikveh*), Jewish ritual baths, at the bottom of the steps, are a visual reminder of the purification rites once demanded of Jews before they entered the Temple Mount. ✉ *Dung Gate,* ☎ *02/625–4403.* 🎟 *NIS 14 ($3.50); combined ticket including Ramparts Walk, Damascus Gate, and Hezekiah's Tunnel (☞ below), on same day only, NIS 35 ($8.75).* ☉ *Sun.–Thurs. 9–4, Fri. and Jewish holiday eves 9–2.*

❺ **Pools of Bethesda and St. Anne's Church.** The transition is sudden and complete, from the raucous cobbled streets and persistent vendors to the drooping pepper trees, flower patches, and birdsong of this serene Catholic cloister. The Romanesque Crusader **St. Anne's Church,** built in 1140, was restored in the 19th century, and with its austere and unadorned stone interior, it is one of the finest examples of medieval architecture in the country. According to local tradition, the Virgin Mary was born in the grotto over which the church is built, and the church is named for her mother. It's worth waiting for one of the frequent pilgrim groups, who invariably test the church's extraordinarily reverberant acoustics by singing some hymns.

On the facade of the church, above the main door, is an unexpected five-line inscription in Arabic. After Saladin's defeat of the Crusaders in 1187, the church was turned into a *madrasa,* a Muslim house of study, and despite the Christian restoration, the inscription—a dedication to Saladin—has survived.

In the same compound, and just a few steps from the church, are the excavated **Pools of Bethesda,** a large, double public reservoir in use during the 1st century BC and 1st century AD. The New Testament (John 5) speaks of Jesus's miraculously curing a lame man by "a pool, which is called in the Hebrew tongue Bethesda [the Place of Mercy]." The actual bathing pools were the small ones, east of the reservoir, but it was over the big pools that both the Byzantines and the Crusaders built churches, now ruined, to commemorate the miracle. ⊠ *Al-Mujahideen Rd.,* ☎ *02/628–3285.* ⊠ *NIS 6 ($1.50).* ⊘ *Apr.–Sept., Mon.–Sat. 8–1 and 2–6; Oct.–Mar., Mon.–Sat. 8–1 and 2–5.*

**Temple Mount.** Covering some 35 acres, the Temple Mount (known to Muslims as Haram esh-Sharif) is regarded by some scholars as one of the greatest religious enclosures of the entire ancient world. King Herod the Great (1st century BC) had an immense stone wall built around the hill to retain the rubble used to level off the crest and create the massive plaza. At its center stood Herod's rebuilt Second Temple, a splendid edifice that gained international fame as one of the architectural wonders of its day. (This was the Temple Jesus knew.) The Romans reduced it to ashes in the summer of AD 70. The Temple Mount today is a Muslim preserve (modest dress is essential), administered by the Waqf, the Supreme Muslim Religious Council. In times of political unrest, seek local advice about the advisability of visiting the Temple Mount.

When the Arab caliph Omar Ibn-Khatib seized Jerusalem from the Byzantines in AD 638, he found the Temple Mount covered with rubbish and had to clear the site to expose the great rock at its summit. It is said that Omar asked his aide Ka'ab al'Akhbar, a Jew who had converted to Islam, where he should build his mosque. Ka'ab recommended a spot north of the rock, hoping, the tale suggests, that the Muslims, praying south toward Mecca, would thus include the old temple site in their obeisance. "You dog, Ka'ab," bellowed the caliph. "In your heart you are still a Jew!" Omar's mosque, which he built south of the rock, has not survived, but the splendid gold-domed shrine, completed in AD 691, still stands.

Jerusalem is not mentioned in the Koran, but Muhammad's Night Ride is. Awakened one night by the archangel Gabriel, Muhammad was taken on the fabulous winged horse el-Burak to the *masjad el-aqsa,* the "farthermost place"—hence, the **El-Aqsa Mosque** (☞ *above*). From there he rose to heaven, came face to face with God, received the teachings of Islam, and returned home—all in the same night. The tradition evolved that the masjad el-aqsa was none other than Jerusalem, and the great rock the very spot from which the prophet ascended.

The triumphant Arabs of the generation after Muhammad clearly venerated Jerusalem as the city of biblical kings and prophets. Many modern scholars also postulate, however, that the feeling of being Johnnies-come-lately in the holy city of rival faiths did not sit well with the new masters of Jerusalem. These scholars hold that the masjad el-aqsa tradition and the magnificent Dome of the Rock were designed to proclaim the ascendancy of the "true faith" and the new Arab empire over the rival Byzantine Christians.

The splendid **Dome of the Rock** (☞ *above*) dominates the center of the plaza and, in fact, the entire old cityscape, despite its relatively low elevation.

To the west of the Dome of the Rock is a large *sabil,* a public drinking fountain (now defunct), with an elaborate ornamented stone dome built by the Egypt-based Mamluk rulers in the 14th or 15th century. A large number of the nearby buildings lining the western edge of the Temple Mount date from this period, distinguished by their impressive jigsaws of fitted red, white, and black stone.

Overlooking the plaza from its northwestern corner is a long building, today an elementary school, built on the artificial scarp that once protected Herod's Antonia Fortress. The Christian tradition, probably accurate, identifies the site as the *praetorium* where Jesus was tried.

In the eastern outer wall, facing the Mount of Olives, is the ornate, domed inner **Golden Gate,** or Gate of Mercy, now blocked. The present masonry is restored Byzantine, though the gate—the Eastern Gate of Christian tradition through which Jesus is believed to have entered the area on Palm Sunday—existed in the Second Temple period. In the Jewish tradition, the long-awaited Messiah will one day enter the city through the same gate. ☎ *02/628–3292 or 02/628–3313. ☒ Combined ticket for El-Aqsa Mosque, Dome of the Rock, and Islamic Museum NIS 36 ($9). Buy tickets to the right of El-Aqsa, or at the foot of the western staircase of the Dome of the Rock. Guards will require you to leave shoes, bags, and cameras outside (at your own risk, though theft is rare here); a small purse is usually allowed. ☉ Approximate summer hrs: Sat.–Thurs. 7:30–11 and 1:30–3; winter hrs: 8–10:30 and 12:30–2. Seasonal changes are made without notice to accommodate changing prayer times. Last entry to area 30 mins before closing.*

★ ❻ **Via Dolorosa.** The Way of Suffering—or Way of the Cross, as it's more commonly called in English—is the route Jesus walked, carrying his cross from the place of his condemnation by Pontius Pilate to the site of his crucifixion and burial. The present tradition is essentially 12th-century Crusader, but it draws on older Byzantine beliefs. Some of the incidents represented by the 14 Stations of the Cross are scriptural; some (III, IV, VI, VII, and IX) are not. Some of the stations on the route, which winds through the Muslim and Christian quarters, are marked by tiny chapels; the last five are inside the Church of the Holy Sepulcher. (For walking directions and information, *see* A Good Walk *and* Church of the Holy Sepulcher, *above.*)

**Station I.** Jesus is tried and condemned by Pontius Pilate.

**Station II.** Jesus is scourged and given the cross. This station is at the Monastery of the Flagellation, whose shaded cloister and cool greenery offer some relief from the noisy street. The Roman pavement within the two chapels dates from the century after Christ. At press time it was open daily April to September 8–6 and October to March 8–5. Site may return to closing noon–2 on Monday through Saturday and all day Sunday.

**Station III.** Jesus falls for the first time. (The chapel was built after World War II by soldiers of the Free Polish Forces.)

**Station IV.** Mary embraces Jesus.

**Station V.** Simon of Cyrene picks up the cross.

**Station VI.** A woman wipes the face of Jesus, whose image remains on the cloth. (Her name has come down to us as Veronica, apparently derived from the words *vera* and *icone,* meaning true image.)

**Station VII.** Jesus falls for the second time. (The little chapel contains one of the columns of the Byzantine Cardo, the main street of 6th-century Jerusalem.)

**Station VIII.** Jesus addresses the women in the crowd.

**Station IX.** Jesus falls for the third time.

**Station X.** Jesus is stripped of his garments.

**Station XI.** Jesus is nailed to the cross.

**Station XII.** Jesus dies on the cross.

**Station XIII.** Jesus is taken down from the cross.

**Station XIV.** Jesus is buried.

★ ❷ **Western (Wailing) Wall.** The Wall ("Kotel" in Hebrew), the most important *existing* Jewish shrine, was not itself part of the ancient Second Temple but of King Herod's retaining wall surrounding the Temple Mount (☞ *above*). After the Roman destruction of Jerusalem in AD 70, and especially after the dedication of its pagan successor in 135, the city was off-limits to Jews for generations. Although the general location of the Temple was known (it was in the vicinity of today's Dome of the Rock; ☞ *above*), its precise location was lost. Even when they eventually gained access, Jews avoided ascending the Temple Mount for fear of unwittingly trespassing on the most sacred—and thus forbidden—areas of their ancient sanctuary. With time, the closest remnant of the period took on the aura of the temple itself. The Western Wall is thus really a holy place "by proxy," and in a sense, it is *through* the stones rather than *to* them that devout Jews pray. It is the tears of generations of such worshipers, grieving for the lost temple, to which its Gentile name—the Wailing Wall—refers.

The Western Wall functions under the aegis of the rabbinic authorities, with all the trappings of an Orthodox synagogue: a dress code (modest dress; men are required to cover their heads), segregation of men and women in prayer (men on the left), and prohibition of smoking and photography on the Sabbath and religious holidays. The cracks between the massive stones are stuffed with slips of paper bearing petitions, and the swaying and praying of the devout leave no doubt of the powerful hold this place still has on the minds and hearts of many Jews.

On Monday and Thursday mornings, the place bubbles with often colorful bar-mitzvah ceremonies, when Jewish families celebrate the coming of age of their 13-year-old sons. The fervor is still greater on Friday evenings just after sunset, when the young men of a nearby yeshiva (Jewish seminary) come dancing and singing down to the wall to welcome in the "Sabbath bride." But many people find that it's only when the crowds have gone (the wall is floodlit at night and always open), and you share the warm, prayer-drenched stones with just a handful of bearded stalwarts, that the true spirituality of the Western Wall is palpable.

A long **tunnel** beyond the men's side (north of the plaza) was excavated in recent years, exposing ancient arches and chambers and several courses of the Western Wall along nearly its entire length. Among the masonry were two stones estimated to weigh an incredible 400 and 540 tons, respectively. The tunnel is open only to organized tour groups; you can join a prescheduled local tour. The tour takes about 80 minutes and ends at the beginning of the Via Dolorosa, in the Muslim Quarter. (Call **Western Wall Heritage,** ☎ 02/627–1333, or **Archaeological Seminars,** ☎ 02/627–3515 for details.)

If you're going directly to the Western Wall, you can take Bus 1, which will deposit you inside the Dung Gate. You can also reach the wall by descending from the Jewish Quarter or from the Street of the Chain, in the Arab souk. ⊙ *Daily 24 hrs.*

## Jewish Quarter

When the Crusaders reached Jerusalem in 1099, the Jewish community was concentrated in the northeastern quadrant of the city, which is now the Muslim Quarter of the Old City. The Crusaders' indiscriminate massacre of Jerusalem's population—Muslims, Jews, and eastern Christians—was devastating. The Jewish community only began the slow process of revival in 1267, when the Spanish rabbi Nachmanides (known as the Ramban, an acronym of his name) reached the city and found there "only two Jews, brothers, dyers by trade." The men established themselves in the city's southern quadrant—perhaps on Mt. Zion—eventually occupying the medieval building in today's Jewish Quarter that still bears the Ramban's name. The Ramban Synagogue is on Jewish Quarter Road, adjacent to and south of the Hurva. The community mushroomed with the influx of Sephardic Jews expelled from Spain in 1492, and again with the flow of Ashkenazi Jews from Central and Eastern Europe in the early 18th century. By 1865 more than half the population of Jerusalem was Jewish, most living in the Jewish Quarter in very difficult conditions, some in the Muslim Quarter, and a handful in the new neighborhoods developing beyond the city walls.

During Israel's War of Independence in 1948, the Jewish Quarter was severely damaged, evacuated, plundered, and abandoned for a generation. With the unification of Jerusalem under Israeli rule after the Six-Day War of 1967, the restoration of the quarter began in earnest. With so many buildings little more than rubble, Israeli archaeologists were given a unique opportunity to explore the area systematically, and a decade of frenetic excavation (in order to keep ahead of construction schedules) yielded a harvest of archaeologically important sites. The simultaneous reconstruction of the quarter emphasized the restoration of the old, as well as the design of new buildings that would preserve the neighborhood's original architectural flavor. The result is an eye-pleasing harmony of limestone masonry, arched windows and buttresses, cobblestone alleyways, open archaeological sites, and splashes of greenery that makes the Jewish Quarter the Old City's most attractive.

### A Good Walk

This walk's starting point, the parking lot of the Jewish Quarter, can be reached from a number of directions. You can follow Armenian Orthodox Patriarchate Road from the Jaffa Gate (700 yards) or enter through the Zion Gate and continue right (200 yards). With your back to the bus stop, cross the lot and enter Jewish Quarter Road (there will be a small supermarket on your right). One hundred yards down the road on your left and some 20 ft below you are the excavated and partly restored remains of the **Cardo** ⑩, the colonnaded main street of 6th-century AD Byzantine Jerusalem.

Some 50 yards farther and on the right is the entrance to the ruined **Hurva Synagogue** ⑪, the great landmark of the Jewish Quarter until it was blown up in 1948. Visual aids help reconstruct its past splendor. The second lane to the right beyond the Hurva Synagogue brings you to the **Broad Wall** ⑫, 23 ft thick and 27 centuries old.

Facing the Broad Wall with your back to the Cardo, bear right for 50 yards to Hurva Square, the center of the Jewish Quarter. Here you can duck into a shady spot, take the weight off your feet, and have some refreshments. On the eastern side of the square, take a few steps down the lane that begins some 20 yards to the right of Tony's Deli, where you'll find the **Herodian Quarter/Wohl Archaeological Museum** ⑬, containing the impressive remains of Second Temple–era mansions.

Once outside the Herodian Quarter, you can go down a wide staircase to the Western Wall and the Dung Gate (☞ Old City: The Classic Sights, *above*). To return to Hurva Square, go up the staircase. Just beyond the top of the steps, on your right, is the 2,000-year-old **Burnt House** ⑭, once a basement industrial workshop, destroyed by fire in the great Roman destruction of AD 70.

TIMING
Allow two hours for this walk, though the many good stores and restaurants may tempt you to spend more time. The Herodian Quarter, Burnt House, and all commercial establishments close early Friday afternoon and remain closed on Saturday.

## Sights to See

⑫ **Broad Wall.** The discovery in the 1970s of the rather modest-looking 23-ft-thick foundations of an Old Testament city wall was hailed as one of the most important archaeological finds in the Jewish Quarter. The wall was built in 701 BC by Hezekiah, King of Judah and a contemporary of the prophet Isaiah, to protect the city against an Assyrian invasion (II Chronicles 32). The unearthing of the Broad Wall—a biblical name—resolved a century-long scholarly debate about the extent of Old Testament Jerusalem: a large on-site map shows that the ancient city was far larger than was once thought.

⑭ **Burnt House.** During the Second Temple period, this was the basement industrial workshop of the priestly Bar Katros family, a fact gleaned from inscribed stone weights discovered on the site. The evidence of the city's fiery destruction by the Romans is stronger here than anywhere else, with charred cooking pots and debris giving a vivid sense of the devastation 19 centuries ago. The archaeologists were riveted by the discovery of the skeletal hand and arm of a woman clutching a scorched staircase in a futile attempt to escape the flames. An audiovisual presentation illuminates the period, putting the artifacts in clear context. ✉ *Tiferet Israel St.,* ☎ *no phone.* 🎟 *Combined ticket with Herodian Quarter NIS 19 ($4.75); Burnt House only NIS 9 ($2.25).* ☉ *Sun.–Thurs. 9–4:30, Fri. and Jewish holiday eves 9–12:30.*

⑩ **Cardo.** In AD 135, the Roman emperor Hadrian built his town of Aelia Capitolina on the ruins of Jerusalem, an urban plan essentially preserved in the Old City of today. Hadrian's *cardo maximus* (the generic name for the city's main street) began at the strategic Damascus Gate, in the north, where sections of it have been unearthed. It did not originally run so far south into today's Jewish Quarter, but with the Christianization of the Roman Empire in the 4th century, access to Mt. Zion and its important Christian sites became a priority, and the main street was eventually extended. The original width—today you see only half—was 73 ft, about the width of an eight-lane highway. Some 20 ft below modern ground level, you can walk on the flagstones and among the columns of Byzantine Jerusalem in its heyday.

★ ⑬ **Herodian Quarter/Wohl Archaeological Museum.** Excavations in the 1970s exposed this area's most visually arresting site: the remains of mansions from the luxurious Upper City of the Second Temple period. Preserved in the basement of the modern Jewish seminary built over the ruins, the geometrically patterned mosaic floors, colorful frescoes, and costly glassware, stone objects, and ceramics provide a peek into domestic life at the top in the days of Herod and Jesus. In the first hall, several small stone cisterns have been identified as private *mikva'ot,* Jewish ritual baths; holograms depict their use. A small ascending staircase ends abruptly, a reminder that nothing above ground level survived the Roman devastation of AD 70.

The quality, and even rarity, of some of the goods displayed in the second hall would have been the pride of any aristocratic household in those days: decorated ceramic plates, a ribbed green glass bowl, an imported mottled-alabaster vase. Large stone water jars are just like those described in the New Testament story of the wedding at Cana (John 2; ☞ Nazareth and the Galilee Hills *in* Chapter 5). Rare stone tables resemble the dining-room furniture depicted in Roman stone reliefs found in Europe.

Ancient steps bring you down to the last of the three distinct levels, a mansion with an estimated original area of more than 6,000 square ft. None of the upper stories have survived, of course, but the frescoes (half replaced by the later, more fashionable stucco) and the quality of the artifacts found here indicate a standard of living so exceptional that some scholars have suggested this might have been the long-sought palace of the high priest. At the southern end of the fine reception hall is a badly scorched mosaic floor with a charred ceiling beam lying on it. The Upper City held out against the Roman army for a month after the destruction of the Second Temple, but in September of AD 70, "on the eighth day of [the Hebrew month of] Elul," wrote the Jewish historian Josephus in his contemporary account of Jerusalem's last hours, "the sun rose over a city in flames." Precisely 19 centuries later, the victims' compatriots uncovered evidence of destruction so vivid, wrote archaeologist Nahman Avigad, "that we could almost smell the burning and feel the heat of the flames." ✉ *Hakara'im Rd.,* ☎ *02/628–3448.* 🎫 *Combined ticket with Burnt House NIS 19 ($4.75); Herodian Quarter only NIS 15 ($3.75).* ☉ *Sun.–Thurs. 9–4:30, Fri. and Jewish holiday eves 9:30–12:30.*

**⑪ Hurva Synagogue.** Ruined walls, alcoves that once housed sacred texts, and a modern arch retracing the old are all that remain of what was once the Jewish Quarter's most prominent building. In 1700, a large group of devout Eastern European (Ashkenazi) Jews arrived in the holy city, led by the venerable Rabbi Yehuda Hehassid (Judah the Pious). The old man died days after their arrival, throwing his followers into despair and leaving them with a problem: with the death of the rabbi, the promised funds from the Old Country never materialized, and money for the construction of a synagogue had to be borrowed from the Jews' Muslim neighbors. By 1720 the loan was still outstanding, and the creditors burned down the synagogue, exiling Ashkenazi Jews from the city for more than 100 years. In 1862, a new and splendid synagogue was completed on the ruins—*hurva,* in Hebrew—of the old. It became the preeminent synagogue of the neighborhood, its high dome a Jewish Quarter landmark until the surrender of the quarter in the War of Independence, in 1948, and the destruction of the synagogue by local Arabs.

## Tower of David and Mt. Zion

"From Jaffa Gate to Zion Gate" could be the title of the walk we suggest here. It takes in a fine museum of the history of Jerusalem, a section of the Ramparts Walk, and a clutch of sights, both Christian and Jewish, on Mt. Zion.

## A Good Walk

Begin at the **Jaffa Gate** ⑮, served by Buses 19, 20, 30, 38, and 99. If you have your own car, look for parking in the Mamilla area opposite the walls. Walk to the bottom of the road that leads to Jaffa Gate and pause to look at the **Old City walls.** Above your head is the photogenic Tower of David—actually a Turkish tower and minaret—which has become one of Jerusalem's landmarks.

The road that enters the Jaffa Gate is a mere 100 years old; the gate to your left, which you would enter if you came from the downtown area via Jaffa Road, dates from the 16th century. Inside the gate, the road immediately bends to the right, while directly ahead is David Street, one of the main streets of the **souk,** the Arab bazaar (not to be confused with King David Street, in West Jerusalem). Follow the vehicular road (Armenian Orthodox Patriarchate Road). On your left, 30 yards after the bend, is the entrance to the Anglican Christ Church, a neo-Gothic structure built in the 1840s and the oldest Protestant church in the Middle East. On your right is the platform from which British general Edmund Allenby officially reviewed his victorious troops on December 11, 1917, after the Turkish army had abandoned the city.

Go up the ramp, cross the moat, and enter the **Tower of David Museum** ⑯, a museum of the history of Jerusalem, and one of the city's highlights. From the entrance hall, a winding outside staircase on your right brings you to the roof. Turn left at once to reach the auditorium, where a film is shown, and a second staircase to the top of the great tower. The view is marvelous in all directions but especially looking east across the Old City to the Temple Mount and Mount of Olives. Return to the roof and follow the red signs marked EXHIBIT.

The exit from the museum puts you outside the Jaffa Gate, from which there are two ways to walk to Zion Gate. You can follow the road down to the left, then take an ascending path that hugs the Old City wall; the views across the Hinnom Valley to the Yemin Moshe neighborhood and the New City are splendid. At the southwestern corner of the Old City, turn left and continue 150 yards along the city wall to Zion Gate. Alternately, you can reach the same point by way of the **Ramparts Walk** ⑰, on top of the city walls. As you leave the museum, do not rejoin the road; instead, walk south across the terrace, which only seems like a blind alley. A left at the end brings you to the ticket office for the ramparts. Follow the route—watch the steep steps—and descend at Zion Gate.

Turn right a few steps past Zion Gate and follow the path away from the Old City wall. Bear right at the first fork and turn right at the second. You're now outside the **Dormition Abbey** ⑱; its black conical dome and tall clock tower are Mt. Zion's prominent landmarks. The church preserves the tradition that Mary, mother of Jesus, did not die but fell into "eternal sleep" (hence *dormition*).

Return to the corner on the main path (the second fork) and turn right. Twenty yards on, step through a doorway to your left and climb one flight of steps to the **Room of the Last Supper** ⑲. Also known as "the Upper Room," this site has been enshrined by tradition as the place where Jesus instituted the Eucharist ("This is my body . . . this is my blood") and where his disciples gathered on Pentecost.

The exit leads to a small courtyard. A second, tranquil courtyard (to the left as you go down the stairs), surrounded by flowerpots and a colonnaded corridor, was once the cloister of a medieval monastery. The arched windows of the Room of the Last Supper are above you, and immediately beneath the cloister, in an inner chamber, is the traditional **Tomb of David** ⑳, draped in velvet and silver. As you emerge from the tomb, turn left and leave the cloister from the side opposite where you entered. Across the road is the **Chamber of the Holocaust** ㉑, a small but powerful exhibit dedicated to the Jews killed by the Nazis during World War II. To return to Zion Gate, turn right as you leave the memorial.

TIMING

Allow 1½–2 hours for the Tower of David Museum and a similar amount of time for the rest of the route.

## Sights to See

⑳ **Chamber of the Holocaust.** Not to be confused with Yad Vashem in West Jerusalem, this small museum dedicated to the memory of the 6 million European Jews annihilated by the Nazis in the Second World War contains artifacts salvaged from the death camps, including items that the Nazis forced Jews to make out of sacred Torah scrolls (the Five Books of Moses). With grim humor, one Jewish tailor fashioned the inscribed parchment into a vest, choosing sections that contained the worst of the biblical curses. Ceremonial plaques commemorate some of the 5,000 Jewish communities wiped out by the Nazis. ⊠ *Mt. Zion,* ☎ *02/671–5105.* ☞ *NIS 10 ($2.50).* ☉ *Sun.–Thurs. 8–5, Fri. 8–1:30.*

⑱ **Dormition Abbey.** Built of limestone, with a black dome, ornamented turrets at each "corner," and a tall clock tower, this large German Benedictine church stands on a site given by the Turkish sultan to Kaiser Wilhelm II during the kaiser's 1898 visit to Jerusalem; it was dedicated in 1910. The echoing interior is ringed by six small recessed chapels. At the eastern end is a large Byzantine-style apse with a wall mosaic of Jesus and Mary. The mosaic floor is decorated with expanding circles of names of the Trinity, the evangelists, the disciples, the Old Testament prophets, and the signs of the zodiac. In the basement is a cenotaph with the carved-stone figure of Mary in repose, embracing the tradition of her "dormition," which holds that she did not die but fell into eternal sleep. Among the little chapels on the lower level is one donated by the Ivory Coast, whose wooden figures and motifs are inlaid with ivory. The premises include a bookstore and a pleasant coffee shop. ⊠ *Mt. Zion,* ☎ *02/671–9927.* ☞ *Free.* ☉ *Mon.–Thurs. and Sat. 8–noon and 12:30–6; Fri. 8–noon and 2–6; Sun. 9:30–noon and 12:30–6.*

⑮ **Jaffa Gate.** The gate got its name from its westerly orientation, toward the once-important Mediterranean harbor of Jaffa, now part of Tel Aviv. In Arabic, the gate is called Bab el-Halil, the Gate of the Beloved (referring to Abraham, the "Beloved of God" in Muslim tradition), because from here another road strikes south toward Hebron—El-Halil in Arabic—where Abraham is buried. The vehicle entrance was created by the Ottoman Turks in 1898 to accommodate the carriage of the visiting German emperor, Kaiser Wilhelm II. In December 1917, during the First World War, the victorious British general Allenby had a different approach: he and his staff dismounted from their horses in order to enter the holy city with appropriate humility. The older bent gate is attributed by the Arabic inscription outside it to the Ottoman Turkish sultan Suleiman the Magnificent (1536).

On your left as you enter, a Tourist Information Office offers maps and information; next to the office is a tiny recessed terrace fronted by a grille. Between the two tall cypress trees in the recess are two Muslim tombs, said to be those of the architects of Suleiman's city walls. One story says that the angry Suleiman had them executed for rebuilding the city walls without encompassing Mt. Zion and the venerated Tomb of David. Another version has it that they met their fate for being too good at their jobs: Suleiman wanted to make sure they never built anything grander for anyone else.

Opposite the Tourist Information Office is a huge stone tower built of well-cut stones reminiscent of those in the Western Wall. Built 2,000 years ago by King Herod the Great, and called Phatza'el after his brother, it is the last survivor of the three towers that guarded the gate. It has become known as the Tower of David, but it has as little to do with that biblical king as the photogenic 16th-century Turkish tower, *also* known as the Tower of David, visible from outside Jaffa Gate. Apart from this tower, there are scant remains of Herod's fortress, but in later centuries Crusaders and Muslims continued to fortify this vulnerable spot in the city's defenses, creating the Citadel (as it is still known locally today).

**Old City walls.** Built between 1536 and 1542 by the Ottoman sultan Suleiman the Magnificent, the walls incorporate clearly visible chunks of the so-called First Wall, some 21 centuries old. In some places, the older stones, distinguished by the chiseled border characteristic of the Hasmonean period, project out of the line of the Turkish wall, tracing the foundations of ancient defense towers.

**⑰ Ramparts Walk.** From atop the Old City walls, you'll get to play voyeur as you catch glimpses into the gardens and courtyards of the Armenian Quarter, which occupies the southwestern quadrant of the Old City. As you walk along the narrow stone catwalks and peer through the crenellated shooting niches, you'll also gain some empathy for the medieval soldiers who defended the city under great duress. There are a large number of fairly high steps on this route; the railings are secure, but small children should not walk alone.

The northern section of the Ramparts Walk is accessible at two points—the Jaffa Gate and the Damascus Gate—and you can exit at either of these as well as at the New Gate. There is no connection at the Jaffa Gate between the two sections of the walk. ☎ *02/625–4403.* ✉ *NIS 14 ($3.50); combined ticket with Ophel Archaeological Garden, Damascus Gate, and Hezekiah's Tunnel (on same day only) NIS 35 ($8.75).* ☉ *Sat.–Thurs. 9–4, Fri. and holiday eves 9–2.*

**⑲ Room of the Last Supper.** According to tradition, it was on this location—*inside* the city walls of 2,000 years ago—that Jesus celebrated the Passover seder meal with his disciples. The bread and wine consecrated at the Last Supper became the elements of the Christian Eucharist. Alternately known as the Cenacle or the Coenaculum—the "Upper Room" referred to in the Gospels (Mark 14)—the present room is a large, bare medieval chamber with flagstones and Gothic arches, apparently built in the 14th century. A second tradition identifies the same room with the "one place" of Acts 2, where Jesus's disciples gathered on Pentecost, seven weeks after his death: "They were all filled with the Holy Spirit and began to speak in other tongues . . ."

Incongruously, the chamber has the trappings of a mosque as well: restored stained-glass Arabic inscriptions in the Gothic windows; one window blocked by an ornate mihrab (an alcove indicating the direction of Mecca); two Arabic plaques in the wall; and a Levantine dome. The Muslims were not interested in the site's Christian traditions but in the supposed Tomb of David (☞ *below*) on the level below. ⊠ *Mt. Zion.* ✉ *Free.* ☉ *Sat.–Thurs. 8–5, Fri. 8–1.*

**⑳ Tomb of David.** The Bible refers to Jerusalem, King David's capital in the 10th century BC, as the "City of David," a site that modern archaeologists have identified and excavated to the east of Mt. Zion. Medieval Jewish pilgrims erroneously placed the ancient city on this, the southwestern hill; and because the City of David was also called the "Stronghold of Zion" (II Samuel 5), the hill was named Mt. Zion as well. Since the Bible also relates that David was buried in the City of David, the tomb of the great king was sought—and supposedly found—here. Regardless of its questionable authenticity, at least nine centuries of tears and prayers have sanctified this place.

Enter the antechamber behind the white barred windows (modest dress is required, and men must cover their heads) and pass on to the tomb itself. The cenotaph, a massive stone tomb marker, is draped with a velvet cloth embroidered with stars of David and inscriptions in Hebrew: "David, King of Israel, lives forever" (meaning that David's dynasty, from which the Messiah is to come, is eternal) and "If I forget thee, O Jerusalem, may my right hand lose its cunning" (Psalm 137).

On top of the cenotaph are two beautifully engraved silver canisters, used by Sephardic Jews as containers for Torah scrolls. Behind the cenotaph is an age-blackened stone alcove, thought by scholars to be the oldest remnant of a synagogue in Jerusalem (from about the 5th century AD). In the antechamber opposite the tomb is a mihrab surrounded by green ceramic tiles, which once oriented the Muslim faithful toward Mecca in honor of Nebi Daoud—the prophet David—whom Islam has retroactively beatified. ✉ *Mt. Zion,* ☎ *02/671-9767.* 🎫 *Free.* ☉ *Sun.–Thurs. 8–5, Fri. and Jewish holiday eves 8–2.*

★ ⑯ **Tower of David Museum.** Entered through a gated tower and over a moat, the museum is housed in a series of medieval halls in what is known locally as the citadel (Hametzuda in Hebrew). Confusingly enough, although the name "Tower of David" has traditionally been applied to the 17th-century Turkish minaret at the citadel's southern edge, other traditions attach it to the massive Herodian tower at the opposite end. Neither claimant has the slightest connection to the biblical King David. The museum tells the city's 5,000-year-old history, not with original artifacts but through a variety of interesting visual and audiovisual aids, including models, maps, holograms, and videos. You can rent an audio guide at the entrance. Be sure to inquire about the next screening of the animated introductory film, which has English subtitles.

The site's old stones and arches lend an appropriately antique atmosphere to the entire exhibit, whose galleries are organized by historical period around the citadel's central courtyard. Landscaped archaeological remains in the courtyard form an eye-catching but incomprehensible jumble, except for the massive Herodian tower and the Hasmonean First Wall (2nd–1st centuries BC) to which it is attached. A walk on the citadel's ramparts, with sometimes unexpected panoramas from odd angles, is also worthwhile, though certainly a lesser priority. Ask about the occasional temporary exhibits. ✉ *Jaffa Gate,* ☎ *02/626-5333, 02/626-5310 for recorded info.* 🎫 *NIS 35 ($8.75); electronic audio guide NIS 10 ($2.50).* ☉ *Apr.–Oct., Sun.–Thurs. 9–5, Fri.–Sat. 9–2; Nov.–Mar., Sun.–Thurs. 10–4, Fri.–Sat. 10–2. Free guided tour in English Sun.–Fri. at 11.*

## City of David

The City of David is mentioned in the Bible (II Samuel 5) as a synonym for Jerusalem, once King David had conquered it (1000 BC) from the Jebusites and established it as his capital. In the mid-10th century BC, David's son Solomon expanded the city northward and built the Temple of God on Mt. Moriah, where the Dome of the Rock now stands. In time, Jerusalem spread farther west and north, but in recent years the name "City of David" has been revived to indicate the city's ancient core.

## A Good Walk

Begin at the parking lot outside the Old City walls east of and below Dung Gate. If you're driving, you can park your car here. The entrance to the parking lot is from the steep road that descends at a right angle to the Old City wall. Cross the road, walk 50 yards down it, and take a paved path to your left (east). Fifty yards along, a fence encloses the excavation site known as **Area G** ㉒, one of the areas of the City of David excavated between 1978 and 1985.

The deep Kidron Valley drops sharply away to the east, giving the ancient city its best protection. Close to the present Old City walls was the northern limit of the City of David and the only side not protected by a valley. The city has been conquered at least 35 times in its 5,000-year history, almost always from the north.

From here on, the route is not recommended for visitors who have difficulty with steps. Go down the stairs and follow a small sign on the right to **Warren's Shaft** ㉓, an extraordinary access shaft to the Gihon Spring. Conventional wisdom identifies this as the point where King David's commandos penetrated the city in 1000 BC, though recent excavations near the spring have suggested an alternative route. (At press time, this new excavation, including two massive ancient towers, was being prepared for public opening.) The room at the top of the shaft has several visual aids to help explain the site.

The main stairway continues down to the Kidron Valley. Under a modern building on the right, a short flight of steps descends to the spring itself. This was the original water supply of ancient Jerusalem, and probably the reason the city was first built on this small hill. In 701 BC, in the face of an Assyrian invasion, King Hezekiah built a remarkable water tunnel, a third of a mile long, to bring the spring water to an inner-city reservoir; it's now commonly known as **Hezekiah's Tunnel** ㉔. Walking the tunnel is a memorable experience, but you must bring flashlights or candles and be prepared to walk through thigh-deep water.

The tunnel emerges at a small pool, the "pool of Siloam" in the New Testament story of the healing of the blind man (John 9). Climb the steep road back to the Dung Gate. Bus 1 runs from here to Jaffa Gate and close to the city center.

TIMING

Allow two hours for the walk, three if you walk Hezekiah's Tunnel. The tunnel involves 45 minutes' walking in knee- to thigh-deep water. The sights are closed on Friday afternoon, Saturday, and Jewish religious holidays.

## Sights to See

㉒ **Area G.** Archaeologists, notably Kathleen Kenyon in the 1960s, have sporadically dug up bits of the City of David for more than a century. The most thorough expedition, however, was led by the late Israeli archaeologist Yigal Shiloh from 1978 to 1985. In this sector, he confirmed that the angular pieces of the city wall, seen at the top, dated from the 2nd century BC, but he redated the sloping "stepped structure" to at least the 10th century BC, the time of Israelite kings David and Solomon. It once supported a palace or fortification; in the 7th century BC, a house (now partially restored on a platform) was built against it.

The most intriguing artifacts yielded by the dig were 51 bullae, clay seals used for documents, just as hot wax might be used today. All had personal names impressed on them in ancient Hebrew script. All of the seals were found in one chamber, suggesting that it was used as an archive; and the name on one of the seals—Gemariah ben Shafan, the royal secretary in the days of Jeremiah—reinforces this idea. The clay seals were seared into ceramic permanence, apparently from the fire of the Babylonian destruction of Jerusalem in 586 BC. ✉ *Off Ophel Rd.,* ☎ *02/ 626–2341.* 🎟 *Free.* ☉ *Summer (approximately Apr.–Sept.), Sun.– Thurs. 9–5, Fri. 9–2; winter closes 1 hr earlier.*

NEED A
BREAK?

Immediately opposite the exit from Area G is a vine-shaded **terrace** with a view of the Kidron Valley. The enterprising owner sells soft drinks, fresh orange juice, and Turkish coffee, which you can sip leisurely at one of the stone tables. The toilet facilities are poor, but new ones are available at the visitor center up the hill.

★ ㉔ **Hezekiah's Tunnel.** In 721 BC, the Assyrian Empire destroyed the northern Kingdom of Israel, exiled most of its population into historical oblivion—the so-called Ten Lost Tribes—and subjugated Israel's sister kingdom, Judah, in the south. Twenty years later, Judah revolted against its overlords, triggering a devastating, punitive military invasion. Preparing for an imminent assault by the Assyrians on his capital city of Jerusalem, the Judean king Hezekiah rushed to protect his precious water supply. In the biblical description of the siege, Hezekiah gave instructions to "stop the water of the springs that were outside the city . . . saying, 'Why should the kings of Assyria come and find much water?'" Racing against time, Hezekiah's men dug a water tunnel a third of a mile long through solid rock, one team starting from the Gihon Spring and another from the new inner-city reservoir (called Shilo'ach in Hebrew, Siloam in English). Miraculously, considering the serpentine course of the tunnel, the two teams met in the middle. The chisel marks, the ancient plaster, and the zigzags near the halfway point (each team sought each other by sound) bear witness to the project. Again the Bible: and Hezekiah "closed the upper outlet of the waters of Gihon and directed them down to the west side of the city of David" (II Chronicles 32).

Near the exit of the tunnel (and now in a Turkish museum) an inscription in ancient Hebrew was found in the 19th century: "This is the story of the boring through . . . ," it begins, echoing the biblical account; "the tunnelers hewed the rock, each man toward his fellow, pickax against pickax. And the water flowed from the spring toward the reservoir for 1,200 cubits [577 yards]."

Note the following: there is no lighting in the tunnel, so you must come with a flashlight or a good supply of candles and matches. Because the flow of the spring is unpredictable, the water level varies and can sometimes reach a depth of 3 ft in places. The water is very cool, even in summer. This is no place for very small children or claustrophobes, and although there are guards here, women visiting alone may attract unwanted attention from local youths. ☎ *02/625–4403.* 🎟 *NIS 12 ($3); combined ticket with Ophel Archaeological Garden, Ramparts Walk, and Damascus Gate (on same day only) NIS 35 ($8.75).* ☉ *Sun.– Thurs. 9–4, Fri. and Jewish holiday eves 9–2; last entry to tunnel 45 mins before closing.*

**Kidron Valley.** This valley separates the Old City from the high ridge of the Mount of Olives. Jewish tradition predicts that the Messiah will make his appearance here. The cliff face below the houses on the opposite side of the valley is marked with symmetrical holes, which are mouths of tombs from both the First Temple (Old Testament) and Second Temple (Hellenistic-Roman) periods. From the lookout terrace near the bend in Ophel Road, you can look down and to your left at the impressive group of 2,200-year-old funerary monuments. The huge, square stone structure with the conical roof is known as **Absalom's Pillar**; the one crowned by a pyramidal roof, a solid block of stone cut out of the mountain, is called **Zachariah's Tomb**—but neither has anything to do with the Old Testament personalities for whom they're named. Wealthy Jerusalemites of the Second Temple period had themselves elegantly entombed at the foot of the Mount of Olives to await the Messiah and the resurrection that would follow his coming.

★ ㉓ **Warren's Shaft.** Charles Warren was an inspired British army engineer who explored Jerusalem in 1867. In the City of David he discovered this spacious access shaft, which burrowed under the city wall to a point 40 ft above the Gihon Spring, in the valley. It's assumed that water was hauled up through the shaft in ancient times, perhaps by "the lame and the blind" of II Samuel 5. Conventional wisdom has long maintained that the shaft is pre-Davidic, the actual shaft—called the *tzinnor* (gutter or water shaft) in the Bible—through which David's warriors penetrated the city in 1000 BC. A recent dig around the Gihon spring at the bottom of the hill has uncovered a different access shaft to the spring, protected by two huge towers that date back to the Middle Bronze Age, centuries before David. The biblical story remains intact for the moment, but the famous Warren's Shaft may not have been the place where it occurred.

As you descend into the bowels of the earth, note the ancient chisel marks on the walls. It is now accepted that a good part of the shaft was a natural fissure reamed out by workmen in antiquity. The bottom of the last vertical section is now a dry chamber, walled off from the spring in the Israelite (Old Testament) period. ⊠ *Off Ophel Rd.,* ☎ *02/626–2341.* ✑ *NIS 8 ($2).* ⊙ *Summer, Sun.–Thurs. 9–5, Fri. 9–2; winter, Sun.–Thurs. 9–4, Fri. 9–1.*

# Mount of Olives and East Jerusalem

The sights in this area are for the most part distinctly Christian. Some are well off the beaten path, but the walk, though long, is feasible; you can also cover this route by car or public transportation. A few words of caution: pickpockets continue to be a problem on the Mount of Olives lookout and on the road down to Gethsemane. The walk takes you through East Jerusalem's Arab neighborhoods, areas that Israelis have avoided in recent years because of political tensions. Seek local advice about the advisability of doing this tour at the time you're in the city, and in any event, stick to the main streets and spend your evenings in some other part of town. If you're driving, good parking can be found at the Seven Arches Hotel on the Mount of Olives, the Rockefeller Museum of Archaeology compound, and the American Colony Hotel.

## A Good Drive and Walk

Begin on the **Mount of Olives** ㉕, at the panoramic lookout outside the Seven Arches Hotel. This is the classic picture-postcard view of the Old City, looking west across the Kidron Valley. Below you is a huge and ancient Jewish cemetery; around you are Christian spires and domes.

Leave your car near the Seven Arches Hotel and walk some 150 yards back along the approach road to the hotel. In a bay on your right, through a stone gateway, is a round stone structure about 10 ft in diameter called the **Dome of the Ascension,** built over a rock alleged to bear the foot-

## Exploring East Jerusalem

print of Jesus. Just beyond the dome, the road turns sharply right. Enter the **Pater Noster Convent** ㉖ through a light-gray metal door on your right. Here, it is said, Jesus taught his disciples what is known as the Lord's Prayer, now recalled here in dozens of languages on ceramic tiles.

Walk back toward the hotel. If you're on foot, begin the descent from the Mount of Olives via the steps to your right before the parking lot. If you have a car, you can drive on an asphalt road that breaks off to the right just near the steps, switches back, and then begins a *very* steep descent. Note that despite its narrowness, this is *not* a one-way street!

Just down the steps on the left is a courtyard with a burial complex, said to be the **Tombs of the Prophets** Haggai and Malachi but in reality dating from the Byzantine period.

**Dominus Flevit** ㉗, halfway down the mountain, is a small, modern church that recalls Jesus's sorrowful prediction of the destruction of Jerusalem. The courtyard is a nice place to enjoy the view in peace between waves of tour groups. (Equally worthy of mention are the rest rooms, rare on this route!)

Continue down the hill. This is the traditional Palm Sunday road. The gold onion domes and sculpted white turrets of the Russian **Church of Mary Magdalene,** straight out of a fantasy, can be seen in tantalizing glimpses over a high wall to the right. At the bottom of the road on the left—marked by a platoon of vendors outside—is the **Garden of Gethsemane** ㉘, mentioned in the New Testament as the site of Jesus's arrest. The ancient olive trees and impressive Church of All Nations are the prominent features here.

Gethsemane abuts Jericho Road at the foot of the Mount of Olives. The road bends sharply at this point, and to the right a staircase takes you deep into the subterranean Church of the Assumption, better known by the name of the shrine within it—the **Tomb of the Virgin** ㉙, the presumed burial place of Mary. To the right of the entrance is the Franciscan-administered **Grotto of Gethsemane.**

As you continue toward the Old City, the first left takes you to the City of David, Dung Gate, and Mt. Zion. For this tour, however, continue right. Turn left at the traffic light onto Sultan Suleiman Street. Immediately on your right is a steep driveway leading up to the **Rockefeller Museum of Archaeology** ㉚, with its landmark octagonal tower. Don't park on the street; you can park on the museum grounds. You may want to bring a lunch to enjoy in the shade of the lovely garden.

Continue along Sultan Suleiman Street and turn right at the post office into Saladin Street. Where Saladin Street meets Nablus Road (about 1½ km/1 mi from the Rockefeller Museum of Archaeology), on the right, are the **Tombs of the Kings** ㉛. If you're driving, turn right at the intersection and again into the second street on the right (a dead-end road) to the American Colony Hotel (☞ Lodging, *below*), where you'll find safe parking. If you intend to complete the tour, leave your car here and see the other sights on foot. The immensely impressive tombs, once thought to be of Old Testament vintage, date to the 1st century AD and are the finest such catacombs in Israel.

Continue down Nablus Road, heading back toward the Old City. Almost immediately on your left is the neo-Gothic Anglican St. George's Cathedral, built at the beginning of the 20th century as a copy of New College at Oxford University. Its tower is a landmark in Jerusalem's skyline. Some 500 yards farther, beyond the U.S. Consulate and opposite the bus station, a well-marked narrow lane to the left—Conrad Schick Street—leads to the **Garden Tomb** ㉜.

Back on Nablus Road, turn left and continue for 200 yards. You are now at the Old City walls opposite **Damascus Gate** ㉝. The archaeological remains of the Roman period found beneath the gate are worth your time and the small fee.

You now have several options: return by foot to the American Colony Hotel; take a cab from Damascus Gate to your next destination; walk up Hativat Hatzanhanim Street (outside the Old City, with its walls on your left) toward Jaffa Gate and the New City; walk the Ramparts (☞ Tower of David and Mt. Zion, *above*) to Jaffa Gate; or plunge into the Old City to reach the Via Dolorosa and the Western Wall (left fork inside Damascus Gate) or the Church of the Holy Sepulcher and the Jewish Quarter (right fork).

TIMING

You can easily spend a day on this walk, with a stop for a picnic lunch on the grounds of the Rockefeller Museum of Archaeology. If archaeology is not your thing, you can start early and see most of the sights in time for a leisurely lunch at the American Colony, with just a bit of sightseeing left for the afternoon. The Mount of Olives is best in early morning, when you can see the Old City with the sun at your back, or at sunset on days with some clouds, when the golden glow can compensate for the glare. Several of the Christian sights are closed on Sunday.

## Sights to See

**Church of Mary Magdalene.** Dedicated in 1888, this church is Russian Orthodox and part of the Garden of Gethsemane tradition. It has very limited hours, but its icon-studded interior is well worth a look if you happen to be here at the right time. ✉ *Mt. of Olives*, ☎ *02/628–4371.* 🎟 *Free.* 🕑 *Tues. and Thurs. 10–noon.*

㉝ **Damascus Gate.** The name of the gate reveals its location: it faces north toward Damascus, Syria. Its Hebrew name—Sha'ar Shechem, for the Nablus Gate—delivers the same message. With its tapered carved-stone crenellations and ornamented embrasures, the gate is the most beautiful of the seven still open in the present 16th-century Old City wall. It is also the busiest, the main link between the Old City and the Arab neighborhoods of East Jerusalem.

To the left and below the approach bridge is a surviving arched entrance of the pagan **Roman town** built by Emperor Hadrian in AD 135 on the ruins of its Jewish predecessor. Hadrian's plan to build the town touched off the Jewish Bar Kochba Revolt in AD 132. Excavations just inside the arch (reached by walking to the right of Damascus Gate, then left under the bridge) have brought to light an almost entirely intact Roman tower that connects with the Ramparts Walk (a separate ticket; ☞ Tower of David and Mt. Zion, *above*) and was part of an open plaza from the 2nd-century town. A tall column topped by the emperor's statue once dominated the plaza. With the Christianization of the Roman Empire in the 4th century, the statue was removed; but the column remained, exactly as depicted in the famous 6th-century mosaic floor map of Jerusalem found in Madaba, Jordan (a replica of the map is on view at this site). The column, the point of reference for road distances throughout the country, has not survived, but the Arabic name for the gate—Bab el-Amud, the Gate of the Column—preserves its memory. ✉ *Damascus Gate*, ☎ *02/625–4403.* 🎟 *Roman plaza NIS 8 ($2); combined ticket with Ramparts Walk, Ophel Archaeological Garden, and Hezekiah's Tunnel (on same day only) NIS 35 ($8.75).* 🕑 *Sat.–Thurs. 9–4, Fri. 9–2.*

**Dome of the Ascension.** This building dates from the Crusader period and was once open to the sky. Credulous medieval pilgrims were shown an indentation in the natural rock, said to be the footprint of Jesus as he ascended to heaven, and the identification became part of local lore. The dome is actually Islamic in style, and, curiously, the current caretakers are Muslim. ⊠ *Mt. of Olives.* ⊡ *Small fee, about NIS 4 ($1).* ⊗ *No set hrs; ring bell to enter.*

**㉗ Dominus Flevit.** Designed by Antonio Barluzzi and built between 1953 and 1955, the tear-shape church (whose name means "the Lord wept") provides a potentially tranquil haven—often interrupted by crowds of pilgrims—with a superb view of the Old City. The outstanding feature of the church's simple interior is the picture window facing west, with an iron cross on the altar silhouetted against the Old City and the Dome of the Rock. Although many small archaeological items have been found here, the tradition holding this as the site where Jesus wept over Jerusalem as he prophesied its destruction—"and they shall not leave in thee one stone upon another" (Luke 19)—is apparently no older than the Crusader period. ⊠ *Mt. of Olives,* ☏ *02/627–4931.* ⊡ *Free.* ⊗ *At press time Apr.–Sept., daily 8–6; Oct.–Mar., daily 8–5; site may return to closing 11:45–2:30.*

**㉘ Garden of Gethsemane.** After the Last Supper, Jesus and his disciples came to a "place" called Gethsemane. There he prayed and sweated blood (Matthew 26), and there, in the end, he was betrayed and arrested. The name Gethsemane derives from the Aramaic *gat shamna* or the Hebrew *gat shemanim,* both meaning "oil press." The olive tree, which gives this hill its name (Mount of Olives), grew in greater profusion in antiquity than today, its fruit providing precious lamp oil. The "Garden of the Oil Press" still boasts eight enormous, gnarled trees— still productive—that may, according to some botanists, be as old as Christianity itself.

Within the garden is the **Church of All Nations**, designed by the architect Antonio Barluzzi and dedicated in 1924 on the scanty remains of its Byzantine predecessor. Within each of its interior domes are mosaic symbols of each of the countries that contributed to its building (the seal of the United States is in the first dome as you enter the church; Canada is two up in the same line; and the English dome is the first, nearest the door, in the middle line). The windows are glazed with translucent alabaster in somber browns and purples, creating a mystical atmosphere in the dim interior. At the altar is the so-called Rock of the Agony, where Jesus is said to have endured his Passion, from which comes the older name of the church, **the Basilica of the Agony.** ⊠ *Jericho Rd.,* ☏ *02/628–3264.* ⊡ *Free.* ⊗ *At press time: Apr.–Sept., daily 8–6; Oct.–Mar., daily 8–5; site may return to closing noon–2:30.*

★ **㉜ Garden Tomb.** The theory identifying this site with Calvary and Jesus's burial place goes back to 1883, when the British general Charles Gordon (of later Khartoum fame) spent several months in Jerusalem. From his window just inside the Old City walls, Gordon was struck by the skull-like features of a cliff face north of the Damascus Gate. He was convinced that this, rather than the traditional Calvary, in the Church of the Holy Sepulcher (☞ Old City: The Classic Sights, *above*), was "the place of the skull" (Mark 15) where Jesus was crucified. His conviction was infectious, and after his death a fund-raising campaign in England resulted in the purchase of the adjacent site in 1894. An ancient rock-cut tomb uncovered there some years earlier took on new importance for its proximity to Skull Hill (already becoming known as Gordon's Calvary). Subsequent excavations exposed cisterns and a wine press, features typical of an ancient garden.

The newly formed Garden Tomb Association was jubilant, as all the elements of the Gospel account of Jesus's death and burial were here. Jesus was buried in the fresh tomb of the wealthy Joseph of Arimathea (Matthew 27), and contemporary archaeologists lent their authority to the identification of the tomb as an upper-class burial place of the Second Temple period. Recent research has strongly challenged that conclusion, however. The tomb might be from the Old Testament period, making it too old to have been Jesus's, since his was one "in which no man had yet been laid." It should be noted that the gentle guardians of the Garden Tomb do not insist on the identification of the site as that of Calvary and the tomb of Christ but suggest that (as their brochure puts it) "the features of the Garden . . . provide an atmosphere which brings into focus the relevance of the Death and Resurrection of the Lord Jesus Christ." Indeed, the beautifully tended garden of trees, flower beds, and seats for private meditation makes this an island of tranquillity in the hurly-burly of East Jerusalem. For many Protestant visitors, especially those of Evangelical orientation, this site represents the climax of their pilgrimage to Jerusalem. ⊠ *Conrad Schick St.,* ☏ *02/627–2745.* ⊠ *Free.* ◷ *Mon.–Sat. 8:30–noon and 2–5:30; Sun. service only (nondenominational Protestant in English) at 9.*

**Grotto of Gethsemane.** The rock ceiling in this hewn chapel seems to press down on you. Franciscans identify the *Garden* of Gethsemane with Christ's Passion and this spot with his arrest. ⊠ *Jericho Rd.,* ☏ *02/628–3264.* ⊠ *Free.* ◷ *At press time: Apr.–Sept., daily 8–6; Oct.–Mar., daily 8:30–5; site may return to closing noon–2:30.*

★ ㉕ **Mount of Olives.** The Mount of Olives has been bathed in sanctity—both past and future—since time immemorial. Separating you from the Old City is the Kidron Valley, which continues south for a way before breaking east and beginning its steep descent to the Dead Sea. On the slope beneath you, and spreading off to your left, is the vast **Jewish cemetery,** the oldest cemetery still in use anywhere in the world. Jews have been buried on the Mount of Olives for more than 2,000 years to await the coming of the Messiah and the resurrection to follow. It is said that elsewhere you die and disintegrate; in Jerusalem you die and mingle. The raised structures over the graves are merely tomb markers, not crypts; burial is still below ground.

In the Old City wall facing you, and just to the right of the Dome of the Rock, is the blocked-up, double-arched Gate of Mercy, or Golden Gate. Jewish tradition holds that the Messiah will enter Jerusalem this way; Christian tradition says he already has. To the south of the Dome of the Rock is the black-domed El-Aqsa Mosque, behind which are the stone arches of the Jewish Quarter. Some distance behind the Dome of the Rock is the large, gray dome of the Church of the Holy Sepulcher. To the left of the Old City, the cone-roofed Dormition Abbey and its adjacent tower mark the top of Mt. Zion, today outside the walls but within the city of the Second Temple period.

㉖ **Pater Noster Convent.** The focal point of this Carmelite convent is a grotto, traditionally identified as the place where Jesus taught his disciples the so-called Lord's Prayer: "Our Father [*Pater Noster*], Who art in Heaven . . . " (Mark 11; Luke 11). The site was purchased by the Princesse de la Tour d'Auvergne of France in 1868 and the convent built on the site of earlier Byzantine and Crusader structures. The ambitious Basilica of the Sacred Heart, begun here in the 1920s and designed to follow the lines of Constantine's 4th-century Basilica of Eleona, was never completed; its aisles, open to the sky, are now incongruously lined with pine trees, and its altar is more reminiscent of an Aztec high place than a Catholic church. The princess, entombed in a beautiful marble sarcophagus, lies in state in the cloister, oblivious to the abandonment of the master plan. Ceramic plaques lining the cloister walls quote the Lord's Prayer in some 100 different languages. ⊠ *Mt. of Olives,* ☎ *02/626–4904.* ⬚ *Free.* ☉ *Mon.–Sat. 8:30–12:30 and 3–5.*

③⓪ **Rockefeller Museum of Archaeology.** Built in the 1930s during the British Mandate, the stone halls of this museum still have an old-world atmosphere. The chronological presentation of its fine archaeological collection recalls the British Museum. If you have only a passing interest in archaeology, the Israel Museum's finely presented collection will probably suffice (☞ Center City, *below*); the Rockefeller is for the enthusiast.

The finds are all from Israel, dating from prehistoric times to around AD 1700. Among the most important exhibits are cultic masks from Neolithic Jericho, ivories from Canaanite (Bronze Age) Megiddo, the famous Israelite "Lachish Letters" (6th century BC), Herodian inscriptions, and decorative reliefs from Hisham's Palace, in Jericho, and from the Church of the Holy Sepulcher. ⊠ *Sultan Suleiman St.,* ☎ *02/628– 2251.* ⬚ *NIS 26 ($6.50); combined ticket with Israel Museum (good for 2 wks) NIS 37 ($9.25).* ☉ *Sun.–Thurs. 10–5, Fri.–Sat. 10–2.*

②⑨ **Tomb of the Virgin.** The Gothic facade of the underground Church of the Assumption, which contains this shrine, clearly dates it to the Crusader era (12th century), but the tradition that this is where the Virgin Mary was interred and then "assumed" into heaven apparently goes back to the Byzantine period. In an otherwise gloomy church—hung with age-darkened icons and brass lamps—the marble sarcophagus, thought to date from the 12th century, remains illuminated. The Status Quo Agreement in force in the Church of the Holy Sepulcher and Bethlehem's Church of the Nativity pertains here, too: the Greek Orthodox, Armenian Orthodox, and even Muslims control different parts of the property. The Roman Catholic Franciscans were expelled in 1757, a loss of privilege bitterly recalled to this day. ⊠ *Jericho Rd.* ⬚ *Free.* ☉ *Daily 6–noon and 2:30–5.*

③① **Tombs of the Kings.** These impressive catacombs were explored in the 19th century by the Frenchman Félicien de Saulcy, who accepted the local tradition identifying them with the biblical kings of Judah. Royal tombs they were, but they weren't quite that old. In the 1st century AD, Queen Helene of Adiabene, a country on the border of Persia, converted to Judaism and came to live and die in the holy city. Although she built her palaces in the onetime City of David in the south of the city, she and her descendants were buried here.

Wide, rock-hewn steps descend to rain-catchment pools and into a spacious courtyard, all excavated out of solid rock. The entrance to the tombs is across a porch that once boasted two massive stone columns and still has its Hellenistic-style frieze, above. The "rolling stone" that once sealed the mouth of the catacombs is still in situ, a graphic example of those described in the New Testament.

The "weeping chamber" immediately inside the low doorway has rock benches for mourners and tiny triangular niches for oil lamps. Other chambers branching off this one contain the many alcoves and ledges where the dead were laid, wrapped in shrouds. ⊠ *Saladin St.,* ☎ *no phone.* ⬚ *NIS 3 (75¢).* ☉ *Mon.–Sat. 8–1 and 3–5.*

NEED A
BREAK?

The **American Colony Hotel** (✉ Nablus Rd., ☎ 02/627–9777) is a
19th-century limestone building with cane furniture, Armenian ceramic
tiles, and a delightful courtyard. The food is generally very good, and a
light lunch or afternoon tea in the cool lobby lounge, at the poolside
restaurant, or on the patio can make for a well-earned break.

**Tombs of the Prophets.** The tradition that holds these to be the burial
places of the prophets Haggai and Malachi is spurious, but the site is
interesting in its own right: it's a burial cave from the Byzantine period, about 1,500 years ago. From the round entrance hall, three passages radiate out to meet the two semicircular inner corridors containing
the cave's 26 burial niches. ✉ Mt. of Olives. 🎟 Gratuity for resident
attendant. ⊘ No fixed hrs; usually open.

## West Jerusalem

Understandably, travelers tend to focus on the historical and religious
sights on the eastern side of town; but exploring West Jerusalem gives
more insight into the contemporary life in Israel's largest city. These
attractions are most easily accessible by car or by a combination of buses,
short cab rides, and a little patience.

## A Good Drive

Begin at **Yad Vashem** ㉞, the national Holocaust memorial and museum,
700 yards west of Mt. Herzl. Only Bus 99 stops at the site, but Mt.
Herzl, a 10-minute walk away, is served by many lines (Buses 18, 20
and 27 run from the city center). The experience of the Holocaust is
so deeply seared into the Jewish national psyche that understanding it
goes a long way toward understanding the Israelis themselves.

A good plan for seeing this complex site is the following: walk up the
slope to the right of the bookstore near the entrance to visit the small
but riveting Children's Memorial. Continue past the tall aluminum
memorial to the Jewish resistance to the heavy basalt-and-concrete Hall
of Remembrance. Step down through the carob trees of the Avenue of
the Righteous and turn right onto Warsaw Ghetto Square. Here is the
entrance to the Historical Museum. The Art Museum is in the same
building, accessible from the end of the Historical Museum or by a separate rear entrance. Scattered around the grounds are many impressive sculptures. From the parking lot a road descends (about 1 km/
½ mi) to the Valley of the Communities. If you're on foot, a path to
the left of Warsaw Ghetto Square (opposite the museum entrance) will
lead you down to the valley by a shorter route.

Return toward Herzl Boulevard, but turn left into the large parking
lot that abuts it (*before* you reach the traffic lights). This is the entrance
to **Mt. Herzl (National Memorial Park)** ㉟, named for Theodor Herzl, the
founder of the modern Zionist movement, whose grave is at its summit.
The path that begins at the Herzl Museum entrance eventually turns right
across a huge plaza (used for state ceremonies) to the unadorned, black
stone grave marker. To the left (west) of the grave site, a path leads down
to a section containing the graves of national leaders, among them Golda
Meir and assassinated prime minister Yitzhak Rabin.

Continue west for a few yards, descending to the **Mt. Herzl Military
Cemetery** ㊱. The paths through the cemetery bear around to the right,
double back to the cemetery entrance, and reach Herzl Boulevard 300
yards below the first entrance where you entered Mt. Herzl. An alternative is to enter the military cemetery directly, without going through
the park.

One hundred yards down Herzl Boulevard from the entrance to Mt.
Herzl, turn right at the next traffic light, into Harav Uziel Street. After

2 km (1 mi)—keep bearing left—the road passes the Holyland Hotel, and 150 yards farther is the **Second Temple Period Model** ㊲, a huge open-air scale model of Jerusalem as it existed 2,000 years ago. Park and take the short path on the left.

If you're driving, return to the intersection with Herzl Boulevard and turn left. Stay on the winding main road, the name of which changes several times: Kiryat Hayovel Road, Hantke Street, and Henrietta Szold Road. The road swings sharply right to Hadassah Hospital. There is a relatively remote parking lot on the hospital grounds and a free shuttle bus to the main buildings. What draws visitors here are the world-famous, stained-glass **Chagall windows** ㊳ in the hospital's synagogue. The theme is biblical: Jacob's deathbed blessings on his sons. The effect is magical.

As you leave from the hospital's main entrance, turn right and descend to where the road joins Route 386. Turn right again, reentering Jerusalem through the village of **Ein Kerem.** Dominating the center of the village (on the left as you approach from the west, from the bottom of the village) is the **Church of St. John the Baptist** ㊴, its orange tile roof a distinctive local landmark. Opposite the church, a short street takes you to the small Spring of the Virgin. Turn right and climb a steep, stepped street, past a Russian Orthodox monastery, to the impressive Franciscan **Church of the Visitation** ㊵, said to have been the home of John the Baptist's parents, Zechariah and Elizabeth.

Return to the main road of the village and turn right onto the steep road that emerges at Mt. Herzl.

TIMING

This tour takes a full day, even with the convenience of your own car. Allow two to three hours to do Yad Vashem justice, though you can see its highlights in less time. It's best to visit the Second Temple Period Model *after* you've become familiar with the Old City of today; 45 minutes is the most you need here. Note that Yad Vashem, Mt. Herzl, and the Chagall windows close very early on Friday and are not open on Saturday or on Jewish religious holidays.

## Sights to See

㊳ **Chagall windows/Hadassah Hospital.** Hadassah is one of the two largest general hospitals in the Middle East and is the teaching hospital for Hebrew University's medical and dental schools. When the Hadassah organization approached the Russian-born Jewish artist Marc Chagall in 1959 about designing stained-glass windows for the synagogue at the new hospital, he was delighted and contributed his work for free. Taking his inspiration from Jacob's deathbed blessings on his sons (Genesis 49) and, to a lesser extent, from Moses' valediction to the tribes of Israel (Deuteronomy 33), Chagall created 12 vibrant windows in primary colors, with an ark full of characteristically Chagallian beasts and a scattering of Jewish and esoteric symbols. The innovative techniques of the Reims glassmakers give the wafer-thin windows an astounding illusion of depth in many places. To see them, take the tour of the synagogue, which includes a film about the hospital. Buses 19 and 27 serve the hospital. ⊠ *Hadassah Hospital, Henrietta Szold Rd., Ein Kerem,* ☎ *02/677–6271.* ⊒ *NIS 10 ($2.50).* ◷ *Guided tours of synagogue Sun.–Thurs. at 8:30, 9:30, 10:30, 11:30, 12:30, and 2:30; Fri. and Jewish holiday eves 9:30, 10:30, 11:30.*

㊴ **Church of St. John the Baptist.** The orange tile roof of this large, late-17th-century Franciscan church is a landmark in Ein Kerem (☞ *below*). Though not mentioned by name in the New Testament, the village has long been identified as the birthplace of John the Baptist, a tradition that apparently goes back to the Byzantine period (5th century AD). The church's old paintings and glazed tiles alone make it worth a visit, and you can also see the grotto where John the Baptist is said to have been born. ⊠ *Ein Kerem St., Ein Kerem,* ☎ *02/641–3639.* ⊑ *Free.* ☉ *At press time: Apr.–Sept., daily 8–6; Oct.–Mar. 8–5; site may return to closing Sat., and Sun.–Fri. noon–2:30.*

**⑩ Church of the Visitation.** Built over what is thought to have been the home of John the Baptist's parents, Zechariah and Elizabeth, this church is high up the hillside in Ein Kerem (☞ *below*), with a wonderful view of the valley and the surrounding wooded hills. When Mary, pregnant with Jesus, came to visit her pregnant cousin, the aging Elizabeth, "the babe leaped in [Elizabeth's] womb" with joy at recognizing the unborn Jesus, and Mary pronounced the paean to God known as the Magnificat ("My soul doth magnify the Lord . . . ."—Luke 1). One wall of the church courtyard is covered with ceramic tiles quoting the Magnificat in 41 languages. The upper church is adorned with large wall paintings depicting the various mantles with which Mary has been endowed—Mother of God, Refuge of Sinners, Dispenser of All Grace, Help of Christians—and the Immaculate Conception. Other frescoes depict Hebrew women of the Bible also known for their "hymns and canticles," as the Franciscan guide puts it. ⊠ *Ein Kerem,* ☎ *02/641–7291.* ⊑ *Free.* ☉ *At press time: Apr.–Sept., daily 8–6; Oct.–Mar., daily 8–5. Site may return to closing Sat. and Sun.–Fri. 11:45–2:30.*

**Ein Kerem.** Now part of Jerusalem, this village boasts a mix of its original working-class population along with artists and professionals. Many live in renovated old stone buildings that have become upscale showpieces. Among the landmarks here are the ☞ **Church of St. John the Baptist** and the ☞ **Church of the Visitation.** Ein Kerem is served by Bus 17.

**㉟ Mt. Herzl (National Memorial Park).** The simple grave marker of Theodor Herzl, founder of modern Zionism, lies at the top of Mt. Herzl, inscribed in Hebrew with the name HERZL. The site is beautifully landscaped, with cedars of Lebanon lording it over the native pine and cypress. The **Herzl Museum,** to the left of the entrance, preserves Herzl's Viennese study intact. (The museum was under renovation at press time.)

In 1894, the Budapest-born Herzl was the Paris correspondent for a Vienna newspaper when the Dreyfus treason trial hit the headlines. The anti-Semitic outbursts that Herzl encountered in cosmopolitan Paris shocked him—Dreyfus, a Jewish officer in the French army, had actually been framed and was later exonerated—and thereafter Herzl devoted himself to the problem of Jewish vulnerability in "foreign" host countries, and the need, in his eyes, of creating a Jewish state where Jews could control their own destiny. The result of his activities was the first World Zionist Congress, held in Basel, Switzerland, in 1897. That year Herzl wrote in his diary: "If not in five years, then in 50, [a Jewish state] will become reality." The United Nations approved the idea just 50 years later, in November 1947. Herzl died in 1904, and his remains were brought to Israel in 1949.

To the left (west) of the grave site, a gravel path leads down to a section containing the **graves of national leaders,** among them assassinated prime minister Yitzhak Rabin; his predecessors of the 1960s and '70s Levi Eshkol and Golda Meir; and Israeli presidents Zalman Shazar and Chaim Herzog. ⊠ *Herzl Blvd.,* ☎ *02/651–1108.* ⊑ *Free.* ☉ *Park summer (daylight saving time), Sun.–Thurs. 8–6:45, Fri. and holiday eves 8–1; winter, Sun.–Thurs. 8–4:45, Fri. and holiday eves 8–1.*

**㊱ Mt. Herzl Military Cemetery.** The tranquillity and well-kept greenery of Israel's largest military cemetery almost belie its purpose. Different sections are reserved for the casualties of the various wars the nation has fought. The large number of headstones, all identical, is a sobering reminder of the price Israel has paid for national independence and security. Officers and privates are buried alongside one another, expressing the Israeli approach that lost lives are mourned equally, regardless of rank. ✉ *Herzl Blvd.,* ☏ *02/643–7257.* 🎟 *Free.* 🕑 *Daily.*

**㊲ Second Temple Period Model.** Seven years in the building, this huge open-air model—the size of a tennis court—represents ancient Jerusalem at its largest, in the mid-1st century AD. The scale is 1:50, roughly ¼ inch to the foot. Although built around a concrete core, the miniature structures are faced with the same Jerusalem stone as the originals. The model's designer, the late Professor Michael Avi-Yonah, was guided by ancient literary descriptions of Jerusalem and modern archaeological finds. Public works, such as the city's fortifications and King Herod's great reconstructed marble temple (the Second Temple), are thought to be substantially accurate, although private buildings are more generic, reflecting the known architectural style of the period. The model is constantly evolving; whenever new evidence contradicts old assumptions, elements of the model are changed. Pick up an explanatory booklet in the bookstore, or eavesdrop on one of the many guided tours. Buses 21 and 21A arrive here from the city center and the Central Bus Station. At press time, the admission had been substantially increased to include the temporary but long-running exhibit of scale-models of famous buildings in contemporary Israel, viewed in an adjacent garden. ✉ *Grounds of Holyland Hotel,* ☏ *02/643–7777.* 🎟 *NIS 44 ($11).* 🕑 *Daily 8 AM–11 PM.*

**★ ㉞ Yad Vashem.** It's no accident that Yad Vashem—the world's primary national Holocaust memorial and museum—is a mandatory stop on the itineraries of most official guests of the State of Israel. Created in 1953 by an act of the Knesset, it holds the largest Holocaust archive in the world, with more than 55 million documents. Through its museum, research, and publication departments and its youth-education programs, Yad Vashem attempts not merely to document the Holocaust but to convey the challenge of understanding it, especially to younger generations. The name Yad Vashem—"an everlasting memorial"—comes from the biblical book of Isaiah.

Perhaps the most riveting component of Yad Vashem is the **Children's Memorial.** Of the 6 million Jews murdered by the Nazis in World War II, fully a quarter were children, a fact that emphasizes the single-mindedness of the "Final Solution." In trying to do the seemingly impossible—to convey the enormity of the crime without numbing the visitor's emotions or losing sight of the victims' individuality—architect Moshe Safdie found an ingenious solution. Five candles and some 500 mirrors create an infinity of living flames in the dark interior (there are no steps, and guide rails are provided throughout), while recorded narrators intone the names, ages, and countries of origin of known victims. The effect is electrifying.

The **Avenue of the Righteous,** which encircles the site, contains some 5,500 trees bearing plaques with the names of Gentiles in Europe who risked and sometimes lost their lives trying to save Jews from the Nazis. Raoul Wallenberg, King Christian X of Denmark, Corrie ten Boom, and Oskar Schindler are among the more famous honorees. The **Hall of Remembrance** is a heavy basalt-and-concrete building that houses an eternal flame, with the names of the death and concentration camps inscribed on the floor.

The **Historical Museum,** entered from Warsaw Ghetto Square, is the centerpiece of Yad Vashem. Through artifacts, photographs, videos, recordings, and explanations in English, it documents the period from Hitler's rise to power in 1933 through the following 12 nightmarish years to the postwar turmoil that precipitated the birth of Israel. In the same building is the **Art Museum,** a simultaneously beautiful and heart-wrenching display of art and sculpture by Jewish artists—known and unknown, adults and children—who either perished in the Holocaust (while their work survived) or who survived the period and expressed their experiences in their art.

The **Valley of the Communities** was a project of individual Holocaust survivors and survivors' organizations. Walls of enormous rough-hewn limestone boulders create a series of canyons, each representing a region of Nazi Europe, laid out geographically. The names of 5,000 destroyed Jewish communities are inscribed in the stone, with the largest letters highlighting those that were particularly important in prewar Europe.

There is an information booth next to the bookstore at the entrance. Photography is permitted in the Historical Museum but not in the Children's Memorial or the Art Museum. There is a cafeteria next to the parking lot. ✉ *Near Herzl Blvd.,* ☎ *02/675–1611.* 🎟 *Free.* ⊙ *Sun.–Thurs. 9–4:45, Fri. and Jewish holiday eves 9–1:45.* 🕿

# Center City

West Jerusalem's downtown and near-downtown areas are a mix of old neighborhoods and new limestone edifices, of monuments and markets, of landscapes and peoplescapes. Add the Givat Ram district—readily accessible by foot or a quick bus or cab ride—with the Israel Museum, the Bible Lands Museum, and the Knesset, and you have an absorbing day's sightseeing.

## A Good Walk and Drive

Begin in the **Yemin Moshe** neighborhood at the famous **Montefiore's Windmill** ㊶, named for the Anglo-Jewish benefactor who built it in the mid-19th century. The restored carriage in which Moses Montefiore once traveled the country was on display here until it was torched by vandals some years ago; the one you see now is an exact replica. Walk to the edge of the patio adjacent to the windmill—immediately below you is the long roof of **Mishkenot She'ananim,** the first settlement outside the walls of Jerusalem, built by Montefiore in 1860. Today it's a prestigious guest house for visiting artists, writers, and musicians.

Separating you from Mt. Zion and the Old City is the deep **Hinnom Valley,** mentioned in the Bible (Joshua 15) as the border between the Israelite tribes of Judah (to the south) and Benjamin (to the north) and as the site of renewed pagan sacrifices in the 7th century BC. As you face the valley, look to the right. On a hill just a few hundred yards away is the Scots Church of St. Andrew. Below and to the left of the church, on the bend in the valley known as Ketef Hinnom (the Hinnom Shoulder), an excavation in the late 1970s uncovered a series of tombs. Cut out of the rocky scarp and still visible today, the tombs in turn yielded a treasure trove of archaeological finds.

To your left is the prestigious neighborhood of Yemin Moshe, one of Jerusalem's most affluent. The top of Yemin Moshe is separated from **King David Street** ㊷ by a small park. Follow the street a short distance to the landmark King David Hotel, a handsome, rectangular limestone building with a back terrace overlooking some well-kept gardens and the Old City walls. Across the street is the imposing YMCA; you can take the elevator to the top of its tower for stunning panoramas.

Turn left onto Abraham Lincoln Street, just after the YMCA. From the small intersection 100 yards beyond it, a narrow pedestrian lane (George Eliot Street) continues in the same direction, emerging at Agron Street, next to the U.S. Consulate-General. Cross Agron and enter **Independence Park** by way of the road 100 yards to your right.

The park's crossroad emerges at Hillel Street, to the north. Immediately across the road is Yoel Moshe Salomon Street, and to the right and parallel to it is Yosef Rivlin Street, named after two of the seven founders of **Nahalat Shiva** �43, the second neighborhood built outside the city walls, established in 1869. At the other end of Salomon Street is Zion Square, where Jaffa Road, Jerusalem's main thoroughfare, is met by **Ben Yehuda Street** �44. If you've had enough for one day, turn up Ben Yehuda (on your left) and check out its shops and cafés.

If you still have time, cross Jaffa Road at Zion Square and turn left. The first street on the right is Harav Kook, named after Rabbi Kook, chief rabbi of British Mandate–era Palestine. Two hundred yards up the road on the left, a signposted path takes you to **Bet Ticho** �45, a magnificent limestone house that houses a small art exhibit and a good restaurant. A few blocks away, up Harav Kook St., across Hanevi'im St., and down Ethiopian St., is the fascinating, old-world, ultra-Orthodox neighborhood Me'a She'arim. Keep a low profile here: women's dress must be modest—long skirts and sleeves—and no photography is permitted on Shabbat.

Return to Jaffa Road and turn right. Cross the intersection of King George and Strauss streets and keep going. Six hundred yards farther up Jaffa Road, on your left just beyond the high-rise Clal Center, is the entrance to the **Machaneh Yehuda** �46 produce market. At the opposite end of Machaneh Yehuda is Agrippas Street. Across the street and through an arch is a small, somewhat neglected park where you can sit under a tree and munch on your market buys. A left turn on Agrippas Street, on the other hand, brings you down to King George Street and the city center. Bus 9—make sure you take it in the right direction (outside the Hamashbir department store)—will get you in 10 minutes to Givat Ram, site of the Knesset, the Israel Museum, and the Bible Lands Museum.

To drive to Givat Ram, take the wide, divided Ruppin Road west from the tall, white Wolfson Buildings (on the edge of the Rehavia neighborhood, opposite Sacher Park). Five hundred yards from Sacher Park, at the first traffic light, turn right. The modern, flattop building on the rise to your right is the **Knesset** �47, Israel's parliament. Park on the street, and walk up to the square in front of the Knesset. City Bus 9 drops you right at the main gate. Note: you'll have to produce your passport for identification and will be asked to check your camera before entering the building.

The world-class **Israel Museum** �48 was built in 1965 as a series of glass and white-stone pavilions sprawled over a 22-acre hilltop across Ruppin Road from the Knesset; Buses 9, 17, and 24 stop here. A shuttle bus for passengers with disabilities runs on request from the main gate to the main entrance 200 yards away. The museum's eclectic collection includes the famous Dead Sea Scrolls and extensive art exhibits.

The **Bible Lands Museum** �49, across the Israel Museum parking lot, is highly recommended for the student of ancient cultures.

TIMING

This route can easily be separated into the walk (2–2½ hours, not counting breaks) and the Givat Ram cluster of the Knesset and the two museums. Except for the first part of the route (up to the YMCA), the walk is pointless on Saturday, when the downtown area is dead. Friday is great, but shops close early in the afternoon for the Sabbath. You can *view* the Knesset from the outside any time, but there are tours only Sunday and Thursday morning. Allow at least 1½ hours for the tour, more in summer, when the lines are longer. The museums are closed Friday afternoon and have shorter hours on Saturday; visiting during their weekly evening hours is a time-efficient option. The eclectic Israel Museum demands from two to six hours; the Bible Lands Museum is pure archaeology—conceptually challenging, and best done with a local guide.

## Sights to See

④④ **Ben Yehuda Street.** Ben Yehuda has become the nerve center of downtown Jerusalem. Part of the downtown triangle formed with King George Street and Jaffa Road, the street is named after Eliezer Ben Yehuda, who in the late 19th century almost single-handedly revived Hebrew as a modern spoken language. The open-air mall is called the Midrachov in Hebrew, a combination of *midracha* (sidewalk) and *rechov* (street). Cafés have tables out on the cobblestones; vendors display cheap, arty items like funky jewelry and prints; and buskers are everywhere, playing tunes old and new, good and indifferent. It's a great place to sip coffee and watch the passing crowd.

④⑤ **Bet Ticho.** This fine, large stone house was built by Dr. A. A. Ticho, a renowned early 20th-century ophthalmologist. Ticho married his cousin, Anna, a trained nurse, who had emigrated from Eastern Europe to join him in his pioneering struggle against the endemic scourge of trachoma. Her artistic talent gradually earned her a reputation as a brilliant chronicler—in charcoal, pen, and brush—of the landscape of Jerusalem's hills. Set among pine trees, off the busy streets of downtown, Bet Ticho houses a permanent exhibit of Anna Ticho's works and a very good restaurant serving light fare (☞ *Dining, below*). ⊠ *Ticho La.*, ☎ 02/624–5068. ⊠ *Free.* ⊗ *Sun., Mon., Wed., Thurs. 10–5; Tues. 10–10; Fri. 10–2; Sat. from nightfall to 10 PM.*

④⑨ **Bible Lands Museum.** Most archaeological museums group artifacts according to their place of origin (Egyptian, Babylonian, and so on), but the curators here have abandoned this method in favor of a chronological display. This allows a comparison of objects of neighboring cultures of the same period, the better to explore cross-cultural interactions and influences. The museum was the brainchild of Canadian collector Elie Borowski, whose personal collection of ancient artifacts forms its core.

The exhibits cover a period of more than 6,000 years—from the prehistoric Neolithic period to that of the Byzantine Empire—and sweep geographically from Afghanistan to Nubia (present-day Sudan). Rare clay vessels, fertility idols, cylinder seals, ivories, and sarcophagi fill the soaring, naturally lit galleries. Look especially for the ancient Egyptian wooden coffin, in a stunning state of preservation. ⊠ *Givat Ram*, ☎ 02/561–1066. ⊠ *NIS 28 ($7).* ⊗ *Sun.–Tues. and Thurs. 9:30–5:30, Wed. 9:30–9:30 (Nov.–Mar. 1:30–9:30), Fri. and Jewish holiday eves 9:30–2, Sat. 11–3. Guided tours in English Sun.–Fri. at 10:15 (Wed. at 5:30 in addition), Sat. at 11.*

**Hinnom Valley.** The Hinnom Valley achieved notoriety in the 7th century BC during the long reign of Menasseh (697–640 BC), son of King Hezekiah. Menasseh was an idolater who "burned his sons as an offering [to the god Moloch] in the valley of the son of Hinnom" (II Chronicles 33). The very name of the valley in Hebrew—Gei Ben Hinnom, contracted to Gehennom or Gehenna—has become a synonym for hell in both Hebrew and Yiddish.

At the bend in the valley, below the fortresslike Scots Church of St. Andrew, Israeli archaeologist Gabriel Barkai discovered in the early 1980s a series of Old Testament–period tombs cut out of the rocky scarp. An unplundered pit came to light that contained "grave goods" like clay vessels and jewelry. The most spectacular finds were two tiny rolled strips of silver designed to be worn around the neck as amulets. When experts finally unrolled the fragile pieces, they discovered the biblical priestly benediction inscribed in the ancient Hebrew script: "The Lord bless you and keep you; the Lord cause his face to shine upon you and be gracious unto you; the Lord give you peace." This text dates to the 7th century BC, five centuries earlier than the Dead Sea Scrolls, and is the oldest biblical passage ever found.

**Independence Park.** This is a lovely spot for lounging around, throwing Frisbees, or eating a picnic lunch in warm weather. It also holds a Muslim cemetery with several well-preserved tombs dating from the 13th century. A huge reservoir just below the graves, known as the Mamilla Pool, is probably medieval, though it may have even earlier origins.

★ ㊽  **Israel Museum.** Some of these exhibits are among the best of their kind in the world, especially the ones devoted to archaeology and Judaica. The most distinctive edifice in the museum complex is the white, domelike Shrine of the Book, which houses the famous **Dead Sea Scrolls,** arguably the most important archaeological find ever made in the region. The first of the 2,000-year-old scrolls was discovered by a Bedouin boy in 1947 in the Judean Desert, not far from the Dead Sea. The adventures of these priceless artifacts before they finally came to rest here is the stuff of which Indiana Jones movies are made (☞ Dead Sea Region *in* Chapter 2). The shape of the pavilion in which they're housed was inspired by the lids of the clay jars in which the first scrolls were found.

The scrolls were written in the Second Temple period by a fundamentalist Jewish sect, generally identified as the Essenes. All of the archaeological, laboratory, and textual evidence dates the earliest of the scrolls to the 2nd century BC; none could have been written later than AD 68, the year in which their home community, Qumran, was destroyed by the Romans. Written on parchment, and still in an extraordinary state of preservation because of the exceptional dryness of the Dead Sea region, the scrolls contain the oldest Hebrew manuscripts of the Old Testament ever found, authenticating the almost identical Hebrew texts still in use today. Sectarian literature includes "The Rule of the Community", a constitution of this ascetic group, and "The War of the Sons of Light Against the Sons of Darkness," a blow-by-blow account of a final cataclysmic conflict that would, they believed, presage the messianic age.

Also in the Shrine of the Book, in the basement of the main hall, are artifacts from a slightly later period, that of the Bar Kochba Revolt of AD 132–135. With the collapse of the revolt, Jews fled the Roman legionnaires to remote caves in sheer desert canyons, taking with them their most prized possessions, including woolen blankets, prayer shawls, and a glass bowl of stunning perfection, regarded by scholars as one of the finest examples of ancient glassware ever found.

Next to the shrine is the open-air **Billy Rose Sculpture Garden,** donated by the American impresario and designed by the landscape architect

Isamu Noguchi as a series of semicircular terraces divided by stone walls. Crunch over the gravel amid works by Daumier, Rodin, Maillol, Moore, Lipchitz, Nadelman, and Picasso, among many others, all seen against a Judean Hills cityscape. It's a dreamy setting for a picnic.

In the main building, the **Judaica** section, part of the Jewish Heritage collection, has perhaps the world's greatest collection of Jewish ceremonial art and artifacts. Among the highlights are medieval illuminated *Haggadot* (Passover texts) and *Ketubot* (wedding contracts); a huge collection of Sabbath spice boxes and Hanukkah menorahs; the interior of a 17th-century Venetian synagogue brought here virtually intact; a reconstructed 19th-century German synagogue; and the wonderful, wooden 16th-century Kadavumbagam Synagogue, which served the ancient but now defunct Jewish community of Cochin, in India.

Ethnographic exhibits include dazzling formal costumes and jewelry, as well as everyday objects from Jewish communities throughout the Middle East, North Africa, and Eastern Europe. A modest but high-quality collection of European art includes paintings by Van Dyck, Monet, van Gogh, and Renoir. Period rooms reflecting 18th- and 19th-century European design are an unexpected presence. The adjacent **Cummings 20th-Century Art Building** is dedicated to modern and contemporary art, from Cézanne, Picasso, and Chagall to Dubuffet, Rothko, and Lipchitz.

The **archaeology wing,** in the main building, has a lucid exhibit of objects found in Israel (and some from elsewhere in the Near East). Visitors are often surprised by Israel's *pre*history. Israel lies on the only land bridge between Africa and Asia, and the museum's wealth of important prehistoric objects from across the country attests to significant movement and settlement across it in the misty past. For many, of course, the focal point of this display is the biblical (Old Testament) period. Pots from the time of Abraham, a Solomonic gateway, and inscriptions from Isaiah's day are just a few of the artifacts that help shed light and immediacy on the history of this ancient land. A side hall holds a superb collection of glass, from rainbow-patinated Roman pieces to sleek Art Deco objects.

There's also a **youth wing,** where delightful hands-on exhibits and workshops encourage children to appreciate art—and a changing variety of other subjects—and try their hand at creation in a do-it-yourself crafts workshop. Parents with restless kids will also be grateful for the outdoor play areas. ⊠ *Givat Ram,* ☎ *02/670–8873.* ⊟ *NIS 37 ($9.25), includes admission to Rockefeller Museum of Archaeology.* ☉ *Sun.–Mon. and Wed.–Thurs. 10–5, Tues. 4–10, Fri. 10–2, Sat. 10–4. Call for details on the many free tours in English.* ✑

**42** **King David Street.** The famous **King David Hotel** (⊠ 23 King David St.; ☞ Lodging, *below*) was built in 1931 as the country's premier hotel and is one of the most luxurious in the Middle East. Its guest book lists most of the heads of state and other international personalities who have passed through Jerusalem. The artist who decorated the columns and ceilings that adorn the lobby aimed to capture the spirit of the ancient Near East with a Mesopotamian-style motif.

In the 1940s the hotel acquired a degree of notoriety as the British military headquarters in Jerusalem in the twilight of the British Mandate. Great Britain had governed Palestine since capturing it from Ottoman Turkey in 1918. Initial Jewish enthusiasm for British rule had cooled by 1939, when Britain's "White Paper" outlined a new policy of severely restricted Jewish immigration to Palestine and a ban on Jewish land purchases in the country. Despite the ensuing outcry, the Palestinian Jewish community (the *Yishuv*) put its opposition to the British on hold when World War II broke out and joined ranks with Allied forces. When the war ended and the hoped-for British support for the Jewish state (as envisioned by the League of Nations back in 1922) failed to materialize, the Jewish underground became active. The radical Irgun blew up the south wing of the King David Hotel as a military target in July 1946, with considerable loss of life. The Irgun's claim that its advance warning to evacuate the building had been ignored by the British is still a matter of controversy. The wing was rebuilt and two extra floors were added to the hotel in the 1950s.

The Jerusalem **YMCA** (⊠ 26 King David St.; ☞ Lodging, *below*) was dedicated in 1933. Its almost palatial white-limestone facade and high, domed bell tower often surprise visitors who associate that international organization with modest buildings and sports facilities. The Y has those, too, of course, as well as an auditorium with excellent acoustics, built with a Levantine-inspired dome and decorative motifs. The tower, served by a small elevator, is 150 ft high, giving superb views in all directions; you can ride up to the view Monday through Friday between 8 and 5, Saturday between 8 and 1, for NIS 5 ($1.25).

NEED A BREAK?

The **King David Hotel coffee shop** (⊠ 23 King David St.) is not cheap, but it serves the best cheese blintzes around. In good weather, the ambience on the garden patio, with its view of the Old City walls, is unbeatable. For a simple cold beer and snack, take a seat on the **YMCA patio** (⊠ 26 King David St.), across the street from the King David.

**47 Knesset.** Both the name Knesset and the number of seats (120) in Israel's one-chamber parliament were taken from *Haknesset Hagedolah*, the Great Assembly of the Second Temple period. You may see the building on a 40-minute guided tour (conducted only on Sunday and Thursday), which includes the Knesset session hall and the reception hall, with its three enormous, brilliantly colored tapestries designed by Marc Chagall on the subjects of the Creation, the Exodus, and Jerusalem. On other days, you can attend open sessions of the Knesset (in Hebrew, of course); call ahead for the schedule. You'll need your passport.

"Take two Israelis," runs the old quip, "and you've got three political parties!" The saying is not without truth in a nation where everyone has a strong opinion and will usually not hesitate to express it. The Knesset reflects this rambunctious spirit, sometimes to the point of paralyzing the parliamentary process and driving the public to despair. Israel's electoral system, based on proportional representation, is a legacy of the dangerous but heady days of Israel's War of Independence, in 1948–49. To avoid an acrimonious and divisive election while the fledgling state was still fighting to stay alive, the founding fathers developed a one-body parliamentary system that gave representation to rival ideological factions in proportion to their comparative strength in the country's *pre*-State institutions.

Instead of the winner-takes-all approach of the constituency system, the Israeli system grants any party that wins 1.5% of the *national* vote its first seat in the Knesset. As a result, even fringe parties can have their voices heard. The disadvantage of this system is that it spawns a plethora of political parties, making it virtually impossible for one party to get the majority needed to govern. Israeli governments have thus always consisted of a coalition of parties, often a government of compromise. The smaller parties—whose support is critical for the government to keep its ruling majority—have thus been able to extract major political and material concessions for their own party interests, which are often at odds with those of the nation at large. Extensive discussion, public campaigns, demonstrations, and even proposed legislation to change the system have produced one important result: as of the 1996 general elections, the prime minister is no longer simply the leader of a victorious large party but is elected directly by the voters. This system could produce a deadlock, where the successful candidate for prime minister fails to win a parliamentary majority for his party; already it has produced the unexpected result of strengthening the smaller parties at the expense of the big ones. ⊠ *Givat Ram,* ☎ *02/675–3416.* ▧ *Free.* ☼ *Guided tours Sun. and Thurs. 8:30–2. Call ahead to verify specific tour times in English, arrive early for security checks, and bring your passport.*

Across the road from the Knesset main gate is a 15-ft-high bronze menorah, a seven-branch candelabra based on the one that once graced the First and Second Temples in Jerusalem, and now the official symbol of the State of Israel. Designed by artist Bruno Elkin, and a gift of the British Parliament to the Knesset in 1956, the menorah is decorated with bas-relief depictions of events and personages in Jewish history, from biblical times to the modern day. Behind the menorah (enter below the security barrier) is the Wohl Rose Garden, filled with hundreds of varieties of roses and plenty of lawns for children to romp on.

★ ㊻ **Machaneh Yehuda.** This block-long alley is filled with the brilliant colors of the city's best-quality fruit and vegetables, pickles and cheeses, fresh fish and poultry, and confection stalls and falafel stands. It's riotously busy, especially on Thursday and Friday, when Jewish Jerusalem shops for the Sabbath. ☼ *Sun.–Tues. about 8 AM–sunset (later on Wed. and Thurs.), Fri. and Jewish holiday eves 8 AM–2 hrs before sunset.*

**Mishkenot Sha'ananim.** This building was the first modern neighborhood outside the walls of Jerusalem. Built by Moses Montefiore in 1860, with funds donated by the New Orleans philanthropist Judah Touro, it offered small apartments rent-free to destitute Jews who were prepared to abandon the wretched conditions of the Jewish Quarter and begin a new life. People did not rush to the new project at first, for however dismal life was within the city walls, at least the city gates were shut at night to keep bandits and beasts at bay. In time, however, the neighborhood of Yemin Moshe—named after Moses (Moshe in Hebrew) Montefiore—grew up around it. Today, this splendidly renovated property, with balconies that face the Old City walls, is run by the city-connected Jerusalem Foundation as a retreat for visiting writers, musicians, and artists. It is not open to visitors. ⊠ *Yemin Moshe.*

㊶ **Montefiore's Windmill.** Moses Montefiore was a prominent and wealthy Jew in the financial circles of 19th-century London—a rare phenomenon at the time. He devoted much of his long life to aiding fellow Jews in distress, wherever they might be. To this end he visited Palestine (as this district of the Ottoman Empire was then known) seven times. The windmill was built in 1857 to provide a source of income for Jews in the new planned neighborhood of Mishkenot She'ananim (☞ *above*), but its location in relation to the prevailing winds was ill-chosen. In any event, the windmill was soon superseded by newfangled steam-driven rivals. The narrow interior of the attractive, tapered limestone structure has a small photographic exhibit on Montefiore's life and works. ⊠ *Yemin Moshe,* ☎ *02/625–4321.* ▧ *Free.* ☼ *Sun.–Thurs. 8–4, Fri. 8–1.*

㊸ **Nahalat Shiva.** The name translates roughly as "the Estate of the Seven," for the seven Jewish families that formed an association and established this neighborhood—only the second outside the Old City walls—in 1869. Defying both physical and bureaucratic hostility, they persevered, and they ultimately determined the direction of the growth of the so-called New City. Salomon Street, Rivlin Street, and their adjacent alleys and courtyards have been refashioned as a pedestrian mall and offer the keen photographer and the eager shopper many opportunities. There's a profusion of restaurants and pubs for both a lunch snack and a relaxed dinner.

**Yemin Moshe.** The core of this now-affluent neighborhood is its attractive turn-of-the-20th-century stone buildings. Dangerously near the Jordanian sniper positions on the Old City walls across the valley, the area was largely run-down in the 1950s and '60s, home mainly to families who couldn't afford to move elsewhere. The reunification of Jerusalem under Israeli rule after the Six-Day War in 1967 changed all that. Developers bought up the area, renovated old buildings, and built new and spacious homes in a compatible style. Yemin Moshe is now a place to wander at random. Several artists' galleries are well signposted; the well-known French-style restaurant Mishkenot She'ananim (not part of the original complex) is on your right as you go down the stepped Yemin Moshe Street.

OFF THE
BEATEN PATH

**HAAS PROMENADE –** A great way to get your bearings in Jerusalem is to absorb the panorama from this attractive 1-km (⅔-mi) promenade along one of the city's highest ridges. Hidden behind a grove of trees to the east (your right as you pan the view) is a turreted limestone building, the residence of the British High Commissioner for Palestine in the 1930s and '40s. In Hebrew, the whole ridge is known as Armon Hanatziv (the Commissioner's Palace). When the War of Independence ended, in early 1949, the building became the headquarters of the U.N. Truce Supervision Organization (UNTSO), specially formed to monitor the cease-fire line that divided the city. Until the reunification of the city in the Six-Day War of 1967, the site was an enclave between Israeli West Jerusalem and Jordanian-controlled East Jerusalem. You can see quite a bit of West Jerusalem off to your left; it's the downtown area easily distinguished by its high-rises. The Old City, identified by the walls and golden Dome of the Rock, is directly in front of you. To its right is the ridge of Mt. Scopus–Mount of Olives, with its three towers (from left to right, Hebrew University, Augusta Victoria Hospital, Russian Church of the Ascension), separated from the Old City by the deep Kidron Valley. Between the Kidron Valley, to the east, and the Cheesemakers' Valley (now just an asphalt road), to the west, is a blade-shape strip of land that Jerusalem occupied for its first 2,000 years—the City of David. To get here, drive south along Hebron Road. Turn left at the second traffic light, about 1¼ km (¾ mi) beyond the Ariel Hotel, following signs to East Talpiot and the Haas Promenade. The parking lot is on the left; watch for traffic from your right.

# DINING

Jerusalem's restaurants offer something for every taste and pocket. European and Asian cuisines may be familiar to many visitors, but a brief glossary of *local* culinary terms will help you appreciate the pleasures of the region's specialties. Dairy restaurants are simply those serving meals without meat; many such places serve fish as well. Hummus, a ubiquitous dish in this region, is a creamy paste made from chickpeas, moistened with olive oil and often tahini (a sauce based on ground sesame), and scooped up with pieces of flat pita bread. Have hummus at a place that specializes in Middle Eastern dishes; many "Western" establishments serve poor imitations. Also look for a Kurdish-Iraqi specialty called *koubeh,* seasoned ground meat formed into small torpedo shapes and deep-fried in a jacket of bulgur (cracked wheat).

Falafel, the region's fast food, consists of deep-fried chickpea balls served in pita pockets and topped with a variety of vegetables and sauces. It's filling, nutritious, and cheap. *Shwarma* is grilled meat (traditionally lamb but now more commonly turkey), also served in pita bread with vegetables and sauces. Both falafel and shwarma are sold at stands; try King George Street, the Ben Yehuda Street open-air mall, or the area near the Machaneh Yehuda produce market. A specialty of the grills at Machaneh Yehuda, on Agrippas Street, is *me'oorav yerushalmi* (Jerusalem mixed grill), a deliciously seasoned meal of grilled chicken hearts and other organ meats in pita. This is the area to find authentic back-street eateries, especially for lunch.

Dress codes are pretty much nonexistent in Jerusalem's restaurants (as in the rest of Israel). People tend to dress very casually: jeans are perfectly appropriate in most restaurants, the only possible exceptions being dining rooms at deluxe hotels. Even then it's only a matter of degree; informal dress is acceptable, but a modicum of neatness is expected. Still, if you've taken the trouble to bring your dressy duds, you won't be out of place thus attired in Jerusalem's more exclusive eateries. Remember that kosher restaurants are closed for Friday dinner and Saturday lunch in observation of the Jewish Sabbath.

| CATEGORY | COST* |
| --- | --- |
| $$$$ | over $35 |
| $$$ | $22–$35 |
| $$ | $12–$22 |
| $ | under $12 |

*per person for a three-course meal, excluding drinks and 10%–12% service charge

## Continental

**$$$$** ✕ **Fink.** The dingy facade is part of Fink's mythos. The simple decor hasn't changed much since it was established in 1932, the waiter has been there since 1950, and Moulli, the current owner, will regale you with tales of the internationally famous who have held court here. The great bar and the intimacy (seats 26 *closely*) are what Fink is known for, and the food is excellent to boot. Try the goulash soup or the chopped liver for starters. The veal cordon bleu (with ham and Gruyère) and the fillet steaks are top-notch, but some come for the unusual *Tafelspitz,* Austrian-style baked beef in horseradish sauce. The homemade hazelnut or chestnut ice cream is sublime. ✉ *2 Hahistadrut St.,* ☎ *02/ 623–4523. Reservations essential. AE, DC, MC, V. Closed for 3 wks over Jewish holidays in Sept. or Oct.*

## Eclectic

**$$–$$$** ✕ **Chamomile.** The wide and varied menu is a bit overwhelming at first. It includes fish and Italian dishes, a salad bar, and a variety of strictly vegetarian dishes influenced by the cuisines of India, Thailand, and Mexico. The onion soup is just right, and the chilled, fresh apricot soup (in season) is delightful. The *pasta bianca* is a dreamy combination with ricotta cheese, onions, and spices, and *pasta a la portobello* comes with mushrooms and onions in a rich wine and tomato sauce. The grilled salmon teriyaki is perfection. Many of the vegetarian dishes include tofu, but if that's not your favorite, try the delicious (but spicy) dish called Indian Spice, basmati rice topped with curried vegetables. A great

**84**

Hebrew University

ME'A SHE'ARIM

Strauss
Me'a She'arim
Hanevi'im
Harav Kook   Horkonos
Jaffa Rd.
King George Rd.
Zion Sq.
Yehuda
Salomon
Hillel

Shmu'el Hanavi
St. George
Nablus Rd.
Shivtei Yisra'el
Saladin St.
Jericho Rd.

Sultan Suleiman St.
Damascus Gate
Herod's Gate
MUSLIM QUARTER
Lions' (St. Stephen's) Gate
MOUNT OF OLIVES

New Gate
Church of the Holy Sepulcher
Via Dolorosa
TEMPLE MOUNT
Dome of the Rock

CHRISTIAN QUARTER
Jewish Quarter Rd.
Western Wall

Jaffa Rd.
Independence Park
Mamilla
King David St.
Agron
Keren Hayesod

Jaffa Gate
David St.
JEWISH QUARTER
El-Aqsa Mosque

ARMENIAN QUARTER
Dung Gate
Kidron Valley
Jericho Rd.

Jabotinsky
Hebron Rd.
Sultan's Pool
Zion Gate
CITY OF DAVID
Jewish Cemetery

MT. ZION

GERMAN COLONY
Emek Refa'im
Derech Bethlehem

Agrippas St.
Jaffa Rd.
Harav Kook
Zion Sq.
Eliahu
King George St.
Bezalel
Ben Yehuda
Hahistadrut
Shammai St.
Salomon St.
Hasurei
Shlomzion Hamalka
Narkis
Hillel

alternative drink with your meal is one of the fresh fruit–and–vegetable cocktails. Dessert is a weak point. ⊠ *8 Dorot Rishonim St. (off Ben Yehuda St.), ☎ 02/625–2750. Reservations essential for sushi hour (Sun. 8–9 PM). AE, DC, MC, V. No lunch Sat., no dinner Fri.*

$$–$$$    ✕ **Little Jerusalem ("Bet Ticho").** This is one of downtown Jerusalem's loveliest, most tranquil nooks. Now a national monument, the imposing stone building was built in the 1920s as the home and surgery of the famous ophthalmologist A. A. Ticho and his even more famous wife, artist Anna Ticho, whose evocative drawings of Jerusalem adorn the place. House specialties include sublime salmon blintzes, onion soup served *inside* a crusty loaf of bread, fish in fresh ginger sauce, and a variety of pasta and sautéed veggie dishes. Portions are very generous: share rather than over-order. Desserts are sinfully wonderful, from the apple strudel and various cakes to the ice cream cake topped with hot fudge. On Tuesday night there's a wine-and-cheese buffet, accompanied by a jazz combo (reserve in advance); on Friday at 11 AM, there's live chamber music; and on Saturday night, classical music and a light buffet, with a Viennese accent. Angle for a table on the patio in nice weather. ⊠ *7 Harav Kook St., ☎ 02/624–4186. Dinner reservations essential. AE, DC, MC, V. No lunch Sat., no dinner Fri.*

## Fish

$$$–$$$$    ✕ **Hanevi'im.** Young chef Aviv Moshe creates dishes with a deft touch and changes the menu often enough to keep the locals surprised. Recently featured were a fish soup with root vegetables and Pernod, and a filleted red St. Peter's fish (tilapia) with Portobello mushrooms in a tomato butter sauce. For a leisurely and adventurous treat, the restaurant offers a fixed-price dinner of at least eight small courses, allowing the chef free reign to pamper you as his culinary mood dictates. The restaurant occupies a renovated old stone building with interior arches and a tea shop at the back. ⊠ *54 Hanevi'im St., ☎ 02/624–7433. Reservations essential. AE, DC, MC, V. No lunch Sat., no dinner Fri.*

$$$–$$$$    ✕ **Michael Andrew.** In a stone building overlooking the Old City (ask
★    for a window table), this fine restaurant defines itself as Belgian. Chef-owner Michael, half-Belgian himself, spent several years working in highly rated Brussels restaurants and now blends his imported skills with local produce. The results are impressive and the menu changes completely every two months. Fish is complemented by delectable, imaginative, and well-balanced sauces, lighter and more subtle than their French counterparts. Try the fish soup, typically a consommé in summer, a piquant tomato-based chowder in winter. Those avoiding fish can choose from a few vegetable-based entrées. The superb crème brûlée, when available, is the dessert of choice. For an intimate dinner for two in good weather, ask for the balcony table off the kitchen, where the ethereal views of the illuminated Old City walls create an unmatched ambience (just dress warmly). The staff is charming, and the business lunch is a good deal. ⊠ *12 Emil Botta St. (in Zionist Confederation House, in the park), ☎ 02/624–0090. Reservations essential. AE, DC, MC, V. In summer: closed Sat., no dinner Fri. In winter: closed Fri., no lunch Sat.*

$$$–$$$$    ✕ **Rienzi.** In a renovated 1868 stone building, with a courtyard for outside dining, this gourmet fish-and-pasta restaurant is one of Jerusalem's best-kept secrets. At once subtle and sensual, the gastronomic influence is part French, part Italian. For starters, go for the light and delicate cream of garlic soup or the roasted pepper gratin. Standouts among the scrumptious pasta dishes are the fettuccine Piemonte with mushrooms and the spaghetti Toscana with sun-dried tomatoes, pine nuts, and pesto. Fresh, in-season fish is creatively presented. Try the

*tricolata* for dessert—a pyramid of milk and white chocolate in a light caramel sauce. Service is charming and impeccable. ⊠ *10 King David St.,* ☎ *02/622–2313. Reservations essential. AE, DC, MC, V. Closed Fri. No lunch Sat., no dinner Sat. in summer).*

## French

**$$$$** ✕ **Arcadia.** You're unlikely to stumble on this place, but it's worth hunting for, housed in an old stone-arched building (with a garden courtyard for outdoor dining) in a narrow alley between Agrippas Street and Jaffa Road. The menu is imaginative and the service excellent. Two tiny complimentary appetizers and a basket of fresh rolls set the tone. From the regular appetizer menu, try the calf's brain with sun-dried tomatoes and garlic, or any of the shrimp dishes. The main courses change from time to time, depending on seasonal fresh produce and the chef's inspiration; there are typically half a dozen fine beef, lamb, and fish combinations to choose from. Save space for the exceptional desserts, like *pithiviers* (puff pastry and almond cream cake) with figs and cheese or an Earl Grey–scented cold soufflé with honey-lemon sauce and caramelized bananas. ⊠ *Off 10 Agrippas St.,* ☎ *02/624–9138. Reservations essential. AE, DC, MC, V. Closed Sun.*

**$$$$** ✕ **Mishkenot Sha'ananim.** With a picture window overlooking the illuminated Old City walls, this veteran restaurant is a landmark in its own right. It has one of the region's best wine cellars, extensive if expensive. Melt-in-the-mouth rolls start you off well, but you can pass on the mixed hors d'oeuvres. Excellent main courses include duck à l'orange, veal marsala, and several steak options. Desserts are good, not exceptional. ⊠ *Yemin Moshe St., below the Windmill,* ☎ *02/625–4424. AE, DC, MC, V.*

**$$$$** ✕ **Shonka.** The floors of hewn wood add a nice balance to the modern decor as you walk through the bar area to your table (though the acoustics make conversation difficult with any but your immediate neighbors). Great starters are the shrimp in Cajun butter and the grouper seviche with lime and vanilla. There are several excellent fish and seafood entrées, or try the veal fillet in a red wine and shallot sauce, or the breast of mallard in a coffee and cardamom sauce. Desserts are uneven, but you'll enjoy the tart Tatin (caramelized apple tart) or the fruit sorbets. ⊠ *1 Hasoreg St. (off Jaffa Rd.),* ☎ *02/625–7033. Reservations essential. AE, DC, MC, V.*

## Grills

**$$$** ✕ **Stanley's.** Stanley combines a native South African's respect for good meat (aged steaks, slow cooking) with some French kitchen techniques and sauces to produce a satisfying dining experience. The arches and niches of the old stone building break the room into intimate sections, and the wooden-roof deck is wonderful in nice weather. Excellent appetizers include a foie-gras terrine, a skewer of Portobello mushrooms, chicken wings in an orange sauce, and delicious South African *boerewors* (beef sausage). The best meats are the sirloin steaks and barbecued ostrich, but you can't go wrong with any of the other carnivorous choices, and there are fish and salad options if you eschew the meat. Desserts are a bit less reliable. The "Struggling Artist Lunch Menu" is a real find, with a good steak meal for NIS 35 ($8.75). A good bar attracts those looking for a drink and a light bite. ⊠ *3 Horkanos St.,* ☎ *02/625–9459. AE, DC, MC, V.*

**$$–$$$** ✕ **El Gaucho.** It's all about red meat at this Argentinian grill in the Nahalat Shiva neighborhood. To a stone building with interior arches and a flagstone floor, El Gaucho adds rustic wooden tables, lattice screens, and artifacts from the Argentinian pampas. Munch a delicious beef empanada while you wait for your steak. Best here are the steak entrecôte and the steak chorizo (no relation to the sausage of the same name, though it's also available) with a parsley-based *chimichurri* (herbs with olive oil and vinegar) sauce. The grilled udders and innards are very much an acquired taste. There is a separate children's menu and a few fish dishes and a vegetarian platter for the steak avoider. ⊠ *22 Rivlin St.,* ☎ *02/624–2227. AE, DC, MC, V. Closed Fri. No lunch Sat.*

## Indian

**$$–$$$** ✕ **Kohinoor.** Graciousness and impeccable service are the hallmarks
★ of this national tandoori chain, and the Jerusalem branch is no exception. Low lighting and Indian ornaments and background music set a tone of quiet yet informal elegance. The cuisine is northern Indian, subtler and less fiery than the curries of the south. Best of the appetizers are the chicken wings marinated in ginger, garlic, and spices, then deep-fried. The breads, served with piquant chutneys and sauces, are great—just don't fill up on them. Try the tandoori-baked *kulcha,* stuffed with a nondairy "cheese." For the main course, try the wonderfully flavored lamb dishes—the *bhuna gosht* or the *rogan gosht*—or the succulent marinated chicken chunks baked to redness in a tandoor (clay oven). Vegetarians are far from neglected; the vegetable curries, *sabzi* pilaf, and spinach pureed with a cottage-cheese substitute will have meat eaters reaching across the table. End the meal with one (or all) of the fragrant *kulfi*-type ice creams. The lunch buffet is an excellent value. ⊠ *Crowne Plaza Hotel, Givat Ram,* ☎ *02/658–8867. Reservations essential for dinner Thurs. AE, DC, MC, V. No lunch Sat., no dinner Fri.*

## Italian

**$$$** ✕ **Spaghettim.** In an old stone building tucked into a downtown side street, Spaghettim's decor is spare, pastel, and attractive. In summer, the courtyard is filled with tables for alfresco meals. The restaurant is popular with the fashionable young set, but you can still take the family without breaking the bank. Sauces are grouped in three categories: tomato-, oil-, and cream-based. The Bolognese (meat) sauce is ordinary, but the *arrabbiata* (fiery tomato sauce flavored with chili peppers) is good; the smoked salmon (with optional asparagus), delicious; and the fresh mushrooms (with optional bacon), sublime. Some of the oil-based sauces are quite spicy. The pasta portions are generous; two youngsters can easily share one. Friendly and efficient service adds a final welcoming touch. ⊠ *8 Rabbi Akiva St.,* ☎ *02/623–5547 or 02/623–5548. AE, DC, MC, V.*

**$$** ✕ **Focaccia.** The smallish interior in an old stone building is pleasant enough, but the spacious patio just off the street is where the action and the atmosphere are. A popular haunt of the twenties crowd, this "focaccia bar" (as it defines itself) offers good value. There is a variety of focaccia toppings (don't miss the black olive spread), and some tasty antipasti (go for the vine leaves stuffed with goat cheese, but steer clear of the beef carpaccio). Chicken livers stir-fried with apples, shallots, and nuts are delicious. There are great sandwich options, like sirloin strips, and several pasta dishes. Desserts are good, with an excellent tart Tatin. ⊠ *4 Rabbi Akiva St.,* ☎ *02/625–6428. AE, DC, MC, V.*

**$$** ✕ **Mamma Mia.** A nicely renovated stone building with a shady courtyard houses a restaurant that virtually pioneered the concept of vegetarian Italian food in Jerusalem. For an appetizer, try the *insalata alla siciliana* (salad of tomato and grated mild feta cheese with a basil dressing) or the minestrone. The cannelloni entrées and the lasagna are excellent, as are the spinach and cheese ravioli; or you can choose from a wide selection of (homemade) pasta and pizza. A refreshing summer offering is spaghetti primavera, with an uncooked sauce of tomatoes, olive oil, and garlic. The hot apple potpie and the homemade ice cream are the best desserts. ⊠ *38 King George St., behind parking lot,* ☎ *02/624–8080. AE, DC, MC, V. No lunch Sat., no dinner Fri.*

## Korean

$$ ✕ **Korea House.** Tucked into a corner of the marvelous, restored 130-year-old neighborhood of Nahalat Shiva, the restaurant combines a charming decor (including murals of ancient Korean and Chinese texts) with gracious service. The set menu is good value, but if you order à la carte, start with the sushilike *modeum kim bab,* or the *goo jul pan,* do-it-yourself paper-thin crepes with meat and raw vegetables. Recommended entrées include the delicate *saeng sun zim* (stewed Nile perch) or the dishes of chopped roast beef, chicken, or shrimp in a special brown sauce. Vegetarians will find several tempting alternatives. ⊠ *7 Ma'alot Nahalat Shiva St.,* ☎ *02/625–4756. Reservations essential on weekends. AE, DC, MC, V.*

## Mediterranean

$$$ ✕ **Le Tsriff.** This very Jerusalemite restaurant, on a downtown back-
★ street, occupies an old house with a stone patio. It has cultivated a faithful local clientele, from students to celebrities, and earned its early reputation with savory pies encased in great crusts: chicken with nuts and raisins; veal and prunes; and vegetable combinations. Try as well the marvelous Moroccan *harira* (chickpea and coriander) soup. Owner-chef Michal has stirred the menu even further by introducing flavors from her native southern France. For starters, try the hot breaded goat cheese on a bed of leafy salad, or the grilled calamari. Specialty entrées include succulent seafood offerings, tender sirloin with a French-style wine sauce, and roasted sea bream (known locally as "denise") in a delectable citrus-ginger sauce. The house dessert is a hot sweet pie, but the pear tart Tatin and the crème brûlée with ginger are excellent, too. ⊠ *5 Horkonos St.,* ☎ *02/625–5488 or 02/624–2478. AE, DC, MC, V.*

## Middle Eastern

$$–$$$ ✕ **Barood.** Owner Daniella Lerer fiercely preserves the culinary traditions of her Sephardic forebears, a family exiled from Spain 500 years ago, and settled in Jerusalem for some 10 generations. The fixed-price "sampler's" menu is a taste adventure, though all items can be ordered à la carte. Homemade olives, marinated green almonds, and the sweet-onion house bread are followed by *pastilikos* (meat and pine-nuts muffin) and *prasa* (leek patties with yogurt) and more. Standouts among the entrées are meat balls with plums and wine, *medias* (tomatoes stuffed with meat), and a beef, leek, and plum stew. For dessert, look for the traditional *sutlach,* a cold rice and milk pudding topped with cinnamon, nuts, and the jam of the day. Barood's other face is its well-stocked bar, with more familiar fare like spareribs and sausages. From 4:30 to 7 PM on Friday afternoons the place sways to the rhythms of live Balkan music. ⊠ *In courtyard off 31 Jaffa Rd.,* ☎ *02/625–9081. Reservations essential Fri. afternoon and Sat. AE, DC, MC, V. Closed Sun.*

$$–$$$ ✕ **Eucalyptus.** The traditional cooking of yesteryear's Israel is the passion of owner Moshe Basson, who has rambled across the country quizzing old-timers and searching for wild greens that few people use anymore. The result is an intriguing experience for adventurous palates (and there's good, more typical Middle Eastern fare for their less curious companions). For appetizers, try the salty mixture of *sabanach* (wild spinach) with *postulaka* or *hobeiza* greens (depending on the sea-

son); fried koubeh; and either the almond or the Jerusalem-artichoke soup. Stuffed leaves (grape, cyclamen, and many others) come in both meat and vegetarian versions. Recommended among the meat dishes are the lamb offerings, quail breast in date syrup, and figs stuffed with meat and nuts. Basson's prize-winning couscous is not listed but is generally available. A "banquet" choice allows you to sample just about everything, a great way of spending the evening if you come with good company, a hearty appetite, and a bigger budget. Arched windows, vaulted ceilings, and early 20th-century artifacts give the meals an apt period setting. The tree-shaded tables on the adjacent square are a treat in good weather. ⊠ *4 Safra Sq. (next to City Hall complex; opposite 19 Jaffa Rd.),* ☎ *02/624–4331. AE, DC, MC, V. No lunch Sat., no dinner Fri.*

**$$** ✕ **Ima.** It's pronounced "*ee*-mah," means "mom," and is named for Miriam, the owner's Kurdish mother, who still does all the cooking. This restaurant, at the bottom of the Nahla'ot neighborhood, opposite Sacher Park, serves traditional, plentiful, very good Middle Eastern food. First courses include a modest meze of some half dozen salads, such as hummus and *baba ghanoush* (eggplant dip), as well as the excellent koubeh and stuffed vine leaves. Try the tangy koubeh soup, full of dumplings—it's almost a meal in itself. The entrée, which could be *shishlik* (shish kebab) or a Jerusalem mixed grill, is accompanied by *majadra* (rice and lentils). ⊠ *189 Agrippas St.,* ☎ *02/624–6860. AE, DC, MC, V. Closed Sat. No dinner Fri.*

**$$** ✕ **Nafoura.** Just inside the Jaffa Gate, Nafoura is a welcome addition to the local scene. There's an attractive tranquil courtyard for alfresco dining, where your table might lean against the Old City's 16th-century wall. Start with the traditional meze, an array of salads: the smaller version is enough for two people. Insist on the excellent local dishes only (hummus, eggplant dip, tahini, carrots, etc.) and skip the mushrooms and corn. Ask for the unusual *sujuk,* tiny chunks of a piquant Armenian sausage. From the typical selection of entrées, try the lamb cutlets or the sea bream (called "denise"). ⊠ *18 Latin Patriarch Rd.,* ☎ *02/626–0034. Dinner reservations essential. AE, DC, MC, V.*

**$–$$** ✕ **Mifgash Ha'esh.** Here's a good example of the wisdom of eating where the locals eat. When the restaurant opened a few years ago in the Romema industrial zone behind the Central Bus Station, it gained an almost instant reputation for good food and good value and began attracting Jerusalemites from farther afield—and even the occasional tourist. People flock here for the skewers of grilled meat and the house specialty, succulent grilled pieces of marinated chicken. Appetizers include particularly good hummus and koubeh. Pass on the baklava for dessert. ⊠ *23 Yirmiyahu St., Romema,* ☎ *02/538–8888 or 02/528–8889. Reservations not accepted. AE, DC, MC, V. No lunch Sat., no dinner Fri.*

## Moroccan

**$$$$** ✕ **Darna.** Darna's Moroccan-born owner has indulged his nostalgia for his native land and brought an architect from back home to re-create the "real" Morocco here. The results are delightful: a vaulted peach-painted tunnel deposits you in a corner of Morocco, an asymmetrical arrangement of different-size rooms with stone arches and decorative motifs of wood, copper, pottery, brass, and fabrics. The set menu is a good value, but ordering à la carte gives you more flexibility if you're not up to the generous portions. There's a great selection of salads, with a quite different range of tastes than those in the local Arabic mezes. Another excellent starter is *pastilla,* thin phyllo pastry stuffed with almonds, cinnamon, and Cornish hen; there are both vegetarian and fish versions. The couscous is competent, and the various *tagines,* or Moroccan stews, are very good. End the meal with refreshing, green mint tea (served with fine ceremony), and, if you have room, the candied fruits or the exquisite *toubkal* delight, a sweet phyllo pie done in cinnamon and (nondairy) almond milk. ⊠ *3 Horkonos St.,* ☎ *02/624–5406. AE, DC, MC, V. Closed Fri. No lunch Sat.*

## Vegetarian

**$$–$$$** ✕ **Te'enim.** The name means "figs," and if you're a vegetable lover— let alone a card-carrying vegetarian—the Garden of Eden association is inescapable. The sunny yellow decor creates a cheerful atmosphere. Check the soup of the day, and try the savory tomato and tarragon soup, when available. In addition to the good green salads, more "ethnic" options are available: the Indian salad of curried lentils, yogurt, and chutney stands out. Hot quiches and pies change constantly and are generally excellent. In addition to the regular menu, every weekday has offerings from a different culinary tradition—Mexican, Japanese, Indonesian, Indian, Chinese, and Moroccan—and many regulars choose their day accordingly. Desserts are good; try the chocolate parfait in orange sauce. ⊠ *21 Emek Refa'im St.,* ☎ *02/563–0048. AE, DC, MC, V. No lunch Sat., no dinner Fri.*

**$–$$** ✕ **Village Green.** Right near the downtown Zion Square, this airy, vegetarian restaurant offers a good variety of soups, quiches, pies, and wonderfully fresh vegetable salads, with a choice of great dressings. It's strictly self-service, and you pay by weight. Vegans (the management proudly points out) are well catered to. Every meal comes with homemade bread. The dessert pies are worth trying. ⊠ *33 Jaffa Rd.,* ☎ *02/625–3065. AE, DC, MC, V. Closed Sat. No dinner Fri.*

## Cafés

Sitting down for coffee and cake in one of Jerusalem's fine cafés is something of a tradition. The selection of sweets includes the gooey, cream-filled pastries many Israelis favor; more sophisticated cheesecakes and pies; and yeast cakes and strudels, a Central European inheritance.

The downtown **Midrachov,** the open-air mall of Ben Yehuda Street and its side lanes, has several venerable hangouts from an earlier era, but a new generation of cafés offers a more sophisticated menu and better coffee. Two neighborhood arteries—Azza Street, in **Rehavia,** and Emek Refa'im Street, in the **German Colony**—are well stocked with popular watering holes, a few of which serve decent light meals as well. On summer evenings in particular, these places teem with the young set; arrive in mid-evening to beat the after-show crowd.

In the downtown area, the self-service **Aroma** (⊠ 18 Hillel St., ☎ 02/625–5365) is brash and young and almost never closes. The croissants and the coffee are good and prices are reasonable. The fashionable **Hillel** (⊠ 8 Hillel St., ☎ 02/624–7775) has a spacious interior, a breakfast menu, and good prices. Opposite, and in a wide alley, is **Second Cup** (⊠ 4 Shammai St., ☎ 02/623–4533), with good muffins, a remarkable selection of coffees, and some upholstered armchairs in the no-smoking section.

**Conus** (⊠ 18 King George St., ☎ 02/625–5317), next to the Hamashbir department store, is the outlet for a local maker of excellent Italian-style ice cream and gelato.

A sign of the times is **Netcafe** (⊠ 9 Helene Hamalka St., ☎ 02/624–6327), where you can surf the Net and check your e-mail over a good cup of coffee.

**Paradiso** (⊠ 36 Keren Hayesod St., ☎ 02/563–4805) does light meals, coffee, and exceptional cakes.

**Jan's** (⊠ 20 Marcus St., ☎ 02/561–2054), under the plaza of the Sherover (Jerusalem) Theater, is a one-of-a-kind café. You sit or lounge on soft pillows and rugs, with low lights and Asian ornaments adding to the mysterious atmosphere. The menu isn't extensive—the ambience is all—but what's served is very good (and not cheap). It's better for romantic assignations than clubby conversation.

# LODGING

Some travelers insist on a hotel in a central location; others prefer to retreat to a haven at the end of the day, with ambience more important than accessibility. Jerusalem has more of the first kind of hotel than the second; even hotels once considered remote are now no more than 10 minutes by cab or hotel minibus from the city center. In truth, with only a few exceptions, most hotels are modern, with little claim to old-world charm.

Many Jerusalem hotels can be grouped by the following locations: on or near the downtown triangle formed by King George Street, Jaffa Road, and Ben Yehuda Street (Sheraton Jerusalem Plaza, Lev Yerusha-layim, Jerusalem Tower, Kikar Zion, Zion); near the city center (and most convenient to Jaffa Gate and the Old City), near the intersection of King David and Keren Hayesod streets (King David, Eldan, Inbal, King Solomon, Dan Panorama, Mt. Zion, Windmill, Ariel, YMCA [West], St. Andrew's Scottish Hospice); in West Jerusalem between the Central Bus Station and Givat Ram, on major city bus routes (Mer-cure-Jerusalem Gate, Park Plaza, Four Points Jerusalem). A few defy the above categories (Hyatt Regency, Olive Tree, Yitzhak Rabin Guest House, Ramat Rachel, Louise Waterman-Wise). An interesting alternative is a kibbutz guest house in the forested hill country, a 20-minute drive from the city center (Neve Ilan, Ma'aleh Hahamisha, Kiryat Anavim, and Shoresh); it's best to have a car to reach these (☞ West of Jerusalem *in* Chapter 2).

Hotels in Arab East Jerusalem, which are generally in the less-expensive categories, were seriously affected by Palestinian street violence in the late 1980s and early '90s. The ensuing shrinkage of hotel occupancy there has, unfortunately, led to a widespread decline in standards as well. The unrest at press time hasn't helped, but we still recommend the American Colony, the renovated Ambassador, and the new Addar.

Rates quoted by hotels are the maximum regular-season rates, but remember that it's quite common to get a room at a price below the published rate, especially off-season. The high season typically includes 10 days to a month around the Jewish holiday of Passover (March–April), a similar period over the Jewish holidays in September and October (High Holy Days and Sukkoth), part of the summer, and, for some hotels, the Christmas season. Because there is considerable variation in what different hotels consider high season, and because the dates of Jewish holidays shift annually in accordance with the Jewish calendar, the difference in room rates can be significant; it's worth confirming the rate before making a firm reservation.

All hotels are heated, and all in the $$$$ and $$$ categories (as well as some of those more moderately priced) have air-conditioning, TV, and telephones in the rooms.

| CATEGORY | COST* |
|---|---|
| $$$$ | over $200 |
| $$$ | $100–$200 |
| $$ | $60–$100 |
| $ | under $60 |

*All prices are for two people in a standard double room, including breakfast and 15% service charge.

$$$$ ⊞ **Addar.** This brand-new all-suite hotel is located on the "seam" between East and West Jerusalem. The red marble floor, gilded columns, wooden lattices, and wrought-iron work of the lobby could have been gaudy but manage to be stylish instead. The elegant suites, furnished in antique style and upholstered in deep blue and silver, have kitchenettes and whirlpool baths. Another 11 royal and presidential suites are expected to be completed by early 2001. ⊠ *53 Nablus Rd. (opposite American Colony),* ☎ *02/626–3111,* FAX *02/626–0791. 81 suites. Restaurant, business services. AE, DC, MC, V.*

$$$$ ⊞ **American Colony Hotel.** This onetime pasha's palace, a cool lime-
★ stone oasis with a flower-bedecked inner courtyard, has been a hotel for more than a century. It's a 10-minute walk from the Damascus Gate, in East Jerusalem, but worlds away from the hubbub of the Old City. A favorite haunt of American and British expats, foreign journalists, and diplomats, the hotel (now affiliated with Relais & Châteaux) is noted for its service and ambience (turquoise-and-blue tilework, Damascene wood inlay, potted palms). Guest rooms in the old wing are comfortable but not sumptuous; the better rooms are spacious and more individualized, usually topped with vaulting or an antique painted-wood ceiling. Planned major renovations of the new wing (completion by mid-2001)—with European theme floors, such as 19th-century English—are expected to produce more luxurious results. The in-house Arabesque restaurant has a good local reputation. ⊠ *Nablus Rd., Box 19215, 97200,* ☎ *02/627–9777,* FAX *02/627–9779. 77 rooms, 7 suites. 3 restaurants, bar, pool. AE, DC, MC, V.* ✎

$$$$ ⊞ **Crowne Plaza.** A quintessential business and convention hotel, the Crowne Plaza is a tower block that dominates the city's western skyline, giving almost all of the rooms—and particularly those on the top five floors—sweeping views of some part of Jerusalem. Rooms are not especially large, but their decoration, in tasteful pastels and light earth tones, makes them feel light and airy. The lobby-level dairy restaurant–bar–coffee shop has an eclectic menu, and the Kohinoor Indian and Oasis fish restaurants are real treats. The small, informal health club is privately owned, but guests of the hotel enjoy a special rate. ⊠ *Givat Ram (West Jerusalem), 91130,* ☎ *02/658–8888,* FAX *02/651–4555. 397 rooms. 4 restaurants, bar, pool, hot tub, sauna, miniature golf, 2 tennis courts, health club, playground, business services. AE, DC, MC, V.*

$$$$ ⊞ **Dan Panorama.** The old Moriah has been taken over by the prestigious Dan chain and been given a significant face-lift. At press time almost half the guest rooms had been been refurbished in pleasing earth colors, and the reception-lobby area was newly renovated (all work was scheduled for completion by summer 2001). Some rooms tend to be a bit compact: ask for one of the bigger ones (the front desk is generous with upgrades, when available). Advantages are the excellent location, convenient to downtown and the Old City; the pleasant atmosphere; and a friendly staff. ⊠ *39 Keren Hayesod St., 94188,* ☎ *02/569–5695,* FAX *02/623–2411. 292 rooms. 3 restaurants, bar, in-room data ports, pool, beauty salon, health club, business services. AE, DC, MC, V.* ✎

**$$$$** 🏨 **Hyatt Regency.** Cascading down Mt. Scopus, the Hyatt Regency has the most dramatic setting of any hotel in Jerusalem, and the boldest design (it's built around seven courtyards). The lobby is a stylish combination of stone and greenery. The spacious guest rooms, about one-third of which have views of the Old City, are decorated in light colors and are looking especially spruced up after recent renovations. The pool area, with an adjacent playground, is a cool enclave of palms and plants. The sophisticated, independently owned Jerusalem Spa offers cosmetic and therapeutic treatments in addition to the standard facilities, and hotel guests receive a discounted day rate. Valentino's, the in-house Italian-Mediterranean restaurant, is recommended. ✉ *32 Lehi St., 97856,* ☎ *02/533–1234,* ℻ *02/581–5947. 502 rooms. 4 restaurants, bar, 1 indoor (fee) and 1 outdoor pool, beauty salon, hot tub, sauna, steam room, 2 tennis courts, health club, nightclub, business services. AE, DC, MC, V.* 🐢

**$$$$** 🏨 **Inbal.** A low-rise building of Jerusalem stone wrapped around a central courtyard and atrium, the Inbal, formerly the Laromme, is more appealing for its architecture and friendly, energetic staff than for its decor. Recent refurbishing has improved the guest rooms, some of which have balconies and fine views. The pool is chlorine-free, kept clean by a newfangled substitute. Its location next to the playgrounds of Liberty Bell Garden is a plus for families. ✉ *3 Jabotinsky St., 92145,* ☎ *02/675–6666,* ℻ *02/675–6777. 294 rooms. 3 restaurants, bar, pool, beauty salon, hot tub, sauna. AE, DC, MC, V.* 🐢

**$$$$** 🏨 **Jerusalem Hilton.** This hotel makes a powerful first impression with its stonework and arches, and the fine aesthetics are carried over into the spacious guest rooms. Furnishings are in soft tones of beige and cream; wall hangings include stone mosaics in an ancient style; and bathrooms are well appointed. The lobby, however, is somewhat cold, a monument to the architect rather than a welcoming vestibule. ✉ *7 King David St., 94101,* ☎ *02/621–1111,* ℻ *02/621–1000. 381 rooms. 3 restaurants, bar, pool, sauna, exercise room, business services. AE, DC, MC, V.* 🐢

**$$$$**
**★** 🏨 **King David.** The grande dame of Israeli luxury hotels opened in 1931 and has successfully defended its title ever since. The lobby, whose ceilings, columns, and walls are covered with "ancient" geometric decoration, is comfortable but bustling, very much a part of the nearby reception area. Recent renovations have transformed the already spacious and elegant rooms into symphonies of tasteful cream and brown, with old-fashioned writing tables a gracious addition. The pricier rooms have views of the Old City. The large pool, in a beautifully landscaped garden behind the hotel, may tempt you away from your touring in hot weather. The in-house French-style grill restaurant, La Régence, is highly regarded locally. ✉ *23 King David St., 94101,* ☎ *02/620–8888,* ℻ *02/620–8882. 237 rooms. 3 restaurants, bar, pool, tennis court, shops, business services. AE, DC, MC, V.* 🐢

**$$$$** 🏨 **Sheraton Jerusalem Plaza.** Not far from the lively shopping area on Ben Yehuda Street, the 22-story Sheraton looks like a big business hotel anywhere, complete with look-alike guest rooms (big beds, big closets), but it actually has more to recommend it. The balcony views are impressive; the nonmeat Italian restaurant, Primavera, has won kudos locally; and the expensive French restaurant, Cow on the Roof, is considered the hotel's calling card. ✉ *47 King George St., Box 7686, 91076,* ☎ *02/629–8666,* ℻ *02/623–1667. 300 rooms. 4 restaurants, bar, pool, beauty salon, massage, sauna. AE, DC, MC, V.* 🐢

**$$$–$$$$** 🏨 **Olive Tree.** Aesthetics are the strong point of this brand-new property. Stone arches behind the reception, old flagstones in the lobby, stone columns and wood latticework in the atrium, stonework in the guest bathrooms—even the staff uniforms—combine to create a distinctly regional ambience. Guest rooms are not huge, but comfortable enough.

At press time, a pool was under construction, and a spa and health club in the planning stage. ✉ *23 St. George St.,* ☎ *02/541–0410,* ℻ *02/541–0411. 304 rooms. 2 restaurants, bar. AE, DC, MC, V.*

$$$ 🏨 **Ambassador.** One of East Jerusalem's veteran hotels, the Ambassador has been transformed by thorough and tasteful renovations. Throughout the hotel the use of Jerusalem limestone and beige-and-cream decor gives a marvelous feeling of light and airiness. For the extra space, upgrade from a regular to a junior guest room, and ask for an Old City view. The two specialty restaurants—one Italian-French in a skylit room of cherry wood and deep reds and greens, the other Middle Eastern with a garden extension and a Bedouin tent—will tempt you to eat in. ✉ *Nablus Rd.,* ☎ *02/541–2222,* ℻ *02/582–8202. 118 rooms. 3 restaurants. AE, DC, MC, V.*

$$$ 🏨 **Ariel.** The Ariel was originally conceived as an apartment hotel, so an early change in plans left it with a good number of spacious guest rooms, some large enough to accommodate families. About a third of the rooms have excellent views of Mt. Zion. Extensive bathroom renovations and some new bedroom furniture have raised the comfort level. The public areas—lobby, bar, and dining room—balance marble with copious plants. ✉ *31 Hebron Rd., 93546,* ☎ *02/568–9999,* ℻ *02/673–4066. 128 rooms. Restaurant, bar. AE, DC, MC, V.*

$$$ 🏨 **Eldan.** Completely renovated, renamed, and under new management, this hotel is an excellent value. It is centrally located, just 10 minutes' walk from downtown or the Jaffa Gate, and the rooms are airy, spacious, and decorated in cheerful colors. Every night you stay at the hotel gives you a day of free car rental (excluding insurance) from the Eldan company. ✉ *24 King David St.,* ☎ *02/567–9777,* ℻ *02/624–9525. 76 rooms. Restaurant. AE, DC, MC, V.*

$$$ 🏨 **Four Points Jerusalem.** Although there's nothing particularly remarkable in the look of this hotel on Jerusalem's west side, its recreational facilities make it a standout in its price category. The health club—complete with indoor pool, exercise room, sauna, and whirlpool bath—and the grassy outdoor pool area provide delightful, relaxing environments at the end of an intense day of sightseeing. The hotel is managed by the Sheraton chain. ✉ *4 Vilnai St., 91036,* ☎ *02/655–8888,* ℻ *02/651–2266. 200 rooms. Restaurant, bar, 1 indoor and 2 outdoor pools, hot tub, sauna, exercise room, health club. AE, DC, MC, V.*

$$$ 🏨 **Jerusalem Tower.** This hotel is in a choice location: bang in the center of downtown. The stone floor of the lobby is studded with replicas of ancient mosaics. Guest rooms are small, but have large wall mirrors above the wood-paneled headboards to enhance the sense of space. Ask for a room above the sixth floor to guarantee a view. ✉ *23 Hillel St., Box 2656, 94581,* ☎ *02/620–9209,* ℻ *02/625–2167. 120 rooms. Restaurant, bar, café. AE, DC, MC, V.*

$$$ 🏨 **Kikar Zion.** Although this seven-story building dominates downtown Zion Square (Kikar Zion in Hebrew), the entrance is a very modest doorway off Shammai Street a half block away, where the elevator takes you up to the huge lobby. High above street level, the guest rooms are quiet and spacious. The rooms wrap around the building, affording good views of the city; insist on a high floor facing either the Old City or Independence Park. Guests pay a nominal fee to use the privately owned health club. ✉ *25 Shammai St., 94631,* ☎ *02/624–4644,* ℻ *02/624–4136. 120 rooms. 2 restaurants, bar, pool, health club. AE, DC, MC, V.*

$$$ 🏨 **King Solomon.** The centerpiece of the lobby is a huge, spherical sculpture of Jerusalem by Frank Meisler. A split-level atrium reveals shops one floor down and restaurants below that. The standard guest rooms are not spacious, but the more deluxe ones are quite large. The rooms are attractive, with brown and tan predominating, enhanced by sepia

prints above the beds. The well-equipped bathrooms are more spacious than most. Rates are at the upper end of the price range, but the deluxe aesthetic makes them a good value. ⊠ *32 King David St., 94101,* ☎ *02/569–5555,* FAX *02/624–1774. 142 rooms, 6 suites. 2 restaurants, bar, pool, beauty salon. AE, DC, MC, V.*

**$$$** 🏨 **Lev Yerushalayim.** A good bargain for its price category, especially for families, this all-suite hotel is in the heart of the city center. You leave the heat and noise behind as you enter the stone-walled, plant-filled lobby and suites decorated in pleasing blues and pastels. Please note that service and amenities can be uneven. Prices are per suite for two guests; additional guests using the sofa beds pay an extra $75 per night for an adult and $50 per night for a child under 12. Deluxe suites are defined by an additional room with sofa beds—for a family, easily worth the small extra charge—not by a higher grade of furnishings. Breakfast is included, but you can make other meals in your kitchenette. The use of the on-site Samson's Gym is free to hotel guests. ⊠ *18 King George St., 91079,* ☎ *02/530–0333,* FAX *02/623–2432. 57 suites, 27 deluxe suites, 2 royal suites, 6 penthouses. 2 restaurants, kitchenettes, hot tub, sauna, exercise room, health club, coin laundry. AE, DC, MC, V.*

**$$$** 🏨 **Mercure–Jerusalem Gate.** The Jerusalem Gate caters to business travelers and tour groups. It's adjacent to the old Central Bus Station and on many convenient bus routes, though not a short walk to anywhere in particular. Recent refurbishing of the guest rooms have introduced attractive wood furniture and sunny upholstery. For a view across the hills, ask for a room facing north or west. The attractive bar on the mezzanine overlooking the lobby has a copper ceiling. The rooftop sundeck is a welcome haven. ⊠ *43 Yirmiyahu St., 94467,* ☎ *02/500–8500,* FAX *02/500–2121. 298 rooms. Restaurant, bar, business services. AE, DC, MC, V.*

**$$$** 🏨 **Mount Zion.** The core of the Mount Zion is a renovated 19th-cen-
★ tury building that once served as a British eye hospital. To this a new, similar wing was added in the 1970s. Columns, arched doorways, and windows in Jerusalem stone all frame ethereal views of Mt. Zion and create attractive nooks filled with wall hangings, Armenian tiles, and plants. New ownership and management have gone a long way toward realizing the hotel's phenomenal potential. The rooms in the newer wing have been renovated, but the rooms in the old wing are still superior; they have character and better views. The swimming pool and children's pool overlook the Hinnom Valley. The gym (with its own picture window) is free to guests; the charming "water spa" (hot pool, sauna, and both indoor and outdoor whirlpool baths) asks a nominal fee. ⊠ *17 Hebron Rd., 93546,* ☎ *02/568–9555,* FAX *02/673–1425. 140 rooms. 2 restaurants, bar, pool, hot tub, sauna, health club. AE, DC, MC, V.* 🐾

**$$$** 🏨 **Park Plaza.** This West Jerusalem hotel has a good local reputation. Its rooms are small and its facilities limited, but renovations have added a touch of class to both guest rooms and public areas. ⊠ *2 Vilnai St., Box 3835, 95435,* ☎ *02/658–2222,* FAX *02/658–2211. 217 rooms. Restaurant, bar. AE, DC, MC, V.*

**$$$** 🏨 **Prima Kings.** The Kings—the name by which it's still known—is on a busy intersection (insulated from noise) less than 10 minutes' walk from the city center. Cane furniture and deep sofas create comfortable, if not particularly intimate, public areas. Most of the guest rooms are fairly spacious, an effect that's enhanced by light colors. ⊠ *60 King George St. (entrance on Ramban St.), 94262,* ☎ *02/620–1201,* FAX *02/ 620–1211. 187 rooms. 2 restaurants, bar. AE, DC, MC, V.*

**$$$** 🏨 **Ramat Rachel.** As a rustic kibbutz hotel less than 15 minutes' drive
★ from downtown, at the southern end of the Bus 7 route, Ramat Rachel enjoys the best of both worlds. Most rooms have stunning views of Bethlehem and the Judean Desert. The pleasant if unexceptional decor

is offset by the brilliant colors of Calman Shemi quilted "soft art" originals above each headboard. With its fine pool and other sports and health facilities, all free to guests, Ramat Rachel feels like an isolated resort. ⊠ *Kibbutz Ramat Rachel, Jerusalem 90900,* ☎ *02/670–2555,* ℻ *02/673–3155. 164 rooms. Restaurant, bar, pool, beauty salon, hot tub, saunas, 3 tennis courts, basketball, exercise room, playground. AE, DC, MC, V.*

$$$ 🏨 **Windmill.** This hotel is comfortable but fairly nondescript, with unobtrusive decor other than an abundance of plants in the public areas. Its rates are high for what it offers, but the location—on a side street opposite the Dan Panorama, near the city center and on good bus routes—counts for something. ⊠ *3 Mendele St., off Keren Hayesod, 92147,* ☎ *02/566–3111,* ℻ *02/561–0964. 133 rooms. Restaurant, bar. AE, DC, MC, V.*

$$$ 🏨 **YMCA (West)–3 Arches.** Built in 1933, this limestone building with its famous domed bell tower is a Jerusalem landmark. Stone arches, exotic murals, wooden cupboards, and Armenian tiles give it charm and character. The guest rooms are not large, but they're attractive, comfortable, and air-conditioned. These and an excellent location make the Y an attractive deal at the upper end of this price category. On the premises are excellent sports facilities, an auditorium for concerts and folkloric performances, and the privately run Le Tsriff restaurant (☞ *Dining, above*). ⊠ *26 King David St., Box 294, 91002,* ☎ *02/659–2692,* ℻ *02/623–5192. 56 rooms. Restaurant, café, pool, sauna, 4 tennis courts, basketball, exercise room, indoor track, squash. AE, DC, MC, V.*

$$ 🏨 **Bet Shemuel.** This stone building, with cool inner courtyards and fabulous views of the Old City from the roof and almost half the rooms, was built not just as a guest house but as a cultural and educational center of the World Union for Progressive Judaism. Its spacious rooms, which can sleep six, are bright and pleasant, if a little spare. Rooms come with shower only. The location is excellent: only 5 minutes' walk to the Old City, 10 minutes to the center of town. There's just one drawback: in good weather the central courtyard is used for Friday-night concerts and occasional receptions, rendering the guests in many rooms involuntary participants; opt for an outside room. A new wing (under construction at press time) will add 11 more intimate and higher-grade rooms. ⊠ *13 King David St. (entrance on Sham'a St.), 94101,* ☎ *02/620–3456,* ℻ *02/620–3467. 41 rooms. Restaurant, coffee shop. AE, DC, MC, V.*

$$ 🏨 **Christ Church.** This is the guest house of the adjacent Anglican church, the oldest Protestant church (1849) in the Middle East. Rooms in the old stone buildings (once a pilgrim hospice) are comfortably furnished, if not exactly luxurious; the eight newer rooms are air-conditioned. The courtyard and garden make a nice retreat. The location, in the Old City just inside Jaffa Gate, is excellent for sightseeing, though many people are more at ease in modern West Jerusalem. ⊠ *Jaffa Gate, Old City, Box 14037, 91140,* ☎ *02/627–7727 or 02/627–7729,* ℻ *02/628–2999. 32 rooms. Coffee shop, dining room. MC, V.*

$$ 🏨 **St. Andrew's Scottish Hospice.** Part of the St. Andrew's Church complex, the Presbyterian-operated hospice—a guest house, not a medical facility!—is as much a retreat as a place to stay overnight. Opened in 1930, the building has the pleasing stone arches, alcoves, and atriums that characterize the local architecture of that period. The rooms are small, somewhat sparsely furnished, and not air-conditioned (though they have overhead fans), but most compensate with views of the garden, and some have views of Mt. Zion. Rooms have showers only. Meals are available upon request. ⊠ *Off corner of King*

*David and Emek Refa'im Sts., opposite rail station, Box 8619, 91086,* ☎ *02/673–2401,* FAX *02/673–1711. 17 rooms. AE, DC, MC, V.*

**$$**   ⌨ **Zion.** This Parisian-style hotel occupies a 140-year-old stone building right in the center of town, its little balconies overlooking a pedestrian-only side street off the Ben Yehuda mall. Rooms at the front of the building get some street noise until late hours, but new air-conditioning has alleviated the problem, and planned double glazing should solve it altogether. Rooms are simply but pleasantly furnished (and have cable TV). Ten rooms have showers only. Note: there is no elevator, and only four rooms are on the first floor. ✉ *10 Dorot Rishonim St., 94625,* ☎ *02/625–9511,* FAX *02/625–7585. 25 rooms. Bar. AE, DC, MC, V.*

**$–$$**   ⌨ **Louise Waterman-Wise.** Once a youth hostel, now upgraded to a guest house (in keeping with the Youth Hostel Association's successful attempt to march with the times), this large facility offers simply but neatly furnished rooms. They vary in size, sleeping anywhere from one to six, but all have en-suite bathrooms. The setting, opposite Mt. Herzl in the Bayit Vegan area of West Jerusalem, has sweeping views of the Judean Hills yet is only a 10-minute cab ride (there's a taxi stand next door) or a 20-minute bus ride from downtown. Guests have access to a garden and other common rooms and to occasional evening activities. Meals are substantial and very cheap. The rate jumps on weekends. ✉ *8 Hapisgah St., Bayit Vegan, Box 16350, 91162,* ☎ *02/642–3366,* FAX *02/642–3362. 80 rooms. AE, DC, MC, V.*

**$–$$**   ⌨ **Yitzhak Rabin Guest House.** Part of the official Youth Hostel Association, this new facility is an example of how far "popular" accommodations have come. It's not quite a hotel, but it's no longer a dormitory-style hostel either. Furnishings are a bit spare (though there are some better-grade rooms), but rooms are spacious (they sleep from two to five, two in fold-up bunks) and showers and toilets are private. The building faces the greenery of Hebrew University's Givat Ram campus; the Israel Museum is a short walk away; and there is a bus route to the downtown and the Central Bus Station. ✉ *1 Nahman Avigad St., Givat Ram, 91390,* ☎ *02/678–0101,* FAX *02/679–6566. 77 rooms. Restaurant, cafeteria. AE, DC, MC, V.*

# NIGHTLIFE AND THE ARTS

## Nightlife

Jerusalem's nightlife is a great deal more limited than Tel Aviv's—almost provincial—but some lively spots do keep late hours.

### Bars and Lounges

All the major hotels have bars, of course, but none of them are particularly distinctive. The legendary **Fink's** (✉ 2 Hahistadrut St., ☎ 02/623–4523) has been a hangout of the famous and the infamous since 1932 and is known for its well-stocked bar and skillful mixes.

### Dance Clubs

Primarily the preserve of the 17- to 21-year-old crowd (Israel's drinking age is 18), Jerusalem dance clubs come alive on Thursday, Friday, and Saturday nights. Don't even *think* about going before midnight. Admission ranges from NIS 40 to NIS 52 ($10 to $13).

The veteran downtown **Underground** (✉ 1 Yoel Salomon St., off Zion Sq., ☎ 02/625–1918) looks like something out of Dante's *Inferno,* with rough black walls, murals, and sculptures of prisoners. The bar, up at street level, is only marginally saner. You can also have a drink at the upper level, where the dance floor is free. The **Orient Express** nightclub (✉ 32 Lehi St., ☎ 02/581–1334), at the entrance to the Hyatt

Regency Hotel on Mt. Scopus, is decorated to recapture the bygone era of that famous train, but the sound system is marvelously state-of-the-art. Some evenings are reserved for 1960s and '70s nostalgia and draw a more mature crowd; other nights attract students from the Hebrew University campus next door.

The **Talpiot Industrial Zone,** 4 km (2½ mi) south of city center, may seem an unlikely place to find a clutch of discos, but it makes sense in a city where the Jewish Sabbath is sacrosanct to so many. Nothing much happens before midnight, but by then parking is tight on Yad Harutzim Street and the adjacent side streets and the snack bars are crowded. Most places are geared to the college-age set, a few to a slightly older crowd. Individual clubs appear and disappear with such bewildering speed that specific listings have little long-term significance; ask your hotel staff for recommendations.

### Folk-Music Clubs

Jerusalem has a modest folk scene, with performances by local artists and occasional visits by international performers. Watch for listings, usually under "Entertainment" in the *Jerusalem Post* and elsewhere, or call folk singer Jill Rogoff (☎ 02/679–0410) for connections with the local folk community.

### Jazz Clubs

The **Pargod Theater** (✉ 94 Bezalel St., ☎ 02/623–1765) hosts a regular jam session on Friday afternoon and features evening programs of jazz, rock, world music, and country.

### Pubs

A half dozen nondescript pubs populate a courtyard off **31 Jaffa Road,** where a drink is just a drink and the ambience seems to be secondary. There's another cluster of pubs in and around the **Russian Compound.**

## The Arts

For schedules of performances and other cultural events, consult the Friday weekend section of the *Jerusalem Post* and its insert *In Jerusalem;* Friday's "The Guide" of *Ha'aretz*'s English edition (which comes with the *Herald Tribune*); the Ministry of Tourism's monthly bulletin, *Events in Jerusalem;* and the free weekly booklets *This Week in Jerusalem* and *Hello Israel;* all in English.

The main ticket agencies for performances in Jerusalem are **Ben-Naim** (✉ 38 Jaffa Rd., ☎ 02/623–1273), **Bimot** (✉ 8 Shammai St., ☎ 02/624–0896), and **Kla'im** (✉ 12 Shammai St., ☎ 02/625–6869).

Student discounts are sometimes available; present your card at the ticket office.

Top Israeli and international orchestras, choirs, singers, theater companies, dance troupes, and street entertainers participate in the **Israel Festival,** usually held in May or early June. All of the performing arts are represented, and offerings range from the classical to the avant-garde.

### Dance

The **Israel National Ballet** and the modern **Bat-Dor** have a varied performance record. The better-known **Batsheva** modern-dance troupe is the one to look out for.

### Film

The usual Hollywood fare is available at the comfortable modern cinemas clustered in the center of town, in the Jerusalem Mall, and south of the city in the Talpiot Industrial Zone. They're closed Friday night. Movies are subtitled in Hebrew and, when appropriate, English. The

**Jerusalem Cinemateque** (⊠ Hebron Rd., ☎ 02/672–4131) specializes in old, rare, and art films, but its wide-ranging programs often include current offerings. Its monthly series focuses on specific directors, actors, or subjects, and its annual **Jerusalem Film Festival,** held in July, is a must for film buffs. The theater is open Friday night.

## Music

Classical music abounds in Jerusalem, with Israeli orchestras and chamber ensembles performing year-round and a trickle of international artists passing through. The **International Convention Center,** or ICC (☎ 02/655–8558), still known locally by its old name Binyanei Ha'ooma, is opposite the Central Bus Station and is the local venue for occasional concerts by the world-renowned **Israel Philharmonic Orchestra.** For tickets, contact the orchestra's offices in Tel Aviv (⊠ Hechal Hatarbut, 1 Huberman St., ☎ 03/525–1502). The **Jerusalem Center for the Performing Arts** (⊠ 20 Marcus St., ☎ 02/560–5757), still best known as the Jerusalem Theater, houses the Jerusalem Sherover Theater, the Henry Crown Auditorium, and the more intimate Rebecca Crown Theater. All in all, this is Jerusalem's most active and interesting venue.

**Bet Ticho,** or Ticho House (⊠ Off Harav Kook St. near Zion Sq., ☎ 02/624–5068), holds intimate recitals on Friday mornings in a charming setting. The atmosphere is rustic at the **Targ Music Center,** in Ein Kerem (⊠ Hama'ayan St., ☎ 02/641–4250), 7 km (4½ mi) from the city center, where noontime chamber-music performances are common on Friday and Saturday. The popular (and free) **Etnacha** series of concerts, produced by Israel Radio's classics station, takes place Monday at 5 PM, generally from October through June, at the Henry Crown Auditorium (⊠ 20 Marcus St., ☎ 02/560–5757). Always check listings before you make plans.

Hearing music in one of Jerusalem's many churches can be a moving experience. The **Church of the Redeemer** (⊠ Muristan, in the Old City's Christian Quarter, ☎ 02/627–6111) is a favorite venue. **Dormition Abbey** (⊠ Mt. Zion, ☎ 02/565–5330) also offers concerts.

A rousing concert of Israeli folklore—mostly singing and folk dancing—is presented at the **YMCA (West)** (⊠ 26 King David St., call Zion at ☎ 050/233–210 or 052/233–210), usually on Monday, Thursday, and Saturday evenings. Call ahead to confirm. Reservations are advised; but as the 500-seat hall is generally inundated by tour groups and seats are unmarked, it's recommended that you arrive early. The cost is $15.

The **Bible Lands Museum** (⊠ Givat Ram, next to Israel Museum, ☎ 02/561–1066) hosts Saturday-evening concerts, preceded by cheese and wine in the foyer. The delightfully eclectic programs range from chamber music to jazz and gospel to folk music and country-and-western. An added attraction: the museum's galleries are open to concertgoers for half an hour before and after the concert.

To rub shoulders with the locals, look into the Friday-night Oneg Shabbat series at **Bet Shemuel** (⊠ Eliyahu Shama'a St., off King David St., ☎ 02/620–3456), which typically hosts some of the top performers on the Israeli pop scene. The evening will be in Hebrew, of course, but the music and the atmosphere may speak to you in an international language of good feelings.

## Theater

Most plays are performed in Hebrew, but there is the odd offering in English. Some performances have simultaneous translation. Your best bet for plays in English is the **Khan Theater** (⊠ 2 David Remez Sq., near the railway station, ☎ 02/671–8281), but check newspaper listings for other venues as well.

# OUTDOOR ACTIVITIES AND SPORTS

For a change of pace from sightseeing, keep in shape or pursue a favorite sport.

## Bicycling

The informal **Jerusalem Bicycling Club** (☎ 02/561–9416; ask for Benny) leads rides on Saturday morning at 7 starting from the International Convention Center, Binyanei Ha'ooma (opposite the Central Bus Station). The club is a good source for information on bike rentals and can recommend routes within the city.

## Bowling

The **Jerusalem Bowling Center** (⊠ Achim Yisrael Mall "Kenyon Talpiot," 18 Yad Harutzim St., Talpiot Industrial Zone, ☎ 02/673–2195) has 10 lanes, a small cafeteria, and billiard tables. The center is open daily 10 AM–2 AM (Saturday from 11 AM). From Sunday through Thursday, the cost per game (including shoe rental) is NIS 20 ($5) 10 AM–6 PM and NIS 25 ($6.20) 6 PM–2 AM; from Friday evening through Saturday night the cost is NIS 28 ($7). Play two games and get the third free.

## Health Clubs

The best health clubs in Jerusalem are in hotels; some are privately run concessions. All welcome health seekers who are not hotel guests. The most comprehensive facilities are at the **Crowne Plaza** (⊠ Givat Ram, ☎ 02/658–8888), **Hyatt Regency** (⊠ 32 Lehi St., Mt. Scopus, ☎ 02/533–1204), and **Renaissance Jerusalem** (⊠ 6 Wolfson St., ☎ 02/659–9999).

## Horseback Riding

A number of stables offer lessons and trail riding, including those suitable for children, as well as longer (and more interesting) trails. Rates vary, so call ahead.

Try **King David's Riding Stables** (⊠ Neve Ilan, north of Rte. 1, ☎ 02/534–0535), in the wooded Judean Hills, is 16 km (10 mi) west of Jerusalem. **Meir Mizrachi Stables** (⊠ Kfar Adumim, north of Rte. 1, ☎ 02/535–5419 stables, 02/535–4769 Meir Mizrachi's home) is in the Judean Desert, 17 km (11 mi) east of Jerusalem. The **Riding Club** (⊠ Kiryat Moshe, behind Angel's Bakery, ☎ 02/651–3585) breeds Arabians; do not call between 1 and 3 PM.

## Squash

The **YMCA (West)** (⊠ 26 King David St., ☎ 02/569–2692) has three squash courts for rental. They're available for NIS 40 ($10) for 45 minutes, 7:15 AM–8:45 PM, Monday–Saturday.

## Swimming

The enthusiast can swim year-round at these pools (those at hotels welcome nonguests). Indoor: **Bet Hano'ar Ha'ivri** (or YMWHA; ⊠ 105 Herzog Blvd., ☎ 02/678–9441), **Djanogly** (⊠ Bet Avraham Community Center, Ramot Allon, ☎ 02/586–8055), and **Renaissance Jerusalem Hotel** (⊠ 6 Wolfson St., ☎ 02/659–9999). Outdoor (covered and heated in winter): **Inbal** (⊠ 3 Jabotinsky St., ☎ 02/675–6666).

Other recommended outdoor pools (except in winter) include the public **Jerusalem Pool** (⊠ 43 Emek Refa'im St., ☎ 02/563–2092), which gets very crowded in July and August, and the beautifully landscaped facilities at the following hotels:

**Crowne Plaza** (⊠ Givat Ram, ☎ 02/658–8888); **Hyatt Regency** (⊠ 32 Lehi St., Mt. Scopus, ☎ 02/533–1234); **King David Hotel** (⊠ 23 King David St., ☎ 02/620–8888); and **Renaissance Jerusalem** (⊠ 6 Wolfson St., ☎ 02/659–9999). A little less expensive are the facilities at the **Four Points Jerusalem** (⊠ 4 Wolfson St., ☎ 02/655–8888) and **Mt. Zion Hotel** (⊠ 17 Hebron Rd., ☎ 02/568–9555), also in attractive locations.

## Tennis

Tennis is now very popular in Israel. Advance reservations are always required.

**Hebrew University at Mt. Scopus** (☎ 02/581–7579 or 02/588–2796) has 10 lighted courts and rental equipment. Courts go for NIS 35 ($8.75) an hour in daylight and NIS 40 ($10) an hour in evenings and are open Sunday–Thursday 8 AM–10 PM, Friday 7–6, and Saturday 7–5. Call ahead, especially during campus recess. The **Israel Tennis Center** (⊠ 5 Almaliach St., Katamon Tet, ☎ 02/679–1866 or 02/679–2726) has 18 lighted courts, available for NIS 35 ($8.75) per hour Sunday–Thursday 7 AM–4 PM, NIS 40 ($10) per hour Sunday–Thursday 7 PM–10 PM, Friday 7–5, and Saturday 7–2. Equipment rental is sometimes available; call ahead. The **YMCA (West)** (⊠ 26 King David St., ☎ 02/569–2692) has four courts that rent for NIS 40 ($10) per hour; they're open Monday–Saturday 8 AM–8 PM. Several major **hotels** have their own courts, but they often restrict usage to guests or club members. Ask your concierge to make inquiries if you want to play at a particular hotel.

# SHOPPING

Jerusalem has good shopping, for everything from jewelry and art to crafts and souvenirs. The several distinct shopping areas make it easy to plan expeditions. Prices are generally fixed in the city center and the Jewish Quarter of the Old City, though you can sometimes negotiate for significant discounts on expensive art and jewelry. Shopping in the Old City's colorful Arab bazaar, or souk (pronounced "shook" in Israel—rhymes with "book"), is fascinating but can be a trap for the unwary. Avoid buying gold, silver, or gem-studded jewelry here. Sporadic Palestinian Arab unrest has reduced the tourist flow in the bazaar, though most everything remains open. You're advised to evaluate the current political climate before spending time in the area.

Stores generally open by 8:30 or 9 AM, and some close between 1 and 4. Some also close on Tuesday afternoon, a traditional but not mandatory half day. Jewish-owned stores (that is, all of West Jerusalem—the "New City"—and the Old City's Jewish Quarter) close on Friday afternoon at 1 or 2, depending on the kind of store and the season (food and souvenir stores tend to stay open later), and reopen on Sunday morning. Some stores geared to the tourist trade, particularly downtown, reopen on Saturday night after the Jewish Sabbath ends, especially in summer. Arab-owned stores in the Old City and East Jerusalem are busiest on Saturday and quietest on Sunday, when many (but not all) Christian storekeepers close for the day.

# Shopping Streets and Malls

**Arts and Crafts Lane** (known in Hebrew as Hutzot Hayotzer), opposite and downhill from the Jaffa Gate, has goldsmiths and silversmiths specializing in Judaica, generally done in an ultramodern, minimalist style. The work is exquisite and is priced accordingly. You can also find excellent jewelry, weaving, fine art, and musical instruments.

The **Cardo,** in the Old City's Jewish Quarter, began life as the main thoroughfare of Byzantine Jerusalem, was a street during the Crusader era, and has now been converted into an attractive shopping area. Beyond discovering souvenirs and Judaica, you'll find good-quality jewelry, art, and objets d'art here.

**Hatachana** (the Mill) is a small arcade on Ramban Street, near the intersection with King George Street. Built around an old windmill, the complex houses expensive boutiques and an excellent beauty salon.

The **Jerusalem Mall,** known locally as Kenyon Malcha, is—at 500,000 square ft not counting parking—the largest in the Middle East. It includes a department store, a supermarket, eight cinemas, and almost 200 shops and eateries (Pizza Hut and Burger King among them). The interior is an attractive mix of arched skylights and wrought-iron banisters in a quasi–art deco style. The mall is clearly signposted from the Begin Boulevard, via Eliyahu Golomb Street, and from the Pat Junction–Gilo Road.

**King David Street** is lined with a sizable number of prestigious stores, with the emphases on art, Judaica, antiquities, and interesting jewelry.

The pedestrian-only **Midrachov** is simply downtown Ben Yehuda Street, the heartbeat of West Jerusalem (the New City). The selection of clothing, shoes, jewelry, souvenirs, T-shirts, and street food is prodigious here. You'll be serenaded by street musicians at every turn. It's a real scene, best appreciated from one of the many outdoor cafés. Summer evenings are lively, as the mall fills with peddlers of cheap jewelry and crafts, and young shoppers admiring them.

**Salomon Street,** in the old neighborhood of Nahalat Shiva, just off Zion Square, has also been developed as a pedestrian mall. Here and in adjacent alleys and courtyards, eateries abound, but you'll also find some attractive crafts galleries and arty jewelry and clothing shops.

# Specialty Stores

## Art Galleries

Several galleries representing a range of Israeli artists are close to the city's premier hotels, on **King David Street.**

For large wall decorations (with prices to match), check out the appliqué-like "soft art" of **Calman Shemi** (⊠ 22 King David St., ☎ 02/624–9557), whose marvelous effects must be seen to be appreciated. **Frank Meisler** (⊠ 21 King David St., ☎ 02/624–2759) has an original and whimsical sense of humor; his caricaturish silver-plated pewter sculptures cover subjects from Noah's ark and Jerusalem cityscapes to Freud and animal figures that seem to be sharing Meisler's secret joke.

## Clothing

Clothing tends to be expensive in Israel, and in Jerusalem you have to search for really fashionable clothes. One homegrown women's clothing store with definite style is **A.B.C.** (⊠ 33 King George St., ☎ 02/623–4934). The very pricey **Lagotte Studio,** in the Hatachana arcade

(✉ 8 Ramban St., ☎ 02/566–5059), stocks well-designed imported women's wear, with the adjacent **Lagotte Plus** (☎ 02/561–2113) specializing in large sizes. In the same building, **Oui Set** (☎ 02/563–8365) stocks more casual but still elegant merchandise of a similar standard.

SWIMWEAR

Israeli swimsuits and beach accessories have revolutionized the market overseas with their dazzling designs and colors. Gottex swimwear is available at the downtown department store **Hamashbir** (✉ 28 King George St. ☎ 02/624–9069).

## Crafts

For ceramics, glass, jewelry, wooden objects, and embroidery, try the **Jerusalem House of Quality** (✉ 12 Hebron Rd., ☎ 02/671–7430), which presents the work of some excellent Israeli craftspeople. Their studios are on the second floor, so you can often see them at work.

For Armenian hand-painted pottery—predominantly blue and brown, with geometric or stylized natural motifs—one of the best artisans is Stefan Karakashian of **Jerusalem Pottery** (☎ 02/626–1587) at the VI Station of the Cross, on the Via Dolorosa in the Old City. Karakashian's work is of a particularly high standard and includes plates, plaques, and bowls. Just inside Zion Gate in the Old City **Hagop Antreassian** (☎ 02/627–2584) makes Armenian pottery as well. You can often catch him painting or firing his clay creations.

Drop in at **Cadim** (✉ 4 Salomon St., ☎ 02/623–4869), in Nahalat Shiva, for a selection of interesting contemporary Israeli ceramics. **Shemonah Beyachad** (✉ 11 Salomon St., ☎ 02/624–7250) displays the work of several artists. At **7 Artists** (✉ 6 Salomon St., ☎ 02/623–4210), pottery shares the showcases with embroidered and woven fabrics. Feast your eyes at the **Guild of Ceramicists** (✉ 27 Salomon St., ☎ 02/624–4065), where artistic designs are applied to pottery both functional and decorative. **Danny Azoulay**'s store (✉ 5 Salomon St., ☎ 02/623–3918) has fine porcelain items; many are traditional Jewish ritual objects—some of which are expensive—but you can also find less pricey items, such as napkin rings and bottle stoppers, all beautifully hand-painted in rich blues, reds, and golds.

Opaque, smoky Israeli **glass** is available in both decorative and practical items in many tourist shops. The miniature vases, sometimes decorated with silver, are particularly attractive.

**Kakadu** (✉ 1 Rivlin St., ☎ 02/625–6412) manufactures and sells exciting modern "art and design in wood," colorful items that range from desktop paraphernalia to full-size mirrors. **Klein** (✉ 3 Ziv St., off Bar Ilan St., ☎ 02/538–9992 or 02/538–8784), in northern Jerusalem, has some of the highest-quality olive-wood objects in the country. This is actually the factory, so the showroom stocks everything they make, from bowls and yo-yos to attractive trays of Armenian pottery tiles framed in olive wood; picture frames; boxes; and desktop paraphernalia.

Paper cutting was a well-established Jewish art form until about 100 years ago. **Yehudit Shadur** (✉ 12 Hovevei Zion St., ☎ 02/566–3217), who has been primarily responsible for the Israeli revival of this traditional craft, makes pieces in styles that range from simple contrasts to richly colored and varied textures; call for an appointment. Working with traditional motifs, **Archie Granot** (✉ 1 Agron St., ☎ 02/625–2210) has evolved his own complex, multilayered style of paper-cut Judaica. Some of his work is included in museum collections around the world. Call ahead.

**G.R.A.S.** (✉ 20 King George St., adjacent to Hamashbir department store, ☎ 02/625–6599) sells its own special line of pillow covers and curtains in its distinctive, Israeli-made fabrics in exotic patterns. The pillow covers are an especially good value and make great, easy-to-pack gifts. **Charlotte** (✉ 4 Coresh St., ☎ 02/625–1632) carries a rich variety of colorful good-quality items: ceramics, weavings, painted silks, jewelry, and fashion accessories. **Amnon & Tamar** (✉ 8 Rivlin St., ☎ 02/622–1674) sells a bit of everything, from Judaica, glassware, and weaving, through jewelry, painted silk, and wood and ceramic ornaments, to herbs and fruit preserves—all in good taste.

A very different emporium is **Marvels of the Orient** (✉ 9 Safra Sq., Shop No. 6, ☎ 050/561–150), where Nuha Muslel displays the acquisitions of her collector husband, Hader—Asian carpets and tapestries, Palestinian costumes and embroidery, Damascene inlay furniture, and Islamic art and ethnic jewelry. Many are true collector's items and are priced accordingly.

## Harps

The **House of Harrari,** (☎ FAX 02/570–9075) is in the village of Ramat Raziel, a 25-minute drive from downtown Jerusalem, west of Ein Kerem. The selection of beautiful harps, ranging from decorative door harps to 22-string folk instruments, is inspired (the makers say) by the Bible. The workshop displays the instruments in different stages of production. You can choose from a variety of ornamentation, and the little door harps can be decorated with an appropriate inscription. The gallery will ship your purchase home. Call for directions.

## Jewelry

Jewelry in Israel is of a high international standard.

**Meshulash** (✉ Arye Leib Hurwitz Alley, off Salomon St., ☎ 02/624–1762) makes and sells exquisite ultramodern pieces, characterized by their clean, almost minimalist lines. The very affordable **G.R.A.S.** (☞ Crafts, *above*) creates modern adaptations of traditional Yemenite silver jewelry. **Pick** (✉ 11 Ben Hillel St., ☎ 02/623–2859) specializes in modern silver jewelry—the earrings are especially good—at reasonable prices. **Idit** (✉ 21 King George St., ☎ 02/622–1911) has fine merchandise in a more formal style. One particularly outstanding craftsman is **Danny Alsberg** (☎ 02/628–9275), in the Arts and Crafts Lane (Hutzot Hayotzer), outside the Jaffa Gate. Not to be missed is **Sarah Einstein** (✉ 7 Ma'alot Nachalat Shiva, off Salomon St., ☎ 02/622–1151), with a collection of one-of-a-kind necklaces and earrings made from antique silver, amber, and other materials.

The ubiquitous **H. Stern** (✉ Just inside Jaffa Gate and at many major hotels) has high-quality, conventional pieces. **National Diamond Center (NDC)/Caprice** (✉ 143 Bethlehem Rd., ☎ 02/673–3770), a large diamond manufacturer, has a factory and showroom for jewelry and loose-cut gems. **Adipaz** (✉ 20 Pierre Koenig St., ☎ 02/678–3887) is a similar large diamond manufacturer. You can take guided tours of both companies' facilities upon request.

## T-Shirts

Tourist shops all stock the same range of machine-stamped shirts, but most stores will also decorate shirts from a selection of designs. There are several on Ben Yehuda Street: Army/Navy Surplus (also on Ben Hillel Street, adjacent to Ben Yehuda), Sweet, and Happening. Mr. T. and Lord Kitsch, on Zion Square, also stock a good selection.

## Street Markets

Jerusalem's first and foremost market, of course, is the **souk** in the Old City. Spreading through a warren of intersecting streets, the souk is primarily for the Old City's Arab residents. It's awash with color and redolent with the clashing scents of exotic spices. Village women's baskets of produce vie for attention with hanging shanks of lamb, fresh fish on ice, and fresh-baked delicacies, and food stalls are interspersed with those selling fabrics and shoes. The baubles and trinkets of the tourist trade often seem secondary, except along the well-trodden paths of the Via Dolorosa, David Street, and Christian Quarter Road.

Haggling with merchants in the Arab market—a time-honored tradition—is not always the good-natured experience it once was. Unless you know what you want, know how much it's *really* worth, and enjoy the sometimes aggressive give-and-take of bargaining, you're better off just enjoying the local color (stick to the main streets, and watch your wallet or purse) and doing your shopping in the more modern and familiar New City.

Off Jaffa Road, near the Clal Center office buildings, is the **Machaneh Yehuda** produce market, a block-long alleyway that becomes a blur of brilliant primary colors as the city's best-quality fruit and vegetables, pickles and cheeses, fresh fish and poultry, confections, and falafel await inspection. The busiest days are Thursday and Friday, when Jews shop for the Sabbath; the market is closed on Saturday along with the rest of Jewish West Jerusalem.

On Thursday and Friday, **Hamartef** (the Cellar) arcade, beneath City Tower (⊠ Corner of King George and Ben Yehuda Sts.), hosts jewelers and vendors of bric-a-brac and secondhand books. It's fun just to browse here, but sometimes the wares are really worth buying.

# JERUSALEM A TO Z

## Arriving and Departing

### By Bus

The **Egged** National Bus Cooperative (☎ 03/694–8888) serves Jerusalem's **Central Bus Station** (⊠ 224 Jaffa Rd.) with comfortable, air-conditioned buses from all major cities in Israel. Egged buses in and out of Jerusalem stop running about a half hour before sunset on Friday and Jewish religious holiday eves and resume after dark on Saturday or religious holidays. The **East Jerusalem Bus Station** (⊠ Sultan Suleiman St., opposite Damascus Gate) is the terminus for private Arab-run lines serving West Bank towns such as Bethlehem.

### By Car

**Route 1** is the chief route to Jerusalem from both the west (Tel Aviv, Ben Gurion Airport, Mediterranean Coast) and the east (Galilee via Jordan Valley, Dead Sea area, Eilat). From Tel Aviv, Route 1 becomes Jaffa Road, which runs into the city center. The road from Tel Aviv is a divided highway that presents no problems except at morning rush hour (7:30–9), when traffic backs up at the entrance to the city.

### By Plane

INTERNATIONAL FLIGHTS

Most visitors entering Israel fly into **Ben Gurion International Airport** (☎ 03/971–0000 for information), 16 km (10 mi) east of Tel Aviv and 50 km (31 mi) west of Jerusalem.

**Egged** Buses 423, 945, and 947 run from the airport to Jerusalem's Central Bus Station on a reasonably frequent schedule (you'll seldom wait more than 30 minutes), except in the evenings, and cost NIS 18.50 ($4.60). You need Israeli currency. There is no bus service from Friday afternoon to Saturday night, or on Jewish religious holidays. For bus schedules, call ☎ 03/694–8888.

The **drive** from the airport, on Route 1 east, takes about 35 minutes. A "special" taxi (as opposed to a shared one, a *sherut*) should cost (at press time) NIS 140–NIS 154 ($35–$39), NIS 175 ($44) after 9 PM and on Saturday and holidays.

Seven-seat **sherut** taxis (limo-vans; ☞ *below*) depart when they fill up and drop passengers off at whatever Jerusalem address they request for NIS 40 ($10). To get *to* Ben-Gurion Airport from Jerusalem the same way, call **Nesher** (☎ 02/625–3233 or 02/623–1231) to book a place, preferably a day in advance. They'll pick you up at any address in Jerusalem.

### By Sherut

Seven-seat sheruts (stretch cabs or minivans) ply the same routes as the Egged buses to and from Tel Aviv and Haifa and charge about the same fares (25% more on Saturday and holidays, when the buses don't run). In Jerusalem, **Ha'ooma/Habira** (⊠ 1 Harav Kook St., near Zion Sq., and adjacent to the Central Bus Station, ☎ 02/538–9999) goes to Tel Aviv. Sheruts from Tel Aviv to Jerusalem congregate at Tel Aviv's New Central Bus Station. Sheruts to Jerusalem from Haifa leave from the Hadar district.

## Getting Around

### By Bus

The **Egged** National Bus Cooperative (☎ 02/530–4704 for local information; note that it's very difficult to reach) enjoys a monopoly on bus lines within Jerusalem. Routes within the city are extensive. Service begins at 5:30 AM and ends around midnight, depending on the route. Service stops half an hour before sunset on Friday (or on the eve of a religious holiday) until half an hour after sundown on Saturday. The fare on all routes is NIS 4.70 ($1.20), and you need to use Israeli money, but you don't need exact change. There are no transfers. Buses do not automatically stop at every bus stop; you need to signal the driver. Bus schedules are available at the Central Bus Station, on Jaffa Road in West Jerusalem, and some commercial maps show the bus routes. If you need bus advice, your best bet is to inquire at your hotel or ask the locals.

The two small, Arab-run bus stations in **East Jerusalem** primarily serve routes to towns in the West Bank (☞ Around Jerusalem A to Z *in* Chapter 2).

Egged's **Bus 99** runs a loop that sets out from the small terminal on Ha'emek Street (near Jaffa Gate) and takes about 1½ hours to complete. The 27 stops include City Hall, King David and Inbal hotels, the Jerusalem Mall, the Biblical Zoo, Holyland Hotel (with its scale model of ancient Jerusalem), Mt. Herzl, Yad Vashem, the hotel district near the Tel Aviv exit, Israel Museum, the Knesset, the Supreme Court, the Central Bus Station, Hyatt Hotel, Hadassah Hospital-Mt. Scopus, and a half-circuit of the Old City walls, including stops at Lions' (St. Stephen's) Gate, Dung Gate (Western Wall), and Mt. Zion, returning to the departure point near Jaffa Gate. The route stops at sites that are otherwise difficult to reach except by taxi. Buses leave the Jaffa Gate station Sunday–Thursday every half hour, from 9 AM to 4:30 PM. On

Friday and eve of Jewish holidays, the last bus leaves at 1 PM. There is no service on Saturday or Jewish religious holidays. The cost is NIS 40 ($10) for a one-day ticket, with unlimited transfers on this route.

## By Car

Navigating a rental car through unfamiliar territory and looking for legal parking make driving in Israel's big cities a dubious pleasure. A combination of walking and taking cabs or a guide-driven tourist limo-van is often more time-effective—and even more cost-effective. In Jerusalem the only sights that might be easier to reach by car are West Jerusalem and the panoramic overlooks, which are a bit out of the way.

Note that curbs painted with alternate bands of blue and white indicate legal parking, but only with the use of inexpensive parking cards (available for purchase at post offices and at many refreshment stands or curb vendors in or near the downtown area) or of pay-and-display parking ticket machines that are usually within sight of your parking place.

Gas stations are easy to find, and some never close, but gasoline is expensive in Israel—about NIS 16.70 ($4.20) a gallon. Drive defensively: many local drivers take hair-raising risks on the road.

## By Taxi

Taxis can be flagged on the street, ordered by phone, or picked up at a taxi stand or at major hotels. There are usually taxis waiting outside the Israel Museum and Yad Vashem. The law requires taxi drivers to turn on their meters, so you can insist on it, but if you want the cab badly you might need to compromise. Negotiating the fare puts you at a disadvantage unless you're familiar with the distance involved. A 10- to 15-minute ride (day rates until 9 PM) should cost between NIS 16 and NIS 24 (between $4 and $6). The fare is 25% higher after 9 PM and on Saturday and holidays. Any serious problem with the cabbie can be reported to the Ministry of Tourism: be sure to note the number on the illuminated yellow sign on the roof of the cab.

# Contacts and Resources

### Car Rental

**Avis** (✉ 22 King David St., ☎ 02/624–9001). **Budget** (✉ 23 King David St., ☎ 02/624–8991). **Eldan** (✉ 24 King David St., ☎ 02/625–2151). **Europcar (National)** (✉ 8 King David St., ☎ 02/625–5467). **Hertz** (✉ 18 King David St., ☎ 02/623–1351; ✉ Hyatt Regency Hotel, 32 Lehi St., ☎ 02/581–5069). **Sixt** (✉ 14 King David St., ☎ 02/624–8204; ✉ Hilton Hotel, 7 King David St., ☎ 02/624–8886).

### Consulates

**United States Consulate-General** (✉ 18 Agron St., West Jerusalem, ☎ 02/625–3288; for consular services: ✉ 27 Nablus Rd., East Jerusalem, ☎ 02/622–7200). **British Consulate-General** (✉ Tower House, next to St. Andrew's Church, Remez St., West Jerusalem, ☎ 02/671–7724; for consular services: ✉ Sheikh Jarrah, East Jerusalem, ☎ 02/541–4100). This consulate also serves citizens of New Zealand.

### Doctors and Dentists

The privately run, 24-hour **Terem Emergency Care Center** (✉ 7 Hamag St., Romema, ☎ 02/652–1748) offers first aid and other medical attention. **Yad Sarah** (✉ 124 Herzl Blvd., ☎ 02/644–4444) is a voluntary organization that lends medical equipment and accessories such as wheelchairs, crutches, and canes. There is no charge, but a contribution is expected. It's open Sunday–Thursday 9–7 and Friday 9–12:30.

A private **dental clinic** offers an emergency service (⊠ 1 Mendele St., at 24 Keren Hayesod St., opposite Dan Panorama Hotel, ☎ 02/563–2303) Sunday–Thursday 8 AM–midnight, Friday 8 until just before sundown, and Saturday evening. Call first: when the office is closed, the call is automatically transferred to an on-call dentist. It's closed on Sabbath and Jewish holidays.

## Emergencies

**Ambulance** (☎ 101 or 02/652–3133). The ambulance service, Magen David Adom, is the Israeli version of the Red Cross. **Police** (☎ 100 or 02/539–1111). **Fire** (☎ 102).

### HOSPITAL EMERGENCY ROOMS

Emergency rooms in major hospitals are on duty 24 hours a day in rotation; the schedule is published in the daily press. In an emergency, call Magen David Adom (☎ 101) to find out which hospital is on duty that day for your specific need (orthopedic or gastric, for example). Be sure to take your passport with you. There will be a fee. The major hospitals in Jerusalem are **Bikur Holim** (⊠ Strauss St., ☎ 02/670–1111); **Hadassah** (⊠ Ein Kerem, ☎ 02/677–7111, 02/677–7222 emergency room, 02/677–7444 children's emergency room); **Hadassah** (⊠ Mt. Scopus, ☎ 02/584–4111); **Sha'arei Tzedek** (⊠ Bayit Vegan, ☎ 02/655–5111, 02/655–5509 emergency room).

## Guided Tours

### ORIENTATION

Two tour operators offer half- and full-day tours of Old and New Jerusalem, with different itineraries on different days of the week:

**Egged Tours** (⊠ 8 Shlomzion Hamalka St., ☎ 02/622–2929) and **United Tours** (⊠ King David Hotel Annex, 23 King David St., ☎ 02/625–2188 or 02/625–2187).

A tour costs about $24 for a half day and $46–$56 for a full day, depending on itinerary. The price includes pickup and drop-off at your hotel. You can reserve directly or through your hotel concierge.

### PERSONAL GUIDES

At press time the daily rate for a private guide with an air-conditioned car or limousine was $300–$400, depending on the size of the vehicle. Many guides will offer their services without a car for about $170–$200. The customary rate for a half day is 60% of the full-day rate. For private guiding, contact **Eshcolot Tours** (⊠ 36 Keren Hayesod St., ☎ 02/563–5555). Or contact Fodor's writer Mike Rogoff, a licensed guide (☎ FAX 02/679–0410, rogoff@netvision.net.il).

### SPECIAL-INTEREST TOURS

The **Society for the Protection of Nature in Israel** (⊠ 13 Helene Hamalka St., ☎ 02/624–4605), or SPNI, emphasizes nature, often trekking off the beaten path. Tours in English cater to tourists, but sometimes the experience matters more than the explanations, so you might want to consider the richer menu of tours in Hebrew. Itineraries change throughout the year; call for details.

### WALKING TOURS

**Archaeological Seminars** (☎ 02/627–3515) specializes in visiting sites of archaeological importance. Tours are preceded by a slide lecture, and the guides are generally excellent. The Western Wall Tunnel walk is offered Sundays, Tuesdays, and Wednesdays throughout the year. The group added three other Old City routes and has greater frequency in the summer. Tours last two to three hours and cost $18. Prior reservation is recommended. All tours depart from 34 Habad Street, in the Jewish Quarter of the Old City. Ask about the Dig-for-a-Day program, a three-hour excavation at Bet Guvrin-Maresha National Park, outside of Jerusalem.

**Zion Walking Tours** (⊠ Inside Jaffa Gate, opposite police station, ☎ 02/628–7866) has eight different itineraries, each running twice a week. Tours last about three hours and cost $10–$20.

## Late-Night Pharmacies

The daily press publishes the addresses of pharmacies on duty at night, on Saturday, and on holidays. This information is also available from Magen David Adom (☎ 02/652–3133).

**SuperPharm** (⊠ 5 Burla St., Nayot, ☎ 02/678–4139) is open Sunday–Thursday 8:30 AM–midnight, Friday 8:30 AM–3 PM, and Saturday 9 PM–midnight. Its downtown location (⊠ 3 Hahistadrut St., ☎ 02/624–6249) closes at 11 PM.

## Taxis

Twenty-four-hour service:

**Hapalmach** (☎ 02/679–2333 or 02/679–3333); **Hapisgah** (☎ 02/642–1111, 02/642–2222 except on the Sabbath); **Rehavia** (☎ 02/625–4444 or 02/622–2444).

## Travel Agencies

**American Express** (⊠ 19 Hillel St., ☎ 02/625–4171 or 02/624–0830). **ISSTA** (⊠ 31 Hanevi'im St., ☎ 02/621–3600), for students and academics. **Vaintours** (⊠ 33 King George St., ☎ 02/625–2984). **Ziontours** (⊠ 19 Hillel St., ☎ 02/625–4326 or 02/625–4327).

## Visitor Information

The **Tourist Information Office** at the Jaffa Gate of the Old City (☎ 02/628–0382) is open Sunday–Thursday 8–7, and Friday 8–3.

The **Christian Information Center** (⊠ Jaffa Gate, Old City, ☎ 02/627–2692) is open Monday–Saturday 8:30–1, except Christmas, New Year's Day, and Good Friday.

# 2 AROUND JERUSALEM

*Including Bethlehem,*
*Masada, and the Dead Sea*

West of Jerusalem, rugged pine-forested hills fold down to a green region of soft landscapes, biblical echoes, and chalk caves. To the east, in stark contrast, you plunge at once through the Judean Desert to Masada and the Dead Sea, the lowest spot on earth, with dramatic, bleak vistas punctuated by brilliant green oases. And just south of the Holy City is Bethlehem, birthplace of Jesus. Travelers based in Tel Aviv can easily reach these areas with just an hour's additional travel in each direction.

By Mike Rogoff

JERUSALEM'S LOCATION IN THE HEART of Israel's central mountain range makes it an excellent base for day tours in the area. Furthermore, many people find visiting Jerusalem so intense that they need excursions like these for a change of pace and scenery.

By far the most interesting and dramatic sights are those in the Judean Desert–Dead Sea region. This is a rocky desert of extraordinary barrenness, throwing into brilliant relief the waterfalls and greenery of Ein Gedi, the springs and reed thickets of Ain Fashkha, and the sprawling oasis of the town of Jericho.

The road skirting the Dead Sea (Route 90) is hemmed in by awesome, fractured brown cliffs that soar in many places to heights of more than 1,600 ft. Slicing through these immense desert crags are Ein Gedi's two canyons, Nahal David and Nahal Arugot, both refreshing surprises of rivulets, pools, waterfalls, and subtropical vegetation. Wildlife abounds here, particularly the ibex (wild goat) and the hyrax (coney), though you can't rely on seeing them.

The Dead Sea itself—actually a lake—is a unique phenomenon: it is the saltiest body of water in the world, at the lowest point on earth. You can feel the tension seep away as you float in the balmy brine or as you smooth mineral-rich black mud all over your body. Bathing options range from free public beaches with minimal facilities to well-equipped spas; the best are in the Ein Bokek hotel district, at the southern end of the Dead Sea (☞ Chapter 7).

Masada, the great mountaintop palace-fortress built 2,000 years ago by King Herod, overlooks the Dead Sea. Its palaces, mosaics and frescoes, ingenious water system, and baths are a tribute to Herod's grand style; the remote location and almost unassailable position are evidence of his paranoia. Add the human drama of Masada's defense and fall during the Jewish revolt against Rome a century later, and it's easy to understand why this is one of the most visited sites in Israel.

Bethlehem, a stone's throw from Jerusalem, is a major place of pilgrimage for Christians. The cavernous and colonnaded Church of the Nativity, the oldest standing church in the country, is built over the grotto where Jesus is believed to have been born. Today's town is a West Bank Arab community of some 35,000 souls, one-third Christian, two-thirds Muslim, straddling the ancient high road through the rocky, olive-groved Judean Hills.

Still on the trail of the Bible, you'll find echoes of Joshua (though not his walls) at the palm-studded oasis of Jericho, to the east; and topographical detail that identifies the dueling ground of David and Goliath in the Elah Valley, to the west.

The planted pine and cypress forests west of Jerusalem have an abundance of delightful views and picnic spots, and a few nature reserves. Don't miss the Sorek Cave, an almost fantastical cavern of stalagmites and stalactites; or the extraordinary network of ancient man-made chalk caves—the huge "bell caves" of Bet Guvrin and the adjacent underground complexes of Maresha.

## Pleasures and Pastimes

### Bird-Watching

Israel's varied climate and its position on major migratory routes make it a fascinating place for bird-watchers. Especially interesting in this region are the raptors in the skies of the Judean Desert.

## Dead Sea Beaches, Spas, and Mineral Pools

You cannot actually swim in the briny Dead Sea; you simply float in it. The incredible density of its water—about 10 times that of the ocean—makes it impossible to sink here. The Dead Sea area is recognized as one of the world's primary health retreats for sufferers of psoriasis and various rheumatic and arthritic ailments. But the hale, too, will enjoy the benefits of the incredible mineral concentration in the Dead Sea water and mud, the natural warm mineral springs, and the oxygen-rich atmosphere at the lowest point on earth. There are several places to swim along the Dead Sea and the Ein Gedi Spa. (For the sophisticated spas and therapeutic facilities of the Ein Bokek area, *see* Chapter 7.)

Doctors recommend remaining in the water for no more than 15 minutes at a time because of the enervating effect of the brine; and if you have a heart condition or high blood pressure, you should not bathe here at all. Avoid the discomfort of getting the salt water in your eyes and mouth, although you can rinse off at the outdoor showers and faucets found at recognized beaches. It's imperative to drink a lot of fresh water, especially in the hot season (April to October). Many beaches are rocky (and hot in summer), so it's a good idea to wear protective rubber sandals, shoes, or sneakers. Don't leave your possessions unguarded on the beach.

## Dining

Beyond some passable lunch cafeterias, and a couple of better eateries in which to laze over a midday meal, there are few restaurants in this area to tempt you out in the evening. Most tours bring you back by nightfall to Jerusalem or Tel Aviv, where your options are plenty (☞ Dining *in* Chapters 1 and 3). For price-category definitions, *see* Dining *in* Chapter 1.

## Hiking and Rappelling

The Judean Desert has some excellent hiking trails. Ein Gedi's two nature reserves, Nahal David and Nahal Arugot, are the best for beginners. Serious hikers can seek out more challenging walks in spectacular canyons but should only pursue these with expert local guidance. The combination of heat and dryness can be dangerous, so bring a hat and copious amounts of water when hiking in this region.

## Lodging

The lodgings of the Dead Sea region are heavily used by visitors, both local and international, who come to "take the waters." Many enjoy the quiet ambience between cliffs and coastline. Others just make this a convenient base from which to strike out over the Judean Desert. Facilities range from youth hostels to the luxury hotels of the nearby Ein Bokek area (☞ Chapter 7).

People typically explore the area west of Jerusalem as a day trip from Jerusalem or Tel Aviv. The only decent lodgings here are some fine guest houses 15–20 minutes outside the capital. Bethlehem, now governed by the Palestinian Authority, has a few unprepossessing hotels; Jerusalem, only 10 minutes away, is a far more convenient and congenial base. For price-category definitions, *see* Lodging *in* Chapter 1.

# Exploring Around Jerusalem

This area offers day-trip options in three different directions. The Dead Sea has the richest fare and takes the most time, but you can see some of its sights en route to the Galilee via the Jordan Valley. The other two areas—west of Jerusalem, and Bethlehem—are closer to Jerusalem and can be combined with Jerusalem sights or, even, with each other.

## Great Itineraries

To explore the **Dead Sea region,** you journey east through the arid Judean Desert to Qumran, where the Dead Sea Scrolls were found; the salty Dead Sea, the lowest point on earth; the canyons and waterfalls of Ein Gedi; and the ancient palace-fortress of Masada. An interesting side trip (political climate permitting) includes the oasis town of Jericho, the oldest city known.

With an early start, you can see most of these sights in one day. A good combination is Masada (with its dramatic history and interesting archaeological remains), the Dead Sea (total relaxation), and one of the nature reserves at Ein Gedi (a refreshing antidote to the heat and brine of the Dead Sea). From April to October, later closing times allow a visit to Qumran as well. You can see Jericho (again, if accessible from the point of view of security) as a tag-on to this day, as a day tour from Jerusalem, on the way to an overnight trip along the Dead Sea, or en route to the Jordan Valley and Galilee.

The area **west of Jerusalem** encompasses part of the Judean Hills and, farther southwest, the lowland area known as the Shefelah. Highlights include the exquisite Sorek stalactite cave; the Elah Valley, where David and Goliath clashed; and the intriguing man-made caves of Bet Guvrin and Maresha. It's a full but comfortable day trip.

**Bethlehem,** with its famous Church of the Nativity, is no more than a 10-minute drive south of Jerusalem (though sporadic unrest makes it necessary to check the political climate before considering a visit). You can see the church and be back in the city within two hours. Continuing deeper into the West Bank is not recommended at press time.

## When to Tour Around Jerusalem

The Dead Sea region is pleasant in the cool season (October–April) but often very hot the rest of the year. Getting a very early start and beginning the day with Masada can help beat the heat and the crowds. *Ending* the day with Masada often achieves the same result, but stay aware of closing times. Bethlehem is best first thing in the morning or late in the afternoon if you want to avoid the crowds, especially the seasonal cruise-boat traffic; but do note the hours for the Grotto of the Nativity. The area west of Jerusalem is good anytime, although the Sorek Cave has limited hours and no guided tour on Friday.

*Numbers in the margin correspond to points of interest on the Around Jerusalem map.*

# DEAD SEA REGION

From the ridges of Jerusalem's Mt. Scopus and Mount of Olives, the view to the east is of barren hills that cascade almost 4,000 ft down to the Dead Sea. Clouds off the Mediterranean warm and disperse as they cross the high ridge and descend toward the chasm of the Dead Sea, creating what is called a "rain shadow." Within a map distance of about 24 km (15 mi), the average annual rainfall drops from 22 inches in Jerusalem to 2 inches at the Dead Sea. This "shadow" region is the Judean Desert, and its proximity to Jerusalem has always made it part of that city's consciousness. Refugees fled to it; hermits sought its solitude; and in ancient times, before the Jewish Day of Atonement, the scapegoat symbolically bearing the sins of the people was driven into oblivion among its stark precipices.

Important words of caution: it is vital to wear a hat and drink plenty of water here in hot weather. Approach the desert with respect—do not attempt unfamiliar trails without expert guidance.

Route 1 leaves Jerusalem just north of the French Hill neighborhood, runs east, swings back below the eastern slopes of Mt. Scopus and the Mount of Olives (look for their distinctive towers on your right), and begins its steep descent to the Dead Sea. Some 8 km (5 mi) on, ahead and above you, is the edge of the town of Ma'aleh Adumim, built in the 1970s and '80s as a bedroom community of Jerusalem. This and the handful of small Jewish villages in the Judean Desert are some of what are commonly called the West Bank settlements that so often make the news. Because of their isolation, however, they have been spared the constant friction with Palestinian Arab neighbors typical of such settlements in the mountain region.

On both sides of the road you'll see encampments of tent-dwelling Bedouins (Arab nomads) still clinging to their ancestors' way of life and eking out a livelihood by herding sheep and goats. Yet they have made concessions to modernity; water tanks and tractors, synthetic fabrics flapping on clotheslines, and even the occasional TV antenna sprouting from a tent bear witness to a culture in flux.

## Inn of the Good Samaritan

**❶** *20 km (13 mi) east of Jerusalem on Rte. 1, 500 yards east of the junction with Rte. 458.*

The lone one-story building, its courtyard surrounded by a low stone wall, was a Turkish police fort a century ago, the halfway point on what was then a two-day journey between Jerusalem and Jericho. Known in the Hebrew Bible as Ma'aleh Adumim (the Red Ascent) because of its distinctive patch of red limestone, this spot was once the border marker between the biblical Israelite tribes of Benjamin, to the north, and Judah, to the south (Joshua 15). (Don't confuse it with the town of the same name closer to Jerusalem.)

The popular name of the site, the Inn of the Good Samaritan, is not necessarily spurious. The New Testament (Luke 10) relates the parable of a man ambushed on the Jericho road and helped only by a Samaritan (a member of a people hostile to the Jews), who lodged him at the nearby inn. Because Jesus's parables used images familiar to his listeners, it's entirely possible that he had a specific inn in mind and that the inn was at this perennially strategic spot. The original Jericho road, now tarred but not much used, is off to the left of the highway as you continue east.

No remains of a 1st-century inn have been found, but other ages have left their mark. If you're energetic, turn your back on the once-commercialized (and now abandoned) "Inn," cross the road *very, very* carefully, and climb the dirt track to the top of the hill opposite. Amid the scanty ruins of the small 12th-century Crusader fort of Maldoim—from which you can see the outskirts of both Jerusalem and Jericho—the Gospel passage comes alive. The medieval Burchard of Mt. Sion wrote that the Red Ascent (called the "Blood Ascent" by Arabs) got its name "from the frequent blood shed there. Of a truth it is horrible to behold and exceedingly dangerous! . . ."

## Jericho

**★** *45 km (28 mi) northeast of Jerusalem.*

The oasis town of Jericho, immortalized as the place where "the walls came tumblin' down" at the sound of Joshua's trumpets, is the oldest city in the world, and at 850 ft below sea level, it's (currently) the lowest as well. It may be worth a trip through Jericho just to be able to

**Around Jerusalem**

DESERT

SHEFELA

WEST BANK BORDER

Neot Kedumim

Modi'in

Hulda

Neve Shalom

Nahshon

Latrun Armored Corps Museum

Trappist Abbey of Latrun

Canada Park

Emmaus

Shaʻar Hagai

Eshtaʻol

Tel Bet Shemesh

Elah Valley

Kesalon

Zova

Bet Shemesh

Beit Jimal

Nes Harim

Sorek Cave

Shoresh

Neve Ilan

Abu Ghosh

Maʻaleh Hahamisha

Kiryat Anavim

Ein Hemed

Mevo Betar

Alon Shevut

Kfar Etzion

Elazar

Efrat

Beit Fajjar

Solomon's Pools

Beit Jala

Rachel's Tomb

Bethlehem

Herodion

Kubeibe

Givat Zeʻev

Bet Horon

Horon Junction

Ramot

Atarot

Airport

Bira

Ramallah

Mukhmas

El-Azariya

Maʻaleh Adumim

Jerusalem

Inn of the Good Samaritan

Monastery of St George

Qarantal

Jericho

Hisham's Palace

Tel Jericho

Almog

Kalia

Qumran

Einot Zukim (Ain Fashkha)

① Inn of the Good Samaritan
② Tel Jericho
③ Hisham's Palace
④ Qumran
⑧ Sorek Cave
⑨ Emmaus
⑩ Latrun Armored Corps Museum
⑪ Trappist Abbey of Latrun
⑫ Tel Bet Shemesh
⑬ Elah Valley
⑯ Bethlehem

TO TEL AVIV

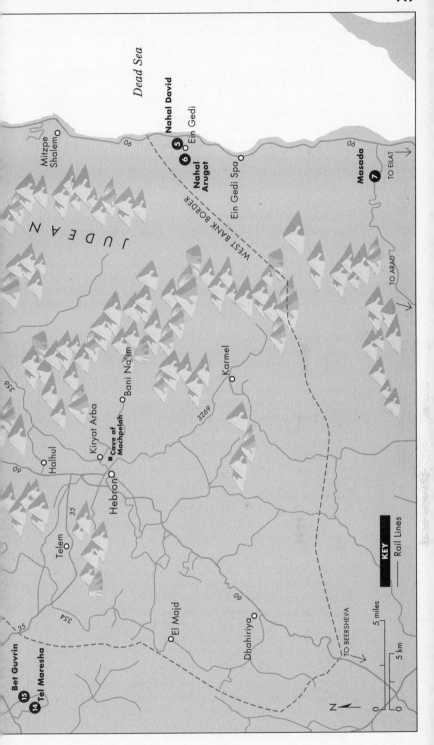

*Dead Sea*

Mitzpe Shalem

J U D E A N

Nahal David

**5** Ein Gedi

**6** Nahal Arugot

Ein Gedi Spa

WEST BANK BORDER

90

90

TO EILAT

**7** Masada

TO ARAD

Bani Na'im

Karmel

3269

Kiryat Arba

■ Cave of Machpelah

Halhul

60

356

Hebron

35

Telem

354

El Majd

Dhahiriya

60

Bet Guvrin **15**

**14** Tel Maresha

35

TO BEERSHEVA

**KEY**
— Rail Lines

5 miles

5 km

N

0

0

say "I was there," but the town does have enough to hold you a little longer. The wide, tree-lined main artery is more country lane than city street. The riot of greenery—date palms, orange groves, banana plantations, bougainvillea, and papaya trees—takes the edge off the neglect and dilapidation that are still apparent, despite the many new buildings that are beginning to give the town a fresher look. The Arab population of about 20,000 is mostly Muslim, with a tiny Christian minority.

Jericho has been under autonomous Palestinian control since April 1994. At press time, the generally relaxed atmosphere of recent years was shattered by anti-Israel riots, and Jericho was closed to visitors. Check the current situation before you plan your tour, asking as well about any restrictions on tourists in private cars visiting the town.

Entering the town from the south, you are met (on your right) by the Oasis Casino, alongside the new Inter-Continental Hotel, Jericho's most prominent landmark. At press time both were closed due to political unrest.

Take the left fork at the traffic island. A few hundred yards farther, the road swings sharply to the left. To the right of the bend and one block down a no-entry street is a huge, fenced-off sycamore tree, which tradition (and the postcard vendors) identifies as the very one Zacchaeus climbed to watch Jesus pass by (Luke 19).

**②** **Tel Jericho** is the mound of accumulated earth that entombs the legendary ancient city. Archaeologists have extensively excavated it, looking for its most famous ruins, the Canaanite walls that fell to the blast of Israelite rams' horns when Joshua stormed the city in the mid-13th century BC. Those walls have not been found, but remains of the world's oldest walled city have. An excavation pit at the top of the *tel* (hill) reveals a massive, round stone tower 30 ft in diameter, preserved to a height of 25 ft and attached to a 10-ft-thick wall. The structures predate the invention of pottery, and carbon-14 tests have placed human skulls and bones found here in the Neolithic period (Late Stone Age) between 6500 and 7800 BC. Little is known about who these early urbanites were, or why they needed such stout fortifications thousands of years before they became common in the rest of the region, but a wealth of artifacts, most displayed in the Israel and Rockefeller museums in Jerusalem (☞ Exploring Jerusalem *in* Chapter 1), helps us imagine their domestic life and customs.

From the sun shelter at the top of the tel, there is a fine sweeping view of Jericho, the biblical "City of Palms." The generous spring that was always the secret of its fecundity is across the road, capped today by a pump house. It is known as **Ain es-Sultan,** the Sultan's Spring, or Elisha's Spring, in recognition of the Old Testament prophet's miracle of sweetening the water with a bowl of salt (I Kings 2). In the distance to the east are the high mountains of the biblical kingdoms of Ammon and Moab, now in Jordan, among them the peak of Mt. Nebo, from which Moses viewed the Promised Land.

To the south, among the banana trees some 3 km (2 mi) away, is a small but distinctive mound of earth. This is **Tel Abu Alaik,** where archaeologists' spades have uncovered the remains of the royal palace of the Jewish Hasmonean dynasty (2nd–1st centuries BC), described by the Jewish historian Josephus Flavius (AD 37–circa 100). In the last decades of the 1st century BC, Mark Antony gave the valuable oasis of Jericho to his beloved Cleopatra; the humiliated King Herod, Antony's local vassal, was then forced to lease the property back from the Egyptian queen. Herod expanded and improved the palace, turning it into his winter retreat. He died there in 4 BC.

To the west is the **Mount of Temptation,** identified by tradition as the "exceedingly high mountain" from which Satan tempted Jesus with dominion over "all the kingdoms of the world" (Matthew 4). The peak is surrounded by a modern wall. Halfway down the mountain and a bit to the left is the remarkable Greek Orthodox monastery of Qarantal, the name being a corruption of *quarantena*—a period of 40 days (the source of the English word *quarantine*)—the period of Jesus's temptation. Built right into the cliff face on Byzantine remains, it is flanked by many caves, which once housed hermits. From a station opposite the tel, a brand-new **cable car** takes you to the foot of the stairs leading up to the monastery. The upper station is served by a restaurant and a spectacular view. ⊠ *Turn left at sharp bend in the main road through town; enter the parking lot of the tel from the west.* ☎ *Tel Jericho NIS 10 ($2.50).* ⊙ *Daily 8:30–5 (often closes later in summer months); subject to change.* ☎ *Cable car NIS 32 ($8)* ⊙ *8:30–6:30.*

NEED A BREAK?

The **Temptation Restaurant,** next to the Tel Jericho parking lot, has excellent *bourma*, a honey-rolled pastry filled with whole pistachio nuts. The lunches offer good value, with tasty *mezes* (Middle Eastern salads) and meats. The nearby fruit stands tend to overcharge, but try the pomelo (related to the grapefruit), in season from December to March.

❸ A spacious site in pastoral surroundings, the remains of **Hisham's Palace** (Hirbet el-Mafjar, in Arabic) have some interesting stonework and a spectacular mosaic floor. Hisham was a scion of the Ummayad dynasty, which built the Dome of the Rock and El-Aqsa Mosque, in Jerusalem. Like Herod eight centuries earlier, he was attracted by the balmy winter climate of the Jericho oasis. While still under construction, the palace was badly damaged by the great earthquake of AD 749 and never completed, but the high quality of the mosaics and stone and plaster reliefs that survive is evidence of its splendor.

To get here from Tel Jericho, go north for 2 km (1 mi) and turn right at the sign. After that, the left turn toward the site itself is another kilometer (½ mi) down the road but is marked only by a low stone pillar on the right. The site is adjacent to Muslim neighborhoods: given the unstable political situation (at press time) you should check at the tel to see if the site is accessible at all.

You enter the ruins through a small gatehouse, which leads into a wide plaza dominated by a large, star-shape stone window that once graced an upper-floor chamber. The basement bathhouse and one of the palace's two mosques (open to the sky) are an interesting juxtaposition of both the worldly and the spiritual character of the Arab empire of the time. North of the plaza is a series of columns—some artless reconstructions in concrete—that supported the roof of a large bath and recreation area. Several sections of the fine geometric mosaics have been left exposed; others are covered by sand.

The most impressive part of the complex is the reception room, off the plaza. Its intricate **mosaic floor,** depicting a lion hunting a stag, is one of the most beautiful in the country, the tiny colored tesserae producing a realism astonishing for this medium. You can still see fragments of ornate stucco reliefs on some of the walls, but the best examples found here are now in Jerusalem's Rockefeller Museum (☞ Exploring Jerusalem *in* Chapter 1). The balustrade of an ornamental pool reflects the artistic influences of both East and West. ⊠ *Jericho,* ☎ *02/*

232–2522. ✆ NIS 10 ($2.50). ☉ *Daily 8:30–5 (often closes later in summer months); subject to change.*

*En Route* Route 90 south brings you back toward the **Dead Sea.** A milestone by the side of the road just before the gas station (at the Kalia Junction) announces that you have now reached the bottom of the world. The Dead Sea has shrunk in recent years, so the shore at this point is a good kilometer (over ½ mi) away. You'll see heaps of white potash, the primary product of the Dead Sea, off to the left, though today all extraction of potash, bromine, and magnesium takes place at the huge plant at Sodom, at the southern end of the lake.

# Qumran

**④** *6 km (4 mi) south of the Kalia Junction on Rte. 90, 20 km (13 mi) south of Jericho, 50 km (31 mi) east of Jerusalem.*

The ancient remains of Qumran are not especially impressive to the layperson, but caves in the cliffs west of the small site yielded the most significant archaeological find ever made in Israel: the **Dead Sea Scrolls.** They were found under extraordinary circumstances. In 1947, a young Bedouin goatherd stumbled on a cave containing a cache of the now-famous scrolls, hidden in earthen jars. Because the scrolls were written on parchment—treated animal hide—one of the nomads sought out a Bethlehem shoemaker to turn them into sandals! The shoemaker alerted a local antiquities dealer, who brought them to the attention of Professor Eliezer Sukenik of the Hebrew University of Jerusalem. Six other major scrolls and hundreds of fragments came to light in subsequent years, some from pirate digs conducted by the Bedouin themselves in other caves in the area, others from methodical archaeological excavations.

The scrolls were written by an ultradevout Jewish sect generally identified as the Essenes, who had set up a monastic community at Qumran in the late 2nd century BC. During the Great (Jewish) Revolt against Rome (AD 66–73), they apparently hid their precious scrolls in the caves in the cliffs behind the town. Their fears were well founded—Qumran was destroyed in AD 68, giving scholars a "terminus" date for the age of the scrolls.

The Dead Sea Scrolls include books of the Old Testament and sectarian literature of the Qumran community. Among the Hebrew biblical scrolls is one containing the full 66 chapters of the Book of Isaiah, almost identical to the text used in Jewish communities to this day, putting to rest any doubts about the authenticity of the modern version. Sectarian texts include the constitution or "Rule of the Community"; a description of an end-of-days battle ("The War of the Sons of Light Against the Sons of Darkness"); and the "Thanksgiving Scroll," containing hymns reminiscent of biblical psalms.

Apart from the bonanza the scrolls represented for Bible scholars and students of ancient Hebrew, they gave researchers rare insights into this previously shadowy Jewish sect. Christian scholars in particular have long been intrigued by the suggestion that John the Baptist, whose lifestyle seems to have paralleled that of the Essenes, may have been a member of the Qumran community. Several of the scrolls are on display in the Israel Museum in Jerusalem (☞ Exploring Jerusalem *in* Chapter 1).Qumran sits on a small plateau between the craggy limestone cliffs to the west and the narrow shores of the Dead Sea to the east. The site was excavated in the 1950s by British and French archaeologists. A short film at the entrance to Qumran introduces the visitor to the mysterious sect that once lived here. Climb the tower for a good view, and note the unusual number of water channels and cisterns that gathered runoff winter floodwater from the cliffs to the west. Just below the tower (in front of you as you look toward the Dead Sea) is a long room identified as the **scriptorium**. A plaster writing table and bronze and ceramic inkwells found here confirm that this was where the scrolls were written. A good air-conditioned cafeteria and gift store serve the site. ⊠ *Rte. 90,* ☎ *02/994–2235.* ⊠ *NIS 14 ($3.50).* ☉ *Apr.–Sept., daily 8–5; Oct.–Mar., daily 8–4.*

## Beaches and Pools

**Attraktzia** offers a Dead Sea beach, freshwater pools with water slides, and full facilities. ⊠ *3 km (2 mi) north of Qumran off Rte. 90,* ☎ *02/ 994–2393.* ⊠ *Water park and beach NIS 67 ($16.75), after 2 PM NIS 42 ($10.50); beach only (Nov.–Mar.) NIS 15 ($3.75).* ☉ *Water park and beach Apr.–Oct., daily 9–5; beach only, Nov.–Mar., daily 9–5.*

**Einot Zukim (Ain Fashkha)** is a nature reserve, with fresh (though brackish) springs, and a variety of trees and reeds rare in the arid Judean Desert. Unfortunately the most beautiful part of the reserve is closed to the general public to preserve its fragile ecosystem, but there is a Dead Sea beach, and picnic and changing facilities. Avoid Friday and Saturday, when it's especially crowded. ⊠ *3 km (2 mi) south of Qumran on Rte. 90,* ☎ *02/994–2355.* ⊠ *NIS 22 ($5.50).* ☉ *Apr.–Sept., daily 8–5; Oct.–Mar., daily 8–4.*

**Siesta Beach** has good access to the Dead Sea, free black mud, showers, and changing rooms. You can buy disposable or regular towels (with soap and shampoo). ⊠ *3 km (2 mi) north of Qumran off Rte. 90,* ☎ *02/994–4111.* ⊠ *NIS 20 ($5).* ☉ *Daily 8:30–5:30 (often later in the summer months).*

## Shopping

**Kibbutz Mitzpe Shalem** (⊠ 20 km, or 12½ mi, south of Qumran on Rte. 90, ☎ 02/994–5117) manufactures the excellent Ahava line of skin- and hair-care products based on (but not smelling like!) the Dead Sea minerals. The factory outlet here is open Sunday–Thursday 8–6, Friday and holiday eves 8–4, and Saturday 8:30–6, but the products are sold elsewhere (at Masada, Qumran, and the Ein Gedi Spa, for example) and at pharmacies in major cities.

# Ein Gedi

★ *33 km (21 mi) south of Qumran, 20 km (12½ mi) north of Masada, 83 km (52 mi) east and south of Jerusalem.*

The wondrous oasis of Ein Gedi—two nature reserves and a verdant kibbutz-type village—bursts upon you with a splash of vivid green against the burnt browns and beiges of the desert rock.

**⑤ Nahal David** (David's Stream), where, 3,000 years ago, David hid from the wrath of King Saul (I Samuel 24), is a marvelous nature reserve, with cliffs soaring to more than 1,600 ft above the streams, waterfalls, and tropical reeds. This would be a delightful spot anywhere, but in the middle of a harsh desert, it's nothing short of spectacular. As you reach Ein Gedi from the north, the first turnoff to the right takes you to the parking lot at the entrance to Nahal David.

The clearly marked trail takes you past several pools and small waterfalls to the beautiful top waterfall. There are many steps, but it's not too daunting. Allow at least 1¼ hours to include a refreshing dip under one of the lower waterfalls. Look out for ibex (wild goat), especially in the afternoon, and for the small, furry hyrax, often seen on tree branches. Leopards were rediscovered in this area some years ago but face extinction again because of breeding problems; they're seldom seen nowadays, and never in the reserve.

If you're a hiker, don't miss the trail that breaks off to the right some 50 yards down the return path from the top waterfall. It passes the remains of Byzantine irrigation systems and offers breathtaking views of the Dead Sea. The trail doubles back on itself toward the source of Nahal David. Near the top, a short side path climbs to the remains of a 4th-millennium BC Chalcolithic temple. The main path leads on to the streambed, again turns east, and reaches Dudim (Lovers') Cave, formed by boulders and filled with the crystal-clear spring water. You are directly above the waterfall of Nahal David (don't throw stones—there are people below). Since this trail involves a considerable climb (and hikers invariably take time to bathe in the "cave"), access to the trail is permitted only up to 3½ hours before closing time. ✉ *Ein Gedi,* ☎ *08/658–4285.* ✉ *NIS 18 ($4.50), includes Nahal Arugot (☞ below) on same day only.* ☉ *Sat.–Thurs. 8–4, Fri. 8–3 (closes 1 hr later during daylight saving time, late spring and summer); last admission 1 hr before closing.*

**❻ Nahal Arugot,** like Nahal David to its north, is a splendid nature reserve. Aside from its natural beauty—though perhaps because of it—Ein Gedi has attracted settlement for thousands of years. Near the mouth of the canyon is a small mound known as **Tel Goren,** where excavations in the 1960s exposed five noncontinuous strata of settlement from the 7th century BC (Israelite period) to the 6th century AD (Byzantine period). An intriguing Hebrew and Aramaic inscription removed from a 6th-century AD mosaic synagogue floor nearby invokes the wrath of heaven on troublemakers of different stripes, including "whoever reveals the secret of the town to the Gentiles." The "secret" is believed to refer to the revived cultivation of the balsam tree, which produced the prized perfume for which the town was once famous.

Although not quite as green as Nahal David, the deep canyon of Nahal Arugot is, if anything, more spectacular. Enormous boulders and slabs of stone on the opposite cliff face seem poised in mid-cataclysm, and the whole effect is powerfully primordial. The hour-long hike to the **Hidden Waterfall** (quite a lot of steps, but not especially steep) takes you by delightful spots where the stream bubbles over rock shelves and shallow pools offer relief from the heat. The Hidden Waterfall is reached by a short marked trail down to the left. Do not continue on the trail beyond the waterfall without prior arrangement with the Nature Preservation Authority. From the waterfall, if you're adventurous and have appropriate footwear, you can return through the greenery of the streambed, leaping the boulders and wading the pools. ✉ *Ein Gedi,* ☎ *08/658–4285.* ✉ *NIS 18 ($4.50), includes Nahal David (☞ above) and the synagogue floor on same day only; synagogue floor only NIS 9 ($2.25).* ☉ *Sat.–Thurs. 8–4, Fri. 8–3 (closes 1 hr later during daylight saving time, late spring and summer); last admission 2 hrs before closing.*

## Beaches and Pools

**Ein Gedi Spa** offers good facilities (indoor showers and changing rooms with lockers), access to the Dead Sea, a freshwater pool, free Dead Sea mud, and marvelously relaxing, warm indoor sulfur pools. There's a restaurant downstairs from the changing rooms. Massages are available, advance reservation recommended. ✉ *3 km (2 mi) south of Ein Gedi gas station,* ☎ *08/659–4813.* ✉ *NIS 50 ($12.50), NIS 55 ($13.75) Sat. and holidays; NIS 48 ($12), including light lunch, if accompanied by licensed guide.* ☉ *Months of daylight saving time (late spring and summer), daily 7–6; rest of year, daily 7–5.*

A somewhat rocky **public beach,** 200 hundred yards south of Nahal David behind the gas station, has free access to the Dead Sea, freshwater showers (absolutely essential) by the water's edge, and basic changing facilities for NIS 6 ($1.50). Don't leave valuables unguarded.

## Lodging

**$$$** 🏨 **Kibbutz Ein Gedi.** A motel-style guest house on the kibbutz grounds is set between 1,600-ft-high cliffs and the Dead Sea and surrounded by subtropical landscaping. There is no maid service and rooms come with showers only. Prices per double range, according to season, from $146 to $178 and include breakfast, another full meal, and unlimited entry to the nearby spa, to which there's a free shuttle throughout the day. ⊠ *Rte. 90, M.P. Dead Sea 86980,* ☎ *08/659–4222,* 𝔽𝔸𝕏 *08/658–4328. 120 rooms. Kitchenettes, pool, 2 tennis courts. AE, DC, MC, V.*

**$** 🏨 **Bet Sarah.** This newly expanded lodging belongs to the official YHA network. It has 208 beds in either dormitory or (far better) guest-house configurations, all with facilities en suite. ⊠ *Rte. 90, M.P. Dead Sea 86980,* ☎ *08/658–4165,* 𝔽𝔸𝕏 *08/658–4445. 208 beds. Cafeteria. AE, DC, MC, V.*

## Outdoor Activities and Sports

The newcomer to Ein Gedi will have no problem hiking the area alone, on well-marked trails through magnificent scenery. For advice on more serious trails and information on organized hikes, contact the **Society for the Protection of Nature in Israel** (⊠ 13 Helene Hamalka St., Jerusalem, ☎ 02/624–4605; ⊠ 3 Hashefela St., Tel Aviv, ☎ 03/638–8677; or the Society's field school in ⊠ Ein Gedi, ☎ 08/658–4288).

# Masada

★ ❼ *19 km (12 mi) south of Ein Gedi on Rte. 90, 103 km (64 mi) east and south of Jerusalem, 20 km (12½ mi) north of Ein Bokek.*

The great, isolated flattop rock of Masada is visible to the west of the highway long before you reach it. Built in the 1st century BC by Herod the Great—King of the Jews by the grace of Rome—it was designed as an impregnable yet palatial refuge, to which he could escape, if necessary, his hostile subjects or the military threats of Cleopatra, Queen of Egypt. Nowhere in the land are both his paranoia and sense of grandeur more evident.

Masada entered history as the site of the dramatic last stand of Jewish rebels against the legions of Rome. With Herod's death in 4 BC and the exile of his son, Archelaus, 10 years later, the central districts of Judea and Samaria (south and north of Jerusalem, respectively) came under direct Roman control. Decades of oppression and misrule precipitated the Great Revolt of the Jews against Rome in AD 66. Masada fell to the rebels early on, but with the Roman reconquest of the country and the fall of Jerusalem in AD 70, the fortress became the last refuge for almost a thousand men, women, and children. The new Roman governor, Silva, came down with a full legion of troops and thousands of slaves to crush the last vestige of resistance. The long Roman siege wall at the foot of the mountain and the eight square Roman camps in strategic locations on all sides attest to the thoroughness of the siege.

The 1st-century Jewish historian Josephus Flavius sets the final scene. Despite the Jews' vigorous defense, the Romans succeeded in constructing a massive earth assault ramp from the high western plateau to the very summit of the mountain. Seeing that the battle was lost, the rebel leader, Elazar Ben Yair, assembled his warriors and exhorted them to "at once choose death with honor, and do the kindest thing we can for ourselves, our wives and children" rather than face the brutal consequences of capture. The decision was not an easy one, relates Josephus, but once taken, it impelled each man to "carry out his terrible resolve" without delay. Having dispatched their own families, the men then drew lots to select 10 executioners for the rest; and the 10 similarly chose the last man, who would kill them all and afterward take his own life.

Josephus, and his melodramatic account, have been suspect in the eyes of some modern historians, not least of all because he had gone over to the Romans in the course of the revolt. His description of Masada has been borne out by archaeologists, however, and the human skeletal remains and inscribed potsherds (the lots, perhaps?) seem to give weight to his story as well.

Most visitors ride up to Masada on the large **cable car** (three minutes), with a scheduled run every half hour starting at 8 AM, and intermediate runs depending on demand. The intrepid climb the **Snake Path** (up to one hour of steep walking), some even going before dawn to watch the sunrise. Others take the easier, western Roman Ramp path, accessible only from Arad (☞ Exploring Eilat and the Negev *in* Chapter 7). The desert climate makes it imperative to drink lots of water and wear a hat. Running water (but no other refreshments) is available on Masada itself, so save your bottles for refilling. Allow 1½ to 2 hours to explore the site. Maps, brochures, and a very useful electronic guide are available at the top entrance.

The entire mountaintop—an area of more than 20 acres—is surrounded by a 4,250-ft-long **casemate**, a double wall that included living quarters and guardrooms. Most of the important buildings are concentrated in the site's high northern area. A street passes between long storerooms, where quantities of broken jars, seeds of grain, and dried fruit pits were found, bearing out Josephus's story that the Jews burned their possessions but spared their food supply in order to show the Romans that they did not die of want.

At the highest and most northerly point of Masada stands the **Northern Palace,** an extraordinary structure that seems to hang off the mountain. The panoramic effect is awesome: baked brown precipices and bleached valleys shimmering in the midday glare, or awash in the gentler light of the early morning or late afternoon. Designed to serve as an inner citadel in time of crisis, the palace is protected by an outer plastered wall.

Clearly visible from the upper terrace of the palace are the Roman camps and "runner's path" (used for communication between the camps), as well as the Ein Gedi oasis, 16 km (10 mi) to the north, from which the Romans had to haul their water. The Jewish defenders could mock them: using Herod's old system of trapping the winter floodwaters in streambeds west of the mountain, they had diverted the runoff to huge cisterns in the slope of the mountain, and then hauled the water to the top by hand. By the time the Romans came they had their supply "on tap."

Facing you as you return from the upper terrace is the **bathhouse,** a state-of-the-art facility in Herod's time, with its *apodyterium* (changing room), *frigidarium, tepidarium,* and *caldarium* (cold, lukewarm, and hot rooms, respectively). Frescoes and floor tiles are evidence of the Herodian opulence; intrusive benches and a pool represent alterations by the later occupants. The caldarium was once a closed room, heated, sauna-style, from below, and through wall pipes by hot air pumped in from an outside furnace. West of the bathhouse, steps descend to the middle and lower terraces of the Northern Palace—interesting, but a long climb back up.

Two *mikvehs*, or Jewish ritual baths, from the time of the revolt were found on Masada, creating a sensation in Israel's ultra-Orthodox circles, especially after a rabbinic inspection team confirmed that the mikvehs had been built in precise obedience to Jewish law.

The **synagogue**, one of only four ever found from this period, can be seen in the western casemate. The building's orientation toward Jerusalem suggested its function, but the stone benches (synagogue means "place of assembly") and the man-made pit for damaged scrolls (a *geniza*) confirmed it. It was likely here, in the community's spiritual center, that Elazar's men made their fateful decision.

At a break in the walls of the western edge, a modern winch marks the place where the Roman legionnaires broke into Masada. The original wedge-shape **ramp** is below, though its upper part has since collapsed. Here, too, is the Western Gate, from which a modern trail takes you down this side of the mountain (access via Arad only).

The small **Byzantine chapel,** complete with mosaic floor and wall designs, comes as something of a surprise on Masada. The monastic movement of the 5th century swirled and eddied into the most remote corners of the Byzantine Empire and found solitude here, too. South of the chapel is the **Western Palace,** the largest structure on Masada and originally its residential and administrative center. Its most interesting features are two colorful Herodian mosaics, the larger with especially meticulous geometric and fruit motifs.

The message of the Jews' last stand on Masada was not lost on Palestinian Jews fighting for independence in the 1930s and '40s, or on the modern Israel they created. "Masada shall not fall again!" became not just a rallying cry but a state of mind. It reflected the resolve of many Jews (made more poignant by the Nazi Holocaust) for self-determination in their own country.

If you have time and energy, explore the sparser, southern part of Masada, with its huge water cistern and spectacular view from the southern citadel. Test the echoes here as you face the great canyon to the south.

The new visitor center, alongside the lower cable-car station, offers a short movie, a model of Masada, a photo gallery of the archaeological dig, a cafeteria, and a store.

A fine summer-night diversion is the **sound-and-light show** at Masada's western base, accessible from Arad.

✉ *Off Rte. 90,* ☎ *08/658–4207 or 08/658–4208.* ▧ *Site and cable car (round-trip) NIS 50 ($12.50); site and cable car (1-way) NIS 37 ($9.25); site only (for walkers) NIS 18 ($4.50).* ☉ *Apr.–Sept., Sat.–Thurs. 8–5 (last car up at 4, last down at 5), Fri. and Jewish holiday eves 8–3 (last car up at 2, last down at 3), eve of Yom Kippur until noon. Oct.–Mar., Sat.–Thurs. 8–4 (last car up at 3, last down at 4), Fri. and Jewish holiday eves 8–2 (last car up at 1, last down at 2).* ▧ *Sound-and-light show (access only from Arad [☞ Exploring Eilat and the Negev in Chapter 7]) NIS 33 ($8.25).* ☉ *Mar.–Aug., Tues. and Thurs. 9 PM, Sept.–Oct., Tues. and Thurs. 7 PM.* ▧ *Translation headsets (from Hebrew) NIS 13 ($3.25).* ▧ *Shuttle bus, by prior reservation through your hotel (or ☎ 052/562–563), NIS 52 ($13) from Arad, NIS 62 ($15.50) from Ein Bokek (Dead Sea); call ahead to verify show times.*

### Beaches and Pools

The **Ein Bokek** hotel district, about 10 minutes' drive south of Masada, has a free public beach with showers (between Kapulsky's and Hordos restaurants). There are better facilities at the adjacent **Hammei Zohar** (☎ 08/658–4161). Nonguests can pay to use the beaches and freshwater pools at the **Lot** (☎ 08/658–4321 or 08/658–4324) hotel and the **Tsell Harim** (☎ 08/658–4121) hotel. Also available to nonguests are the beaches, pools, and full spa facilities at the more expensive **Caesar Premier** (☎ 08/668–9666), **Crowne Plaza** (☎ 08/659–1919), **Grand Nirvana** (☎ 08/668–9444), **Hod** (☎ 08/658–4644), **Hyatt Regency** (☎ 08/659–1234), and **Sheraton Moriah** (☎ 08/659–1591) hotels. For more information on Ein Bokek, *see* Chapter 7.

### Lodging

One inexpensive option at the foot of Masada itself is the 140-bed **Taylor Hostel,** part of the YHA network, with a few dormitories and 20 "family rooms," all with facilities en suite (✉ Rte. 90, M.P. Dead Sea 86935, ☎ 08/658–4349, ℻ 08/658–4650). About 15 km (9 mi) south of Masada are the excellent hotels of **Ein Bokek** (☞ Beersheva to Ein Bokek *in* Chapter 7).

# WEST OF JERUSALEM

The rugged and reforested Judean Hills tumble down to the west, eventually easing into the gentler landscapes of the Shefelah lowlands. This is not a region of towns but of rural landscapes, biblical ghosts, and ancient fingerprints. There are a variety of approaches from Jerusalem (though all sites are of course accessible from Tel Aviv as well). One route takes in the exquisite Sorek stalactite cave in the Avshalom Nature Reserve, before bringing you down to Bet Shemesh and points south. From Mt. Herzl, in West Jerusalem, take the steep descent to Ein Kerem and out the other side. One kilometer (½ mile) beyond the neighborhood is the Kerem Junction. Continue straight (left fork) on Route 386. On the hills to your left is the Hadassah Hospital complex (☞ West Jerusalem *in* Chapter 1), one of the largest in the Middle East. Most of these hillsides have the terraced effect of the natural strata of sedimentary limestone; many were laboriously widened by farmers over the centuries by enclosing them with drystone walls. One of the landscape's dominant features is the reforestation—mostly pines and cypresses—of the hills, an attempt to reverse the decimation of ancient woodlands, provide recreation areas, and restore something of the habitat of animals such as the gazelle, which is now seen again near Jerusalem itself.

The road crosses the defunct Jerusalem–Tel Aviv railway line, where the Refaim Valley merges with Nahal Sorek, and at once begins climbing, offering fine views of the deep gorge below. At the Bar Giora Junction (a T-junction) turn right onto Route 3866 and follow the signs to the cave. After your visit, back up the road again, and turn down Route 3855 to Bet Shemesh, to join Route 38 south.

An alternate route is to take Route 1, the main Jerusalem–Tel Aviv highway, which will bring you to Latrun where you turn south to Bet Shemesh and beyond. Ten kilometers (6 miles) west of Jerusalem, Route 425 turns off to the Arab village of Abu Ghosh and to some of the guest houses recommended below. Abu Ghosh itself offers several excellent Middle Eastern restaurants on its main street. Farther down Route 1, in several places by the roadside, are derelict trucks and armored cars dating back to the 1948 War of Independence. Many supply convoys attempting to relieve the siege on the Jewish side of

Jerusalem in that war were ambushed and stopped on what was then a narrow and winding road. The old vehicles have been preserved as memorials for those who died in the attempt.

Twenty kilometers (13 miles) west of Jerusalem is the Sha'ar Hagai Interchange, where the rugged Judean Hills suddenly give way to the low hills of the Shefelah. There is a gas station on the right. To the left of the road are two restored old buildings, once the overnight caravansary or inn for two-day journey from Jaffa to Jerusalem in the mid-19th century. Behind the gas station is a small tower, one of 17 built in 1869 to guard travelers from the robbers that plagued this route. To avoid Latrun, and continue via Bet Shemesh to Bet Guvrin, turn off onto Route 38. Latrun itself is 5 km (3 mi) farther on. If you visit the sites of Latrun, Route 3 south and Route 44 east will bring you back to Route 38, the road to Bet Shemesh and Bet Guvrin.

## Sorek Cave

★ ⑧ *25 km (17 mi) southwest of Jerusalem on Rtes. 386 and 3866, 16 km (10 mi) east of Bet Shemesh on Rte. 3855.*

The Avshalom Reserve contains the justly renowned Sorek Cave, a stalactite cave that is small in comparison with similar caverns elsewhere, but is said to include every type of formation known. It was discovered in 1967, when a routine blast in the nearby quarry tore away the rock face, revealing a subterranean wonderland never seen before.

In developing the site, the Nature Reserves Authority (as it was then known) faced the problem of how to allow public access to the cave yet minimize impact on its unique environment. The Authority's sensitive solutions have generally won kudos. Colored lights have been eschewed in favor of white ones, which highlight the stones' natural whites and honey browns. The cave's forms have names like "macaroni," "curtains," and "sombreros," the products of tour guides vying with each other to find imaginative familiarity in the shapes of the formations. In a series of "interfaith" images, some guides find rocky evocations of Moses, the Madonna and Child, Buddha, and the Ayatollah Khomeini. Photography is allowed only on Friday morning, when there are no guided tours. Despite the almost 100% humidity, the temperature and the atmosphere in the cave are very comfortable year-round.

A stepped path winds down to the cave entrance—visitors with medical problems should bear in mind the climb back to the parking lot. Local guides take groups into the cave every 15 minutes for a 30-minute tour (English tours on request and dependent on demand). A video in an acclimatization room (English version available) explains how the cave was formed. ⊠ *Avshalom Reserve, Rte. 3866,* ☎ *02/991–1117.* ✆ *NIS 18 ($4.50).* ☉ *Summer (daylight saving time), Sat.–Thurs. 8–4, Fri. 8–3; winter, Sat.–Thurs. 8–3, Fri. 8–1; eve of Passover and Yom Kippur 8–11:30 AM, all other holiday eves 8–noon; last entry 30 mins before closing.*

### Lodging

There are four very good kibbutz guest houses in wooded enclaves of the Judean Hills, 15–20 minutes' drive west of Jerusalem. All have commanding hilltop views, quiet surroundings, rural ambience, very comfortable if not luxurious accommodations, and good swimming pools. Bed-and-breakfast for two runs $90–$170, depending on the season.

🏨 **Kiryat Anavim.** This is the smallest of the area's guest houses, a little more intimate, and a little less expensive. All the rooms are in one main building in a classic hotel configuration. ⊠ *8 km (5 mi) west of*

*Jerusalem, north of Rte. 1, M.P. Judean Hills 90833,* ☎ *02/534–8999,* ☎ *02/534–8848. 50 rooms. AE, DC, MC, V.*

🏨 **Ma'aleh Hahamisha.** In this large guest house, new additions have provided a health club, including an indoor heated pool, gym, saunas, and whirlpool baths. Some rooms lead to a garden patio. A few have shower only. ⊠ *12 km (7 mi) west of Jerusalem, north of Rte. 1, M.P. Judean Hills 90835,* ☎ *02/533–1331,* ☎ *02/534–2144. 231 rooms. AE, DC, MC, V.*

★ 🏨 **Neve Ilan.** A cut above its neighbors, this hotel has larger and better-furnished rooms. You can also reserve superior-grade rooms, and minisuites with their own whirlpool baths. The pool is covered year-round and heated in winter, and there is a well-equipped exercise room. ⊠ *15 km (10 mi) west of Jerusalem, north of Rte. 1, M.P. Judean Hills 90850,* ☎ *02/533–9339,* ☎ *02/533–9335. 160 rooms. AE, DC, MC, V.*

🏨 **Shoresh.** Recent renovations have diversified the offerings of this guest house. Options include relatively simple budget arrangements, hotel rooms in a central building, and a few new and more luxurious suites. The pool is covered and heated year-round. ⊠ *15 km (8½ mi) west of Jerusalem, south of Rte. 1, 88 M.P. Judean Hills, 90860,* ☎ *02/533–8338,* ☎ *02/534–0262. 24 B&Bs, 70 rooms, 5 suites. AE, DC, MC, V.*

## Swimming
Several villages have beautiful pools in wooded parts of the Judean Hills, to the north of the Sorek Cave (☞ Lodging, *above*).

**Kiryat Anavim.** ☎ *02/534–8999.* ☑ *Sun.–Fri. NIS 40 ($10), Sat. and holidays NIS 45 ($11.25).* ☉ *May–Sept., Sun.–Fri. 10–6:30, Sat. 10–7.*

**Ma'aleh Hahamisha.** ☎ *02/533–1331.* ☑ *Sun.–Fri. NIS 42 ($10.50), Sat. and holidays NIS 49 ($12.25).* ☉ *June–Aug., daily 9–6.*

**Neve Ilan.** ☎ *02/533–9339.* ☑ *Sun.–Fri. NIS 45 ($11.25), Sat. and holidays NIS 55 ($13.75).* ☉ *Mon.–Thurs. 5:30 AM–9 PM, Fri. 7–6, Sat. 8–6, Sun. 8 AM–9 PM.*

# Latrun

*25 km (16 mi) west of Jerusalem on Rte. 1.*

Latrun is the name given to the salient of high ground that projects into and dominates the Ayalon Valley to the west of it. A natural passage between the Mediterranean coastal plain and the Judean Hills to the east, the valley has been a battleground throughout history, from the conquests of the biblical Israelite leader Joshua in the 13th century BC, through the Maccabean campaigns of the 2nd century BC, to the conflicts of modern times.

Coming from Jerusalem on Route 1, exit onto Route 3 (the Ramallah and Ashkelon-Beersheba road), about 5 km (3 mi) west of the Sha'ar Hagai gas station. At the T-junction, turn right for Emmaus and Canada Park, left for the Trappist Monastery of Latrun and the Latrun Armored Corps Museum.

The New Testament (Luke 24) records one of Jesus's appearances ❾ after his resurrection on the road to **Emmaus.** The traditional text places the site "60 stadia" (about 11 km, or 7 mi) from Jerusalem, but other ancient sources talk of "160 stadia" (about 29 km or 18 mi), a confusion that has spawned several rival sites. The enduring Arabic name of this place—Imwas—seems to echo the ancient name and may strengthen its claims of authenticity. Within the remains of Byzantine mosaic floors and a 5th-century basilica is the ruined but better-preserved Crusader church of the 12th century. ✉ *Rte. 3, 100 yards towards Ramallah from the junction with Rte. 1 W* ☎ *02/274–2486.* 🎫 *Free.* ⊘ *Mon.–Sat. 8:30–noon and 2:30–5:30.*

NEED A
BREAK?

On Route 3 north (toward Ramallah), 400 yards from Emmaus, is **Canada Park**, a woodland area straddling the highway, that is built on the site of two Palestinian villages that were evacuated in the 1967 war. The small western section is primarily a picnic site, with tables, toilets, and playground equipment. The far larger eastern section has similar facilities, as well as some springs, remains of the old agricultural installations, and fine views from the higher points (accessible from a network of roads). Entrance is free, and the park is open 7 AM to sunset.

The name Latrun is thought to derive from "La Toron de Chevaliers" (the Tower of the Knights), the French name of the Crusader castle that occupied the crest of the hill (behind the present Trappist monastery) in the 12th century. Eight centuries later, the British erected a concrete fortress for much the same reason: to secure the road to Jerusalem. Jordanian troops took the site in the 1948 war but lost it to Israel in 1967. ❿ Today it is the flag-bedecked national memorial site of the **Latrun Armored Corps Museum,** offering visitors grand views, a movie (check for English), and an outside exhibit of some 100 varieties of tanks that have fought in the region. The site is about 1 km (½ mi) south of Route 1, on Route 3 (the Ashkelon–Beersheba highway). A decent cafeteria serves the site. ☎ *08/925–5268.* 🎫 *NIS 20 ($5).* ⊘ *Sun.–Thurs. 8:30–4:30, Fri. and Jewish holiday eves 8:30 AM–12:30 PM, Sat. and Jewish holidays 9–4.*

In dramatic contrast to the angular raw concrete of the fortress are the ⓫ graceful facade and soft green groves and vineyards of the **Trappist Abbey of Latrun,** built in the early 20th century. The interior of the church (access only to the entrance) is an odd mix of round neo-Byzantine arches and apses and the soaring ceiling that seems Gothic in inspiration. Survivors of the Cistercian Order suppressed in the French Revolution, the Trappists keep a vow of silence, with exceptions made for the monks who run the monastery's wine and olive oil operation. ✉ *Rte. 3 South, 2 km (1.5 mi) off Rte. 1,* ☎ *08/922–0065.* ⊘ *Mon.–Sat., church 8–11 and 2:30–4, wine shop 8:30–noon and 1–6.*

OFF THE
BEATEN PATH

**NEOT KEDUMIM** – In the lowland hills (the Shefelah) halfway between Jerusalem and Tel Aviv, a 625-acre "Biblical landscape reserve" awaits those with a feel for the past and a love of nature. It is a truism that the Bible, from the Old Testament psalms to the parables of Jesus, draws heavily on images of the land to convey its message. Since 1965, the founders of the Neot Kedumim ("Oasis of Antiquity") reserve have invested enormous effort in re-creating something of the country's ancient scenery, both natural and agricultural. They have trucked in vast loads of soil, restored ancient terraces and old wine and oil presses, planted thousands of trees and shrubs, dug pools and cisterns, and developed infrastructure for visitors. A network of roads and walking paths (most of them paved and wheelchair-accessible) allows a leisurely exploration of the site. Take one of the self-guided tours (brochures and maps in English provided), or inquire ahead of time about guided tours in English. Allow two hours minimum for the visit. The reserve is closed Saturday and Jewish holidays and closes at 1 PM the previous day. Call 08/977–0777 for further information. Neot Kedumim is on Route 443, about 4 km (2½ mi) east of the Ben Shemen Interchange (take the Modi'in turnoff coming from Tel Aviv), or most easily reached from Jerusalem by way of the

Ramot neighborhood and Givat Ze'ev. To continue the tour via Latrun
and Bet Shemesh, drive west to the Ben Shemen Interchange, and turn
east on Route 1.

## Bet Shemesh

*12 km (7½ mi) west of Sorek Cave on Rtes. 3855 and 38, 35 km (22
mi) west of Jerusalem.*

The modern town of Bet Shemesh takes its name from its ancient predecessor, now entombed by the *tel*, or archaeological mound, on a rise
on Route 38, 2 km (1 mi) south of the town's main entrance. This is
Samson country. Samson, one of the judges of Old Testament Israel,
is better known for his physical prowess and lust for Philistine women
than for his shining spiritual qualities, but it was here, "between Zorah
and Eshta'ol," that "the Spirit of the Lord began to stir him" (Judges
13). Today, Eshta'ol is a moshav a few minutes' drive north, and Tzora
(Zorah) is the kibbutz immediately to the west.

NEED A     Just 300 yards south of the main entrance to Bet Shemesh is the turnoff
BREAK?     to **Kibbutz Tzora** (*Zora* on the sign), west of the highway. Once within
           the village, follow signs to the right to the winery. In addition to tasting
           the very drinkable wines, enjoy a light meal of fresh bread, fresh vegeta-
           bles, and a variety of sheep cheeses. The wine store sells olives, olive
           oil, and some unusual homemade deli items. It's open 10–5 (10–2 on
           Friday and eve of Jewish festivals), but call 02/990–8261 to verify.

On Route 38 south, and under 2 km (1 mi) from the Tzora turnoff,
⑫ the road rises to (and over) the low-profile **Tel Bet Shemesh.** There is
a clearing to pull off the road on your right (only southbound). From
the top of the tel there is a fine view of the fields of Nahal Sorek, where
Samson dallied with Delilah (Judges 16). The city of Bet Shemesh controlled access through the valley to the mountains of Judah, to the east.
According to the Bible, when the Philistines captured the Israelite Ark
of the Covenant in battle (11th century BC), they found that their prize
brought divine retribution with it, destroying their idol Dagon and af-
flicting them with tumors and their cities with rats (I Samuel 5). In con-
sternation and awe, the Philistines rid themselves of the jinxed ark by
sending it back to the Israelites at Bet Shemesh.

## Elah Valley

⑬ *10 km (6 mi) south of Bet Shemesh, 42 km (26 mi) west of Jerusalem.*

The Elah Valley is one of those delightful places—not uncommon in
Israel—where you can relate the scenery to a specific biblical text and
confirm the maxim that once you've visited this country, you'll never
read the Bible the same way again.

Just beyond the junction of Route 38 with Route 383, and up to your
right above the pine-wooded slopes, is a distinctively bald flattop hill, **Tel
Azekah,** the site of an ancient Israelite city. The hills are crisscrossed by
dirt roads, especially delightful in spring when the wildflowers are out.

You are now in the Elah Valley. The road crosses a usually dry
streambed; 200 yards beyond it is place to pull off and park. If you
have a Bible with you, open it to I Samuel 17 and read about the dramatic duel between David and the giant Philistine champion Goliath.
The battle probably took place within a half mile or so of where you're
standing. Skeptical? Review the following passage:

*Now the Philistines gathered their armies for battle; and they were gath-ered at Socoh, which belongs to Judah* [identified by a mound 800 yards east of the junction ahead of you], *and encamped between Socoh and Azekah* [your location] . . . *And Saul and the men of Israel were gath-ered, and encamped in the valley of Elah, and drew up in line of bat-tle against the Philistines. And the Philistines stood on the mountain on the one side, and Israel stood on the mountain on the other side, with a valley between them.*

Try this: as you look east up the valley (across the road), you'll see the mountains of Judah in the distance and the road from Bethlehem— now, as then—by which David reached the battlefield. The white northern ridge, a spur of the mountains of Judah, may have been the emplacement of the Israelite army; the southern ridge (where the gas station is today)—including Tel Socoh, where, as the Bible says, the Philistines gathered—ascends from the Philistine territory to the west. And the creek you crossed is the only one in the valley: "And David . . . chose five smooth stones from the brook . . . ; his sling was in his hand, and he drew near to the Philistine." The rest, as they say, is history: Goliath was slain, the Philistines were routed, and David went on to become the darling of the nation and eventually its king.

## Dining

$$$ ✕ **Kela David.** This is a restaurant to plan your day around. In an airy, bright, art-filled setting, surrounded by vineyards, the farmer-owners offer a wide menu enhanced by homegrown olives and herbs and homemade wine and bread. Appetizers show imagination and a light touch: try the lightly smoked salmon or the marinated zucchini. Main courses include baked lamb, steaks, baked fish, several pasta dishes, a good spicy chicken steak (steak-like cuts of chicken), and delectable slices of goose liver in a sauce of dried fruit and cassis. Desserts change, but the mousse and the cheesecake are great choices. The restaurant is in a tiled-roof building, just off Route 38, 2 km (1 mi) south of Elah Junction. ⊠ *Givat Yishayahu, Rte. 38,* ☎ *02/999–4848 or 02/999– 2710. Reservations essential Fri. and Sat. AE, DC, MC, V. Closed Sun.*

$$–$$$ ✕ **Mitzpeh Massua.** The chef describes the restaurant as "Mediter-ranean" or "Israeli," and the grilled meats and fish are prepared with local herbs and farm produce. The house salads are more a selection of regional antipasti, and these alone, with some good bread and draft beer, make a satisfactory light lunch. On Friday only a dairy-based brunch is served. The pine forest and the fabulous panoramic view are free. Mitzpeh Massua is west of Route 38, 2 km (1 mi) south of Elah Junc-tion, on the top of the hill, next to the watchtower. ⊠ *Off Rte. 38,* ☎ *02/991–2464. AE, DC, MC, V. No dinner Fri., Sat., Jewish holiday eves, and Jewish holidays.*

*En Route* Between the Elah Junction (Routes 38 and 375) and Bet Guvrin, some 10 km (6 mi) to the south, the sharp eye can pick out evidence of the 2nd–3rd century AD Roman road that ran from coastal Ashkelon through the Elah Valley to Bethlehem and Jerusalem, which at that time was called Aelia Capitolina. Look for small standing milestones above the road to the right, about 1½ km (1 mi) south of the Elah Junction, and another group of stones and long sections of the terrace where the road once ran, to the left of the road farther south.

## Tel Maresha and Bet Guvrin

★ *21 km (13 mi) south of Bet Shemesh, 52 km (33 mi) southwest of Jerusalem.*

The Bet Guvrin-Maresha national park is a wonderland, both under the ground and above it.

The flattop mound of ancient Maresha, known today as **Tel Maresha,** was already the site of an important city in the Israelite period (early 1st millennium BC); but it was during the Hellenistic period (4th–2nd centuries BC) that the endless complexes of chalk caves that riddle the site—and make it so delightful—were excavated. Maresha was finally destroyed by the Parthians in 40 BC, and its place was subsequently taken by the new nearby Roman city of Bet Guvrin.

Even before you enter the park, the antiquities greet you: sprawled around the kibbutz of Bet Guvrin, just beyond the junction of Routes 30 and 35, are bits and pieces of the 2nd- to 3rd-century AD "free city" of Bet Guvrin, renamed (around the year 200) Eleuthropolis, "the city of free men." A particularly great find was the amphitheater, an arena for blood sports, one of only a handful discovered in Israel. (The ruins of a 12th-century church are virtually the only evidence of the Crusader town of Bethgibelin.)

The layout of the park's roads encourages but does not compel you to begin with its older sites. Nothing remains of earlier excavations that unearthed the Hellenistic city on the tel's top, but more recent digs have exposed the masonry of ancient fortifications from the Old Testament period at the corner of the mound. The view from the tel is worth the short climb.

The main reason to visit Tel Maresha, however, is a vast series of underground chambers carved out of the soft chalk by the Hellenistic citizens more than 2,000 years ago. One impressive complex (to the right before you reach the tel) is the so-called **Columbarium,** a huge underground chamber some 30 ft deep, hewn out in the shape of a double cross, and lined with symmetrical niches. The shape of the chamber is of no religious significance; this is older than Christianity. The Latin word *columba* means dove or pigeon, and a leading theory about the purpose of the complex is that these birds were raised here primarily as ritual sacrifices, though their usefulness as carriers, as food, and as producers of fertilizer from the droppings cannot be ignored. Other scholars question the pigeon theory because chemical analysis of the surrounding chalk has failed to support it; they suggest instead that the niches contained urns of cremated human remains. The term *columbarium* has nevertheless entered the archaeological lexicon to describe this style of niche-filled walls, whatever their purpose.

The most interesting and extensive of the mazes is just off the road on the opposite side of the tel (at a parking lot, the trail begins through the posts, and down to the left). Here, under their houses, the ancient Mareshans dug their own personal water cisterns and storerooms. The excitement of exploration makes this sight a must for kids (with close parental supervision, though the safety features are good), but the many steps are physically demanding. The last chamber of the maze route displays a restored ancient olive press in situ, where an estimated 9 tons of that precious commodity were processed each year.

Warning: other fascinating but undeveloped complexes of caves near the tel have dangerous pits and are off-limits to visitors. Keep to the marked sites only. The leaflet you're given with your ticket has a good map of the site.

On a ridge to the north of Tel Maresha, look for a large apse standing in splendid isolation. Known as Santahanna in Arabic, it has been identified by scholars as a remnant of the Crusader Church of St. Anne.

Archaeological Seminars, in Jerusalem (☎ 02/627–3515), runs a "Dig for a Day" program at the park (actually only about 3 hours), which includes supervised digging in a real excavation inside a cave, into which local inhabitants dumped earth and artifacts 21 centuries ago. Participants then sift the buckets of dirt they have hauled out of the cave, looking for "finds." Some museum-quality finds of the 3rd–2nd centuries BC (Hellenistic Period) have been found here. (No, you can't take home what you find!) The participants (who wish to) are then led on a 30-minute exploration (a lot of fun) through unexcavated caves not yet open to the public. This involves some crawling, because some places are too tight or too low to do anything else. Those who prefer to pass on that experience just wait for the last component—a short talk in the "pottery shed" about how clay vessels are restored from shards. Individuals can join this program on Fridays by prior reservation, though groups are sometimes organized on other days if there is a demand. The cost per person is $25, not counting the entrance fee to the park itself.

**15** The great "bell caves" of **Bet Guvrin** date from the Late Roman, Byzantine, and even Early Arab periods (2nd century–7th century AD), when the locals created an ecologically sound quarry to extract lime for cement. These caves are very different from the functional underground chambers of Maresha. At the top of each "bell" is a hole through the 4-ft-thick hard stone crust; the moment they reached the soft chalk below, the diggers began reaming out their quarry in the structurally secure bell shape, each bell eventually cutting into the adjacent one. The effect of the soaring domed ceilings and the interplay of shadow with shafts of sunlight is awesome.

Although not built to be inhabited, the caves may have been used as refuges by early Christians. In the North Cave (currently closed for restoration), a much later cross high on the wall, at the same level as an Arabic inscription, suggests a degree of coexistence even *after* the Arab conquest of the area in AD 636. ✉ *Rte. 35,* ☎ *08/681–1020.* 🎥 *NIS 18 ($4.50).* ⊙ *Apr.–Sept., Sat.–Thurs. 8–5, Fri. and Jewish holiday eves 8–4; Oct.–Mar., Sat.–Thurs. 8–4, Fri. and holiday eves 8–3.*

An attractive alternative route back to Jerusalem is east from the Elah Valley on Route 375, past Israel's main satellite communications receiver, and up through fine, wooded hill country to Tzur Hadassah (look out for the rock-hewn Roman road on the right). Route 386 heads off to the left and runs north to Jerusalem through rugged mountain scenery, emerging in the Ein Kerem neighborhood on the city's western edge. Bearing right (continuation of Route 375) takes you to Bethlehem, or on to Jerusalem along the faster "tunnels" route, entering the city at the southern Gilo neighborhood. **Warning: use this route only if the Bethlehem area itself is peaceful.** For reasons of security, avoid Route 35 from Bet Guvrin to Hebron.

# BETHLEHEM

**Warning:** Most travelers to this West Bank area confine themselves to Bethlehem and the immediate vicinity, and that only if political and security conditions permit. Because of extensive Arab unrest at press time, you are *strongly* urged to avoid other Arab parts of the West Bank entirely.

The West Bank is that part of the onetime British Mandate of Palestine, west of the Jordan River, that was occupied by the Kingdom of Transjordan in its war with Israel in 1948 and unilaterally annexed shortly afterward. That country then changed its name to the Hashemite Kingdom of Jordan to reflect its new territorial reality. The territory was lost to Israel in the Six-Day War of 1967 and, with the exception of recently autonomous areas (mostly urban), has remained under Israeli military administration ever since. In Israel itself, the region is often referred to as "the territories" or "over the Green Line." The term *Green Line* denotes the pre-1967 border between the West Bank and Israel proper. Many Israelis refer to the region by its ancient biblical names *Yehuda,* or Judea, for the area south of Jerusalem, and *Shomron,* or Samaria, for the much larger area north of it.

The West Bank is a kidney-shape area, a bit larger than the U.S. state of Delaware and almost half the size of Northern Ireland. The Arab population of over 1 million is more than 90% Muslim, with the Christian minority living mostly in the Greater Bethlehem area (in Judea) and in Ramallah (in Samaria).

In the mid- and late-1990s, a series of negotiated agreements between Israel and the Palestinians transferred most of the Gaza Strip and all the West Bank Arab towns and some hinterland to Palestinian control. The much sought-after "Final Status Agreement" proved elusive, however, as seemingly irreconcilable rival stands on the thorny questions of land, refugees, and Jerusalem produced more rhetoric than dialogue. At the end of September 2000, the simmering crisis exploded with lethal ferocity as young Palestinian Arabs took to the streets. At press time, security for visitors to the West Bank and the future of the peace process were equally uncertain.

The Jewish population in the West Bank numbers more than 160,000, dispersed in a handful of small towns and more than 100 villages. Although some of the towns are really suburbs of Jerusalem and Tel Aviv, other settlements were set up by fiercely nationalist Israelis—the majority of them religious Jews—who see the region as an integral and inalienable part of their ancient homeland and who consider the almost miraculous "homecoming" of 1967 as nothing less than a first rumble of the messianic age. With its mountain heights dominating Israel's main population centers and the area thrusting to within 14 km (9 mi) of the Mediterranean Sea, the West Bank has a strategic value that has convinced even many moderate Israelis that it would be folly to relinquish it all to potentially hostile Arab control. A person's attitude toward the questions of continuing settlement in the West Bank and the ultimate status of the region is an important touchstone of political affiliation in Israel, and the country is completely divided on these issues.

Bethlehem is a mere 10 minutes' drive from Jerusalem. As you leave Jerusalem, look for the large buildings of Kibbutz Ramat Rahel on the hill to your left. This was an important Israeli position in the War of Independence of 1948, and then a border outpost in the years that followed, when the Green Line ran through the valley immediately below it. The next ridge is capped by the Greek Orthodox monastery of Mar Elias (St. Elijah)—once a Jordanian stronghold—and immediately beyond is your first view of Bethlehem.

Way off on the eastern horizon is a prominent flattop hill. This is Herodion, one of Herod's great palace-fortresses, later used by the Zealots in the Great Revolt against Rome (AD 66–73) and by Bar Kochba's fighters in the 2nd century AD. Today it is a national park.

**Rachel's Tomb,** on your right as you enter Bethlehem, is the only Israeli enclave in a Palestinian area, its once-landmark white dome now invisible behind a security wall. The Bible relates that the matriarch Rachel, second and favorite wife of Jacob, died in childbirth on the outskirts of Bethlehem, "and Jacob set up a pillar upon her grave" (Genesis 35).

The present building, behind the security wall, is probably medieval, with 19th-century additions made by the renowned British Jewish philanthropist Sir Moses Montefiore. There is no vestige of Jacob's original pillar, of course, but the large, velvet-draped, blocklike cenotaph inside the building has been hallowed by observant Jews for centuries as the very site of Rachel's tomb. The interior is decorated with Hebrew biblical quotations referring to Rachel. People come to pray here for good health and fecundity (Rachel was long barren), and some pilgrims wind a red thread seven times around the tomb marker, then take it off, and give away snippets of it as talismans to cure all ills.

Rachel is respected by Islam as well. Next to the tomb is a Muslim cemetery, reflecting the Middle Eastern tradition that it is a special privilege to be buried near a great personage. ⊠ *Rte. 60.* 🎟 *Free.* ☉ *Sun.– Thurs. 8–5, Fri. and Jewish holiday eves 8–1.*

Even from a distance, Bethlehem is easily identified by the minarets and church steeples that struggle for control of its skyline. Immediately beyond Rachel's tomb, the road forks; the right fork goes toward the Etzion Bloc and Hebron, the left into Manger Street and on to Manger Square. Note that Bethlehem is now an autonomous Palestinian enclave, with all security and tourism matters in the hands of the Palestinian Authority.

The wide Manger Street winds into town past large gift shops and the high stone walls of various religious institutions. To the east are occasional panoramas of what geographers call "marginal land"—still more or less arable, but very close to the desert. Fields that now belong to the adjacent town of Beit Sahour are traditionally identified with the biblical story of Ruth the Moabite, daughter-in-law of Naomi, who "gleaned in the field" of Boaz, Naomi's kinsman. Boaz eventually "took Ruth and she became his wife" (Ruth 4); and it was in Bethlehem that their great-grandson, King David, was born.

The same fields are identified by Christian tradition as those where shepherds "keeping watch over their flock by night" received word of the birth of Jesus in Bethlehem. Several denominations maintain sites in the valley, which they venerate as the authentic "Shepherds' Fields."

★ Manger Square is Bethlehem's central plaza and the entrance to its primary sight, the **Church of the Nativity,** built over the grotto thought to be the birthplace of Jesus. The square has a tourist-information office, a few restaurants, and some shops. At press time Bethlehem was closed to visitors because of local rioting, but the importance of tourism in the town's economy allows for optimism that this, too, shall pass. Check the political situation before you set out. Even in calm periods, most visitors take in the Church of the Nativity and avoid the *souk* (market) and narrow alleys beyond Manger Square.

The unprepossessing stone exterior of the Church of the Nativity is crowned by the crosses of the three denominations sharing it: the Greek Orthodox in the center, the Latins (Roman Catholic, represented by the Franciscan order) on the left, and the Armenian Orthodox on the right. The blocked square entranceway dates from the time of the Byzantine emperor Justinian (6th century AD), the arched entrance (also now blocked) within the Byzantine one is 12th-century Crusader, and the current low entrance (watch your head) was designed in the 16th century to protect the worshipers from attack by hostile Muslim neighbors.

The church interior is vast and gloomy. In the central nave, a wooden trapdoor reveals a remnant of a mosaic floor from the original church, built in the 4th century by Helena, mother of Constantine the Great, the Roman emperor who first embraced Christianity. Emperor Justinian's rebuilding two centuries later enlarged the church, creating its present-day plan and structure, including the high columns that run the length of the nave in two paired lines.

This is the oldest standing church in the country. When the Persians invaded in AD 614, they destroyed every Christian church and monastery across the land except the Nativity. The story holds that the Byzantine church that greeted the Persians in Bethlehem was adorned with a wall-painting depicting the Nativity tale, including the visit to the infant Jesus by the Three Wise Men of the East. For the local artist, "east" meant Persia, and he had thus dressed his wise men in Persian garb. The Persians understood nothing of the picture's significance, but they "recognized" themselves in it and spared the church.

The church was pillaged by the early Muslims in the 7th century (much of the marble used at the Temple Mount in Jerusalem came from here), but the patches of 12th-century mosaics high on the walls and the faded burned-wax figures of saints on the Corinthian pillars hint at its revived medieval splendor. The ceiling beams are medieval English oak and are said to have been covered by lead, which the Turks later melted down for bullets in their wars with the Venetians.

The elaborately ornamented front of the church serves as the parish church of Bethlehem's Greek Orthodox community. The right transept is theirs, too, but the left transept belongs to the Armenian Orthodox. All three "shareholders" in the church have vied for centuries for control of the holiest Christian sites in the Holy Land. The 19th-century Status Quo Agreement that froze their respective rights and privileges in Jerusalem's Church of the Holy Sepulcher and the Tomb of the Virgin pertains here, too: ownership, the timing of ceremonies, the number of oil lamps, and so on are all clearly defined.

You descend to the **Grotto of the Nativity** from the right transept at the front of the church. Once a cave—precisely the kind of place that might have been used as a barn—the grotto has been reamed, plastered, and decorated beyond recognition. Immediately on your right as you enter is a small altar, and on the floor below it is the focal point of the entire site: a 14-point **bronze star** with the Latin inscription HIC DE VIR-GINE MARIA JESUS CHRISTUS NATUS EST (Here of the Virgin Mary, Jesus Christ was born). The original star was placed here in 1717 by the Latins, who lost control of the altar 40 years later to the more influential Greek Orthodox. In 1847 the star mysteriously disappeared, and pressure from the Turkish sultan compelled the Greeks to allow the present Latin replacement to be installed in 1853. The Franciscan guardians do have possession, however, of the little alcove a few steps down on your left as you enter the Grotto, said to be the manger where the infant Jesus was laid. There is clear evidence of the fire that gutted the grotto in the 19th century; the asbestos wall hangings were a French gift to prevent a recurrence. ✉ *Manger Sq.*, ☎ *02/274–1020.* ▣ *Free.* ☉ *Apr.– Sept., daily 6:30 AM–7:30 PM; Oct.–Mar., daily 5:30–5; grotto closed Sun. morning; access to grotto restricted other mornings until about 9 AM for Armenian mass.*

The **Church of St. Catherine,** adjacent to the Church of the Nativity and accessible by a passage from its Armenian chapel, is Bethlehem's Roman Catholic parish church. Completed in 1882, and renovated in time for Christmas 1999, the church incorporates remnants of its 12th-century Crusader predecessor. It has fine acoustics but is otherwise unexceptional. It is from this church that the midnight Catholic

Christmas mass is broadcast around the world. Steps descend from within the church to a series of dim grottoes, clearly once used as living quarters. Chapels here are variously dedicated to Joseph; to the Innocents killed by Herod; and to the 4th-century St. Jerome, who wrote the Vulgate, the Latin translation of the Bible, supposedly right here. At the end of a narrow passage, a small wooden door (kept locked) connects the complex with the Grotto of the Nativity.

✉ *Manger Sq.,* ☎ *02/274–2425.* ✆ *Apr.–Sept., daily 6–noon and 2– 7; Oct.–Mar., daily 5:30–5:30.*

**Manger Square** is brilliant with lights and bursting with life on Christmas Eve (December 24; the Greek Orthodox celebrate Christmas Day on January 7, the Armenian Orthodox on January 19). Traditionally, choirs from around the world perform carols and sacred music in the square between 8:30 PM and 11:30 PM, and at midnight the Roman Catholic mass from the Franciscan Church of St. Catherine is simultaneously relayed on closed-circuit television onto a large outside screen and, via satellite, to all parts of the globe.

For information, contact the **Office of Tourism of the Palestinian Authority** in Bethlehem (☎ 02/277–0603 or 02/277–0604). Regarding the Christmas mass, contact the **Christian Information Center** at Jerusalem's Jaffa Gate (☎ 02/627–2692). General advice: you'll probably need to leave your car in Jerusalem and take public transportation to Bethlehem; there is no seating in Manger Square; very warm clothing is essential; you should have your passport with you; you may not bring in alcohol; and it's not ideal to carry large bags (because of security checks). The Israel Ministry of Tourism extends its patronage to parallel Christmas celebrations in Nazareth.

## Shopping

Bethlehem craftspeople make carved olive-wood and mother-of-pearl objects, mostly of a religious nature, but the many stores along the tourist route in town sell jewelry and a range of baubles and notions as well. For quality and reliability, most of the half dozen or so large establishments on Manger Street, where the tour buses stop, are worth investigating, but some of the merchants near the Church of the Nativity, on Manger Square, have good-quality items as well.

# AROUND JERUSALEM A TO Z

## Arriving and Departing

The points of departure for the three areas explored in this chapter are Jerusalem and Tel Aviv. For information about arriving and departing, *see* Jerusalem A to Z *and* Tel Aviv A to Z *in* Chapters 1 and 3, respectively.

## Getting Around

### By Bus

With few exceptions, the **Egged Bus Cooperative** enjoys a nationwide monopoly on intercity bus routes. Buses are modern, comfortable, airconditioned, and reasonably priced. Service is solid on main routes but infrequent to outlying rural districts. For fares and schedules, call 03/ 694–8888 (Tel Aviv).

Jerusalem's **Central Bus Station** is in the city's northwestern corner, on Jaffa Road. Give yourself ample time to buy a ticket and get in line for the often crowded Dead Sea routes.

Since Jericho became autonomous under the Palestinian Authority, Egged no longer serves it. For the Dead Sea area (Qumran, Ein Gedi, Masada, and Ein Bokek), take Bus 421 or 486 (or 487 only as far as Ein Gedi). Service is approximately hourly. The crowded Bus 444 to Eilat (which does not drive into Masada) runs four times a day. Only one bus departs daily from Tel Aviv to the Dead Sea area—Bus 421, currently at 8:30 AM.

You can get to Rachel's Tomb (when politics permit) on the infrequent Bus 163 from Jerusalem's Central Bus Station, but you can also pick it up near downtown Jerusalem, on **Keren Hayesod Street** opposite the Dan Panorama Hotel, and at the **Jerusalem Train Station.** From the **East Jerusalem Bus Station,** on Sultan Suleiman Street near the Damascus Gate, an Arab company operates Bus 22 to Manger Square, in the heart of Bethlehem. There is no direct bus service from Tel Aviv to Bethlehem.

The sights west of Jerusalem are difficult to reach by public transportation. The only bus going to Bet Guvrin (Bus 011) leaves at 8 AM from the town of Kiryat Gat. There are frequent buses to Kiryat Gat: Bus 446 from Jerusalem and Bus 369 from Tel Aviv.

## By Car

Driving is much better than relying on public transportation here, as many of the sights in this chapter are on secondary roads, where bus services are infrequent or in some cases nonexistent. Roads range in condition from fair to excellent, and most destinations are clearly marked. Drive defensively—many Israeli drivers are frustrated fighter pilots. Gas stations are plentiful, and some are open 24 hours a day. Still, it's wise to play it safe and keep your tank at least half full at all times. Pay special attention to keeping the radiator topped in the hot Israeli summer. In times of political unrest check with local authorities to confirm safety of roads that pass through the West Bank.

Masada, the farthest of the Dead Sea sites in this chapter, is 100 km (62 mi) from Jerusalem, about 1½ hours' drive, on Routes 1 and 90 south; add one hour from Tel Aviv. Jericho, which is 40 km (25 mi) from Jerusalem, can be reached in 35 minutes via Routes 1 and 90 north. As you head southwest from Jerusalem, it takes 40 minutes to get to the Sorek Cave via Route 386 (about 24 km, or 15 mi) and another 30 minutes' driving time (about 30 km, or 19 mi) to Bet Guvrin via Route 38. Latrun, on Route 1, is 20 minutes from Jerusalem (25 km, or 16 mi); Bet Guvrin, via Bet Shemesh, is another 35 minutes on Routes 3, 44, and 38 (40 km, or 25 mi). From Tel Aviv (east on Route 1, south on Route 38), you can reach Bet Shemesh in about 40 minutes. Bethlehem is a mere 8 km (5 mi) from downtown Jerusalem, a 15-minute drive. Driving your own car in other areas of the West Bank is not recommended.

## By Guide-Driven Limousine/Minivan

This is by far the best way (if not the cheapest) to see the areas covered in this chapter. With a private licensed guide in a 4-, 7-, or 10-passenger, air-conditioned limousine/minivan, *you* determine the tour's character and pace (☞ Guided Tours *in* Contacts and Resources, *below*).

## By Sherut and Taxi

A *sherut* is a shared taxi (seating up to seven passengers) that runs along a set route. Usually it follows a major bus route and charges a comparable fare. From Jerusalem you can get an Arab sherut to West Bank towns such as Bethlehem and Jericho, which will give you some local flavor—and sometimes a hair-raising driving experience. An Arab taxi is likely to be delayed at military checkpoints, however. Depending on the destination, Egged buses (☞ By Bus, *above*) are a more comfortable and reliable alternative.

Using a regular **taxi** to tour is not cheap. Define your itinerary, get a quote from one of the main West Jerusalem taxi companies, and use that as a starting point for negotiating a better deal with an individual cabbie (outside your hotel, or the Arab cabbies at the Jaffa Gate). Hiring a taxi for seven hours to Ein Gedi, the Dead Sea, and Masada, for example, costs about NIS 800 ($200). Hiring a qualified tour guide with an air-conditioned vehicle for the same trip is a far better value for the money.

## Contacts and Resources

### Bird-Watching

For more information on birds in this area, contact the **Society for the Protection of Nature in Israel** (SPNI), which has a bird-watching center and a center for raptors, based in Tel Aviv (☎ 03/644–9622, FAX 03/644–9625).

### Car Rental

JERUSALEM

**Avis** (✉ 22 King David St., ☎ 02/624–9001). **Budget** (✉ 23 King David St., ☎ 02/624–8991). **Eldan** (✉ 24 King David St., ☎ 02/625–2151). **Europcar** (National; ✉ 8 King David St., ☎ 02/623–5467). **Hertz** (✉ 18 King David St., ☎ 02/623–1351; ✉ Hyatt Regency Hotel, 32 Lehi St., ☎ 02/581–5069 [open on Saturday]). **Sixt** (✉ 14 King David St., ☎ 02/624–8204; ✉ Hilton Hotel, 7 King David St., ☎ 02/624–8886).

TEL AVIV

**Avis** (✉ 113 Hayarkon St., ☎ 03/527–1752). **Budget** (✉ 99 Hayarkon St., ☎ 03/524–5233). **Eldan** (✉ 112 Hayarkon St., ☎ 03/527–1166). **Europcar** (National; ✉ 126 Hayarkon St., ☎ 03/524–8181). **Hertz** (✉ 144 Hayarkon St., ☎ 03/522–3332). **Sixt** (✉ 155 Hayarkon St., ☎ 03/524–9794; ✉ Hilton Hotel, 7 King David St., ☎ 02/624–8886).

### Emergencies

**Ambulance and medical emergencies—Magen David Adom** (☎ 101).

The major **hospitals** in Jerusalem are as follows: **Bikur Holim** (✉ Strauss St., ☎ 02/670–1111); **Hadassah** (✉ Ein Kerem, ☎ 02/677–7111, 02/677–7215 for emergency room, 02/677–7204 for children's emergency room); **Hadassah** (✉ Mt. Scopus, ☎ 02/584–4111); **Sha'arei Tzedek** (✉ Bayit Vegan, ☎ 02/655–5111, 02/655–5508 for emergency room).

**Police** (☎ 100).

### Guided Tours

"Regular" bus tours, as they're known locally (as opposed to charter tours), pick you up at your hotel and bring you back there at the end of the tour. Guided bus tours departing from Tel Aviv offer the same itineraries as those leaving Jerusalem. There are discounts for children. One of the main operators is **Egged Tlalim Tours** (✉ 8 Shlomzion Hamalka St., Jerusalem, ☎ 02/622–1999 or 02/622–2929; ✉ 59 Ben Yehuda St., Tel Aviv, ☎ 03/527–1212, 03/527–1213, 03/527–1214, or 03/527–1215). Another major operator is **United Tours** (✉ 9 Coresh St., Jerusalem, ☎ 02/625–2187 or 02/625–2188; ✉ 113 Hayarkon St., Tel Aviv, ☎ 03/522–2008 or 03/693–3412). Most hotels carry the tour companies' brochures and can book tours for you.

Both companies offer full-day tours of Masada, the Dead Sea, Ein Gedi, and sometimes Jericho. Tours cost $70 per person from Jerusalem (slightly more from Tel Aviv), not including lunch, and depart daily. The Church of the Nativity, in Bethlehem, and sometimes Rachel's Tomb can be seen as part of half-day or full-day Jerusalem tours (daily departures, $26 to $56 per person depending on itinerary).

Touring in a private **guide-driven limo/van** is comfortable and convenient (☞ Getting Around, *above*), and for four or more people, it's cost effective as well. Current recommended rates are $300–$320, $340–$365, and $385–$415 per day for 4-, 7- and 10- passenger vehicles respectively. Rates include all guiding and car expenses (up to 200 km/120 mi per day, averaged out over the days of the tour). There is a charge for the guide's expenses for overnights away from the home base.

Some guides have organized into cooperatives, but all are essentially freelancers. In Jerusalem, try **Eshcolot Tours** (✉ 36 Keren Hayesod St., ☎ 02/563–5555, FAX 02/563–2101). In Tel Aviv, call **Twelve Tribes** (✉ 29 Hamered St., ☎ 03/510–1911, FAX 03/510–1943). **Tar-Hemed** (✉ 59 Hayarkon St., ☎ 03/517–6101, FAX 03/510–0165) is another Tel Aviv–based option.

You can get advice and guiding service info from three of Fodor's infield writers, themselves qualified guides: **Mike Rogoff** (☎ FAX 02/679–0410, rogoff@netvision.net.il), **Judy Goldman** (☎ 02/624–5827, FAX 02/623–3834, judebob@netvision.net.il), and **Miriam Feinberg Vamosh** (☎ FAX 02/534–5071, mim@netvision.net.il).

Hotel concierges can usually recommend guides as well.

JEEP TOURS

**Israel Adventure Tours** (✉ 10 Ben Tabai St., Jerusalem, ☎ 02/679–9140) offers Jeep day tours to the Judean Desert. Each vehicle can take up to seven passengers and costs $350. A roughly five-hour moonlight tour costs $260.

SPECIAL-INTEREST TOURS

**Archaeological Seminars** (☎ 02/627–3515) in Jerusalem offers a Dig-for-a-Day program, a three-hour excavation at Bet Guvrin-Maresha National Park, outside of Jerusalem. The cost is $25, not counting the entrance fee to the park itself.

The **Society for the Protection of Nature in Israel** (✉ 13 Helene Hamalka St., Jerusalem, ☎ 02/624–4605, FAX 02/625–4953; ✉ 3 Hashefela St., Tel Aviv, ☎ 03/638–8677, FAX 03/688–3940), also known as SPNI, runs several off-the-beaten-track excursions, with an emphasis on nature and some hiking. Their English-speaking tours in this region include Masada, the Dead Sea, and the Ein Gedi Nature Reserve (including hiking); a trip into the Judean Desert in a go-anywhere vehicle (no hiking); a more energetic trip into Wadi Kelt, with its marvelous desert spring and St. George's Monastery; and a monthly moonlight hike into the same area, timed for a bright moon. An occasional tour to the area west of Jerusalem includes the Neot Kedumim Biblical Landscape Reserve, the Sorek Cave, and Bet Guvrin. Day tours range from $59 to $72; the two-day Masada–Ein Gedi combination costs $185 (including lodging and some meals); and longer, more complex packages are available.

## Visitor Information

There are **Tourist Information Offices** (TIOs) at the following locations: ✉ Manger Sq., Bethlehem, ☎ 02/277–0603, FAX 02/277–0604; ✉ Jaffa Gate, Jerusalem, ☎ 02/628–0382 or 02/628–0457; ✉ 2 Luntz St., Jerusalem, ☎ 02/625–8908; ✉ Shop No. 6018, 6th floor, New Central Bus Station, Tel Aviv, ☎ 03/639–5660.

# 3   TEL AVIV

Although it's not the official capital of Israel—a right reserved for age-old Jerusalem—Tel Aviv is the country's pulse, the center for Israel's economy, business, culture, and cuisine. Brash and unlovely at first glance, this teeming, cosmopolitan city on the Mediterranean has fine sandy beaches, excellent restaurants and nightlife, and a serious performing-arts scene. It's hard to believe that less than a century ago, these streets were nothing but sand dunes.

By Lisa Perlman

Updated by
Linda Yachbes
and
Karen Bressler

**P**ROUD RESIDENTS CALL IT the city that never stops, and if you don't believe them, just come around at 4 AM, when you may find yourself waiting in line for a table at a café or stuck in a traffic jam on Hayarkon Street. True, there are no buses at that hour, but that doesn't stop the young and the restless of surrounding towns from finding their way to the country's throbbing heart.

Next to the magical holy city of Jerusalem, Tel Aviv seems more like the city of sin. Your first reaction to it may be negative—to the newcomer it appears muggy, congested, ill planned, and scarred with boxy, concrete buildings. But what it lacks in grandeur, Tel Aviv makes up for in vitality. One-third of Israel's population—a number approaching 2 million—lives in this 138-square-km (55-square-mi) metropolis. Half a million cars enter and leave the city every day. Residents of other towns swell the population further on weekends, when they make Tel Aviv their playground. The city is Israel's center of commerce and culture, and it bustles with restaurants, art galleries, museums, and beaches.

Having risen from empty sand dunes less than a century ago, Tel Aviv could never hope for the ancient beauty of Jerusalem. Still, the city's southern border, the port of Jaffa, is as old as they come: Jonah set sail from here for what turned out to be his journey to the belly of a whale. The cedars of Lebanon that were used to build Solomon's Temple arrived in Jaffa before being transported to Jerusalem. According to archaeologists, Jaffa was founded in the Middle Canaanite period, around 1600 BC. For the next thousand years it was dominated by one ancient people after another: Egyptians, Philistines, Israelites, Phoenicians, and Greeks. After being taken by Crusaders twice, in the 11th and 12th centuries, Jaffa was recaptured by the Muslims and remained largely under Arab control until the 20th century. During much of this time it was abandoned; it did not regain its importance as a port until the 19th century.

In the second half of the 19th century, Jewish pioneers began immigrating here from other parts of the world, and their numbers strained the capacity of the small port. By the late 1880s, Jaffa was overcrowded, rife with disease, and stricken with poverty. A group of Jewish families moved to the empty sands north of Jaffa to found Neve Tzedek, the first specifically Jewish neighborhood. This was followed by Ahuzat Bayit (literally, "housing estate"), an area to the north of Neve Tzedek that became the precursor of Tel Aviv. The city was named Tel Aviv in 1909; Arab riots in Jaffa in the 1920s then drove more Jews to Ahuzat Bayit, spurring further growth. These Jews were joined by immigrants from Europe, mostly Poland, and a decade later by an influx of German Jews fleeing the Nazis. These new, urban arrivals—unlike the pioneers from earlier immigrant waves—brought with them an appreciation for the arts and a passion for the sidewalk cafés that began to sprout like mushrooms in this city. It was they who made the strongest social and cultural impact on Tel Aviv.

The fact that Tel Aviv began as separate neighborhoods helps to explain its eclectic (some would say discordant) appearance, its Mediterranean-style buildings jostling each other in the shadow of towering skyscrapers. In the 1930s and '40s, the city became known as the "white city," because it was the only one in the world dominated by the International Style of Le Corbusier and Mies van der Rohe—an aesthetic of functional forms, flat roofs, and whitewashed exteriors. By the 1950s, however, shoddy imitations of this style led to its decline, and many of its buildings fell into disrepair. Happily, recent efforts by preservationists are helping to reclaim these architectural treasures.

The Tel Aviv of today is already vastly different from the Tel Aviv of 50 years ago. Although northern Tel Aviv has traditionally been the city's flashy, affluent half, it's the oft-neglected south that gets attention now. Here, gentrification projects in many neighborhoods are changing the area's face; each week the scaffolding rises on another building, and new restaurants and shops appear. Tel Aviv has come a long way in its short life; look around and try to imagine the scene just 90 years ago, when this teeming metropolis was nothing but sand.

## Pleasures and Pastimes

### Beaches

Tel Aviv's western border, an idyllic stretch of Mediterranean sand, has miles of beaches and a beachfront promenade. Sunsets here are spectacular. Still, the Med can be moody; the lapping of gentle waves offers respite and relaxation for most of the year, but it's not always as uplifting as you might expect. Because the Med is a closed sea, its water turns warm and decidedly unrefreshing in the dead of summer. If the jellyfish are out in force—as they are in July and August—you may find that an air-conditioned café with a view of the sea is a more pleasurable place to be.

### Cultural Activities

As Israel's undisputed cultural capital, Tel Aviv puts on a pretty good show, even at the street level. There's a stimulating range of museums; dance and music of all kinds are popular; opera is budding; and theater (almost all in Hebrew) is prolific. As for pop culture—well, it's all around you.

### Dining

Tel Aviv's culinary scene has improved radically in the last few years, so that the city's cosmopolitan character is now happily represented in its food. That's not to say that you can't still enjoy the Middle Eastern fast foods for which this part of the world is famous—falafel and *shwarma* (spit-grilled meat) stands still occupy countless street corners. But beyond these are restaurants serving everything from American burgers to Chinese dim sum. In contrast to Jerusalem, Tel Aviv makes you really search to find a kosher restaurant outside the hotels (where all restaurants are required to be kosher).

Tel Aviv is also very much a café society. The murmur of varied languages and the range of exotic coffees at the scores of cafés across town will convince you as nothing else will that you are in a world-class cosmopolitan city.

Tel Aviv's restaurants are concentrated in several areas: Sheinkin and Rothschild streets, Basel, Ibn Gvirol Street, and Little Tel Aviv, near the old port. In addition, there are numerous establishments along the seafront south of Little Tel Aviv—all the way to Jaffa, at the city's southern end—and in the inner city. In Herzliya Pituach, a suburb north of Tel Aviv, most restaurants are housed in one complex, about a 10-minute walk from the Herzliya hotels.

### Lodging

Nothing stands between Tel Aviv's luxury hotels and the Mediterranean Sea except the golden beach and the Tayelet (promenade), outfitted with chairs and gazebos. Even the small hotels are only a short walk from the water. Tel Aviv's hotel row is on Hayarkon Street, which becomes Herbert Samuel Esplanade as you proceed south between Little Tel Aviv (the old port area) and Jaffa. This means that no matter where you stay, you're never far from the main thoroughfares of Ben Yehuda and Dizengoff streets, with their shops and outdoor cafés, or the city's major concert hall, museums, art galleries, and open-air Carmel Market.

Note that in the winter (mid-November to March), Tel Aviv hotels close their outdoor pools, and the lifeguards at the public beaches take a break as well. And aside from the Hilton, most hotels don't have room for tennis courts. Hotel health clubs are open to anyone over age 18 but often charge an entrance fee.

Because of low occupancy rates at press time, a few Tel Aviv hotels had closed temporarily. Please call ahead to assure that a hotel is open.

## Water Sports

Tel Aviv has no shortage of water-sports opportunities, even some that may come as a surprise. In addition to enjoying the more obvious swimming, sailing, and windsurfing, you can rent pleasure boats on the Hayarkon River, and also water-ski—not in the sea but on a cable in a man-made lake.

# EXPLORING TEL AVIV

Tel Aviv is an eclectic collection of neighborhoods—from gentrified Florentine in the south to Ramat Aviv in the north—bordered on the west by the Mediterranean Sea. The beachfront Tayelet (promenade) runs from north Tel Aviv to Jaffa, some 4 km (2½ mi) to the south, and provides a great walk, especially at sunset. The city's main north–south thoroughfares of Hayarkon, Ben Yehuda (which becomes Allenby), Dizengoff, and Ibn Gvirol streets run more or less parallel to the shore. The hotels are almost all concentrated on the seafront, along Hayarkon Street, which is also bursting with cafés, restaurants, and pubs. Allenby Street, one of the oldest in the city, crosses Hayarkon and Ben Yehuda streets and becomes the latter at its southern terminus. The change in affluence is as immediate as the change in street name: you'll see shabbier buildings and more budget-oriented shops along Allenby. You might say that the "border" between south and north is Carmel Market, a real junction of East-meets-West and old-meets-new. In the north, the business center dwindles north of Arlosoroff Street, which runs east–west near Kikar Hamedina (Hamedina Square). The residential area continues north and takes in the Yarkon River, once the city's northern boundary and now a popular recreational spot. South of Mercaz Ha'ir (city center) is Jaffa, once a separate city but now part of the municipality of Tel Aviv. An ancient port, Jaffa contains an impressively restored section known as Old Jaffa.

Technically, there are boundaries between Tel Aviv and the numerous towns and cities that surround it, but the urban sprawl is so great that residents of these surrounding municipalities will often tell you they live in Tel Aviv.

*Numbers in the text correspond to numbers in the margin and on the Exploring Tel Aviv map.*

## Great Itineraries

Spending three or four days in Tel Aviv is ideal. You'll have time to explore a variety of neighborhoods and museums and still have time left over to cool off on the beach. A shorter stay will require a lot of action, though you'll still be able to catch the highlights.

Begin in Old Jaffa, wandering around the restored section and delving into the small galleries and shops. Enjoy a meal of fresh fish on the waterfront at the port, and walk along the coastal Tayelet (promenade) back to central Tel Aviv. Head for the Sheinkin Street area (Israel's wanna-be Greenwich Village) to get a feel for the contemporary Israeli lifestyle. This area is a meeting point between the city's trendiest trendy and a local ultra-Orthodox (Hasidic) Jewish community. Nearby Rothschild Boulevard has good examples of the city's various architectural styles and periods, from Middle East–influenced to Bauhaus to latter-day steel and glass, and some of the city's best restaurants and cafés.

On the second day, take in a museum on a subject that interests you: the Tel Aviv Museum of Art; the Eretz Israel Museum, with its excellent archaeological exhibits; or Beth Hatefutsoth (Diaspora Museum), which depicts Jewish life around the world throughout the ages. You may want to squeeze in some shopping after that, then spend a few hours doing what Tel Avivians do best—*beten-gav* (tummy-back, in Hebrew)—cooling off on the beach.

If your first day is a Tuesday or a Friday, head straight for the Nahalat Binyamin street fair and the Carmel produce market. From there, it's a hop, skip, and a jump to Sheinkin Street for a coffee break. Spend the afternoon at the Tel Aviv marina, either on the port or on the Mediterranean (rent a small boat with or without a captain). The next day, walk through Old Jaffa and Neve Tzedek, where you'll get an excellent idea of Tel Aviv's origins. Rest up in the late afternoon and go out for a late dinner on Ha'arba'a Street, which is lined with bars and eateries. Begin the third day on the beach, and then hit a museum (☞ If You Have 2 Days, *above*). Spend the evening in Jaffa; the atmosphere is very different at night. Leave the last day for wandering around the city center—browsing and shopping. Stroll the Tayelet again before you leave.

# From the Market to the Theater

It's only 2 km (1 mi) from the *shuk* (marketplace) to the national theater, yet this walk traverses a good part of the city's nine-decade history, its ethnic mix, and its various social strata.

## A Good Walk

Begin at **Bialik Street** ① (off Allenby Street), one of the city's quaintest corners, with well-preserved architecture characteristic of Tel Aviv's early years. The change from bustling, polluted Allenby to Bialik is striking: quiet descends upon you in an instant. Walk to the end of the street and you'll find a mosaic and a fountain (which rarely flows). Strolling from the fountain back toward Allenby Street, stop in at Number 22, **Bet Bialik** ②, the home of the "father of Hebrew poetry." Three doors down, at Number 14, is **Bet Rubin** ③, an art gallery that houses painter Reuven Rubin's works as well as changing exhibits.

Return to Allenby Street, cross at the traffic light, and head south (left). In less than a minute you'll be at the entrance to the **Carmel Market** ④; soak up the lively atmosphere and perhaps purchase some dry goods or samples of Israel's fresh produce. On Tuesday and Friday, Tel Aviv's artisans create a street fair along **Nahalat Binyamin** ⑤, east of the market.

Nahalat Binyamin forms a V with the marketplace at Allenby Street, at **Kikar Magen David** ⑥. Cross Allenby at this intersection by taking the underpass (otherwise you risk life and limb), and you'll end up on

the corner of Sheinkin and Allenby streets. Cross narrow Sheinkin Street to King George Street and make your way downhill. Halfway down King George Street, on the right, the alley called **Simtat Plonit** ⑦ is identifiable by the two obelisk-style plaster structures at its entrance; pop in here to see some of the city's older architecture.

**Gan Meir** ⑧, a park that's a bit farther along on the other side of King George, is a nice place to rest your feet. Walk north from the park and turn right onto Ben Zion Boulevard. It's a few minutes' walk up a slight incline to the culturally rich **Kikar Habimah** ⑨, a square containing the **Habimah National Theater**; the **Helena Rubinstein Pavilion,** an annex of the Tel Aviv Museum (TAM); and the **Mann Auditorium.** A 1-km (½-mi) detour northeast to Shaul Hamelech Boulevard would bring you to another cultural highlight, the **Tel Aviv Museum of Art.**

Ben Zion Boulevard swings right (south) at Kikar Habimah to become **Rothschild Boulevard.** It's a 15-minute walk south to the **Independence Hall Museum** ⑩; you'll see it on your left after you cross Allenby. Israel's statehood was announced here in 1948. Nearby, in the middle of the boulevard, stands the stark, square **Founders' Monument and Fountain** ⑪.

TIMING

This walk can take the better part of the day, if you include time spent at the Nahalat Binyamin street fair and stops for coffee and a light meal along the way. Allow about three hours for a straight stroll.

## Sights to See

★ ❷ **Bet Bialik.** Bialik House is the charmingly restored home and library of Chaim Nachman Bialik (1873–1934), the national poet who is considered the father of Hebrew poetry. Bialik was already a respected poet and publisher by the time he moved to Tel Aviv from Russia in 1924; in the remaining 10 years of his life, his house became the intellectual center of Tel Aviv, and Bialik himself became the city's inspiration. His two-story, cream-color house, with its pointed arches and turrets, is a harmonious blend of Mediterranean and European styles. Built in 1927, it was almost palatial by the harsh standards of the time: mosaic-tile floors; Islamic-style arches and pillars; a small tower for meditating; sturdy, dark wood; and European-style furniture, including shelves for some 3,000 books. All labels are in Hebrew (an explanatory pamphlet is available in English), but the house is still a highly recommended stop. ⊠ *22 Bialik St.,* ☎ *03/525–4530.* ☜ *NIS 6 ($1.50).* ☉ *Sun.–Thurs. 9–5, Sat. 11–2.*

❸ **Bet Rubin.** Recognized as one of Israel's major painters, Reuven Rubin (1893–1974) bequeathed his house to Tel Aviv along with 45 of his works, which make up the permanent collection here. Unlike the still-furnished Bet Bialik (☞ *above*), this house functions solely as an art gallery, with changing exhibits by Israeli artists in addition to the great Rubin's work. Upstairs, there is a small but well-stocked art library where you can pore over press clippings and browse through art books. Note that on most days the museum has limited hours. ⊠ *14 Bialik St.,* ☎ *03/525–5961.* ☜ *NIS 15 ($3.75).* ☉ *Sun., Mon., Wed., Thurs. 10–2; Tues. 10–1 and 4–8; Sat. 11–2.*

❶ **Bialik Street.** This area has been more successful than many other Tel Aviv neighborhoods in maintaining its charming older buildings. Bialik has long been a popular address with many of the city's artists and literati, so it's not surprising that some of the houses have been converted into small museums. One end of the street has a fountain and a **mosaic,** designed by painter-cum-writer Nahum Gutmann, which depicts the history of the city from the ancient days of Jaffa to the rise of Tel Aviv. Gutmann was among the elite group of Tel Aviv's first artists. His writer father, Simcha Ben Zion, had a special place in the city's beginnings, too, and a boulevard, Ben Zion, is named for him.

★ ❹ **Carmel Market.** Consisting of one long street and numerous short streets branching off it in both directions, the Carmel Market (commonly referred to as the *shuk*) is invariably crowded on weekdays from about 9 through the afternoon, especially on Friday, as people rush to finish the shopping before Shabbat and the weekend. Take a deep breath before you dive in.

The first section is devoted mainly to dry goods and assorted items. If you're looking for, say, a pair of slippers or a can opener, you'll find it here. A little farther down is the fruit and vegetable section, where everyone yells. Here, Israel's famous oranges, avocados, and mangoes are as fresh as they get, and if you think the vendor is insulting you for not taking a large enough quantity, he probably is—but it's all part of the show. With prices fixed, the days of market-style bargaining are over, but all the atmosphere and vigor of the past are retained.

If you feel like trying something new, stop at one of the stalls that sell dried fruit and ask for *ledder* (a variation on the English *leather*). It's a Moroccan version of the dried apricot, beaten to a pulp and rolled out into a superthin, square sheet that resembles . . . leather.

NEED A BREAK? | The Carmel Market borders the **Yemenite Quarter,** which hides a score of delicious and cheap little eateries (closed Friday night and Saturday) offering shwarma and barbecued skewered meats, all kosher. Dig into any that catch your fancy, and wash them down with a cold beer.

⓫ **Founders' Monument and Fountain.** Dedicated in 1949, the Founders' Monument names those who founded Tel Aviv. This large slab of stone also encapsulates the city's past in three bas-relief panels representing the earliest pioneer days of planting and building as well as modern structures and houses. ⊠ *Rothschild Blvd. on the island at Nahalat Binyamin St.*

❽ **Gan Meir.** In this park you can rest on one of the benches and take in a free performance by city birds. It's something of a green haven in muggy Tel Aviv, and although also favored by local derelicts, it is perfectly safe.

You are now close to the Dizengoff Center, Israel's first shopping mall (☞ Shopping, *below*). Before the center opened in the early 1980s, this area was known as the **Nordiya Quarter,** a neighborhood set up in the 1920s by Jewish refugees seeking a home in the wake of Arab attacks in Jaffa. If you proceed north from Meir Park, you'll reach Bograshov Street, named for the man who founded the Nordiya Quarter and served as one of the headmasters of Tel Aviv's first school.

**Habimah National Theater.** The origins of Israel's national theater are rooted in the Russian Revolution, when a group of young Jewish actors and artists in Russia established a theater company that performed in Hebrew—this at a time when Hebrew was barely a living language. Subsequent tours through Europe and the United States in the 1920s won wide acclaim. In the late 1920s and '30s, many of the group's members moved to Israel and helped to establish the theater here. The cornerstone was laid in 1935; the current large, rounded glass-front building dates from 1970. ⊠ *Kikar Habimah,* ☎ *03/526–6666.*

NEED A
BREAK? Stop in for some stargazing at **Cafe Habimah** (⌧ 2 Tarsat St., ☎ 03/
620–4113), near the wide, round window in the Habimah National
Theater complex. If you attend a play at the Habimah, you might see
some of the actors here afterward. In any case, this café is something of
a theater in itself, with many of the Who's Who of Tel Aviv vying for the
spotlight.

**Helena Rubinstein Pavilion.** This annex of the Tel Aviv Museum of Art
(☞ *below*) houses changing contemporary-art exhibitions. ⌧ *6 Tarsat
St.,* ☎ *03/528–7196.* ▣ *Combination ticket with Tel Aviv Museum
of Art NIS 30 ($7.50).* ☾ *Sat.–Mon. and Wed. 10–4, Tues. and Thurs.
10–10.*

🔟 **Independence Hall Museum.** This impressive structure was originally
the home of longtime mayor Meir Dizengoff; he donated it to the city
in 1930 for use as the first Tel Aviv Museum. More significantly, the
settlement's leaders assembled here in May 14, 1948, to announce to
the world the establishment of the State of Israel. Today the museum's
**Hall of Declaration** stands as it did on that dramatic day, with the original microphones on the huge table where the dignitaries sat. Behind
the table is a portrait of the Zionist leader Herzl. ⌧ *16 Rothschild Blvd.,*
☎ *03/517–3942.* ▣ *NIS 12 ($3).* ☾ *Sun.–Thurs. 9–2:30, Fri. 9–1.*

9️⃣ **Kikar Habimah.** Habimah Square is a center of culture in Tel Aviv—
home of the **Habimah National Theater** (☞ *above*), the **Mann Auditorium** (☞ *below*), and the **Helena Rubinstein Pavilion** (☞ *above*), an
annex of the Tel Aviv Museum. Nestled between the theater and the
museum is a charming little junglelike garden, **Gan Ya'akov,** whose centerpiece is a sycamore that's been here almost longer than the city itself. Legend has it that camels were brought here to relax in the shade
of the sycamore and drink from the nearby well.

6️⃣ **Kikar Magen David.** This meeting point of six streets is named for the
six-point Magen David, or Star of David. The intersection gives you
an all-too-close look at the Israelis' hair-raising driving style; if you need
to cross the street here, use the underpass.

OFF THE
BEATEN PATH **SHEINKIN STREET –** This street off Kikar Magen David recalls New York's
Greenwich Village, with its artists and would-be artists, trendoids and
wanna-bes, and endless cafés. Shopping here is fun, too, if you're not
looking for anything in particular. Half the street is closed to vehicular
traffic on Friday afternoons, allowing for street performances in good
weather (though it's hard to see much through the crowds).

**Mann Auditorium.** One of the several cultural centers on Kikar Habimah
(☞ *above*), Mann Auditorium is Israel's premier concert hall and the
home of the Israel Philharmonic Orchestra, led by maestro Zubin
Mehta. The low-slung gray building, among the most distinguished and
sophisticated cultural buildings in the country, has excellent acoustics
and a seating capacity of 3,000. It also hosts pop and rock concerts
(☞ Nightlife and the Arts, *below*).

★ 5️⃣ **Nahalat Binyamin.** The selection at this street market, open Tuesday
and Friday, is broad—ranging from tacky plastic trinkets to sophisticated crafts such as hand-carved wooden boxes and attractive glassware—
but the real drawing card is the handmade silver jewelry. Nahalat
Binyamin is further enlivened with a profusion of street performers and
buskers. For a finishing touch of local color, cafés serving cakes and light
meals line the street. At the end of the fair is a large Bedouin tent where
you can treat yourself to a *laffa* with *lebane* and *za'atar* (large pita bread
with tangy sour cream, sprinkled with hyssop, a mintlike herb).

# MODERN ISRAELI LITERATURE AND THE ARTS

**T**HE PEOPLE OF THE BOOK has lived up to its name. Israel has one of the highest per capita book consumption rates in the world. Moreover, recent years have seen something of a surge in the quality of Israeli literature, as a number of exciting writers (David Grossman, Meir Shalev, Orly Castel-Bloom) have come to the fore.

The revival of Hebrew as a modern spoken language paralleled the development of Zionism. The early proponents of modern Hebrew, led by national poet Haim Nahman Bialik and S.Y. Agnon (to date Israel's only winner of the Nobel Prize for Literature), breathed modernity, power, and richness into the ancient tongue. No longer shackled solely to religious contexts, early modern Hebrew writing depicted the pioneering era, the struggle for independence, state building, mass immigrations, the quest for peace, and a host of other contemporary issues.

A number of Israeli writers have taken their place in the international arena, including A.B. Yehoshua, Amos Oz, S. Yizhar, Shulamit Hareven, Ruth Almog, and Batya Gur. English translations of their works are widely available. Today's Israeli writers have broken away from the previous generation's predominant themes of pioneering, heroism, and spiritualism; they embrace a new individuality and explore more cosmopolitan subjects in their work.

For a tiny nation, Israel has a thriving and abundant arts scene. The country is home to thousands of classical musicians. The mass immigration from the former Soviet states has, in fact, created something of a glut of musical talent. The Israel Philharmonic Orchestra has a world-class reputation, and Israeli soloists such as Pinhas Zuckerman, Shlomo Mintz, Daniel Barenboim, and Yitzhak Perlman regularly share the stage with the IPO.

A number of music festivals are held annually (☞ Festivals and Seasonal Events in Smart Travel Tips A to Z), many of them drawing international crowds—from the Red Sea Jazz Festival, in the south, to the Voice of Music chamber music event and Jacob's Ladder folk festival, in the north.

Israeli theater, too, enjoys a significant following. There are six professional repertory theaters and dozens of regional and amateur companies performing throughout the country. They perform almost exclusively in Hebrew. Habimah is the national theater; it began in 1917 Moscow, under the guidance of the Russian director Stanislavsky, before establishing its permanent home in Tel Aviv in 1931. The Cameri Theater in Tel Aviv was the first company to stage realistic portrayals of Israeli life. Israel's leading playwrights include Yehoshua Sobel, Hillel Mittelpunkt, Ephraim Kishon, and the late Hanoch Levine.

Professional dance companies also abound in Israel today. The Suzanne Dellal Center for Dance and Theater in the Neve Tzedek quarter of Tel Aviv is the primary venue for dance events.

Folk dancing has always been unusually popular in Israel, where it is, in fact, an evolving art form. As well as "Israeli" folk dancing (really a blend of Jewish and non-Jewish folk dance forms from around the world), some of Israel's different ethnic groups have preserved their traditional dances: a number of troupes specialize in the dances of Yemen, Kurdistan, India, Georgia, and Ethiopia, and there are also Arab, Druze, and Circassian dance ensembles.

Enthusiasm for the visual arts can be seen in all walks of Israeli life, with artists and craftspeople widely represented in the country's many museums and private galleries. A good viewing of the breadth of Israeli art can be made at both the Israel Museum (in Jerusalem), the Tel Aviv Museum, and, for modern Israeli art, the Ramat Gan Art Museum.

**Rothschild Boulevard.** Half a century ago, this was the most exclusive street in the city, and its real estate still commands astronomical prices. Many of the 1940s buildings have been allowed to deteriorate; others have been restored. Still others are examples of the International Style, a look that's charming on this tree-lined street but poorly imitated elsewhere in the city.

**➐ Simtat Plonit.** It's worth a wander down this alley to see old Tel Aviv decorative (now derelict) architecture at its best. Note the stucco lion in front of **Number 7,** which used to have glowing eyes fitted with lightbulbs. The tract of land that incorporates Simtat Plonit was bought in the 1920s by an outspoken builder from Detroit named Meir Getzel Shapira. (He established what is still known as the Shapira Quarter, just south of the Central Bus Station and now one of the city's seedier neighborhoods.) After buying the land, Shapira insisted that this pint-size street be named after him, and the story goes that he fought furiously with Tel Aviv's first mayor, Meir Dizengoff, to get his way. (Dizengoff had already planned to name another street Shapira, after a different Shapira.) The mayor emerged victorious and named the alley Plonit, meaning "What's-His-Name."

**Tel Aviv Museum of Art.** The TAM houses a fine collection of Israeli and international art, including works by Israeli artist Reuven Rubin and a Roy Lichtenstein mural commissioned for the museum in 1989. There's also an impressive French Impressionist collection and an extensive collection of sculptures by Aleksandr Archipenko. ✉ *27 Shaul Hamelech Blvd.,* ☎ *03/696–1297.* ✆ *NIS 30 ($7.50), includes entry to Helena Rubinstein Pavilion (☞ above).* ☉ *Mon., Wed., and Sat. 10–4; Tues., Thurs. 10–10; Fri. 10–2.*

# Jaffa

The origin of Jaffa's name is unclear: some say it derives from the Hebrew *yafeh* (beautiful); others claim the town was named after its founder, Japhet, son of Noah. Nor is it known exactly when Jaffa was established. What is certain is its status as one of the oldest ports in the world—perhaps the oldest. Excavations have turned up artifacts up to 4,000 years old. The Bible mentions Jaffa in connection with a number of significant events: the cedars used in the construction of the Temple passed through Jaffa on their way to Jerusalem; the prophet Jonah set off from Jaffa before being swallowed by the whale; and St. Peter raised Tabitha from the dead here. In the ancient world, Jaffa was an important stop on the Via Maris, the trade route that extended from Egypt to Mesopotamia.

Jaffa's history has been one of fits and starts. The city has been razed and rebuilt scores of times as various powers fought to control it. Napoléon was but one of a succession of invaders who brought the city walls down; these walls were rebuilt for the last time in the early 19th century by the Turks and torn down yet again as recently as 1888.

By that time, Jaffa was a thriving cosmopolitan center, host to international businesspeople, bankers, and diplomats. Christian and Jewish pilgrims on their way to Jerusalem were a familiar sight. Jewish immigrants lived peacefully with Arabs here until the riots of 1921, when discord sent most of Jaffa's Jews fleeing to the sandy north that would become Tel Aviv. Now part of the municipality of Tel Aviv, Jaffa has a Jewish majority (most hailing from North Africa and from other Middle Eastern countries) and is also home to many Arab Christians and Muslims.

The restored section, Old Jaffa, is only a small part of this fascinating port; it caters primarily to tourists and fishermen. Beyond the restored section, a visit to Jaffa can take in the city's shabbier side, where trading, bargaining, and arguing are as much a part of life as ever.

## A Good Walk

To get to Jaffa, you can take Bus 8, 10, 25, 46, or 90 from downtown Tel Aviv. If you're driving, you can park for free during the day on weekdays and Sunday; there's a charge on weekday evenings and Saturday.

A good starting point is the northwestern corner of Jaffa's main square—known familiarly as the "clock square"—in front of the **police station** on Yefet Street. On the empty patch of land across the road, you can see the remains of what used to be Jaffa's northern wall. This patch was the *saraya* (administrative center) of the Turkish government in the early 20th century and was one of the corners of what was later called Government Square (its official, though rarely used, name is Jewish Agency Square). The square was eventually destroyed by a Jewish underground group seeking to root out Arab terrorist gangs.

Head south on Yefet for about 100 ft, passing the **clock tower** ⑫, on an island in the middle of the street—a popular meeting place for anyone with any kind of rendezvous in Jaffa. On the southwestern corner of the square is the beautifully preserved **El-Mahmoudiye Mosque** ⑬.

Turn onto Beit Eshel Street, opposite the mosque, and wander through what was a bustling business district some 300 years ago: the old Jerusalem Road, with handy access to the harbor. Number 11, which you'll recognize by the numerous arches forming its facade, was the local *khan,* the rough equivalent of a motel, built in the early 18th century by an Armenian family named Manouli. The ground floor was used as stables, with rooms upstairs for travelers. Today the building houses a furniture store. Any of the small streets leading south from Beit Eshel Street will take you into the **shuk hapishpeshim** ⑭, a flea market where you can find anything from silver earrings and Indian-style clothes to a kilo of shrimp. The ambience seems a world away from modern Tel Aviv.

Return to Yefet Street, south of the clock tower. Cross the street and enter the passage between Numbers 10 and 12: this used to be the local fish market. The aroma lingers—there are still a few excellent fish stores and restaurants in the vicinity—but these days you'll find more shoe stores than seafood here.

You are now very close to the ancient port. Walk south (you'll be going uphill) on Mifratz Shlomo Street until you come to a square on the left. Note the fountain here: when it was built by Turkish governor Mohammed Abu Najat Aja in the early 19th century, the fountain had six pillars and an arched roof, providing shade as well as water. The archway just beyond formed the entrance to the *hamam,* or old Turkish baths. Today archaeologists are digging beneath the floor of what is now an events hall here in search of ancient artifacts. Their finds—most of which were parts of Jaffa's ancient fortifications dating from the town's beginnings around 2000–1500 BC—have been preserved beneath the building's center stage as well as in the **Jaffa Museum** ⑮, also on Mifratz Shlomo Street.

Before you continue up the hill to the main square of Old Jaffa, cast your gaze north to see the dramatic contrast between the ancient and the modern, linked by the soft waves of the Mediterranean. As you make your way toward **Kikar Kedumim**, Old Jaffa's central plaza, you'll see the beautiful ocher-and-russet **St. Peter's Monastery** ⑯, on the right.

Before leaving the square, go through the restaurant Yamit (it's on an outdoor terrace, with a narrow walkway beside the tables), on the western side, for the best view of an unassuming but legendary piece of rock that rises from the sea here and is known as **Andromeda's Rock** ⑰. Now climb the hill from Kikar Kedumim, passing wide, shady yucca and fig trees, and cross the wooden bridge to a park called **Gan Hapisga** ⑱—literally "Summit Garden."

Return to Kikar Kedumim and follow one of the stepped alleyways leading down to the **Jaffa Port** ⑲, which makes for pleasant exploring. If you have the energy to continue walking, some very interesting sights and sounds remain. You can either follow the coast north for about five minutes to return to the clock tower or take the official port exit, walk a few steps up the hill, and turn left onto Louis Pasteur Street. About 300 ft ahead, you'll notice a bronze sculpture of a roly-poly little whale by sculptor and jewelry maker Ilana Goor, a resident of Old Jaffa. (Goor's house, 4 Mazal Dagim Street, is open as a museum. It's worth a stop inside to get a feel for modern Israeli artistry.) The whale keeps watch over a small parking area, beyond which stands a remnant of the city's ancient wall.

Continue on Louis Pasteur Street and return to **Yefet Street,** a few strides ahead, which links Jaffa sights both old and new. The **St. Louis French Hospital** ⑳ can be found at the T-junction where these two streets meet. A little farther south, on the left at Number 51, is the **San Antonio Roman Catholic Church** ㉑.

A few steps farther south, turn right into Sha'arei Nicanor Street and wander down to the charming little **Hadolphin Street** ㉒. The sightseeing walk ends here. To the south is the **Ajami Quarter** of Jaffa, one of many neighborhoods around the country benefiting from a rejuvenation program known as Project Renewal, financed by Jewish communities around the world.

TIMING

Allow about three hours for a daytime walk around Jaffa. Jaffa Port and restored Old Jaffa are good for a stroll at any time; consider coming at night for a romantic dinner.

## Sights to See

⑰ **Andromeda's Rock.** To look at this rock from Kikar Kedumim (☞ *below*) is to see the stuff of Greek myth and legend: Nireus, father of mermaids, was incensed that Andromeda, daughter of King Copeus of Ethiopia and his queen, Xaiopa, was more beautiful than the mermaids. He implored Poseidon, the god of the sea, to intervene. Poseidon obligingly set the sea astorm and sent a monster to eat whatever approached. In an attempt to restore calm, the people tied Andromeda to this rock. Only Perseus, riding the winged horse Pegasus, dared to save her. Soaring down from the sky, he beheaded the monster, rescued the lovely Andromeda, and promptly married her.

⑫ **Clock tower.** The tower is the focus of Jaffa's central square and stands at the center of town, with restored Old Jaffa to the west and the flea market to the east. The clock tower was completed in 1906, in time to mark the 30th anniversary of the reign of Sultan Abdul Hamid II; similar clock towers were built for the same occasion in Akko and in Jerusalem. The four clock faces stood still for many years until 1965, when the city renovated the tower and set them in motion again; the renovation also added stained-glass windows depicting events in Jaffa's history. ⊠ *Yefet St.*

---

NEED A
BREAK? There's always a line outside **Abulafia Bakery** (⊠ 7 Yefet St.), south of the clock tower. The Middle East's answer to pizza goes like hot cakes here—literally. For a simple snack with an exquisite flavor, order a pita topped with the herb *za'atar* (hyssop), or stuffed with salty cheese, calzone-style. Abulafia is a good place to try *sachlab*, a warm drink sprinkled with coconut and cinnamon.

---

**⓭ El-Mahmoudiye Mosque.** Built in 1809, the mosque was renovated for the first time in 1812 by Turkish governor Mohammed Abu Najat Aja. The governor rebuilt much of the city during his rule (1807–22), including the city walls that Napoléon's army had torn down in 1799.

The mosque managed to escape the fate of other sites in Jaffa that were destroyed during the War of Independence. In the late 19th century a separate entrance was built into the east wall to save the governor and other dignitaries the bother of having to push through the market-square crowds at the main entrance, on the south wall. With a minaret and two colorful domes, this is one of the local Muslim community's most important mosques and is not usually open to the general public.

The original mosque had a huge, splendid **drinking fountain** built into its southern wall, where travelers refreshed themselves after long journeys. In recent times, however, the Suleiman Fountain has lost its glory, and it sits sadly between two soft-drink stores that offer today's wanderers a less romantic means of quenching their thirst. ⊠ *Yefet St.*

**⓲ Gan Hapisga.** You might have to vie for space in the Summit Garden with a long line of newlyweds, who come here to be photographed in their wedding garb at sunset. Seven archaeological layers have been unearthed in a section of the park called Ramses II Garden. The oldest sections of wall (20 ft thick) have been identified as part of a 17th-century BC Hyksos city. Other remains include part of a 13th-century BC city gate inscribed with the name of Ramses II; a Canaanite city; a Jewish city from the time of Ezra and Nehemiah; Hasmonean ruins from the 2nd century BC; and traces of Roman occupation. At the summit, disturbing the ancient aura, is a kitschy stone sculpture—the Statue of Faith—from the 1970s, in the shape of a gateway.

**⓴ Hadolphin St.** This enclave is a hive of activity, with an art gallery, a French restaurant, a Greek Orthodox church dating from 1924, one of the best hummus joints in the city (open only in the morning), and a ceramics store run by local potter Eytan, all within a stone's throw of one another.

**⓯ Jaffa Museum.** This building has a lengthy history. It was first built during the Crusades; in the 18th century, the Turks added to what was left of the original building and used it as their Government House until 1897. In the first half of the 20th century it was a soap factory, and since 1961 the upper level has been operating as the Jaffa Museum, displaying many of the finds unearthed during archaeological digs here and in other parts of Tel Aviv. ⊠ *10 Mifratz Shlomo St.,* ☎ *03/ 682–5375.* 🎫 *NIS 10 ($2.50).* ☉ *Sun.–Thurs. 9–1.*

★ **⓳ Jaffa Port.** A great many fishing boats are stuffed into this small marina, as well as a handful of houseboats. Along the waterfront are a plethora of restaurants, all expensive but most pretty good.

**Kikar Kedumim.** This is Old Jaffa's central plaza. Old Jaffa used to be Tel Aviv's red-light district, plagued with crime of all kinds and raw sewage in the streets. Today, however, thanks to efforts begun by the Tel Aviv municipality in the late 1950s, the square is chockablock with excavation sites, restaurants, expensive gift and souvenir shops, and galleries. The artists who live here complain that there's too much noise on summer nights; some visitors say it's too touristy. But Old Jaffa is indisputably charming and should not be missed. The labyrinthine network of tiny alleys snakes in all directions from Kikar Kedumim down to the modern port. The focus of Kikar Kedumim is an archaeological site that exposes 3rd-century BC catacombs; the site has been converted into an underground visitor center with large, vivid, illustrated descriptions of Jaffa's history. Admission is free.

**Police station.** On the whole it's an uninteresting structure, but the station has an Ottoman-designed arch above its entrance. The design over the door is the seal of Turkish sultan Abdul Hamid II. During the British Mandate, the British used the building to intern both Arabs and members of the Zionist group Irgun. ✉ *Yefet St.*

**㉚ St. Louis French Hospital.** This building was named for Louis IX, leader of the Seventh Crusade, who landed in Jaffa in 1251. Established by Roman Catholic nuns in the late 19th century, it was Jaffa's first modern hospital. Its neo-Renaissance style, popular in Europe at the time, includes high ceilings and tall arched windows. The building also had strategic importance, occupying the southwestern corner and highest point of Jaffa's encircling wall. It's now a community health center. ✉ *Yefet St.*

**⑯ St. Peter's Monastery.** Established by Franciscans in the 1890s, St. Peter's was built over the ruins of a citadel that dates from the Seventh Crusade, which was led by King Louis IX of France. It remained Jaffa's principal Roman Catholic church until the church of San Antonio was built in 1932. A monument to King Louis stands today at the entrance to the friary. Napoléon is rumored to have stayed here during his Jaffa campaign of 1799. To enter, ring the bell by pulling the string on the right side of the door; you will probably be greeted by one of the custodians, most of whom speak Spanish and some English. ☎ *03/682–2871; call ahead if you want to visit.*

**㉑ San Antonio Roman Catholic Church.** Although it looks quite new, with its clean white-stone bricks, this church actually dates from 1932, when it was built to accommodate the growing needs of Jaffa's Roman Catholic Church. (St. Peter's, ☞ *above,* was in a heavily populated Muslim area and was unable to expand due to lack of land.) The church is named for St. Antonius of Padua, friend and disciple of St. Francis of Assisi. ✉ *51 Yefet St.*

**★ ⑭ Shuk hapishpeshim.** The flea market actually began as one of many small bazaars that surrounded the clock tower in the mid-19th century, and it's now the only survivor of that era. The market's main street is **Olei Zion,** but there are a number of smaller streets and arcades to explore at your leisure, so take your time. Today there's more junk than there are treasures, and bargaining is not as vigorous as it once was; but it's still important to play the game, so don't agree to the first price the seller demands.

**Yefet Street.** Think of Yefet as a sort of thread between eras: beneath it is the old market area, while all around you stand the Christian and Western schools and churches of the 19th and 20th centuries. Numbers 21, 23, and 25 deserve mention. The first is the **Tabitha School,** established by the Presbyterian Church of Scotland in 1863. Behind the school is a small cemetery where some fairly prominent figures are buried, including Dr. Thomas Hodgkin, the personal physician to Sir

Moses Montefiore and the first to define Hodgkin's disease; he died in Jaffa in 1866. **Number 23** was a French Catholic school (it still carries the sign COLLÈGE DES FRÈRES) from 1882 but has long since been used by the French Embassy for administrative purposes. And next door, the neo-Tudor, fortresslike **Urim School**, with its round tower, was set up as a girls' school in 1882 by nuns of the same order that built the St. Louis French Hospital. It's now a local school.

# Neve Tzedek

In 1887 a small group of Jewish families concentrated their efforts to get out of crowded, poverty-stricken Jaffa and began creating an infrastructure on the sand to the north of the mainly Arab port town. Building at a rate of 10 houses a year, they laid the cornerstone for Neve Tzedek (Dwellings of Justice) in 1890. This was the forebear of Tel Aviv. The area is off the beaten path for most tourists, but as time and money are invested in its restoration, it attracts renewed interest. Today Neve Tzedek is the home of many of Tel Aviv's artists, rich and poor; it also has a splendid dance and arts complex (the Suzanne Dellal Center) and a growing number of small trendy galleries, gift stores, and restaurants. Though bordered on three sides by major thoroughfares (Eilat Road to the south, Herzl Street to the west, and Kaufman Street along the sea), this little quarter is very tranquil. Made up of only about a dozen tiny streets stuffed with one- and two-story dwellings in various stages of either depressing disrepair or enthusiastic renovation, Neve Tzedek is rich with tales of 100 years ago.

## A Good Walk

Begin your visit at the corner of Eilat Road and Chelouche Street. Get used to the name Chelouche: as one of the quarter's founding families, the Chelouches are remembered all over Neve Tzedek. The shell of Aaron Chelouche's house—the first in the quarter—still stands at what later became **32 Chelouche Street.**

Cross the Chelouche Bridge and continue past the old and newly renovated pastel buildings, which are representative of the neighborhood's style, until you see the plaza of the **Suzanne Dellal Center for Dance and Theater** ㉓ on the left. The two buildings dating back to the early 20th century are now venues for a wide range of performances. At the main entrance you will find yourself on the corner of Yehieli and Shabazi streets. Turn right on Shabazi, following the street to its end, and delight in the area's art galleries, antiques shops, boutiques, and cafés.

Turn right on Neve Tzedek Street and continue to the intersection of Rokach and Neve Tzedek streets. On the northwestern corner, where the cream-color bomb shelters stand today, were Neve Tzedek's wells; here residents waited eagerly for their "water man," a Yemenite by the name of Yosef Minz, who pumped the water and even offered home delivery. Toward the end of the century people began digging their own wells; running water did not start to flow until after World War I.

At **36 Rokach Street** is the house of another of Neve Tzedek's founders, Shimon Rokach; family members still live here. A few steps on, you'll come to Pines Street. To the left and across the road, on the corner of Pines and Lilienblum streets, the pink-and-yellow shell of a building was the Eden Cinema, the first movie house in the country and a curious phenomenon altogether in 1914, set up as it was in the middle of the sand. The Eden became a cultural center, hosting the city's earliest opera and theater performances as well as films.

Continue up Lilienblum to Herzl Street and turn left. End your walk at the huge, ungainly **Shalom Tower** ㉔, where the view from the rooftop observatory takes in both the sprawling city and the Mediterranean.

TIMING

Allow around two hours for this walk, including time for coffee or a light meal. There are few sites to enter, but these are closed on Friday afternoon and Saturday, so it's better to visit on a weekday.

## Sights to See

**32 Chelouche St.** Aaron Chelouche, who began his career as a money changer, was prominent in Jaffa's Jewish community, but he was intent on setting up a Jewish town elsewhere. He thus built the first house here, in 1887. The shell of the huge house still stands, with hints of its grandeur in the arched terrace that spans the facade on the second floor. It held more than just the Chelouche clan (including Aaron's two daughters, three sons, and their families): by the time Aaron "persuaded" other Jews to come here to live—by selling them cheap plots—the house was doubling as a community center. There was even a synagogue out back. The dynasty would continue, and one of Aaron's grandsons—Moshe—even became mayor of Tel Aviv, albeit only for a day. Following the 1936 death of the city's first mayor, Meir Dizengoff, Moshe was elected to replace him; but he was quickly deposed by the city's rightist bloc, backed by the ruling British, who preferred another son of Neve Tzedek, Yisrael Rokach.

**35 Chelouche St.** Drawn to this quarter like so many other Israeli literati and artists, writer S. Y. Agnon lived here from 1909 to 1912. At the time, the young Agnon was working as a literary assistant to the more senior writer Simcha Ben Zion, the namesake of the boulevard leading from King George Street to Habimah Square; his first story was published in literary journals produced by Ben Zion. Much of Agnon's writings reflects these very surroundings.

**36 Rokach St.** Shimon Rokach moved to the area from Jerusalem in 1884, and his son was born here three years later. This grandiose house changed the face of the street; it was designed by an Austrian architect whose touches included a bronze dome at the rear. Rokach became known as the Parisian Street because of its obvious grand-European influence.

Rokach the younger was already ensconced in politics by the time he was 28. After Mayor Dizengoff died in 1936, Rokach bumped out Moshe Chelouche as the preferred choice to succeed him. He served as mayor until 1952. In 1953, he became Israel's interior minister. The house is still occupied by the family; Shimon's sculptor granddaughter renovated it and now opens it up to the public on Saturday from 10 to 2.

㉔ **Shalom Tower.** Israel's first skyscraper stands on the site of the first high school ever to hold its classes entirely in Hebrew: the Herzliya Gymnasium (named, like the street, for the founder of the Zionist movement, Theodor Herzl). The building is your basic office block, but there is a photograph exhibit and models of old and new Tel Aviv in the lobby. The rooftop observatory is well worth a visit for its magnificent city and sea views. ✉ *Herzl St.,* ☎ *03/517–0991.* 🎫 *NIS 15 ($3.75).* ☉ *Sun.–Thurs. 10–6, Fri. 10–2, Sat. 11–4.*

㉓ **Suzanne Dellal Center for Dance and Theater.** The two large whitewashed buildings that make up this attractive complex started as schools, one built in 1892 and the other in 1908. Both were used for education until the 1970s, though they also served as headquarters for the political force Etzel and the underground military group Haganah, which marched on Arab Jaffa in the 1940s, when Arab residents terrorized Jewish neighborhoods. The complex was always something of a meeting place for theater folk, and it opened as a dance center after extensive renovations in 1990 (☞ Nightlife and the Arts, *below*). The halls are only open for performances, but you can walk around the attractive grounds. There are two cafés, an Italian restaurant, and an ice cream shop on the premises. ⊠ *6 Yehieli St.,* ☎ *03/510–5656.*

## Northern Tel Aviv

Among the sights north of the Yarkon River are two important museums. The Eretz Israel Museum is close to Tel Aviv University; Bet Hatefutsoth (Diaspora Museum) is farther north, on the university campus. The museums are about 8 km (5 mi) from the downtown hotels; Buses 24, 25, 27, 45, or 49 will take you to both. Allow at least two hours for each.

### Sights to See

★ **Beth Hatefutsoth (Diaspora Museum).** Presented here are 2,500 years of Jewish life in the Diaspora (the settling of Jews outside Israel), beginning with the destruction of the First Temple in Jerusalem and chronicling such major events as the exile to Babylon and the expulsion from Spain in 1492. Also covered is the world of Eastern Europe before the Holocaust. Photographs and text labels provide the narrative, and films and music enhance the experience. One highlight is a replica collection of miniature synagogues throughout the world, both those destroyed and those still functioning. Another is the computerized genealogy section, where it is possible to look up Jewish family names to determine their origins. ⊠ *Tel Aviv University Campus (Gate 2), Klausner St., Ramat Aviv,* ☎ *03/646–2020.* ⊡ *NIS 20 ($5).* ☉ *Sun.–Tues. and Thurs. 10–4, Wed. 10–6, Fri. 9–3.*

★ **Eretz Israel Museum.** This national museum comprises eight pavilions that present such facets of Israeli life as ethnography and folklore, ceramics and other handicrafts, and coinage; the displays span 3,000 years of history. In the center of the complex is the ancient site of Tel Kassile, where archaeological digs have so far uncovered 12 layers of settlements. There is also a daily sound-and-light show in the adjacent planetarium with Hebrew narration (call to verify hours). ⊠ *2 Levanon (University) St.,* ☎ *03/641–5244.* ⊡ *Museum NIS 28 ($7), planetarium NIS 20 ($5).* ☉ *Sun.–Tues. and Thurs. 9–3, Wed. 9–5, Fri.–Sat. 10–4.*

# DINING

Most Tel Aviv restaurants are open throughout the day and well into the night year-round, except Yom Kippur. Keep in mind that many serve business lunches at reasonable prices, making them less-expensive options than the price categories suggest. (Eating well in Tel Aviv can be very expensive.) Like many of their counterparts around the Mediterranean, Israelis dine late; chances are you'll have no trouble getting a table at 7 PM, whereas at 10 you may face a long line. Casual attire is always acceptable in Tel Aviv, even in the poshest restaurants.

Although the quality of Tel Aviv's cuisine has improved significantly, be warned that the same cannot be said about service. Even in good restaurants, staff members may make you feel as though they're doing you a favor by waiting on you. It's customary to leave a 10%–15% tip, but don't feel obliged to do so if you've received poor service. Occasionally, the service charge is added to the bill, so look for it; this is uncommon enough that it generally goes unnoticed, and diners end up paying twice for service.

| CATEGORY | COST* |
|----------|-------|
| $$$$ | over $35 |
| $$$ | $22–$35 |
| $$ | $12–$22 |
| $ | under $12 |

*per person for a three-course meal, excluding drinks and 10%–15% service charge

# American

$$$   ✕ **Dixie.** This bar and grill is away from the main tourist areas and mostly serves the surrounding offices and commercial centers. But grab a taxi and go (any time—it's open 24 hours a day). There's no place like Dixie for a hearty American-style breakfast of eggs Benedict or a stack of pancakes. The dinner menu includes prime ribs, Cajun veal, and a selection of burgers. There is a minimum charge to sit at the comfortable leather couches in the main dining area, but feel free to sit at the bar with an order of spicy chicken wings, the house specialty. ⊠ *120 Yigal Allon St.,* ☎ *03/696–6123. AE, DC, MC, V.*

# Barbecue

$$   ✕ **Dita.** Inside, the massive square bar dominates the main dining area. Outside, the tables line the entrance along Rothschild Boulevard. Both settings provide a loud, lively atmosphere to accompany the large portions of meat such as spareribs in pear sauce or grilled kebabs. The main dishes come with a side order of potatoes, freshly baked bread, and a house salad. ⊠ *61 Rothschild Blvd.,* ☎ *03/528–4866. AE, DC, MC, V.*

# Cafés

$$   ✕ **Café Cazeh.** This stalwart survivor of Tel Aviv's capricious restaurant scene is also one of the few kosher places in the trendy Sheinkin street area with an official license from the Israeli Rabbinate. No meat is served, but the vegetable pies and quiches are hearty and come with fresh salads. Desserts are the real specialty here—you may have trouble deciding among lemon-meringue or pecan pie, apple cake, and brownies. In addition to the two separate, intimate sitting rooms, there is a pleasant garden in the back of the restaurant where you can temporarily escape the noisy street. ⊠ *19 Sheinkin St.,* ☎ *03/629–3756. No credit cards. Closed Sat. No dinner Fri.*

$$   ✕ **Café Tnuva.** This dairy restaurant is a good place to take a break from "Dizengoffing" (the act of strolling along Dizengoff Street). Tnuva is one of Israel's leading dairy companies, and the milk- and cheese-based items on the menu are made from its products. The hearty salads, such as the Soho (penne, cherry tomatoes, lettuce, and cashews in herb dressing), cheese toasts, pastas, and fish meals all satisfy. There are also natural fruit shakes and a range of tasty desserts: check out the cheesecake. ⊠ *34 Ben-Gurion Blvd.,* ☎ *03/527–2972. AE, DC, MC, V.*

$$   ✕ **Orna and Ella.** Consistently good for light meals and excellent for cakes and desserts, Orna and Ella is worth several trips. Have the sweet-potato latkes, but don't leave here without trying something from the dessert corner, such as a *tarte Tatin* (apple tart) or pear pie. There is often a long wait for tables, especially Friday afternoons and after 9 PM on weekdays. ⊠ *33 Sheinkin St.,* ☎ *03/620–4753. Reservations not accepted. AE, DC, MC, V.*

**ONE LAST TRAVEL TIP:**

# Pack an easy way to reach the world.

Wherever you travel, the MCI WorldCom Card℠ is the easiest way to stay in touch. You can use it to call to and from more than 125 countries worldwide. And you can earn bonus miles every time you use your card. So go ahead, travel the world. MCI WorldCom℠ makes it even more rewarding. For additional access codes, visit **www.wcom.com/worldphone**.

## EASY TO CALL WORLDWIDE

1. Just dial the WorldPhone® access number of the country you're calling from.

2. Dial or give the operator your MCI WorldCom Card number.

3. Dial or give the number you're calling.

| | |
|---|---|
| Argentina | 0800-222-6249 |
| Belize (A) | 557 or 815 |
| Brazil | 000-8012 |
| Chile | 800-207-300 |
| Colombia ◆ | 980-9-16-0001 |

| | |
|---|---|
| Costa Rica (A) ◆ | 0800-012-2222 |
| Ecuador ÷ | 999-170 |
| Egypt ◆ | 7955770 |
| El Salvador (A) | 800-1567 |
| Guatemala ◆ | 99-99-189 |
| Honduras (A) ÷ | 8000-122 |
| Israel | 1-800-920-2727 |
| Mexico | 01-800-021-8000 |
| Nicaragua | 166 |
| Panama (A) | 00800-001-0108 |
| Turkey ◆ | 00-8001-1177 |
| Venezuela ◆ ÷ | 800-11140 |

**(A)** Calls back to U.S. only.  ◆ Public phones may require deposit of coin or phone card for dial tone.  ÷ Limited availability.

## EARN FREQUENT FLIER MILES

 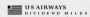

Limit of one bonus program per customer. All airline program rules and conditions apply. © 2000 WorldCom, Inc. All Rights Reserved. The names, logos, and taglines identifying WorldCom's products and services are proprietary marks of WorldCom, Inc. or its subsidiaries. All third party marks are the proprietary marks of their respective owners.

**Bureau de change**

**Cambio**

**外国為替**

# In this city, you can find money on almost any street.

---

NO-FEE FOREIGN EXCHANGE

---

The Chase Manhattan Bank has over 80 convenient
locations near New York City destinations such as:

> Times Square
> Rockefeller Center
> Empire State Building
> 2 World Trade Center
> United Nations Plaza

**Exchange any of 75 foreign currencies**

THE RIGHT RELATIONSHIP IS EVERYTHING.®

©2000 The Chase Manhattan Corporation. All rights reserved. The Chase Manhattan Bank.
Member FDIC.

**$  ✕ Ashtur.** A popular hangout among locals, this corner café in the heart of the Basel area is a great place "to see and be seen," a favorite Tel Aviv pastime. The coffee is good, the snacks are light, and the service is helpful. ✉ *37 Basel St.,* ☎ *03/546–5318. AE, DC, MC, V.*

**$  ✕ Ilan's Coffee Shop.** The exclusively developed "Angelo Mio" is considered the best espresso in town. But this intimate café, as well as Ilan's other three Tel Aviv locations, also offers 20 other blends of coffee, a selection of teas, and specialty sandwiches. Don't leave without trying a dessert. Especially recommended is the heated *jocolada*—a doughy cake that oozes melted white chocolate from the center. ✉ *90 Ibn Gvirol St.,* ☎ *03/523–5334. AE, DC, MC, V.*

## Contemporary

**$$$$  ✕ Tamuz.** Tucked away in a quiet corner of the city, where downtown Tel Aviv becomes Neve Tzedek, this so-called "bistro-bar" offers an eclectic menu that varies from season to season. Sauces are very much emphasized, most of them a tad sweet. Highlights include a beef fillet in light pickle; goose thigh cooked with port, onions, and dried fruit; salmon in orange sauce; and risotto with calamari in tomato butter. For dessert, try the sumptuous baked pears and marzipan coated with white chocolate. The decor is in warm tones, with Santa Fe–style terra-cotta stucco walls complementing old-style Mediterranean tile floors. Live jazz sessions on Friday afternoons help to welcome in the weekend. ✉ *6 Ahad Ha'am St.,* ☎ *03/516–7888. Reservations essential. AE, DC, MC, V.*

**$$$  ✕ Kachol.** Were it not for the crowd of trendy Tel Avivians here, you could forget you were still in the city. *Kachol* means "blue," and the restaurant has a suitably romantic and relaxing setting on the Tel Baruch beach, in north Tel Aviv. During the day, sit outside to soak up the sunshine and the sea view. Come evening, there's nothing like a Mediterranean sunset with your glass of wine. For starters, dip into the scrumptious salmon pâté with fresh bread, or *halumi* salad (fresh vegetables dotted with deep-fried goat's cheese); for dinner itself, lean toward the baked fish. ✉ *Tel Baruch Beach,* ☎ *03/699–6574. AE, DC, MC, V.*

## Eastern European

**$$  ✕ Bebale.** With its old-style Jewish food amid photographs and mementos from the past, Bebale now serves young, hip Israelis newly appreciative of their Eastern European roots. Specialties include gefilte fish, chopped liver, meatballs in tomato sauce, and cold cherry soup. ✉ *42 Montefiore St.,* ☎ *03/560–2228. AE, DC, MC, V. No dinner Fri.*

**$$  ✕ Café Batia.** The simple decor of this Dizengoff Street institution hasn't been changed in years and the menu is similarly filled with old-fashioned, Eastern European favorites. Try a bowl of matzoh-ball soup or stuffed cabbage for a nostalgic reminder of the kind of meal that Grandma used to prepare. If the weather allows, sit outside to enjoy a dose of people-watching. ✉ *197 Dizengoff St.,* ☎ *03/522–1335. AE, DC, MC, V.*

## French

**$$$$  ✕ Kapot Tmarim.** Over the years, a small number of restaurants have been credited with turning Israel's culinary tide, and Kapot Tmarim is one of them. The pleasant ambience and friendly staff enhance a compelling French menu with contemporary influences, from hot goose liver with onions and dates right down to the restaurant's own ice cream. The more reasonably priced lunch menu is one of the best deals in town. ✉ *60 Ahad Ha'am St.,* ☎ *03/566–3166. Reservations essential. AE, DC, MC, V. Closed Sat.*

## Tel Aviv Dining and Lodging

Mediterranean
Sea

163

**Dining**

| | |
|---|---|
| Ashtur | 26 |
| Bebale | 15 |
| Big Mama | 4 |
| Café Batia | 30 |
| Café Cazeh | 10 |
| Café Tnuva | 33 |
| Chimichanga | 14 |
| Dita | 32 |
| Dixie | 37 |
| | 38 |

| | |
|---|---|
| Giraffe Noodle Bar | 8 |
| Ilan's Coffee Shop | 36 |
| Kachol | 4 |
| Kapot Tmarim | 30 |
| Keren | 10 |
| Mongolian Grill Bar | 33 |
| Mul-Yam | 14 |
| Orna and Ella | 32 |
| Pastalina | 37 |

| | |
|---|---|
| Shipudei Hatikva | 26 |
| Shtupak | 15 |
| Suzanna | 35 |
| Tabun | 43 |
| Tamuz | |
| Tandoori | 34 |

| | |
|---|---|
| Shipudei Hatikva | 45 |
| Shtupak | 6 |
| Suzanna | 41 |
| Tabun | 46 |
| Tamuz | 42 |
| Tandoori | 23 |

**Lodging**

| | |
|---|---|
| Adiv | 22 |
| Aviv | 27 |
| Basel | 13 |
| Carlton | 11 |
| Center | 24 |
| City | 19 |
| Dan Accadia | 3 |
| Dan Panorama | 40 |
| Dan Tel Aviv | 21 |

| | |
|---|---|
| Daniel | 1 |
| David Intercontinental | 39 |
| Dizengoff Circle/ Dizengoff Square Apartments | 25 |
| Grand Beach | 7 |
| Grand Deborah Hotel | 17 |
| Hilton | 9 |
| Maxim | 28 |

| | |
|---|---|
| Prima Astor | 20 |
| Regency Suites | 29 |
| Renaissance Tel Aviv | 16 |
| Sharon | 2 |
| Sheraton Moriah Tel Aviv | 12 |
| Sheraton Tel Aviv Hotel & Towers | 18 |

$$$$ ✕ **Keren.** Ranked among the finest restaurants in Israel, Keren is housed in the only fully restored building in Jaffa's run-down American Colony. The bar downstairs proves a restful spot after the inevitable daytime traffic jam on Eilat Street. You'll forget the state of the neighboring buildings when you enter the upstairs dining room, with its smooth wood floors and welcoming armchairs. Foie gras features prominently on the menu, in various forms; but the range is wide. ✉ *12 Eilat St. (at Auerbach St.), Jaffa,* ☎ *03/681–6565. Reservations essential. AE, DC, MC, V. No lunch Sun.*

# Indian

$$$ ✕ **Tandoori.** This veteran restaurant—the oldest of the Tandoori chain, ★ which introduced Israelis to fine Indian cuisine—has maintained the high quality of its food and service over the years, which in Tel Aviv is noteworthy in itself. The curries come in three strengths, but tandoori chicken is the specialty: it comes to the table sizzling hot, and finger bowls of rose water mean you can dig in with abandon. ✉ *2 Zamenhoff St. (Kikar Dizengoff),* ☎ *03/629–6185. AE, DC, MC, V.*

# Italian

$$$$ ✕ **PastaLina.** One of the most innovative restaurants in Tel Aviv, PastaLina is worth the trek to this less-well-known corner of Jaffa, near the American Colony. Antipasti cover a large table by the entrance, and you're served generous samples upon sitting down. The fixed-price menu, which changes daily, includes antipasti and a pasta, meat, or fish dish. Glass bricks in the front wall allow natural light to highlight the russet walls and wood furniture. ✉ *16 Elifelet St., Jaffa,* ☎ *03/ 683–6401. Reservations essential. AE, DC, MC, V. No dinner Fri.*

$$ ✕ **Big Mama.** This spot is off the beaten path, near the Carmel Market, ★ but it's well worth looking for. The thin-crust pizza is excellent, and the owners use only the freshest ingredients. Toppings range from the traditional basil to more unusual ideas, such as zucchini or prosciutto and egg. There are some great pastas on the menu, including pumpkin ravioli in cream sauce, and seafood specialties, such as oysters in wine and garlic. ✉ *13 Nagara St.,* ☎ *03/517–5096. AE, DC, MC, V. Closed Sun. No lunch.*

# Mediterranean

$$$ ✕ **Suzanna.** This century-old building once housed the first coffee shop in Tel Aviv, and Suzanna's owners retained the early Israeli furnishings, such as decorative ceramic floor tiles, when they renovated several years ago. A pleasant café and eatery by day, the restaurant bustles by night, when it's especially nice to sit on the leafy terrace. The menu is odd but very successful, drawing on both traditional and contemporary cuisines. Do you feel like Iraqi *koubeh* (meat-filled semolina dumplings) and pumpkin soup, or Moroccan silk soup with chickpeas, veal, and coriander? If you're still in a Middle Eastern mood, will it be lamb in yogurt, grilled chicken salad with pine nuts and shallots, or couscous-stuffed chicken with a sweet date-and-plum sauce? The choices don't end there: for dessert, there's home-style sorbet, ice cream, and cakes: pear-and-apple tart, chocolate cake with cream and biscuits, and chocolate fudge cake. ✉ *9 Shabazi St., Neve Tzedek,* ☎ *03/517–7580. AE, DC, MC, V.*

# Mexican

$$$$ ✕ **Chimichanga.** Located in a light-industrial area, this New Mexican restaurant joins the ranks of Tel Aviv eateries that stay alive and hopping long after everything—and everyone—else has gone to sleep. It's

large but friendly. Start with a margarita; then tuck into a meal of chicken in tequila and lime, all sautéed in clarified butter and served with grilled vegetables. ⊠ *6 Kriminitzky St.,* ☎ *03/561–3232. Reservations essential. AE, DC, MC, V. No lunch Fri.*

## Middle Eastern

$ ✕ **Shipudei Hatikva.** This family-style restaurant chain is one of many grills along Ha'etzel Street, in the Hatikva Quarter. The Las Vegas–style lights along the street contrast with the plain Formica tables and fluorescent lighting inside. There is a selection of salads and spreads to begin with, including eggplant in mayonnaise and hot Turkish salad, as well as hummus and pita. For the main course, you can pick from a range of sumptuous skewered meats grilled over hot coals. The specialty is barbecued goose liver. ⊠ *37 Ha'etzel St.,* ☎ *03/687–8014. AE, DC, MC, V. No lunch Sat., no dinner Fri.*

## Pan-Asian

$$$ ✕ **Giraffe Noodle Bar.** Generous portions of noodles in a variety of Japanese, Thai, and other Asian styles attract a loyal clientele to this crowded, lively restaurant. There's a selection of soups and sushi for starters. And save room for something sweet from the classic European dessert menu, such as the meringue-based, berry-topped Pavlova. Check out the worthwhile lunch deal. ⊠ *49 Ibn Gvirol St.,* ☎ *03/691–6294. AE, DC, MC, V.*

$$ ✕ **Mongolian Grill Bar.** Fill a bowl with your favorite vegetables and cubes of raw ostrich meat, chicken breast, or salmon. Add some red wine, soy sauce, shredded coconut, chopped peanuts, and ginger. Then hand it over to the chef behind the barbecue and watch as he grills your mixture, turning it into a savory meal. The fixed menu includes an "all you can eat" special, so if you are not satisfied with your first ensemble, go back and try again. The Grill Bar is a fun place for kids. ⊠ *62 Hayarkon St.,* ☎ *03/517–4188. AE, DC, MC, V.*

## Seafood

$$$$ ✕ **Mul-Yam.** This is Israel's first true-to-life oyster and seafood bar. Every-
★ thing is flown in fresh from abroad—including Nova Scotia lobsters—so the prices are not low. Still, it's a true pleasure: the dishes are tasty and well presented, and the great location, in the old port by the Mediterranean, adds to the flavor. ⊠ *Tel Aviv Port,* ☎ *03/546–9920. Reservations essential. AE, DC, MC, V. No dinner Sat.*

$$$$ ✕ **Tabun.** The fishing boats docked along the water's edge and the salty smells of the sea are enchanting, and the whitewashed walls as well as the crisp, white linen tablecloths and turquoise trimmings lend sophistication to the Mediterranean ambience. Your best bet here is the catch of the day, lightly herbed and baked in olive oil in the *tabun* (stone) oven, which imparts a rich and faintly barbecued flavor. If you can't wait for the main course—ideally, baked sea bass or bream with herbs—the carpaccio of salmon and grouper is delectable, and the bouillabaisse is excellent. ⊠ *Main Gate, Jaffa Port (turn left at pier),* ☎ *03/681–1176. Reservations essential. AE, DC, MC, V.*

$$ ✕ **Shtupak.** There is usually a line at this popular fish restaurant because the food is good and reasonably priced. Fish entrées come with an assortment of salads and spreads for starters. For the main course, there is a daily selection of fresh "catches of the day," which may include whole trout, fried calamari, or oysters in cream sauce. There is a good selection of wines to choose from. For dessert, try the cappuccino parfait. ⊠ *256 Ben Yehuda St.,* ☎ *03/544–1973. AE, DC, MC, V.*

# LODGING

Hotel reservations are essential during all Jewish holidays and are advised throughout the year. Keep in mind that most hotels (except as noted) include breakfast in the price: fresh vegetables, salads, and fruit; cereals and pastries; and eggs and cheeses are usually among the options.

Tel Aviv is known for a dearth of middle-price hotels, but the few hotels listed in the $$ and $ categories are generally clean and comfortable, with friendly employees who create a warm atmosphere.

At press time, a few Tel Aviv hotels had closed temporarily. Please call ahead to assure that a hotel is open.

| CATEGORY | COST* |
| --- | --- |
| $$$$ | over $120 |
| $$$ | $80–$120 |
| $$ | $60–$80 |
| $ | under $60 |

*All prices are for a standard double room, including breakfast and excluding 15% service charge.

## Tel Aviv

**$$$$** ★ 🏨 **Carlton.** The newly renovated Carlton fancies itself a boutique hotel, and with good reason. The lobby is made up of several intimate sitting areas, each of which features the works of a different artist. Fresh flowers and bowls of fruit can be found on every floor. Wake-up calls are accompanied by fresh juice and newspapers upon request, and milk and cookies are delivered in the evening. The rooms are elegantly designed in muted colors with dark wood furniture. Guests on the "royal" floors have a private lounge, and Nintendo and CD players in the room (there's a library in the lobby). The hotel also has a rooftop pool and glass-enclosed gym and two conference rooms with state-of-the art equipment. Service is efficient and personal. ⊠ *10 Eliezer Peri St., 61064,* ☎ *03/520–1818,* 𝖥𝖠𝖷 *03/527–1043. 284 rooms. 2 restaurants, bar, 2 coffee shops, minibar, pool, beauty salon, chapel, parking (fee). AE, DC, MC, V.* 🐾

**$$$$** 🏨 **Dan Panorama.** This high-rise hotel is located at the southern end of the Tel Aviv beachfront, adjacent to the new business district and a close walk to Jaffa. Each of the attractive rooms has a balcony overlooking the sea, either facing south toward Jaffa or north toward the hub of Tel Aviv. Poolside barbecues in the summer are a plus. Some rooms have Internet data ports. ⊠ *10 Y. Kaufman St., 68012,* ☎ *03/519–0190,* 𝖥𝖠𝖷 *03/517–1777. 504 rooms. Restaurant, bar, coffee shop, pool, massage, sauna, exercise room, health club, parking (fee). AE, DC, MC, V.* 🐾

**$$$$** ★ 🏨 **Dan Tel Aviv.** Despite its reputation for exclusivity, this landmark hotel has a warm, congenial atmosphere. Patterned coverlets decorate olive-green furniture in the rooms; the bathrooms have hair dryers, phones, and radios. Rooms are larger in the luxurious King David wing and have panoramic sea views as well as double-glazed windows to muffle city noise; however, none of these have balconies. Guests have access to both the beach below and free golf at the Dan Accadia hotel (☞ *below*), about 25 km (15½ mi) north of Tel Aviv. Tel Avivians themselves come to La Regence, the hotel's restaurant, for elegant dining. ⊠ *99 Hayarkon St., 63903,* ☎ *03/520–2525,* 𝖥𝖠𝖷 *03/524–9755. 238 rooms, 50 suites. 3 restaurants, bar, café, minibars, pool, sauna, steam room, health club, parking (fee). AE, DC, MC, V.*

**$$$$** ⊞ **David Inter-Continental.** At the southern end of the Tel Aviv coastline, the newest and most luxurious of Tel Aviv's deluxe hotels is quickly becoming the preferred place to stay for many business travelers, vacationers, and celebrities. The spacious rooms are decorated in warm, pastel shades and the hotel staff is especially helpful and professional. The impressive, grand atrium lobby—a massive and elegant room with high ceilings and marble floors—has four restaurants, including the Aubergine, which specializes in French and Italian cuisine, and the IM@C Cafe, where guests can surf the Net as they face the sea. There's a sophisticated cigar bar on the lobby level. All rooms feature individually controlled air-conditioning, and most overlook the sea. The hotel's top floors are reserved for club-room guests, who have use of a private lounge. ⊠ *12 Kaufman St., 68012,* ☎ *03/795–1111,* FAX *03/795–1112. 559 rooms. 4 restaurants, bar, café, sushi bar, 3 pools, spa, shops, children's programs, business services, parking (fee). AE, DC, MC, V.* 🍴

**$$$$** ⊞ **Grand Beach.** All of these rooms are decorated in turquoise, gray, and yellow and have unusually good reading lamps. There is a rooftop pool, and the beach is a five-minute walk away. The main dining room has a view of city streets, and light food is served in the large lobby lounge. ⊠ *250 Hayarkon St., 63113,* ☎ *03/543–3333,* FAX *03/546–6589. 212 rooms. Bar, lobby lounge, in-room safes, pool, chapel. AE, DC, MC, V.* 🍴

**$$$$** ⊞ **Hilton.** Overlooking the Tel Aviv Marina and bordered on three sides by Independence Park, the Hilton is a luxury hotel that caters directly to business travelers. It offers a state-of-the-art business center, meeting rooms, and Japanese-language services. The hotel's large seawater pool is the best in town and, together with the spa and all the guest rooms, has recently been completely renovated. In addition to enjoying the excellent, eclectic cuisine at the intimate King Soloman Grill, you can grab a bite at the Mediterranean Café Med or at the sushi bar overlooking the sea. ⊠ *Hayarkon St., Independence Park, 63405,* ☎ *03/520–2222,* FAX *03/527–2711. 582 rooms. 2 restaurants, 2 bars, sushi bar, saltwater pool, tennis court, health club, beach, parking (fee). AE, DC, MC, V.* 🍴

**$$$$** ⊞ **Regency Suites.** This Best Western hotel is made up entirely of well-equipped one-bedroom suites, each of which comes with a small living area and kitchenette. The decor is tasteful and the atmosphere is homey, and the suites can accommodate up to four people. The hotel has a sundeck and hot tub on the roof and a lovely breakfast room. Full, daily cleaning services are provided. ⊠ *80 Hayarkon St., 63432,* ☎ *03/517–3939,* FAX *03/516–3276. 30 suites. Breakfast room, kitchenettes, hot tub, free parking. AE, DC, MC, V.* 🍴

**$$$$** ⊞ **Renaissance Tel Aviv.** All rooms have balconies with sea views at this comfortably informal luxury hotel. Club-floor guests enjoy a private lounge that offers refreshments throughout the day. Restaurants include the Jaffa Terrace, a dairy coffee shop, and the Sabres Brasserie, for Israeli cuisine. The hotel has direct access to the beach and one of the few indoor heated swimming pools in Tel Aviv. ⊠ *121 Hayarkon St., 63453,* ☎ *03/521–5555,* FAX *03/521–5588. 330 rooms, 10 suites. 2 restaurants, 2 bars, coffee shop, minibars, 1 indoor and 1 outdoor pool, hot tub, sauna, Turkish bath, exercise room, beach, parking (fee). AE, DC, MC, V.* 🍴

**$$$$** ⊞ **Sheraton Moriah Tel Aviv.** In this 17-floor hotel, all rooms (except singles) have sea views from their balconies. Public areas are freshly decorated in earth tones and rooms have Mediterranean color schemes. The outdoor saltwater pool (with daily children's activities in summer) overlooks the beach, to which you have direct access. ⊠ *155 Hayarkon St., 63453,* ☎ *03/521–6666,* FAX *03/527–1065. 355 rooms. 2 restau-*

*rants, bar, patisserie, in-room safes, minibars, saltwater pool, beauty salon, health club, business center, meeting rooms, parking (fee). AE, DC, MC, V.* ✑

**$$$$**  ⚏ **Sheraton Tel Aviv Hotel and Towers.** Combining a personal touch
★  with the efficiency and experience of the international Sheraton chain, this is one of the most attractive lodging options in Tel Aviv. An excellent lobby design allows for private areas within the public space, and there's a lounge bar with a view of the sea. The rooms are decorated in soft hues and color-coordinated fabrics. The well-run executive Sheraton Towers floors have their own check-in and private lounge, which serves refreshments throughout the day. The new Olives restaurant offers Mediterranean-inspired cuisine with a French accent. ✉ *115 Hayarkon St., 61032,* ☎ *03/521–1111,* FAX *03/523–3322. 345 rooms. 2 restaurants, bar, minibars, 2 pools, health club, nightclub, business services, parking (fee). AE, DC, MC, V.* ✑

**$$$**  ⚏ **Basel.** It's not on the beach side of Hayarkon Street, but this seven-story hotel lives up to its reputation as a good deal. All but five rooms on each floor have sea views; their decor includes well-designed wooden furniture and patchwork-style fabrics. Expect personalized service—probably the legacy of the original Swiss owners. The lobby, with a corner bar, overlooks the small swimming pool. ✉ *156 Hayarkon St., 63451,* ☎ *03/520–7711,* FAX *03/527–0005. 120 rooms. Bar, coffee shop, room service, pool, parking (fee). AE, DC, MC, V.* ✑

**$$$**  ⚏ **City.** On a quiet street near the beach, this six-story hotel is at the bottom of its price range. The light, airy lobby has a small sitting area on one side, a cozy dining room on the other. The basic but pleasant outdoor café, which faces the neighbor's hedge across the street, consists of a dozen plastic chairs and tables under a sidewalk canopy. The rooms have blond-wood furniture and TVs. The City is known for its fine food, including an acclaimed Israeli breakfast and a Friday-night Shabbat dinner with gefilte fish. ✉ *9 Mapu St., 63577,* ☎ *03/524–6253,* FAX *03/524–6250. 96 rooms. Restaurant, café, room service, free parking. AE, DC, MC, V.* ✑

**$$$**  ⚏ **Grand Deborah Hotel.** The bar and the lobby share one relatively small space here, so you can have a drink as you check in. The pleasant guest rooms are decorated with warm colors and wood trim. Location is a big plus here, with easy access to both the city center and the beach. Internet access is available in the lobby. ✉ *87 Ben Yehuda St.,* ☎ *03/527–8282,* FAX *03/527–8304. 63 rooms. Lobby lounge, free parking. AE, DC, MC, V.* ✑

**$$$**  ⚏ **Prima Astor.** Built on a rise on the corner of Frishman and Hayarkon streets, the Astor has an excellent view of the sea. The rooms in this 30-year-old hotel have recently been enlarged, and many have sea views. The small, homey lobby has prints of Israeli scenes and a coffee bar. The restaurant, Shangri-La, serves kosher Thai cuisine and sushi and has a beautiful canopied terrace that faces seaward. ✉ *105 Hayarkon St., 63903,* ☎ *03/520–6666,* FAX *03/523–7247. 70 rooms. Restaurant, bar, in-room data ports, business services, free parking. AE, DC, MC, V.* ✑

**$$**  ⚏ **Center.** This is one of the new breed of tourist-class hotels in Tel Aviv—simple rooms, warm but basic service, and far more reasonable prices than the luxury properties on the beach, which is just a 15-minute walk from here. The Center, well situated in town, just off Dizengoff Square, is newly renovated with a pleasant sitting area in the lobby and small dining area where breakfast is served. Rooms are small and tasteful. Most have balconies facing the Square, though there is no Mediterranean view. ✉ *2 Zamenhoff St.,* ☎ *03/629–6181,* FAX *03/629–6751. 56 rooms. AE, DC, MC, V.* ✑

**$$** ☷ **Dizengoff Circle/Dizengoff Square Apartments.** These two apartment complexes, which face each other on opposite sides of the Agam Fountain in the heart of Dizengoff Square, provide a comfortable, reasonably priced alternative to Tel Aviv's more expensive hotels. The studios, rooms, and suites all have kitchenettes and come in a variety of sizes and prices. Rooms are small and homey—simply decorated but comfortable. The amiable owner will take the time to personally offer travel advice. ⊠ *4 Dizengoff Circle, 61111,* ☎ *03/524–1151,* 𝔽𝔸𝕏 *03/523–5614. 51 rooms, 6 suites. AE, DC, MC, V. www.hotel-apt.com.*

**$$** ☷ **Maxim.** Moderately priced amid pricier accommodations, Maxim is a good value. The rooms are basic, but most have sea views. Europeans like to stay here, and there is indeed a kind of Continental atmosphere about the place, due in part to the many languages heard in the lobby. The lobby café is a popular place to relax. ⊠ *86 Hayarkon St.,* ☎ *03/517–3721,* 𝔽𝔸𝕏 *03/517–3726. 60 rooms Bar, café, kitchenettes (some). AE, DC, MC, V.*

**$** ☷ **Adiv.** This five-floor amiable hotel is on a side street off Hayarkon Street. Rooms have pleasing modern furnishings and pastel-print bedspreads and curtains, although most have no sea view. The fifth floor has five suites, with kitchen facilities. The staff is polite. ⊠ *5 Mendele St., 63907,* ☎ *03/522–9141,* 𝔽𝔸𝕏 *03/522–9144. 79 rooms. Bar, café, kitchenettes (some), room service. AE, DC, MC, V.*

**$** ☷ **Aviv.** This three-story 1950s building was renovated when the trendy Picasso restaurant opened on its ground floor. You enter through the restaurant and register at a desk behind the kitchen. There's no elevator, and the decor is spare; don't expect air-conditioning, telephones, or TVs. The rooms in back are said to be quiet, but their location on Hayarkon Street and over the restaurant (which is open until 5 AM) is not ideal for those who seek serenity. The front rooms, however, which face the sea, have a view of the Mediterranean. A real plus here is the breakfast (omelet, salad, juice, and bread) at Picasso, which is included in the room rate. ⊠ *88 Hayarkon St., 63432,* ☎ *03/510–2784,* 𝔽𝔸𝕏 *03/510–2785. 20 rooms. Restaurant. DC, MC, V.*

## Herzliya Pituach

Herzliya Pituach, or Herzliya-on-the-Sea, is a resort area 12 km (7½ mi) up the coast from Tel Aviv. It has a number of beachfront hotels, a wide range of eating options (some on the beach but most a short distance inland), public squares with outdoor cafés and shops, and a marina. Affluent suburbanites live here, as do diplomats and foreign journalists; there's a cosmopolitan, holiday air to the place. An express tourist bus (Bus 90) plies the route between the Herzliya hotels, the center of Tel Aviv, and ancient Jaffa.

**$$$$** ☷ **Dan Accadia.** This well-known seaside hostelry opened in 1956 and is still going strong. Its two buildings are surrounded by plant-filled lawns, which in turn surround a pool overlooking the sea. Sixty rooms face the pool, with direct access to the beach; others face the marina. The rooms are not huge, but they have balconies with sea views; interior decor includes quilted bedspreads and matching blue-and-pink drapes. Organized activities help keep children and teenagers amused on Friday and Saturday. Guests have access to the adjacent tennis courts, to the nine-hole executive Ga'ash golf course (a 10-minute drive), and to the golf course at the Dan Caesarea, farther north. The dining room has a glass wall looking out to sea, and a second, poolside restaurant is open for lunch. The Wednesday-night poolside barbecue, complete with a band and dancing, has been a local fixture for years. ⊠ *Herzliya-on-the-Sea 46851,* ☎ *09/959–7070,* 𝔽𝔸𝕏 *09/959–7091. 185 rooms. 2 restaurants, bar, coffee shop, pool, beauty salon, mas-*

*sage, sauna, 6 tennis courts, exercise room, children's programs, free parking. AE, DC, MC, V.* 🕸

$$$$  🏨 **Daniel.** Almost anywhere you stand (or recline) in the Daniel, you can see the Mediterranean: from the rooms, restaurant, and lobby. One of the bonuses here is the state-of-the-art spa, whose facilities include an indoor pool, wet and dry sauna, and single and double treatment rooms. All rooms look onto the Mediterranean; the deluxe rooms have balconies. The decor is a tasteful mixture of sea-blue and mustard hues. Business-club floors offer office services and access to a plush lounge that serves light refreshments. The hotel has a movie theater and a synagogue. ⊠ *60 Ramot Yam, Herzliya-on-the-Sea 46851,* ☎ *09/952–8282,* ℻ *09/952–8288. 200 rooms. 2 restaurants, bar, sushi bar, room service, 1 indoor and 1 outdoor pool, saunas, spa, 2 tennis courts, shops, business services, parking (fee). AE, DC, MC, V.* 🕸

$$$$  🏨 **Sharon.** The newly renovated Sharon first opened its doors in 1948. Today the rooms have light-color furniture and pink-and-gray color schemes, and most have balconies that overlook the sea. The garden rooms are near the outdoor seawater pool. The Sharon's health club (popular with Tel Avivians) has a heated indoor pool, a workout room, dry and wet saunas, massage, and Dead Sea mineral baths. The Sharon Kiddy Club runs during the summer months, on holidays, and weekends. ⊠ *5 Ramot Yam, Herzliya-on-the-Sea 46748,* ☎ *09/957–5777,* ℻ *09/956–8741. 170 rooms. Restaurant, bar, room service, indoor pool, saltwater pool, beauty salon, tennis court, health club, children's programs, free parking. AE, DC, MC, V.* 🕸

# NIGHTLIFE AND THE ARTS

## Nightlife

"The city that never stops" stays up later than many of the world's capitals. Peak hours on Hayarkon Street on a Friday or Saturday night continue until about 3 AM, when things finally begin to wind down. On Allenby Street, the clubs are still crowded at 5 AM. Partygoers are not daunted by the fact that nightspots come and go about as quickly as the tides.

Bars and nightspots in Tel Aviv usually open in the daytime, long before the night owls descend; typically, they offer either full dinners, beer and fries, or, at the very least, the coffee and cake they've been serving throughout the afternoon.

### Bars, Pubs, and Nightclubs

**Buzz Stop** (⊠ 86 Herbert Samuel St., ☎ 03/510–0869) is the closest thing to a wild Irish pub this side of the Mediterranean. It's crowded with beer-drinking tourists and English-speaking waiters. But the location, across the street from the beach, gives the place a local flavor.

**Cafe Noga** (⊠ 4 Pinsker St., ☎ 03/629–6457) is a bar that doubles as a pool hall. The music ranges from oldies to ambient, with a hint of local sound tossed in the mix. The hummus and fries are among the best in the city.

**Camelot** (⊠ 16 Shalom Aleichem St., ☎ 03/528–5222) has been described as "neo-yuppie" by the local newspaper. Quiet jazz is the main item on the menu, with some blues thrown in; the bar is upstairs, the music downstairs.

**Eurobar** (⊠ 35 Allenby St.) is one of Tel Aviv's trendiest places for drinks, but it also has a full food menu. Metallic tables and red neon dominate the decor.

**Hakossit** (✉ 6 Kikar Rabin, ☎ 03/522–3244) appears to be nothing more than a simple pub, but some of Israel's most successful jazz musicians began their careers on a wooden bar stool here.

**Hamisba'a** (✉ 344 Dizengoff St., ☎ 03/604–2360) is usually packed, and people really do dance on the tables here. Be sure to call and reserve one.

**Hashoftim** (✉ 39 Ibn Gvirol St., at the corner of Hashoftim St., ☎ 03/695–1153), one of Israel's first pubs, has stood the test of time. Longtime regulars still hang out here, and newcomers will enjoy the atmosphere.

**Joey's Bar** (✉ 42 Allenby St., ☎ 03/517–9277) is Tel Aviv's ultimate dive joint. Visitors who arrive early can enjoy a drink at the bar, but by midnight, it's a wild, crowded dance party.

**Lemon** (✉ 17 Hanagarim St., ☎ 03/681–3313) is a small place with a nice bar, showcasing a variety of music and often attracting an over-30 crowd (unlike many other Tel Aviv nightspots). It sometimes organizes parties.

**Logus** (✉ 8 Hashomer St., corner of Nahalat Binyamin, ☎ 03/516–1176) has live music inside, for which there's a cover charge, but it's usually loud enough to hear from the mall outside, where food and drinks are also served.

**Lola** (✉ 54 Allenby St., ☎ 03/516–7803) features alternative and electronic music, and a crowd to match.

**My Coffee Cup/Bar 39** (✉ 39 Allenby St.) is an outdoor café by day and a bar by night. It's a great place to check out the fervor of Allenby Street's nightlife scene while being able to hold a conversation.

**Paco** (✉ 87 Yehuda Halevy St., ☎ 03/560–7345) is all bar, but you can get Spanish-style ham and sausages with your drinks.

**Rose** (✉ 147 Yehuda Halevy St., ☎ 03/685–0340) is one of the chicest bars in town. There's good music, too, and an over-30 crowd.

**Scene** (✉ 56 Allenby St., ☎ no phone) is a bar–dance club that specializes in house and techno. The long, dimly lit bar separates the lounge in the front from the dance area in the back. Monday is Gay Night, and on Wednesday internationally known DJs are featured. It's closed on Sunday and Tuesday.

**Swing** (✉ 52 Nahalat Binyamin St., ☎ 03/510–0865) is known for its large, round bar downstairs. Music is generally light.

**Yuazar** (✉ 2 Yuazar Ish Habira, near clock tower, Jaffa, ☎ 03/683–9115), a posh wine bar, is owned and operated by one of Israel's best-known gourmets.

## Gay Bars

Tel Aviv has a thriving gay scene. Independence Park, next to the Hilton Hotel, is one of the hot spots for gay men. It's a perfectly acceptable place to meet, and there is also a gay beach just below the park. The floating, weekly FFF ("Friendly Freedom Friday") parties happen on Friday nights—the location changes from week to week, so ask around at the bars for information. Gay bars come and go even faster than other bars and restaurants, though a few seem to be standing the test of time.

**Cafe Nordau** (✉ 145 Ben Yehuda St., ☎ 03/524–0134) is one of the oldest establishments around, with especially good cakes.

**HESHE** (✉ 8 Hashomer St., ☎ 03/510–0914) attracts a younger crowd, mostly 18–25, with its informal atmosphere and popular music.

**Minerva** (✉ 20 Beit Hamoshava St., ☎ 03/566–6051) is a fashionable lesbian bar with its own art gallery and a decent menu.

**Out Bar** (✉ 45 Nachlat Binyamin St., ☎ 03/560–2391) is a two-floor bar and club, popular among the over-25 crowd and best known for its nightly theme parties.

# The Arts

Tel Aviv is Israel's cultural capital, and it fulfills this role with relish. Like New York, the city is full of people who devote their lives to the arts without necessarily getting paid for it. It's entirely likely that your waitress, taxi driver, or salesperson is also a struggling actor, painter, or musician.

You can purchase tickets to events at the box office or through one of Tel Aviv's three major ticket agencies:

**Hadran** (✉ 90 Ibn Gvirol St., ☎ 03/527–9955), **Castel** (✉ 153 Ibn Gvirol St., ☎ 03/604–4725), and **Le'an** (✉ 101 Dizengoff St., ☎ 03/524–7373).

All accept major credit cards. You must pick up your tickets in person. Although there is never a shortage of events in Tel Aviv, some of the arts—opera in particular—are still developing. The Friday editions of the English-language *Jerusalem Post* and *Ha'aretz* contain extensive entertainment listings for the entire country.

## Dance

Most of Israel's dance groups, including the contemporary Bat Sheva Dance Company, perform in the **Suzanne Dellal Center for Dance and Theater** (✉ 6 Yehieli St., Neve Tzedek, ☎ 03/510–5656), and Neve Tzedek itself is home to artists and a growing number of trendy galleries and gift shops. A visit here is a cultural experience, as the complex itself is an example of new Israeli architectural styles used to restore some of the oldest buildings in Tel Aviv. (For more about Neve Tzedek, *see* Exploring Tel Aviv, *above*.)

## Music

The **Enav Cultural Center** (✉ Gan Ha'Ir [roof level], 71 Ibn Gvirol St., ☎ 03/528–9163) is a more intimate venue, also with eclectic fare.

**Bet Mayumana** (✉ 15 Louis Pasteur St., Jaffa, ☎ 03/681–1787) is home to Israel's answer to Stomp, a troupe of drummers who bang in perfect synchronicity on anything from garbage pails to the floor. Performances are held on Friday and Saturday, and tickets cost NIS 125 ($30).

The **Mann Auditorium** (✉ 1 Huberman St., ☎ 03/528–9163), Israel's largest concert hall, is home to the Israel Philharmonic Orchestra from the end of October through the beginning of August. Concert prices range from NIS 120 to NIS 290 ($29 to $71; for tickets, call 03/621–1777). It is also possible to catch an occasional rock, pop, or jazz concert here.

Large outdoor concerts are held in the open air in **Hayarkon Park** (☎ 03/642–2828); within the park is a smaller venue called the Wohl Amphitheater.

## Opera

The **Tel Aviv Performing Arts Center** (✉ 28 Leonardo da Vinci St., ☎ 03/692–7700) is home to the budding New Israeli Opera during the October-to-June season. Tickets are available at the box office (☎ 03/692–7777).

## Theater

Performances are almost always in Hebrew.

Most of the plays at **Bet Liessin** (✉ 34 Weizmann St., ☎ 03/695–6222) are by Israeli playwrights. The **Cameri Theater** (✉ 101 Dizengoff St., ☎ 03/524–5211) sometimes offers simultaneous (taped) English translations. **Habimah** (✉ Habimah Sq., ☎ 03/526–6666) is the national theater; plays here are all in Hebrew, but some have simultaneous translation. **Hasimta Theater** (✉ 8 Mazal Dagim St., ☎ 03/681–2126), in Old Jaffa, features avant-garde and fringe performances.

# OUTDOOR ACTIVITIES AND SPORTS

## Beaches

Beaches in the heart of the city are free. Hatzuk, on the northern edge of Tel Aviv, charges an entrance fee, as do the beaches in Herzliya (except Sidney Ali).

Beaches are generally named after something nearby—a street or a hotel, for example. Thus, you have Hilton Beach in front of the hotel of that name, Gordon Beach at the end of Gordon Street, and likewise Bograshov Beach. Sometimes, however, this gets a bit confusing: Sheraton Beach is at the site of the first Sheraton Hotel in Tel Aviv, about 1 km (½ mi) north of today's Sheraton; and Jerusalem Beach, at the bottom of Allenby Road, is named after the city, not after something in Tel Aviv.

When choosing a beach, look for one with timber lifeguard huts, where first aid is available. Lifeguards are on duty from roughly May to October, from 7 AM until between 4 PM and 7 PM, depending on the month (check with your hotel's concierge). Be forewarned: Tel Aviv's lifeguards are fond of yelling commands over the loudspeakers if they think swimmers are misbehaving. Most beaches have public amenities, including bathrooms and changing rooms, and many have kiosks and the omnipresent ice cream man, who paces up and down the sand proffering his treats throughout the summer.

## Participant Sports

### Boating

**Yehoshua Gardens (Hayarkon Park)** (☎ 03/642–0541), in the northern part of the city, rents out pedal boats and rowboats (NIS 50, or $12.50, per hour) and motorboats (NIS 70, or $17, per half hour). You can also opt for pleasure boats, which take up to 100 people for 15-minute rides (NIS 8, or $2, per person); bicycles; or tandems that take up to six people.

### Health Clubs

Most of the city's luxury hotels have health clubs, normally free for guests.

The Cybex Spa at the **Hilton** (✉ Hayarkon St., ☎ 03/520–2291) has the largest gym and is open to nonguests; the fee for each visit is NIS 102 ($25). The club is open Sunday–Thursday 6:30 AM–11 AM and 1 PM–9 PM (Friday 1–5 PM).

The **Gordon Health Club** (✉ 165 Hayarkon St., at the end of Gordon St., ☎ 03/527–1555), a Tel Aviv institution since the 1950s, includes an outdoor Olympic-size saltwater pool, a gym, and a sauna. Entrance to the health club, including use of the pool, costs NIS 85 ($20.75). Admission to the pool alone costs NIS 45 ($11). You must present a passport. It's open Sunday to Thursday 6:30 AM–10 PM, Fri. 6:30 AM–7 PM, and Sat. 6:30 AM–4 PM; the pool is open daily, 5 AM–7 PM.

### Sailing

The **Sea Center** (✉ Tel Aviv Marina, ☎ 03/522–4079, with another branch at the Hilton) rents out sailboats and windsurfing equipment by the hour. Windsurf rentals cost NIS 80 ($20) per hour; kayaks, NIS 70 ($17) per hour; sailboats, NIS 185 ($45) per hour; and catamarans, NIS 250 ($61) per hour. The unskilled can take private windsurfing lessons or a one-hour surf-kayaking course for NIS 150 ($36.60).

### Scuba Diving

The **Dugit Diving Center** (✉ Tel Aviv Old Port, ☎ 03/546–8498) is located at the end of the Old Port and serves as a popular meeting place for veteran divers. Although the view beneath the surface of the Mediterranean Sea doesn't offer as breathtaking an array of fish and coral as the Red Sea, it's a good place to start. A one-hour introductory course costs NIS 150 ($36.60). Diving equipment is available for rent on a daily basis to licensed divers.

### Swimming

The **Gordon Health Club** (☎ 03/527–1555) has an Olympic-size saltwater pool, a real Tel Aviv landmark (☞ Health Clubs, *above*). The pool is open daily 5 AM–7 PM; admission is NIS 45 ($11).

### Waterskiing

**Park Darom** (☎ 03/739–1168), in southern Tel Aviv, runs waterskiing without boats: cables attached to a revolving crane pull you around an artificial lake, a system that holds no appeal for some but is particularly good for beginners. Costs are around NIS 55 ($13.40) for half an hour, including instruction. It's open daily from April through October, but hours vary, so call in advance.

## Spectator Sports

**Yad Eliyahu Stadium** (☎ 03/537–6376) is the place to go for basketball games. **Bloomfield Stadium** (✉ 1 Hatehiya St., Jaffa, ☎ 03/682–1276) hosts soccer matches. The **Israel Football Stadium** (✉ Abba Hillel Rd., ☎ 03/579–9966), in nearby Ramat Gan, is another venue for soccer.

# SHOPPING

Tel Aviv's shopping scene has made rapid advances in recent years, as prosperous Israelis have begun demanding higher-quality goods.

## Department Stores

The French **Galleries Lafayette** now has a branch in the Azrieli Center, but unlike its "parent" in Paris, it stocks only clothes and cosmetics.

**Hamashbir** (✉ Dizengoff Center, Dizengoff and King George Sts., ☎ 03/528–5136) carries, for the most part, a rather banal selection of goods, often at prices a little higher than those in smaller stores. On the second floor, however, its Designer Avenue features women's clothing by local designers, who also have boutiques at the northern end of Dizengoff Street or in the surrounding area—sample the range here, and then ask for the address if you'd like to see more of a particular designer's line.

## Shopping Districts and Malls

**Allenby Street,** a less affluent strip in the southern part of the city, offers some real bargains on clothes, jewelry (especially gold), and Judaica (religious and decorative objects).

**Dizengoff Center** (✉ Dizengoff and King George Sts.), Israel's first shopping mall, is multilevel and somewhat confusing to navigate at first.

It bursts with stores selling everything from air conditioners to camping equipment, with many a fashion boutique and gift shop in between.

The northern end of **Dizengoff Street** is lined with the avant-garde bridal shops and the boutiques of some of Israel's most innovative designers. There are also several suit stores for men in this area. Clothing stores become trendier and less expensive as you head south.

**Kikar Hamedina,** in northern Tel Aviv, is arguably the most expensive real estate in the country; this is where the wealthy shop. Hit the shops on this circular street for, say, a Sonia Rykiel or Chanel suit, perhaps a Kenzo creation, or a pound of Godiva chocolates. The middle of the square is an unkempt plaza that, alas, is the perfect foil to the luxury surrounding it but does nothing to bring prices down.

**Opera Tower** (✉ 1 Allenby St.), near the sea, has a small but eclectic range of stores. It's particularly good for jewelry. The Tower Records on the ground floor is a great place to find local music.

Malls have mushroomed here in recent years. They include **Gan Ha'Ir** (✉ 71 Ibn Gvirol St.), **Azrieli Center** (✉ Hashalom Rd., above the railway station), **Ramat Aviv Mall** (✉ 40 Einstein St.), and **Canion Ayalon** (✉ Ramat Gan).

## Specialty Stores

### Jewelry, Judaica, and Ethnic Crafts

**Ben Yehuda Street** is lined with gift shops that specialize in Judaica, especially between Gordon and Bograshov streets. You can find good prices on gold in the many hole-in-the-wall jewelry stores on **Allenby Street.** For silver, hit the **Nahalat Binyamin** street fair on Tuesday or Friday (☞ Street Markets, *below*). Shop for sophisticated gems and jewels at **H. Stern,** with branches in the David Inter-Continental, Daniel, Sheraton Tel Aviv, Hilton, and Dan hotels.

### Swimwear

Although swimsuits and accessories sometimes cost less in the United States than in their country of origin, it's worth checking out the stores here.

Tel Aviv–based **Gideon Oberson** (✉ 36 Gordon St., ☎ 03/524–3822) is well known. **Gottex** (✉ 148 Dizengoff St., ☎ 03/524–5383) is internationally known for its designer swimwear. For more of a bargain, visit Tel Aviv's three bathing-suit factory outlets, in Yad Eliyahu near the Cinerama arena: **Gottex** (✉ 62 Anilvich St., ☎ 03/688–8476), **Oberson** (✉ 8 Nirim St., ☎ 03/537–5784), and **Pilpel** (✉ 3 Nirim St., ☎ 03/639–6151).

## Street Markets

At the **Nahalat Binyamin** street fair, held Tuesday and Friday, local crafts ranging from handmade puppets to olive-wood sculptures and silver jewelry attract throngs of shoppers and browsers (☞ Exploring Tel Aviv, *above*). The **shuk hapishpeshim,** in Jaffa, is mostly full of junk these days, but you can still find a bargain, even if it's not an authentic antique. The flea market has a wide selection of reasonably priced Middle Eastern–style jewelry that uses chains of small silver coins and imitation stones.

# TEL AVIV A TO Z

## Arriving and Departing

### By Bus

Bus travel in Israel is generally very convenient. The main interurban bus company, **Egged** (☎ 03/694–8888), operates primarily from Tel

Aviv's **Central Bus Station** (⊠ Levinsky St.) but also from the **Central Railway Station** (⊠ Arlosoroff St.). The Central Bus Station may look like a big, confusing marketplace, but the bus service is actually very efficient. (Buses leave for Jerusalem every 15 minutes throughout most of the day.) You can purchase your ticket at the booth on each platform (signs at each platform indicate destinations) or, if your booth is closed, from the driver on the bus. Only the Eilat line requires advance reservations—particularly necessary in peak season.

## By Plane

Israel's international airport is **Ben-Gurion** (☎ 03/971–0111), 16 km (10 mi) southeast of Tel Aviv. All international flights to Israel land here, except for charters to Eilat. The airport is modern and efficient and is served by most major American and European carriers, with frequent and convenient connections to major cities around the world.

From **Sde Dov Airport** (☎ 800/444–888), 4 km (2½ mi) north of the city center, the domestic airline Arkia flies to Eilat (some 10 flights per day), Jerusalem (3 flights), Haifa (3 flights), and the Upper Galilee (2 flights or more).

### BETWEEN BEN-GURION AND CITY CENTER

**United Bus 222** (☎ 03/971–1711) runs between the airport and the city roughly every hour from 4 AM to midnight on weekdays and on Saturday at 45-minute intervals from noon to midnight. From the airport it stops at the Central Railway Station (⊠ Arlosoroff St.), the youth hostel (⊠ Weizmann St.), and numerous points along the promenade, Tel Aviv's main hotel strip. The fare is NIS 16 ($4) from downtown Tel Aviv and NIS 12 ($3) from Arlosoroff.

**Bus 475,** a local, runs to the Central Bus Station (Platform 613) from 5:30 AM to 11:30 PM. The fare is NIS 10 ($2.50). Like all state-run buses, it does not run on the Sabbath (Friday afternoon to Saturday evening) or on holidays.

**Tal Limousine Service** (⊠ Ben-Gurion Airport, ☎ 03/972–1701, FAX 03/972–1705) can supply a limousine (that is, a van that can hold up to seven people) and driver for the trip into Tel Aviv for NIS 134 ($32.70). It's slightly cheaper to go from Tel Aviv to the airport, because the driver has to pay taxes only to exit the airport.

There is a fixed tariff for **taxis** from the airport into town (and vice versa); it's printed in a booklet that the driver carries. Verify the price before you get in, and don't let the driver switch the meter on: the rate is NIS 75 ($18.30), going up to NIS 85 ($20.75) after 9 PM and on the Sabbath. The price includes one piece of baggage per person; for each additional piece there is a baggage charge of NIS 2.50 (70¢). The airport has a supervised taxi stand. To arrange for a taxi from Tel Aviv to the airport, call **Castel Taxi** (☎ 03/699–2233), or check with your hotel.

### BETWEEN SDE DOV AND CITY CENTER

City **Bus 26** runs between Sde Dov and the Central Bus Station every 10–15 minutes, following Ibn Gvirol Street. The fare is NIS 4.70 ($1.15). There is no service on the Sabbath or on holidays. Taxi is the most convenient way to get from Sde Dov to the center of town; the fare is determined by the meter (unlike from Ben-Gurion, where it's a fixed rate) but should be about NIS 25 ($6.20), excluding baggage charge.

## By Sherut

*Sherut* taxis are a fleet of stretch Mercedes-Benzes at the Central Bus Station that run the same routes as the buses, at comparable one-way prices (unlike buses, sheruts do not offer round-trip tickets). The "schedule" of arrivals and departures is determined by how long it takes to fill all seven seats of each car. You'll find sheruts at various points (depending on destination) in front of the bus platforms; you can usually hear someone yelling the destination before you even approach. (If you don't, try yelling yourself—someone is sure to point you in the right direction.) Sheruts do run on Saturday, but for more money.

### By Train
Train travel is not as common as bus travel in Israel, yet this is one of the most scenic and relaxing ways to travel between Tel Aviv and cities and towns to the north, such as Netanya, Hadera, Haifa, and Nahariya. The northbound train leaves the **Central Railway Station** (✉ Arlosoroff St., ☎ 03/577–4000). The information office is open Sunday to Thursday 6 AM–9 PM and Friday 6–2. Trains run roughly every hour on weekdays from 6 AM to 8 PM; there are fewer trains on Friday and holiday eves and no service on Saturday or on holidays. There is also a line to and from Beersheva. Timetables are available in English at all rail stations. Note that the Tel Aviv–Jerusalem line is undergoing renovations and is currently out of service.

## Getting Around

### By Bus
The city bus system is well developed, with lines run primarily by the Dan bus cooperative, as well as by Egged. The fare is a fixed NIS 4.70 ($1.15) within the city center, and you buy your tickets on the bus. If you think you might use the buses between 21 and 25 times during your stay, you can buy a *kartisia,* which offers 11 journeys for the price of 10. Remember, however, that Dan's kartisia is only good for Dan lines and Egged's for Egged (but you'll be able to use the Egged ticket in other cities).

Two of the major lines, Bus 4 (Ben Yehuda and Allenby streets) and Bus 5 (Dizengoff Street and Rothschild Boulevard), are also serviced by privately run red minibuses. You can flag these down and ask to get off at any point along their routes; the fare is the same as on regular buses. Minibuses also run on Saturday, when regular buses do not.

### By Car
Driving in Tel Aviv is not recommended, especially if you get nervous on the road. Aside from the aggressive tactics of other drivers, Tel Aviv's layout seems more the creation of an absentminded philosopher than a city planner. Moreover, many of Tel Aviv's main streets are only accessible to taxis and public transportation vehicles during the day. Some street names may not be marked in English—or, indeed, at all—which makes getting to your destination nothing short of a headache. Parking is yet another problem, and the last thing you want is to deal with the Israeli bureaucracy if your illegally parked car has been booted (clamped) or towed.

Tel Aviv is more fun on foot, anyway. Most attractions and sights are in the heart of the city within walking distance of one another; and when you get tired, a bus or taxi is never far away.

### By Taxi
Taxis here can be any car model or color; they're identified by lighted signs on top. Cabs are plentiful, even in bad weather; drivers will honk their horns to catch your attention, even if you're not trying to catch theirs. If you're traveling within the metropolitan area, make sure the driver turns the meter on when you get into the car. Rates are NIS 7.70 ($1.90) for the first 18 seconds and 30 agorot (7¢) in increments thereafter. For interurban trips, there is a fixed tariff; if you think you're being quoted a price that's too high, ask to see the tariff in the

booklet each driver carries. Expect night rates to be about 25% higher than day rates. Tipping taxi drivers is not customary in Israel.

# Contacts and Resources

## Car Rental

Rental agencies include **Budget** (⊠ Dan Hotel, 99 Hayarkon St., ☎ 03/523–1551); **Eldan** (⊠ 112 Hayarkon St., ☎ 03/527–1166), Israel's largest rental company; and **Hertz** (⊠ Sheraton Hotel, 115 Hayarkon St., ☎ 03/527–1881)

## Dentists

**Ichilov Hospital** (⊠ Weizmann St., ☎ 03/697–3696 or 03/697–3676) has dental service Sunday, Monday, and Wednesday 8–7, Tuesday and Thursday 8–1. The **dental clinic** inside the Dizengoff Center (⊠ Gate 3, 50 Dizengoff St., ☎ 03/629–6716 or 050/502–050) is open daily from 8 AM to 10 PM.

## Embassies

**U.S. Embassy** (⊠ 71 Hayarkon St., ☎ 03/519–7575). **U.K. Embassy** (⊠ 1 Ben Yehuda St., ☎ 03/510–0166). **Canadian Embassy** (⊠ 9 Hashlosha St., ☎ 03/636–3300). **Australian Embassy** (⊠ Europe House, 37 Shaul Hamelech St., ☎ 03/695–0451). **New Zealand Honorary Consulate** (⊠ 3 Daniel Frish St., ☎ 03/695–1869).

## Emergencies

**Ambulance** (☎ 101). **Fire** (☎ 102). **Police** (☎ 100).

**Magen David Adom** (⊠ 2 Alkalai St., ☎ 03/546–0111) provides 24-hour emergency first aid.

**Emergency calls** are free at public phones; no tokens or telecards are necessary.

### HOSPITAL

The casualty ward of **Ichilov Hospital** (⊠ Weizmann St., ☎ 03/697–4444) has 24-hour emergency service. Bring your passport.

### POLICE

The main **police stations** are at 14 Harakevet Street, near the Central Bus Station (☎ 03/564–4444), and 221 Dizengoff Street (☎ 03/545–4444). Harakevet Street also has a lost-and-found.

## English-Language Bookstores

**Steimatzky** (⊠ 107 Allenby St., ☎ 03/566–4277; ⊠ 109 Dizengoff St., ☎ 03/522–1513) is Israel's best-known chain, with several Tel Aviv locations and a large selection of books in English.

## Guided Tours

### BOAT TOURS

**Kef** (⊠ Jaffa Port, ☎ 03/682–9070) and **Sababa 5** (⊠ Jaffa Port, ☎ 03/681–6739) run hourly boat tours (weekends and summer evenings) from the Jaffa Port to the Tel Aviv Marina and back. Fare is around $4.90.

### ORIENTATION TOURS

**Egged Tlalim** (⊠ 59 Ben Yehuda St., ☎ 03/527–1212) and **United** (⊠ 113 Hayarkon St., ☎ 03/522–2008) bus companies offer half-day tours of Tel Aviv for $30 per person. The tour takes in Old Jaffa and the flea market, the Mann Auditorium, Yitzhak Rabin Square, the Oppenheimer Diamond Museum, and the Eretz Israel Museum.

### PERSONAL GUIDES

**Twelve Tribes** (⊠ 29 Hamered St., ☎ 03/510–1911, FAX 03/510–1943) provides personal guides, usually with a car, who will take you anywhere in the city and even around the country. Personal guides can also be arranged through most hotels.

WALKING TOURS

The Tel Aviv–Jaffa municipality has laid out four self-guided tours of the city called the **Tapuz (Orange) Routes**; these take in both historic and current cultural sites. Maps are available from the Tel Aviv Tourist Information Office in the Central Bus Station (☞ Visitor Information, *below*). Free, city-sponsored walking tours of **Old Jaffa** begin at the clock tower on Wednesday at 9 AM; no prior registration is required.

## Late-Night Pharmacies

Pharmacies take turns keeping late hours, and the duty roster changes daily. Check the *Jerusalem Post* or *Ha'aretz* for those currently on call.

## Travel Agencies

Ben Yehuda Street, in central Tel Aviv, is full of travel agencies large and small. Among the biggest are the following:

**Diesenhaus** (⊠ 21 Ben Yehuda St., ☎ 03/517–2140) and **Ophir Tours** (⊠ 32 Ben Yehuda St., ☎ 03/526–9777). **Issta** (⊠ 128 Ben Yehuda St., ☎ 03/521–0555) specializes in student travel.

## Visitor Information

The **tourist bureau** at Ben-Gurion Airport is open 24 hours. You'll find the latest local information at the **Tel Aviv Tourist Information Office** (⊠ Store No. 6108, Central Bus Station, Levinsky St., 6th floor, ☎ 03/639–5660, FAX 03/639–5659), open Sunday to Thursday 9–5, Friday 9–1. They can also provide a list, albeit not comprehensive, of *zimmerim* (bed-and-breakfast-type accommodations) and youth hostels.

# 4 NORTHERN COAST AND WESTERN GALILEE

*Including Haifa, Caesarea, and Akko*

North of Tel Aviv and up to the border with Lebanon lies the only part of Israel where you can drive for long stretches with unimpeded views of the Mediterranean. Coastal cities speak from the past: Caesarea, a 2,000-year-old port, was built by King Herod, and the vast underground ruins of the ancient walled city of Akko hark back to Crusader victories. Mt. Carmel meets the sea in the city of Haifa, where steep streets climb to sharp, white hotel towers at the crest of Mt. Carmel, a backdrop for the sparkling golden dome of the Baha'i Shrine.

By Karen
Wolman

Updated by
Judy Stacey
Goldman

**S**TRETCHED TAUT ON A NARROW COASTAL STRIP between Tel Aviv and the chalky cliffs of the Lebanese border, this region offers more than just balmy Mediterranean beaches. Sand and sea meet archaeology here—historical sights line the shore along with the gently undulating dunes, fields, and citrus groves of the Sharon Plain, a fertile swath encompassing Netanya, Hadera, and Caesarea that was converted from a wasteland of malarial swamp early in the 20th century by Jewish pioneers. Today, Caesarea is a delightful resort full of whitewashed villas and romantically crumbling Roman and Crusader ruins. The arches of an ancient aqueduct disappear into the sand, and Israeli children splash in the cove in summertime, heedless of the feats of King Herod's engineers.

It was in the softly contoured foothills and valleys at the base of Mt. Carmel that the philanthropic Baron Edmond de Rothschild came to the Jews' succor in helping Israel create a wine industry, still one of its most successful enterprises. The Carmel range rises dramatically to its pine-covered heights over the coast of Haifa, a friendly, hardworking, thoroughly modern port city. Haifa was the site of some heartrending and historic scenes in the decade prior to Israel's independence: scores of ragtag ships filled with Jewish refugees fleeing Nazi persecution were turned away by the British just off the shore of Haifa, within view of relatives and residents. North of Haifa is the Western Galilee, which runs along a fertile plain up to the Lebanese border. Just across the sweeping arc of Haifa Bay lies Akko, a jewel of a Crusader city that combines Romanesque ruins, Muslim domes and minarets, and swaying palms. To the north are the resort town of Nahariya, popular with Israelis and, just under the Lebanese border, the amazing seaside caves at Rosh Hanikra, scooped from the cliff by the pounding waves.

As the scenery changes, so does the ethnic mix of the residents and their ancestors: Druze, Carmelite monks, Ottomans, Baha'is, Christian and Muslim Arabs, and Jews. Paleontologists continue to study on-site the artifacts of the most ancient natives of all, the prehistoric people of the caves of Nahal Me'arot, on Mt. Carmel. In Haifa, a city of Jews and Arabs, you'll also meet the region's latest arrivals, Jews from the former Soviet Union. The Baha'is, whose universalist religion embraces the teachings of many others, dominate Haifa's mountainside. Their golden temple gleams, and their terraced gardens decorate the slopes like bright jewels. Robed Carmelite monks preside quietly over their monasteries in Haifa and in Mukhraka, on Mt. Carmel, next door to the Druze villages. Although the north-coast Druze consider themselves an integral part of Israeli society, they maintain a unique cultural and religious enclave on Mt. Carmel, with the secret rites and rituals of their faith and the distinctive handlebar moustaches and white head scarves favored by the older men. Arabs and Jews live side by side in Akko, whose dilapidated, cramped, and dusty old quarter belies its pristine, picture-postcard reputation. Yet Akko's vast subterranean Crusader vaults and halls, Ottoman skyline of domes and minarets, and outdoor *shuk* (market), awhirl with fascinating colors and sounds, can still enchant. After two centuries of rule, the warriors' tenuous hold over Palestine came to a close when they were chased out in 1291 with the fall of Akko to Egypt's powerful Mamluk dynasty.

Running the length of the region up to Haifa are two main highways: Route 2, a multilane thoroughfare that gets you from Tel Aviv to Haifa in just over an hour, and the inland Route 4, otherwise known as the Old Haifa Road. Route 4 continues all the way to the border. Most sights are a short drive from one of these roads. In the spring, you'll pass fields ablaze with the color of wild anemones, tulips, and butter-cups; cyclamen and narcissus grow higher up. And you don't have to be an ornithologist to appreciate the variety of birds here, sometimes perched casually on telephone wires. Flocks of storks, pelicans, herons, cormorants, and ducks pass through every spring and fall on their migratory routes between Europe and Africa.

# Pleasures and Pastimes

## Archaeology

It's said that wherever you put down a shovel in Israel, you'll find ancient ruins. Even onetime visitors to Caesarea have found old coins after a rainfall, when the surface earth is washed away. Archaeologists continue to uncover history, while restorers lovingly assemble shards and patch up ancient buildings. Caesarea and Akko are two of Israel's star archaeological sites, where even repeat visitors are amazed to find new and stunning discoveries each time. Such museums as the underwater archaeology museum at Nachsholim-Dor and the Hecht Museum at Haifa University display finds in unusually engaging style. And Herod's fabulous port, which subsided beneath the Ceasarea waters 2,000 years ago, beckons scuba divers to an underwater tour.

## Arts

On many a balmy summer night in towns up and down the coast, you're bound to find an outdoor concert or dance performance. In summer, the performances held under the stars on the reconstructed stage of Caesarea's are particularly memorable; in other seasons, catch chamber music in Ein Hod and Zichron Ya'akov. For printed listings, check the Friday issue of the *Jerusalem Post* or pick up a copy of the monthly brochure "Events in Haifa and the Northern Region," available at hotels and tourist offices.

## Beaches

Between Tel Aviv and the Lebanese border are miles of beautiful sandy beaches, most of them public and attended by lifeguards from early May to mid-October. Many Israeli beaches are left untended off-season and get pretty grubby as a result, but they're generally cleaned up and well maintained once warm weather returns. *Never* swim in the absence of a lifeguard, as the currents and undertows can be dangerous.

## Dining

You won't have to look hard in this region for a restaurant with either a striking view of the Mediterranean or good fresh fish, or both. These range in style from fishing-shack to chic. The fish you'll most often find on your menu—served grilled or baked, with a variety of sauces—are *locus* (grouper), *mulit* (red mullet), *churi* (red snapper), and *farida* (sea bream). Also fresh, but hailing from commercial fishponds and the Sea of Galilee, are *buri* (gray mullet) and the ubiquitous *tilapia* (St. Peter's fish), as well as the hybrid *iltit* (salmon-trout). Fresh seafood, such as shrimp and calamari, is also to be found in restaurants along the coast.

Until recently, coastal restaurants weren't as refined as those in Tel Aviv, with a few exceptions. But a change has taken place in the last year or so. Hilly Haifa, now firmly on the tourist track with the opening of the new Baha'i Garden terraces and the newly restored German Colony, has several brand-new, upscale restaurants with creative young chefs, delicious food, and good wine lists. Wine bars with wine tastings, tasty food, and cigars are also on the Haifa scene. In the village of Zichron Ya'akov, there are no fewer than five classy restaurants on its short, cobblestoned main street. Eating ethnic food is always a pleasure: you can sample the locally famous falafel in the Druze village of Daliyat el Carmel or try hearty dishes at down-home, family-run eastern European restaurants in Haifa. Netanya has the region's highest concentration of kosher establishments.

Even at the most expensive restaurants in this region, dress is informal (but tasteful). Ties are never required.

| CATEGORY | COST* |
|---|---|
| $$$$ | over $35 |
| $$$ | $22–$35 |
| $$ | $12–$22 |
| $ | under $12 |

*per person for a three-course meal, excluding drinks, service, and sales tax

## Hiking and Walking

Magnificent parks and nature reserves grace the coastal area, both along the Mediterranean shore and in the hilly areas to the east. The largest of these is the flourishing Carmel Park, which comprises 20,000 hilly acres and covers the top of Mt. Carmel. Several parks and reserves have visitor centers, where staff can explain maps and trails, and all have parking lots, rest rooms, and picnic areas. Though parks and reserves are generally not signposted from the road in English, you can spot the entrances by looking for distinctive dark wooden boards with white or yellow letters.

## Lodging

Options range from small and spare to luxury hotels, though you won't find nearly the selection and quality of deluxe accommodations comparable to those in, say, Tel Aviv. The region does have a splendid spa hotel near Haifa. In some places, such as Akko, the pickings are slim indeed; but because this region is so compact, you can cover many sights along the coast from a single base.

The chart below lists peak-season prices, which normally kick in for July and August; Passover, Rosh Hashanah, and Yom Kippur; and Hanukkah (☞ National and Religious Holidays *in* Chapter 9). There are variations, however, so be sure to inquire at each hotel. In addition, many hotels are considerably less expensive—sometimes 40% less— during low season, from November through February.

Camping facilities, including some bungalows and cabins, dot the coastline north of Netanya. Note that the wooded slopes of Carmel National Park, however inviting, do not have facilities. Contact the tourist office in Tel Aviv or Haifa (*see* Visitor Information *in* Northern Coast and Western Galilee A to Z, *below, and in* Tel Aviv A to Z *in* Chapter 3 for complete lists of campgrounds and maps as well as a brochure on "Isra-chalets" and bungalows).

| CATEGORY | COST* |
|---|---|
| $$$$ | over $120 |
| $$$ | $80–$120 |
| $$ | $55–$80 |
| $ | under $55 |

*All prices are for a standard double room, including breakfast and excluding service charge.

## Wine

Wine lovers, take note: this is one of the country's prime wine-growing areas (its classification is "Shomron"). Though wine has been produced in Israel for thousands of years, and the Rothschilds updated viniculture around Zichron Ya'akov some 120 years ago, truly high-quality wines have appeared on the market only in the last decade or so. The Zichron Ya'akov Carmel Winery's best (and most expensive) wines are those in the Rothschild series, whose best vintage, in turn, is the 1985 cabernet sauvignon. Also distinctive are the wines of the less exclusive Selected series, especially the chardonnay. Israelis enjoy the semi-dry Emerald Riesling, fruity and aromatic.

# Exploring the Northern Coast and Western Galilee

Starting from Tel Aviv, Route 2 (the Coastal Road) hugs the coast, introducing travelers to the northern coast via Netanya, Caesarea, and Haifa, with archaeological sites Nachsholim-Dor and Atlit in between. Zigzagging along to the east, parallel to Route 2 (at the most about 10 km, or 6 mi, away), is Route 4, also known as the Old Road. Just off Route 4 is the Rothschild wine country—the scenic back-door route to Haifa—which meanders through the foothills and up the spine of Mt. Carmel, taking in Shuni, Zichron Ya'akov, the Carmel Park, the Carmelite monastery at Mukhraka, and two Druze villages near Haifa. (A branch of Route 4, going north and then inland, winds through the huge Carmel National Park and later connects with Route 672, leading to the Druze villages.) Haifa is Israel's third-largest city and is a good base for two other sights to the south, Ein Hod and the Carmel Caves. The Western Galilee is the area north of Haifa, including Akko, Nahariya, and Rosh Hanikra, with several sights along the way and inland. All sights in this region are within easy driving distance of Caesarea and Haifa, the former a quiet overnight spot and the latter a thriving city.

## Great Itineraries

Remember to allow time for swimming, hiking, or golfing if you're so inclined. Here the Mediterranean coast is lined with beaches, the land is packed with scenic trails, and Caesarea has Israel's only golf course. Less-conventional sporting options include paragliding and underwater diving to shipwrecks.

*Numbers in the text correspond to number in the margin and on the Northern Coast and Western Galilee map.*

IF YOU HAVE 2 DAYS

For a quick tour of the highlights, start with King Herod's port city, **Caesarea** ②, bursting with Roman, Byzantine, and Crusader ruins. Then travel through Rothschild wine country, in the rolling Carmel Hills, and **Benyamina** ⑱, one of the area's first settlements. Set aside several hours to half a day for the pioneer village of **Zichron Ya'akov** ⑳ and the picturesque Druze villages of **Daliyat el Carmel** ㉓ and **Isfiya** ㉔. Stay overnight in modern 🕅 **Haifa** ⑤–⑰, atop Mt. Carmel. The next day, get an early start so you can see the Baha'i Shrine and Gardens on your way down the hill and out of Haifa. Head north to the walled Crusader city of **Akko** ㉗–㉟, and after a late lunch, head up to the Lebanese border and watch the waves crash through the caves at **Rosh Hanikra** ㊴.

IF YOU HAVE 3 DAYS

Start with a visit to the **Carmel Wine Cellars** (reserve a tour in advance) and **Zichron Ya'akov** ⑳; then head through the hilly wine country to see the Carmelite Monastery at **Mukhraka** ㉒. Stop at **Daliyat el Carmel** ㉓ en route to 🕅 **Haifa** ⑤–⑰. Bright and early the next morning, visit the Baha'i Shrine and Gardens; then head north to **Akko** ㉗–㉟ and zip up the coast to **Rosh Hanikra** ㊴. Return to Haifa for the night. On the third day, explore the artists' village of **Ein Hod** ㉕ and **Caesarea** ②.

IF YOU HAVE 5 DAYS

On a hot summer's day, stop at **Netanya** ① for a swim beneath the cliffs. Then drive through Rothschild wine country to the restored Roman theater and Ottoman fortress at **Shuni** ⑲, and continue on to the **Carmel Wine Cellars** and the pioneer town of **Zichron Ya'akov** ⑳. Travel through the foothills of Mt. Carmel to the Carmelite Monastery at **Mukhraka** ㉒ and the Druze villages of **Daliyat el Carmel** ㉓ and **Is-fiya** ㉔. Spend the night in 🏨 **Haifa** ⑤–⑰, and devote the next day to exploring the city. On day three, leave Haifa early for the walled Crusader city of **Akko** ㉗–㉟, the Holocaust memorial museum at **Lochamei Hageta'ot** ㊲, and the seaside town of **Nahariya** ㊳. Now that you're almost at the Lebanese border, a short drive north brings you to the incredible sea caves at **Rosh Hanikra** ㊴. If you have energy left, walk up to the medieval castle of **Montfort,** perched high on a wooded mountain. (If not, you can see it long distance from Goren Park.) You can spend the night in Haifa, but you may want to move on to tomorrow's stomping ground, **Caesarea** ②. After exploring the myriad ruins, head south to **Nachsholim-Dor** ③ to see the intriguing Underwater Museum. From here you'll zigzag between Route 2 and Route 4 to see the reconstructed British detention camp at **Atlit** ④, the artists' village of **Ein Hod** ㉕, and the prehistoric **Carmel Caves.** Nearby is the entrance to the **Nahal Me'arot Nature Reserve** ㉖, where you might want to set aside a few hours for a hike on the wooded slopes of Mt. Carmel.

## When to Tour the Northern Coast and Western Galilee

Summer (June–September) is hot here, but there's no humidity, and soft sea and mountain breezes cool things down. Spring (April–May) and fall (October–November) are balmy and crisp. Winter (late December, January, February, and into March) brings cold weather (sun interspersed with rain), while the sea makes the wind chilly. If you have warm clothes, you can wander with impunity.

As in the rest of Israel, hotels and other lodgings tend to fill up on weekends. On Saturdays and national holidays, Israelis themselves hit the road, so it's best to avoid north-to-south travel out of Tel Aviv or Jerusalem altogether, and prepare for big crowds at beaches and sights. If you're taking a two-day trip, and if you have the option, the weekdays (Sunday to Thursday) will give you peace and quiet at hotels and sites. If you can only go on Friday and Saturday, make reservations well in advance.

Summer brings theater and dance to Caesarea's Roman theater and a blues festival to Haifa, usually in July.

# THE NORTHERN COAST

## Netanya

❶ *30 km (18 mi) north of Tel Aviv, off Rte. 2; take second exit (Central Netanya).*

Netanya is a seaside resort, with cliffs above a pristine beach, and the geographic capital of the Sharon Plain. Once a sleepy town of farmers and orange groves, Netanya, named after Jewish philanthropist Nathan Strauss, steadily burgeoned to its present population of 180,000 from a few settlers in 1929.

Though citrus farming is still evident on Netanya's outskirts, there are few traces of small-town charm and few sights to see in the rambling clusters of apartment buildings, some built on the coast itself. Travel-

**Northern Coast and Western Galilee**

Mediterranean Sea

LEBANON

GOLAN HEIGHTS

Jordan R.

Sea of Galilee (Lake Kinneret)

Rosh Hanikra 39
Achziv National Park
Nahariya 38
Kibbutz Lochamei Hageta'ot 37
Baha'i Gardens and Shrine 36
Akko (Acre) 27 — 35
Haifa 5 — 17
Atlit 4
Nachsholim-Dor 3

Montfort
Ma'alot Tarshia
Yechi'am
Meron
Zfat
Hazor HaGelilit

Kiryat Bialik
Kiryat Ata
Neshet
Mt. Carmel
Carmel National Park
Tirat Carmel
Ein Hod 25
26
Daliyat el Carmel 22
Isfiya 24
23
Mukhraka
Nahal Me'arot Nature Reserve 21
Bat Shlomo
N. Oshkon

Karmi'el
Sakhnin
Arraba
Tamra
Shefar'am
Nazareth
Afula
Tiberias
Degania

90
91
89
88
8833
85
85
70
70
79
75
65
77
767
90
87
60
66
4
2
721
672

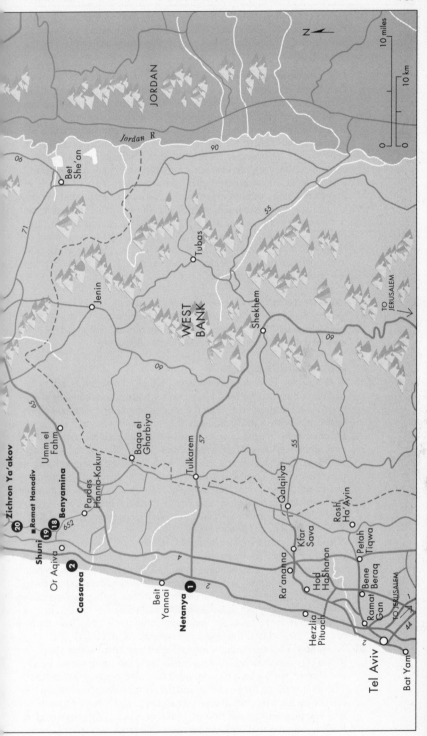

ers come here to revel in consistently sunny days and the sandy public beaches just below the cliffs—ideal for swimming, sunbathing, windsurfing, and paragliding—and the pleasant outdoor cafés on the pedestrian mall.

Lively **Ha'atzmaut Square,** near the beach, is the city's heart, along with the adjoining pedestrian mall. Both are packed with open-air cafés and restaurants that are crowded late into the night, often in the mornings, and all day Friday. The square has just been repaved, and new benches sit among the flower beds and palm trees. A Tourist Information office is located close to the entrance to the beach. Saturday nights are enlivened by folk dancing here, and the amphitheater hosts free concerts in summer and an arts-and-crafts fair on Friday mornings and several other late afternoons each week. Netanya attracts droves of French travelers, and in the summer their lilting tones float above the café au lait and croissants (now popular all over Israel) served in the outdoor cafés. The overall atmosphere is laid back, with nothing buttoned up, and everyone having a good time. To get to your hotel or the beach, drive down the town's main artery, Herzl Street, which ends at the pedestrian mall and Ha'atzmaut Square; access to the beaches is south and north of the mall.

| | |
|---|---|
| OFF THE BEATEN PATH | **FIELDS OF FLOWERS –** In February and March, detour a few kilometers south of the city to see fields carpeted with a rare, exotic variety of deep-indigo **wild iris** indigenous to this area. Marked paths lead the way, and there's a parking lot on Ben-Gurion Boulevard. |

## Dining and Lodging

**$$$$** ✕ **El Gaucho.** Tucked into the Carmel Hotel, El Gaucho is one of Israel's few high-quality (and kosher) steak houses. Decorated in a rustic style, the restaurant is nonetheless dominated by a dramatic view of the sea, with a picturesque garden below. Professional grill man Ernesto, from Uruguay, cooks South American–style meat specialties over embers on a giant grill that forms part of the restaurant. Juicy steaks, grilled chicken, and fish are highlights and are served by very professional waiters. Ask for the extensive wine list. Eating here during daylight hours, or at sunset, is especially recommended because of the breathtaking view of sea and sky. ⊠ *Carmel Hotel, Jabotinsky St.,* ☎ *09/884–1263 or 09/884–1264. Reservations essential. AE, DC, MC, V. No lunch Sat., no dinner Fri.*

**$$$** ✕ **Lucullus.** Tunisian owner Bernard Gabay has run this reliable French restaurant on the southern edge of town for 25 years. (There's also a kosher version, at 5 Ha'atzmaut Square.) Although the menu is French, the ambience is Israeli. Candles and fresh flowers add a touch of class, and there's a pianist in the bar on Friday nights. Gabay recommends his Mediterranean fish dishes, coquilles St. Jacques, or chateaubriand and for dessert the chocolate mousse or profiteroles. ⊠ *2 Jabotinsky St.,* ☎ *09/861–9502. Reservations essential. AE, DC, MC, V.*

**$$** ✕ **Apropo.** This restaurant—something of a glorified coffee shop—is in King George Park and serves a buffet breakfast (until noon), lunch, and dinner overlooking the scalloped coastline below a jutting cliff. There's something for everyone (and the portions are generous) on the eclectic menu: fresh fish, Italian pastas, soups and salads, a variety of omelets, plus a large selection of Thai specialties. All dishes are glatt kosher, meaning that meal preparation undergoes very strict supervision by the *kashrut* authorities. There's a pianist every evening after 9. ⊠ *Gan Hamelech park, at end of Ha'atzmaut Sq.,* ☎ *09/862–4482 or 09/862–4483. Reservations essential. AE, DC, MC, V. No lunch Sat., no dinner Fri.*

$$ ✕ **Yotvata.** Here's the *original* Yotvata, opened 13 years ago and named for the Negev kibbutz whose dairy products are famous nationwide. Farm-fresh products are what you get: salads large enough to be shared by two people, fish dishes, cheeses, sandwiches, and blintzes help stuff the menu, which lists a whopping 200 items. Also available is a special fish business lunch—served all day. The desserts are huge; even the most voracious sweet-lovers will be able to share their portions. The fresh juice drinks (a mixture of several fruits is tasty) and drinks made with yogurt, milk, or cream are generous and refreshing. ⊠ *3 Ha'atzmaut Sq.,* ☎ *09/862–9151. Reservations essential. AE, D, MC, V.*

$$$ 🏨 **Carmel.** Built on a cliff overlooking the Mediterranean, the Carmel makes the most of its beautiful views—the lobby has floor-to-ceiling windows; glass elevators serve the 20 stories; and the decor in the guest rooms reflects the blues and greens of the sea outside. It's attractive and well kept up. Most of the rooms have sea views, each has its own air conditioner, and most have kitchenettes (with dishes, pots, and utensils furnished upon request). The swimming pool, which includes a whirlpool, is covered and heated in winter. It's fun to sit on the lawn and watch the paragliders, who use the the grass as their springboard into the blue. ⊠ *Jabotinsky St., south of Ha'atzmaut Sq.,* ☎ *09/860–1111,* 𝔽𝔸𝕏 *09/860–1171. 200 rooms. Restaurant, lobby lounge, pub, pool, 2 saunas, health club, children's programs. AE, DC, MC, V.*

$$$ 🏨 **Seasons.** Just outside the city center, with stair access to the beach
★ below, the Seasons is well maintained and provides consistently good service. At the lower end of this price range, it's a good value. The hotel was built 30 years ago, but most of the rooms and all of the public areas have been redecorated in the last few years. The bedrooms are quite spacious, with private terraces and sea views; the newer ones, decorated in pleasing pastels, are especially comfortable, and their baths are luxurious. The pool overlooks the sea and is surrounded by gorgeous flower beds and bright yellow chaises. The dining room also has a view of the blue. ⊠ *Nice Blvd., 42269,* ☎ *09/860–1555,* 𝔽𝔸𝕏 *09/862–3022. 94 rooms. Restaurant, coffee shop, pool, hot tub, massage, sauna, tennis court, exercise room. AE, DC, MC, V.* 🐾

$$ 🏨 **Blauweiss.** An imposing building houses this six-year-old hotel, with a white stone Roman motif of columns and pediments on the facade. The beige marble lobby shows a bas-relief of an ancient menorah on one wall, and another of Jerusalem's Old City on another. Guest rooms are in suite style: the "Junior" is one room with sitting area, sleep area, and kitchenette; and the "Suite" has the same facilities, divided into two rooms. Furnishings are modern though simple, and all rooms have balconies with stunning sea views. The lobby opens on to the city's garden promenade, and access to the beach is a stone's throw from the hotel. Though there's no outdoor pool here, the spa is definitely an attraction, and it does have a small indoor pool. The Roman motif continues into the spa, which offers Dead Sea mineral and mud treatments and a full range of massages. ⊠ *22 Gad Machness St., 42279,* ☎ *09/860–3939,* 𝔽𝔸𝕏 *09/860–3940. 8 rooms, 45 suites. Restaurant, lobby lounge, piano bar, kitchenettes, beauty salon, hot tub, massage, 2 saunas, spa, exercise room. AE, DC, MC, V.*

## Outdoor Activities and Sports

Much of the sophisticated equipment at the **Wingate Institute,** Israel's national Center for Sports and Physical Education, 8 km (5 mi) south of Netanya (☎ 09/863–9521), is now available to the public, albeit generally early morning, late afternoon, and late evening. Facilities include a 25-meter pool with a retractable roof, squash courts, tennis courts, and a fitness center. You can even get a full medical checkup in the sports-medicine division.

BEACHES

Standard facilities, including lifeguards, first-aid station, showers, toilets, and changing rooms, are available free at all of Netanya's beaches, which cover 12 km (7 mi) of soft, sandy coastline. Most beaches also rent beach chairs and umbrellas. The main beach, **Sironit,** is open year-round; the parking lot is on the beach, just off Jabotinsky Street south of the main square, and costs NIS 12 ($3) per car. The beach has volleyball nets and two snack bars. South of town is the Orthodox beach **Kiryat Sanz,** where men and women have different bathing days and hours. There's another beach near the **Seasons Hotel,** with a restaurant and refreshment stand as well as standard facilities. **Herzl** is right in front of Ha'atzmaut Square and has a water slide, restaurant, and refreshment stand. **Argamon** has a refreshment stand but no chair or umbrella rentals.

There's a lovely **private beach** (☎ 09/866–6230) 5 km (3 mi) north of Netanya, next to Moshav Bet Yannai. Amenities include grills, picnic tables, a lifeguard in season, toilets, cold showers, and chair and umbrella rentals. There is no entrance fee, but parking costs NIS 16 ($4) per car Sunday–Thursday and NIS 25 ($6.20) on Friday, Saturday, and holidays. Because this beach is only 2,400 ft long and cannot comfortably accommodate crowds, it's wise to come on a weekday.

The beach at **Mikhmoret,** 7½ km (4½ mi) north of Netanya, is very popular. The huge dirt parking lot, which charges NIS 20 ($5) per car, is 1 km (½ mi) after the turnoff from Route 2. There are three lifeguard stations, a restaurant, a café, and chair and umbrella rentals.

HORSEBACK RIDING

The **Ranch** (☎ 09/866–3525) is in northern Netanya, 2 km (1 mi) up the road from the Blue Bay Hotel. It's wise to reserve for Saturday or for moonlight rides on the beach (you'll need at least eight people to make a reservation); you can also take a pastoral ride though orange groves. The stables are open daily 9–6; the cost is NIS 80 ($20) per hour.

PARAGLIDING

If you're between 6 and 60 and want to fly without an engine or a cockpit but with an instructor beside you, call **Dvir Paragliding** (☎ 09/899–0277 or 052/546–077) for a thrilling experience.

## Shopping

Netanya is known for quality diamonds. Shoppers will be dazzled by the profusion of gold and diamond jewelry such as earrings, necklaces, bracelets, and loose stones with international diamond certificates. **Caprice** (✉ 90 Herzl St., ☎ 09/862–4770) is a reliable shop that also sells watches and semiprecious stones. A jewelry store worth visiting is **Inbar Jewelry** (✉ 1 Ussishkin St., ☎ 09/882–2233), known for its special in-house designs. Prices are competitive. The tourist office may be able to recommend other firms currently known for fairness and authenticity.

## Caesarea

❷ *16 km (10 mi) north of Netanya, 49 km (29½ mi) south of Haifa.*

By turns ancient Roman port city, Byzantine capital, and Crusader stronghold, Caesarea marks the northern tip of the Sharon Plain. Chock-full of Roman, Byzantine, and Crusader ruins, it's a delightful place to spend half a day sightseeing followed by a leisurely lunch or a swim at the beach. (Swim only if a lifeguard is on duty.) Stretched out over 3 km (2 mi) are a Roman theater, a Crusader city, and recently discovered Roman-Byzantine remains that include a bathhouse complex, a Herodian amphitheater, parts of Herod's port, and, in the sand dunes themselves, an ancient aqueduct.

Herod the Great gave Caesarea its name, dedicating the magnificent Roman city he built to his patron Augustus Caesar: he called the port itself Sebastos, the Greek translation of Augustus. It was the Roman emperor who had crowned Herod—born to an Idumean family that had converted to Judaism—King of the Jews around 30 BC. Construction began in 22 BC at the site of an ancient Phoenician and Greek port called Strato's Tower. Herod spared nothing in his elaborate designs for the port—a major engineering feat at the time—and the city itself, which included palaces, temples, a theater, a marketplace, a hippodrome, and water and sewage systems. When Caesarea was completed, 12 years later, it was outshone only by Jerusalem. Its population under Herod grew to around 100,000, larger than that of Jerusalem, and the city covered some 164 acres.

In AD 6, a decade after Herod died, Caesarea became the seat of the Roman procurators. Herod's kingdom had originally been divided among his surviving sons, with his eldest, Archelaus, getting Judea and Samaria; but the Romans were unhappy with Archelaus's rule and banished him to Gaul. With Jerusalem predominantly Jewish, the Romans preferred the Hellenistic Caesarea, with its Jewish minority, as the seat of their administration.

Religious harmony did not prevail here. The mixed population of Jews and Gentiles (mainly Greeks and Sytians) repeatedly clashed, with hostilities exploding in the Jewish revolt of AD 66. The first Jewish rebellion was squelched by Vespasian, who was proclaimed emperor here by his legions in AD 69. A year later, his son and co-ruler, Titus, captured and razed Jerusalem and celebrated his brutal suppression of the Jewish revolt. Henceforth Caesarea was a Roman colony and the local Roman capital of Palestine for nearly 600 years. It was here that Peter converted the Roman centurion Cornelius to Christianity—a milestone in the spread of the new faith—and where Paul preached and was imprisoned for two years. In the 2nd century, Rabbi Akiva, the spiritual mentor of the Bar Kochba Revolt, was tortured to death here.

Caesarea is distinguished by well-marked signs in English. The **Roman theater,** along with the port area, is under the aegis of the National Parks Authority. One ticket admits you to both the theater and the Crusader city, so save your stub. At the entrance you can pick up a free brochure with a basic map and layout of the sites. (Be sure to lock your car and keep valuables out of sight.)

Entry to the theater is through one of the vomitoria (arched tunnels that led the public into Roman theaters). Herod's theaters—here and elsewhere in Israel—were the first of their kind in the ancient Near East. Although smaller than the better-preserved Roman theater at Bet She'an (☞ Chapter 5), Caesarea's has become famous in its own right. The theater today seats 3,600 and is a spectacular venue for summer concerts and dance performances (☞ Nightlife and the Arts, *below*). The backdrop of the sea steals any show, especially when set ablaze by the setting sun.

What you see today is predominantly a reconstruction. Only a few of the seats of the *cavea* (where the audience sat) near the orchestra are original, in addition to some of the stairs and the decorative wall at the front of the stage. Just inside the main gate is proof that one of the Roman rulers who spent time here was Pontius Pilate, governor of Judea when Jesus was crucified; it's the only archaeological evidence of the governor's presence in Palestine. The fragmented Latin inscription on a mounted plaque (a replica of the original, which is in the Israel Museum in Jerusalem) is believed to say that "Pontius Pilate, the prefect of Judea, built and dedicated the Tiberieum [probably a temple or shrine dedicated to the Emperor Tiberius] to the Divine Augustus." ☎ 04/636–1358. 🎦 *Theater and Crusader city NIS 18 ($4.50). ☉ Winter, daily 8–4; summer, daily 8–5. Arrive well before closing time.*

In the large area of **ongoing excavations** along the shore, you'll see the streets of a Roman-Byzantine administrative area built over vaults that served as storehouses. Worth a special look are the beautiful and imaginative mosaic floors in the bathhouse complex. The huge, horseshoe-shape "entertainment area," its sloping sides filled with rows of stone seats, was an amphitheater built by Herod (most likely the one mentioned by 1st-century AD historian Flavius Josephus in both *The Jewish War* and *The Antiquities of the Jews*), where some 10,000 spectators watched horse races, chariot races, and various sporting events some 2,000 years ago.

★ The walls that surround the **Crusader city** were built by King Louis IX of France. They enclose both the remains of the Herodian port and the Crusader city itself, which was actually only one-third the size of Herod's original city. The bulk of what you see today—the moat, escarpment, citadel, and walls, which once contained 16 towers—dates from 1251, when the French king actually spent a year pitching in with his own two hands to help restore the existing fortifications. The Crusaders first besieged and conquered Caesarea in 1101 after it had been ruled for nearly five centuries by Arabs, who had allowed the port to silt up. As a reward for furnishing the fleet that was instrumental in the victory, the Genoese were awarded a green glass vessel found in Caesarea by the Crusaders and believed to be the Holy Grail.

You enter the Crusader city over a dry moat. However impressive, the 42-ft-deep moat was of little use in repelling an attack under Sultan Baybars in the late 13th century. The invading Mamluks then destroyed the city to prevent its resettlement by the Christians. Still, the fortifications and the gatehouse (at the entrance) are fine examples of medieval architecture. Note the sloping glacis against the outer wall, the shooting niches, and the groined vaults of the gatehouse.

Arrows and signs direct you on a designated walking tour. Especially after heavy rains, keep a vigilant eye out for old bronze coins, some smaller than a dime. As you walk under a series of four arches, spanning a ruined Crusader street, you can see just to your right the remains of a Frankish house. At the southeast corner of the fortress is a postern gate, designed for counterattack against an enemy. You're on the high area above the remains of the harbor—walk toward the sea and the observation point to find the remains of the unfinished Crusader cathedral. It's built on the site of a Byzantine church; the three graceful curves of its apses stand out. Both churches stood on the ruins of the temple Herod dedicated to Augustus on this promontory dominating the port. The collapse of the underlying vaulted chambers halted construction of the cathedral.

At the railing in front of the church ruins, there's a lookout over the ancient port, now under water, as well as a view up the coast to Zichron Ya'akov and Haifa. On a clear day, you can see the shadowy outlines of the submerged harbor constructions from the top terrace of the tower, now the Citadel restaurant. The diving center in Caesarea's port offers underwater tours with marked maps of the port area (☞ *Outdoor Activities and Sports, below*).

Even today, **Herod's port** can be regarded as an awesome achievement. Flavius Josephus described the wonders of the port in glowing terms, comparing it to Athens's port of Piraeus. Once archaeologists explored the underwater ruins, beginning in the 1960s and continuing sporadically into the 1990s, it became clear that what had been long dismissed by many historians as hyperbole was exactly as Josephus described it.

The port's construction was an unprecedented challenge—there was no artificial harbor of this size anywhere in the world. There were no islands or bays to provide natural protection, and the work itself was hindered by bad weather. During preliminary underwater digs in 1978, archaeologists were stunned to discover concrete blocks near the breakwater offshore, indicating the highly sophisticated use of hydraulic concrete (which hardens underwater). Historians knew that the Romans had developed such techniques, but before the discoveries at Caesarea, they never knew hydraulic concrete to have been used on such a massive scale. The main ingredient in the concrete, volcanic ash, was probably imported from Mt. Vesuvius, in Italy, as were the wooden forms. Teams of professional divers actually did much of the trickiest work, laying the foundations hundreds of yards offshore. To inhibit the natural process of silting, engineers designed sluice channels to cut through the breakwaters and flush out the harbor. Herod's engineers also devised underwater structures to break the impact of waves.

Once finished, two massive breakwaters—one stretching west and then north from the Citadel restaurant some 1,800 ft and the other 600 ft long, both now submerged—sheltered an area of about 3½ acres from the waves and tides. Two towers, each mounted by three colossal statues, marked the entrance to the port; and although neither the towers nor the statues have been found, a tiny medal bearing their image was discovered in the first underwater excavations here, in 1960. The finished harbor also contained the dominating temple to Augustus and cavernous storage facilities along the shore. The port was devastated by an earthquake in AD 130. The Crusaders only reutilized a small section of the harbor when they conquered Caesarea in 1101. ☏ 04/636–1358. *www.infotour.co.il/TourismArea/74001.html* . ▨ *Theater and Crusader city NIS 17 ($4.25).* ☉ *Sat.–Thurs. 8–4, Fri. and holiday eves 8–3.*

| | |
|---|---|
| NEED A BREAK? | Relax in the shadow of the vaulted remains of Herod's inner harbor, on the raftered **patio** in the middle of the Crusader city (near the rest rooms). The kiosk sells hot and cold drinks, snacks, and ice cream, and souvenir shops and restaurants hug the water's edge. |

East of the main entrance to the site (across the road), a small, sunken, fenced-in area encloses Caesarea's **Byzantine street.** It was during the Byzantine period and in late Roman times that Caesarea thrived as a center of Christian scholarship and as an episcopal see; in the 7th century, Caesarea had a famous library of some 30,000 volumes that originated with the collection of the Christian philosopher Origen (185–254), who lived in Caesarea for two decades. Eusebius, who was an ecclesiastical advisor to Emperor Constantine and is known as the Church's first historian, became Caesarea's first bishop in the 4th century. Once lined with workshops and stores, the street is paved with marble slabs. The inscription you see dates the area to the late 6th or early 7th century. Towering over the street are two monumental marble statues that face each other, both probably carted here from nearby Roman temples. The provenance of the milky white one is unknown; the purple porphyry figure might have been commissioned by the Emperor Hadrian when he visited Caesarea. In Byzantine times, the city's area grew an estimated eight times the size of the fortified Crusader city. The Byzantine street is just across the street from the entrance to the Crusader city.

The **Caesarea Museum** houses many of the artifacts found by kibbutz members as they plowed their fields in the 1940s. The small museum has arguably the best collection of late-Roman sculpture in Israel; impressive holdings of rare Roman and Byzantine gemstones; and a large variety of coins minted in Caesarea over the ages, as well as oil lamps, urns excavated from the sea floor, and fragments of jewelry. ⊠ *On grounds of Kibbutz Sdot Yam, about 600 ft south of entrance to theater,* ☎ *04/636–4367.* ⊠ *NIS 12 ($3).* ⊘ *Sat.–Thurs. 10–4, Fri. 10–1.*

A wonderful finale to your trip to Caesarea (especially at sunset) is the ★ **Roman aqueduct** on the beach. The chain of arches tumbling north toward the horizon, where they disappear beneath the sand, is a captivating sight and forms a unique backdrop for a swim at the pretty beach (☞ *Beaches, below*). During Roman times, the demand for a steady water supply was considerable, but the source was a spring about 13 km (8 mi) away in the foothills of Mt. Carmel. Workers had to cut a channel approximately 6½ km (4 mi) long through solid rock before the water was piped into the aqueduct, whose arches spanned that entire length. In the 2nd century, Hadrian doubled its capacity by adding a new channel. Today you can walk along the sea side of the aqueduct and see marble plaques dedicated to the support troops of various legions who toiled here. On your way back to the road, you might want to drive around the villa area and admire some of Israel's tonier homes, some brand new and many covered with swaths of brilliant bougainvillea. ⊠ *Villa area, north of Crusader city.*

## Dining and Lodging

$$$$  ✕ **Wine Cellar.** Among the trees near the Byzantine street with the headless stone statues of once-glorious rulers sits a domed building that houses a small wine cellar, plus walls of bottles from the major wineries in Israel. With a glass of the house wine (or a choice from farther afield), you may dine on a tasty antipasti of grilled vegetables and country-style bread, followed by baked, grilled or deep-fried fish, or a hefty grilled entrecôte steak served with chicken livers and a sauce of onions, mushrooms, and red wine, with spinach soufflé or ratatouille on the side. Or you could have a fresh Greek salad, made with local feta, thus saving enough room for rich pecan pie or the delicious house specialty— a phyllo pastry base topped with meringue, wild berries, and vanilla ice cream. ⊠ *Opposite the main entrance to the Caesarea site,* ☎ *04/ 626–4644. Reservations essential. AE, D, MC, V. No lunch Sun.*

$$$$  ✕ **Zafran.** If you have the time one evening (say a few hours), and are interested in a special dining experience, visit the small, charming dining room of Benita's lovely home in the residential area of Caesarea. You'll be served a set eight-course dinner that blends French Provençal and Mediterranean cooking. Wine is extra and the list is good; on Thursday nights a guided wine tasting accompanies your meal. The menu changes often and usually starts with bite-size flaky pastries filled with goat cheese and chutney or wild mushrooms. The courses that follow might include rare fillets of lamb with asparagus, a crisp salad of various lettuces with fresh mint and sage, icy sorbet in between, and a hot chocolate soufflé to end the meal on a high note. Vegetarians can consult with Benita on their very own menu. The minimum number of diners is four; you must call two days ahead to reserve. ⊠ *12 Narkis St., Cluster 5, Villa Area,* ☎ *04/626–4889. Reservations essential. AE, D, MC, V.*

$$$  ✕ **Charley's.** It's a delight to eat on one of Charley's several patios on a clear day. Located under the stone watchtower in the Crusader city's port, right above the sandy cove beach, Charley's is especially known

for its way with fresh seafood, grilled or baked. Depending on the catch of the day—supplied by fishermen from a neighboring Arab village—you might choose from red snapper, mullet, or grouper, or simpler and cheaper alternatives such as a Middle Eastern salad or just coffee and crème caramel or cheesecake. ⊠ *Crusader city,* ☎ *04/636–3050. Reservations essential. AE, D, MC, V.*

$$$ 🏨 **Dan Caesarea.** Quiet comfort is combined here with accessibility
★ to a range of sports facilities, the beach, and the famed site of ancient Caesarea with its Roman, Byzantine, and Crusader archaeological remains. Adjacent to the hotel's 15-acre gardens lies Israel's only 18-hole golf course, which offers Dan guests a discount. The four-story hotel, built in 1958, is unobtrusively set in attractively landscaped grounds and is located halfway between Tel Aviv and Haifa. All the rooms have balconies, overlooking either the sea or the open countryside. Especially recommended are the comfortable deluxe doubles, with marble bathrooms and modern decor in cheerful hues. ⊠ *North of Crusader city (opposite entrance to villa area), Caesarea 30600,* ☎ *04/626–9111,* FAX *04/626–9122. 114 rooms. Restaurant, bar, café, pool, hot tub, sauna, 18-hole golf course, 2 tennis courts. AE, DC, MC.* 🐾

For a longer vacation, you can rent a villa, one of the modern white-washed houses near the beach. Contact **Chana Kristal Real Estate** (⊠ 23 Hamigdal St., Cluster 8, Caesarea 36060, ☎ 04/636–3896 or 051/ 813–131, FAX 04/636–0212).

## Outdoor Activities and Sports

### BEACHES

Bathers have three choices here. In the Old City, in a sandy cove in Herod's ancient harbor, is the small **Caesarea Beach Club,** where the admission charge of NIS 30 ($7.50) includes chairs, umbrellas, and the use of hot showers. The beach has a diving platform, and you can also rent kayaks. The Gal-Mor Diving Center is right next door. The largest and most popular beach in the area is **Hof Shonit** (☎ 04/636–2927), just south of Caesarea—from Route 2, turn left instead of right toward the Old City. The parking lot here accommodates a hefty 400 vehicles and charges NIS 12 ($3). There are lifeguards in season, a refreshment stand, and a restaurant, as well as toilets and cold showers. At the **Roman aqueduct,** just north of the Crusader city in the residential area, is a considerably more spacious beach with the dramatic backdrop of Roman arches disappearing into the sand. The amenities, however, are few: toilets, and a lifeguard in season. There is no entrance fee, and there's plenty of parking. The beach and swimming area have been cleared of rocks and debris, but swimming outside the designated, guarded area is prohibited (never swim at all unless the guard is on duty).

### GOLF

Both Israeli and foreign golfers flock to the **Caesarea Golf Club** (☎ 04/ 636–1172); it's the only 18-hole course in Israel. Adjacent to the Dan Caesarea hotel, the club is open from sunrise to sunset, and the course is built on sandy soil so that you can even play after heavy rainfall. Reservations are advisable. The club is closed on Monday. The greens fee is NIS 340 ($85) from Sunday to Thursday and NIS 400 ($100) on Friday and Saturday (it's a per-day fee; you can play twice if you'd like). After 2 PM, the "twilight" fee is NIS 180 ($45) on weekdays and NIS 220 ($55) on Friday and Saturday. Golf-club rentals run NIS 100 ($25), electric-car rentals are NIS 115.50 ($33). There is a French bistro on the premises.

SCUBA DIVING

The **Old Caesarea Diving Center,** in the Crusader city (☎ 04/626–5898), runs a teaching program for nondivers with one- to seven-day trips. Licensed divers can go on diving tours of the submerged port built by King Herod 2,000 years ago.

### Nightlife and the Arts

Caesarea's **Roman theater** (☎ 02/500–5444 parks authority for general information; ⊠ Le'an ticket agency, 101 Dizengoff St., Tel Aviv, ☎ 03/524–7373) hosts evening performances of the highest caliber, by both local and international artists and troupes. The season runs from May to mid-October; the box office is open on performance days.

## Nachsholim-Dor

❸ *20 km (12 mi) north of Caesarea. Travel east at Zichron Ya'akov turnoff until the Fureidis Junction (marked "to Haifa"), turn south, and travel 1 km (½ mi) to sign for Nachsholim-Dor. Turn west and drive 3 km (2 mi).*

Founded 3,500 years ago, biblical Dor was once the maritime capital of the Carmel coast. Its small bay made it the best harbor between Jaffa and Akko and thus a target for many imperial ambitions, from the ancient Egyptians and the "Sea Peoples" through King Solomon and on down. It was renowned in antiquity for its precious purple dye, called Tyrian purple; reserved for royalty, this hue was extracted from a mollusk that was abundant along the coast. During the Arab period, the town was renamed Tantura, which is also the name of the town's popular beach today.

★ Well worth a visit is the **Nachsholim-Dor Museum** (or Hamizgaga Museum); turn in at the sign for the Nachsholim Guest House, which is also the Center for Nautical and Regional Archaeology. It's housed in the partly restored former glass factory opened by Baron Rothschild in 1893 to serve the wineries of nearby Zichron Ya'akov. (Run by Meir Dizengoff, the first mayor of Tel Aviv, the glass enterprise failed after only two years because the poor quality of the sand used made the bottles black.) The museum is a rich trove of finds from both local nautical digs and excavations at nearby Tel Dor. The sequence of peoples who settled, conquered, or passed through Dor—from the Phoenicians to Napoléon—can be traced through these artifacts. Of particular interest is the bronze cannon that Napoléon's vanquished troops dumped into the sea during their retreat from Akko to Egypt in May 1799. An interesting film in English illuminates the seminal work of Kurt Raveh, a Dutch-born member of the kibbutz who spearheaded many of the underwater digs. ⊠ *Kibbutz Nachsholim,* ☎ *04/639–0950.* ☜ *NIS 10 ($2.50).* ☉ *Sun.–Thurs. 8:30–2, Fri. 8:30–1, Sat. and holidays 10:30–3.*

NEED A BREAK?

The decor is fishing-shack and the music is loud at **Bar Dag** (☎ 04/630–1641). Children run around, and it's right on the beach. If you'd like a round of good hummus and some plain fresh fish, an icy beer, and a chocolate ice cream while staring at the beach and the blue Med, walk about 110 yards to the right of the Dor Beach entrance (☞ *below*) for all the above.

### Outdoor Activities and Sports

BEACHES

**Dor Beach** (☎ 04/630–7180), also known as Tantura Beach, is one of the most popular in Israel thanks to the fine sand lining its 1½ km (1 mi) of coastline. It's right beside Kibbutz Nachsholim. Amenities are ample: parking, lifeguards in season, a snack bar and restaurant, a first-aid station, a trampoline (fee), and chair and umbrella rentals, as well as changing rooms and showers. At press time, the changing rooms and other facilities were in need of renovation, but the sand was still soft and alluring.

DIVING

Kurt Raveh, a diver-archaeologist and resident of Kibbutz Nachsholim, runs the **Underwater Archaeological Center** (☎ 052/796–695) on Dor Beach. Kurt conducts underwater expeditions and "dives into history" where divers (even those without experience) get to tour ancient shipwrecks under his experienced eye.

## Atlit

**❹** *9 km (6 mi) north of Nachsholim-Dor, 15 km (9 mi) south of Haifa.*

Atlit is a peninsula with the jagged remains of an important Crusader castle. Of more recent vintage, to the west (about 1,500 ft from the highway), is the **Atlit detention camp,** used by the British to house refugees smuggled in during and after World War II. The reconstructed barracks, fences, and watchtowers stand as reminders of how Jewish immigration was practically outlawed under the British Mandate after the publication of the infamous White Paper in 1939. More than a third of the 120,000 illegal immigrants to Palestine passed through the camp from 1934 to 1948. The 45-minute tour includes the living quarters, complete with laundry hanging from the rafters. The authenticity of the exhibit is striking: it was re-created from accounts of actual detainees and their contemporaries. Call ahead to make sure the site is open. ⊠ *Rte. 2,* ☎ *04/984–1980.* ☜ *NIS 12 ($3).* ۞ *Sun.–Thurs. 9–4, Fri. 9–12:30, Sat. 10–3.*

# HAIFA

Spilling down from the pine-covered heights of Mt. Carmel to the blue Mediterranean is Haifa, whose vertiginous setting has led to perhaps hyperbolic comparisons with San Francisco. Israel's largest port and third-largest city, Haifa was ruled for four centuries by the Ottomans and gradually grew up the mountainside into a cosmopolitan city whose port served the entire Middle East. In 1902, Theodor Herzl enthusiastically dubbed it "the city of the future."

Haifa was already a center for science and technology by 1924, when the Technion Institute opened. The Turks' construction at the turn of the 20th century of the Hijaz Railway—which stretched from Constantinople via Damascus to the Muslim holy cities of Mecca and Medina—proved a boon to Haifa, which had its own branch of the new line to Damascus. Under the British Mandate, a deep-water port was dug and opened to world traffic in 1933, and Haifa was linked to Iraq by an oil pipeline the following year. After Israel's independence, Haifa's links with neighboring Arab states were broken, but today cruise ships from abroad ply its waters, and the Technion is still the nation's citadel of scientific research.

First mentioned in the Talmud, the area around Haifa had two settlements in ancient times. To the east, in what is today a congested industrial zone in the port, lay Zalmona, and 5 km (3 mi) west around the cape was Shiqmona. The Crusaders conquered Haifa while it was an important Arab town and maintained it as a fortress along the coastal road to Akko for 200 years; like much of the Crusader kingdom, it was lost and repeatedly regained by the Christians. During this period, in 1154, the Order of Our Lady of Mount Carmel (the Carmelite order) was founded on the slopes of Mt. Carmel by a group of hermits following the principles of the prophet Elijah and the rules of poverty, vegetarianism, and solitude. After Akko and Haifa succumbed to the Mamluk Sultan Baybars in 1265, Haifa was destroyed and left derelict, just as it had been at the end of Byzantine rule. It was a sleepy fishing village for centuries thereafter.

The city reawakened under the rule of Bedouin sheikh Dahr el-Omar, who had rebelled against direct Ottoman rule in the mid-18th century and independently governed Akko and the Galilee. Dahr recognized that Haifa's location left it vulnerable to attack; in 1761 he ordered the city to be demolished and moved about 3 km (2 mi) to the south. The new town was fortified by walls and protected by a castle, and its port began to compete with that of Akko across the bay—for while its harbor was not as good as Akko's, Mt. Carmel offered a natural barrier against the strong southwesterly winds and thus a comfortable anchorage.

Napoléon, too, came to Haifa, though only briefly, and en route to ignominious defeat at Akko during his Eastern Campaign. Napoléon left his wounded at the Carmelite Monastery (☞ *below*) when he beat a retreat in 1799, but the French soldiers there were killed and the monks driven out by Ahmed el-Jazzar, the victorious pasha of Akko.

Today, the metropolis is divided into three main levels that run parallel to the harbor, crisscrossed by parks and gardens. The downtown port encompasses the largely uninhabited Old City; the midtown area, called Hadar HaCarmel (Hadar for short), was one of the early Jewish neighborhoods and is now a bustling shopping area; and Central Carmel, or Mercaz HaCarmel, on top, includes upscale residential developments and the posher hotels. The most striking landmark on the mountainside is the gleaming golden dome of the Baha'i Shrine.

Haifa is a city of fairly steep slopes, which reward the visitor not only with sites to see amidst pine trees and blossoming foliage but vistas of the Mediterranean at every turn, all accompanied by hillside breezes. And thanks to the beneficence of the Baha'is you will soon be able to walk down the whole mountainside from the crest of the city at Mt. Carmel through the stunning terraces that lie like multicolored jewels all the way to the German Colony below.

*Numbers in the margin correspond to points of interest on the Haifa map.*

## A Good Walk

Start with a short taxi ride (or the infrequent Bus 31) down to the **Carmelite Monastery** ⑤, and the **Stella Maris lighthouse,** on a promontory overlooking Haifa Bay.

It's about a 20-minute walk until you reach the **Clandestine Immigration and Naval Museum** ⑥ on Allenby Road, which tells the story of the efforts to bring European Jewish refugees to Palestine around the time of World War II. Up the road is the **National Maritime Museum** ⑦, which brings 5,000 years of maritime history to life via model ships, coins with nautical motifs, and other artifacts, including underwater finds from nearby excavations and shipwrecks.

For great views of Haifa and the Mediterranean below, stroll scenic **Yefe Nof Street** ⑧, starting behind the Dan Panorama Hotel. (You'll be happy to know that this walk is all downhill). At 89 Yefe Nof Street is the **Mané Katz Museum** ⑨, the lattice-windowed former home of the Ukrainian-born Expressionist painter Emmanuel Katz. Parallel to and west of Yefe Nof is Hanassi Avenue; Number 88 is the **Tikotin Museum**

**of Japanese Art** ⑩. Back on Yefe Nof Street, walk west (accompanied by great vistas, and passing the black-gate entrance to the upper terraces of the Baha'i Gardens) to the intersection of Yefe Nof and Hanassi streets.

Across the street, just down from the intersection, on your left, is the entrance to a **sculpture garden** ⑪ that overlooks Haifa Bay. Walk through, and continue downward to **Sderot Hatziyonut** (Zionism Boulevard), where you'll turn right, passing under the new bridge above. This street was originally named after the United Nations, but following the 1975 passage of a U. N. resolution that equated Zionism with racism, the city government quickly changed it (the resolution was rescinded in 1992). A bit farther along, you'll come upon the ornately carved gates that lead to the **Baha'i Shrine and Gardens** ⑫, the dazzling gold dome of the Shrine of the Bab is the mainstay of Haifa postcards. Keep heading down the hill to the intersection of Sderot Hatziyonut and Shabbetai Levy, where you'll see the **Haifa Museum** ⑬. Turning left, onto Sderot Hagefen, walk three blocks to Ben-Gurion Boulevard, whereupon you'll turn right into what's known as the **German Colony** ⑭, a late-19th-century colony established by the German Templar religious reform movement. This is a lovely way to end your (long) walk, strolling past the renovated stone, red-roofed buildings with their stern demeanor, now softened by pretty landscaping. The new City Mall, with shops and restaurants, concludes the walk.

Three additional sights are a bit farther afield. The closest, still downtown, is the **National Museum of Science and Technology** ⑮, with hands-on exhibits. Bus 30 takes you to Haifa University and the **Hecht Museum** ⑯, known for its archaeological collections. Bus 31 takes you to the **Technion** ⑰ scientific research center.

## Sights to See

★ ⑫ **Baha'i Shrine and Gardens.** The most striking feature of the stunning gardens is the Shrine of the Bab, whose gilded dome dominates as well as illuminates Haifa's skyline. Haifa is the world center for the Baha'i faith, which was founded in Iran in the 19th century and holds as its central belief the unity of mankind. Religious truth for Baha'is is not doctrinaire; rather, it consists of progressive revelations of a universal faith. Thus the Baha'is teach that great prophets have appeared throughout history to reveal divine truths, among them Moses, Zoroaster, Buddha, Jesus, Mohammed, and, most recently, the founder of the Baha'i faith, Mirza Husayn Ali, known as Baha'u'llah—the Glory of God. Baha'u'llah (1817–1892) was exiled from his native Persia by the Shah and then by the Ottomans to Akko, where he lived as a prisoner for almost 25 years. The Baha'is' holiest shrine is on the grounds of Baha'u'llah's home, where he lived after his release from prison and where he is now buried, just north of Akko (☞ *below*).

Here in Haifa, at the center of the shrine's pristinely manicured gardens, is the mausoleum built for the Bab (literally, the "Gate"), the forerunner of this religion, who heralded the coming of a new faith to be revealed by Baha'u'llah. The Bab was martyred by the Persian authorities in 1850. The gardens and shrine were built by Baha'u'llah's son and successor, who had the Bab's remains reburied here in 1909. The building, made of Italian-cut stone and rising 128 ft, gracefully combines the canons of classical European architecture with elements of Eastern design and also houses the remains of Baha'u'llah's son. The dome glistens with some 12,000 gilded tiles imported from the Netherlands. Inside, the floor is covered with rich Oriental carpets, and a filigree veil divides visitors from the inner shrine.

**200**

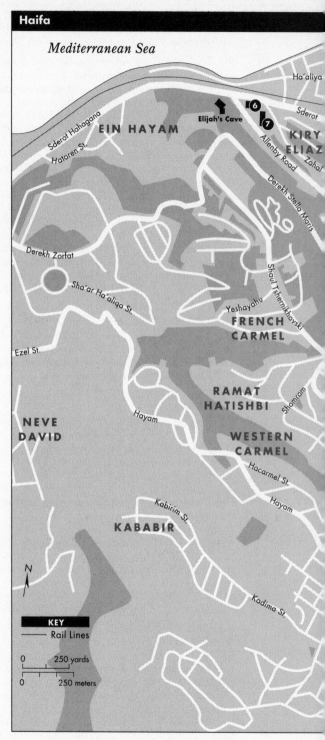

Haifa

*Mediterranean Sea*

Ha'aliya

Sderot

Sderot Hahagana

**EIN HAYAM**

Hatoren St.

Elijah's Cave

**6**

**7**

**KIRY
ELIAZ**

Allenby Road

Zahal

Dereth Stella Maris

Derekh Zorfat

Sha'ar Ha'aliqa St.

Shaul Tshernikhovski

Yeshayahu

**FRENCH
CARMEL**

Ezel St.

**RAMAT
HATISHBI**

Shomram

Hayam

**NEVE
DAVID**

**WESTERN
CARMEL**

Hacarmel St.

Hayam

Kabirim St.

**KABABIR**

N

Kadima St.

**KEY**
Rail Lines

0        250 yards

0        250 meters

The magnificent gardens are a sight to behold. Since 1987, work has been underway on 18 wonderfully landscaped circular terraces, extending from Yefe Nof Street for a kilometer (½ mi) all the way down the slope to Ben Gurion Boulevard to the German Colony (☞ *below*). The terraces are a harmony of color and form—pale pink and gray stone staircases and carved urns overflowing with red geraniums delineate perfect cutouts of emerald green grass and floral borders, dark green trees and wildflowers, with not a leaf out of place anywhere. At present, two of the terraces can be explored on foot via the ornate black and gold gate (also connected by tunnel to the Louis Promenade) on Yefe Nof. In May 2001 the inauguration of the opening from Ben Gurion Boulevard will be celebrated, and the terraces will then be open to the public from the German Colony.

The Shrine of the Bab (along with the Shrine of Baha'u'llah north of Akko) are sites of pilgrimage for the worldwide Baha'i community; visitors to the shrine are asked to dress modestly, no shorts. ✉ *Entrance to the Shrine: 65 Sderot Hatziyonut,* ☏ *04/835–8358.www.bahai.org* ✉ *Free.* ◷ *Shrine daily 9–noon; gardens daily 9–5.*

**❺ Carmelite Monastery and Stella Maris lighthouse.** During the Crusader period, groups of hermits emulating the life of the prophet Elijah lived in caves on this steep mountain slope. In the early 13th century they united under the leadership of the Italian pilgrim (later saint) Berthold, who petitioned the patriarch of Jerusalem for a charter for the group. Thus was born the Carmelite order, which spread across Europe, and esteems the prophet Elijah, the order's patron. The Carmelite monks were forced to leave their settlements on Mt. Carmel at the end of the 13th century, when Akko fell to the Mamluks, and did not return until nearly four centuries later. When they found Elijah's cave inhabited by Muslim dervishes, they set up a rudimentary monastery nearby. Dahr el-Omar drove them out again in 1767.

The church of the present monastery dates from 1836 and was built with the munificence of the French monarchy, hence the name of the surrounding neighborhood: French Carmel. The French connection is explained by a small pyramid, topped with an iron cross, that stands before the entrance of the basilica-style church. The monument commemorates those French who were slaughtered here by the Turks in 1799 after the retreating Napoléon left his ailing troops behind to be treated in what was then a military hospital at the monastery. Inside, the academic paintings in the dome depict Elijah in the chariot of fire in which he ascended to heaven, and other Old Testament prophets. The small cave a few steps down at the end of the nave is traditionally associated with Elijah and his pupil, Elisha. A small museum near the entrance contains some fossils and Byzantine artifacts discovered in the area. Across the street from the church, at the tip of the promontory, is the Stella Maris (Star of the Sea) lighthouse, built in the 19th century to guide the Turkish fleet to safe harbor and still in use. It is not open to the public. ✉ *Carmelite Monastery, Stella Maris Rd.,* ☏ *04/833–7758.* ✉ *Free.* ◷ *Daily 6:30–1 and 3–6.*

**❻ Clandestine Immigration and Naval Museum.** The rather dull name of this museum belies the dramatic nature of its contents. The Clandestine Immigration and Naval Museum tells the story of the often heroic efforts to bring Jewish immigrants to Palestine from war-torn Europe in defiance of British policy. In addition to a clearly marked map showing the immigration routes, there are video presentations, photographs, and documents recording both deportations and successful missions. The exhibits are labeled in English.

Emigration to Palestine was well nigh impossible after the British imposed a naval blockade, bowing to pressure by Arabs opposed to Jewish immigration. In 1939, on the eve of World War II, the British issued the so-called White Paper, which effectively strangled Jewish immigration to Palestine and prohibited Jews from buying land there. Small boats sometimes managed to elude the vigilant British warships and unload their human cargoes at secret landing beaches; but for bigger ships the odds were daunting. Out of 63 clandestine ships that tried to run the blockade after the war's end, all but five were intercepted, and their passengers were deported to Cyprus.

The museum is full of moving stories of courage, tenacity, and disaster. A photomural of the celebrated ship the *Exodus* recalls the story of the 4,530 refugees aboard who were forcibly transferred back to Germany in 1947, but not before the British forces opened fire on the rebellious ship, convincing the passengers and crew to surrender. Another tragic episode befell the *Struma,* a leaky vessel that was forced to anchor in Istanbul for repairs in 1941. The Turks refused to assist the ship after warnings from the British; so, unable to continue but unwilling to return, the boat wallowed in Istanbul harbor for two months and finally sank a few miles offshore. Of the 767 on board, one person survived.

One of the blockade runners was an old American tank-landing craft renamed *Af-al-pi-chen* ("Nevertheless," in Hebrew), which serves as the museum's centerpiece. (It's accessible from the roof.) This ship left Italy in 1947 for Palestine and was intercepted by the British, at which point its 434 passengers, all survivors of the Holocaust, were sent to internment camps in Cyprus. ⊠ *204 Allenby Rd.,* ☎ *04/853–6249.* ⌑ *NIS 8 ($2).* ⊙ *Sun.–Thurs. 9–4, holiday eves 9–1.*

**Elijah's Cave.** This site is considered sacred by Jews, Christians, and Muslims; an early Byzantine tradition identified it as the cave in which Elijah found refuge from the wrath of Ahab, king of Israel from 871 to 853 BC. Graffiti from pilgrims of various faiths and different centuries are scrawled on the right wall, and written prayers are often stuffed into crevices. Some supplicants come to ask for fertility, others for better fortune or a cure for an illness. Modest dress is requested. The cave is a 20-minute walk down the fairly steep path across from the entrance to the Carmelite Monastery and church; you can also reach it by walking about 100 ft up from Allenby Road. ⊠ *230 Allenby Rd.,* ☎ *04/ 852–7430.* ⌑ *Free.* ⊙ *Sun.–Thurs. 8–5, Fri. and holiday eves 8–1.*

⓮ **German Colony.** Ben-Gurion Boulevard, ruler-straight, was the heart of a late-19th-century colony established by the German Templar religious reform movement. Neglected for years, the German Colony is a prime example of meticulous renovation that gives Haifa, in any case a city of beautiful walks, one of its loveliest strolls. Ben-Gurion starts at the bottom of the magnificent Baha'i Gardens (footpath access is slated to be completed in May 2001) and winds up three blocks later at Yaffa Street. It's only one street—actually a broad boulevard—but it packs in history, interesting architecture, several coffee houses, greenery and trees, shaded benches for people-watching, the tourist office, and several top restaurants. Along the way, note the robust two- and three-story stone houses, with red-tile roofs typical of the neighborhood; some houses still bear German names and inscriptions on the lintels above the doors. Old wooden shutters highlight the unique character of the houses, and balconies here and there showcase intricate metalwork. The street ends (or starts, depending where you're coming from) at City Centre, a two-story shopping mall containing two upscale restaurants.

The Templars' colony in Haifa was the most important one in the Holy Land. The early settlers formed a self-sufficient community and enjoyed quite a comfortable standard of living; by 1883 they had built nearly 100 houses and filled them with as many families. They introduced several improvements in transportation to Haifa, including the horse-drawn wagon, unknown until their arrival. They started to make wagons locally and then built with their own funds a pilgrimage road from Haifa to Nazareth. The Germans' labors gave rise to modern workshops and warehouses, and it was under their influence that Haifa began to resemble a modern Western city, with well laid-out streets, gardens, and attractive homes.

Haifa's importance to Germany was highlighted in 1898, when Kaiser Wilhelm II sailed into the bay, his first stop on the first official visit to the Holy Land by a German emperor in more than 600 years. The ruling Turkish sultan ordered a new jetty built for the occasion. During World War II the Germans who lived in the colony were expelled, suspected of being Nazis.

The German Templars and the French Carmelite monks on the hill were on no better terms than their compatriots back home. A nationalistic battle arose in 1885, when the Germans bought some acreage on the mountain and the French monks refused to let them cross their land to get there. The case ended up in a Haifa court, and the monks were ordered to allow the Germans access.

⑬ **Haifa Museum** (Museum of Modern Art). Until recently, this was three "museums" in one building; now Ancient Art is housed at the National Maritime Museum (☞ *below*), while Music and Ethnology has yet to find a home. One admission ticket is good for both Modern Art and Ancient Art, as well as the Tikotin Museum of Japanese Art (☞ *below*), also under the auspices of the Haifa Museum.

The Museum of Modern Art displays work from all over the world, dating from the mid-18th century to the present. It's also a good place to learn about modern Israeli art: the many pieces include 20th-century graphics and contemporary paintings, sculpture, and photography. The print collection is of special note, and international photography shows are mounted several times a year. ⊠ *26 Shabbetai Levy St.,* ☎ *04/852–3255.* ☜ *NIS 24 ($6), includes all 3 museums.* ☉ *Mon., Wed., Thurs. 10–5; Tues. 10–2 and 5–8; Fri. 10–1; Sat. 10–2.*

⑯ **Hecht Museum.** It's worth the trip to Haifa University for these fine archaeological holdings. At the summit of Mt. Carmel, in the main campus tower (designed by Brazilian architect Oscar Niemeyer), the collection spans the millennia from the Chalcolithic era to the Roman and Byzantine periods, concentrating on "The People of Israel in Eretz Israel". The artifacts range from religious altars and lamps to two coffins and figurines from the Early Bronze Age. Featured prominently are finds from the excavations of Jerusalem's Temple Mount. A separate wing displays a small collection of paintings, mostly impressionist and Jewish School of Paris, with works of Monet, Soutine and Pissarro, among others. To get here, take Bus 37 from the Nof Hotel. ⊠ *Abu Hushi St.,* ☎ *04/824–0577.* ☜ *Free.* ☉ *Sun., Mon, Wed., Thurs. 10–4; Tues. 10–7; Fri. and holiday eves 10–1; Sat. 10–2.*

NEED A
BREAK? **Gan Ha'em** (Mothers' Park), opposite the Dan Panorama Hotel, has a small and happy collection of zoo animals and reptiles, along with a botanical garden, a picnic area, park benches, and a snack bar.

**⑨ Mané Katz Museum.** This is the house and studio where the Expressionist painter Emmanuel Katz (1894–1962) lived and worked for the last four years of his life. Katz spent the 1920s in Paris, where he exhibited with a group of Jewish artists from the École de Paris; as in the canvases of fellow members Marc Chagall and Chaim Soutine, a recurring theme in his work is the village life of Jews in Eastern Europe. A whitewashed building with ornamental grillwork on the windows, this intimate museum houses a collection of Katz's paintings, drawings, and sculptures, the Ukrainian-born artist's legacy to the city. The artist was an avid collector of rugs and 17th-century antiques from Spain and Germany, and these are also on display along with objects from his Judaica collection. ☒ *89 Yefe Nof St.,* ☎ *04/838–3482.* ☜ *Free.* ⊙ *Sun.–Thurs. 10–4; Tues. 2–6; Fri. 10–1; Sat. 10–2.*

**⑦ National Maritime Museum.** Here 5,000 years of maritime history is told (and made more interesting than it sounds) with model ships, archaeological finds, coins minted with nautical symbols, navigational instruments, and other artifacts. There are also a number of intriguing underwater finds from nearby excavations and shipwrecks. The ancient-art collection, formerly housed in the Haifa Museum, is one of the finest in the country; it comprises mostly Greek and Roman stone and marble sculpture, Egyptian textiles, Greek pottery, and encaustic grave portraits from Fayyum, in Lower Egypt. Particularly rare are the figures of fishermen from the Hellenistic period. Among numerous terracotta figurines from Syria and Egypt are several curious animal-shape vessels—once used as playthings, incense burners, or funerary gifts—from Haifa's nearby Shiqmona excavation. Also from Egypt are a group of finely carved alabaster vessels and funerary masks. ☒ *198 Allenby Rd.,* ☎ *04/ 853–6622.* ☜ *NIS 24 ($6), including Museum of Modern Art (☞ above) and Tikotin Museum of Japanese Art (☞ below).* ⊙ *Mon., Wed., Thurs. 10–5; Tues. 10–2 and 5–8; Fri. 10–1; Sat. 10–2.*

**☝ ⑮ National Museum of Science and Technology (Technoda).** Children and adults alike will be captivated by the hands-on chemistry and physics exhibits in this beautifully designed building, the original home of the Technion (☞ *below*). ☒ *Balfour St.,* ☎ *04/862–8111.* ☜ *NIS 24 ($6).* ⊙ *Sun., Mon., Wed., Thurs. 9–6; Tues. 9–7; Fri. and holiday eves 10– 3; Sat. 10–5.*

**⑪ Sculpture garden.** From one of the benches on a winding path through the garden, you can contemplate the life-size bronzes of humans and animals by sculptor Ursula Malbin, who came to Israel as a refugee from Nazi Germany. ☒ *Just west of Baha'i Shrine.*

**⑰ Technion.** Israel's foremost center for applied research, the 300-acre Technion City was relocated to this area in 1953. The original institute (known as the Technoda) was founded in 1912 and opened its doors in midtown 12 years later, due in part to the hardships of an intervening world war. Today, the Technion is highly fertile ground for Israel's scientific innovations: two-thirds of the nation's university research in such fields as science, technology, engineering, medicine, architecture, and town planning takes place here. Visitors can get an idea of the vast scope of these studies, plus the goals for the future, at the Coler-California Center, housed in a concrete-and-glass building. A 20-minute English-language film called "Vision" is an introduction to the multimedia touch screens and Internet stations available in the comfortable lounge. Laser-disc videos describe the various Technion departments. To get here, take Bus 31 from the Nof Hotel or the Dan Panorama Hotel. ☒ *Kiryat Ha-Technion (Technion City), Neve Sha'anan,* ☎ *04/832–0664.* ☜ *Free.* ⊙ *Sun.–Thurs. 8:30–3.*

⑩ **Tikotin Museum of Japanese Art.** Established in 1957 by Felix Tikotin, this graceful venue adheres to the Japanese tradition of displaying beautiful objects that are in harmony with the season, so exhibits change frequently. The Japanese atmosphere, created in part by sliding doors and partitions made of wood and paper, accompanies you through a display of scrolls, screens, pottery and porcelain, lacquer and metalwork, paintings from several schools, netsuke and inro, and fresh-flower arrangements. ✉ *88 Hanassi St.,* ☎ *04/838–3554.* ✉ *NIS 24 ($6), including Museum of Modern Art and National Maritime Museum (☞ above).* ⊙ *Mon., Wed., Thurs. 10–5; Tues. 10–2 and 5–8; Fri. 10–1; Sat. 10–2.*

⑧ **Yefe Nof Street.** Also known as Panorama Road, this curving street high above the city skirts the backs of Haifa's biggest hotels, providing superlative views. Part of the walk (through the black iron gate) takes you past two magnificent terraces of the Baha'i Gardens. Enjoy the beauty of the lushly planted Louis Promenade, with shaded benches along the way, beginning behind the Dan Carmel Hotel. On a clear day, from any of several lookouts, the naked eye can take in the port below; Akko, across the bay; and the cliffs of Rosh Hanikra, with Lebanon in the distance. Panorama Road is beautiful during the day and at night.

NEED A BREAK? In a city known for its falafel, we can still highly recommend a **falafel joint** just around the corner from the Wadi Nisnas market, on a small street parallel to St. John's. Turn left at the mall's end onto Khouri Street, and then take the first left. Some 300 ft up on your right is a tidy stand with fresh, steaming chickpea balls; warm pita bread; and all the toppings, as well as soft drinks to wash them all down.

## Dining

$$$$ ✕ **Isabella.** At first glance you'd think you were in Manhattan: the decor is sleek and ultramodern, with tiny lights in the ceiling; walls and curving surfaces in muted gray tones; dark wood tables with sleek leather chairs; and an industrial brushed cement floor. The hip, young waitstaff wear white T-shirts and jeans or go all in black. Opened in spring 2000 by the chef of a famous Tel Aviv upscale pizza place, Isabella is Haifa's first high-tech-style restaurant. The food is a modern interpretation of Italian cuisine, with choices such as salad cacciatore (bite-size pieces of meat stir-fried in olive oil and herbs on a bed of sautéed vegetables); excellent "stuffed" pizza (filled with, among other choices, mushrooms, mozzarella, arugula, and marinated zucchini); and veal or chicken scaloppine in lemon, garlic, white wine, and green onion. Grilled steak is a specialty here; try the veal or beef T-bone with rosemary and lemon sauce. A wise choice for dessert is an individual chocolate cake with hot chocolate sauce and forest berries. An extensive wine list is available. ✉ *6 Ben Gurion Blvd., City Center Mall,* ☎ *04/855–2201. Reservations essential. AE, D, MC, V.*

$$$$ ✕ **Old Man and the Sea.** As the name suggests, this seafood restaurant is inspired by writer Ernest Hemingway. It would make Papa happy to think he'd been remembered so creatively: he would certainly love the glass floors, with colorful fish and crabs swimming beneath, as well as the Hemingway posters that decorate the soft-pink and red walls. This inventive restaurant was opened in spring 2000, and the chef is proud to serve at least six different specials every day. In the center of the room, a wooden fishing boat acts as a salad bar, with a wide variety of vegetables and antipasti. Creamed crab soup makes a perfect starter. If you like sushi (nigiri and sashimi), you're in for a treat; the maki sushi plate is a house specialty. Other main courses include baked sea bream in fresh herbs, spaghetti with mullet in lemon and cream

sauce, seafood in a pot (shrimp, calamari, and mullet) with cream and herbs, and sea fish stroganoff (various sea fish, sliced and stir-fried with mushrooms, cream, garlic, and herbs). Don't pass up the vanilla ice cream with tropical fruit sauce before you order coffee. ⊠ *6 Ben Gurion Blvd., City Center Mall, 2nd floor,* ☎ *04/850–7777. Reservations essential. AE, D, MC, V.*

**\$\$\$\$**  ✕ **Restaurant 1873.** The name indicates when the house was built and suggests that you'll enjoy a bit of history with your meal. This charmingly renovated house has several small rooms, each with wooden floors and an intimate air. The French-Italian chefs create admirable dishes such as, for starters, crabs with rouille and homemade bread, or goose liver on green lentils with caramelized pears. For the main course, choose from fillet of salmon *en choucroute* in white butter and chive sauce, duck for two à la 1873, Cornish hen stuffed with chicken mousse and smoked goose breast, or fillet of veal with Wellington rack of lamb in port sauce. Vegetarians will enjoy the spinach-filled pastry, asparagus tempura, and zucchini blossoms stuffed with mushrooms. A crepe filled with rich pastry cream in toffee sauce makes a grand finale. If you can't wait until dinner, try the business lunch. There's also a pleasant wine bar upstairs. ⊠ *102 Jaffa St.,* ☎ *04/853–2211. Reservations essential. AE, D, MC, V. No lunch Fri.*

**\$\$\$\$**  ✕ **Special Reserve.** You can discover new gustatory experiences in this spacious, informal setting: an excellent bistro, a deli counter loaded with fine local cheeses and meats, plus a high-quality wine shop, and a cigar shop. (Ask if there will be any wine tastings during your stay.) It's a pleasure to dine on the curving balcony, with its creamy yellow walls decorated with artwork by Haifa artists. Start with goat cheese terrine and move on to goose leg confit with fennel salad or spareribs *satay* (marinated, cooked, then served in a peanut, lemon, and chili pepper sauce). Nondieters will enjoy halvah and date parfait for dessert. Small groups can rent the upstairs room, with its wine "cellar" and cigar humidors, for private dining. ⊠ *109 Hanassi Blvd., in the Dan Panorama Mall, ground floor,* ☎ *04/837–9750. Reservations essential. AE, D, MC, V.*

**\$\$\$**  ✕ **Jacko.** If ever there was an eating place that's loved and well known, Jacko is it. Say the name to your taxi driver, and he'll nod approvingly and gun the motor. You'll be dropped in front of a nondescript building with a Hebrew sign, in a crowded, downtown area. Since 1976, this family-run restaurant has been serving up delicious food in a crowded, informal setting (you may end up sharing your table with other diners, many of them regulars). The specialties here are fish and seafood (grilled or fried); the daily catch might be snapper, red mullet, or grouper, and there's seafood pasta, and piles of crab, mussels, or calamari with sauces, as well as large shrimp grilled in their shells, and Mediterranean lobster (in summer). For dessert try the Turkish cookies, semolina and coconut cake, or *travados*—a sticky, dripping-with-syrup, cinnamony confection, accompanied by mint tea. Wine and draft beer are available. ⊠ *12 Hadekalim St.,* ☎ *04/866–8813. Reservations essential. AE, D, MC, V. No dinner Sat.*

**\$\$\$**  ✕ **Karyola.** A Mediterranean-style bistro, this lively restaurant is on a busy main street but it's set back from the traffic. Inside, swathes of floaty white material billow dramatically from the ceiling. The terrace is a pleasant venue for dinner on a warm summer night. Service here, under the eye of chef and owner Liora, is friendly. For starters, try the "cigars," deep-fried crispy cylinders stuffed with ham and spiced cheese, or a dish of shrimp satay. Main courses include Español crab, sautéed in olive oil, fresh tomatoes, garlic, and fish stock; fish baked with herbs, sun-dried tomatoes, garlic, and white wine; salmon fillet in butter served on peppers with garlic; and sautéed chicken breast with ham, pine nuts, garlic, and lemon. Poached pears in wine and saffron is a tasty and light dessert. The wine list offers Israeli and Chilean selections. ⊠ *117 Moriah Blvd.,* ☎ *04/826–5827. AE, D, MC, V. No lunch Sun.*

$$$    ✕ **Mayan HaBira.** If you're a vegetarian, forget it. But if you're looking for meat with a capital "M," you've found the place. Like its neighbor, Jacko (☞ *above*), this restaurant is in the traffic-ridden downtown area, with a sign in Hebrew only outside. It's a highly esteemed Haifa institution, so just ask anyone for directions. The restaurant is divided into three sections, and tables are shared, so you may be eating with strangers. The decor is informal: beer kegs are piled up in a corner; and the walls are covered with photos of politicians, restaurant reviews (glowing), and a mural of their customers painted by an art student in 1989. The family's been in business since 1962; today the son, Reuven, holds forth, and he, his children, and his Romanian mother do all of the excellent cooking. To start, savor meat kreplach, chopped liver, jellied calf's foot, gefilte fish, or oxtail soup. Then go to work on delectable spareribs or goose or beef pastrami, which they smoke themselves. Grilled rabbit is also a good choice. Mother's yummy Bavarian cream makes the perfect finale. ⊠ *4 Nathanson St.,* ☎ *04/862–3193. AE, D, MC, V. Closed Sat. No dinner.*

$$    ✕ **Taiwan.** One of Haifa's best Chinese restaurants, this family-owned place in the German Colony has been in business since the 1970s. The chef is, fittingly enough, from Taiwan. House specialties are lemon chicken and meat and seafood with satay sauce. It's closed between 4 and 7. ⊠ *59 Ben-Gurion Blvd.,* ☎ *04/853–2082. Reservations essential. AE, DC, MC, V.*

## Lodging

$$$$    🏨 **Carmel Forest Spa Resort.** Set in the Carmel Forest, the Spa is lo-
★    cated 25 km (about 14½ mi) from Haifa. It's the ultimate escape: a handsome, top-of-the-line spa in a tastefully appointed hotel designed to pamper its guests in a calm and healthful setting (no cell phones or children under 16). The hotel is located on a hillside, with stunning views of trees and the Mediterranean Sea. Inside the spa there are 25 different treatment rooms dedicated to your well-being. Choose from a variety of massages, from aromatherapy to shiatsu; facials; body peels; seaweed wraps; and such treatments as hydrotherapy, mind-body harmony, reflexology, and body sculpture. (Reserve treatments in advance.) Green wicker chaises face the forest and the Mediterranean coast through the solarium windows. A sample day? Consult the nutritionist, strike out on a forest walk, have a sesame-oil massage, and then sit down to a meal prepared with all-natural ingredients. Other comforting amenities include an authentic Turkish bath, a reading room, and a music room with stuffed armchairs in front of the fireplace. Weight-loss and anti-stress packages are also available. The hotel rate includes full board (while treatments are extra). Day guests are welcome. ⊠ *Carmel Forest, Box 90000, Haifa 31900,* ☎ *04/832–3111,* 𝖥𝖠𝖷 *04/832–3988. 126 rooms. Restaurant, lobby lounge, pool, beauty salon, hot tub, massage, sauna, spa, exercise room. AE, D, MC, V.* ✆

$$$$    🏨 **Dan Carmel.** The Dan is beautifully located on the heights of the Carmel. One of Haifa's first hotels, this thirtysomething institution still has a charm of its own, and the staff is devoted. The premises could use a renovator's touch, but the deluxe rooms on the upper floors are nicely furnished, with wooden bureaus and satin bedspreads. The other doubles are less luxurious, but they're cheerfully decorated in pastels. All guest rooms have balconies with stunning views over the city or the curving shore. The large garden around the pool, landscaped

with potted geraniums and surrounded with fir trees, is always breezy and pleasant. ⊠ *85–87 Hanassi Ave., 31060,* ☎ *04/830–6211,* 𝐅𝐀𝐗 *04/838–7504. 219 rooms. Restaurant, café, pool, beauty salon, sauna, exercise room. AE, DC, MC, V.*

**$$$$** 🏨 **Dan Panorama.** Another member of the Dan hotel chain, this one is glitzier than its sister down the road. It's run by a competent staff, several of whom have been with the hotel for many years. The winding Louis Promenade, which overlooks the city, is a few minutes' walk from the entrance. The rooms are spacious; the blue-and-yellow color scheme, like the light-wood furnishings, is serene. Some rooms look out onto the gold-topped Baha'i Shrine and the bay; the rest have lovely city views. The in-house Vienna Cafe is a fine place to linger over coffee and cake. The hotel is connected to the Panorama Center shopping mall, filled with small restaurants and boutiques. ⊠ *107 Hanassi Ave., 31060,* ☎ *04/835–2222,* 𝐅𝐀𝐗 *04/835–2235. 266 rooms. 2 restaurants, 3 cafés, lobby lounge, pool, children's pool, sauna, aerobics, exercise room, baby-sitting, parking (fee). AE, DC, MC, V.*

**$$$$** 🏨 **Holiday Inn Haifa Bayview.** On the Carmel heights, in the hotel neighborhood, the newest addition to Haifa's lodging facilities opened its doors in December 1999. The well-designed and comfortable hotel is built into a pine-treed slope (guests enter at the ninth floor). The glass-domed lobby has tawny gold-and-green sofas, set off by floral arrangements in clay pots. The business floor has a fully equipped business center. Food is served throughout the day until 8 PM. If you have your computer with you, the Executive rooms are equipped with modem linkups and faxes, plus a trouser press to keep you spiffy for business appointments. Views from the guest rooms are gorgeous, and 10 rooms on the sixth floor have balconies. At press time, an exercise room was being built. ⊠ *111 Yefe Nof St., 31061,* ☎ *04/835–0835,* 𝐅𝐀𝐗 *04/835–0836. 100 rooms. Restaurant, pool, 2 saunas, parking (fee). AE, D, MC, V.*

**$$$** 🏨 **Nof.** The rooms in this small, pleasant hotel are done up in turquoise and are adequately comfortable. What's unbeatable is the location, and the view of the city spilling down to the sea from the top of Mt. Carmel. The modest guest rooms take full advantage, with large windows all facing the sea. The lobby lounge, which opens onto the Promenade, also has superb views. The front-desk staff and room service are friendly and efficient. The on-site Chinese restaurant makes for a convenient, and rewarding, dining experience. ⊠ *101 Hanassi Ave., 31063,* ☎ *04/835–4311,* 𝐅𝐀𝐗 *04/838–8810. 93 rooms. Restaurant, bar, lobby lounge, dance club. AE, DC, MC, V.*

**$** 🏨 **Port Inn Hostel Guest House.** Located in lower Haifa, two bus stops from the beach and near the train to Akko, this haven for those on a budget was opened in winter 1999. In an old neighborhood, it's an old house beautifully redone by owner-manager Rachel's son in quiet shades of pale yellow, with plants and bric-a-brac that lend a decorative touch. The dormitories won't interest most travelers (one is for women, one for men; each sleeps 14), but there are five double rooms with private bath, and one without. Reserve early for this good value, complete with a small outside patio, kitchen facilities, a tasty breakfast, and a helpful staff. ⊠ *34 Jaffa Rd., Haifa 33261,* ☎ *04/852–4401. 6 doubles, 5 with bath. Lounge, air-conditioning, in-room data ports, laundry service. AE, DC, MC, V.*

## Nightlife and the Arts

For the latest information on performances, festivals, and other special events in and around Haifa, check Friday's *Jerusalem Post* or the monthly brochure "Events in Haifa and the Northern Region," available at hotels and tourist offices. In balmy weather, a stroll along the Louis

Promenade and then along Panorama Road is a relaxing way to end the day. For a more festive evening, try the wine bars and restaurants in the newly spruced-up German Colony. Nightspots in Haifa come and go, and some open only on certain evenings, so call first if possible.

### BARS

Two pubs of the moment are **Migdalor** (⊠ At Stella Maris, ☎ 04/833–6292) and **Shmura** (⊠ 38 Pica Rd., ☎ 04/834–7727).

### DANCE CLUBS

In the basement of the Dan Panorama hotel is the **Chaplin Club** (☎ 04/835–2206), a disco catering to the thirtysomething crowd. There's no cover charge and no minimum on weekdays; on Friday the minimum per person is NIS 60 ($16) plus a 10% service charge. The club is open from 10:30 PM to 2 AM daily. On Friday, call for reservations. **Fever** is a club that's hot with the younger crowd and is conveniently located in Gan Ha'Em, opposite the Dan Panorama hotel.

### FILM

In October, around the time of the holiday Sukkoth, Haifa hosts an **international film festival.** Contact the **Haifa Cinemateque** (☎ 04/835–3530) for schedules and venues.

### MUSIC

A **blues festival** takes place in July in Haifa's port; for information call ☎ 04/837–4010 or inquire at the tourist office (☎ 04/853–5606). The **Israel Philharmonic Orchestra** gives approximately 30 concerts at the Haifa Auditorium (⊠ 138 Hanassi Ave., ☎ 04/838–0013) from October through July. Ticket prices range from NIS 105 ($30) to NIS 280 ($80) and are generally sold only at Philharmonic box offices in Jerusalem, Tel Aviv, and Haifa (in Haifa, ⊠ 16 Herzl St., ☎ 04/866–4167). Concerts start at 8:30 PM or 9 PM, and the box office opens one hour before performances. The **Haifa Symphony Orchestra** also performs at the Haifa Auditorium four times a week, one week of every month. It's best to buy tickets about 30 minutes before the performance, which generally begins around 8:30 PM; ticket prices range from NIS 40 ($10) to NIS 80 ($20). Contact the box office for more information (⊠ 50 Tezner St., ☎ 04/862–1973).

### WINE BARS

A lovely way to reflect on the day's touring is to settle down over a glass of wine at a local wine bar. Indeed, good food is served at all the places listed below (at lunchtime as well). **Batzir** (⊠ 44 Jaffa St., ☎ 04/853–5668) is a small place whose ceiling is plastered with wine labels—it's filled with old wooden cupboards and shelves of wine bottles; clusters of grapes decorate the exterior (the sign's in Hebrew only). Tasty accompaniments to *vino* are bruschetta with prosciutto ham and tapenade or smoked goose and Portobello mushrooms in wine and almonds. The upper floor of the old stone building housing **Restaurant 1873** (⊠ 102 Yaffa St., ☎ 04/853–2211), in the lively German Colony, is open Thursday, Friday, and Saturday nights; reservations are a good idea. An extensive choice of local and imported wines is available, along with two types of fondue: pieces of beef fillet dipped in hot wine, or chunks of bread with vegetables in hot cheese. **Special Reserve** (⊠ 109 Hanassi Blvd., Dan Panorama Mall, ground floor, ☎ 04/837–9750) is a well-organized store with a huge selection of wine, in a gracious setting that also includes a restaurant. Owner and wine expert Andre hosts wine tastings and complements his wares with fine cheeses and local foie gras from the shop on the premises.

## Outdoor Activities and Sports

BEACHES

Haifa's coastline is one fine, sandy public beach after another. From south to north, **Dado, Zamir, Carmel, and Bat Galim beaches** (☎ 04/852–4231) cover 5 km (3 mi) of coast, with many lifeguard stations among them. Entrance and parking are free. The beaches have sports areas, changing rooms, showers, toilets, refreshment stands, many restaurants, and a winding stone promenade that connects them. On Saturday afternoons at Dado Beach (near the Hof HaCarmel train station at the city's entrance) Israelis of all ages come and folk dance, to onlookers' delight.

BOWLING

It's hardly the national sport, but **Bowling,** under the Super Sol supermarket (✉ 124 Hanassi Blvd., ☎ 04/810–1188), is open from 10 AM until midnight, seven days a week. One game costs NIS 21 ($5.25), including shoe rental.

DIVING

If you'd like to learn to dive, **Val Tal** diving club (✉ 2 Hubert Humphrey St., ☎ 04/851–1523) gives lessons. If you already know how and would like to explore 20th-century wrecks off the Haifa coast (for instance, an Italian submarine sunk by the British), look for Val Tal at the bottom station of the cable car, near the Yotvata restaurant. Rental equipment is available, and it's open from 9 to 5 every day.

ICE-SKATING

One of Israel's few ice-skating rinks is in the **Lev Hamifratz** shopping center (☎ 04/841–5388), in northern Haifa on the road to Akko. The rink is open daily from 10 AM to 10 PM, but call ahead, as practice sessions sometimes tie up the rink in the afternoons. Admission, which includes skate rental, is NIS 40 ($10).

## Shopping

Haifa is studded with modern indoor shopping malls replete with boutiques, small restaurants, and movie theaters. Convenient to the hotels on Mt. Carmel is the **Horev Center,** on Horev Street at Pica Street, in the Ahuza district. The **Panorama Center,** next to the Dan Panorama hotel, is also conveniently close to Haifa's hotels. In the German Colony, the new **City Center** (6 Ben Gurion St.) offers internationally known designer clothing and shoe shops, plus coffee shops and two upscale restaurants. The huge **Grand Canyon,** a bit out of the way in Neve Sha'anan, has more than 100 shops.

Duck into **Sara's Gift Shop,** in the Dan Carmel hotel (☎ 04/830–6238), to pick up gifts for everyone, including yourself, at reasonable prices. It's crammed with jewelry made exclusively for these displays; the silver and Roman glass pieces are particularly seductive. Other items include Judaica, souvenirs such as the *chamsa* (a hand for warding off the evil eye), and handmade textile hangings.

# THE ROTHSCHILD WINE COUNTRY AND MT. CARMEL

This is the back-door route to Haifa, one that wanders through the foothills and up the spine of Mt. Carmel through Druze villages. Route 4 is smooth sailing, with the Carmel looming to the east beyond cultivated fields and huge banana plantations (though you may not see the bananas, as they're usually bagged in blue or gray plastic). The road leads through undulating countryside dotted with cypresses, palms, and vineyards.

# Benyamina

**⑱**  *55 km (34 mi) north of Tel Aviv on Rte. 652.*

Coming from the south, you'll drive through Benyamina, the youngest settlement in the area. Founded in 1922, it was named after Baron Edmond de Rothschild (1845–1934), the head of the French branch of the famous family, who took a keen interest in the welfare of his fellow Jews in Palestine. (His Hebrew name was Benyamin.) With his prestige, vision, and financial contributions, Rothschild laid the foundations in the late 19th century for Zichron Ya'akov and Bat Shlomo, as well as other towns along the coastal plain and in the Upper Galilee.

The advice of the viniculture experts Rothschild hired in the 1880s paid off handsomely, at least in this region—after years of adversity and setbacks, the fruit of the vines flourished in the 1890s. Rothschild's paternalistic system was not without its pitfalls, however; some of his administrators ruled his colonies like petty despots, trying, for instance, to impose use of the French language on the local settlers, who wished to speak Hebrew. Note that in Benyamina, as in other Rothschild towns, the signs of early settlement are respectfully preserved: rows of lofty, willowy Washingtonian palms introduced to the area by the local hero and agronomist Aaron Aaronson, of neighboring Zichron Ya'akov; and modest, one-story stucco homes capped with terra-cotta roofs, inspired by towns in Provence.

## Dining

**$$$**  ✕ **Shuni Castle.** After pleasing customers for 14 years in nearby Shuni, the Castle relocated in the winter of 1999 to a small neighborhood near the railway station in this early settlement town. The restaurant is located in a one-story old wooden house with a black pointed roof, set in a garden. The warm country charm is still the same, with artfully arranged baskets of red peppers, chunky dried sausage, and chubby loaves of homemade bread on the wooden tables. Also the same is the cheery welcome proferred by chef and proprietor Antoine, who will suggest such tasty dishes as homemade goose liver pâté, leg of duck with honey and fruit, boeuf bourgignon with mushrooms, veal with white wine and artichokes, and braised entrecôte with peppers and tomatoes. Consider apple-filled crêpes Normande with caramel sauce for dessert. Local red and white wines are served. ⊠ *Hamesilla St.,* ☎ *04/638–0227. Reservations essential. DC, V. Closed Sun.*

# Shuni

**⑲**  *At railroad tracks in Benyamina, turn left onto Rte. 652, then drive 1 km (½ mi) north.*

This stone fortress was built by effendis in the 18th and 19th centuries, on the site of existing ruins, because of its sweeping command over the surrounding lands, some planted with grain (*shuni* is Arabic for granary). Now the landscaped **Jabotinsky Park,** this area was part of a parcel purchased by Rothschild in 1914, but its chief attractions today are Shuni (the Ottoman fortress) and the Roman theater. You can also dine in the fortress. The spring at present-day Shuni was also the source of the spring water that was tapped for the aqueducts of ancient Caesarea. In the 1930s and '40s, the site was chosen for its remote location as a training ground for members of self-organized units inspired by Ze'ev Jabotinsky (1880–1940), the right-wing Zionist leader who was the spiritual head of the Jewish underground organization Irgun Zvai Leumi. Armed Irgun units later launched attacks from here.

Excavations of the well-preserved, 2nd-century **Roman theater** (which you enter through the fortress) have revealed the remains of bathing pools lined with 2nd-century Roman mosaics and a marble statue of the Greek god of medicine, Aesculapius, both now in storage at the Rockefeller Museum, in Jerusalem. These finds support the theory that this was once a sacred spa whose waters had healing powers—indeed, an early 4th-century pilgrim mentioned in his writings that women who bathed here always became pregnant, like it or not. The theater also contains an ancient olive press, carved lintels, and fragments of columns. On the right, before you enter the fortress, you can still see part of a mosaic floor. Call ahead to arrange a guided tour of the site. ⊠ *Rte. 652,* ☎ *04/638–9730.* ≦ *NIS 12 ($3).* ⊙ *Sun.–Thurs. 9–4, Fri. and holiday eves 9–12:30, Sat. 9–4.*

NEED A BREAK?    Shortly after passing Shuni, turn left past the olive trees and into the **Tishbi Estate Winery** (☎ 04/638–0434) for a look at one of the country's most esteemed wineries. "Tishbi Estate" is the premier label (the sauvignon blanc and chardonnay are among the best in Israel), while "Tishbi" and "Baron" are the others. Call ahead to reserve a wine tasting and a tour of the old buildings—the Tishbi family's great-grandfather planted the first vineyards in the area almost 120 years ago. Tishbi's is open Sunday to Thursday 8–4 and Friday 8–3.

## Zichron Ya'akov

★ ⓴   *61 km (40 mi) north of Tel Aviv.*

The planted roundabout marks the entrance to Zichron Ya'akov, a town named by its original settlers in honor of Rothschild's father, James. Pick up a town map in the tourist office just opposite, next to the Founders' Monument and the central bus station. Most of the main sights are signposted in English. You can visit Zichron Ya'akov in an hour or so if you're on your way elsewhere; it also makes a nice day trip from Tel Aviv or Haifa, including a relaxing lunch at one of the town's new restaurants (make reservations if you're coming on Saturday).

Founded in 1882 by Romanian pioneers, this settlement nearly foundered until rescued by Edmond de Rothschild. A decade later, however, the town's winery took off, the same **Carmel Mizrachi Wine Cellars** that you'll find by veering to the right from the roundabout and driving down Jabotinsky Street. At the end of Jabotinsky, turn right on Hanadiv Street. Today the winery is Israel's largest, producing more than 160 different wines and spirits. The old wooden buildings house a wine shop, and a homey restaurant where local cheeses and pasta are served, on weekdays. The original storage vats and oak barrels are still on view, though wine is now stored mostly in stainless-steel vats and concrete tanks. A guided one-hour tour outlines the stages of local wine production, from the weighing-in of tractors laden with grapes to grape pressing and the aging of wine in caves. Included in the tour are a tasting of some four varieties, and a seven-minute audiovisual presentation screened in a 100-year-old wine cellar. Tours leave at various times between 9 AM and 4 PM, and it's a good idea to reserve one in advance. The finest Carmel Mizrachi wines are the Rothschild vintages: merlot, chardonnay, cabernet sauvignon, sauvignon blanc, and sweet wine. Carmel gin, vodka, and brandy are also available at the shop. An autumn wine festival takes place here after the harvest, around the time of the Sukkoth holiday. ☎ *04/629–0977.* ≦ *NIS 12 ($3).* ⊙ *Sun.–Thurs. 9–4, Fri. 9–1.*

To visit the town itself, retrace your way up Jabotinsky Street to the town's entrance. The main street, **Hameyasdim,** starts at the stone arch with the red-tile roof, just past the Founders' Monument. Residents have made every effort to maintain the original appearance of this short thoroughfare, and the cobblestone street is lined, for the most part, with restored, small, red-roof 19th-century homes. In those days, people needed courtyards behind their homes to house animals, carts, and farm equipment; several of these have been restored to look exactly as they did then. These days, upscale restaurants, historical sites, and offbeat shops occupy the courtyards and are interspersed with the old houses on the main street.

About halfway down the street is **Bet Aaronson** (Aaronson's House), whose late-19th-century architecture successfully combines Art Nouveau and Middle Eastern traditions. This museum was once the home of the accomplished agronomist Aaron Aaronson (1876–1919), who gained international fame for his discovery of an ancestor of modern wheat, a wild and hardy strain that grew in the surrounding mountains. The house remains as it looked after World War I, with family photographs and French and Turkish furniture. The museum also houses the library, diaries, and letters of Aaronson, who in his youth was sent by Rothschild to France to study agriculture.

Aaronson and his sisters became local heroes as leaders of the spy ring called the NILI (an acronym for a quotation from the Book of Samuel: "The Eternal One of Israel will not prove false")—a militant group dedicated to ousting the Turks from Palestine by collaborating with the British during World War I. They were spurred on by such Turkish policies as the expulsion of Russian Jews from Palestine (the Russians were enemies of the Turks during World War I) and the confiscation of Jewish property.

Both sisters, Sarah and Rebecca, were in love with Aaron's assistant, Absalom Feinberg. A double agent was disrupting NILI's communications with the British, so Feinberg set off to cross the Sinai desert to make contact. He was killed in an ambush in the Gaza Strip. His remains were recovered some 50 years later from a grave marked simply by a palm tree, the tree having sprouted from some dates in Feinberg's pockets. (After the Six Day War, Feinberg's body was reburied in Jerusalem.) Sarah Aaronson was captured by the Turks and committed suicide in her brother's house after being tortured. Other NILI leaders were executed by the Turks upon discovery. Aaron returned to Zichron Ya'akov with the victorious British in 1918, but the following year his plane mysteriously vanished en route from London to the Paris Peace Conference. A tour in English is provided; the last one takes place at 2:15 PM. ✉ *40 Hameyasdim St.,* ☎ *04/639–0120.* 💵 *NIS 12 ($3).* 🕙 *Sun.–Thurs. 8:30–2:15 (last tour), Tues. 8:30–3, Fri. 8:30–noon.*

A few doors up the street is **Binyamin Pool,** a misnomer because it's actually the town's original water tower, built in 1891. Zichron was the first village in Israel to have water piped to its houses; Meir Dizengoff, the first mayor of Tel Aviv, even came to town to see how it was done. The facade resembles that of an ancient synagogue.

Farther on, at the corner of Hanadiv and Hameyasdim streets, stands the old synagogue, **Ohel Ya'akov,** built by Rothschild in 1886 to satisfy the settlers' first request.

Turn left onto Hanadiv Street, at the end of which stands the **First Aliya Museum,** located in the former Administration House. Commissioned by Baron de Rothschild, it is a fine example of late-19th-century Ottoman-style architecture, built of white stone with a central pediment capped by a tile roof. The museum is dedicated to the lives of immigrants who came to Israel with the First Aliya (a period of settlement from 1882 until 1904). Life-size model displays of local immigrants (like Zachariya, the seed vendor and Izer, the cobbler) help illustrate how life was lived at that time. One film, among others, traces a family who came from Europe to follow a vision and describes the struggle encountered in a difficult, not-so-dreamlike period of Israel's modern history.

| | |
|---|---|
| NEED A BREAK? | An inviting place to relax and watch the action in this still-rural town is the sweet little **park** on Hanadiv Street, opposite the old synagogue and the First Aliya Museum. In the spring it's filled with multicolored roses and all year round flowers blossom vibrantly. |

## Dining

**$$$$** ✕ **Il Bacio (Ha Neshika).** Walk in off the main street until you spy an old one-story farmhouse—one section is the young chef-owner's home (he's the fourth generation); the other is this charming restaurant. The place is small and cozy, with wooden window frames, dark metal rafters, charming old family photos, and an open kitchen that allows you to see the staff at work. The chef is very conversant and attentive; he'll happily explain the menu to you. The food is delicious and creative. Start with the grouper fish soup, homemade sausage, or stuffed cabbage with bacon and mushrooms. Served with your meal is homemade bread, with lentils in balsamic vinegar. Main courses might include baked crabs in sweet and hot chili sauce, pork roll made with roasted baby onions, lamb casserole, or quail with a root vegetable sauce. Two types of sea fish are always available. A vegetable tasting menu including steamed asparagus, black olive and lemon salad, and artichoke with fresh fava beans. The chocolate tart and the creamy white chocolate mousse with berries are both mouthwatering indeed. ⊠ 37 Hameyasdim St., ☎ 04/639–0133. Reservations essential. AE, D, MC, V. Closed Sun. No lunch Mon.

**$$$$** ✕ **Picciotto.** Not so long ago, Zichron was a sleepy village, and many
★ of its old houses sat shuttered and closed. One of these, on the main street, retains its original wood shutters and warm clay color but has been restored inside. The ceiling is original, made of wood brought from the Carpathian mountains; settlers peer sternly out from photos on the pale-pink walls; and the dishes are ocher-color pottery decorated with green palm trees. The young chef creates an eclectic menu depending on what's fresh in the market. Both the pumpkin soup with ginger and the cauliflower with goat cheese merit mention. Each makes a fine introduction to main courses such as quail breast baked with rosemary, grilled fillet of pork with balsamic vinegar and olive oil, or grilled drumfish in a sauce of shallots and butter. For dessert, try the chocolate custard or tarte Tatine with vanilla ice cream. ⊠ 41 Hameyasdim St., ☎ 04/629–0646. Reservations essential. AE, D, MC, V. Closed Sun.

**$$** ✕ **Hatemaniya shel Santo.** Settle down on this wooden porch, in a courtyard well off the main street, for a tasty and authentic Yemenite meal. There's no menu—the waiter brings you soft pita bread, country black bread, and a large, fresh vegetable salad along with a rugged hummus dripped with olive oil. You can order stuffed vegetables or chicken, but make sure you also try the potato cakes and a plate of the small meat patties flavored with cilantro. It's all delicious, and nicely washed down by Yemenite coffee or cold water with lemon and mint. ⊠ 52 Hameyasdim St., ☎ 04/639–8762. AE, DC, MC, V. Closed Sat.

## Lodging

**$$$$** ☷ **Baron's Heights and Terraces.** Built in 1989, and spread over the hillside on 14 terraced levels facing the coast, this hotel was designed with clean, modern geometric lines. The rooms are furnished in pastels with terra-cotta tiles and carpeting, and each has a terrace (with a nice view), a separate living area, and a kitchenette. The specially designed mountain elevator reaches all levels. The pool, which adjoins the large coffee shop, overlooks the sea from the 15th floor. ⊠ *Box 332, Zichron Ya'akov 30900,* ☎ *04/630–0333,* FAX *04/630–0325. 154 rooms. Restaurant, bar, café, pool, hot tub, sauna, steam room, exercise room, children's programs. AE, DC, MC, V.*

**$$$$** ☷ **Carmel Gardens.** This large hotel, 1 km (½ mi) from Zichron Ya'akov and occupying most of a mountainside, has stunning views of the Mediterranean coast sloping down to the sea. Its newest wing, surrounded by trees and gardens, is very large and very contemporary. The public rooms are pleasingly furnished with heavy, off-white wooden pieces plumped with seat covers and lots of white pillows dappled with blue, brown, or beige. Polished stone floors set off the modern look. Outdoors, on the terrace, a waterfall splashes down the hill to a pool below, surrounded by olive trees and pretty gardens. The guest rooms (up 10 steps) are functional rather than fancy, but each has a smashing view. The hotel is geared for conventions, but the common areas are so large and spread out that crowds are not likely to disturb those traveling independently. The work of Israeli artists is displayed in the lobby. ⊠ *1 Etzion St. (at western entrance to Zichron Ya'akov), 30900,* ☎ *04/630–0111,* FAX *04/639–7030. 112 rooms. Lobby lounge, pool, massage, playground. AE, DC, MC, V.*

**$$** ☷ **Bet Daniel.** In a verdant park near the town center, this guest house was founded in 1938 as a retreat for musicians. Its guests came to include artists and writers, and today it is open to the public. If you place a premium on quiet and charm, you'll love it. The living room boasts a 1905 Steinway and other antiques from England; old photographs hang on the walls; and the library is well stocked with books in German, Yiddish, French, and Hebrew. The rooms in the stone building were recently redecorated. If you want to stay here during the biannual chamber-music festival (☞ The Arts, *below*), reserve well in advance. Good home cooking is available under various meal-plan options including breakfast, half-board, and full board. ⊠ *Box 13, 30900,* ☎ *04/639–9001,* FAX *04/639–7007. 14 rooms. DC, V.*

**$$** ☷ **Bet Maimon.** This family-run hotel on the western slopes of Zichron Ya'akov has a spectacular view of the coastal valley and the sea. The terrace restaurant serves both Middle Eastern and Eastern European cuisine. Inquire about the special health-vacation packages. The rooms have been recently redecorated in a gentle pastel yellow. Guests who are less than fit will feel the climb to the sundeck on the roof; the three-story building has no elevator. ⊠ *4 Zahal St., 30900,* ☎ *04/639–0212,* FAX *04/639–6547. 23 rooms. Restaurant, hot tub, sauna. AE, DC, MC, V.*

## The Arts

The pastoral musicians' and artists' retreat, Bet Daniel (☎ 04/639–9001) is a perfect setting for the two **chamber-music festivals** held here during Sukkoth and Passover, which generally fall in October and April, respectively. The programs feature open rehearsals and discussions by musicians and teachers as well as alternating afternoon and evening concerts. Between concerts, you can walk around the lovely landscaped grounds, set in the woods with a fine view of Mt. Carmel. Try to reserve a room well in advance if you want to stay at Bet Daniel itself.

## Bat Shlomo

**㉑** *5 km (3 mi) northeast of Zichron Ya'akov on Rte. 4, then Rte. 70 (toward Yokneam).*

Bat Shlomo was established in 1889 and named after the Baron de Rothschild's mother, Betty, daughter of Solomon ("bat Shlomo" in Hebrew). Established for the children of Zichron Ya'akov's farmers, this tiny hamlet failed to grow, and the town remains virtually unchanged. The oldest part of the village has only one street; it's a charming stroll past small, square houses with red-tile roofs, the space between them leaving just enough room for the farmer's horse and wagon. The old synagogue is in the middle of the street. A few of the owners still cultivate the land and sell locally made cheese, olive oil, and honey, much like their forebears. The short walk ends with a dramatic view of vineyards below and, opposite, the lushly forested hill of a nature reserve established by the British in 1941.

## Mukhraka

★ **㉒** *18 km (11 mi) northeast of Bat Shlomo, on Rte. 70, then Rte. 672. Drive 3 km (2 mi) east on bumpy 672, then turn at sign for Mukhraka.*

Past open, uncultivated fields and a goatherd's rickety shack is the **Carmelite Monastery** at Mukhraka. The monastery stands on the spur of the Carmel range, at an altitude of 1,580 ft, on or near the site where the struggle between Elijah and the priests of Ba'al is believed to have taken place. *Mukhraka* is the Arabic word for a place of burning, referring to the fire that consumed the offering on Elijah's altar. The conflict developed because the people of Israel had been seduced by the pagan cults introduced by King Ahab's wife, Jezebel; Elijah demanded a contest with the priests of Ba'al in which each would erect an altar with a butchered ox as an offering and see which divinity sent down fire. Elijah drenched his altar with water, yet it burst into flames. On his orders, the priests were taken down to the Brook of Kishon and executed.

The stark stone monastery was built in 1883 over Byzantine ruins. Records show that the site was revered as early as the 6th century, when hermits dwelled here. The Carmelites, a Roman Catholic monastic order established in the 13th century, look to Elijah as their role model (Muslims revere Elijah as a prophet). (The courtyard contains a statue of a fearless Elijah brandishing a knife.) The monks who live here have no telephones and only a generator for power. Climb to the roof for an unforgettable panorama: to the east stretches the Jezreel Valley and the hills of Nazareth, Moreh, and Gilboa. On a clear day you can even see Jordan's Gilead Mountains beyond the Jordan River and Mt. Hermon. ☎ No phone. ⌦ NIS 2 (50¢). ☉ Mon.–Sat. 8–1:30 and 2:30–5.

## Daliyat el Carmel

**㉓** *2 km (1⅓ mi) west of Mukhraka (at junction with Rte. 672).*

Daliyat el Carmel is Israel's largest Druze village. The Druze are a close-knit, Arabic-speaking people who practice a secret religion; they form one of the most intriguing entities in the mosaic of Israel's population (of which they number 2%). So exclusive is this sect that only around 6% of the community is initiated into its religious doctrine, one tenet of which is a belief in reincarnation. The Druze broke away from Islam about 1,000 years ago, believing in the divinity of their founder, al Hakim bi Amir Allah, the Caliph of the Egyptian Fatimid dynasty from AD 996 to 1021. The Druze who live in the two existing villages on Mt. Carmel (the other is Isfiya; ☞ *below*) serve in the Israeli Army, a sign of their loyalty to Israel. Though many of the younger generation wear jeans and T-shirts, some older men and women are easily recognizable in their traditional garb. Head coverings indicate the degree of religious belief, from high white turban (resembling a fez) to white kerchief covering the head and shoulders. Many men sport a bushy, walruslike moustache, a hallmark of the Druze, and some older ones wear flowing dark robes and black pantaloons. Although many women wear Western garments, they retain the diaphanous white headdress, often worn with an embroidered dress.

About 1 km (½ mi) inside town, take a right turn into the marketplace, a colorful jumble of shops lining the street. You can be assured of eating excellent falafel at any of the roadside stands or restaurants.

### Dining

**$$** ✕ **House of Druze Heritage.** The Druze are famous for their hospitality. Here you get not only a warm welcome and a good, solid meal but a look at the accoutrements of the Druze way of life. The traditional meal begins with an assortment of appetizers, such as hot-pepper salad, pickles, tahine (sesame paste), and hummus with big, flat Druze pita bread. The main course consists of skewers of grilled lamb or steak; baklava and Turkish coffee provide the finishing touch. The museum in the back displays Druze clothing and an intriguing array of farm implements, household objects, handicrafts, and photos. ⊠ *4 Ahat St.,* ☎ *04/839–3242. AE, D, MC, V.*

### Shopping

Along a brief stretch of the main road that winds through Daliyat el Carmel are shops selling lightweight throw rugs, handwoven baskets, brightly colored pottery, brass dishes, characteristic woven wall hangings, and embroidered skullcaps (for men). Bargaining is expected. Some shops close on Friday; the strip is crowded on Saturday.

## Isfiya

**㉔** *1 km (½ mi) north of Daliyat el Carmel on Rte. 672.*

Isfiya is very similar to neighboring Daliyat el Carmel, with flat-roof homes built closely together into the hillside, many of them raised on pillars and cut with arched windows. Hospitality is second nature to the Druze; you may be able to visit a village home and watch as the woman of the house bakes crispy-thin pita bread in the courtyard, then eat it with yogurt cheese and spices while hearing about Druze life from an ornate sofa in the living room (☞ Guided Tours *in* Northern Coast and Western Galilee A to Z, *below*). As you leave the village, at the top of the hill, note the vista of the Jezreel Valley opening suddenly on your right. The final approach to Haifa also affords a magnificent view of the coast stretching up to Akko, across the bay.

### Dining

**$$** ✕ **Nof Carmel.** Don't bother to look for an English sign; this Druze
★ restaurant is identifiable by the ubiquitous red Coca-Cola logo. Drive to the northern edge of the village and it's on your left, encircled by a picket fence. People come for the fine Middle Eastern fare, especially the thick homemade hummus with pine nuts or *foule* (a baked broadbean concoction seasoned with oil, garlic, and lemon juice), and the well-seasoned kebab. Those with a sweet tooth will want to sample the *sahlab* (a warm, custardlike winter drink or pudding of crushed orchid bulb with thickened milk and sugar, topped with raisins, almonds, cinnamon, or ginger) or the scale-bending baklava. ⊠ *Rte. 672,* ☎ *04/ 839–1718. Reservations not accepted. AE, MC, V.*

# Ein Hod

⓯ *5 km (3 mi) west of Isfiya.*

To get to the artists' village of Ein Hod, head east straight past the coastal highway to Route 4, where you turn right. The exit ramp, climbing through olive trees and scrub, will be on your left. You can also get there with Bus 921 or 202 from Haifa. Today, Ein Hod is home to around 135 families of sculptors, painters, and other artists. The setting is an idyllic one, with rough-hewn stone houses built on the hillside with sweeping views. As the Dadaist painter Marcel Janco (1895–1984) wrote of the deserted Arab village slated for demolition after his first trip there, in 1950: "The beauty of the place was staggering." Though the place was ruled by scorpions and snakes and was without water or electricity, Janco and a group of 20 artists set up a colony here two years later.

Parking is across the road, opposite the entrance to Ein Hod. Climbing up the hill, you'll soon come to a winding street on the left that starts a lovely walk that encircles the small village. Signs indicate studios and workshops where artists paint, sculpt, and make jewelry, pottery, silkscreen prints, and clothing.

The town square is bordered by a restaurant and a large gallery where works by present and past Ein Hod artists are exhibited (☞ Shopping, *below*). Across the street is the **Janco-Dada Museum.** As one of the founders of the Dada movement, the Romanian-born Janco already had, of course, a well-established professional reputation when he immigrated to Israel in 1941. The museum, which opened in 1983, houses a permanent collection of works in various media by the artist, reflecting Janco's output in both Europe and Israel. A 20-minute slide show chronicles the life of the artist and the Dada movement. Also exhibited are works by other Israeli modern artists. Don't miss the view from the rooftop before leaving. ☎ *04/984–2350.* ☐ *NIS 10 ($2.50).* ☉ *Sun.– Thurs. and Sat. 9:30–5, Fri. and holiday eves 9:30–4.*

## Dining

$$ ✕ **Restaurant Ein Hod.** After all that walking, and all that art, you might like to relax on the terrace and enjoy an appetizing lunch under the trees. Antipasti is a fine way to start off; your plate will include lentil salad, celery root cooked with lemon, homemade olives, and French country bread. Main courses include ravioli stuffed with salmon in a fresh tomato, cream, and vodka sauce and moussaka made with beef, eggplant, and sun-dried tomatoes with an arugula salad. Nothing beats the chocolate truffles or panna cotta with orange syrup for dessert. ☒ *Main Sq.,* ☎ *04/954–1254. AE, DC, MC, V. No dinner Sun.*

## Nightlife and the Arts

Ein Hod's **Gertrud Kraus House** (☎ 04/984–1058 or 04/984–2018), just off the main square, features chamber music on occasional Saturday evenings at 6:30 between October and June. Admission is NIS 40 ($10), and coffee and cake are on the house.

## Shopping

The best place in this region for quality handicrafts is the **Gallery** (☎ 04/984–2548), on Ein Hod's main square. Arrayed in the front room of the village's official gallery are silver, enamel, and gold jewelry; hand-blown glass; and ceramic jugs, mugs, and teapots. Three other rooms are devoted to paintings, watercolors, sculptures, and graphic works by resident artists, some of them internationally known. Tourists can ask for a small discount. The gallery is open Sunday–Thursday and Saturday 10–4:30, Friday and holidays 10–2.

The gallery **Silver Print** (☎ 04/984–1067), run by Vivienne and Roy Silver, a four-minute walk from the main square, is devoted to Israeli photography. Ask to see the lovely old photos, many taken by Vivienne's grandfather. A subspecialty is greeting cards, some of which are old photos of the Holy Land. The Silvers also sell a map (NIS 20, or $5) with a walking tour of Ein Hod and stickers with photos of the 18 sites along the way. Call ahead for an appointment.

## Nahal Me'arot Nature Reserve

㉖ *3 km (2 mi) south of Ein Hod, 1 km (½ mi) east of Rte. 4.*

The prehistoric **Carmel Caves** are in the Nahal Me'arot Nature Reserve. The three excavated caves are up a steep flight of stairs, on a fossil reef that was covered by the sea 100 million years ago. The first discoveries of prehistoric remains were made when this area was being scoured for stones to build the Haifa port. In the late 1920s, the first archaeological expedition was headed by Dorothy Garrod of England, who received assistance from a British feminist group on condition that the dig be carried out exclusively by women. It was. In the Tannur cave, the first on the tour, the strata Garrod's team excavated are clearly marked, spanning about 150,000 years in the life of early man. The most exciting discovery made in the area was the existence of both Homo sapien and Neanderthal skeletons; evidence that both lived here has raised fascinating questions about the relationship between the two and whether they lived side by side. A display on the daily life of early man as hunter and food gatherer occupies the Gamal cave. The last cave you'll visit, called the Nahal, is the largest—it cuts deep into the mountain—and was actually the first discovered. A burial place with 84 skeletons was found outside the mouth of the cave, where you can see a hunched-up skeleton.

The bone artifacts and stone tools discovered in the Nahal cave suggest that people who settled here, about 12,000 years ago, were the forebears of early farmers with a modified social structure more developed than that of hunters and gatherers. There is also evidence that the Crusaders once used the cave to guard the coastal road. Inside, an audiovisual show sheds light on how early man lived here. There's a snack bar and parking lot at this site. ☎ *04/984–1750 or 04/984–1752.* ▣ *NIS 16 ($4).* ☉ *Sun.–Thurs., Sat., and holidays 8–4; Fri. and holiday eves 8–1.*

### Outdoor Activities and Sports

At the entrance to the Carmel Caves is the stone office of the **Nature Reserves Authority** (☎ 04/984–1750), where trained staff provide maps and information about two well-marked nature walks that leave from this point. The route of the "Botanical Path" takes two hours, while the "Geological Path" takes 40 minutes; both include specially built lookout points.

# THROUGH WESTERN GALILEE, FROM AKKO TO ROSH HANIKRA

## Akko

★ *22 km (13½ mi) north of Haifa.*

The walled Old City of Akko (also known as Acre), located in the modern town of Akko, is an enchanting mix of mosques, markets, khans (Ottoman inns), and vaulted Crusader ruins (many of which are underground) at the northern tip of Haifa Bay. You can approach it from

Haifa on Route 4. A much slower but far prettier inland route takes you north on Route 70, a scenic drive that runs roughly parallel to Route 4 about 7 km (4½ mi) to the east, through rolling hills, avoiding the unattractive industrial pockets and drab satellite towns of Haifa. Continue north past a small jog in the road that you'll encounter 10 km (6 mi) ahead. Take Route 85 west some 14 km (9 mi) later to reach Akko's walled Old City, where you'll start your visit. Plan on at least three hours here, half a day if you want to see everything.

*Numbers in the margin correspond to points of interest on the Akko Old City map.*

You approach the Old City on Weizman Street (watch for signs that say "Old Akko"), proceeding through a breach in the surrounding walls. Once inside, park at the Knights parking lot, where you'll start a walking tour (the circular route brings you back to your car). Double back a few steps to the entrance to the Old City at the walls and climb the signposted blue-railing stairway on your right for a stroll on the **ramparts.** Walking right, you can see the stunted remains of the 12th-century walls built by the Crusaders, under whose brief rule—just under two centuries—Akko flourished as never before or since. The indelible signs of the Crusaders, who made Akko the main port of their Christian empire, are much more evident inside the Old City itself.

The wide wall you are walking on, which girds the northern part of the town, was built by Ahmed el-Jazzar, the Pasha of Akko, who added these fortifications following his victory over Napoléon's army in 1799. With the help of the British fleet, which sunk the French heavy artillery sent by sea, el-Jazzar turned Napoléon's attempted conquest into a humiliating rout. Napoléon had dreamed of founding a new Eastern empire, thrusting northward from Akko to Turkey and then seizing India from Great Britain. His defeat at Akko hastened his retreat to France, thus changing the course of history.

History clings to the stones of old Akko, with each twist and turn along its warren of streets telling another tale. The city's history begins 4,000 years ago, when Akko was first mentioned in Egyptian writings that refer to the mound, or tel, northeast of the walls you are standing on. The Old Testament describes in Judges 1 that after the death of Joshua the tribe of Asher was unable to drive the Canaanite inhabitants from Akko and so lived among them there. Akko was a prize worth fighting for throughout the course of history. It had a well-protected harbor, a well-watered and fertile hinterland, and a strategic position on the coastal road that links Egypt and Phoenicia (present-day Lebanon). In the 4th century BC, Akko eclipsed Tyre and Sidon as the principal port of the eastern Mediterranean. Alexander the Great's high regard for Akko is reflected in the fact that in the 3rd century BC he set up a mint in the city; it remained in operation for six centuries. For long periods Akko was a Phoenician city, but when the Hellenistic king Ptolemy II of Egypt gained control of the country in the 2nd century BC, he renamed it Ptolemais, the name it retained through the Roman and Byzantine periods.

Walk around to the guard towers and up an incline just opposite; there's a commanding view of the moat below and Haifa across the bay. Turn around and let your gaze settle on the exotic skyline of Old Akko, the sea-green dome of the great mosque its dominating feature. Walk down the ramp, crossing the Moat Garden at the base of the walls, and continue alongside the round arches on the backside of Shuk el Abiad (White Market). This market was built by Dahr el-Omar, the Bedouin sheikh who defied Turkish rule and set up his own fiefdom

# Akko—Old City

Napoleon Bonaparte St.

Chaim Weizman St.

El Jazzar Wall

**HOSPITALLERS' QUARTER**

Moat Garden

El-Jazzar Wall

35

29

28

*i*

Mausoleum

Bus Station

Majdala Mosque

31

El-Jazzar

Salach E Din St.

Shazalia Mosque

30

Parchi Sq.

Shuk el-Abiad (White Market)

El-Zituneh Mosque

A-Ramal Mosque

Yonatan Hachashmonai

Mediterranean Sea

Narco Polo

Hachomot Beach

BinyaminMitudela

32

St. George's Church

Ramchal Synagogue

Sha'ar Nikanor

Akko Bay

Baha'i House

ZalmanHatzoref

Hagana St.

Sinan Basha Mosque

Maronite Church

Mu'allek Mosque

Venezia Sq.

St. Andrew's Church

Pisa Sq.

33

Khan A-Shuna

Akko Port

Church of St. John

Salach Ravtziri

34

Lighthouse

Southern Promenade

N

0       110 yards
0       100 meters

Crusader Vaults and Halls . . . . . . . **29**

El-Jazzar Mosque . . . **28**

Khan el-Umdan . . . **33**

Museum of the Underground Prisoners . . . . . . . . **35**

Pisan Harbor . . . . . . **34**

Ramparts . . . . . . . . **27**

Refectory . . . . . . . **31**

Souk . . . . . . . . . . **32**

Turkish Bathhouse . . . . . . . . **30**

in the Galilee in the 18th century. In 1749 he moved his capital from Tiberias to Akko and rebuilt the walls of the city. Dahr el-Omar's rule here ended more than four centuries of desolation and isolation that had beset Akko after the Mamluks drove the Crusaders out in 1291. He rebuilt the port and also built access roads to the city. Continue along a pedestrian walkway, with a bank on your right.

★ **28** The **El-Jazzar Mosque** is considered one of the most magnificent in Israel. Ahmed el-Jazzar, who succeeded Dahr el-Omar simply by having him assassinated, ruled Akko from 1775 to 1804. During his reign he built this mosque along with other public structures. The Albanian adventurer's cruelty was so legendary that he earned the epithet "the Butcher." (He is buried next to his adopted son in a small white building to the right of the mosque.)

Just beyond the entrance, in the middle of the courtyard, is a pedestal mounted with a marble reproduction of a seal. Engraved with graceful calligraphy, it re-creates the seal of a 19th-century Ottoman sultan. Some of the marble and granite columns that adorn the mosque and courtyard were plundered from the ruins of Caesarea. On your left is the entrance to the underground reservoir; the ornate fountain with eight slender columns opposite the entrance to the mosque is used by the faithful for ritual washings of hands and feet. Bordering the courtyard are outbuildings once used as a religious school. Inside the mosque, enshrined in the gallery reserved for women, is a reliquary containing a hair believed to be from the beard of the prophet Muhammad; it is removed only once a year, on the 27th day of Ramadan.

The reservoir dates from the Crusader period and was actually a cathedral until converted into cisterns by Ahmed el-Jazzar. You can traverse the cavernous depths on a wooden walkway (children like this, but do keep an eye on them); the cisterns still fill up with rainwater. The mosque closes five times a day for prayers, so you might have a short wait. Dress modestly. ✉ *Off El-Jazzar St., opposite entrance to Crusader Vaults and Halls.* 🔖 *NIS 4 ($1).* ☉ *Sat.–Thurs. 8–5, Fri. 8–11 and 1–5.*

| NEED A BREAK? | In the plaza outside the mosque are several **outdoor restaurants** where you can enjoy a falafel in a pita, fresh-squeezed orange juice, or coffee while sunning yourself and watching the world go by. |

★ **29** Across from the mosque is the entrance to the **Crusader Vaults and Halls.** Your ticket also gets you into the Turkish Bathhouse and the Refectory (☞ *below*), so hang on to it. You can pick up the headphones for a guided tour here (price included in admission), as well as brochures and maps. There's a post office along one wall, and a tourist information office beside the admission desk.

Here you begin a tour of the 12th-century subterranean city, which unfolds beneath the 18th- and 19th-century buildings you see today. Deep inside is a series of barrel-vaulted rooms known as the Crusader Vaults and Halls (one of which is sometimes used for chamber-music concerts). Six such halls have been discovered thus far. Arrows point the way through dimily lit vast rooms filled with on-going reconstruction work, huge marble columns, and myriad archaeological pieces from the past. Above this part of the Crusader city stands the Ottoman citadel, which you can glimpse from the courtyard. Raised by Dahr el-Omar on the rubble-filled Crusader ruins, the citadel was the highest structure in Akko. It was later converted by the British into a prison (☞ Museum of the Underground Prisoners, *below*), and in order to unearth the Crusaders Halls, the former prison courtyard was completely dug out. Archaeologists are always busy delving into the mysteries of Akko, but signs keep you on a safe path.

The Crusaders who conquered Akko in 1104 were led by King Baldwin I and assisted by the Genoese fleet. The port city, which the victorious French Hospitallers, the Knights of St. John, renamed for their patron saint—Jeanne d'Arc (Joan of Arc)—was the Crusaders' principal link to their homeland. Commerce thrived, and the European maritime powers Genoa, Pisa, Venice, and Marseilles developed separate quarters here. After the disastrous defeat of the Crusader armies at the Horns of Hattin in 1187, Akko surrendered to the victorious Saladin without a fight, but England's Richard the Lionheart recaptured the Crusader stronghold four years later. In the 13th century, after the capture of Jerusalem by the Muslims, Akko became the effective capital of a shrunken Latin kingdom. In its Crusader heyday, Akko had about 40 churches and monasteries and a population of 50,000. Today its residents number 45,000, an ethnic mix of Jews and Arabs.

The seeds of the Crusaders' downfall in Akko were probably sown by the divisive factions within its walls. The Hospitallers and Templars, the so-called fighting monks, also had separate quarters (the Templars, also French, lived near the lighthouse by the western Crusader sea wall). By the mid-13th century, open fighting had broken out between the Venetians and Genoese. When the Mamluks attacked with a vengeance in 1291, the Crusaders' resistance quickly crumbled, and the city's devastation was complete. It subdued the city for centuries, and even today Akko retains a medieval cast. ⊠ *Opposite El-Jazzar Mosque,* ☎ *04/991–1764. www.infotour.co.il/TourismGeneralInfo/39012.html* ▣ *Crusader Vaults and Halls, Turkish Bathhouse, and Refectory NIS 24 ($6).* ☉ *Nov.–Mar., Sun.–Thurs. 9–4:15, Fri. and holiday eves 9–1:15, Sat. 9–4:15; Apr.–Oct., Sun.–Thurs. 9–5, Fri. and holiday eves 9–2:15, Sat. 9–5.*

★ ⑳ Akko's remarkable **Turkish Bathhouse,** built for Pasha el-Jazzar in 1781, was in use until 1947, when it was damaged by the explosion at the British prison nearby. The bathhouse has been restored to a pristine condition and is slated to become a museum, with displays of copper objects, jewelry, coins, and other artifacts from both the city's collection and the latest archaeological digs. You'll notice colored glass bubbles protruding from the roof domes, sending a filtered green light to the steam rooms below; these skylights were actually made by the same Hebron workshop that made the originals a century ago. The dressing room is decorated with colorful handmade Turkish tiles and topped with a cupola; note the inlaid marble floors. For admission and hours, *see* Crusader Vaults and Halls, *above*.

㉛ The **Refectory** was once known as the Crypt of St. John—before excavation it was erroneously thought to have been an underground chamber (diggers thought the high-up windows were the doors). The dimensions of the colossal pillars that support the roof (note that they're girdled with metal bands for extra support) make this one of Israel's most monumental examples of Crusader architecture and one of the oldest Gothic structures in the world. In the right-hand corner opposite the entrance is a fleur-de-lis carved in stone—the crest of the French House of Bourbon—which has led some scholars to postulate that this was the chamber in which Louis VII convened the knights of the realm.

At the wooden stairs descending from the base of one of the columns, there's an opening to an extremely narrow subterranean passageway. Cut from stone, this was a secret tunnel that the Crusaders probably used to reach the harbor when besieged by Muslim forces. (Those who are claustrophobic can take an alternate route, which goes back to the entrance of the Turkish bathhouse and continues straight.) You'll emerge to find yourself in the cavernous vaulted halls of the Posta, the fortress guardpost, with a 13th-century marble Crusader tombstone and map of the Crusader city at the exit. Go up the stairs to the left and turn right into the covered market, where artisans beat pieces of copper into bas-relief plates and bowls and sell other handcrafted items. Exit to the left.

Continue through a square with the whitewashed El-Zituneh Mosque on your right, and wend your way to the left through the angular streets ㉜ to the local **souk** (market). Stalls heaped with fresh produce alternate with specialty stores: a pastry shop with an astonishing variety of exotic Middle Eastern delicacies; a spice shop filled with the aromas of the East; a bakery with steaming-fresh pita. You'll often see fishermen sitting on doorsteps, intently repairing their lines and nets to the sounds of Arabic music blaring from the open windows above.

NEED A BREAK?
Here in the souk, duck into the **Oudah Brothers Cafe** (☎ 04/991–2013) and enjoy a coffee, hummus, or kebab in the courtyard of the 16th-century Khan el-Faranj, or Franks' Inn. Note the 18th-century Franciscan monastery and tower to your left.

Exiting the Khan el-Faranj from the south, you'll pass the Sinan Basha mosque on your left as you enter Venezia Square, in front of the port. ㉝ On your right is the **Khan el-Umdan,** or Inn of the Pillars. Before you visit this Ottoman *khan*—the largest of the four in Akko—and the Pisan Quarter beyond, take a stroll around the port, with its small flotilla of fishing boats, yachts, and sailboats. Then walk through the khan's gate beneath a square clock tower, built at the turn of the 20th century. The khan served vast numbers of merchants and travelers during Akko's golden age of commerce, in the 18th century. The 32 pink-and-gray granite pillars that give it its name are compliments of Ahmed el-Jazzar's raids on Roman Caesarea. There was once a market at the center of the colonnaded courtyard.

㉞ You can walk along the sea walls at **Pisan Harbor.** Start at the café perched on high—a great lookout (boys dive off the rocks into the sea in summer)—and head west in the direction of the 18th-century Church of St. John. You'll end up at the southwestern extremity of Akko, next to the lighthouse. The Templars once occupied this area. Head north along Haganah Street, which runs parallel to the crenellated western sea wall. After five minutes you'll reach the whitewashed, blue-trimmed Baha'i house (not open to the public), where the prophet of the Baha'i religion, Baha'u'llah, spent 12 years of his exile. His burial site is just north of Akko (☞ Baha'i Founder's Shrine and Gardens, *below*).

㉟ The **Museum of the Underground Prisoners** is housed in several wings of the citadel built by Dahr el-Omar and then amended by Ahmed el-Jazzar in 1785. It became a British prison during the Mandate. On the way in, you pass the citadel's outside wall; the difference between the large Crusader building stones and the smaller Turkish ones above is easy to spot. Prison life is illustrated by the original cells and their meager contents, supplemented by photographs and documents that reconstruct the history of the Jewish resistance to British rule in the 1930s and '40s. During the Mandate, the citadel became a high-security prison whose inmates included top members of Jewish resistance organizations, among them Ze'ev Jabotinsky. In 1947 a dramatic prison breakout by leaders of the

Irgun captured headlines around the world and provided Leon Uris's novel *Exodus* with one of its most dramatic moments.

As you leave the museum, turn right after 60 ft and follow the massive walls around the northern part of town to the breach at Weizman Street and the parking lot where you entered the Old City. ⊠ *Haganah St. (a few mins north of the lighthouse),* ☎ *04/991–8264.* ⊡ *NIS 8 ($2).* ☉ *Sun.–Thurs. 9–3, Fri. 9–1.*

## Dining

$$$$ ⨉ **Uri Buri.** If you're in Akko at mealtime, you're in luck: Uri's famous
★ fish and seafood restaurant was relocated from Nahariya to Akko in the summer of 1998. It's now housed in an old stone Turkish building, with three arches, and one room is furnished in old Arab style, with sofas, copper dishes, and *nargillas* ("water pipes"). Everything on the menu is seasonal, i.e., very fresh, and the fish is steamed, baked, or grilled (one delicious dish is fish in mustard and honey sauce). Allow time for a meal here, as it's not your everyday fish fry. Two house specialties are gravlax and Thai-style fish; seafood soup is another fixture. Or have a go at baby calamari with kumquats and pink grapefruit, or anchovy fillets in lemon, oil, and hot pepper. Look for the restaurant near the lighthouse, on one edge of the coast-side parking lot. ⊠ *93 Haganah St.,* ☎ *04/955–2212. Reservations essential. AE, D, MC, V. Closed Tues.*

$$ ⨉ **Abu Christo.** This popular waterfront fish restaurant at the north-
★ ern edge of the Crusader port actually stands at one of the original 18th-century gates built by Pasha Ahmed el-Jazzar when he fortified the city after his victory over Napoléon. A family business opened in 1948 and passed from father to son, Abu Christo serves up the daily catch—often grouper, red snapper, or sea bass—prepared simply, either grilled or deep fried. Shellfish and a selection of grilled meats are also available. The covered patio on the water is idyllic in summer. ⊠ *Crusader Port,* ☎ *04/991–0065. Reservations essential July–Sept. AE, DC, MC, V.*

$$ ⨉ **Galileo.** Here you can sit on a terrace alongside the Old City's ancient walls and dine on fresh fish, grilled meats, or Middle Eastern salads. You'll be right on the water in the Pisan Harbor, with nothing but a few ruins and an expanse of blue before you. The view, which often includes young boys diving off the rocks into crashing water below, compensates for the standard fare. ⊠ *Crusader Port,* ☎ *04/991–4620. Reservations essential Fri., Sat. AE, DC, MC, V.*

## Lodging

$$$ ⌸ **Hofit.** Eight kilometers (5 miles) north of Akko, not far from Nahariya (☞ *below*), the Hofit (formerly Beit Hava) is a country hotel at Moshav Shavei Zion, a communal settlement founded in 1938 by German Jews. The extensive lawns invite strolls; the beach is 5 minutes from your front door, and a lovely private beach (with lifeguard) is only 10 minutes away. The spacious guest rooms are adequate, though almost spartan. Each room has a double bed plus two sofa beds, and all have striking views of the Moshav and the sea. The buildings of the hotel are almost in the settlement itself, which gives it a cozy, rural touch. Nearby farms and cow sheds—though not visible from the hotel—only add to the pastoral feeling. The lobby and lounge areas are spacious, and so is the adjoining dining area, one wall of which faces a verdant setting of trees and garden. The large, well-kept pool is open from April to October. The Hofit is perfectly located for touring the western coast; sites such as Akko, the Baha'i Gardens, and Rosh Hanikra are easily accessible. The staff can arrange horseback riding, Jeep trips, and donkey rides. Families with children will appreciate all the kid-friendly activities nearby. ⊠ *Box 82, Shavei Zion 25227,* ☎

*04/982–0391,* FAX *04/982–0519. 90 rooms. Dining room, lobby lounge, pool, 2 tennis courts, baby-sitting. AE, MC, V.*

**$$$**    ⊞ **Nes Ammim Guest House.** Founded in 1964, Nes Ammim is an ecumenical Christian settlement of about 90 people, where life and study center on the furthering of mutual respect and tolerance. Lodging options are two: double rooms, or family apartments with fully equipped kitchens. The furnishings are pleasant, and the setting, 10 km (6 mi) north of Akko, is picturesque and rural, providing pastoral views. Guests are invited to chat with members of the community, stroll the grounds, and visit the botanical garden and the hothouse, blooming with roses. In the summer, classical music is performed in the serene chapel, or near the large pool (drawing local music lovers as well as guests), often after a barbecue meal. To get here, drive north from Akko on Route 4. ⊠ *D. N. Western Galilee, 25225,* ☎ *04/995–0000,* FAX *04/995–0098. 48 rooms, 13 apartments. Grocery, lounge, pool. AE, D, MC, V.*

**$$$**    ⊞ **Palm Beach.** The Palm Beach is on Route 4 just south of Akko—right on the beach, with a fine view of Haifa Bay and the rooftops of the Old City. Guests have access to the facilities of the adjoining country club, which include a pool and a whirlpool bath. Rooms are modest, but all face the sea. ⊠ *Rte. 4,* ☎ *04/981–7777,* FAX *04/991–0434. 120 rooms. Restaurant, dance club. AE, MC, V.*

### Outdoor Activities and Sports

BEACHES

Just south of the Old City on the Haifa–Akko road is a sandy stretch of municipal beach in Akko Bay, with parking, showers, toilets, and chair rentals. Admission is NIS 8 ($2).

SCUBA DIVING

In Akko's marina is the **Ramy Diving Center** (☎ 04/834–3006 or 052/667–835). Ramy, a former navy diver, runs the diving school and offers guided dives. The three local dives explore the reef (NIS 140, or $40), the submerged city wall (NIS 120, or $30), and the wreck of an Italian submarine from World War II (NIS 240, or $60). Prices include equipment rental.

### Shopping

**I. E. Dany's Archaeological Galleries** (⊠ 13/3 Salah Adin, ☎ 04/981–3770), in the Old City, is a fascinating place to browse. (It's on your left before the plaza of the El-Jazzar Mosque.) The shop is lined with glass cases whose contents, some more than 4,000 years old, range from ancient coins to small statuary, delicate Roman glass, and urns and pottery. The pieces carry government-issued certificates, and those for sale are officially approved for export. Prices start around $50 and go into the thousands.

## Baha'i Founder's Shrine and Gardens

★ ③⑥    *Rte. 4, 1 km (⅔ mi) north of gas station at northern edge of Akko.*

For the Baha'is, this is the holiest place on earth, the site of the tomb of the faith's prophet and founder, Baha'u'llah (☞ Sights to See *in* Haifa, *above*). First you'll pass the west gate of the gardens, open only to Baha'is. Take the first right (no sign) and continue to the unobtrusive turn, 500 yards up, to the north and main gate. Baha'u'llah lived in the red-tile mansion here after he was released from jail in Akko and was buried in the small building next door, now the Shrine of Baha'u'llah. Visitors to the shrine are asked to dress modestly. The gardens and terrace are exquisitely landscaped. ▨ *Free.* ⊙ *Gardens daily 9–4; tomb Fri.–Mon. 9–noon.*

*En Route* To the west of the highway, as you travel north, stands a segment of the multitiered aqueduct built by Ahmed el-Jazzar in the late 18th century to carry the sweet waters of the Kabri springs to Akko.

## Lochamei Hageta'ot

③⑦ *2 km (1 mi) north of Akko, 6 km (4 mi) south of Nahariya.*

Kibbutz Lochamei Hageta'ot ("Ghetto Fighters") was founded in 1949 by survivors of the German, Polish, and Lithuanian Jewish ghettos and veterans of the ghetto uprisings against the Nazis. To commemorate their compatriots who perished in the Holocaust, and to perpetuate the memory thereof, the kibbutz members set up a **museum,** which you enter to the right of the main gate. Exhibits include a vast collection of photographs documenting the Warsaw Ghetto and the famous uprising, and halls devoted to different themes, among them Jewish communities before their destruction in the Holocaust; the death camps; and deportations at the hands of the Nazis. You can also see the actual booth in which Adolf Eichmann, architect of the "Final Solution," sat during his Jerusalem trial.

Opened in 1996, **Yad Layeled** (Children's Memorial), a white, cone-shape building, is dedicated to the memory of the 1½ million children who perished in the Holocaust. It's designed for young visitors, who can begin to comprehend the events of the Holocaust through a series of tableaux and images accompanied by recorded voices, allowing them to identify with individual victims without seeing shocking details. There is a small restaurant on the premises. ☎ *04/995–8080.* ✉ *Free; donation appreciated.* ☉ *Sun.–Thurs. 9–4, Fri. 9–1, Sat. 10–5.*

## Nahariya

③⑧ *8 km (5 mi) north of Akko.*

Nahariya was the first Jewish settlement in the Western Galilee. It was founded in 1934 by German Jews who had fled the Nazis and come to eke out a living by farming in what was then termed a communal village for agricultural settlement. Eventually these pioneers turned from the soil to what they realized was their greatest natural resource—some of the country's best beaches—for a more lucrative livelihood. Thus a popular seaside resort was born. The *yekke* (Jews of German origin) spirit lingers on in the clean and orderly boulevards and streets. Nahariya's main thoroughfare, Haga'aton Boulevard, was built along the banks of a river, now dried up, lined with shady eucalyptus trees; the town's name comes from *nahar,* the Hebrew word for "river."

Although German was once the language of these streets, you're now just as likely to hear Russian or Amharic (spoken by Ethiopians), and blue-bereted U.N. soldiers from bases to the north are frequent visitors. In July and August, there's dancing in the amphitheater at the mouth of the river, and Israeli stars come out to perform on the beach and in the town square.

The **Byzantine church** has an elaborate, 17-color mosaic floor, discovered in 1964, that depicts peacocks, other birds, hunting scenes, and plants. It was part of what experts consider one of the largest and most beautiful Byzantine churches in the Western Galilee, where Christianity rapidly spread—as in the rest of Israel—from the 4th to the 7th century. Call the tourist office (☎ *04/987–9800*) to arrange a visit, as the church is not always open. To get here, head east on Haga'aton to Route 4, making a left at the stoplight and then the first right onto Yechi'am Street.

From here take the third left and then an immediate right onto Bielefeld Street. The church is next to the Katzenelson school. ⊠ *Bielefeld St.* ✆ *NIS 2 (50¢).*

## Dining and Lodging

$$ ✕ **Penguin.** This casual, main-street institution opened its doors in 1940, well before the state of Israel was even created. Three generations of the same family work here, and the walls carry enlarged photographs of how the place looked when it was just a hut. Stop off for coffee and cake, or make a meal of fresh spinach blintzes with melted cheese; pasta; hamburger platters; or Chinese dishes. Management swears that the schnitzel gets accolades from Viennese visitors. All main dishes come with salad, rice, french fries, and vegetables. Finish off with a frozen yogurt from the adjacent stand, under the same venerable ownership. ⊠ *31 Haga'aton Blvd.,* ✆ *04/992–8855. V.*

$$$ ▥ **Carlton.** The best (and only) traditional hotel in town, this centrally located, six-story hotel, built in 1970, is blessed with a staff that will go the extra mile. The guest rooms are spacious, and many have sea views or a view of the mountain range rearing up to the northeast. Furnishings are not exceptional, but they're comfortable enough. The La Scala dance club attracts revelers from all over the north with live music in the summer. ⊠ *23 Haga'aton,* ✆ *04/900–5555,* ℻ *04/982–3771. 198 rooms. Restaurant, lobby lounge, pool, hot tub, 2 saunas, night-club, baby-sitting. AE, D, MC, V.*

$$$ ▥ **Club Med Arziv.** *Chic alors!* Overhauled in 1998, and celebrating its 40th anniversary right now, this Club Med (Israel's only other is in Eilat) lays claim to one of the most beautiful locations in the country, a gentle rise with the sparkling sea stretching toward the horizon below. It's open from mid-June to mid-October, depending on when the Jewish holidays take place. The grounds are crowded with flowering bushes and palm trees and include old, stone Turkish-style buildings. Club rules apply: the price is all-inclusive and includes everything from your straw hut (which sleeps two or three) to excellent food and wine (three meals a day), nightly entertainment, and all sports activities. Special prices are available midweek. The pool is especially lovely— you're looking at the sea as you dip and dive. In the Unusual Perks department, the in-house circus school gives trapeze and juggling lessons. The hotel is 6 km (4 mi) north of Nahariya, near the caves of Rosh Hanikra. ⊠ *Box 34, Achziv, Nahariya,* ✆ *03/521–2525 for reservations, 04/982–1203 on site,* ℻ *03/527–1345 for reservations, 04/982–4417 on site. 276 huts. Restaurant, pool, aerobics, archery, basketball, exercise room, jogging, boating, dance club, children's programs. MC, V.*

## Nightlife and the Arts

Nahariya's flashiest disco is **La Scala** (✆ 04/900–5555), which draws the over-30 crowd for standard dance tunes with a throbbing beat. It's in the passageway just west of the Carlton. The cover charge on Friday is NIS 50 ($12.50); doors open at 10 PM.

## Outdoor Activities and Sports

BEACHES

Nahariya's public bathing facilities, at **Galei Galil Beach,** just north of Haga'aton Boulevard, are ideal for families and not far from most hotels. Beyond the lovely beach, facilities include an Olympic-size pool, a wading pool, and playground for children, and changing rooms and showers, plus a snack bar. In peak season, the beach offers exercise classes early in the morning. The entrance fee is NIS 12 ($3) for children.

Beautifully maintained because it's in the Achziv National Park just north of Nahariya, **Achziv Beach** is great for kids, with a protected man-made lagoon, lifeguards, and playground facilities. You can picnic on the grassy slopes or make use of the restaurant. Admission, which is NIS 16 ($4), includes the use of showers and toilets. **Betzet Beach,** a bit farther north, is part of a nature reserve and offers abundant vegetation, trees, and the ruins of an ancient olive press. There's a lifeguard on duty in season.

SCUBA DIVING

**Trek Yam Ltd.,** also known as Sea Treks (☎ 04/982–3671 or 04/982–5089), takes scuba divers to explore the Achziv Canyon ($40, including tank and weight belt), and the caves at Rosh Hanikra ($30, including tank and weight belt) along the northern coast. The outfit also offers Jeep tours from two hours to a full day, with a price range from $150 to $450.

## Rosh Hanikra

**39**   *7 km (4½ mi) north of Nahariya.*

The dramatic white cliffs on the coast signal both Israel's border with Lebanon and the sea **grottoes** of Rosh Hanikra. Even before you get in line for the two-minute cable-car ride down to the grottoes, take a moment to absorb the stunning view back down the coast. Still clearly visible is the route of the railway line, now mostly a dirt road, built by the British through the hillside in 1943 to extend the Cairo–Tel Aviv–Haifa line to Beirut. After the descent, you can see the new 12-minute audiovisual presentation called "The Sea and the Cliff." The incredible caves beneath the cliff have been carved out by relentless waves pounding away at the white chalky rock for countless years. Footpaths inside the cliff itself lead from one huge cave to another, while the sound of waves echoes among the water-sprayed rocky walls. Huge bursts of seawater plunge into pools at your feet (behind protective rails). It's slippery, so hold your children's hands. ☎ 04/985–7109. ☛ NIS 36 ($9). ☺ Sun.–Thurs. and Sat. 8:30–4 (July–Aug., 8:30–11 PM); Fri. and holiday eves 8:30–4 (Apr.–June, 8:30–6). Sept. and Oct. open until 6. Call to verify hrs.

NEED A BREAK?

The **cafeteria** perched on top of the Rosh Hanikra cliff may not be a gourmet's dream, but you'd be hard pressed to find a more fabulous view. It's bright and breezy, with a wide range of snacks, drinks, and ice cream as well as hot meals. It's fun to take a photo outside at the sign on the cafeteria wall, which indicates the distance from there to Beirut.

OFF THE BEATEN PATH

**YEHIAM** – This kibbutz, set in a wooded area, has an unusual attraction, the ruins of the medieval **Castle Judin.** The memorial that you pass on the way commemorates the convoy that set out to bring fresh supplies and reinforcements to the besieged kibbutz in Israel's War of Independence, in 1948. Apparently built by the Templars in the late 12th century, Castle Judin was destroyed by the Mamluk sultan Baybars in the 13th century, but its ruins so impressed the 18th-century Bedouin sheikh Dahr el-Omar that he transformed it into a palatial citadel 500 years later. You can see the remains of a large reception hall and mosque, as well as a tower and bathhouse. There are picnic facilities on-site. The site is 12 km (8 mi) east of Nahariya: at Hanita Junction, turn south onto Route 70; then at Kabri Junction, head east 7 km (4½ mi) on Route 89. ☎ 04/985–6004. ☛ NIS 8 ($2). ☺ Daily 8–4.

# NORTHERN COAST AND WESTERN GALILEE A TO Z

## Arriving and Departing

### By Bus

The Egged bus cooperative (☞ Getting Around, *below*) serves the coastal area from Ben-Gurion Airport and from the Jerusalem and Tel Aviv central bus stations. Service to Netanya, Hadera, Zichron Ya'akov, and Haifa from both cities starts before 8 AM and usually ends around 8 PM. A bus leaves Tel Aviv for Haifa every 20 minutes between 5:20 AM and 11 PM. Travel to Caesarea requires a change at Hadera; service from Hadera to Caesarea runs only until 12:30 PM. You must change buses at Haifa to get to Akko and Nahariya. Keep in mind that Egged buses do not operate between late Friday afternoon and Saturday evening (sometimes Sunday morning). One exception is Haifa, where some buses do run on Saturday. For fares and information, call 03/694–8888 (Tel Aviv) or 02/530–4704 (Jerusalem).

### By Car

You can take either Route 2 or Route 4 north along the coast from Tel Aviv to Haifa, continuing on Route 4 all the way up to the Lebanese border. From Jerusalem follow Route 1 to Tel Aviv and then connect through the Ayalon Highway to Herzliya, where you can pick up Route 2.

### By Plane

Most travelers from abroad arrive at **Ben-Gurion International Airport,** at Lod on the outskirts of Tel Aviv. The airport is 105 km (65 mi) from Haifa, about a 90-minute drive. At the airport you can catch Bus 945 or 947 (on Saturday only after 9 PM) to Haifa. Or share a sherut taxi, which costs NIS 30 ($7.50).

### By Ship

Many cruise ships that tour the Mediterranean stop at Haifa. You'll exit the docks area through either Gate 5 or the Passenger and Customs Terminal, depending on whether or not you're required to go through customs. Taxis are usually waiting at the exits. You can catch buses nearby for the central bus station, the Hadar district, and Mt. Carmel.

### By Train

A train line connects Tel Aviv's Rakevet Zafon's station (Northern Train Station) with Netanya, Haifa, and Nahariya, with stops along the way. There is no train service from Jerusalem. The trip from Tel Aviv to Haifa takes 90 minutes and costs NIS 21 ($5.25). Trains depart every half hour starting at 6 AM until 10:30 PM; on Friday from 6 AM until 3:20. On Saturday trains do not run, though there are four departures after 9:30 PM. There is also a fast (one-hour) direct train that runs twice a day from Tel Aviv to Haifa. Haifa has several train stations; the main one is **Haifa Bat Galim,** located at the central bus station (☎ 04/856–4564). The **Netanya train station** is on Ha'Rakevet Road, just east of Route 2 (☎ 09/823–470). For all train information, call 03/577–4000 (closed on Saturday and holidays during the day; reopens after sunset).

## Getting Around

### By Bus

The **Egged** network will get you just about anywhere in the region. Most buses depart hourly on weekdays. For information on routes and schedules, call ☎ 02/530–4704 Jerusalem, 03/694–8888 Tel Aviv, 04/854–9131 Haifa.

## By Car

Driving is probably the most comfortable and convenient way to tour this region, and it allows you to explore some of the more scenic back roads. The distances are short: for example, 29 km (18 mi) from Tel Aviv to Netanya, 22 km (15 mi) from Haifa to Akko, 37 km (23 mi) from Haifa to Zichron Ya'akov.

Traffic gets particularly snarled along the coast at rush hour, especially entering and exiting major cities. The worst times are weekdays after 4 PM and Saturday evenings, also after 4 PM. Expect gridlock in Haifa's port area during morning and evening rush hours. Even at the best of times, Haifa traffic is heavy, and because of the city's steep layout, streets zigzag up the slope and are difficult to negotiate. Remember to pay attention to Haifa's street signs indicating which streets close on Saturday.

## By Train

The North Coast and Western Galilee is, aside from Tel Aviv and Jerusalem, the one part of Israel with rail service. You can reach many of the region's main cities and towns by train, including Netanya, Hadera, Benyamina, Zichron Ya'akov, Haifa, Atlit, Akko, and Nahariya.

Haifa has Israel's only subway system: the six-station Carmelit subway runs from Gan Ha'em Park on Hanassi Avenue (opposite the Dan Panorama) in Central Carmel down to Kikar Paris in the port area in six minutes. The fare is NIS 4 ($1), and the train operates Sunday–Thursday 6 AM–10 PM, Friday 6–3, and Saturday 7 PM–midnight. Though the Carmelit doesn't serve the tourist sites, children enjoy this ride (it's so short you just travel both ways).

# Contacts & Resources

## Car Rentals

**Haifa: Avis** (⊠ 7 Ben-Gurion St., ☎ 04/851–3050); **Budget** (⊠ 46 Histadrut St., ☎ 04/842–4004); **Eldan** (⊠ 95 Hanassi Ave., ☎ 04/837–5303); **Hertz** (⊠ 33 Histadrut St., ☎ 04/840–2127); **Reliable** (⊠ 33 Histadrut St., ☎ 04/850–7907). **Nahariya: Budget** (⊠ 62 Weizman St., ☎ 04/992–9252). **Netanya: Avis** (⊠ 34 Lochamei Hageta'ot St., ☎ 09/833–0618); **Budget** (⊠ 2 Gad Machness, ☎ 09/861–4711); **Eldan** (⊠ 2 Gad Machness, ☎ 09/861–6982); **Hertz** (⊠ 8 Ha'atzmaut Sq., ☎ 09/882–8890).

## Consulate

**Haifa:** Jonathan Freidland, **U.S. Consular Agent**, ⊠ 6 Ben-Gurion Blvd., German Colony, ☎ 04/853–1446. ☉ Sun.–Thurs. 9–1.

## Emergencies

AMBULANCE

**Akko** (⊠ 101 Magen David Adom, ☎ 04/991–2333); **Haifa** (☎ 101); **Nahariya** (☎ 101 or 04/823–332); **Netanya** (☎ 101).

HOSPITALS

**Carmel** (☎ 04/825–0211). **Haifa: Rambam Hospital** (☎ 04/854–3111). **Nahariya: Western Galilee Regional Hospital** (☎ 04/985–0766). **Netanya: Laniado Hospital** (☎ 09/860–4666).

POLICE

**Akko** (☎ 100); **Haifa** (☎ 100); **Nahariya** (☎ 100 or 04/992–0344); **Netanya** (☎ 100).

## Guided Tours
### GENERAL INTEREST
You can usually arrange to be picked up at your hotel for the following tours which depart from Tel Aviv and Jerusalem, and often Nahariya and Haifa, on Sunday, Tuesday, and Friday. Two tour operators organize these one-day trips, which take in the ancient port cities of Caesarea and Akko, and go north to Rosh Hanikra: **Egged Tours** cost between $66 and $70; you can reserve in Tel Aviv (☎ 03/527–1212), Netanya (☎ 09/860–6206), or Jerusalem (☎ 02/622–1999). Similar rates can be found at **United Tours** in Tel Aviv (☎ 03/693–3412 or 03/522–2008) or Jerusalem (☎ 02/625–5013).

Israel's **Society for the Protection of Nature** (SPNI) offers expertly guided, off-the-beaten-track nature tours where walking and hiking (with bus travel as well) help you get to know the country on a first-hand basis. The **one-day** tour (which costs $59) departs from Tel Aviv and Netanya every Sunday and visits Caesarea, Hod, and a nature reserve on the Carmel. The **two-day** trip covers western Galilee including Akko, a nature reserve walk, and a visit to a Druze village. The price is $185, including overnight stay at a kibbutz. Both trips depart from Tel Aviv, while the Caesarea trip also has a departure from Netanya; 8 AM is the starting time. The SPNI office (☎ 03/638–8674 in Tel Aviv, 02/624–4605 in Jerusalem) will provide details about what you should bring.

The **Haifa Tourist Board** (☎ 04/853–5606) conducts a free 2½-hour walking tour that departs on Saturday at 10 AM from the corner of Yefe Nof (Panorama Road) and Sha'ar Ha'levanon streets. The itinerary generally includes the Mané Katz Museum and the Baha'i Shrine and ends at Haifa Museum, but it may change slightly; call ahead to confirm.

### BOAT TOURS
**Carmelit** (☎ 04/841–8765) offers boat tours of Haifa Bay from Magan Hadayag, beside the airport. The ride lasts one hour and costs $5. Call ahead for departure times. From Akko's Crusader port, the *Princess of Akko* (☎ 04/991–0606) ferry makes a 40-minute jaunt around the bay, setting out whenever the boat fills up, year-round. The cost is $5. From a location 5 km (2½ mi) north of Nahariya, **Trek Yam** (☎ 04/982–3671 or 04/982–5089) takes you on an exciting 30-minute ride up the coast in a high-speed motorboat, the *Tornado,* for $15.

### DRUZE HOSPITALITY
For an ethnic adventure in a Druze village in the Carmel, call **El Carmel** (☎ 04/839–0412 or 052/645–100) and ask Amit to make the arrangements. You'll be invited into a private home, usually one with a courtyard where pita bread is baked over a traditional stove; and the head of the house will discuss the distinctive life of the Druze. The cost is $25 with lunch, $18 without.

### PERSONAL GUIDES
Caesarea resident and authorized tour guide **Illana Berger** (☎ 04/636–3936 or 050/624–710) provides an upbeat 2½-hour walking tour through Caesarea for $50. **Mitzpe Tours** (☎ 04/867–4341) offers custom-tailored tours in a private car, limousine, or quality 4 x 4 vehicle, for individuals or small groups.

## Taxis
**Akko: Akko Zafon** (☎ 04/981–6666). **Haifa: Carmel-Ahuza** (☎ 04/838–2727); **Mercaz Mitzpe** (☎ 04/866–2525). **Nahariya: Kefarim** (☎ 04/992–3333). **Netanya: Hasharon** (☎ 09/833–3338).

## Travel Agencies

**Akko: Shefi Tours** (⊠ 37 Ha'Arba'a St., ☎ 04/991–2730). **Haifa: Histour** (⊠ 6 Derech Hayam, ☎ 04/836–2696). **Nahariya: Ler Tours** (⊠ 19 Ha'Ga'aton Blvd., ☎ 04/982–5636). **Netanya: Atlas Tours** (⊠ 29 Herzl St., ☎ 09/834–5183).

## Visitor Information

The following towns and cities have tourist offices:

The **Akko Tourist Information Office** (⊠ El Jazzar St., just inside Knights Hall, opposite mosque, ☎ 04/991–1764) is open Sunday–Thursday 9–5 (9–6 in winter), Friday 9–2.

The **Haifa Tourist Board** (⊠ 48 Ben-Gurion Blvd., German Colony, ☎ 04/853–5606) is open Sunday–Thursday 9–5:30, in summer until 6:30; Friday 9–2); a second office, at the Central Bus Station (⊠ Haganah Blvd., ☎ 04/851–2208), is open Sunday–Thursday 9:30–4:30, Friday 9:30–2.

The **Nahariya Tourist Information Office** (⊠ 19 Ga'aton Blvd., ☎ 04/987–9800) is open Sunday–Thursday 8–1 and 4–7, Friday 8–1.

The **Netanya Tourist Information Office** (⊠ Next to amphitheater on Ha'atzmaut Sq., ☎ 09/882–7286) is open Sunday–Thursday 8:30–6 (8:30–4 in winter), Friday 9–noon.

The **Zichron Ya'akov Tourist Office** (⊠ Next to central bus station, Gidonim, ☎ 04/639–8811) is open Sunday–Thursday 9–1.

# 5 LOWER GALILEE

*Including Nazareth,
Tiberias, and the Sea of Galilee*

Nowhere does the Bible resonate more powerfully than in this land of soft cultivated valleys, rocky hills, and the freshwater Sea of Galilee. The Jezreel Valley is the land of Deborah, Gideon, King Saul, and Elijah. Nazareth and the Sea of Galilee are rich with significance for the Christian pilgrim. Yet this is also a region of parks, one of Israel's most popular playgrounds.

By Mike Rogoff

**T**O MOST ISRAELIS, THE GALILEE is synonymous with "the North," a land of mountains and fertile valleys, nature reserves and national parks. In short, they would claim, it's a great place to visit, but they wouldn't want to live there: it's provincial, rustic, and remote. Although much of the wild scenery associated with the North—rugged highlands, waterfalls, and panoramas that seem to go on forever—is in the Upper Galilee, the Lower Galilee has its own quiet beauty, varied landscape, and, more than anything else, rich history.

On a map, the Lower Galilee fits into a frame about 50 km (31 mi) square, divided into valleys, hill country, and the Sea of Galilee. To the south is the fertile Jezreel Valley, known in Hebrew simply as Ha'emek—the Valley—and sentimentally, if not scientifically, perceived by many Israelis as distinct from the rest of the Lower Galilee. To the east, the boundaries are easily defined by the Jordan Valley and the eastern shore of the Sea of Galilee (the Kinneret in Hebrew). To the north, the steep hillsides above the lake merge into the Upper Galilee, while Route 85 west follows the Bet Hakerem Valley, the natural division between the two regions. Toward the Mediterranean Sea, the hills flatten out as you reach the coastal plain; Route 70 follows the region's western edge. Farming forms the economic base: fruit orchards; fishponds; field crops such as wheat and cotton in the valleys; olive groves in the hills; livestock everywhere. The valley towns of Afula and Bet She'an are little more than small, nondescript rural centers, while the larger hill town of Nazareth, the region's automotive-service center, has more character—a noisy clash of pistons and politics. Tiberias, on the Sea of Galilee, depends on tourism for its livelihood, but its location is more impressive than the town itself.

Ancient history abounds here. In the Jezreel Valley, filled with Old Testament lore, you come face-to-face with Deborah, Gideon, King Saul and Jonathan, King Solomon, the prophet Elijah, Ahab, and Jezebel. After the Assyrian devastation of the northern kingdom of Israel in the 8th century BC, the region declined as the stream of history was diverted elsewhere; but in the late Roman and Byzantine periods (1st century BC–6th century AD), the vibrancy and wealth returned. The magnificent city of Scythopolis/Bet She'an, the opulent spa of Hammat Gader, the exquisite mosaics of Hammat Tiberias and Zippori, and the synagogues of Bet Alfa and Capernaum all illustrate this period.

For Christian pilgrims, of course, there is nothing more compelling than exploring the landscape where Jesus of Nazareth lived, walked, and forged his ministry. Although Nazareth and Cana play crucial roles in the Gospel stories, it is the Sea of Galilee and the many New Testament sites near its shores that have the most powerful resonance. Here Jesus called his disciples, wrought miracles, cured the sick, and taught the multitudes.

But the Galilee is not all ancient history. Twentieth-century Jewish pioneers first tamed hostile ground here, draining malarial swamps and clearing boulders to transform the region into some of Israel's richest farmland. Here, too, they invented a new way of living together in perfect equality—the kibbutz.

The region's *kibbutzim* and a smaller number of *moshavim* (Jewish family-farm settlements) are concentrated in the Jezreel and Jordan valleys and around the Sea of Galilee. The rockier hill country is predominantly Arab (*Israeli* Arab; this is not disputed territory). Although Arabs and other Arabic-speaking minorities are only 21% of Israel's general population, they were long the majority in the Galilee.

The demographics have shifted over time, however, so that half a dozen small Jewish towns and several dozen rural villages have brought the two communities to numeric parity.

Whatever your agenda in the Lower Galilee, take time to savor the region's natural beauty. Follow a hiking trail above the Sea of Galilee or drive up to Belvoir, a mountaintop Crusader fortress; wade through fields of rare irises in the spring; bathe in warm mineral spas and spring-fed swimming pools; water-ski on the lake; canoe on the Jordan River; or slip down a water slide.

Culture and entertainment are not this region's strong suits. A number of annual festivals and other events are the highlights. Tiberias's pubs and restaurants probably come closest to providing lively nightlife; but there are worse ways to spend an evening than sitting by a moonlit lake washing down a good St. Peter's fish, lamb *shishlik* (grilled skewered meat), or a Chinese meal with an excellent Israeli wine.

## Pleasures and Pastimes

### Biblical History
Biblical echoes are what make the Lower Galilee unique. The Jezreel Valley is saturated with Old Testament sites; and the hill country and the Sea of Galilee witnessed the beginnings of the ministry of Jesus and are second only to Jerusalem in its importance to the Christian story.

### Dining
Tiberias, as the center of gravity for Lower Galilee tourism, used to have a monopoly on good restaurants. No longer. There are some places out in the countryside worth going out of your way for, a few really good cafeterias, and many satisfying if unmemorable local eateries. St. Peter's fish (also known as *tilapia*) is a regional specialty. Restaurant attire, even at dinner, is strictly casual.

| CATEGORY | COST* |
| --- | --- |
| $$$$ | over $35 |
| $$$ | $22–$35 |
| $$ | $12–$22 |
| $ | under $12 |

*per person for a three-course meal, excluding drinks and 10%–12% service charge

### Festivals
Ein Gev, on the eastern shore of the Sea of Galilee, has an Israeli-music festival in the spring. The Misgav area, at the region's western edge, is more eclectic: small and larger events alike take place during the week of Passover in a widespread series of venues, the better to encourage the Israeli public to mix their music with some sightseeing. Bet She'an has revived its ancient Roman theater for a short series of events in October, and in May, Jacob's Ladder—the annual "Anglo" folk festival—fills the air above Karei Deshe, on the Sea of Galilee, with the traditional folk and country music of the British Isles and North America.

### Lodging
Tiberias, the region's tourist center, has a large number of hotels for every budget, from deluxe (though not top-drawer) to moderate—and even cheaper hostelries for those traveling on a shoestring. Within a radius of 20 to 30 minutes' drive from Tiberias are a number of excellent motel-type guest houses, some run by kibbutzim and some on the shore of the Sea of Galilee itself. A few of these also rent out cheaper huts or small mobile homes called caravans, with access to the same facilities as the better accommodations.

Nazareth has a few new deluxe hotels, and several older inexpensive ones (not all recommended), that cater primarily to organized Christian pilgrim groups but are starting to attract individual travelers and Israeli vacationers as well. Tiberias, just 45 minutes away, has far more to offer after hours. Also in Nazareth, and to a lesser extent around Tiberias, are a number of hospices run by one or another Christian denomination or order. (In the Holy Land, a hospice is a hotel for pilgrims, not a facility for the ill.) At press time a few Nazareth and Tiberias hotels had closed temporarily. Please call ahead to check that a hotel is open.

Bed-and-breakfasts have sprung up in such profusion in recent years that it's hard to keep track of them. Many are in or adjacent to private homes in rural farming communities; others are within kibbutzim, where the collective has renovated older buildings, creating units with a kitchenette and a bath. These are usually good value for money, especially for families.

The Sea of Galilee is a magnet for Israeli vacationers, especially during the two major Jewish-holiday seasons: Passover (March–April) and the High Holidays and Sukkoth (September–October). Because they're based on the Hebrew lunar calendar, the dates of these holidays shift from year to year; be sure to verify the dates before you decide when *not* to stay in the area. The weather is normally great during these periods, but everything is crowded, and rates soar. Some hotels charge high-season rates for part of the summer and during the week of Christmas. Some hotels raise weekend rates substantially.

Youth hostels aren't what they used to be. Gone are the days of 10 people to a room with iron beds and communal showers. The Youth Hostel Association has seriously upgraded its facilities (including five in this region alone), with many hostels offering suite-type arrangements suitable for families. These are generally the cheapest deals around.

| CATEGORY | COST* |
|---|---|
| $$$$ | over $200 |
| $$$ | $120–$200 |
| $$ | $60–$120 |
| $ | under $60 |

*All prices are for a standard double room, including breakfast and 15% service charge.

## Swimming and Water Sports

The Jezreel Valley has two fine pools (one actually a river) in national parks with delightful natural surroundings. The Sea of Galilee—really a freshwater lake—is a refreshing but rocky place for a swim. You can recline on pleasant commercial beaches with shaded lawns, facilities, cafeterias, and the occasional water park, or on free beaches with minimal facilities, particularly south of Tiberias.

At several locations around the Sea of Galilee you can hire pedal boats, rowboats, kayaks, and motorboats and arrange to water-ski. Serious kayakers convene for an annual international competition in March. Water slides are available at some of the private beaches just south of Tiberias and some of the beaches on the northeastern shore, north of Ein Gev.

## Walking, Jogging, and Running

Two annual *Tza'adot* (Big Walks) take place in March or April, one along the shore of the Sea of Galilee (with distances from 3 km/2 mi to 20 km/12½ mi), the other along the trails of Mt. Gilboa (two routes: 11 km/7 mi and 40 km/25 mi). These mass scenic rambles attract folks from all over the country and abroad. A promenade suitable for jogging follows the lakeshore for about 5 km (3 mi) from Tiberias south. Dedicated runners might want to participate in the Sea of Galilee Marathon, which takes place in December or January. A triathlon takes place at the beginning of May.

## Exploring the Lower Galilee

The Lower Galilee embraces three distinct subregions: the Jezreel and Jordan valleys, which traverse the southern part of the region from Mt. Carmel, in the west, to the Jordanian border, in the east; Nazareth and the rugged hill country north of the Jezreel Valley and west of the Sea of Galilee; and the Sea of Galilee itself.

The Jezreel Valley is most easily entered from the Mediterranean coast by Route 65 (the Wadi Ara Pass), which runs northeast from Caesarea. From Jerusalem, you're more likely to come up the Jordan Valley (politics permitting) and begin exploring the area from the east. You'll find echoes of Old Testament stories throughout the area, but the most compelling attractions include fine natural sites as well as archaeological ones.

The hill country is permeated with the history of the New Testament, but it still defies a simple label. Olive groves dominate the landscape like scriptural illustrations. You can cover this whole area comfortably in a day if you time it right.

The third part of this chapter takes you clockwise along the shores of the entire Sea of Galilee starting at Tiberias, the main town. The shores are dotted with sites hallowed by Christian tradition, but there are also important ancient synagogues at Capernaum and Hammat Tiberias. Tiberias itself is one of Judaism's four holy cities. Those whose interests lie elsewhere will find plenty of ways to relax in, on, and around the water.

*Numbers in the text correspond to numbers in the margin and on the Lower Galilee map.*

### Great Itineraries

It's possible to get a feeling for this region in a few days, but you may want to expand your trip to include some highlights of the Upper Galilee and the Golan (☞ Chapter 6).

IF YOU HAVE 2 DAYS

Use Tiberias or the Sea of Galilee region as a base. Explore the archaeological excavations of **Megiddo** ① and/or **Bet She'an** ⑥ on the way into or out of the area. In hot weather, take a dip at Gan Hashelosha (Sachne). Visit the Church of the Annunciation in **Nazareth** ⑨ and the fine mosaics of **Zippori** ⑪, nearby. A Christian itinerary might also include **Mt. Tabor** ⑫ and **Yardenit** ㉑, on the Jordan River. For a more general approach, visit the ancient synagogue mosaics of **Bet Alfa** ⑤ or **Hammat Tiberias** ㉓, the Crusader fortress of **Belvoir** ⑦, and the **cemetery of Kibbutz Kinneret** ㉒.

If you want to concentrate on Christian sights, spend the second day around the Sea of Galilee. Join a boat ride, admire the ancient boat at **Ginosar** ⑭, contemplate the multiplication of the loaves and fishes at **Tabgha** ⑯, eat St. Peter's fish near the water, explore the ruins of **Capernaum** ⑰, and end the day in the panoramic tranquillity of the **Mount of Beatitudes** ⑮. For a more general experience, ascend the Golan Heights via **Hammat Gader** ⑲ for a spectacular view, and in the Upper Galilee explore the nature reserves of Banias and Tel Dan (with a trout lunch along one of the rivers) or the synagogues and cobblestone lanes of Zfat (☞ Chapter 6).

## Lower Galilee

Akko (Acre)

Ahihud

Karmi'el

_Mediterranean
Sea_

85

784

Misgav

Sakhnin

11

Manof

Arraba

Kiryat
Bialik

Kiryat
Motzkin

Kiryat
Haim

Shefar'am

70

Kiryat
Ata

TO
HAIFA

70

Hamovil Jct.

Zippori

79

Zippori

754

Nesher

75

Kiryat
Tivon

77

Bet
She'arim

75

Nazareth

9

Daliyat
el Karmil

70

Nahalal

Migdal
Ha'emek

Nazera
Illi

(Upper Nazareth)

75

Yokne'am

73

_Jezreel
Valley_

66

Hill of
Moreh

Nair

8

65

Afula

70

TO
TEL AVIV

Megiddo

1

675

Tel Yizre'el

Ma'ayan
Harod

Megiddo
Junction

65

60

Umm el Fahm

WEST BANK BORDER

66

TO
CAESAREA
AND TEL AVIV

Jenin

71

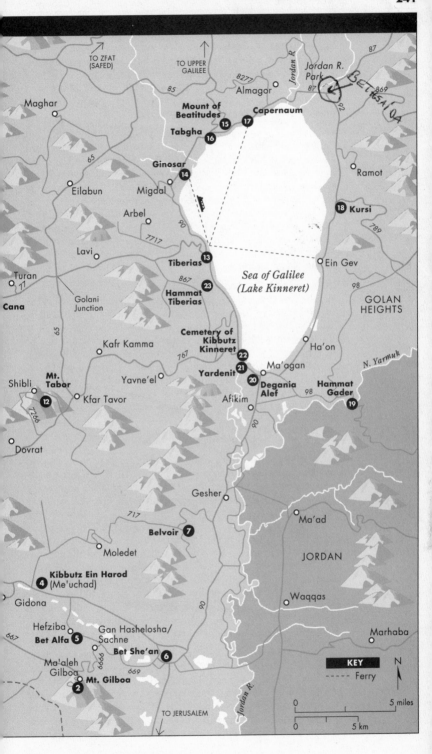

TO ZFAT (SAFED)

TO UPPER GALILEE

Jordan R.

Jordan R. Park

BETHSAIDA

87

869

92

85

8277

Almagor

Maghar

Mount of Beatitudes **15** **17** Capernaum

Tabgha **16**

Ginosar **14**

Eilabun

Migdal

Arbel

Lavi

7717

90

Ramot

**18** Kursi

789

Tiberias **13**

Turan

11

867

Hammat Tiberias **23**

*Sea of Galilee (Lake Kinneret)*

Ein Gev

98

GOLAN HEIGHTS

**Cana**

Golani Junction

65

Kafr Kamma

767

Cemetery of Kibbutz Kinneret **22**

Yardenit **21**

**20**

Ma'agan

Ha'on

N. Yarmuk

**Mt. Tabor**

Shibli **12**

7266

Yavne'el

Kfar Tavor

Degania Alef

Afikim

98

**Hammat Gader**

**19**

Dovrat

90

Gesher

Ma'ad

717

**Belvoir** **7**

Moledet

**JORDAN**

**Kibbutz Ein Harod (Me'uchad)** **4**

Gidona

667

Hefziba

**Bet Alfa** **5**

Gan Hashelosha/ Sachne

6666

**Bet She'an** **6**

669

Waqqas

Marhaba

Ma'aleh Gilboa

**Mt. Gilboa** **2**

Jordan R.

TO JERUSALEM

**KEY**

N

- - - Ferry

0        5 miles

0        5 km

Spend the first day in the Jezreel Valley, including **Megiddo** ①, visiting the scenic attractions of **Mt. Gilboa** ②–⑤, **Bet She'an** ⑥, and, time permitting, either the catacombs of **Bet She'arim** ⑧, in the west, the Crusader castle of **Belvoir** ⑦, in the east, or the church and fine views atop **Mt. Tabor** ⑫. Stay overnight in ⓣ **Tiberias** or one of the kibbutz guest houses in the Galilee. (The sequence of the following days will be determined to some extent by where you stay.)

The Christian explorer should spend the second day around the Sea of Galilee (☞ If You Have 2 Days, *above*). On the morning of the third day, drive up to Banias and Caesarea Philippi, in the Upper Galilee (☞ Chapter 6), and then head south via the Church of the Annunciation in **Nazareth** ⑨ and the mosaics of ancient **Zippori** ⑪. A more general approach might include a more leisurely outdoor exploration of the Golan Heights and Upper Galilee on the second day (eat some trout, go boating, or inner-tube the Jordan River in season; ☞ Chapter 6). On the third day, explore the old synagogues and artists' quarter of the mystical mountaintop city of Zfat, in the Upper Galilee, and **Nazareth** ⑨ and **Zippori** ⑪ on the way south.

## When to Tour the Lower Galilee

By far the best time to tour the Galilee (and Israel in general) is the spring—March, April, and early May—when the weather is usually excellent (though March is a bit less reliable) and the countryside is blanketed with wildflowers. At 700 ft below sea level, the Sea of Galilee region is very hot in summer. Avoid the week of Passover, when half the country is vacationing there; weekends in general (Thursday night through Saturday night) are more crowded as well. Autumn—late September, October, early November—is fine, though the Jewish holidays bring crowds and high-season prices.

# JEZREEL AND JORDAN VALLEYS

"Highways of the world cross Galilee in all directions," wrote the eminent Victorian scholar George Adam Smith in 1898. The great international highway of antiquity, the Via Maris (Way of the Sea), swept up the Mediterranean coast from Egypt and broke inland along three separate passes through the hills to emerge in the Jezreel Valley before continuing northeast to Damascus and Mesopotamia. The west–east through-road that began at the Mediterranean coast just north of Mt. Carmel and led to the Jordan Valley (at Bet She'an) ran through the Jezreel Valley as well. And then, as now, roads connected the valley with the hill country of the Galilee to the north, and Samaria to the south. Its destiny as a kind of universal thoroughfare and its flat terrain made the Jezreel Valley a frequent and easy battleground, so much so that the Book of Revelation identified it—by the name Armageddon—as the stage for humanity's apocalyptic finale.

On a topographical map, the Jezreel Valley appears as an equilateral triangle, each side about 40 km (25 mi) long, edged by low mountains. The narrow Harod Valley extends the Jezreel southeast to Bet She'an, in the Jordan Rift. Your first impression will be one of lush farmland as far as the eye can see, but as recently as 50 years ago, malarial swamps still blighted the area; some early pioneering settlements had cemeteries before their first buildings were completed.

The sights in this section are covered from west to east (though they can easily be explored in the reverse order). Begin with the ancient city of Megiddo; continue to the clutch of diverse attractions on or near Mt. Gilboa; go through the famous dig at Bet She'an; and end (if time permits) at the Crusader castle of Belvoir, overlooking the Jordan River. There are no fewer than six national parks here, making the Nature Protection and National Parks Authority's two-week pass (☞ Nature Parks and Reserves *in* Smart Travel Tips A to Z) a worthwhile investment. Most people spend less than a day in these valleys, but a more leisurely pace will pay off.

With a few good exceptions, restaurants in this rustic area are confined to roadside cafeterias; lunch-only places next to archaeological sites and parks such as Megiddo and Sachne/Gan Hashelosha; and small restaurants and snack bars in the towns of Afula (especially) and Bet She'an.

## Megiddo

★ ❶ *2 km (1¼ mi) north of the Megiddo Junction, where Rtes. 65 and 66 meet; 12 km (7½ mi) west of Afula.*

Since the beginning of the 20th century, several archaeological expeditions have exposed no fewer than 25 strata of civilization—from the 4th millennium BC to the 4th century BC—in the historical urban layer cake (known to archaeologists as a *tel*) of Megiddo. The ancient city owed its great importance to its strategic position at the mouth of a pass, the main branch of the international highway between Egypt and Mesopotamia. Megiddo's coveted location made it as much a target for foreign conquest as it was the center of power of its own small region.

A tiny museum at the site's entrance offers some good visual aids, including maps, a video, and a model of the tel itself. There is an unremarkable cafeteria.

The ramp up to the flattop mound brings you through the partially restored remains of a Late Canaanite (Late Bronze Age) gate, quite possibly the very one that unsuccessfully defended Megiddo against the Egyptian pharaoh Thutmose III in 1468 BC, as described in his victory stele. Above this is a larger and later gate, almost identical to those found at Hatzor, in the north, and Gezer, to the south. Long identified with King Solomon (10th century BC)—the three cities were his regional military centers—the gate has been redated by some scholars to the time of Ahab, king of Israel a century later.

Evidence has indicated prehistoric habitation here as well, but among the earliest remains of the *city* of Megiddo are a round altar dating from the Early Bronze Age and the outlines of several Early Bronze Age temples, almost 5,000 years old, visible in the trench between the two fine lookout points.

The connection to King Ahab (9th century) is strong at Megiddo. Ruins of stables, also once thought to have been Solomon's, are now definitively dated to the reign of Ahab, who is known to have had a large chariot army. But nothing else at Megiddo is as impressive as the water system. Before its construction (again apparently by Ahab), residents had to leave the safety of the city walls to draw water from the subterranean spring. In a masterful stroke, the Israelite engineers dug a deep shaft and a horizontal tunnel through solid rock to reach the spring from within the city. With this access, the spring could be permanently blocked outside the defensive walls, securing the city's vital water supply. The spring, at the end of the tunnel, is no more than a trickle today, perhaps blocked by earthquakes of later centuries. As you descend 180 steps through the shaft, traverse the 65-yard-long tunnel under the ancient city wall, and climb up 83 steps at the other end, look for chisel marks and ancient steps hewed from the rock.

The Jezreel Valley has so often heard the clash of arms that the very name of the site that commands it—Har Megiddo, Mt. Megiddo, or Armageddon (Revelation 16)—has become synonymous with the final cataclysmic battle of all time. In 1918, General Allenby swept up the pass by way of Megiddo to outflank the Ottoman Turks and seal the British victory; he was subsequently elevated to the peerage, taking as his title Viscount of Megiddo. ✉ *National Park, Rte. 66,* ☎ *04/652-2105.* 🎫 *NIS 18 ($4.60).* 🕐 *Apr.–Sept., Sat.–Thurs. 8–5, Fri. and holiday eves 8–4; Oct.–Mar., Sat.–Thurs. 8–4, Fri. and holiday eves 8–3; water tunnel closes 30 mins before rest of site.*

### Shopping

A small **jewelry shop** at Megiddo (☎ 04/642–0314) specializes in handsome and reasonably priced silver and gold items, some incorporating pieces of ancient Roman glass in attractive combinations.

*En Route*    From the Afula road (Route 65), Route 675 breaks southeast through a small farming region called the Ta'anach. On the left, 500 yards beyond the intersection with Route 60 and just after the entrance to Kibbutz Yizre'el, is the low-rise **Tel Yizre'el,** site of the Old Testament city of Jezreel. A short dirt road leads to a rise with a small thicket of trees. Here Ahab coveted Naboth's vineyard (I Kings 21), and his Phoenician wife, Jezebel, met the gruesome death predicted by the prophet Elijah (II Kings 9). From among the indecipherable ancient ruins, you have a magnificent view of the valley below and a great place to sit and read those biblical passages.

Five hundred yards farther, on the right, the scenic Route 667 strikes up through the pine forests of Mt. Gilboa, eventually descending to Route 669 just east of Bet Alfa.

## Mt. Gilboa

★ ❷    *17 km (10½ mi) from Megiddo (on Rte. 675) to Rte. 667, descending via Rte. 6666 to Rte. 69, just east of Bet Alfa.*

Mt. Gilboa—actually a small, steep mountain range rather than a single peak—is geographically a spur of the far greater Samaria Range (the biblical Mt. Ephraim) to the southwest. Literally half the mountain is freshly reforested with evergreens, while the other half is left in its pristine rockiness; environmentalists prefer the latter, as it protects the profusion of wildflowers that splatter the slopes with color every March and April. From the gravel parking area off Route 667 on the summit of the ridge, easy and well-marked trails wind through the natural habitat of the rare black (actually purple) iris, which draws hordes of Israelis every spring. Years of tireless efforts by environmental groups, such as the Society for the Protection of Nature in Israel (SPNI), have paid off, to the extent that preschoolers will tell you imperiously that you are not allowed to pick the wildflowers! The views of the valley below and the hills of Galilee beyond are great year-round, but on a good winter or spring day they're amazing, reaching as far as the snowcapped Mt. Hermon, far to the north. Afternoon is the best time to come.

Three thousand years ago, the Israelites were routed by the Philistines on Mt. Gilboa, and King Saul, mortally wounded, took his own life on the battlefield. "On the morrow, when the Philistines came to strip the slain, they found Saul and his three sons fallen on Mt. Gilboa. And they cut off his head, and stripped off his armor, and sent messengers throughout the land of the Philistines to carry the good news to their idols and the people . . . and they fastened his body to the wall of Bethshan"—thus the Bible (I Samuel 31) describes the aftermath of the debacle. The battle was presumably fought on the mountain's lower slopes, as the upper reaches are too craggy and steep; but from a vantage point on the crest, you can easily conjure up the din of a battle beneath you. Saul's death sowed panic in the ranks, and the Israelites "forsook their cities and fled; and the Philistines came and dwelt in them." In his lyrical eulogy, king-to-be David curses the battlefield— "Let there be no dew or rain upon you"—where "thy glory, O Israel" was slain (II Samuel 1).

**❸ Ma'ayan Harod** (the Spring of Harod), at the foot of Mt. Gilboa, is a small national park with an attractive spread of lawns, huge eucalyptus trees, and a big swimming pool (open in summer) fed by a spring. Today it's a bucolic picnic spot, but almost 3,200 years ago, Gideon, the reluctant hero of the biblical Book of Judges, organized his troops to fight the Midianite desert invaders: "And the camp of Midian was north of them, by the Hill of Moreh, in the valley" (Judges 7). At God's command—in order to emphasize the miraculous nature of the coming victory—Gideon dismissed more than two-thirds of the warriors and by, selecting only those who lapped up water from the spring "as a dog laps," further reduced the army to a tiny force of 300. Equipped with swords, ram's horns, and flaming torches concealed in clay jars, the army divided into three companies and surrounded the Midianite camp across the valley in the middle of the night. At a prearranged signal, the Israelite warriors shouted, blew the ram's horns, and smashed the jars. Waking to the commotion and the sudden appearance of flaming torches, the Midianites were panicked into flight, and the victory was won.

The spring has seen other armies in other ages. It was here in 1260 that the Mamluks stopped the invasion of the hitherto invincible Mongols. And in the 1930s, the woods above the spring hid clandestine Jewish self-defense squads training in defiance of British military law. ⊠ *National Park off Rte. 71, next to Gidona,* ☎ *04/653–2211.* ⛨ *NIS 27 ($6.75).* ⊙ *Summer (approximately Apr.–Sept.), Sat.–Thurs. 8–5, Fri. and holiday eves 8–4; winter (approximately Oct.–Mar.), Sat.–Thurs. 8–3, Fri. and holiday eves 8–2.*

**🐚 ❹ Kibbutz Ein Harod (Me'uchad),** across the highway from Mt. Gilboa, has an **art museum** with a permanent collection that showcases Jewish artists past and present. Temporary exhibits are more general, spanning cultures and genres. Don't confuse the place with its immediate neighbor to the west, Kibbutz Ein Harod (Ichud).

Also on the kibbutz is **Bet Sturman,** a museum of the region's natural history and human settlement. ⊠ *Rte. 71 opposite gas station,* ☎ *04/ 653–1670 art museum, 04/653–3284 Bet Sturman.* ⛨ *Art museum NIS 14 ($3.50); Bet Sturman NIS 15 ($3.75).* ⊙ *Art museum Sun.–Thurs. 9–4:30, Fri. and holiday eves 9–1:30, Sat. and holidays 10–4:30. Bet Sturman Sun.–Fri. 9–3, Sat. and holidays 11–3 (last entry 1 hr before closing). A video in English is included. An English-speaking guide can sometimes be arranged; call ahead.*

---

NEED A
BREAK?

The **Gan Hashelosha** National Park (⊠ Off Rte. 669, ☎ 04/658– 6219), commonly known as Sachne, has won international recognition for its natural beauty. The name, Gan Hashelosha—the Garden of the Three—remembers three Jewish pioneers killed here by a land mine in 1938. The park is developed around a warm spring (28°C, or 82°F, most of the year) and a deep stream (actually a small river deep enough to dive into at spots, with artificial cascades in others). Admission is NIS 27 ($6.75). The park is open April to August, Saturday to Thursday 7:30–5, Friday and holiday eves 7:30–4; from September to March closing times are one hour earlier. Facilities include changing rooms for bathers and a good cafeteria at the east end. In good weather, the park is especially crowded on Friday and Saturday. Don't leave your possessions unattended on the lawns.

To the left before you enter Gan Hashelosha is **Gan-Garoo,** a 4-acre zoo of exclusively Australian wildlife. Different kinds of kangaroo and wallaby, and the kookaburra, the emu, and a host of other exotic birds will delight children and please their parents. Call ahead for English-speaking guides (☎ 04/648–8060). A fun maze enhanced by distorting mirrors ends in a clearing with playground equipment. Admission (adults *and* children) is NIS 24 ($6) on weekdays, NIS 27 ($6.75) on weekends. The zoo is open Sunday to Thursday 9–4, Friday 9–1, Saturday 9–5. In July and August it is usually open into the evening, but call ahead to verify.

**❺** The ancient synagogue of **Bet Alfa** was accidentally discovered in 1928 by members of Kibbutz Hefziba who were digging an irrigation trench. Their tools hit a hard surface, and careful excavation uncovered a lovely, multicolored mosaic floor, almost entirely preserved. The art is somewhat childlike, but that, too, is part of its charm. An Aramaic inscription dates the building to the reign of Byzantine emperor Justinian, in the second quarter of the 6th century AD; a Greek inscription credits the workmanship to one Marianos and his son, Aninas. In keeping with Jewish tradition, the synagogue faces Jerusalem, with an apse at the far end to hold the holy ark. The building faithfully copies the architecture of the Byzantine basilicas of the day, with a nave and two side aisles; and the doors lead to a small narthex and a onetime outdoor atrium. Stairs indicate there was once an upper story.

The large mosaic in the nave is divided into three panels. The top one leaves no doubt that the building was a synagogue, as all the classic Jewish symbols are here: the holy ark flanked by lions; the *menorah,* a seven-branch candelabra; the ram's horn, called a *shofar;* the incense shovel once used in the Temple; and the *lulav* and *etrog,* the palm frond and citron used in the celebration of Sukkoth, the Feast of Tabernacles. The middle panel, however, is the most interesting: it's filled with human figures depicting the seasons, the zodiac, and—even more incredibly for a Jewish house of worship—the Greek sun god, Helios. Clearly these were more liberal times theologically; and perhaps the prohibition on making graven images didn't apply to two-dimensional art then. Scholars agree that the mosaic's motifs do not suggest a divergent Jewish sect or regional apostasy but a convenient artistic convention to symbolize the orderly cycles of the universe, since the Creator himself could not be represented graphically. The last panel tells the story of Abraham's near-sacrifice of his son Isaac (Genesis 22), again captioned in Hebrew. Take the time to watch the lighthearted but informative film. ⊠ *National Park on Kibbutz Hefziba, Rte. 669,* ☎ *04/653–2004.* ☐ *NIS 9 ($2.25).* ☉ *Apr.–Sept., Sat.–Thurs. 8–5, Fri. and holiday eves 8–4; Oct.–Mar., Sat.–Thurs. 8–4, Fri. and holiday eves 8–3; last entrance 30 mins before closing.*

### Dining

**$$$** ✕ **Herb Farm on Mt. Gilboa.** The sweeping view of the Jezreel Valley ★ from the wooden deck or the picture windows is reason enough to come here, but this restaurant glories in the myriad tastes of fresh herbs (25 in use at any one time) and good produce. The homemade bread and spreads and the "salad basket" of flavorful cold appetizers make delicious basic starters, but you can also branch out to a chives crepe stuffed with chicken liver or the excellent house Farm Salad. Entrées include a delicious tart of shallots, forest mushrooms, and goat cheese; ostrich breast stuffed with smoked goose breast and *kashkeval* cheese and served with a pesto sauce; and the unique chicken in plum, blackberry, and cardamom sauce. The less adventurous palate can choose from a good selection of steak and other grilled meats and several fish and pasta dishes. For dessert, agonize between tiramisu, hot apple cake, and crème brûlée. ⊠ *Rte. 667,* ☎ *04/653–1093. Reservations essential for Sat. lunch. AE, DC, MC, V. Closed Sun.*

## Outdoor Activities and Sports

### KITE FLYING

The **Janusz Korczak Kite-Flying Competition** is an annual event at Ma'ayan Harod, drawing contestants from throughout Israel and abroad. The less serious kite flier can buy a kite on the spot, or join a kite-building workshop. The event is named after the great Polish-Jewish educator, who visited the nearby kibbutz in 1930 and subsequently perished in the Holocaust. The event takes place on the first day of Rosh Hashana, the Jewish New Year, usually in September or early October. For details, contact Hagilboa Community Centers (⊠ M. P. Gilboa 18120, ☎ 04/653–3242).

### WALKING

The annual **Gilboa Big Walk** (Tza'adat Hagilboa in Hebrew) takes place in March, when the famous wild black irises are in bloom. There are two routes along Mt. Gilboa, a one-day walk of 11 km (7 mi), and a two-day hike covering 20 km (12½ mi) each day. Transportation to the starting point is provided from Ma'ayan Harod. The views are delightful, and the weather, though still unstable in this season, can be superb. For details, contact Hagilboa Community Centers (⊠ M. P. Gilboa 18120, ☎ 04/653–3242, FAX 04/653–3362).

# Bet She'an

★ ❻   *23 km (14 mi) east of Afula, 39 km (24 mi) south of Tiberias.*

At the intersection of the Jordan and Jezreel valleys and surrounded by farming settlements and fishponds, Bet She'an has one spectacular site and no other attractions. Once in town, follow signs to the national park or the Roman theater. The theater was exposed in the 1960s, but the rest of the great Roman-Byzantine city of Scythopolis, as the city was known in antiquity, came to light only in the more recent excavations.

The high tel dominating the site to the north was the location of **Canaanite/Israelite Bet She'an** three to four thousand years ago. There is no visible evidence of the partial excavation undertaken by a University of Pennsylvania group in the 1920s, but a team of Israeli archaeologists has reworked this area. The climb to the top for the fine panoramic view of the surrounding valleys and a superb bird's-eye view of the excavated area is a bit strenuous but worth every gasp.

The impressive, semicircular **Roman theater** was built of contrasting black basalt and white limestone blocks around AD 200, when Scythopolis was at its height. Although the upper *cavea*, or tier, has not survived, the theater is the best preserved and largest in Israel, with an estimated original capacity of some 10,000 people. The large stage and part of the *scaena* (backdrop) behind it have been restored, and Bet She'an hosts autumn performances as in days of yore (☞ Nightlife and the Arts, *below*).

The excavations have systematically exposed the downtown area of one of the region's greatest and most cosmopolitan cities during the Late Roman and Byzantine periods (2nd–6th centuries AD). Masterfully engineered colonnaded main streets, complete with storm drains and lined with shops, converge on a central plaza that once boasted a pagan temple, a decorative fountain, and a public monument. An elaborate Byzantine bathhouse, covering 1¼ acres in area and built with *caldaria* (steam rooms) and mosaic-floored porticoes, once pampered the town's worthies. And the enormous haul of marble statuary and friezes says much about the opulence of Scythopolis in its heyday. One of the most interesting finds was a multicolored mosaic floor in a small room near the ancient *odeon* (a small auditorium for chamber music), showing Tyche (Fortuna), Greek goddess of good fortune, holding a cornucopia. The original was plundered by a local fortune-seeker; there is a replica in its stead. A lack of funds has halted further excavation, but restoration of what has already been unearthed continues.

On the main thoroughfare, Sha'ul Hamelech (King Saul) Street (a few hundred yards east of Bank Leumi), are the impressive remains of Scythopolis's **amphitheater,** where blood sports and gladiatorial combats were once the order of the day. ⊠ *National Park off Sha'ul Hamelech St., at Bank Leumi,* ☎ *04/658–7189.* ◪ *NIS 18 ($4.60).* ☉ *Apr.–Sept., Sat.–Thurs. 8–5, Fri. and holiday eves 8–4; Oct.–Mar., Sat.–Thurs. 8–4, Fri. and holiday eves 8–3.*

### Nightlife and the Arts
**Gesher Leshalom** (Bridge to Peace; ☎ 04/658–6597 or 04/658–8220) is the name of the arts festival that enlivens Bet She'an each October. The emphasis is on Israeli song and dance. The main venue is the marvelous Roman theater, but secondary locations elsewhere in town spotlight local talent as well.

# Belvoir

❼ *Rte. 717; turnoff 12 km (7½ mi) north of Bet She'an; continue 5 km (3 mi) to site. The road from Ein Harod via Moledet is passable but in very bad condition in places.*

The Crusaders chose their site well: Belvoir, they called it—"beautiful view"—and it was the most invincible fortress in the land. The Hebrew name Kochav Hayarden (the Star of the Jordan) and the Arabic Kaukab el Hauwa (the Star of the Wind) merely underscore the splendid isolation. The breathtaking view of the Jordan River valley and southern Sea of Galilee, some 1,800 ft below you, is best in the afternoon.

The mighty castle was completed by the Hospitallers (the Knights of St. John) in 1173. In the summer of 1187 the Crusader armies were crushed by the Arabs under Saladin at the Horns of Hattin, west of Tiberias, bringing to an end the Latin Kingdom of Jerusalem. Their remnants struggled on to Tyre (in modern Lebanon), but Belvoir alone refused to yield; 18 months of siege brought the Muslims no further than undermining the outer eastern rampart. The Crusaders, for their part, even sallied out from time to time to battle the enemy, but their lone resistance had become pointless. They struck a deal with Saladin and surrendered the stronghold in exchange for free passage, flags flying, to Tyre.

Don't follow the arrows from the parking lot; instead, take the wide gravel path to the right of the fortress. This brings you right to the panoramic view, and the best spot from which to appreciate the strength of the stronghold, with its deep, dry moat; massive rock and cut-stone ramparts; and gates. Once inside the main courtyard, you're unexpectedly faced with a fortress within a fortress, a scaled-down replica of the outer defenses. It's little wonder the Muslims couldn't force its submission. Not much remains of the upper stories; in 1220, the Muslims system-

atically dismantled Belvoir, fearing another Crusade and the renewal
of the fortress as a Frankish base. Once you've explored the modest
buildings, exit over the western bridge (once a drawbridge) and spy
on the postern gates (the protected and sometimes secret back doors
of medieval castles). ✉ *National Park, Rte. 717, 5 km (3 mi) west of
Rte. 90,* ☎ *04/658–1766.* 🎫 *NIS 14 ($3.50).* ⊙ *Apr.–Sept., Sat.–
Thurs. 8–5, Fri. and holiday eves 8–4; Oct.–Mar., Sat.–Thurs. 8–4, Fri.
and holiday eves 8–3.*

# NAZARETH AND THE GALILEE HILLS

Remove the modern roads and power lines, and this region's landscape
is an illustration of the Bible. Unplanned villages are splashed seemingly haphazardly on the hillsides, freeing the valleys for small-scale
agriculture. Acres of olive groves, the source of the region's wealth in
antiquity, are still harvested by whacking the trees. New Testament settings abound here: Nazareth, where Jesus grew up; Cana, with its miraculous wedding feast; Mt. Tabor, identified with the Transfiguration;
and more. Jewish history resonates strongly, too: Tabor and Yodefat
were fortifications in the Great Revolt against the Romans (1st century AD); Shefar'am, Bet She'arim, and Zippori were in turn the headquarters of the Sanhedrin, the Jewish high court, between the 2nd and
4th centuries AD; and latter-day Jewish pioneers, attracted to the region's wild scenery, put down roots where their ancestors farmed.
Our suggested route reflects the area's diversity, moving from the catacombs of Bet She'arim to Nazareth, Cana, and Zippori and detour-
ing to Mt. Tabor before descending to Tiberias and the Sea of Galilee.

## Bet She'arim

❽ *20 km (12½ mi) southeast of Haifa, 25 km (15½ mi) west of Nazareth.*

The chalk slopes are honeycombed with catacombs around the attractively landscaped site of ancient Bet She'arim. A Jewish town flourished here after (and to some extent because of) the eclipse of Jerusalem.
The little that was left of Jerusalem after Titus's legions sacked it and
razed the Second Temple in AD 70 was plowed under by Hadrian in
AD 135, following the Second or Bar Kochba Revolt of the Jews against
Rome. Hadrian built in its stead the pagan town of Aelia Capitolina,
and the Jews were denied access to their holy city and the venerated
burial ground of the Mount of Olives for generations. The center of
Jewish life and religious authority retreated first to Yavne, in the southern coastal plain, and then for several centuries to the Lower Galilee.

By around AD 200 the unofficial Jewish capital had shifted to Bet
She'arim, a city that owed its brief preeminence to the enormous
stature of one man who chose to make it his home: Rabbi Yehuda
Hanassi, the Patriarch—or, as he's sometimes called, the Prince. The
title was conferred on the nominal leader of the Jewish community,
who was responsible both for its inner workings and for its relations
with its Roman masters. Alone among his contemporaries, Yehuda
Hanassi brought to his dual office both a worldly understanding of the
ways of diplomacy (he was a personal friend of one of the emperors,
possibly Marcus Aurelius) and an awesome reputation as the foremost
Jewish religious scholar and spiritual leader of his day.

The rabbi eventually moved east to Zippori (☞ *below*) because of its
more salubrious climate, and there he gathered the great Jewish sages of
his day and compiled the Mishnah, which remains the definitive interpretation of biblical precepts for religious Jews. Nonetheless, it was in his
hometown of Bet She'arim that Yehuda Hanassi was finally laid to rest.

If Bet She'arim was a magnet for scholars and petitioners in Yehuda Hanassi's lifetime, it became a virtual shrine after his death. With Jerusalem still off-limits, Bet She'arim became the most prestigious burial site in the Jewish world. The town's prominence lasted until AD 352, when Gallus destroyed it in suppression of yet another Jewish revolt.

Two major expeditions in the 1930s and '50s uncovered a huge series of 20 **catacombs.** The largest of these is open to the public, with 24 chambers containing more than 200 stone sarcophagi and *arcosolia* (arched burial niches). A wide range of both Jewish and Roman symbols are carved into the sarcophagi, and more than 250 funerary inscriptions in Greek, Hebrew, Aramaic, and Palmyrene throughout the site testify to the great distances some people traveled—from Yemen and Mesopotamia, for instance—to be buried here. Without exception, the sarcophagi were plundered over the centuries by grave robbers seeking the possessions with which the dead were interred. ✉ *Follow the signs in Kiryat Tivon, off Rte. 75 or 722,* ☏ *04/983–1643.* ☑ *NIS 14 ($3.50).* ☉ *Apr.–Sept., Sat.–Thurs. 8–5, Fri. and holiday eves 8–4; Oct.– Mar., Sat.–Thurs. 8–4, Fri. and holiday eves 8–3.*

## Nazareth

★ ❾  *30 km (19 mi) east of Bet She'arim; about 56 km (35 mi) east of Haifa; 15 km (9½ mi) north of Afula.*

The Nazareth where Jesus grew up was an insignificant village nestling in a hollow in the Galilean hills. Today's city of 70,000 has burst out of the hollow with almost frenetic energy. It's a slightly bemusing and dissonant experience for the Christian pilgrim who seeks the spiritual Nazareth among the horn-blowing cars, vendors, and donkeys (at least *they* add some scriptural authenticity!) plying Paulus VI Street. The scene is hardly quieter even on Friday, the holy day of the Muslim two-thirds of the Arab population, but it calms down somewhat on Wednesday afternoon, when many businesses close for a midweek sabbatical; and on Sunday, the day of rest for the Christians who make up the other third of the town, it's positively placid. If you're out for local color (and traffic jams), come on Saturday, when Arab peasants come to town to sell produce and buy goods and Jewish families from the surrounding area come looking for bargains in the *souk* (market).

A newly developed site called Nazareth Village tries to reconstruct life of 2,000 years ago, with guided tours of its indoor visual aids and its outdoor replicas of buildings, crafts and artifacts. (For details call 04/ 645–6042.)

If you're coming from Bet She'arim, Route 77 breaks off to the north—to Zippori, the Golani Junction, and Tiberias. Route 75 skirts the north side of the picturesque Jezreel Valley as it climbs into the hills toward Nazareth; at the crest of the hill, it's joined by Route 60 from Afula. A turn to the left takes you down to Paulus VI, Nazareth's main drag.

★  The Franciscan **Church of the Annunciation,** the largest church in the Middle East, dominates the lower part of the town. Consecrated in 1969, it enshrines the Roman Catholic belief that the angel Gabriel visited Mary here to announce that she would give birth to Jesus. (Casa Nova Street climbs steeply to the entrance of the church. Parking is hard to find here; try Paulus VI Street, in the direction of the Galilee Hotel.)

The artwork in and around the church is eclectic in the extreme, but the more interesting for it. The portico around the courtyard just inside the main gate is decorated with striking contemporary mosaics, most depicting the Madonna and Child, donated by Catholic communities around the world. Many carry the names of their countries of origin; for others you must rely on the script (such as Korean or Gaelic) or the artistic style (such as Thai) to tell you the provenance.

The church's main entrance is marked by massive bronze doors, made in Germany, that relate in bronze relief the central events of Jesus's life. Here you can enter the dimly lighted lower church, with its brilliant, abstract stained-glass windows. The focal point of the entire church is the grotto, a small, sunken cave dwelling. The New Testament (Luke 1) relates, "The angel Gabriel was sent from God to a city of Galilee named Nazareth, to a virgin . . . and the virgin's name was Mary. And he came to her and said, 'Hail, O favored one, the Lord is with you! . . . And behold, you will conceive in your womb and bear a son, and you shall call his name Jesus.'" This event is known to Christians as the Annunciation, and Roman Catholic tradition identifies the grotto as the former home of Mary and the place where the angel appeared to her. Crusader-era walls still stand beneath the modern windows, and there are some restored Byzantine mosaics near the grotto.

Just inside the entrance, a spiral staircase leads to the vast upper church, some 70 yards long and 30 yards wide, the parish church of Nazareth's Roman Catholic community. Note that the beautiful Italian ceramic reliefs on the huge concrete pillars representing the Stations of the Cross are captioned in the Arabic vernacular. The cupola, which soars 195 ft above the grotto of the lower church (seen down through a well), is formed by ribs representing the petals of an upside-down lily chalice rooted in heaven. The lily, a symbol of purity, represents Mary's unblemished nature, and the petals are repeatedly inscribed with the letter *M*. The huge mosaic behind the altar shows Jesus and Peter at the center and an enthroned Mary behind them, flanked by figures of the hierarchical church (to your right) and the charismatic church (to your left). The modern concrete trusses over the nave evoke the wooden roofs of the early Christian basilicas.

On the walls of the upper church are the so-called banners, large panels of mosaics and ceramic reliefs contributed by Roman Catholic communities abroad. Among the countries represented are the United States (a piece inspired by Revelation 12:1–2), Canada (a fine terracotta), England, and Australia. Particularly interesting are the Madonna and Child gifts from Japan (made with gold leaf and real pearls), Venezuela (a carved-wood statue), and Cameroon (a stylized painting in black, white, and brick red). In the courtyard, a glass-enclosed baptistery is built over what is thought to have been an ancient *mikveh*, a Jewish ritual immersion bath.

In the same complex as the Church of the Annunciation is the small **Church of St. Joseph,** just past Terra Sancta College, built over a complex of rock-hewn chambers traditionally identified as the workshop of Joseph the Carpenter. ☒ *Casa Nova St.,* ☎ *04/657–2501.* ▣ *Free.* ☉ *At press time: Apr.–Sept., daily 8–6, Oct.–Mar., daily 8–5. Site may return to closing 11:45–2 and Sun. morning.*

NEED A BREAK?  Try the Arab pastries at the **Mahroum** confectionery, at the corner of Casa Nova and Paulus VI streets. It's clean, has bathrooms, and serves wonderful *bourma,* a honey-soaked cylindrical pastry filled with whole pistachio nuts. Don't confuse this place with another one nearby: look for the Arab pastries, not the gooey Western cakes.

The Greek Orthodox **Church of St. Gabriel,** about 1 km (½ mi) north of the junction of Paulus VI and Casa Nova streets, contains a spring that the Greek Orthodox, citing the noncanonical Gospel of St. James, believe to be the site of the Annunciation. (At the bottom of the short approach to the church, on Paulus VI Street, is a round, white, stone structure marked MARY'S WELL—but this is merely a modern fountain.) One may question the validity of that tradition—though evidence of an earlier structure, perhaps a medieval church, suggests the tradition is not new—but one thing is certain: this is the only natural water source in Nazareth, and Mary must have come here almost daily to draw water.

The ornate church was built in 1750 and contains a fine carved-wood pulpit and iconostasis (chancel screen), with painted New Testament scenes and silver-haloed saints in the niches. The walls are adorned with frescoes of figures from the Bible and the Greek Orthodox hagiography. A tiny "well" stands over the running spring, and a modern aluminum cup on a cord gives a satisfying plop as it drops into the sacred water. (The water is pure; the cup's sanitary condition is more suspect.) ⊠ *Off Paulus VI St.* ⊡ *Small donation expected.* ⊙ *Daily 8–5 (expect delays on Sun. because of services).*

Christianity speaks with many voices in Nazareth. The **Baptist Church,** a few hundred yards north of the Church of St. Gabriel, along Paulus VI Street, is affiliated with the Southern Baptist Convention of the United States.

For unobstructed **panoramas** of the town, drive up to Upper Nazareth, on the eastern ridge, a Jewish town of about 35,000 founded as a separate municipal entity in the 1950s; or drive to the St. Gabriel Hotel on the western ridge (accessible from the police station at the town's northern exit, where the road heads for Tiberias).

## Dining

Travelers tend to hit the sights in Nazareth and move on, and the result is a dearth of good restaurants. There is, however, a clutch of fairly decent little Arab restaurants on Casa Nova and Paulus VI streets, frequented mostly by locals. Dinner here means hummus, shish kebab, baklava, Turkish coffee, and the like. Decor is incidental, atmosphere a function of the clientele of the moment, and dinnertime early. Needless to say, reservations are not necessary, and dress is casual.

## Lodging

Tourist Nazareth has been transformed by several new hotels, and some old ones are slated for renovation. At press time, several hotels had closed temporarily. Please call ahead to assure that a hotel is open. Roman Catholic **hospices** (which are hostelries, not sanatoria) cater primarily to pilgrim groups, though some welcome individual travelers. Contact the **Government Tourist Office** (⊠ Casa Nova St., ☎ 04/657–3003) for listings.

$$$$ 🏨 **Marriott.** White and soft-pink stone interiors give the first good impression that Nazareth has at last acquired an upscale hotel; the dark wood fittings and good bathrooms of the guest rooms confirm it. Many rooms enjoy the fine view of Old Nazareth. The dining room does a very good job, and at press time the Terra Cotta Italian-French specialty restaurant had just opened. The hotel offers its guests a free Saturday morning tour of Old Nazareth. ⊠ *2 Hermon St., Upper Nazareth 17000,* ☎ *04/602–8200,* ☏ *04/602–8222. 272 rooms. 3 restaurants, bar, hot tub, sauna, exercise room, children's programs. AE, DC, MC, V.*

$$$$ 🏨 **Renaissance.** The airy stone-walled and wooden-beamed lobby of this brand-new hotel offers great views of the Jezreel Valley from its huge picture window (though not all guest rooms face that direction). There are some nice touches in the guest rooms: poster beds, stone tables, and decorative bathroom tiles. The hotel is currently managed by the Marriott chain. Guests can sign up for a free Saturday-morn-

ing tour of Old Nazareth. ✉ *Mt. of Precipitation, Box 2015, 16000,* ☎ *04/602–8600,* FAX *04/602–8666. 245 rooms. 2 restaurants, bar, hot tub, 2 saunas, exercise room. AE, DC, MC, V.*

**$$** 🏨 **St. Gabriel.** Sitting high on the ridge that overlooks Nazareth from the west, this hotel began life as a Catholic convent, as one is reminded by the charming neo-Gothic church still in use today. Renovations extended the nuns' old cells, and half the rooms enjoy one of the city's greatest views. All rooms have private showers. The reception area is furnished with inlaid tables, chairs, and mirrors in the old Damascene style, and the dining room prides itself on its local dishes. The garden and the view make for a perfect sundowner option. ✉ *2 Salesian St., Box 2318, 16000,* ☎ *04/657–2133 or 04/656–7349,* FAX *04/655–4071. 60 rooms. 2 restaurants, bar. AE, DC, MC, V.*

## Cana

🔟 *8 km (5 mi) north of Nazareth on Rte. 754, 1 km (½ mi) south of the junction of Rtes. 77 and 754; 50 km (31 mi) east of Haifa.*

Most scholars identify the ancient Jewish village of Cana with the modern Arab village of Kafr Kanna. According to the New Testament (John 2), it was here that Jesus reluctantly performed his first miracle, turning water into wine at a wedding feast. He thus emerged from his "hidden years" to begin a three-year ministry in the Galilee. Approaching the village from Nazareth, the road winds down through typical Galilean countryside. The profusion of olive groves, pomegranates, grapevines, fig trees, and even the occasional date palm (unusual at this altitude) is a reminder of how much local scenery is described in the Bible. Even the clutter of modern buildings, power lines, and industrial debris cannot ruin the impression.

Within the village, red signs on the right lead to two rival churches— one Roman Catholic (Franciscan), the other Greek Orthodox—that enshrine the scriptural tradition. The alleyway to these churches was once just barely passable for cars, and you could park in the courtyard of the souvenir store opposite the Franciscan **Cana Wedding Church** (☎ 04/651–7011). If ongoing road repairs make this impossible, find parking on the main road and walk the short distance.

The present Catholic church was built in the 1880s on what the Franciscans believe to be the very spot where the wedding took place. Completely renovated recently, it is worth a short visit. Admission is free. At press time, it was open daily 8–6 from April to September, and 8–5 from October to March. It may return to closing noon–2, as well as on Saturday afternoon and all day Sunday.

## Zippori

★ 1️⃣1️⃣ *Village, 5 km (3 mi) west of Nazareth off Rte. 79; site, 4 km (2½ mi) farther; 47 km (29 mi) from Haifa.*

For years the main attraction of Zippori was its charming hilltop location, surrounded by planted pine and cypress woods, cultivated fields, and a fine view of the valley below. The site has been transformed into a national park, where archaeologists have unearthed much of the large and prosperous city of the Roman period, including a most impressive water system and several mosaic floors of sometimes extraordinary fineness (at press time, not all had yet been opened to the public).

A Jewish town stood here from at least the 1st century BC through the early Middle Ages. Known also by its Greek name, Sepphoris, it is identified in some Christian traditions as the birthplace of the Virgin Mary. In the Great Revolt of the Jews against the Romans (AD 66–73), the citizens of Zippori opted out of the struggle and sued for peace with Vespasian, thus creating a serious gap in the rebel defenses in the Galilee and earning the ire of their compatriots but sparing their town the vengeful destruction the Romans inflicted on those that opposed them.

In the late 2nd or early 3rd century AD, the legendary sage Rabbi Yehuda Hanassi (the Patriarch) moved here from Bet She'arim (☞ *above*) for health reasons. His enormous prestige and official status as the head of the Jewish community made the subsequent relocation of the Jewish high court, the Sanhedrin, to Zippori an obvious move. It was apparently here (the sources are equivocal) that Rabbi Yehuda convened the greatest Jewish sages of the time and compiled the Mishnah, the codification of Oral Law. For centuries, rabbis had given learned responses to real-life questions of civil and religious law, basing their judgments on the dos, don'ts, and between-the-lines principles of the Torah (the biblical Five Books of Moses, and the foundation of Judaism). These rabbinic opinions had been transmitted orally from generation to generation and, like court decisions, had become legal precedents and the heart of Jewish jurisprudence. Further commentary was added to the Mishnah in later centuries to produce the Talmud, the primary guide to Orthodox Jewish practice to this day.

Zippori was clearly a town with a cosmopolitan soul, however. Jewish, pagan, and (apparently) early Christian communities coexisted for some time around the 3rd century AD. A relatively small **Roman theater**—capacity about 4,000, its stone seats long since stolen by local villagers for their own building projects—tells mutely of the town's cultural life, and the mosaic floors bespeak the opulence that could support it. One mosaic is made up of Egyptian motifs, including the famous lighthouse at Alexandria and a mythological depiction of the source of the Nile River. Another mosaic, once a synagogue floor, rather surprisingly depicts the signs of the zodiac, just like those found in Bet Alfa (☞ Jezreel and Jordan Valleys, *above*) and Hammat Tiberias (☞ Tiberias and the Sea of Galilee, *below*). The finest mosaic floor of all reveals a series of Dionysian drinking scenes as well as the exquisite face of a woman, which the popular press at once dubbed "the Mona Lisa of the Galilee." Situated on the crest of the ridge, that floor must have been the centerpiece of the town's most prominent villa, perhaps the governor's residence. The mosaics have been restored and an air-conditioned structure built over them, with useful explanations of the various panels.

Alongside the villa is a **watchtower,** Zippori's landmark. The lower, Crusader part of the structure reused Roman sarcophagi as cornerstones. The upper, Turkish levels have been renovated, and the roof offers superb views. Within the tower, a good video and, upstairs, a small museum that includes interactive CD-ROMs along with archaeological artifacts add an extra dimension to your visit. East of the villa, and leading to the Nile Mosaic, is an impressive Roman colonnaded street, possibly the *cardo maximus* (main north–south thoroughfare) of the 3rd-century town.

One kilometer (½ mile) east of the main site—but still within the park—is a huge section of ancient Zippori's **water system,** fed by springs just north of Nazareth. The ancient aqueduct is in fact a deep, man-made, plastered canyon, and the effect is extraordinary. ⊠ *Beyond the village of Zippori, off Rte. 79,* ☎ *04/656–8272.* 🖃 *NIS 18 ($4.60).* ☼ *Apr.–Sept., Sat.–Thurs. 8–5, Fri. and Jewish holiday eves*

8–4; Oct.–Mar., Sat.–Thurs. 8–4, Fri. and Jewish holiday eves 8–3; last
entry 45 mins before closing.

## Golani Junction

6 km (4 mi) east of Cana at intersection of Rtes. 77 and 65, 50 km (31
mi) from Haifa.

One of the most important crossroads in the Lower Galilee, the Golani
Junction was captured by the Golani Brigade of the Israel Defense Forces
in the War of Independence in 1948. A monument, a museum, and a
McDonald's stand on the east side.

All around the Golani Junction are new groves of evergreens planted
by visitors as part of the project "Plant a Tree with Your Own Hands."
Over the last 90 years or so, the **Keren Kayemet** (also called the Jewish National Fund, or JNF) has worked to redeem a neglected land,
including an attempt to restore the forests that once covered the hills
of Israel. More than 230 million trees have been planted nationwide.
Jewish tradition elevates the act of planting a tree to the level of a *mitzvah*,
a good deed given authority by the Bible. If you want to leave something living behind you, look for the Planting Center (open Sunday–
Thursday), to the left of the Tiberias Road (Route 77), a few hundred
yards from the junction (but accessible from the Lavi turnoff slightly
farther east. For NIS 40 ($10) you can pick out a sapling, dedicate it
to someone if you wish, and plant it yourself.

At the Horns of Hattin, a small double hill that is an extinct volcano,
Saladin crushed the Crusader army in 1187, bringing to an end the Latin
Kingdom of Jerusalem. Richard the Lionhearted's Third Crusade, a few
years later, restored some parts of the country to Christian control, but
the power and glory of the Latin Kingdom were gone forever. The hill
is just beyond Lavi (☞ Lodging, *below*), about 2½ km (1½ mi) east of
the Golani Junction on Route 77.

### Lodging

$$–$$$ 🏨 **Lavi Kibbutz Hotel.** The guest house at Kibbutz Lavi is designed like
a hotel, with all the units in one building. The community is Jewish
Orthodox, so there is no vehicular traffic into or out of the village (and
thus no check-ins or checkouts) on the Sabbath, from sunset on Friday until after dark on Saturday. Schedule aside, the atmosphere at the
is warm and welcoming, and many Christian pilgrim groups make it
their Galilee base. Two-thirds of the rooms have recently been renovated, and a new wing with 60 additional rooms and gym and spa facilities are slated for completion in 2001. Twelve of the rooms have
showers; the rest have bathtubs. The experience of waking to rural surroundings has much to recommend it, and you're only 15 minutes from
Tiberias. ✉ *Rte. 77, 11 km (7 mi) west of Tiberias, Lower Galilee 15267,*
☎ *04/679–9450,* 📠 *04/679–9399. 124 rooms. 2 restaurants, pool, 2
tennis courts. AE, DC, MC, V.*

## Mt. Tabor

★ ⑫ 16 km (10 mi) south of the Golani Junction off Rte. 7266, 17 km (10½
mi) northeast of Afula.

Mt. Tabor and the nearby areas are rich with biblical history. The large
village of **Kfar Tavor,** a veteran pioneering community from the late
19th century, is dominated to the west by the domed mountain that
gave it its name.

The modern kibbutz of **Ein Dor,** a mile or so past Kfar Tavor, is the
biblical Endor of I Samuel 28. Three thousand years ago King Saul com-

muned here with the spirit of the prophet Samuel before his fateful battle against the Philistines. Saul got little consolation. "The Lord has torn the kingdom out of your hand, and given it to your neighbor, David," cried Samuel, "and tomorrow, you and your sons shall be with me . . . ." At the subsequent battle on Mt. Gilboa (☞ Jezreel and Jordan Valleys, *above*), Saul and his three sons were killed and the Israelite army was routed. "How are the mighty fallen . . . ," lamented David when the news reached him.

**Shibli,** on Route 7266 at the very foot of the mountain, is a village of Bedouin who abandoned their nomadic life a few generations ago and became farmers. The narrow switchback road up Mt. Tabor begins from a clearing beyond Shibli and between Shibli and the next village of Dabouriya. Nazareth-based taxis are usually waiting at the bottom of the mountain to provide shuttle service to the top.

As far back as the Byzantine period, Christian tradition has identified Mt. Tabor as the "high mountain apart" that Jesus ascended with his disciples Peter, James, and John. "And he was transfigured before them, and his garments became white as light. And behold there appeared to them Moses and Elijah, talking with him" (Matthew 17). Early churches on the mountain were designed to represent the three tabernacles Peter had suggested to Jesus that they build, one for Moses, one for Elijah, and one for Jesus himself. The altar of the present imposing **Church of the Transfiguration** (☎ 04/673–2283), which was consecrated in 1924, represents the tabernacle of Jesus; those of Moses and Elijah are represented as chapels at the back of the church. The church is open Sunday–Friday 8–noon and 2–5; admission is free.

Thirty-two centuries ago, somewhere near the foot of the mountain, the Israelite conscripts of the prophetess-judge Deborah and her general, Barak, routed the Canaanite chariot army. From the terrace of the Franciscan hospice next to the church, you see the Jezreel Valley to the west and south; and from a platform on the Byzantine and Crusader ruins to the left of the modern church (watch your step), there is a panorama east and north over the Galilean hills. No wonder the Jewish general Yosef Ben Matityahu (Josephus Flavius) fortified the hill in the 1st century AD during the Great Revolt against the Romans.

NEED A
BREAK?

The **Dovrat Inn** (✉ Rte. 65, ☎ 04/659–9520) is a rather good cafeteria, now part of the Mövenpick chain, offering a wide range of attractively presented food. It's at the gas station, about 5 km (3 mi) from the Shibli turnoff (Route 7266), toward Afula.

## Dining

$$$ ✕ **Tzela Hatavor.** This restaurant lies "in the shadow of Mt. Tabor"
★ (a fair translation of the name), but it's not a roadside diner. Split-pane arched windows and solid wood tables create a fashionably rustic ambience. The menu is wide-ranging—soups, salads, pastas, fish, fine steaks, and a kids' meal. The best appetizers are mallard in orange sauce (also available as a main dish); eggplant and Roquefort cooked in tomato sauce and herbs; the stuffed Portobello mushrooms; and the house salad (but not the house dressing). Fish and steak are good here (for the latter, go with the Dijon-mustard sauce). The fettuccine Alfredo is excellent. For dessert, try the crème brûlée or the mousse cake. ✉ *Rte. 65 (next to gas station), Kfar Tavor,* ☎ *04/676–9966. Reservations essential weekends and holidays. AE, DC, MC, V.*

$$–$$$ ✕ **Sahara.** The menu of this Middle Eastern restaurant is a bit more sophisticated than its nearby roadside rivals. Look for a new stone building with a landmark round tower. Inside it is spacious, with stone floors

and arches, wooden tables, and a centerpiece water cascade. Follow the excellent fresh *meze* (local salads) with traditional skewers of grilled meat; one of the fish, lamb, baby chicken, or quail dishes; or the (unlisted) moussaka. A Jordanian connection has added a few unusual items to the menu. ✉ *Rte. 65 (next to gas station),* ☎ *04/642–5959. Reservations essential Fri. and Sat. AE, DC, MC, V.*

*En Route* If you're heading to the Sea of Galilee, take Route 767, which breaks off Route 65 at Kfar Tavor. It's a beautiful drive of about 25 minutes. The first village, **Kafr Kamma,** is one of two in Israel of the Circassian (*Cherkessi*) community, Muslims from the Russian steppes who were settled here by the Ottoman Turks in the 19th century. The decorative mosque is just one element of the tradition they continue to preserve.

On the descent to the lake, there is a parking area precisely at sea level. The Sea of Galilee is still more than 700 ft below, and the view is superb, especially in the afternoon. You meet Route 90 at the bottom of the road.

# TIBERIAS AND THE SEA OF GALILEE

The great American writer and humorist Mark Twain was unimpressed by the Sea of Galilee region. He passed through in 1867 in the company of a group of pilgrims and Arab dragomans (interpreters) on horseback and found "an unobtrusive basin of water, some mountainous desolation, and one tree." He would scarcely recognize it now. Modern agriculture and forestation projects have made the plains and hills green; the handful of "squalid" and "reeking" villages of his day have been supplanted by a string of thriving and well-landscaped kibbutzim; and the "unobtrusive basin of water" has become a lively resort.

The Sea of Galilee is in fact a freshwater lake, 21 km (13 mi) long from north to south and 11 km (7 mi) wide from east to west. The Jordan River feeds the lake from the north, then leaves it from the south to meander to the Dead Sea. Almost completely ringed by cliffs and steep hills, the lake lies in a hollow about 700 ft below sea level, which accounts for its warm climate and subtropical vegetation.

The city of Tiberias provides a sort of anchor for the region and the logical starting point for exploration. Thereafter, we describe sights in sequence as you circumvent the Sea of Galilee clockwise (via Routes 90, 87, 92, and 98), ending at Hammat Tiberias, at the city's southern edge. It's worth crossing the lake by boat if someone can bring your car around. Note that several of the Christian sites demand modest dress.

## Tiberias

★ ⑬ *38 km (23½ mi) north of Bet She'an, 36 km (23 mi) east of Nazareth, 70 km (43 mi) from Haifa.*

As the only town on the Sea of Galilee, Tiberias has become the natural center of the region. It is not a town with class, however; almost 2,000 years old, Tiberias still has the atmosphere of a community yet to come of age. It is at once brash and sleepy, a provincial town where falafel is far more popular than foie gras and where a few pubs with loud recorded music constitute the entertainment menu most nights. Its reputation as a resort town is based more on its great location and some decent hotels than on the town's own attractions.

Today's Tiberias, with a population of 40,000, spreads all the way up the slope behind it, from about 700 ft below sea level, at the lake, to 800 ft above sea level, in its highest hilltop neighborhoods—a difference big enough to create a serious temperature differential in mid-summer. Tiberias itself is not lovely; it deserved better than the sort of development it has experienced. Most travelers, however, see little of the town proper and confine themselves to the lakeshore district, where most of the hotels and all of the pubs and restaurants are clustered. Tourism, as much Israeli as foreign, is one of the mainstays of the town's economy—you can eat well here, boogie a bit, and drink late along an incomparable subtropical lake.

Tiberias has an almost invisible history. Much has happened here, but you'll find few footprints of the past. Part of the black-basalt medieval city wall crosses Habanim Street just south of the Sheraton Moriah Hotel; the Tourist Information Office, on Habanim Street opposite the hotel, is framed by restored Crusader arches; and massive Crusader towers and ramparts behind the Scottish Centre dominate Dona Gracia and Gedud Barak streets. Near the promenade, between the Sheraton Moriah and Caesar hotels, is a cluster of old basalt synagogues and mosques and a 19th-century church (some of the synagogues date from the Aboulafia period of the 18th century). The Franciscan Church of St. Peter commemorates the events described in John 21, in which Jesus entrusted Peter with the continuation of his ministry ("Feed my sheep").

In AD 18, the town was completed by Herod Antipas, son of the notorious Herod the Great, and dedicated to Tiberius, emperor of Rome at the time. Although Antipas, with the title of tetrarch, was able to surround himself with ambitious courtiers and functionaries, many common folk shunned the new town because it had been built on an old cemetery and was therefore considered unclean.

Rich men make poor rebels, and the Tiberians seem to have had little stomach for the Jewish war against Rome that broke out in AD 66. They surrendered to the Romans in 67, thus saving themselves from the vengeful destruction visited on so many other Galilean towns. In the 2nd century, the revered Rabbi Shimon Bar Yochai ceremonially purified Tiberias, opening the way for a wave of settlement and development that transformed the city. Jerusalem, devastated by Titus's legions in AD 70, lay in ruins, the Jews banished from the city. The center of Jewish life in Israel gradually gravitated to the Galilee. By the 4th century, the Sanhedrin had established itself in Tiberias. It was here, around AD 400, that the Jewish Oral Law was finally compiled into what became known as the Jerusalem Talmud.

This was something of a golden era in Tiberias, assuring it a place among Judaism's holy cities in the Land of Israel (together with Jerusalem, Hebron, and, later, Zfat). The community knew hard times under the Byzantines, stabilized under more-tolerant Muslim dynasties (the Arabs conquered the region in the 7th century), and declined again under the hostile Crusaders, who made Tiberias the capital of their Principality of Galilee. The Arab Saladin besieged the city in 1187 and, at the nearby Horns of Hattin, routed the Crusader army that was on its way to relieve it. Crusader fortifications remain a prominent feature of the cityscape.

Tiberias's decline was almost total after the debacle at Hattin. It was not until 1562, when the Ottoman sultan Suleiman the Magnificent gave the town to the Jewish nobleman Don Joseph Nasi, that an attempt was made to revive the community. Don Joseph resettled the town and planted mulberry trees in the hope—the vain hope, as it turned out—of developing a silkworm industry.

In the 18th century, Tiberias was expanded and fortified by renegade Bedouin governor Dahr el-Omar, who invited a group of Jews from

Izmir, in Turkey, to settle it. In conflict with the Ottomans, and unable to trust his own subjects, this cunning ruler decided to populate his capital city with a citizenry loyal to him personally. The leader of the new settlers was Isaac Aboulafia, perhaps still the best-known family name in Tiberias today. The Jewish community swelled further with the arrival in 1777 of a group of Hasidim, members of a devout, charismatic sect from Eastern Europe.

In 1833 the Egyptian nationalist leader Ibrahim Pasha, enjoying his short-lived independence from Turkey, built the town up further, but a cataclysmic earthquake just four years later left Tiberias in ruins with (it is said) 1,000 dead.

Relations between Jewish and Arab Tiberians were generally cordial until the Arab riots of 1936, in which some 30 Jews were massacred. Confrontation during the 1948 War of Independence had a different consequence. An attack by local Arabs in anticipation of an imminent Syrian invasion brought a counterattack from Haganah forces (the Jewish army before Israeli statehood), and the Arab population abandoned the town.

Among the many tombs in Tiberias is that of its most famous denizen, the great 12th-century sage Moses Maimonides (1135–1204). To get to the **tomb of Moses Maimonides** from the tourist office, walk north up Habanim Street and take a left at Hayarden Street. Walk two blocks, and then turn right onto Ben Zakkai Street. A short way up, you'll see the tomb on your right.

Born in Córdoba, Spain, Maimonides won renown as a philosopher, as physician to the royal court of Saladin in Egypt, and, in the Jewish world, as the greatest religious scholar and spiritual authority since the Talmudic period of the 4th and 5th centuries AD. To his profound knowledge of the Talmud, Maimonides brought an incisive intellect honed by his study of Aristotelian philosophy and the physical sciences. The result was a rationalism unusual in Jewish scholarship and a lucidity of analysis and style admired by Jewish and non-Jewish scholars alike.

After his death, in Egypt, Maimonides's remains were interred in Tiberias, one of four Jewish holy cities (although he never lived here). His whitewashed tomb has become a shrine, dripping with candle wax and tears. Marble plaques on either side of the path approaching the tomb recall the many disciplines in which Maimonides distinguished himself. Less tasteful is the stall at the entrance selling cheap religious trinkets. ⊠ *Ben Zakkai St.* ▨ *Free.* ☉ *Sun.–Thurs. daylight hrs, Fri. and holiday eves until 2* PM.

## Dining and Lodging

Tiberias and the Sea of Galilee are a much livelier proposition than other parts of Lower Galilee. Because most travelers to this region actually stay overnight here, there are a few very good restaurants in Tiberias proper, and a few of the daytime watering holes on the lake stay open into the evening. The local specialty is St. Peter's fish (tilapia), which is native to the Sea of Galilee, but demand far outstrips supply, so the fish most restaurants serve is pond-bred. Meat dishes tend to be more Middle Eastern: shishlik and kebabs accompanied by hummus, pickles, and the ubiquitous french fries. A string of virtually indistinguishable restaurants with this menu lines the promenade.

At a right angle to the promenade is the *midrachov* (pedestrian mall), between the Sheraton Moriah and Caesar hotels, with a wide range of affordable eating options: hamburger joints, pizzerias, ice cream parlors, and restaurants serving light meals. Among the last is a member of the nationwide Kapulsky chain, known for its sinfully rich cakes. Perhaps because of the competition, the "regular" restaurants, with their fish, grills, schnitzel, and *shwarma* (slices of spit-grilled meat served in pita bread with salads and condiments), have kept their prices down; if you're not looking for a gourmet experience, you can eat quite well for $10 or less. Another genre that has gained popularity is the pub, with wood-paneled rooms and smoky atmosphere, and meals to mitigate the effect of the excellent local Goldstar draft. Try Big Ben, on the mall, and Le Pirate Pub, below the Caesar hotel.

If you have a hankering for falafel, that classic Middle Eastern fast food (deep-fried chickpea balls and salad in pita bread), rub shoulders with the locals on Hagalil Street. In fact, if you're into local color, look for the tiny, modest restaurants (where English really *is* a foreign language) on Hagalil Street and in the little streets that connect it to Habanim Street. The menus predictably emphasize fish and Middle Eastern salads and meat dishes. It's possible to strike culinary gold here, often at very reasonable prices. A good bet is the small, pedestrian-only Kishon Street, opposite the Carmel Jordan River Hotel, which houses the well-considered El Gaucho, part of a national chain of Argentinian grill restaurants; the vegetarian A Taste of Life (run by former Americans), with veg-based shwarma and homemade nondairy ice cream; and several fish-and-meat establishments popular with the locals.

At press time, a few Tiberias hotels had closed temporarily. Please call ahead to assure that a hotel is open.

**$$$** ✕ **Decks.** Built right on a pier, Decks is at its best in fine weather. Begin with a (shared) focaccia and the unusual fried onion loaf. The kitchen specializes in good meat—steak, goose liver, or long skewers of veal and vegetables—grilled slowly over hickory wood. Fish and large salads make excellent noncarnivorous alternatives. An apple tartin panbaked at your table is the house dessert. ✉ *Lido complex, Rte. 90, at the exit from Tiberias north,* ☎ *04/672–1538. AE, DC, MC, V. Closed Fri. No lunch Sat.*

**$$–$$$** ✕ **Pagoda and The House.** These Chinese-Thai restaurants (under one ★ management) are part of the Lido Beach complex, which includes other eateries and a small harbor. Pagoda, in a faux Chinese temple with wraparound windows, is spacious, with a generous patio for outdoor dining overlooking the lake. The House, across the road, has a maze of smaller, more intimate rooms entered through a delightful garden. The restaurants have identical menus, with one difference: Pagoda is kosher and is closed on the Sabbath and on Jewish religious holidays. The House is open only when Pagoda is not. Neither serves pork or shrimp. The food is in general exceptionally good. Try the spicy Thai soups (coconut based, or hot-and-sour), the (lamb) spareribs, and strips of beef sautéed in satay (peanut) sauce. ✉ *Gedud Barak St. (Rte. 90),* ☎ *04/672–4488 or 04/679–2564. Reservations essential. AE, DC, MC, V. Pagoda: no lunch Sat., no dinner Fri.; The House: no dinner Sat.–Thurs., no lunch Sun.–Fri.*

**$$$$** 🏨 **Caesar.** Part of a small national chain, the Caesar faces the lake, with views from all rooms. The public areas are all white marble and polished brass; the guest rooms have tasteful, if unexceptional, furnishings. Every suite has a whirlpool bath. There's a large outdoor swimming pool, but the area would have been enhanced by more grass and less concrete. A spa offers a warm indoor pool and treatments. The dining room does a very respectable job. ✉ *The Promenade, Box 275, 14102,* ☎ *04/672–7272,* 🆉 *04/679–1013. 227 rooms. Bar, coffee shop, dining room, 1 indoor and 1 outdoor pool, sauna, spa, exercise room. AE, DC, MC, V.*

$$$$ 🏨 **Gai Beach.** Many regard the Gai Beach as the current leader among
★ Tiberias's upscale hotels. Its rare lakeshore location is a big plus, and,
for some, so is its distance from the noisy downtown promenade. The
marble lobby is large, with comfortable armchairs for a touch of intimacy. Guest rooms are well designed and tastefully furnished, if small-
ish; some face the lake. The hotel owns the adjacent water park, with
its beach, water slides, and wave pool, and all are free to guests. At
press time, a spa was under construction, to include an indoor pool,
sauna, gym, and whirlpool bath. The attractions are undeniable, though
the rates are a bit high for a hotel of this class. ⊠ *Rte. 90, Box 274,
14102,* ☎ *04/670–0700,* ℻ *04/679–2776. 196 rooms, 2 suites. Restaurant, bar, pool. AE, DC, MC, V.*

$$$$ 🏨 **Sheraton Moriah.** The lobby and bar of this modern hotel are bright,
cozy places to relax. Rooms are comfortable but fairly ordinary, with
darkish furnishings that emphasize the relative lack of space. The service is generally professional and accommodating. The hotel overlooks the lake but does not have lake frontage. The Texas restaurant
and bar imports a touch of the American West in both its grill menu
and its decor. ⊠ *Just off Habanim St., 14103,* ☎ *04/679–2233,* ℻ *04/
679–2320. 272 rooms. 3 restaurants, bar, pool, beauty salon, hot tub,
sauna, exercise room. AE, DC, MC, V.*

$$$ 🏨 **Four Points Tiberias.** Lording it high above the city, this Sheraton
★ property compensates for its distance from the town center with a quiet
location and superb lake views from every room. The guest rooms are
fairly spacious, though the bathrooms are small; half the rooms have
balconies. The Lodge Bar, with its wide picture windows, is a cozy evening
hangout despite some bizarre touches of decor. A children's club, with
diversions and scheduled activities, is staffed in summer daily 9 AM–8
PM. ⊠ *18 Hashomer St., 14102,* ☎ *04/679–1484. 218 rooms. 2 restau-
rants, bar, pool, hot tub, 2 saunas, exercise room, children's programs.
AE, DC, MC, V.*

$$$ 🏨 **Ron Beach.** The last hotel in Tiberias on Route 90 north, the fam-
★ ily-run Ron Beach has rare private frontage on the lake. The ameni-
ties—high-quality mattresses, TVs, and hair dryers—are impressive in
this price category (at the low end of the range). In addition to the main
building, two rows of 27 rooms each open onto the lawn and the beach;
those at ground level have their own patio. There are several enormous
family rooms. All in all, it's a great value. ⊠ *Gedud Barak St. (Rte.
90 N), 14101,* ☎ *04/679–1350,* ℻ *04/679–1351. 74 rooms. Restaurant, pool, beach. AE, DC, MC, V.*

$$ 🏨 **Astoria.** One of Tiberias's better moderately priced hotels, the As-
toria is set away from the lake, halfway uptown, with few views from
guest rooms; but what it lacks in aesthetics it makes up for in quality.
It's comfortable, clean, and family-run, with furnishings in attractive
pastels. Large family rooms are available. Prices jump in August and
during the main Jewish holidays. ⊠ *13 Ohel Ya'akov St., 14223,* ☎
*04/672–2351,* ℻ *04/672–5108. 88 rooms. Restaurant, bar, coffee
shop, pool, hot tub, sauna. AE, DC, MC, V.*

$$ 🏨 **Church of Scotland Centre.** Built in 1893 as a hospital of the Free
★ Church of Scotland, this building was ultimately converted into a pil-
grim hospice. Today it welcomes all visitors, professing a commitment
"to build bridges of trust and respect among our neighbors, whoever they
are and wherever they come from." The two-story stone buildings, with
their deep porches and high-ceilinged rooms, are a pleasant change from
the sterility of many modern hotels. The rambling, slightly wild gardens
make a challenging adventureland for kids and a pastoral refuge for their
elders. The outer gate is closed at 7 PM, but your key lets you in at your
convenience, as well as providing access to the private beach across the
road. The location could not be more central. ⊠ *Gedud Barak and*

*Hayarden Sts., Box 104, 14100,* ☎ *04/672–3769 or 04/672–1165,* FAX *04/679–0145. 47 rooms. Beach. AE, DC, MC, V.*

**$$** ✕🍴 **YMCA Peniel-by-Galilee.** One of the area's more unusual hostelries, Peniel-by-Galilee was built as a retreat in the late 1930s by Archibald Harte, founder of the famous Jerusalem YMCA. It occupies a low cliff just north of Tiberias, where you can enjoy unobstructed lake views and a pebbly but clean beach. The common room is lined with 180-year-old Damascene wood and inlaid panels. The guest rooms and family-size apartments are less inspiring, though spacious and comfortable enough; apartments have kitchen facilities. Most units have views of the lake. Dinner is served only when there's group demand (at least eight people; call ahead to verify), and it's worth trying to round up the quota. ⊠ *Off Rte. 90, 3 km (2 mi) north of Tiberias, Box 192, Tiberias 14101,* ☎ *04/672–0685,* FAX *02/623–5192. 12 rooms, 3 apartments. Dining room, beach, playground. V on-site; AE, DC, MC, V when reserved at YMCA Jerusalem.*

**$** 🍴 **Berger Hotel.** Run by the family of that name, this two-wing hotel
★ has spacious, well-furnished rooms, most with a balcony. It's uptown, and more convenient if you have a car, but buses to the downtown area are frequent (except on weekends). Meals are generally not served (unless there's a group in the house), but the supermarket across the road makes it easy to stock your kitchenette. Renovated sections, and frills such as satellite TV, have lifted the hotel's quality above its price category. More than half of the rooms have bathtubs; the rest have showers. The management is quick to upgrade you to a larger room at the same price when rooms are available and offers a further discount if you produce your Fodor's guide. ⊠ *27 Neiberg St., Box 535, 14105,* ☎ *04/671–5151,* FAX *04/679–1514. 45 rooms, 2 apartments. Kitchenettes. AE, DC, MC, V.*

**$** 🍴 **Meyouhas Youth Hostel.** This large basalt building fronted by a lawn and trees is in the heart of downtown Tiberias, a minute's walk from the lake, the promenade, and the mall. The term "youth" is inaccurate, and so is the term "hostel": the place is open to all and is more like a guest house, with new pine furniture and en-suite facilities for half the rooms. Meals are cheap and frills are few, but it's an excellent value for the budget conscious. ⊠ *Corner of Gedud Barak and Hayarden Sts., Box 81, 14100,* ☎ *04/672–1775 or 04/679–0350,* FAX *04/ 672–0372. 56 rooms, 24 with bath. Restaurant. AE, DC, MC, V.*

## Nightlife and the Arts

As you might expect in a resort area, entertainment is more plentiful than culture. Much of it, especially in the larger hotels in Tiberias, is of the live-lounge-music variety: piano bars, dance bands, and crooners. Thursday and Friday are "nightclub" nights at some hotels, with dance music for the weekend crowds. The clientele tends to be a bit older. Generally speaking, the younger set wouldn't be caught dead here, preferring to hang out at the pubs along the midrachov and the promenade, where the recorded rock music is good and loud and the beer is on tap.

Some boat operators use their larger boats as floating dance clubs in the summer, usually departing from the piers at the promenade for 30- to 45-minute cruises. The cost is about NIS 20 ($5). **Lido** also occasionally offers a two-hour dinner-and-disco cruise for $40 to $50; for details call **Lido Kinneret** (☎ 04/672–1538 or 04/679–2564) or **Kinneret Sailing** (mid-July and Aug. only, disco only: ☎ 04/655–8008 or 04/655–8009).

The Ministry of Tourism sometimes sponsors a free **Israeli folklore evening** at one of the major hotels; call the tourist-information number (☎ 04/672–5666) for schedules. Sometimes a classier act comes through, often performing on one of the local kibbutzim, and if it's not too language-specific (a Hebrew comedian, for example), the performance can be a tasty slice of Israeli culture.

## Outdoor Activities and Sports

### SWIMMING

There's good swimming at a number of beaches near Tiberias.

**Blue Beach** (⊠ Rte. 90 at northern exit from Tiberias), **Sironit** (⊠ Rte. 90 at southern exit from Tiberias), and **Gai Beach** (⊠ next to Sironit) are all options.

### WALKING AND JOGGING

A promenade follows the lakeshore for about 5 km (3 mi) to the south of Tiberias.

### WATER SPORTS

For waterskiing, inquire at the **Tourist Information Office** (☎ 04/672–5666).

Water slides are available at the **Sironit and Gai beaches,** south of Tiberias.

## Shopping

Tiberias relies heavily on tourism, but despite its developing infrastructure, it has little in the way of shopping. The exceptions are jewelry and, of course, souvenirs.

A large, established diamond factory, **Caprice/NDC,** has two outlets here, showing a video about the industry before releasing you into its showrooms (⊠ Rte. 90, just south of Tiberias, opposite Tiberias Hot Springs, ☎ 04/672–6930 or 04/671–6262; ⊠ Tabor St., ☎ 04/679–2616), which also gives a tour of its workshops and small museum. There are a few smaller **jewelry stores** near the intersection of Habanim and Yarden streets and in some of the better hotels.

# Ginosar

 *10 km (6 mi) north of Tiberias.*

Perhaps the site of the New Testament's Gennesaret, Ginosar is now a veteran kibbutz in a glorious lakeside location. Many Israelis know it as the home of the late Yigal Allon (1918–80), commander of the crack Palmach battalions in the War of Independence and deputy prime minister in the 1970s under Golda Meir and Yitzhak Rabin. The settlement's favorite son is immortalized in **Bet Allon** (Allon House), a basalt-and-concrete eyesore of a building that houses a museum of the region's natural and human history. It's a good rainy-day option.

For the traveler, however, the site is intriguing for the brilliant archaeological find made on its shore: a 2,000-year-old wooden boat, the most complete boat of this age ever found in an inland lake. In January 1986, after three years of poor rainfall had lowered the level of the lake, fishermen from the adjacent kibbutz spotted the boat's prow in the mud. Excavated in a frenetic 11 days, the 28-ft-long boat became an instant media sensation. Considering its age and the frequency of nautical references in the New Testament stories that took place around here, the popular press immediately dubbed it "the Jesus Boat." For a reader of the Gospels, it's a startlingly vivid relic.

The ancient boat was amazingly intact but extremely fragile, its timbers sodden like wet cardboard. To move it, experts sprayed the vessel inside and out with a polyurethane mixture, giving it a buoyant "straitjacket." It was then towed a few hundred yards by rowboat and lifted by crane to a small building between the lake and the museum. The plastic was removed, and for almost a decade, the boat lay in a specially constructed bath filled with a wax-based preservative solution, to displace the water molecules in the wood. Today the boat is dry and can be seen in all of its modest but remarkably evocative glory in a specially built pavilion. Bet Allon screens an excellent video, filmed during the excavation, that explains the boat's unique features. ⊠ *Rte. 90,* ☎ *04/672–2905.* 🎫 *Museum and boat NIS 15 ($3.75); boat only (including video) NIS 9 ($2.25).* ⊙ *Sat.–Thurs. 8:30–5, Fri. and holiday eves 8:30–1 (boat only, 8:30–4). Last entry to museum 1 hr before closing; last entry to boat 30 mins before closing.*

### Lodging

**$$$** 🏨 **Nof Ginosar Guest House.** This is one of the largest and best established of the Galilee's kibbutz guest houses. Its location—right on the Sea of Galilee, with a private beach—makes Nof Ginosar especially popular. There are evening lectures on kibbutz life and a morning tour. Also on the grounds are a spectacular, 2,000-year-old fishing boat; the small natural-history and anthropological museum at Bet Allon; and kayak, pedal-boat, and rowboat rentals. The decor is rustic-resort, with good motellike accommodations. Rooms are comfortable and airy, if not overly spacious. The large dining-room buffet alternates between decent meat-based meals and meatless offerings, which include tasty salads, hot fish, and outstanding blintzes with sweetened cheese. ⊠ *Rte. 90, M. P. Jordan Valley 14980,* ☎ *04/670–0300,* 📠 *04/679–2170. 170 rooms. Restaurant, bar, coffee shop, pool, beach. AE, DC, MC, V.*

*En Route* Just north of Ginosar, on Route 90 on your right, is an electric substation that powers huge water pumps buried in the hill behind it. The Sea of Galilee is Israel's primary freshwater reservoir and the beginning of the National Water Carrier, a network of canals and pipelines that integrates the country's water sources and distribution lines. On the hill above this is the small tel of the Old Testament city of **Kinneret,** which dominated the main highway of the ancient Near East, the so-called Via Maris (Way of the Sea). Scholars assume that the Hebrew name for the lake—Kinneret—comes from that of the most important city on its shores in antiquity. Romantics contend that the name derives from the lake's shape, which resembles the biblical *kinnor,* or lyre.

## Mount of Beatitudes

★ ⑮ *8 km (5 mi) north of Ginosar; 3 km (2 mi) north of Capernaum Junction, where Rtes. 90 and 87 meet.*

Well-tended gardens and spreading ficus trees make a tranquil setting for contemplating the New Testament "Sermon on the Mount," with which this hill is identified. "And seeing the multitudes, he went up into a mountain; and when he was set, his disciples came unto him. And he opened his mouth, and taught them, saying: 'Blessed are the poor in spirit, for theirs is the kingdom of Heaven . . .'" Thus the Gospel of Matthew (5:1–7:29) begins the record of Jesus's most extensive teaching. It was higher up this same hill that Pope John Paul II celebrated mass with some 100,000 faithful in April 2000.

The domed **Roman Catholic church** (of the Italian Franciscan Sisters), built by the famous architect Barluzzi, was completed in 1937. The marble walls carry quotations from the Beatitudes, the initial "Blessed are they . . ." verses from the Sermon on the Mount. The terrace surrounding the church offers a superb view of the Sea of Galilee (best in the afternoon, when the diffused western sun softens the light and height-

# KIBBUTZ LIFE

**T**HE FOUNDING FATHERS and mothers of yore would probably look on in bewilderment at life on the 21st-century kibbutz. But as any "kibbutznik" will tell you—times change!

From a deeply ideological beginning, inspired by Zionist and socialist ideals, the kibbutz has undergone a metamorphosis in the last decade, paralleling the changes experienced by the rest of Israel, right down to privatization and the widespread use of personal credit cards, even to pay for meals in the communal dining room.

The original kibbutznik was a member of an egalitarian community, sharing ownership of the means of production, the chores, and the overall responsibility. So successful was the concept that the kibbutz movement grew to become the largest communitarian movement in the world. It peaked in 1990, when the number of kibbutzniks living on the 270 kibbutzim (plural for "kibbutz") around Israel exceeded 125,000 (the number of members can range from less than 100 to more than 1,000). Those figures have since been on the wane. Despite the changes, however, city folk, volunteers, and tourists are still drawn to this unique rural-like environment—often not far from bustling centers—which still offers a slower pace, the experience of a communal meal, and an ambience of serenity.

The kibbutz had its beginnings in 1909, on the shores of the Sea of Galilee, where a handful of spirited pioneers toiled the land. They were motivated by their idealism and a political goal of establishing Jewish settlements in Palestine. Many of the original kibbutzniks were immigrants from Russia who came imbued with the spirit of the time in that country, the same spirit that led to the Russian Revolution. Life was tough—the work was arduous and malaria was rampant—but they endured and their numbers grew. By 1950, two years after Israel gained independence, there were more than 200 kibbutzim dotted around the land.

The kibbutzim played a considerable role in the molding of the fledgling state (and prior to that), absorbing immigrants, developing agriculture, and sometimes serving as border demarcations. In addition to agriculture, many introduced light industry, and some became highly successful businesses. (The Kibbutz Contemporary Dance Company and the Kibbutz Orchestra were two cultural offshoots of the movement.) The standard of living improved phenomenally, and kibbutzim borrowed funds to increase their development. Then came the financial crisis of the 1980s, which brought many of these communities to the brink of economic ruin. New ideas had to be sought, and quickly, to keep from going under.

Most kibbutzim have survived these pressures and others brought on, for example, by the emergence of the global economy, which has had a direct impact on these once self-contained communities. Though some 15% of members still work in agriculture, accounting for a significant proportion of the national agriculture activity, industry, services, and tourism now command the greater chunk of income. Wage systems have been introduced by most kibbutzim and unemployment is growing. Foreign laborers are often found in the many areas of menial labor, in fields and factories.

Interestingly, however, in 1997 the United Kibbutz Movement established a new kibbutz, the first in a decade. Kibbutz Eshbal, in the Western Galilee, with 50 young and enthusiastic—indeed, pioneering—members, is Israel's first kibbutz ever to start off without means of production other than the skills of its members. Its economy is based almost solely on teaching and educational counseling.

Thus, Israel's kibbutzim are—individually and collectively—experiencing a wave of soul searching as they reexamine basic principles and values with the aim of finding an identity that suits their unique lifestyle and meets the challenges of a new era.

ens colors). In keeping with the spirit of the place, this is one of the few Christian holy sites in the country where Catholics and Protestants seem to feel equally at ease.

The sisters run a newly renovated pilgrim hospice (hostelry) on the site. ⊠ *Rte. 8177 off Rte. 90,* ☎ *04/679–0978.* ⊘ *Apr.–Sept., daily 8–noon and 2:30–5; Oct.–Mar., daily 8–noon and 2:30–4.*

## Tabgha

⓰  *14 km (8 mi) north of Tiberias, at Capernaum Junction (Rtes. 90 and 87).*

The German Benedictine **Church of the Multiplication,** a large building on the west side of Tabgha, marks the place identified by tradition as the "deserted place" of Matthew 14. Here, toward evening, the gospel relates, Jesus miraculously multiplied two fish and five loaves of bread to feed the crowds that followed him. "And they did all eat, and were filled . . . And they that had eaten were about 5,000 men, beside women and children." This event is known as the miracle of the Multiplication of the Loaves and Fishes.

The church, dedicated in 1981, is built in the Byzantine-basilica style—it's an airy limestone building with a wooden truss ceiling—and incorporates some remains of its 5th-century predecessor. Most impressive is the beautifully wrought Byzantine mosaic floor depicting flora and birds, and curiously including Egyptian motifs such as the Nilometer, a graded column once used to measure the water level of the Nile. In front of the altar is the small and simple mosaic of the Loaves and Fishes, perhaps the most famous mosaic in Israel. ⊠ *Rte. 87.* ⊘ *Mon.–Sat. 8:30–5, Sun. 10–5.*

The austere, black basalt **Church of the Primacy of St. Peter,** 200 yards east of the Church of the Multiplication, is built on the water's edge, over a flat rock known as Mensa Christi (the Table of Christ). After his resurrection, says the New Testament (John 21), Jesus appeared to his disciples by the Sea of Galilee and breakfasted with them on a miraculous catch of fish. Three times Jesus asked the disciple Peter if he loved him, and after Peter's reply of "You know that I love you," Jesus commanded him to "Feed my sheep." Some scholars see this affirmation as Peter's atonement for having thrice denied Jesus in Jerusalem after Jesus's arrest. The episode is seen as establishing Peter's "primacy" and, in the Roman Catholic tradition, that of his spiritual descendents, the bishops of Rome. Part of the Franciscan "Custody of the Holy Land," the site was included in the itineraries of both Pope Paul VI in 1964 and Pope John Paul II in 2000. ⊠ *Rte. 87.* ⊘ *At press time: Apr.–Sept., daily 8–6; Oct.–Mar., daily 8–5. Site may return to closing noon–2.*

## Capernaum

⓱  *3 km (2 mi) east of Tabgha and the Capernaum Junction, 17 km (10½ mi) northeast of Tiberias.*

Capernaum (Kfar Nahum in Hebrew) was once a thriving town of merchants, farmers, and fishermen; today it contains an archaeological site and two monasteries. The easterly one, distinguished by its red-dome, whitewashed church, is Greek Orthodox and is seldom visited, since its own antiquities have not been developed for tourists. The westerly, Franciscan (Roman Catholic) one, at the first turnoff after Tabgha, is what you come to see, along with the nearby excavations.

The prosperity of this ancient Jewish community is immediately apparent from the remains of its synagogue. Excavations by the Franciscan friars in the early 20th century exposed a large lakeside town that had thrived from the Second Temple–Early Roman period (about the 1st century BC) to the Byzantine period (5th–6th centuries AD). It was here that Jesus established his base for the three years of his ministry in the Galilee. Here, the New Testament relates, he called many of his disciples ("Follow me, and I will make you fishers of men"), healed the afflicted, taught in the synagogue . . . and ultimately cursed the city for not heeding his message.

To the right of the cashier as you enter the site is a display of finely carved stones showing the typical range of Jewish artistic motifs of the time, including the native fruits of the land: grapes, pomegranates, figs, dates, and olives. A dedication to a donor of the synagogue's building fund, one "Alpheus the son of Zebedah the son of John," is in Aramaic, the language spoken by Jews in the region at the time (compare the Gospel of Mark 15:34) and strong proof that this was a Jewish community. A horizontal stone—a lintel—shows an artist's depiction of the biblical Ark of the Covenant, typically carried on shoulders in Old Testament times but here shown on wheels, perhaps a reference to the two such instances recorded (I Samuel 6 and II Samuel 6).

Immediately before you is a modern church, suspended from its outer support pillars over the scanty remains of Capernaum's central Christian shrine, the **House of St. Peter.** The church follows the octagonal outline of the Byzantine basilica that once encompassed the house Jesus is supposed to have visited.

The partly restored **synagogue** dominates the complex. The ancient Jewish community went to the expense of transporting white limestone blocks from afar to set the synagogue off from the town's crudely built black-basalt houses. Stone benches line the inside walls, recalling the building's original, primary function as a place of assembly where the Torah was read and explained on Sabbaths and holidays. (The fixed synagogue liturgy used today was a later development.)

The age of the Capernaum synagogue is still contested—it's thought to date from sometime between the 2nd and 5th centuries AD—but one thing is certain: this is not the actual synagogue of Mark 1 where Jesus taught. Nevertheless, consecrated ground was often reused, so the small structure in the excavation pit in the present building's southeastern corner may be the remains of that 1st-century synagogue.

Near the deep shade of the ficus trees, look for the remains of a fine olive-oil press and some small hand mills made from hard and durable volcanic basalt. Basalt's advantages over the limestone found in the rest of Israel gave the Sea of Galilee region the raw material for an important export commodity in ancient times: agricultural equipment. Such mills have been found as far afield as Masada, Jerusalem, and the Mediterranean coast. To the right of the olive-oil press is the capital of a column with Jewish symbols in relief—a seven-branched menorah, a *shofar* (ram's horn), and an incense shovel—to preserve the memory of the Temple, with which they were associated. A small 1st-century mosaic from Magdala shows a contemporary boat, complete with oars and sails—a dramatic illustration of the many New Testament and Jewish references to traffic and fishing on the lake. ✉ *Rte. 87,* ☎ *04/ 672–1059.* ✆ *NIS 3 (75¢).* ☉ *Daily 8:30–4.*

*En Route*  Route 87 continues east past Capernaum and crosses the **Jordan River**—somewhat muddy at this point—at the Arik Bridge. Those raised on spirituals extolling the Jordan's width and depth are often surprised to find how small a stream it really is. Seldom more than 30 ft wide, it's often shallow enough to wade in. (Record-breaking rains in the winter of 1991–92 did swell the river, flooding fields and threatening homes farther south.) The Jordan enters the Sea of Galilee just a few hundred yards to your right. In this wetland part of the Jordan Delta, archaeologists have finally identified, excavated, and opened for tourism the elusive site of the ancient Jewish town of Bethsaida, Peter's birthplace, according to the New Testament.

## Kursi and the Eastern Shore

⓲ *Kursi is 17 km (10½ mi) from Capernaum and 5 km (3 mi) north of Ein Gev.*

Route 92 skirts the lake's eastern edge under the imposing cliffs of the southern Golan Heights. Kursi, at the foot of the steep Golan Heights, where Route 789 breaks east from 92, is linked with the New Testament, which tells the story of a man from Gadara who was possessed by demons (Matthew 8, Mark 5, and Luke 8 have him from Gerasa). Jesus miraculously exorcised the evil spirits, causing them to enter a herd of swine grazing nearby, which then "ran violently down a steep place into the lake, and were choked." Fifth-century Byzantine Christians identified the event with this spot, at the foot of the steep Golan Heights, and built a monastery here. Those were days of frequent pilgrimage to holy places, and the monastery prospered from the gifts of the devout. The partly restored ruins of a fine Byzantine church are a classic example of the basilica style common at the time; the remains of the monastery are perched higher up the hillside behind it. ⊠ *Rte. 92,* ☎ *04/673–1983.* ☜ *NIS 9 ($2.25).* ☉ *Summer (daylight saving time), Sat.–Thurs. 8–5, Fri. and holiday eves 8–4; winter, Sat.–Thurs. 8–4, Fri. and holiday eves 8–3.*

### Dining and Lodging

If you're interested in **camping,** this area has two campgrounds with full cooking and washing facilities, beach access, and stores: **Ein Gev** (⊠ Ein Gev 14940, ☎ 04/665–8199) and **Ha'on** (⊠ M. P. Jordan Valley 15170, ☎ 04/665–6555).

$$　✕ **Ein Gev Fish Restaurant.** This lunch institution on the eastern shore serves dinner year-round. Known for its St. Peter's fish (pay the higher price for a large fish to ensure moist meatiness), it also serves alternative, light entrées such as pizza, pasta, salads, and omelets. The outdoor patio has a view of Tiberias, whose lights twinkle across the lake. ⊠ *Kibbutz Ein Gev,* ☎ *04/665–8036. AE, DC, MC, V.*

$$$　⌂ **Ramot Resort Hotel.** High up in the foothills of the Golan Heights, this hotel affords fabulous views of the Sea of Galilee and is only a few minutes' drive from its good beaches (free entrance to Dugit Beach) and water parks (discount to Lunagal). Its main building has comfortable, air-conditioned guest rooms, each with a very private balcony and a lake view. The cottages, which are less expensive but older, are not as well endowed, but their wooden paneling and shutters and green surroundings give them some charm. Free guided tours of the area are available in summer. ⊠ *East of Rte. 92, 12490,* ☎ *04/673–2636,* 🖷 *04/679–3590. 80 rooms, 40 cottages. Bar, coffee shop, pool. AE, DC, MC, V.*

$$　⌂ **Ein Gev Holiday Village.** The kibbutz at Ein Gev has been in the tourism business for many years and is best known for its fish restaurant (☞ *above*), cruise boats, campground, and air-conditioned caravans. Better-class guest rooms with patios have been added to the motel-style building, all on a palm-shaded lakeside stretch with lawns and beach. Rates go up 25% on weekends and Jewish holidays. ⊠ *Rte. 92, 12 km (7½ mi) from Tzemach Junction, Post Office Ein Gev, 14940,* ☎ *04/665–9800,* 🖷 *04/665–9818. 184 rooms. Restaurant, miniature golf, boating. AE, DC, MC, V.*

**$$**  ▣ **Ma'agan.** This kibbutz on the southern tip of the Sea of Galilee, 12
**★** km (7½ mi) from Tiberias, has gone somewhat upmarket. Choose be-
tween a regular guest room and a spacious suite that includes a living
room (with a lake-view picture window and sofas that become beds),
a small bedroom, bathroom, a kitchenette, a patio, and barbecue fa-
cilities. The kibbutz's sandy beach, swimming pool, and extensive
lawns among the palms and eucalypti make it the best deal in the area.
Kids have a smaller pool and a play area. ⊠ *Rte. 92, 1 km (½ mi) east
of Tzemach Junction, M. P. Jordan Valley 15160,* ☎ *04/665–4411,* FAX
*04/665–4455. 36 rooms, 112 suites. Restaurant, coffee shop, kitch-
enettes (some), pool, windsurfing, boating. AE, DC, MC, V.*

## Nightlife and the Arts

The **Ein Gev Spring Festival** (☎ 04/665–8030 or 04/675–7625, FAX 04/
665–9800), a music festival held within Kibbutz Ein Gev during
Passover, has been going since the 1940s. The festival once hosted the
likes of Bernstein and Rampal, Dietrich and Sinatra, but its direction
today is Israeli music, from traditional to contemporary. Call ahead
for dates.

## Outdoor Activities and Sports

### SWIMMING

**Ma'agan** (☞ Dining and Lodging, *above*) has a shaded lawn and pic-
nic facilities as well as a beach. **Ein Gev, Golan Beach** (parking fee), and
**Lunagal** (parking fee) are good swimming spots on the eastern shore;
all are along Route 92.

### WATER SPORTS

**Golan Beach** (☎ 04/673–1750) has a wide range of attractions, including
powerboat, rowboat, kayak, and pedal-boat rentals; waterskiing; and
the inflatable, power-towed "banana." The on-shore **Lunagal** has
pools, water slides, and other diversions for kids. Open April through
mid-October, the water park has late-evening hours Monday and
Thursday in July and August. Admission to the waterpark is NIS 60
($15) during the months of April, May, June, September, and Octo-
ber. In July and August admission is NIS 65 ($16.25).

# Hammat Gader

**⑲** *10 km (6 mi) east of Zemach Junction, 22 km (14 mi) southeast of
Tiberias, 36 km (22½ mi) northeast of Bet She'an.*

Named for its patron city, Gadara, high up the southern bank of the
Yarmuk, Hammat Gader was in its heyday the second-largest spa in
the Roman Empire (after Baiae, near Naples). The drive to the site is
an absorbing experience in itself. The road clings to the gorge of the
Yarmuk River, crossed by defunct railway bridges that once carried the
narrow-gauge Valley Railroad trains from Haifa via Bet She'an to
Damascus. On the opposite bank is biblical Gilead, now part of Jor-
dan. Just before the descent to Hammat Gader, Route 98 climbs to the
southern Golan Heights in a series of heart-stopping switchbacks.

Built around three hot springs, Hammat Gader's impressive complex
of baths and pools attests to the opulence that once attracted volup-
tuaries and invalids alike. In its time, the entrance corridor was kept
dimly lighted to dramatize the effect of the fine ornamental pool be-
yond—well lighted, in contrast, by high, glass-paned windows. Niches
overlooking the pool are believed to have contained statues of Ascle-
pius, the god of healing, and of Eros, the god of love, representing the
site's two distinct attractions.

The large number of ancient clay oil lamps found in one small pool is proof of nighttime bathing and a hint that this area might have been set aside for lepers, to keep them out of sight. The original "hot tub"—test the water!—is fed by a spring at a temperature of 54°C (129°F). A large, cool pool, once adorned with water-spouting gargoyles, has been partly restored.

Hammat Gader is immensely popular among the locals, who tend to make a day of it, picnicking amid the lawns and large trees near the outdoor warm pool. A spa facility offers treatments (additional fee). Also on hand are a freshwater pool, changing facilities, trampolines and other kids' attractions, an alligator farm, a cafeteria, and Siam, an excellent Thai restaurant. It's delightful as a leisurely visit but pricey if seeing the antiquities is your only purpose. ⊠ *Rte. 98,* ☎ *04/665–9999.* 🎫 *Sun. NIS 45 ($11.25); Mon.–Thurs. NIS 50 ($12.50); Fri., Sat., Jewish holiday eves and holidays NIS 55 ($13.75); after 5 PM (except Fri. and Sun.) NIS 45 ($11.25) (diners at Siam need not buy admission to the whole park).* ⊗ *Sun. 7–4, Mon.–Sat. 7 AM–11 PM. Children's attractions close at 5 PM, alligator farm and antiquities at dusk. Entrance up to 1 hr before closing.*

# Degania Alef

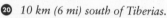 **⑳** *10 km (6 mi) south of Tiberias.*

The collective village of Degania Alef (alef is the *a* of the Hebrew alphabet)—not to be confused with its younger neighbor Degania Bet (for the Hebrew letter *b*)—on the banks of the Jordan River, is distinguished as the world's first kibbutz, founded in 1909 by Jewish pioneers from Eastern Europe and established here on its permanent site the following year. The kibbutz idea—there are now some 280 kibbutzim in Israel—is based on the principle of "from each according to his ability, to each according to his need." Israel's early pioneers needed a unified communal structure to cope with the forbidding terrain and a hostile neighborhood; but more than that, they were seeking the perfect society, based on absolute equality and the subordination of individual desires to the needs of the community.

The principles of the founders remained remarkably resilient for years, but the dream has begun to fade a bit; commitment to the old ideals has become more tenuous and less relevant for a new, more materialistic generation. Still, about 2% of the general population live on kibbutzim; swampland and rocky soil have become fields and plantations, and light industry and tourism are significant additions to the economic profiles of these communities.

Near the entrance to Degania Alef is a small Syrian tank of World War II vintage. On May 15, 1948, the day after Israel declared its independence, the fledgling state was invaded from all sides by Arab armies. Syrian forces came down the Yarmuk Valley from the east, overran two other kibbutzim en route, and were only stopped here, at the gates of Degania, by a teenager with a Molotov cocktail.

Within restored stone buildings of the early kibbutz is the museum of **Bet Gordon** (A. D. Gordon House), named for the white-bearded spiritual mentor of the early pioneers. It houses two fascinating collections: one devoted to the region's natural history, with a renowned collection of stuffed birds, the other examining the history and archaeology of human settlement in the surrounding valleys. Among the prehistoric sites represented is Ubeidiya, just south of the kibbutz and Israel's oldest human settlement, now dated by scholars to 1¼ million years ago. Another **museum** (☎ 04/660–8111), also on Degania Alef, tells the story of the kibbutz; admission is free. There are no English labels here, but the bilingual curator is usually on hand to explain, and the traveler with a taste for modern history and a desire to get off the tourist trail might pass a pleasurable hour here. ⊠ *Near Rte. 90,* ☎ *04/675–0040.* 🖃 *Bet Gordon NIS 8 ($2).* ☉ *Sun.–Thurs. 9–3, Fri. and holiday eves 9–noon.*

### Nightlife and the Arts

**Bet Gabriel** cultural center (☎ 04/675–1175) is located on the southern shores of the Sea of Galilee, near Ma'agan, but only a 10-minute drive from Tiberias. Its fine architecture, beautiful garden setting, and concert facilities have established its popularity in the area.

Tiberias's **Tourist Information Office** (☎ 04/672–5666) and all major hotels carry information on that month's performances and art exhibits.

## Kinneret

*2 km (1 mi) from Degania Alef, 10 km (6 mi) south of Tiberias.*

Kinneret, a kibbutz just across the Jordan to the north of Degania, was founded in 1911 and named for the Hebrew name of nearby Sea of Galilee. Two places in the immediate vicinity are of interest to travelers. On a picturesque stretch of the Jordan, where huge eucalyptus trees droop into the quiet water, is **Yardenit,** developed in recent years as a baptism site for Christian pilgrims. Although the baptism of Jesus by John the Baptist (Matthew 3) is traditionally identified with the southern reaches of the Jordan River, near Jericho, that area was controlled by Jordan from 1949 to 1967 and then became a hostile frontier between Israel and Jordan following the Six-Day War. Pilgrims began to seek out accessible spots near the Sea of Galilee. Here at Yardenit, groups of white-robed pilgrims are often immersed in the Jordan, accompanied by prayers, hymns, and expressions of joy. There are showers and changing facilities, towels and robes for rent in the souvenir shop, and a fairly good cafeteria. ⊠ *Off Rte. 90,* ☎ *04/675–9141.* ☉ *Mar.–Nov., Sat.–Thurs. 8–6, Fri. and holiday eves 8–5; Dec.–Feb., Sat.–Thurs. 8–5, Fri. and holiday eves 8–4:30.*

The serene and somewhat enchanted **cemetery of Kibbutz Kinneret,** at a bend in Route 90 barely 1 km (½ mi) north of the Jordan River bridge, holds the grave of Rachel *Hameshoreret* (Rachel the Poetess), which has become a virtual shrine for many Israelis. An opening in the low stone wall on the right leads by shaded paths to the shore of the Sea of Galilee, with a superb view of the Golan Heights and, rarely, of majestic Mt. Hermon, to the north. Among the other distinguished denizens of this ground are some early philosophers and pioneer leaders of the Zionist movement—Borochov, Hess, Syrkin, Katznelson—better known to most Israelis as street names in almost every city. A few steps down from the clearing to the next path brings you to Rachel's grave, identified (inscriptions are in Hebrew) by the low stone seat attached to it.

The large number of pebbles left on her grave by visitors (a token of respect in the Jewish tradition) is a tribute to Rachel's renown and to the romantic hold she has on the national imagination. Born in Russia, Rachel immigrated to Eretz Yisrael (the Land of Israel) in 1909 at the age of 19, lived in Degania and Kinneret, and was in France studying agriculture when World War I broke out. Unable to get back into Ottoman Turkish Palestine because of her Russian citizenship, she spent the war years working with refugee children in Russia, where she contracted the tuberculosis that eventually took her life. She returned to her beloved lake, but she never regained her health and died in 1931.

Rachel became a poet of national stature in Hebrew, her third language. The modern flavor and immediacy of her poems made them natural lyrics for a whole genre of modern Israeli folk songs. Rachel wrote with great sensitivity of the beauty of this region, and with passion—knowing that her end was near—of her frustrated dream of raising a family. Her tombstone is eloquently devoid of biographical information; it carries the only name by which she is known, Rachel, and four lines from one of her poems: "Spread out your hands, look yonder:/nothing comes./Each man has his Nebo/in the great expanse." (It was from Mt. Nebo that Moses looked into the promised land that he knew he would never enter.) In a recess in the stone seat by the grave site is a weatherproof canister containing a complete volume (in Hebrew) of Rachel's poems, just a few steps from the spot where many were written. ⊠ *Off Rte. 90, 600 yards south of junction with Rte. 767.*

## Hammat Tiberias

★ ㉓ *7 km (4 mi) north of Kinneret, 2 km (1 mi) south of Tiberias.*

Here you'll find Israel's hottest spring, gushing out of the earth at 60°C (140°F). The healing properties of its mineral-rich waters were already recognized in antiquity, as evidenced by the ruins of ancient towns—including an exquisite 4th-century AD mosaic floor of a synagogue. Legend says that Solomon, the great king of Israel, wanted a hot bath and used his awesome authority to force some young devils below ground to heat the water. The fame of the salubrious springs spread far and wide, bringing the afflicted to seek relief. Seeing such gladness among his subjects, Solomon worried about what would happen when he died and the devils stopped their labors. In a flash of the wisdom for which he was renowned, Solomon made the hapless devils deaf. To this day, they have not heard of the king's demise and so continue to heat the water for fear of his wrath.

The scientific explanation is almost tame by comparison. This and other hot mineral springs in Israel (Hammat Gader, Ein Gedi) were created by massive upheavals along the Great Syrian-African Rift, the world's longest fault line. Cracks in the earth's crust allow mineral-rich water to boil to the surface.

By the end of the Second Temple period (the 1st century AD), when settlement in the Sea of Galilee region was at its height, a Jewish town called Hammat (Hot Springs) stood here. With time, Hammat was overshadowed by its newer neighbor Tiberias and became known as Hammat Teverya (Tiberias Hot Springs). The benefits of the mineral hot springs were already legendary: a coin minted in Tiberias during the rule of Emperor Trajan, around AD 100, shows Hygeia, the goddess of health, sitting on a rock with a spring gushing out beneath it.

Parts of ancient Hammat have been uncovered by archaeologists on the mountain side of the road, bringing to light a number of ruined synagogues built one upon the other. The most dramatic dates from the 4th century AD, with an elaborate mosaic floor that uses motifs almost identical to those at Bet Alfa: classical Jewish symbols, human figures representing the four seasons and the signs of the zodiac, and the Greek god Helios at the center (☞ Bet Alfa *in* Jezreel and Jordan Valleys, *above*). The childlike art of Bet Alfa has its charm, to be sure, but the mosaics of Hammat Tiberias are among the finest ever found in Israel. Later cultures exploited the hot springs, too, as the small adjacent Turkish bath attests. Behind Hammat Tiberias, a turquoise dome marks the **tomb of Rabbi Meir Ba'al Ha-Ness,** the "Miracle Worker," a legendary personality who supposedly took a vow that he would not lie down until the Messiah came—and was therefore buried in an upright position. His name has become a sort of emblem for charitable organizations, and many a miracle has been attributed to the power of prayer at his tomb. ⊠ *Rte. 90,* ☎ *04/672–5287.* 🎟 *NIS 9 ($2.25).* ⊘ *Apr.–Sept., Sat.–Thurs. 8–5, Fri. and holiday eves 8–4; Oct.–Mar., Sat.–Thurs. 8–4, Fri. and holiday eves 8–3.*

| NEED A BREAK? | **Tiberias Hot Springs,** on the lake side of the road, is one of the two modern spa facilities fed by the mineral spring (the other, on the mountain side of the road, is exclusively for medical use). In addition to sophisticated therapeutic services and facilities, it has a large, warm indoor mineral pool (35°C or 95°F) and a small outdoor one right near the lake's edge. The restaurant serves lunch. ⊠ *Rte. 90,* ☎ *04/672–8500.* 🎟 *Pools NIS 53 ($13.25); extra for massages and therapies; NIS 35 ($8.75) for weekday entry after 4 PM. Lockers NIS 7 ($1.75). Robe rental NIS 20 ($5) plus deposit of NIS 100 ($25).* ⊘ *Sun., Mon., Wed., and Sat. 8–7:30; Tues. and Thurs. 8 AM–10:30 PM; Fri. 8–4 (inquire about later summer hrs).* |
|---|---|

# LOWER GALILEE A TO Z

## Arriving and Departing

### By Bus

The **Egged** (☎ 03/694–8888) bus cooperative provides frequent service from Jerusalem, Tel Aviv, and Haifa to Bet She'an, Afula, Nazareth, and Tiberias. There is no direct service from Ben-Gurion International Airport; change in Tel Aviv. From Tel Aviv, Buses 824 and 823 run to Afula and Nazareth several times a day; the ride takes 1½ hours to Afula, another 20 minutes to Nazareth. Bus 830 runs from Tel Aviv to Tiberias about every hour; the ride takes 2½ hours. To get from Haifa to Tiberias, take Bus 430, which leaves hourly; the ride is about one hour. From Haifa, take Bus 301 or 302 to Afula (about every 30 minutes); change in Afula for Nazareth or Bet She'an. Buses from Jerusalem to Bet She'an and Tiberias (Buses 961 and 963) depart roughly hourly; change in Bet She'an for Afula, where you change again for Nazareth. The ride to Bet She'an is about two hours, to Tiberias another 25 minutes. Buses 355, 823, and 824 make the 20-minute run between Afula and Nazareth. In any case, call to verify times.

### By Car

From Tel Aviv, the Lower Galilee can be reached by taking Route 2 north (the Tel Aviv–Haifa Highway) and then heading northeast along one of two regional roads: Route 65 (near Caesarea), emerging into the Jezreel Valley at Megiddo (80 km/50 mi; a 1¼-hour drive); or Route 70 (near Zichron Ya'akov), emerging at Yokne'am (90 km/57 mi; a 1½-hour drive). Avoid driving north out of Tel Aviv midday Friday and returning south to Tel Aviv Saturday afternoon and early evening. Access from Haifa is on Route 75 east to Bet She'arim and Nazareth (35 km/22 mi; a 45-minute drive to Nazareth); or from Route 75 onto Routes 70 and 66 south to Megiddo (34 km/22 mi; a 40-minute drive). The best route from Jerusalem is Route 1 east, then Route 90 north to Bet She'an (124 km/78 mi; a 2-hour drive).

## Getting Around

### By Boat

The Ein Gev–based boat company **Kinneret Sailing** (⊠ Rte. 92, Kibbutz Ein Gev, ☎ 04/675–8008 or 04/675–8009) makes regularly scheduled morning, noon, and afternoon runs on the Sea of Galilee between Tiberias (western shore) and Ein Gev (eastern shore) from mid-July through August and during the Jewish holiday seasons (Passover in the spring, Sukkoth/Tabernacles in the autumn). At other times, you can often join a chartered cruise; call close to the time you want to go (office open 8–4:30). The boats are large (100–170 passengers), and the 45-minute crossings are comfortable in almost all weather. Fares are about NIS 24 ($6) for the round-trip, NIS 20 ($5) one-way. You'll probably have time to eat a fish lunch at Ein Gev before sailing back to Tiberias.

**Lido Kinneret** (⊠ Gedud Barak St., ☎ 04/672–1538) specializes in group charters, especially (but not exclusively) between Tiberias and Kibbutz Ginosar or Capernaum.

### By Bus
The most important sights in the region are accessible by bus, but the sometimes infrequent local service and transfers can make bus travel a time-consuming exercise. Bet She'an, Nazareth, Tiberias, and Tabgha are on the main routes; other places, such as Megiddo, the Mount of Beatitudes, and Bet She'arim, are a bit of a walk from a nearby junction—or even a good, long hike, as in the case of Capernaum and Mt. Tabor. Belvoir and parts of Mt. Gilboa are essentially inaccessible without a car.

### By Car
Driving is the best way to explore this region. The main roads are good—some newer four-lane highways are excellent—but some smaller roads are narrow and sometimes in need of repair. Signposting is generally good (and in English), with route numbers clearly marked. Ask directions by destination, because most Israelis have basically ignored the innovation of route numbers. Most sights and accommodations are indicated by brown signs. You'll find gas stations and refreshment stands all over.

### By Limo-Van
Although not cheap for a couple, guide-driven vans can be very efficient and, for a larger party, cost-effective as well. Most people traveling this way reach the region in the company of their Jerusalem- or Tel Aviv–based guide; few guides are actually based in Galilee.

### By Taxi
This is generally an expensive and uninspiring way to travel. For sightseeing you're often much better off hiring a private guide with a car or limousine (☞ *above*). Some of the area's main taxi companies include the following:

AFULA
**Yizre'e** (☎ 04/652–3111).

NAZARETH
**Abu el-Assal** (☎ 04/655–4745); **Diana** (☎ 04/655–5554); **Hashalom** (☎ 04/657–2858).

TIBERIAS
**Hagalil** (☎ 04/672–0353); **Ha'emek** (☎ 04/672–0131).

## Contacts and Resources

### Car Rentals
Agencies close early Friday afternoon and are closed on Saturday (except in Nazareth).

In Tiberias, companies include **Avis** (⊠ Central Bus Station, ☎ 04/672–2766). **Budget** (⊠ Opposite Carmel Jordan River Hotel, Habanim St.,

☎ 04/672–0864), **Eldan** (✉ In Carmel Jordan River Hotel, Habanim St., ☎ 04/672–2831), **Europcar** (National) (✉ Sonol Garage, Alhadeff St., ☎ 04/672–2777), **Hertz** (✉ In Jordan River Hotel, Habanim St., ☎ 04/672–3939), and **Sixt** (✉ 9 Alhadeff St., ☎ 04/672–3464).

## Emergencies

**Ambulance service** (☎ 101). **First aid** (☎ 101). **Pharmacies** with late-night service (☎ 101). **Police** in the Lower Galilee (☎ 100).

## Guided Tours

A free walking tour of Tiberias leaves from the **Sheraton Moriah hotel** (✉ Habanim St., ☎ 04/679–2233) on Saturday at 10 AM. Call ahead to verify.

Few bus tours actually originate in the Lower Galilee; they start instead from Jerusalem, Tel Aviv, Haifa, and Netanya. Most hotels can book a tour for you, and all buses will pick you up and drop you off at your hotel.

Both Egged Tours and United Tours conduct one-, two-, and three-day trips from Jerusalem, Tel Aviv, Haifa, and Netanya several times a week. Itineraries include (in different combinations) the primary sites described in this chapter, a boat ride on the Sea of Galilee, the Upper Galilee and Golan Heights, and (on the three-day tour) a good part of the Mediterranean coast. One-day tours are available from Tel Aviv only. Current prices are $68 for a day trip, $198 for two days, and $298 for three days (the latter two include overnight lodging and dinner). For reservations, contact one of the following:

**Egged Tours,** in Jerusalem (✉ 8 Shlomzion Hamalka St., ☎ 02/622–1999); in Tel Aviv (✉ 59 Ben Yehuda St., ☎ 03/527–1212 or 03/527–1215); in Haifa (✉ 300 Bar Yehuda St., ☎ 04/820–2838 or 04/820–2737); and in Netanya (✉ Central Bus Station, ☎ 09/860–6206 or 09/860–6207). For reservations with **United Tours,** call Jerusalem (✉ King David Hotel annex, ☎ 02/625–2187 or 02/625–2188) or Tel Aviv (✉ 113 Hayarkon St., ☎ 03/522–2008 or 03/693–3412).

**Vered Hagalil,** at Korazim Junction, is an Israeli version of a dude ranch, offering comfortable accommodations and a good restaurant in addition to short and long horseback tours above and around the Sea of Galilee. For more information contact Vered Hagalil (✉ Rte. 90, M. P. Korazim, ☎ 04/693–5785, FAX 04/693–4964).

## Nightlife and the Arts

The best source of information on cultural life in the Lower Galilee is the **Tourist Information Office** on Habanim Street in Tiberias (☎ 04/672–5666), between the Sheraton Moriah and Carmel Jordan River hotels.

Local kibbutzim periodically host theater troupes, dancers, and musicians on tour from the "big cities" in the south; inquire at your hotel or a tourist office for schedules.

## Outdoor Activities and Sports

BICYCLING

There is a bicycle ride around the Sea of Galilee at the end of October or the beginning November, with both popular and competitive categories. There are three distances: 12 km (7½ mi), 25 km (15½ mi), and a complete 64-km (40-mi) ring around the Sea of Galilee. All end at the Tzemach Junction. For details contact the Sports Department of the **Jordan Valley Regional Council** (✉ Tzemach Junction 15132, ☎ 04/675–7630 or 04/675–7631, FAX 04/675–7641).

### HIKING

For information on trails and organized hikes in this region, contact the **Society for the Protection of Nature in Israel** (SPNI; ✉ 3 Hashefela St., Tel Aviv, ☎ 03/638–8677, 𝖥𝖠𝖷 03/688–3940).

### HORSEBACK RIDING

The **Vered Hagalil** ranch (✉ Rte. 90, M. P. Korazim, ☎ 04/693–5785, 𝖥𝖠𝖷 04/693–4964), on Route 90 north of the Sea of Galilee at Korazim Junction, conducts horseback tours (☞ Guided Tours, *above*).

### SWIMMING

Thousands of swimmers take part in the amateur Kinneret Swim in September, a tradition since 1953. There are two distances, 4 km (2½ mi) and 2 km (1 mi). For details, contact the **Jordan Valley Regional Council** (✉ Tzemach Junction 15132, ☎ 04/675–7630 or 04/675–7631, 𝖥𝖠𝖷 04/675–7641).

### WALKING AND RUNNING

The annual Big Walk (Hatza'adah in Hebrew), which takes place in March or April over 12-km (7½-mi), 8-km (5-mi), and 4-km (2½-mi) routes along the Sea of Galilee shore, attracts participants from all over the country. For details contact the **Jordan Valley Regional Council** (✉ Tzemach Junction 15132, ☎ 04/675–7630 or 04/675–7631, 𝖥𝖠𝖷 04/675–7641).

### WATER SPORTS

The so-called kayaks of **Abukayak** (☎ 04/692–2245 or 04/692–1078) are really inflated rubber canoes. Based inside the **Jordan River Park** (✉ Rte. 888, just north of the Sea of Galilee), Abukayak offers a delightfully serene one-hour route (decidedly not white water!) down the lower Jordan River, from April through October. Life jackets are provided, and the trip is entirely appropriate for young children.

## Visitor Information

There are **tourist information offices** in Nazareth (✉ Government Tourist Information Office, Casa Nova St., ☎ 04/657–3003 or 04/657–0555) and Tiberias (✉ Habanim St., between the Carmel Jordan River and Sheraton Moriah hotels, ☎ 04/672–5666).

# 6 UPPER GALILEE AND THE GOLAN

*Including Zfat (Safed)*

With something for everyone, this area draws pilgrims and vacationers, serious hikers and bon vivants. You can walk around Zfat, the mystical hillside city, or kayak on the Jordan. Despite the political heat that pervades the region—the Golan Heights in particular—this part of Israel best represents cool, comfortable relaxation. Its history may date back a million years, but its contemporary culture is geared to the modern traveler, with both traditional and trendy diversions.

SRAELIS CALL IT THE SWITZERLAND OF ISRAEL. The undulating hills of Western Galilee roll into sharper, more rugged limestone and basalt formations, bordered on the north by Lebanon and on the east by the volcanic, mountainous Golan Heights, beyond which lies Syria. The dominant feature of the Upper Galilee and the Golan is Mt. Hermon—Israel's highest mountain (towering 9,292 ft), one of the highest in the Middle East, and the home of Israel's sole ski resort.

By Lisa Perlman

Updated by Miriam Feinberg Vamosh

Most Israelis come here to get away from it all, indulging in everything from hiking and bird-watching to kayaking and wine tasting. Nature trails, rustic restaurants, and kibbutz guest houses make it easy to steer clear of the region's four cities. Two of these, Kiryat Shmona and Ma'alot (both of which began life as development towns designed to absorb Jewish refugees), are actually of little interest to the traveler. The other two, Zfat (Safed) and Katzrin, have unique personalities, the first the result of a long history of Jewish religious mysticism and the second the result of a hardheaded determination to secure Israel's border with Syria.

Mt. Hermon is Israel's "sponge" as well as its ski slope: huge volumes of water from snow and rain soak into the limestone, emerging at the base of the mountain in a series of abundant springs that feed the Jordan River and its tributaries. These rivers, all flowing through the region's Hula Valley, provide half of Israel's water supply. The water sustains gazelles, wildcats, hyraxes and hares, hundreds of species of birds, and lush, verdant foliage that thrives year-round.

More than anything else it is this water that has been the source of political contention since time immemorial. (In second place is the hilltop view, a key factor in the strategic value of the Golan Heights.) Human history in this region began a million years ago. In earliest times, people hunted the rhinos, elephants, and fallow deer that have since roamed to other parts. Later they learned to farm—and to trade, for the Galilee was smack-dab on the Western world's first major trade route, the Via Maris, stretching from Egypt to Mesopotamia.

Consequently, the rivals for this prime real estate have been many. Over the centuries, Egyptians, Canaanites, Israelites, Romans, Ottomans, and Crusaders locked horns here; recently, the borders have been changed by Russia, Britain, France, and, of course, Israel and Syria.

In addition to Jews and Arabs there has always been a small Druze presence here, particularly in the Golan Heights, where they number about 17,000.

Borders are not the only things that have shifted here. A geological fault line, the Syrian-African Rift, cuts straight through the 30-km-long (19-mi-long) Hula Valley. Many extinct volcanic cones daub the Golan; and in 1837 Zfat and Tiberias were razed in an earthquake, though no significant rumbles have been heard since.

With plenty of water and rich fertile soil, the Upper Galilee and the Golan have long been agricultural centers. Since Jewish development resumed here more than a century ago, orange and apple orchards, fish-cultivation ponds, cotton fields, and vineyards have become common sights. These are closely intertwined with the region's other main industry: tourism. Travelers come to see and stay at the many communal settlements—the *kibbutzim* and *moshavim*—that dot the area. They also come to roam the well-watered nature reserves, to witness the seasonal migration of birds that flit between Africa and Europe, and to taste the local wine.

Proximity to Lebanon and Syria does not ordinarily deter people from visiting the Upper Galilee and the Golan. On the contrary, the combination of an exciting past with a gorgeous natural setting draws visitors from all over the world. In times of particular unrest, however, *see* Safety *in* Smart Travel Tips A to Z for travel advisory contact information.

Since their arrival at the turn of the 20th century, the Jews have fought malaria, defended themselves against their enemies, and confronted a host of other hardships and hurdles. Yet the tenacious Galilean will still tell you there's no better place to live. Whether he's a kibbutznik or a town dweller, whether she was born here or chose this corner of the world, the Galilean's pride is palpable and transcends politics. The future of the Golan Heights in the on-again, off-again peace negotiations between Israel and Syria remains unknown. But despite an embattled past and uncertain future, Galileans remain laid-back and friendly. Only four hours' drive from hectic Tel Aviv and visceral Jerusalem, this truly is another world.

# Pleasures and Pastimes

## Dining

Only a few years ago, one hand had too many fingers to count the number of good restaurants in this region. No longer! The inherent attractions of the Upper Galilee and the Golan—its verdant hills, old stone dwellings, and crisp, appetite-whetting air—are an exquisite backdrop for a savory meal. Today many restaurants make the best of this environment. Tuck into hearty steaks in the middle of the forest, fresh grilled Dan River trout in shady groves on the river's banks, Middle Eastern fare prepared by Druze villagers, and home-style Jewish cooking in the heart of the holy city of Zfat. Excellent local wines enhance any meal: try the Mt. Hermon red, Gamla cabernet sauvignon, and Yarden cabernet blanc and merlot. Most restaurants are open every day except Yom Kippur; in a few places, however (Zfat, for example), it's hard to find one on Shabbat (Friday afternoon until Saturday sundown). Attire is always informal, but it's best to dress modestly in Zfat. For women, this means longish skirts or long pants and at least a half-sleeve and, for men, long pants.

| CATEGORY | COST* |
|---|---|
| $$$$ | over $30 |
| $$$ | $22–$30 |
| $$ | $12–$22 |
| $ | under $12 |

*per person for a three-course meal, excluding drinks and service*

## Hiking

Superb nature reserves and national parks make this region a prime destination for hikers. Most trails are well marked; stick to the tracks to avoid any trouble. Always carry water and wear a hat, especially in summer; wear comfortable shoes as well. You may want to take an extra pair of shoes in case you get wet—there's an abundance of water in these parts.

## Horseback Riding

Horseback riding has really taken off in the Upper Galilee. It's an excellent way to see and appreciate Israel's beautiful northern landscape.

## Jeep Tours

Jeep tours are very popular here. Needless to say, Jeeps can cover more distance in less time than your legs or a horse's, and they add a dash of excitement.

## Kayaking and Rafting

One of the more adventurous local sports, and one that's enormously enjoyable for all ages, is skimming the Jordan River in a kayak, raft, or inner tube. Many companies rent the necessary equipment. Novices needn't worry—this is not white-water territory.

## Lodging

There are no grand hotels here, but the ample selection of guest houses and inns ranges from ranch-style to home-style. As the local tourist industry has developed, many communities, especially kibbutzim and moshavim, have added hotels (or guest wings attached to homes) and an extensive range of amenities, including activities for children. Some kibbutz guest houses may offer lectures and tours of the settlement. Many also arrange kayaking and rafting, horseback riding, Jeep tours, and other sports and services for both guests and the general public. The choice can be difficult, as all are in pretty settings and have well-maintained grounds.

| CATEGORY | COST* |
| --- | --- |
| **$$$$** | over $120 |
| **$$$** | $80–$120 |
| **$$** | $55–$80 |
| **$** | under $55 |

*All prices are for two people in a standard double room, including breakfast and 15% service charge.*

# Exploring Upper Galilee and the Golan

The northern Jordan Valley serves as the border between these two regions, with the hilly Upper Galilee lying to the west and the Golan, a basalt plateau, to the east. Together, however, they are still small enough to be combined in a weekend trip.

## Great Itineraries

Tel Avivians do it. Jerusalemites do it. But cramming the Upper Galilee and the Golan into a day trip is far from ideal for the first-time visitor. Although brief visits are certainly possible (a day trip to the Golan Heights from Tiberias, for example), a several-day sojourn here can be as leisurely or as hectic as you wish. In three or four days you can learn about Israel's military history, taste a bit of wine, hike a piece of wilderness, relax over a country meal, try your hand at kayaking, or just kick back in a room with a view.

The more time you have here, the better; there's something about the soft gurgling of the brooks, the lush foliage of the forests, and the crisp mountain air of the Golan Heights that slows the pace. The ideal way to see this area is by car, but local buses will get you almost anywhere you want to go. Towns and sights in this chapter are arranged in the order you would most likely visit them by road, either from Tel Aviv or from Tiberias.

Note: touring in the Upper Galilee and the Golan is usually safe. If, however, security demands unusual caution, certain areas may be temporarily inaccessible to visitors.

*Numbers in the text correspond to numbers in the margin and on the Upper Galilee and the Golan map and the Zfat (Safed) map.*

IF YOU HAVE 1 DAY

If your base is Tiberias or elsewhere in the Lower Galilee (or Western Galilee), spend your day trip in the northernmost part of the country, starting with a walk through the **Tel Dan** ⑰ or **Hermon River (Banias)** ⑱ nature reserve and lunching on Dan River trout. You can then either tackle **Nimrod's Fortress** ⑲ or, in spring and summer, take a chair-lift to the top of **Mt. Hermon** ⑳. In winter, try wine tasting in **Katzrin** ㉑–㉓. Or spend the morning strolling through the Old City in **Zfat** ①–⑨ and the afternoon kayaking on the Jordan River.

IF YOU HAVE 2–3 DAYS

A few days give you a few different options. Tiberias is a good starting point; either spend a morning by the Sea of Galilee or head for **Zfat** ①–⑨ and take a walk through the Old City. Stop in **Rosh Pina** ⑫ for a look at the handicrafts boutiques; then check out the wetlands at the **Hula Nature Reserve** ⑭. Spend the night in a kibbutz guest house; the next day, head for the Golan Heights via Route 98, overlooking the Disengagement Zone between Israel and Syria. The third day is well spent outdoors—horseback riding, kayaking or rafting on the Jordan River, or Jeep touring.

## When to Tour the Upper Galilee and the Golan

The Upper Galilee and the Golan are best in late winter and spring, when the range of floral colors is wondrous. Summer days can be hot, but the region doesn't suffer the humidity of other parts of Israel. Zfat comes alive from July through September, when more galleries are open. There are more activities for travelers then, but also more crowds. In winter, you can expect some rain.

# ZFAT (SAFED) AND ENVIRONS

In the southern part of the Upper Galilee, attractions range from the narrow streets and historic synagogues of Zfat's Old City to the wilderness of the Hula Nature Reserve. Other reserves, like Mt. Meron, have both scenic appeal and spiritual importance. At Rosh Pina you can see where the Galilee's first Zionist pioneers settled. Or you can just relax at an inn or a kibbutz guest house and enjoy the wooded scenery.

## Zfat (Safed)

*33 km (20 mi) north of Tiberias, 72 km (45 mi) northeast of Haifa.*

At 3,000 ft above sea level, Zfat (commonly translated as Safed) is Israel's highest city. Perhaps this proximity to the heavens accounts for its reputation as the center of Jewish mysticism (Kabbala). For although it is one of several holy cities in Israel—along with Jerusalem, Tiberias, and Hebron—Zfat has a spiritual dimension found nowhere else.

The Crusaders built a fortress here, and a thriving Jewish settlement grew up in the shadow of the castle walls. Although it declined with the eclipse of the Crusader presence in the Galilee, the town survived rule by the Ottomans, who retained Zfat as their capital through the 16th century. Soon after their expulsion in 1492, Jews from Spain started streaming in, among them respected rabbis and other spiritual leaders, intellectuals, and poets who gravitated to Zfat as a center of revived Kabbala study.

The Kabbala—whose oral tradition dates to ancient times but gained popularity starting in the 12th century, possibly as a reaction against formal rabbinical Judaism—is about reading between, behind, and all around the lines. Each letter and accent of every word in the holy books has a numerical value with specific significance, offering added meaning to the literal word. During the Middle Ages, Zfat was the heart of the Kabbala, the great rabbis its soul; under their tutelage, religious and mystical schools and meeting places mushroomed here. Some of these leaders would leave their mark on the age, on the generations to follow, and, of course, on Zfat itself.

# Upper Galilee and the Golan

Mediterranean Sea

LEBANON

Liman

899

Dovev

Bar'am
Park

11

Nahariya

Kabri

89

Ma'alot

Hurfeish

Jis

89

Mt.
Meron

Bar

10

Ma'alot-
Tarshiha

Mt.
Peki'in

Meron Mts.

Me

Peki'in

Beit Jann

864

70

4

Kafr Yasif

Rama

866

Akko

85

85

Kiryat Yam

TO HAIFA

TO
TIBERIAS

TO TEL AVIV

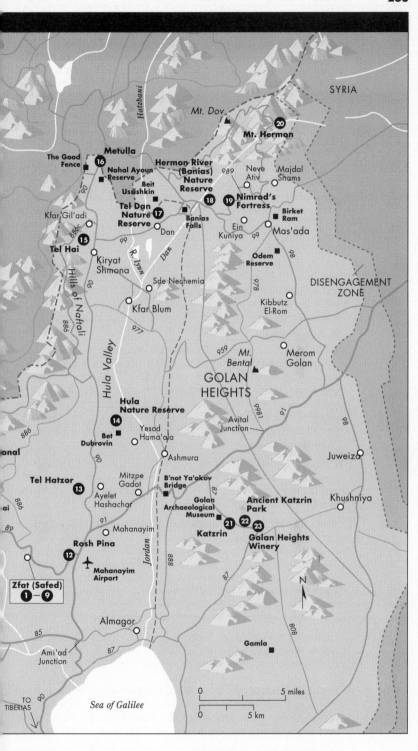

SYRIA

Mt. Dov

Mt. Herman **20**

Metulla

The Good Fence **16**

Nahal Ayoun Reserve

Beit Ussishkin

Hermon River (Banias) Nature Reserve

989

Neve Ativ

Majdal Shams

Nimrod's Fortress **19**

**18**

Tel Dan Nature Reserve **17**

Banias Falls

Birket Ram

Kfar Gil'adi

Dan

Ein Kuniya

Mas'ada

**15**

Tel Hai

Kiryat Shmona

99

Odem Reserve

DISENGAGEMENT ZONE

886c

886

Sde Nechemia

878

Kibbutz El-Rom

Kfar Blum

Hills of Naftali

917

886

959

Mt. Bental

Merom Golan

Hula Valley

GOLAN HEIGHTS

98

Hula Nature Reserve

**14**

Yesod Hama'ala

Avital Junction

9981

16

Bet Dubrovin

Ashmura

98

886

Juweiza

Tel Hatzor **13**

Mitzpe Gadot

B'not Ya'akov Bridge

Khushniya

Ayelet Hashachar

87

Golan Archaeological Museum

Ancient Katzrin Park

91

Mahanayim

**21** **22** **23**

Katzrin

Golan Heights Winery

Rosh Pina **12**

Jordan

87

88

Mahanayim Airport

888

N

Zfat (Safed) **1** – **9**

Almagor

808

85

Gamla

Ami'ad Junction

87

90

5 miles

0

0

5 km

TO TIBERIAS

*Sea of Galilee*

For most of the year, Zfat can be something of an enigma to the traveler: it hibernates from October through June. The city's noted artists move to warmer parts of the country, opening their galleries in Zfat only infrequently, and other sites may also be closed. This does not mean you should leave Zfat off your itinerary during those months; there is enough to occupy the curious wanderer for at least a few hours, and much of it is free. In the summer, especially the school holidays (July and August), Zfat is abuzz with activity: galleries and shops stay open late, klezmer music (Eastern European Jewish "soul music") dances around corners, and the city extends a warm welcome to everyone. Moreover, everyone comes—so avoid Zfat at this time if you don't like crowds.

It doesn't take long to walk all around Zfat's labyrinthine Old City and get a feel for it. Take time to poke around the little cobbled passages that seem to lead nowhere, or linger over some minute architectural detail on a structure from another time. And don't worry if you get lost; you're never far from the center. Yerushalayim (Jerusalem) Street runs through the heart of the Old City, encircling the Citadel, in its center; from here there is easy access to the two main areas of interest, the Old Jewish Quarter and the Artists' Colony. There is no getting around Zfat's hilly topography, so wear comfortable walking shoes. As the town is largely orthodox, modest dress is recommended when visiting synagogues. For women, this means a longish skirt or long pants and at least a half-sleeve and, for men, long pants.

## A Good Walk

Begin by exploring the the **Citadel Park** ①, former site of the largest Crusader fortress in the Middle East. (You can leave your car here.) As you enter the park, on Hativat Yiftah Street, take in the sight of the old houses below and the undulating pastoral scene beyond. This image has inspired many of the paintings and drawings that have emerged from Zfat, and you'll no doubt see numerous modern interpretations of these at the General Exhibition (☞ *below*) and in the rooms of almost every Zfat hotel.

Turn right and walk about 300 ft to the remains of the Citadel tower. It was destroyed over the years, mainly by earthquakes, most recently and devastatingly in 1837. A little farther along on the right is the **Israel Bible Museum,** with its impressive arched entrance.

Walk down the steps and cross Yerushalayim Street. Near No. 24, more steps lead to the parallel Bar Yochai Street. You are now entering the Ashkenazi (Eastern European Jewish) section of the Old Jewish Quarter, distinguished from the Sephardic (Middle Eastern Jewish) section by its wider streets and more subtly colored buildings. Turn left and walk to **Kikar Hameginim** ②. Standing on the square, you'll notice through the arch a stepped street leading down and to the right. This draws you into the 16th century and the Ashkenazi **Ha'Ari Synagogue** ③.

Leaving the synagogue, go down the steps, turn left at Alkabetz Street, and go down again at the first set of steps. Walk under the dome, and you'll soon notice blue window frames and a door next to a little alley. You are now in the heart of Sephardic Zfat. If you haven't found the sign marking the spot, just ask for the **Abouhav Synagogue** ④, whose elements reflect Sephardic traditions. Head back under the arch and up the stairs to Caro Street, with its *souk*-style souvenir stores, and the compact **Caro Synagogue** ⑤, arguably the most charming in the quarter.

A little farther ahead you'll find yourself in the middle of a stairway called **Ma'alot Olei Hagardom.** At this point, you have two options: you can take the stairs down, turn right at the bottom, and follow the road to the **cemetery** ⑥, with its intriguing gravestones old and new.

En route is **Hameiri House** ⑦, a museum devoted to Zfat's history. Or you can continue straight ahead, crossing over the stairway to the **Artists' Colony.** You should make your first stop the **General Exhibition** ⑧, a selection of works by resident artists. A walk down Tet-vav Street brings you to one of the colony's curiosities, the **Museum of Printing Art** ⑨.

## Sights to See

❹ **Abouhav Synagogue.** This large Sephardic synagogue is named in honor of a 14th-century Spanish scribe, one of whose Torah scrolls found its way here with the Spanish Jewish exiles 200 years later. A look around reveals a number of differences between this synagogue and its Ashkenazi counterparts, such as the Ha'Ari (☞ *below*); the walls are painted a lively blue and are richly decorated with religious motifs, the benches run along the walls instead of in rows (so that no man turns his back on his neighbor), and the dome-shape roof rests on four pillars.

Every detail is loaded with significance: there are three arks—for the three forefathers, Abraham, Isaac, and Jacob (the one on the right is said to be the Abouhav original)—and 10 windows in the dome, referring to the Commandments. The charmingly naive illustrations on the squinches include a depiction of the Dome of the Rock (referring to the destruction of the Second Temple) and pomegranate trees, whose 613 seeds are equal in number to the Torah's commandments. The original building was destroyed in the 1837 earthquake, but locals still swear that the southern wall—in which the Torah scroll penned by Abouhav is set—was spared. This scroll is taken out only on Rosh Hashanah, Yom Kippur, and Shavuot (Pentecost). ✉ *Abouhav St.* ✆ *No set visiting hrs.*

**Artists' Colony.** The colony, set in Zfat's old Arab Quarter, was established in 1951 by six Israeli artists who saw the promise beyond Zfat's war-torn and dilapidated condition; for them, the old buildings, the fertile landscape, and the cool mountain air fused to form a magic that would help them create. Others soon followed until, at its peak, the colony was home to more than 50 artists, some of whom are exhibited internationally. The numbers have since dwindled somewhat, and gallery opening hours are unpredictable, especially in winter. In summer, however (July–September), things really come alive as the artists open their doors and display—or work on—their latest pots, paintings, and sculptures.

❺ **Caro Synagogue.** Rabbi Yosef Caro arrived in Zfat in 1535 and led its Jewish community for years. He is the author of the Shulchan Aruch, the code of law that remains a foundation of Jewish religious interpretation to the present day; and this synagogue is said to have been Caro's study hall. It was destroyed in the great earthquake of 1837 and rebuilt in the mid-19th century. If you ask, you can open the ark containing the Torah scrolls, one of which is at least 400 years old. A glass-faced cabinet at the back of the synagogue is the *geniza,* where damaged scrolls or prayer books are stored (because they carry the name of God, they cannot be destroyed). The turquoise paint here—considered the "color of heaven"—is believed to help keep away the evil eye. ✉ *Alkabetz St.* ✆ *No set visiting hrs.*

❻ **Cemetery.** An old and a new cemetery are set into the hillside below the Old Jewish Quarter. The old plots resonate with the names and fame of the Kabbalists of yore, and their graves are identifiable by sky-blue markers. It is said that if the legs of the devout suddenly get tired here, it is because they are walking over hidden graves. The new cemetery holds the graves of members of the pre-State underground Stern Gang and Irgun forces, who were executed by the British in Akko's

# Zfat (Safed)

Ha'ari

Bak

Israel Bible Museum

Central Bus Station

*i*

Ha'ari

Simla Bet

Bar-Yochai St.

Meginei Zfat

Derech Hahasidim

Najara

Yerushalayim St.

Kikar Hameginim

Post Office

Ovruch

**3**

**2**

## OLD JEWISH QUARTER

Alkabelz

Abbo

Yod-alef

Hamekubalim

**4** **5**

Hatam Sofer

Beit Yosef

Tarpat

Ma'alot Olei Hagardom

Montefiore

Ma'alot Moshe

Halivat Yiftah Rd.

**1**

The Citadel

Halivat Yiftah Rd.

## OLD CITY

Pedestrian Mall

Old Jewish Cemetery

**6**

New Cemetery

**7**

**8**

Zvi Levanon

Isackov

Kikar Hama'ayan Haradum

## ARTISTS' COLONY

Arlosoroff

Aliyah Bet

TO MT. MERON

← 

Telxov

Keren Hayesod

Tel-zayin

Telz Shemi

**9**

Merzer

Kikar David Gilboa

Alwail

Hakeren Hakayemet

N

### KEY

▦ Stairs

Zahal

Hehalutz

0 _____ 250 yards

0 _____ 250 meters

prison (☞ Chapter 4). In a separate plot, bordered by cypresses, lie the 24 teenage victims of the 1974 terrorist massacre at Ma'alot.

**❶ The Citadel Park.** In Talmudic times, 1,600 years ago, hilltop bonfires here served as a beacon to surrounding communities heralding the beginning of the lunar month, the basis for the Jewish calendar. In the 12th century, the Crusaders grasped the strategic value of this setting and built the Citadel, scattered sections of which remain. The Muslim ruler Saladin wrenched it from them in 1188, following his victory at the Horns of Hattin, but half a century later the Crusader order of the Templars repossessed it, turning it into the most massive Christian fortress in the region. For decades the Crusaders kept the aggressive Mamluk sultan Baybars at bay, but his army eventually besieged the Citadel in 1266. Having already destroyed many of the cities on the coast, Baybars decided to move his capital from Akko to Zfat.

The Jewish settlements outside the castle walls grew and prospered during and after the Crusader era, with the city becoming a center of Kabbala studies. Zfat remained predominantly Jewish until a devastating earthquake in 1837 razed the town, leaving few survivors. In 1929, Arab riots drove most of these away, and by 1948, only 1,500 Jewish residents remained. The departing British army left the town's key strategic positions to the Arab forces, which set about besieging the Old Jewish Quarter. A handful of Palmach fighters (part of the Jewish clandestine army during the British Mandate) penetrated enemy lines and helped the quarter's (mostly elderly) devout Jews successfully resist the offense in what became known as the Miracle of Zfat. Once again, with its sweeping views and slopes in the heart of Zfat, the Citadel was the focal point of battle. ⊠ *Old City.*

**❽ General Exhibition.** The works inside this large space are a representative sample of the work of Zfat's artists, ranging from oils and watercolors to silk screens and sculptures, both traditional and avant-garde. The permission of the Muslim authorities was required to organize the Exhibition, as it is housed in the old mosque, easily identified from afar by its minaret. The Artists' Colony has recognized the growing presence of artists from the former Soviet Union, and the adjacent building holds the **Immigrant Artists' Exhibition.** In either facility, if any works catch your fancy, just ask directions to the artist's gallery for a more in-depth look at his or her work. ⊠ *Isakov and Zvi Levanon Sts.,* ☎ *04/692–0087.* ☞ *Free.* ☉ *Sun.–Thurs. 9–5, Fri. 9–2, Sat. and holidays 10–2.*

**❸ Ha'Ari Synagogue.** This Ashkenazi synagogue has associations going back to the 16th century. It is named for the renowned Ari, the great rabbi who left an indelible mark on Zfat and on Judaism; his real name was Isaac Luria, but he was known to all as the Ari, Hebrew for "lion" and an acronym for Adoneinu Rabbeinu Itzhak ("our master and teacher Isaac"). In his mere three years in Zfat, he evolved his own system of the Kabbala, which drew a huge following that would influence Jewish teaching and interpretation the world over, right up to the present day. Even more astounding is the fact that he died in his mid-thirties; it is generally said that one should not even consider study of the Kabbala before the age of 40, when one reaches the requisite level of intellectual and emotional maturity.

The pale colors of this tiny Ashkenazi synagogue contrast sharply with its olive-wood holy ark, a dazzlingly carved tour de force with two tiers of spiral columns and vibrant plant reliefs. The synagogue was built after Luria's death, on the spot where he is said to have come with his students on a Friday evening to welcome the Sabbath. It was leveled by the 1837 earthquake and rebuilt in 1857. (The Sephardic

Ari Synagogue, where the rabbi prayed, is farther down the quarter, by the cemetery. The oldest of Zfat's synagogues, this 16th-century structure has especially fine carved wooden doors.) ⊠ *Ha'Ari St.* ☉ *No set visiting hrs.*

❼ **Hameiri House.** This centuries-old stone building houses a museum documenting the life of the Jewish community of Zfat over the past 200 years. ⊠ *Keren Hayesod St.,* ☎ *04/692–1307.* ℻ *04/692–1902* 🖂 *NIS 10 ($2.50).* ☉ *Sun.–Thurs. 9–2, Fri. 9–1, Sat. by appointment.*

**Israel Bible Museum.** This stone mansion was once the home of the Ottoman governor. Today it houses the somewhat dramatic paintings and sculptures of artist Phillip Ratner, all inspired by the Bible. ⊠ *Hativat Yiftah St.,* ☎ *04/699–9972.* 🖂 *Free.* ☉ *Feb.–Dec., Sun.–Thurs. 10–2, Fri. 10–1.*

❷ **Kikar Hameginim.** "Defenders' Square" is the main square of the Old Jewish Quarter and was once its social and economic heart. A sign points to a two-story house that served as the command post of the neighborhood's defense in 1948—hence the plaza's name.

**Ma'alot Olei Hagardom.** Part of Zfat's charm is its setting, on the slope of a hill. This stairway, which extends all the way down from Yerushalayim Street, forms the boundary between the Old Jewish Quarter and the Artists' Colony (formerly the Arab Quarter).

❾ **Museum of Printing Art.** The small but rich collection here spans the history of printing in Israel. On display are the first Hebrew press (operated in Zfat, in 1576), the first Hebrew book (which rolled off press a year later), the first newspaper printed in Israel (1863), and a copy of the May 16, 1948, *Palestine Post* declaring the birth of the State of Israel. ⊠ *Merzer and Alwail Sts.,* ☎ *04/692–0947.* 🖂 *Free.* ☉ *Sun.–Thurs. 10–noon and 4–6, Fri.–Sat. 10–noon.*

## Dining and Lodging

$$$ ✕ **Bat Ya'ar.** This timbered, pub-style, non-kosher restaurant serves tasty steaks and salads and excellent chicken with rosemary, all enhanced by the wooded mountaintop setting, though it takes a little determination to find the place through the winding roads behind Zfat and into the Birya Forest. Outside the restaurant is a play area for children; they'll love the pony rides. Bat Ya'ar is 5 km (3 mi) north of Zfat. It's best to call for directions. ⊠ *Birya Forest,* ☎ *04/692–1788. Reservations essential weekends. AE, MC, V.*

$$ ✕ **Ein Camonim.** The Galilee Hills make perfect pastureland for live-
★ stock—in this case, goats—and in here you can taste the fresh output of Ein Camonim's dairy. The fixed menu contains a platter of goat cheeses, home-baked bread, a wicker basket of raw garden vegetables, a small carafe of local wine, coffee, and dessert. There's a half-price menu for children 12 and under. The retail shop next door sells the cheeses, which are very good but not very cheap. ⊠ *Rte. 85, 20 km (12½ mi) southwest of Zfat, 5 km (3 mi) west of Kadarim Junction (north of highway),* ☎ *04/698–9894. AE, DC, MC, V.*

$$ ✕ **Gan Eden.** The setting, an old stone house, lends great atmosphere to this family-run eatery. Taking in the view of Mt. Meron (the restaurant's name means "paradise"), try the eggplant stuffed with creamed champignons, savory blintzes, vine leaves, salmon steak, or pasta, followed by one of the homemade cakes. The restaurant serves no meat or chicken. The bar in the garden, called the Last Temptation, stays open into the wee hours. This is one of Zfat's few restaurants open on Saturday. ⊠ *Mount Canaan Promenade,* ☎ *04/697–2434. AE, DC, MC, V.*

© 2000 Visa U.S.A. Inc.

Paris, France.

Paris, Texas.

# When it Comes to Getting Local Currency at an ATM,

# Same Thing.

**Whether you're in Yosemite or Yemen, using your Visa® card or ATM card with the PLUS symbol is the easiest and most convenient way to get local currency.** For example, let's say you're in France. When you make a withdrawal, using your secured PIN, it's dispensed in francs, but is debited from your account in U.S. dollars. This makes it easy to take advantage of favorable exchange rates. And if you need help finding one of Visa's 627,000 ATMs in 127 countries worldwide, visit **visa.com/pd/atm**. We'll make finding an ATM as easy as finding the Eiffel Tower, the Pyramids or even the Grand Canyon.

It's Everywhere You Want To Be.

# SEE THE WORLD
# IN FULL COLOR

**Fodor's** Exploring Guides bring all the great sights vividly to life with hundreds of photographs, fascinating historical background, and colorful anecdotes. Detailed maps and practical information keep you headed in the right direction.

Pair a **Fodor's** Exploring Guide with your trusted Gold Guide for a complete planning package.

**Fodor's** EXPLORING GUIDES

*At bookstores everywhere.*

$$ ✕ **Hamifgash.** One of the institutions on pedestrian-only Yerusha-layim Street, Hamifgash (which means "meeting place") has a wide range of dining options from soups and salads to substantial meat dishes. Dining on Friday and Saturday is by reservation only. ✉ *75 Yerusha-layim St.,* ☎ *04/692–0510. AE, DC, MC, V.*

$$$$ ✕⌂ **Ron.** This pleasant but unassuming hotel has a good restaurant with an eclectic menu of European and Middle Eastern dishes. Rooms are spacious, clean, and light-filled, and half have mountain views. The pool is only open in the summer. ✉ *Near Metzuda Park, Hativat Yif-tah, Box 22, Zfat 13214,* ☎ *04/697–2590,* ℻ *04/697–2363. 50 rooms. Restaurant, pool. AE, DC, MC, V.*

$$ ✕⌂ **Habayit Bik'tse Hanof.** The "House at the View's Edge," perched high in the Birya Forest with a stunning vista of the surrounding hills, is run as a holistic center. In addition to a café serving a selection of meat and dairy dishes there is a gallery–gift shop proffering everything from natural soaps to furniture, and four guest rooms for those seek-ing the holistic experience. In contrast to the magnificent surround-ings, the rooms are very utilitarian. One, a separate cottage, has a whirlpool bath and some charm—it's been faced with stone and looks a little like Hansel and Gretl might live there off-season. Shiatsu, re-flexology, and other treatments are available. ✉ *Birya Forest, 7 km (4 mi) from Zfat,* ☎ *04/692–3737. 4 rooms. Café. AE, DC, MC, V.*

$$$$ ⌂ **Howard Johnson Plaza Ruth–Rimonim.** Two hundred years ago, when
★ the Turks were in charge, this gracious old building was the local post office. Rooms were added later, and it became a *khan,* or inn. Since opening in 1961 it has enjoyed a reputation for charm and excellence. The stone-walled rooms have a rustic feel and are tastefully decorated with local art; the former stables serve as the dining room. Half the rooms have views over the mountain and gorges. Children's programs are offered in the summer. ✉ *Artists' Quarter, Box 1011, Zfat 13110,* ☎ *04/699–4666,* ℻ *04/692–0456. 76 rooms. 2 restaurants, bar, pool, sauna, exercise room, children's programs. AE, DC, MC, V.*

$$$$ ⌂ **Sea View (Mitzpe Hayamim).** Halfway between Zfat and Rosh Pina, with a splendid view of the Sea of Galilee, is this serene spot ded-icated to the pampering of both body and soul. The hotel specializes in packages of up to a week that include a medical checkup and diet, massage, reflexology, shiatsu, pedicure, manicure, and hairdressing—as well as full board. For the hale and hearty, there is a guided walk every morning. All rooms share a ban on smoking, and some suites and junior suites have whirlpool baths. The lobby has a "tea corner," with a full range of herbal teas served around the clock. A gallery ex-hibits Israeli works with extremely high prices, and a gift shop sells homemade breads, cheeses, and other local products. ✉ *Box 27, Rosh Pina 12000,* ☎ *04/699–9666,* ℻ *04/699–9555. 84 rooms. Restaurant, pool, no-smoking rooms, beauty salon, hot tub, massage, sauna, ex-ercise room. AE, DC, MC, V.* ✎

$$$$ ⌂ **Vered Hagalil.** Stone and wood cottages, each with a front porch,
★ create a sense of privacy, yet the extremely popular restaurant and sta-bles on this guest farm are only steps away. Owners Yehuda and Yona Avni haven't lost their enthusiasm for the Galilee, which drew them here decades ago (he's from the United States, she's from Jerusalem), and it's reflected in the excellent maintenance of Vered Hagalil. Ac-commodations range from cottage apartments with bedroom, living room, and kitchenette to studios and smaller cabins. All are ranchlike in decor—earth tones, exposed wood, and stone walls, and big picture windows for sea-gazing. Trail-riding packages of up to three days are a specialty. Overnight guests enjoy 10% off riding and meals in the hotel restaurant. ✉ *Rte. 90, 15 km (9 mi) south of Zfat, next to Ko-razim, M.P. Korazim 12385,* ☎ *04/693–5785,* ℻ *04/693–4964. 17*

*units (2 for wheelchair users). Restaurant, bar, pool, kitchenettes (some), horseback riding. AE, DC, MC, V.* 🐾

**$$** 🏨 **Joseph's Well.** Rooms here are like cozy studio apartments, with pine furniture, coordinated tablecloths and sheets, and chintz curtains—each has a coffee corner, with an electric kettle, and tea and coffee. They're all on the ground floor, in clusters of three with a shared patio. The kibbutz dining room—Joseph's Well is on Kibbutz Amiad, 10 km (6 mi) south of Zfat—doubles as the restaurant. Unlike the bigger kibbutz hotels, Joseph's Well offers few activities; guests are here strictly to sleep. Wine, from unusual fruits such as kiwi, is on sale in a shop on the premises, which also peddles a range of local and imported products. ✉ *M.P. Upper Galilee 12335,* ☎ *04/693–3829,* FAX *04/690–9307. 24 rooms. Dining room, pool, horseback riding. AE, DC, MC, V.*

### Nightlife and the Arts

Zfat hosts a **klezmer festival** every summer, and indeed there could be no better setting for three days of "Jewish soul music" than this mystical, cobbled-lane city. Some of klezmer's roots are Hasidic, making it almost prayerlike in tone, especially with its emphasis on wind and string instruments. Many events are street performances and therefore free. Keep in mind, though, that Zfat bursts at the seams at this time, with revelers both religious and secular. The festival is usually held in July; contact the **Zfat Tourist Information Office** (✉ 50 Yerushalayim St., Box 227, Zfat 13010, ☎ 04/692–7474) for details.

### Outdoor Activities and Sports

**Bat Ya'ar** (☎ 04/692–1788), in the Birya Forest 5 km (3 mi) from Zfat, is a steak house that doubles as a sort of ranch, with pony rides for kids and horseback riding for all (☞ Dining and Lodging, *above*).

**Vered Hagalil** (☎ 04/693–5785), a guest ranch at the Korazim Junction at Route 90 (☞ Dining and Lodging, *above*), offers a variety of horseback tours up to three days long, with a specialty in Western riding. Pony rides are available for kids. Prices for guided rides range from NIS 98 ($24.50) for an hour to NIS 400 ($100) for a day.

## Mt. Meron

**⑩** *21 km (13 mi) west of Zfat on Rte. 89.*

The spiritual importance of Zfat extends beyond the city limits to Mt. Meron and its environs, a pilgrimage site for both ultra-Orthodox Hasidic Jews and nature lovers.

Remote as it may seem, the village of Meron has for centuries drawn thousands upon thousands of Orthodox Jews to pay homage to several of the great rabbis of the Roman era who are buried at the eastern foot of the mount. The most important site—and one of the holiest places in Israel—is the **tomb of Rabbi Shimon Bar Yochai,** sage and survivor of the Bar Kochba Revolt of almost 2,000 years ago. Refusing to kowtow to the Romans after they succeeded in taking Jerusalem, Bar Yochai is said to have fled with his son Elazar to a cave at Peki'in, not far from here, where he remained for 13 years. It is believed by the faithful, beginning with the 16th-century mystics who settled in Zfat, that while holed up in the cave, Bar Yochai penned the Zohar (the Book of Splendor), his commentary on the Pentateuch, or the Five Books of Moses, the first five books of the Hebrew Bible. Opponents of this theory claim that the Zohar dates from 13th-century Spain, not 2nd-century Meron, but Hasidic pilgrims continue their annual visits to the great rabbi's tomb. Pieces of cloth and scraps of paper (inscribed with prayers) that hang from trees around the tomb are evidence of the pilgrims' devotion.

The pilgrimage is still celebrated en masse on Lag Ba'Omer, the festive 33rd day of the seven solemn weeks that begin with Passover and end with Shavuot (Pentecost). Mt. Meron comes alive as a grand procession of Hasidic Jews arrive on foot from Zfat, carrying Torah scrolls and singing fervently. Bonfires are lighted, and barbecues follow. Many ultra-Orthodox still uphold the tradition of bringing their three-year-old sons here on Lag Ba'Omer for their first haircuts.

### Dining and Lodging

$$$    ✕ **Hase'uda Ha'aharona.** This restaurant's peculiar choice of name (it mean "The Last Supper") shouldn't stop you from enjoying its magnificent combination of mountaintop location and tasty fare. The vegetarian cuisine, best appreciated by adults, is enriched by any number of the 45 herbs that owner-chef Bella grows in her garden. A savory blend of some of those herbs creates the aroma of Bella's legendary pumpkin soup. Try the scrumptious and beautifully presented phyllo basket, filled with a creamy spinach and asparagus soup. Call ahead for directions. ⊠ *Near the entrance to Moshav Amirim, 4th house on the right,* ☎ *04/698–9788. Reservations essential. No credit cards. Closed weekdays.*

$$$    ▦ **Amirim Holiday Village.** The moshav (communal settlement) of Amirim offers something a little different: almost all of its 300 members are vegetarians. This is a real get-away-from-it-all kind of place, set on top of a hill overlooking Mt. Meron and the Sea of Galilee. Guests have a choice of health and beauty treatments. The lodging units have one or several rooms and are run by different families. Each has a kitchenette, but there is no shortage of external dining options: there are numerous family-run restaurants and café-cum-galleries on-site, with a range of vegetarian fare. Especially good is Hase'uda Ha'aharona (☞ *above*). ⊠ *Moshav Amirim, near Mt. Meron (about 4 km/2½ mi north of the junction of Rte. 89 and Rte. 886), M.P. Carmiel 20115,* ☎ *04/ 698–9571,* ℻ *04/698–7824. 100 units. 6 restaurants, kitchenettes, pool, children's programs. No credit cards. No Sat. checkout in Aug.*

*En Route*    The Arab village of **Jish,** between Mt. Meron and Bar'am off Route 89, was called Gush Halav during the Second Temple period. In those days, it was renowned both for its exceptional olive oil and for the milk from its cattle. Gush Halav translates as "milk bloc," but it's unclear whether the region's name derived from the famous milk or from the whiteness of the chalky limestone that's used in the foundations of local buildings.

## Bar'am National Park

⓫    *15 km (9 mi) northwest of Meron, 40 km (25 mi) northwest of Zfat.*

In an otherwise deserted spot lie the ruins of **Bar'am,** one of the best-preserved ancient synagogues anywhere, dating from the 3rd century AD. Although Bar'am is less grand than the synagogue at Capernaum, on the Sea of Galilee (☞ Chapter 5), the community that built it must have devoted considerable funds and energy to their most important building. Like most other synagogues uncovered in this area, it faces south, toward Jerusalem; unlike any other, however, this one has lavish architectural elements, such as an entrance with a segmental pediment, and freestanding giant columns on the exterior.

The interior, which resembles that of other Galilean synagogues of the talmudic period (3rd–8th centuries AD), is in a worse state of repair than the facade. Rows of pillars in the prayer hall apparently served as supports for the ceiling, and the building may have had a second story. A section of the facade's lintel, now in the Louvre in Paris, contains the Hebrew inscription "May there be peace in this place, and in all the places of Israel. This lintel was made by Jose the Levite. Blessings upon his works. Shalom." ✉ *Rte. 899,* ☎ *04/698–9301.* ☞ *NIS 9 ($2.25).* ☉ *Apr.–Sept., daily 8–4; Oct.–Mar., daily 8–3.*

### Dining

$$ ✕ **Einat.** Although some distance off the main sightseeing tracks, this Romanian restaurant is worth the journey. Owner Moishe smokes his own meats with excellent results; the thick (roughly 1-pound) steaks and kebabs are also excellent. The meats are enhanced by a range of traditional salads, several of them eggplant-based, and pickled vegetables. ✉ *1 Klil Hahoresh (off Rte. 89, next to the tennis courts),* ☎ *04/957–0520. AE, DC, MC, V. No dinner Sun. in winter.*

$$ ✕ **Jascala.** Departing from the usual Middle Eastern plate of hummus and pita with chips, Jascala offers flavors of Lebanon, cooked up with the assistance of the owner's mother. The vine leaves come with or without meat; the fried *koubeh,* a small bulgur wheat pocket, is filled with either meat or hummus; and the pita baked with meat, onion, and hot pepper delivers a kick. ✉ *Jish,* ☎ *04/698–7762. AE, DC, MC, V.*

## Rosh Pina

⑫ *10 km (6 mi) east of Zfat, 25 km (15½ mi) north of Tiberias.*

Rosh Pina—literally, "headstone of the corner"—gets its name from the Bible: "The stone that the builder hath rejected hath become the headstone of the corner" (Psalm 118). This verse inspired the Galilee's first Zionist pioneers, who came from Romania in 1882, determined to build a village. They bought this land, 1,500 ft above sea level at the foot of the mountain ridge east of Zfat, and arrived with all they needed for their new home, right down to the timber for construction. Ironically, the boat that brought them to the Holy Land was called the *Titus,* the name of the Roman general whose destruction of Jerusalem forced the exile of Jews from that city in AD 70.

The Romanians derived their main livelihood at Rosh Pina from the production of silk by silkworms; this industry was encouraged by the great philanthropist Baron Edmond de Rothschild, who gave them the fruit trees they needed for the project. Despite grand efforts, however, the desired results were elusive: residents walked around in silk scarves and socks but had nothing to eat. Slowly, family by family, the immigrants moved away to other settlements, leaving only squatters for decades to follow.

The little village has now been restored and has some lovely gift shops and galleries. To get here, walk for 10 minutes up the path from the modern township of Rosh Pina. The two-story **Schwartz Hotel,** on Ha'elyon Street, built in 1890, was the first rest house in the Galilee. Today it is a mere skeleton of the original, but try to imagine what it was like to check in here after a long, tiring journey on foot and enjoy the tranquil view of the Sea of Galilee below and white-capped Mt. Hermon to the north.

The **synagogue** (✉ Ha'elyon St.) is usually locked. However, someone in the office of Old Rosh Pina (☎ 04/693–6603), a development company, next door to the restaurant at the bottom of Ha'elyon Street, may be able to open it. The interior of the no-longer-functioning synagogue remains as it was when it was built in the mid-1880s; the dark pews and holy ark made of the timber brought from Romania have aged gracefully. Look at the ceiling at the painted depictions of palm trees and biblical motifs.

The **Old Rosh Pina office,** which oversees the restoration and mainte-nance of Old Rosh Pina, occupies the house that belonged to Profes-sor Gideon Mer, a leading expert on malaria in the 1930s. Legend has it that Mer used to inject his wife and children with experimental remedies in his efforts to combat malaria in this region. (All survived.) The British were so impressed with Mer's work that they sent him to Burma to fight malaria epidemics there. Implements and household items from the early days of Rosh Pina are on display. Admission is free. Next door, you can view an outstanding audiovisual presentation about the founding of this pioneering community. (For English viewings, call ☎ 04/693–6603.)

Old Rosh Pina is populated today by some 60 artists, although, un-like their counterparts in the artists' village of Ein Hod (☞ The Roth-schild Wine Country and Mt. Carmel *in* Chapter 4), they do not usually open their homes to visitors. There are, however, a few gal-leries displaying local creations.

## Dining and Lodging

Rosh Pina is a budding center of tourism for this region, and many residents are now opening their homes as bed-and-breakfasts. There is no central reservation center, but the various tourist-information cen-ters (☞ Visitor Information *in* Upper Galilee and the Golan A to Z, *below*) can help you find simple, pleasant accommodations.There are family rooms at the small (100-bed) **youth hostel** (☎ 04/693–7086).

**$$$$** ✕ **Babayit Shel Rafa ("Rafa's").** This inviting stone house in the cen-tury-old upper reaches of rustic Rosh Pina once belonged to the ven-erable Dr. Mer. Owner and chef Rafa infuses the menu with gastronomic memories of his native Argentina, and good service enhances the al-ready comfortable atmosphere. The best starters are the pickled tongue and two kinds of empanadas. Entrées include steaks, chicken, and a choice of fish, but the house specialty is casseroles, hefty meals-in-a-pot with a salad on the side. Try the lamb casserole with celery, rose-mary, lemon, potatoes, and sweet potatoes; or the piquant beef and chorizo *asado* (roasted). Vegetarians will enjoy the rich vegetable, mozzarella, prune, and almond combination, served with polenta. ✉ *Old Rosh Pina restoration site,* ☎ *04/693–6192. Reservations essen-tial Fri. dinner and Sat. lunch. AE, DC, MC, V.*

**$$$** ✕ **Black Steer.** This red-roof steak house is part of a South African chain that has only just arrived in Israel. (True, this seems a strange location for one of a few flagships.) The house specialty is spareribs. Outdoor dining is especially pleasant here, as the garden is leafy and surpris-ingly private; and the location is handy for those on the move. ✉ *Op-posite police station on west side of Rte. 90, at bottom of Rosh Pina,* ☎ *04/693–6250. AE, DC, MC, V.*

**$$$** ✕ **Ja'uni.** Ja'uni is housed in a century-old structure built by Baron Roth-schild, used by the British as a post office and, later, an arms hideout. The menu is seasonal and eclectic, with such options as roast peppers, zucchini in tahini, and a variation on the Spanish tapas. Good service and the separate room for nonsmokers earn extra points. ✉ *30 David Shub St. (next to Beit Ha'am building),* ☎ *04/693–1881. AE, DC, MC, V.*

**$$** ✕ **Indigo.** This easygoing café offers another angle on the changing face of Rosh Pina: youth. With wholesome salads, vegetarian pies, and fon-dues, it's a good place to take a break before or after a walk around Old Rosh Pina, farther up the hill. ✉ *30 Hechalutzim St.,* ☎ *04/693–5333. AE, DC, MC, V. Closed Sat.*

$$$$ ✕🖬 **Auberge Shulamit.** Opened in 1996 by veteran Galilee restaura-
★ teurs, this charming inn takes its name from the original Hotel Shulamit, where the 1948 Armistice Treaty was signed. Among the menu's
delectables—along with home-smoked meats—are chestnut soup (in
season), salmon fillet in Roquefort sauce, and shrimp with wild rice.
The Auberge has four French country–style guest rooms, one with a
whirlpool, for those who really want to indulge for a day or two. ✉
*David Shub St., Box 259, Yesod Hama'ala 12105,* ☎ *04/693–1494,*
*04/693–1495, or 04/693–1485,* 🖹 *04/693–1495. Reservations essen-*
*tial. 4 rooms. Restaurant, minibars. AE, DC, MC, V.*

$$ 🖬 **Village Inn.** These accommodations at Kibbutz Kfar Hanassi give
you a *real* taste of kibbutz life. The one- and two-room units look out
onto a garden, each has a barbecue set, and a few share a kitchenette.
The decor is bright, with boldly colored sheets and cotton dhurrie rugs;
all facilities are spotlessly clean. Meals are in the kibbutz's communal
dining room. Amenities that will appeal to kids include a minizoo, pic-
nic grounds, and a pagoda with a grand view of the Golan and Mt.
Hermon. Several artists live and work at Kfar Hanassi, and you're wel-
come to visit their studios. Guided hikes to the mountainous Jordan
River area northeast of the kibbutz can be arranged. ✉ *Kibbutz Kfar*
*Hanassi, near Mahanayim Airport (10 km, or 6 mi, from Rosh Pina),*
*M.P. Upper Galilee 12305,* ☎ *04/691–4870,* 🖹 *04/691–4077. 28*
*units. Dining room, kitchenettes, pool, massage, miniature golf, 2 ten-*
*nis courts, basketball, travel services. AE, DC, MC, V.* ✑

## Tel Hatzor

⑬ *8 km (5 mi) north of Rosh Pina.*

The large mound of Tel Hatzor, site of the ancient city of Hatzor, is a
good stop for archaeology buffs. Over a period of thousands of years,
the city was built and rebuilt a total of 21 times, allowing latter-day
diggers to slice off layer after layer of differing lifestyles spanning the
ages. Situated on the Via Maris—the most important trade route in
antiquity, since it linked Egypt and Mesopotamia—Hatzor is first re-
ferred to in Mesopotamian documents of the 2nd millennium BC; an
ambassador from Hammurabi's court resided here.

The Book of Joshua (Joshua 11:13) mentions ancient Hatzor as "the
head of all those kingdoms," although Joshua himself destroyed
Canaanite Hatzor in the 13th century BC, and Israelites resettled it. Its
next heyday came three centuries later, when King Solomon decided
it would serve him well as one of his great regional military and ad-
ministrative centers, like Megiddo and Gezer. In 732 BC, Hatzor met
its end when invading Assyrian king Tiglath Pileser III conquered the
Galilee and forced its Israelite inhabitants off the land in chains and
into exile. The city would never regain its former glory.

This site was first identified as the ancient Hatzor in 1928, but the ar-
chaeologist who put it squarely on the modern map, between 1955 and
1959, was the renowned Dr. Yigal Yadin, best known for his excava-
tions at Masada. Excavations and restoration of some antiquities con-
tinue today, with some fascinating results.

The huge site is divided into two areas: the *tel,* or **Upper City,** which
comprised the oldest settlements, and the **Lower City,** first settled in
the 18th century BC. Only the tel, covering less than a fifth of the total
excavation site, is open to the public. The **Hatzor Museum** (on the
grounds of Kibbutz Ayelet Hashachar, across the highway) houses
many of the figurines, weapons, stone pots, and other artifacts unearthed
in the two areas; still others are at the Israel Museum in Jerusalem. ✉

*Tel Hatzor National Park, off Rte. 90, ☎ 04/693–4855. ⊠ NIS 14 ($3.50). ☉ Park and museum Apr.–Sept., Sat.–Thurs. 8–5, Fri. 8–3; Oct.–Mar., Sat.–Thurs. 8–4, Fri. 8–3.*

## Lodging

**$$$$** 🏨 **Ayelet Hashachar Kibbutz Guest House.** The first kibbutz to open a hotel, Ayelet Hashachar stands in a pastoral setting but is run with the efficiency and thoroughness of any urban hotel. The guest quarters, next door to the Tel Hatzor Museum, resemble apartments, with rooms in two-story buildings surrounded by lawn and flower beds. Timber-framed windows add a soft touch. Some facilities are available for people with disabilities. Jeep tours and guided tours of the kibbutz can be arranged; Ayelet Hashachar is one of Israel's biggest honey producers. ⊠ *M.P. Korazim 12200,* ☎ *04/686–8611,* FAX *04/693–4777. 144 rooms. Cafeteria, dining room, pool. MC, V.*

# Hula Nature Reserve

★ ⑭ *8 km (5 mi) north of Tel Hatzor.*

The Hula Nature Reserve contains the last of Israel's wetlands and one of its last vestiges of wilderness. This is no accident: in the first half of the 20th century, British rulers under the Mandate (like the Ottomans before them) repeatedly refused Jewish settlers' requests to drain the swampland in order to limit the growth of Jewish communities in the area, a practice common in other parts of the tiny country as the need for arable land grew. After independence, the Israeli authorities eagerly approved the project almost as soon as they could.

Throughout much of the 1950s, the Hula Valley was drained and dredged again and again, until it was discovered that this was doing grave and irreversible harm to the ecosystem, particularly to the hundreds of thousands of migratory birds that stopped here on their biannual flights between Europe and Africa. This crisis led the International Union for the Conservation of Nature (IUCN) to declare the Hula Valley a reserve of world importance, which it has remained since the early 1970s.

Pelicans, wild geese, storks, cranes, plovers, and a host of exotic birds once again have their sanctuary, but they would not be here were it not also for the swampy waters that abound with carp, catfish, and perch, and a reed habitat boasting rare thickets of papyrus through which you might see a water buffalo or two. Less recognized is the topminnow, an American fish that lives on mosquito eggs and has played a big part in helping rid this region of malaria. The visitor center has complete information about the 800-acre reserve, an observation tower, and a snack bar. Hunting and fishing are strictly forbidden. The main path is wheelchair accessible. ⊠ *East of Rte. 90,* ☎ *04/693–7069.* ⊠ *NIS 18 ($4.50). ☉ Daily 8–4.*

NEED A BREAK? For a rest stop with a bit of history, try **Bet Dubrovin** (⊠ Yesod Hama'ala, ☎ 04/693-7371), near the entrance to the Hula Nature Reserve. This reconstructed farmhouse-cum-museum was once owned by the Dubrovins, immigrant converts from Russia, part of a movement of Christian Russians who converted to Judaism and moved to the Holy Land. Old man Dubrovin brought his family to the swamps of the Hula in 1904, and, despite the hardships, these pioneers set up a model farm on their 173-acre estate, even winning first prize—for cattle in 1922 and for chickpeas in 1927—in the annual agricultural exhibitions in Rosh Pina. The property was eventually donated to the Jewish National Fund and was opened to the public in 1986.

The estate consists of a series of stone buildings built on a square, surrounding a courtyard that holds some old farming equipment and even a few farm animals. An exhibit including an audiovisual presentation in the building where the family lived gives a history of both the family and local area. There is also a ceramics store selling locally made pieces, and a restaurant. The museum entrance fee (NIS 12, or $3) is deducted from the price of a main course at the restaurant and also gets you a 20% discount at the nature reserve, so hang on to your ticket.

### Outdoor Activities and Sports

**Baba Yona's Ranch** (⊠ Yesod Hama'ala Junction, ☎ 04/693–8773), near the Hula Nature Reserve, offers adventure packages that combine kayaking, mountain-biking, and Jeep touring.

# UPPER HULA VALLEY

The sights that hug the border with Lebanon show different sides of Israel. The towns of Kiryat Shmona and Metulla bear eloquent witness to the varying fortunes of Israel's relationships with its Arab neighbors. Tel Dan Nature Reserve, on the other hand, draws visitors with its huge trees, surging river, and wild beauty.

## Kiryat Shmona

*45 km (28 mi) north of Tiberias, 30 km (19 mi) north of Zfat.*

The only urban center in the otherwise agrarian Upper Hula Valley, **Kiryat Shmona** in itself has little to offer travelers aside from burger joints and other fast-food stands in the shopping center on Route 90 and a cable car that journeys between the town and Kibbutz Manara. Like Ma'alot, farther west, Kiryat Shmona made the headlines in 1974 when Arabs infiltrated Israel from Lebanon one night, came down the mountain behind the town, broke into an apartment at dawn, and massacred an entire family. By 1982 the spate of terrorist attacks had reached such proportions that Israel responded by invading Lebanon, the first stage of what would become the war with Lebanon. Kiryat Shmona was again in the news in 1996 when Hezbollah terrorists launched a focused and continued attack on the town and its environs using katyusha rockets. The Israel Defense Forces responded by targeting Hezbollah's bases in southern Lebanon in a campaign that became known as the Grapes of Wrath.

The Kiryat Shmona–Kibbutz Manara **Manara Cable Car** (☎ 04/690–4680; 04/695–9407) runs regularly from 9:30 AM to 6 PM daily (closes 5 PM in winter) and costs NIS 45 ($11.25). There is one station midway on the 1,890-yard trip, where the adventurous can step out and do some rappelling ("snapling" in Hebrew) and dry-sliding (a roller-coaster-like activity). One option is to take the cable car up and mountain bike down. For the brave, there's a 600-ft "zip line"—which is a harnessed, partial free-fall jump down a cable to the ground. If you opt to remain in the cable car, the trip takes eight minutes each way, overlooking cliffs and green hills from a height of some 850 yards. There is wheelchair access to the upper station.

**⑮** Perched on the northern edge of Kiryat Shmona is **Tel Hai,** meaning "hill of life" in Hebrew. In a sense, the hill did become a monument to life after a memorable battle in 1920. In the years immediately following World War I, while Britain and France bickered over who should have final control of the upper Hula valley, bands of Arabs and Bedouins often harassed the tiny Jewish farming settlements. They destroyed one such settlement completely, overran the communal settlement of Tel Hai, and caused the temporary abandonment of the veteran village of Metulla; only Kibbutz Kfar Giladi was successful in defending itself, and it has since gone on to become one of the largest and most prosperous of kibbutzim (☞ Dining and Lodging, *below*).

In the wake of the Tel Hai incident, in which two settlement members were killed, Josef Trumpeldor and seven comrades were called on to defend the place. Trumpeldor had served in the czar's army in his native Russia, and though he had lost an arm fighting, he had already won a reputation as a leader. Fired by Zionist ideals, he moved to Palestine in 1912 at the age of 32 with a group of followers in tow. Soon after, he was fighting with the British against the Turks at the ill-fated battle of Gallipoli. Upon his return to Palestine, he moved to Kibbutz Tel Hai, became its commander, and, like all the other Jewish settlers, was constantly on the alert for Arab infiltrators.

In 1920 the final battle came. Trumpeldor and seven others were killed on the kibbutz grounds, and it is for them that Kiryat Shmona—City of the Eight—is named. It is said that Trumpeldor's last words were "It is good to die for our country." Trumpeldor subsequently became not only a national hero but an inspiration, and he is still referred to with reverence. He is buried not far from here, beneath the stone statue of a roaring lion on the hill behind the museum, once the stockade of Tel Hai. The heroic stand at Tel Hai came to have two important consequences for the area: it was the first modern instance of Jewish armed self-defense, and it did much to change the local image of the Jew as timid and defenseless. Moreover, the survival of at least two of the Jewish settlements this far north determined that when the final borders were drawn by the League of Nations in 1922, these settlements would be included in the British-mandated territory of Palestine and thus, after 1948, in the State of Israel.

The **Tel Hai Courtyard Museum** displays agricultural tools used in Trumpeldor's time. Some of the implements are still put to use (especially during school holidays); you may be able to catch, for example, an old-style pita-making demonstration. A great audiovisual show highlights the history of the place. ✉ *Off Rte. 886,* ☎ *04/695–1333.* 🎟 *NIS 15 ($3.75)* ⏰ *Sun.–Thurs. 8–4, Fri. and holiday eves 8–1, Sat. 10–5 (later in Aug.).*

## Dining and Lodging

In addition to the guest houses here, there is a large (200-bed) **youth hostel** in Tel Hai (✉ Mobile Post, Upper Galilee 12210, ☎ 04/694–0043, 🆅 04/694–1743). For camping or bungalows, head for the **Hurshat Tal National Park** (✉ East of Hagoshrim on Rte. 99, 8 km/5 mi east of Kiryat Shmona, ☎ 04/694–2360, 🆅 04/695–9360), opposite Kibbutz Dafna, but remember that it gets pretty cold here at night once summer is over.

**$$$** ✕ **Dag al Hadan.** Fresh trout and a cool glass of wine in a shady woodlet by the gurgling Dan River—it's as good as it sounds, except on crowded weekends. This was the first restaurant in the region to specialize in the fish the Dan yields in abundance; you can see the trout ponds in a small installation on the grounds. The same management also runs a café next door where light vegetarian meals are served. The restaurant is tucked away behind the main road, but it's large and well signposted. ✉ *Off Rte. 99 near Kiryat Shmona, opposite Kibbutz Hagoshrim,* ☎ *04/695–0225. Reservations essential weekends. AE, DC, MC, V.*

**$$$** ✕🎟 **Jordan Pagoda.** This is an unlikely place for a Chinese-Thai restaurant, perhaps, but somehow sitting in the timber pagoda (imported from Thailand, according to the owners) and eating Southeast Asian delights on the banks of the Jordan River works. The restaurant is part of the Jordan Sources complex (☞ Kayaking *below*), which has 10 very reasonably priced wooden cabins. The complex is on the grounds of Kibbutz Sde Nechemia. ⊠ *Kibbutz Sde Nechemia (8 km, or 5 mi, from Kiryat Shmona), Rte. 918,* ☎ *04/694–7447. AE, DC, MC, V.*

$$$  🏨 **Hagoshrim Kibbutz Hotel.** The waters of the Hermon River flow right through Haoshrim, creating a uniquely natural setting that the residents have wisely exploited in their "pub in nature" (open May to October). While the rooms are simply appointed, the lobby provides very pleasant surroundings decorated with blond wood furniture and colorful cushions and throw rugs. Light meals are served there by a friendly staff. Gosh, the hotel's country-style restaurant, specializes in fish and cheeses. Hagoshrim had an impact on women the world over when it invented the Epilady, a revolutionary depilatory appliance that has won the kibbutz kudos for technological initiative. Kayaking and guided walking tours are available. ⊠ *Rte. 99, east of Kiryat Shmona, Upper Galilee 12225,* ☎ *04/681–0000,* ℻ *04/681–6002. 180 rooms. Restaurant, cafeteria, pub, pool, tennis court, bicycles. AE, DC, MC, V.* 🍴

$$$  🏨 **Kfar Blum Guest House.** Tucked in the northern Hula Valley, Kfar
★    Blum enjoys a reputation for attentive service that surpasses many of its rivals'. The home-style hospitality is enhanced by the garden setting, and period photographs in the rooms depict kibbutz life as it's meant to be. The spacious rooms in their new wing are far above the usual kibbutz hotel standard. Most members of Kfar Blum hail from English-speaking countries, so there are no language barriers here. One of the kibbutz's major attractions is its collection of kayaks—what better way to experience the Jordan River? Kfar Blum hosts an annual chamber-music festival in summer (☞ The Arts, *below*). ⊠ *North of Rte. 977, near Kiryat Shmona, Upper Galilee 12150,* ☎ *04/683–6611,* ℻ *04/683–6600. 133 rooms. Restaurant, bar, pool, sauna, tennis courts, boating, travel services. AE, DC, MC, V.* 🍴

$$$  🏨 **Kibbutz Hotel Kfar Giladi.** Atop a hill behind Tel Hai overlooking the Hula Valley, this is one of the oldest and largest kibbutz hotels in Israel. It's run very efficiently, but it still retains a homey atmosphere. Typical to kibbutz hotels, the rooms are on the plain side, but some have lovely views of the Huleh Valley and Mount Hermon. The gift shop has some unique handcrafted items, many made by senior members of the kibbutz. The lovely woods nearby make for great walks, and the kibbutz grounds contain the Bet Hashomer Museum, which explores the pre-State history of the kibbutz and the vicinity. Kfar Giladi produces sunglasses, which you can buy in the hotel. ⊠ *Rte. 886, Upper Galilee 12210,* ☎ *04/690–0000,* ℻ *04/690–0069. 180 rooms. Snack bar, pool, sauna, tennis court, health club. AE, DC, MC, V.*

## The Arts

For the classically minded, Kibbutz Kfar Blum (⊠ Upper Galilee 12150, ☎ 04/683–6611) hosts **Chamber Music Days** each year in late July and early August, a nationally renowned festival of chamber music in a pastoral setting.

## Outdoor Activities and Sports

A plethora of outfits organize water-sport trips in this region, and almost all hotels can make reservations for you. The minimum age for kayaks and other water "vehicles" is usually six.

### KAYAKING

**Hagoshrim Kayaks** (☎ 04/681–6034; ☞ Dining and Lodging, *above*) has a 5-km (3-mi) "family" course that lasts 1½ hours and a 6-km (4-mi) "stormy" course that expands on the family course to last almost two hours. The family course costs NIS 50 ($12.50) per person, the stormy course NIS 60 ($15) per person.

**Kibbutz Kfar Blum** (☎ 04/694–8755; ☞ Dining and Lodging, *above*) rents two-person rubber kayaks for 1½-hour or 2-hour runs. The cost is NIS 52 ($13) per person for the short course, NIS 84 ($21) per person for the long course. Kayaks are available from March through October; call ahead to inquire at other times of the year.

**Jordan Sources** runs a 3½-hour kayaking trip (this one can be rough) costing NIS 75 ($18.75) per person and a 1½-hour trip for NIS 50 ($12.50) per person (✉ On the grounds of Kibbutz Sde Nechemia, ☎ 04/694–7447).

TUBING

**Sde Nechemia** (✉ Kibbutz Huliot, ☎ 04/694–6010), near Kiryat Shmona along Route 99, rents inner tubes at NIS 40 ($11.40) for an hour or so.

# Metulla

 *7 km (4 mi) north of Kiryat Shmona.*

Israel's northernmost town, Metulla, is so picturesque that it's hard to believe this tranquil spot is just a stone's throw from a foe, Lebanon. And the story of cooperation between the Israelis and the Lebanese at the so-called Good Fence here has drawn visitors from all over the world.

**Metulla** was founded as a farming settlement in 1896 with the aid of Baron Edmond de Rothschild, and in the century since then its residents have shown such tenacity and determination that it has not only survived but thrived. Essentially, it has one thoroughfare, Harishonim Street (though this can hardly be called a main street), where hotels and restaurants are clustered. Somehow the tensions of the Middle East dissipate here, at least briefly; one- and two-story limestone buildings in European-styles line the street, and the Continental atmosphere is enhanced by the numerous signs offering ZIMMER (German for "room") for rent. Even the weather is decidedly un-Mediterranean, with refreshingly cool mountain breezes in summer and snow in winter. Yet the cypresses and cedars provide a whiff of Lebanon.

The **Good Fence** is just a three-minute drive from the town center. This segment of the Israel-Lebanon border has enjoyed its nickname since June 1976, when Israel first sent medical and other aid to residents of southern Lebanon. In one version of the story, Israeli soldiers noticed a Lebanese woman in labor at the border crossing. They rushed her to an Israeli hospital, where she delivered a healthy baby, and within days there were several very pregnant women waiting at the Good Fence. Over the years peaceful interaction blossomed here: first Lebanese citizens with relatives in Israel were allowed to come over to visit, then summer camps were organized for Lebanese schoolchildren and their Israeli counterparts, and eventually, hundreds of southern-Lebanese workers commuted across the border to jobs in the Galilee.

In June 2000 a new chapter of the story (certainly not the last) was written, when the Good Fence was closed in the wake of the pullback of Israeli troops from southern Lebanon. But the souvenir and cold-drink kiosks still mark the spot where thousands have come over the years to take a peek at the border and ponder the complexities of life in the region. In times of political unrest, it's best to check with travel advisories or the local authorities before visiting the border (☞ Safety *in* Smart Travel Tips A to Z).

NEED A
BREAK?
Take a picnic down to the streams and waterfalls that flow year-round in the lush **Nahal Ayoun Nature Reserve,** just south of Metulla next to Route 90.

## Outdoor Activities and Sports

The multistory, multipurpose **Canada Centre** (☎ 04/695–0370), at the top of the hill, has just about everything a sports complex can offer. For the price of admission—NIS 50 ($12.50)—you can spend the whole day here, playing basketball, ice-skating, working out, bowling, swimming, zooming down the water slide, or taking aim on the shooting range. If it gets to be too much, just repair to the sauna or hot tub. The complex is open daily 10–10 and contains a restaurant in case you're afraid you burned too many calories.

The ice-skating rink is one of only two in the Middle East; the other is in Saudi Arabia. But what the Saudis cannot boast are world-class former Soviet skaters, several of whom now live in Metulla and teach the sport at the center. If you're lucky, you might catch a demonstration of their dazzling skills.

# Tel Dan Nature Reserve

★ ⑰ *25 km (15½ mi) southeast of Metulla, 15 km (9 mi) northeast of Kiryat Shmona.*

Tel Dan is hard to beat for sheer natural beauty. A river surges through it, and large, luxuriant trees, including majestic Mt. Tabor oaks, provide shade over wide paths. A host of small mammals live here, many partial to water, such as the otter and the mongoose, while the ubiquitous coney "makes its home in the rocks" as the Bible says. This is also the home of Israel's largest rodent, the nocturnal Indian crested porcupine, and its smallest predator, the marbled polecat, recognizable by its bushy tail, which accounts for about half the creature's 1-ft length. There are wildcats in these parts, too, though you'll rarely see them by day. The reserve has several hiking trails.

A majestic city occupied this land in biblical times; Dan was an urban center second only to Hatzor in importance in northern Palestine. According to Genesis, when Abraham "heard that his brother had been taken captive [by the four kings of the north] he armed his trained servants, born in his own house, three hundred and eighteen, and pursued them up to Dan." Five centuries later, when Canaan extended from Dan (then called Laish), in the north, to Beersheva, in the south, Joshua led the Israelites through the area to victory.

Fine ruins from several epochs lie here. The Canaanite city of Laish existed here 5,000 years ago; its name was changed when the Israelite tribe of Dan captured the tel, sometime in the period of Judges, and it became the northernmost point of the kingdom of Israel. When the kingdom was divvied up, the secessionist King Jeroboam I built a religious center here (and another at Bethel) and erected a cultic golden calf. Among the finds archaeologists have turned up are the city gate and a 9th-century BC paved plaza that was probably the town center. Just inside the city gate the platform for a throne was discovered, together with a long stone bench. This was the likely place where the king of the city pronounced judgment, aided by his town council sitting on the stone bench. One of the site's most extraordinary finds was the arched gateway dating from the 18th century BC, more than a millennium before the time in which scholars had previously thought the arch was invented.

Tel Dan is particularly noteworthy among nature reserves for its wheelchair accessibility: a special raised bridge built for this purpose traverses a small section of the reserve. It also has a pleasant cafeteria-style restaurant, Dan-Eden (☎ 04/695–3826), operated by Kibbutz Dan and serving up delectable fresh trout. ⊠ *North of Rte. 99,* ☎ *04/695–1579.* 🎟 *NIS 15 ($3.75).* ☉ *Daily 8–4.*

## Kibbutz Dan

*1 km (½ mi) from Tel Dan Nature Reserve.*

Adjacent to the Tel Dan Nature Reserve, this kibbutz has an attraction that can really enhance a trip to this area. The **Bet Ussishkin Museum** was founded in 1955 by the Jewish National Fund and is now operated jointly by Kibbutz Dan and the Society for the Protection of Nature in Israel (SPNI). Children will appreciate the displays here, which document the wildlife and natural phenomena found around the Hula Valley, the Golan Heights, and the Jordan River. The audiovisual presentations are concise and informative. ⊠ *Off Rte. 99,* ☎ *04/694–1704.* 🎟 *NIS 13 ($3.25).* ☉ *Sun.–Thurs. 8–4:30, Fri. and holiday eves 8–3:30, Sat. 9:30–4:30.*

# GOLAN HEIGHTS

Geologically distinct from the limestone massif of Mt. Hermon, to its north, the basalt slopes of the Golan Heights extend about 60 km (37 mi) from north to south and between 15 km and 25 km (between 9 mi and 15½ mi) across. The whole region was volcanic in the not-so-distant past, and many symmetrical volcanic cones and pronounced reliefs still dominate the landscape, particularly in the upper Golan. Where the dark basalt rock has weathered or been cleared, the mineral-rich soil supports a wide variety of crops. The Golan's gentle terrain and climate have generally attracted far more settlement than the less hospitable northern Upper Galilee. In spring the region, already greened by winter rains, comes alive with wildflowers; but when the summer heat has frizzled everything to a uniform yellow-brown, it seems a land of desolation. Sights here range from nature reserves, in the north, to a winery and archaeological sites near Katzrin, in the south.

## Hermon River (Banias) Nature Reserve

★ ⑱ *20 km (12½ mi) east of Kiryat Shmona.*

One of the most stunning corners of Israel, this reserve contains gushing waterfalls, dense foliage along riverbanks, and remains of a temple dedicated to the god Pan. There are two entrances, each with a parking lot: the first is indicated on a sign as "Banias Waterfall"; the other is 1 km (½ mi) farther along the same road and marked "Banias." A circular walking trail connects the two. It's an easy walk, but if time is short (the trail takes about two hours), you may prefer to take a brief walk to the falls, return to your car, then drive on to the second entrance to see the caves and the spring where the Hermon River originates. The cost of admission covers entry to both sites.

At the lookout near the **Banias Waterfall,** maps point out the principal mountains and other features on the horizon. The approach to the waterfall, marked by a signpost, is enhanced by huge carob trees, maidenhair ferns, brier ivy, laurel (bay leaf) bushes, and other shrubs. Swimming at the waterfall is prohibited, but don't be surprised to see groups of Israelis splashing around and scrambling to photograph each other against it. There's a tremendous reverence for these unusual 33 ft of cascading water, and people come from all over the country to see them, especially in the rainless summer months.

Backtrack to the signpost and head in the other direction, passing walnut trees, willows, and lemon and fig trees as you head for the riverside walk to the spring and caves. Along the way, the trail passes two abandoned flour mills, and at times you'll be walking on aqueducts that once brought water to these mills. About 1 km (½ mi) from the waterfall, a sign points to **breichat haketzinim** (Officers' Pool), a pool built around the spring by Syrians for the use of their officers (swimming is now prohibited).

The remainder of the trail (about 600 ft) follows and crosses the river before reaching the spring. Note the pungent aroma of mint. There are blackberry bushes here, too, their fruit particularly sweet at the end of summer.

**Banias Spring** emanates at the foot of mostly limestone Mt. Hermon, just where it meets the basalt layers of the Golan Heights. When it rains, or as the snow on the mountain melts, water seeps through the Hermon's crannies and gushes forth at the foot of what is called Pan's Cave.

The name *Banias* is an Arabic corruption of the Greek *Panias*, the original name given to what became a cult center dedicated to the colorful Greek god Pan. (Arabic has no *p* sound, hence the modification.) Pan (son of Hermes), the god of herdsmen, music, and wild nature, and patron of homosexuals and nymphs, was too hedonistic even for the ancient Greeks. In their attempts to keep him at some distance, they eventually built the half man–half goat a temple in this succulent corner of the world.

Take the path that crosses the spring and proceed toward **Banias Cave,** easily identified by the sturdy fig tree at its entrance. Note the five niches hewed out of the rock to the right of the cave; these are what remain of the Hellenistic temple and probably once held statues. Three of the niches bear inscriptions in Greek mentioning Pan, the lover of tunes; Echo, the mountain nymph; and Galerius, one of Pan's priests. Archaeologists are only in the early stages of excavation, but they have already turned up what they believe are the remains of a second temple as well. All early references to the cave identify it as the source of the spring, but earthquakes over the years have changed its formations, forcing the water to emerge at the foot of the cave rather than from within it. (For those in a hiking mood, a long, very steep trail leads from here through the oak and thorny broom forest up to Nimrod's Fortress [☞ *below*], a 40- to 60-minute climb.)

The path continues up to the whitewashed **tomb of Nebi Khader** (nickname in Arabic for the prophet Elijah), built on a ledge of the cliff. The tomb is closed, but from here you have a terrific view of the Hula Valley and the Hermon River. A little farther along are the remains of an ancient wall with a ceramic inlay that archaeologists believe was part of the white marble temple that Herod built as a tribute to Caesar Augustus, who had given him the Hula Valley and Panias in 26 BC.

Herod's son Philip inherited this part of his father's kingdom, and when he made Panias his capital, he changed its name to Caesarea Philippi, to distinguish it from the Caesarea his father had founded on the Mediterranean coast. It was in Caesarea Philippi that Jesus changed Peter's name from Simon and gave him "the keys to the kingdom of heaven" after Peter declared him the Messiah for the first time: "Jesus came here and asked his disciples, 'Who do you say that I am?' and

Peter replied, 'You are Christ, the son of the living God,' to which Jesus responded, 'Blessed are you, Simon, son of Jonah. And I tell you, you are Peter [*petros* means "rock" in Greek], and on this rock I will build my church and the powers of death shall not prevail against it'" (Matthew 16:13–20). Some scholars think Christ may have deliberately selected the heartland of paganism for this great declaration of faith. The small Greek Orthodox church nearby (now closed) was built to commemorate the site.

Though Roman rule in this part of the kingdom would not last another generation past Philip, Panias continued to flourish for more than 1,000 years—and its original name, with only slight modification, has endured.

In the early 12th century, Banias was held by Crusaders, and just outside the second entrance to the reserve (marked BANIAS) are the ruins of what is thought to have been the marketplace of the day: a string of single "rooms" along a well-preserved section of wall might well have been shops. The marketplace sits atop a magnificent palace complex dating back to the reign of Herod's grandson Agrippa II. The remains of this luxurious, 1,613-square-ft facility with its marble floors, mosaics, and a series of subterranean (*under*-underground, if you will) passages can be seen from the road. Access is from within the second entrance, a half hour's walk through a particularly lush section of the reserve. ⊠ *Off Rte. 99,* ☎ *04/695–0272.* ⊡ *NIS 15 ($3.75).* ☉ *Daily 8–4.*

NEED A
BREAK?

A few minutes' walk beyond the Officers' Pool is a little **stall,** where you can buy Druze-style pita (bigger and flatter than the commercial version) not only baked on the premises but also milled here. The ancient flour mill is still powered by water from an aqueduct as it was in days of yore. In fact, until only a few years ago this was where local Druze villagers milled their flour. Now the mill and "bakery" service hungry hikers. Pull up a rock, and for a few shekels you'll be served a large rolled-up pita with *labane* (white goat's cheese) and Turkish coffee.

OFF THE
BEATEN PATH

**TEL FAHER –** The large number of monuments to fallen soldiers in the Golan is a reminder of the region's strategic importance—and the price paid to attain it. Among the easily accessible sites, where old Syrian bunkers give a gunner's-eye view of the valley below, is Tel Faher, in the northern Golan (⊠ Off Rte. 99; turn right just above Banias). At Tel Faher—also known as Mitzpe Golani, for the elite Golani Brigade soldiers who died here in 1967—children can climb onto the tank that now sits passively. *Caution: These sites are safe, but beyond the fences and clearly marked paths are old Syrian minefields that have not been completely detonated.*

# Nimrod's Fortress

★ ⑲ *5 km (3 mi) east of Hermon River (Banias) Nature Reserve.*

The history of Nimrod's Fortress (Kal'at Namrud), the huge, burly limestone fortress perched above Banias, is still vociferously debated. It was built around 1100, but by whom? Muslims? Crusaders? Academic controversy aside, a visit to the fortress is a real treat. Overgrown with scruffy shrubbery, it blends in with the stony mountain terrain and commands superb vistas, especially through the frames of its arched windows or the narrow archers' slits in its walls.

What *is* known about the fortress is that it guarded the vital route from Damascus via the Golan and Banias to Lebanon and to the Mediterranean coast. Although Muslim legend says it was first built by Arabs, it is widely believed to have been a Crusader structure later modified by the Arabs. In any event, it changed hands between Muslims and Christians in the centuries to follow as both vied for control of the region. During one of its more curious periods, from 1126 to 1129, Nimrod's Fortress was occupied by a fanatical sect of Muslims famous as murderers. Before heading out to track down their enemies, the cutthroats would indulge in huge quantities of hashish, thus earning the nickname *hashashin* (hashish users), from which the word *assassin* is derived. Nimrod functioned as a prison during the Mamluk period and was abandoned in the 16th century. Between 1948 and 1967 Syria used it to observe Israeli troop movements.

You enter the fortress through a breach in its western wall. There are several large vaulted cisterns here, which were particularly crucial during a siege: they could store enough water for 500 people for three years. Follow the path through the citadel ruins to the donjon (keep), the fortress's central tower. You may notice that it faces east—the Crusaders expected attacks from this direction. It's possible to climb the donjon, 100 ft above the surrounding castle; this is where the feudal lord would have lived. It forms a kind of fortress within a fortress; the outer wall on the east and south sides is well protected by protruding towers, also equipped with slits. ⊠ *Nimrod's Fortress National Park, Rte. 989 (off Rte. 99)*, ☎ *050/813–227.* ⊡ *NIS 13 ($3.25).* ☉ *Daily 8–4.*

## Mt. Hermon

**⑳**  *12 km (7½ mi) northeast of Nimrod's Fortress, 25 km (15½ mi) northeast of Kiryat Shmona.*

The summit of Mt. Hermon—famous as Israel's highest mountain, at 9,232 ft above sea level—is actually in Syrian territory. Its lower slopes attract Israelis to the country's only ski resort, but the fun is significantly chilled by the high prices (☞ Skiing, *below*). In fact, summer is arguably the most interesting time on the Hermon: after the winter snows melt, hikers can discover chasms and hidden valleys here, the long-term result of extremes in temperature. Moreover, a powerful array of colors and scents emerges from the earth as cockscomb, chamomile, and scores of other flowers and wild herbs are drawn out by the summer sun. Approaching from Nimrod's Fortress, you'll pass the Jewish township of **Neve Ativ,** designed to look like a little piece of the Alps in the Middle East, replete with A-frame chalet-style houses, a handful of which have guest rooms. (The residents of Neve Ativ operate the ski slopes.) You'll also go by the old Druze village of **Majdal Shams,** with a number of good eateries.

### Skiing

Don't compare the slopes of **Mt. Hermon** (☎ 04/698–1337) with those in Europe or the Americas. For Israelis, there is a certain thrill to having a ski resort in a hot Mediterranean country—and it's a bargain compared with flying to the Alps (figure about NIS 288, or $72, per day for admission to the site, lift tickets, and equipment rental). Frankly, though, Mt. Hermon has little to offer the serious, or even the novice, skier. The chairlifts and cafeterias run year-round, the better to enjoy the place in summer, when it's bursting with wildflowers. To get to Mt. Hermon take Rte. 99 east to Rte. 989 north to the village of Neve Ativ.

*En Route*  **Ein Kuniya,** which appears across a valley on your left as you head east into the Golan on Route 99, is the most picturesque of the several Druze villages here. The houses are built of the black basalt so prevalent in the Golan.

# Merom Golan

*20 km (12½ mi) south of Mt. Hermon.*

Kibbutz Merom Golan was the first settlement built in the Golan after the Six-Day War. Its fields and orchards are typical of local kibbutzim. Apples are especially good in these parts, but man cannot live by apples alone, so Merom Golan runs Cowboys' Restaurant (☞ *below*), with good, reasonably priced steaks.

### Dining

**$$** ✕ **Cowboys' Restaurant.** Here's the best corral this side of the Israel-Syria Disengagement Zone. Saddle-shape stools at the bar and cattle hides on the walls contribute to the frontier atmosphere. But it's the grub—specifically the hearty steaks and other meat—that packs 'em in. ⊠ *Kibbutz Merom Golan, off Rte. 959,* ☏ *04/696–0206. AE, DC, MC, V.*

## Mt. Bental Observatory

*3 km (2 mi) north of the Avital junction with Rte. 91; 18 km (11 mi) northeast of Katzrin.*

From the top of this volcanic cone, once a miliary outpost, Mount Hermon rises majestically to the north and the Syrian side of the Golan stretches eastward like it's on the palm of your hand. Opposite is the ruined town of Kuneitra, captured by Israel in 1967, lost and regained in the 1973 Yom Kippur War, and returned to Syria in the subsequent Disengagement Agreement. It is now a demilitarized zone; modern Kuneitra is in the distance. The cluster of white buildings south of old Kuneitra houses the United Nations Disengagement Observer Force. The pine-cabin shop that serves delicious herb teas is the perfect place to get out of the wind that often sweeps this peak. ⊠ *Off Rte. 9981 near Kibbutz Merom Golan, north of the Avital junction with Rte. 91.*

## Katzrin

**㉑** *20 km (12½ mi) south of Merom Golan, 38 km (23½ mi) northeast of Tiberias, 35 km (22 mi) northeast of Zfat.*

The "capital" of the Golan Heights, Katzrin (Qazrin), one of the most appealing residential areas in the north, was founded in 1977 on the site of a 2nd-century town of the same name. To get here from the northern Golan, take Route 91 west, and then go south on Route 87.

Katzrin has a suburban feel, despite its strategic location and attendant sensitivity. It's not unusual to see bomb shelters decorated and converted into recreation centers or into Hebrew classrooms for Russian immigrants. The water here comes straight from the basalt bedrock. It's delicious to drink and makes your skin feel like silk.

Commercial Katzrin has general services—a café (open during the day), a pizzeria (open at night), gift stores, a minimart, and a library. At the **Doll Museum,** some 1,000 handmade dolls serve as the narrators of Jewish history from biblical times until the signing of the Israeli-Jordanian peace treaty. ⊠ *Katzrin,* ☏ *04/696–2982.* ☑ *NIS 14 ($3.50).* ☉ *Sun.–Thurs. 9–5, Fri. 9–2.*

The **Golan Archaeological Museum** has a fascinating collection of animal bones, stones, and artifacts that put the region into historical and geographical perspective. Among the exhibits is a Copper Age dwelling reconstructed from materials excavated nearby. Don't miss the excellent film on the history and last stand of Gamla, the "Masada of the North" (☞ Gamla Nature Reserve, *below*), during the Great Revolt against the Romans (AD 66) and its rediscovery by archaeologists exactly 1,900 years later. The museum is run in conjunction with the Ancient Katzrin Park (☞ *below*). ✉ *Katzrin commercial center,* ☏ *04/696–9637.* ⊡ *NIS 27 ($6.75), including Ancient Katzrin Park (☞ below).* ⊙ *Sun.–Thurs. 8–5, Fri. and holiday eves 8–3, Sat. 10–4.*

㉒ **Ancient Katzrin Park,** 2 km (1 mi) east of Katzrin's business center, is a partially restored Jewish village, dating from the 3rd century, whose economy was based on the production of olive oil. The Katzrin synagogue, a contemporary of those at Bar'am and Capernaum, has decorative architectural details, such as a mosaic pavement and a wreath of pomegranates and amphorae in relief on the lintel above the entrance. The complexity of its ornamentation reflects the importance of the city. Built of basalt, the synagogue was used for 400 years until it was partly destroyed, possibly by an earthquake, in 749.

Since 1967, when the excavations at Katzrin began, 10% of the ancient Jewish village has been uncovered. The park's two reconstructed buildings, the so-called House of Uzi and House of Rabbi Abun (presumably a Talmudic sage), are attractively decorated with rope baskets, weavings, baking vessels, and pottery (based on remnants of the originals) and lighted with little clay oil lamps. ✉ *Rte. 87,* ☏ *04/696–2412.* ⊡ *NIS 27 ($6.75), including Golan Archaeological Museum (☞ above).* ⊙ *Sun.–Thurs. 8–5, Fri. and holiday eves 8–3, Sat. 10–4.*

㉓ The **Golan Heights Winery,** in Katzrin's industrial zone, is one of Israel's top businesses; it launched the country into the international winemaking arena with its Yarden and Gamla labels. (A third label is called, predictably, Golan.) The area's volcanic soil, cold winters and cool summers, and state-of-the-art vinifying techniques have proven a recipe for success. Wine-tasting tours are generally available if reserved in advance. The shop sells the full line of wines, including the Katzrin chardonnay, the Yarden Gewürztraminer, and the Gamla Muscat Canelli, as well as sophisticated accessories for the oenophile. The winery can also give you the business cards of its distributors around the world. ✉ *Rte. 87 (east of town center),* ☏ *04/696–2001, 04/696–8409 for tours.* ⊡ *Tour and tasting NIS 17 ($4.25).* ⊙ *Sun.–Thurs. 9–5, Fri. 9–1:30.* ✍

### Nightlife

Within Katzrin Park, there's a **pub** (☏ 04/696–2521) in a century-old Syrian dwelling. The sheer experience of having a drink among the ancient ruins is worth a detour if you're lodging in this area.

OFF THE BEATEN PATH

**MITZPE GADOT –** If you continue northwest on Route 87 from Katzrin and then west on Route 91, you'll pass this tall, triangular concrete monument to fallen Israeli soldiers. **Caution: The site is safe, but don't explore beyond any marked paths, because there may be undetonated Syrian minefields.**

## Gamla Nature Reserve

*20 km (12 mi) southeast of Katzrin; take Rte. 87 to Rte. 808 and watch for Gamla signpost.*

Aside from its fascinating history of determination and struggle, the "Masada of the North" is truly inspiring in its beauty. Gamla's rugged, hilly terrain is softened in late winter and spring by greenery and wildflowers. You'll probably spot magnificent griffon vultures soaring above you; their nests are clearly visible from the Vultures' Lookout. Keep your eyes peeled for gazelles, porcupines, and foxes, too.

Digs have turned up a fortified town dating from the early Bronze Age, but the main story of the camel-shape Gamla (the name *Gamla* comes from *gamal,* the Hebrew word for "camel") goes back 2,000 years, when Herod encouraged Jews to settle here in order to populate the frontiers of his kingdom. By AD 66, Gamla had joined the Great Revolt against Rome. Herod's great-grandson Agrippa II sided with the Romans and challenged the zealous rebels. When he failed to overpower them, Rome dispatched the general Vespasian with three legions in tow. In AD 67, the Romans launched a bloody attack here that ended seven months later, when the 9,000 surviving Jews flung themselves to their deaths in the abyss below the town.

Flavius Josephus told the story of Gamla in *The Jewish War,* and his vivid descriptions are engraved in stones along the trails throughout the site. "Sloping down from a towering peak is a spur like a long shaggy neck, behind which rides a symmetrical hump, so that the outline resembles that of a camel . . . On the face of both sides it is cut off by impassable ravines. Near the tail it is rather more accessible where it is detached from the hill . . . Built against the almost vertical flank, the town seemed to be hung in the air . . ." This dramatic impression is precisely the first one you have as you approach Gamla from the entrance to the reserve.

It was this steep terrain that almost caused Vespasian's three legions of Roman soldiers to fail in their siege. No sooner had the Romans succeeded in reaching the town than the defenders swung around and counterattacked; the Romans were, Josephus wrote, "swept down the slope and trapped in the narrow alleys." Rallied by Vespasian, the Romans were able to drive the last defenders to the summit. Seeing no escape, the survivors opted for mass suicide.

The town subsequently fell into ruin and oblivion, but because it was never rebuilt, Gamla is the only example of a Roman battlefield whose relics match the vivid stories from the past; among the finds are 2,000 "missile stones" and arrowheads. From a much earlier period (probably the 2nd millennium BC) there are about 200 **dolmens** scattered in the area—strange basalt structures shaped like the Greek letter pi, probably used for burial. The site has three walking trails. A shuttle bus (☎ 053/290–842) also reaches the ruins; call to check on availability. There is an excellent film on the story of Gamla at the Golan Archaeological Museum in Katzrin (☞ *above*). ⊠ *Off Rte. 808,* ☎ *04/682–2282.* 🎟 *NIS 18 ($4.50).* ⊙ *Daily 8–4.*

# UPPER GALILEE AND THE GOLAN A TO Z

## Arriving and Departing

### By Bus
**Egged** buses (☎ 03/694–8888) run daily from Tel Aviv to Kiryat Shmona (Bus 842) and to Zfat (Bus 846); from Jerusalem to Kiryat Shmona (Bus 963) and to Zfat (Bus 964); from Haifa to Kiryat Shmona (Bus 500) and to Zfat (Bus 361); and from Tiberias to Kiryat Shmona (Buses 841 and 963) and to Zfat (Bus 459).

### By Car
The Upper Galilee and the Golan are a three-hour, 180-km (112-mi) drive from Tel Aviv; a 1½-hour, 60-km (37-mi) drive from both Akko and Nahariya; and four hours from Jerusalem, which is 200 km (124 mi) to the south. There are numerous routes to approach the area. From

Tiberias and the Sea of Galilee, Route 90 runs north between the Hula Valley, on the east, and the hills of Naftali, on the west. The more rugged Route 98 runs from the eastern side of the Sea of Galilee up through the Golan Heights to Mt. Hermon. Near the top of Route 98 you can pick up Route 91, which heads west into the Upper Galilee.

From the Mediterranean coast there are several options, but the main one is Route 85 from Akko. Route 89 runs parallel to Route 85 a little farther north, from Nahariya, and has some gorgeous scenery. From Haifa take Route 75 to Route 77, turning onto Route 90 at Tiberias, or Route 70 north onto Route 85 east. If you're starting from Tel Aviv, drive north on Route 4 or 2 to Hadera; from there you'll head northwest on Route 65, exiting onto Route 85 east.

### By Plane
**Arkia Israeli Airlines** (☎ 800/444–888) and **IsraAir** (☎ 03/795–5777) operate several daily flights from Sde Dov Airport in Tel Aviv to the small Galilee airport of **Mahanayim**, part of the township of Rosh Pina. From the airport it is 10 km (6 mi) to Zfat and 30 km (19 mi) to Kiryat Shmona. Arkia also flies from Jerusalem several times a week.

## Getting Around

### By Bus
Local buses stop at all major sights in this region (there is always a kibbutz, a town, or some other small residential settlement nearby), but you should avoid buses if you're on a tight schedule, as they tend to be infrequent. Call **Egged** (☎ 03/694–8888) for schedules. If you have trouble getting through to Egged, you can try the **local depots**: Kiryat Shmona (☎ 04/681–8222), Tiberias (☎ 04/672–9222), and Zfat (☎ 04/692–1122).

### By Car
The state of Israel's roads is generally fair-to-good, but in the Upper Galilee in particular, don't expect wide, even highways. Sometimes the roads are paved, and sometimes, well, they just aren't. This is especially true in the Golan. Drive cautiously! Try to avoid driving during peak hours (usually late Saturday afternoons), when city folk crowd the roads back to Jerusalem and Tel Aviv after a day out in the country.

The main north–south roads in the region are Route 90, which goes all the way up to Metulla at the Lebanese border; the Tiberias–Metulla Road; and the less-traveled Route 98, which runs from the eastern side of the Sea of Galilee through the Golan Heights (along the Disengagement Zone) to Mt. Hermon. The main west–east highways are Route 85, which runs from Akko to Ami'ad, and Route 89, which connects Nahariya and Zfat.

Gas stations are numerous along Route 90 and in the towns, such as Katzrin (Route 87) and Zfat (Route 89). Most are open daily but close by 9 PM, so it's best to fill up during the day.

## Contacts and Resources

### Car Rental
It's much easier to rent a car in Tiberias (☞ Lower Galilee A to Z *in* Chapter 5), Tel Aviv, Jerusalem, or Haifa than to search for a dependable rental agency in the tiny towns of the Upper Galilee. For those flying to the Galilee (☞ Arriving and Departing, *above*), **Arkia Israeli**

**Airlines** (☎ 800/444–888 in Tel Aviv) can arrange for a rental car to be waiting at Mahanayim Airport, outside Rosh Pina.

## Emergencies

**Police** (☎ 100). **Ambulance** (☎ 101). **Fire** (☎ 102). Emergency calls from public phones do not require tokens or telecards.

The main **police station** in the Upper Galilee is in Kiryat Shmona (✉ 1 Salinger St., ☎ 04/694–3444 or 04/694–3445).

The **Magen David Adom** station in Kiryat Shmona (✉ 3 Tchernichovsky St., ☎ 04/694–4334 or 04/694–4335), near the central bus station, handles medical and dental emergencies 24 hours a day.

## Guided Tours

GENERAL INTEREST

Both of Israel's major bus companies, **Egged Tlalim** (✉ 59 Ben Yehuda St., Tel Aviv, ☎ 03/527–1212; ✉ 8 Shlomzion Hamalka St., Jerusalem, ☎ 02/622–1999) and **United Tours** (✉ 113 Hayarkon St., Tel Aviv, ☎ 03/522–2008 or 03/693–3412; ✉ King David Hotel Annex, Jerusalem, ☎ 02/625–2187), offer one- and two-day guided tours of this region, departing from Tel Aviv and Jerusalem.

SPECIAL INTEREST

The **Society for the Protection of Nature in Israel** (SPNI; ✉ 4 Hashfela St., Tel Aviv 66183, ☎ 03/638–8666) sponsors excellent hikes and walking tours in this area. The tours are usually aimed at all ages, so Olympic-level fitness is not required; hikes that require serious physical exertion are clearly described as such.

## Hospital

The largest hospital in the north outside Haifa is the **Rivka Sieff General Hospital**, in Zfat (✉ Harambam Rd., ☎ 04/682–8811). Buses 6 and 7 from the Zfat bus station stop here.

## Kayaking and Rafting

**Jordan River Rafting** (✉ Rte. 91, not far from Mahanayim Junction, ☎ 04/693–6867 or 04/693–4622) operates guided rafting trips through the rapids of the Jordan. White-water rafting begins south of Gadot.

## Lodging

Rooms in kibbutz guest houses can be reserved directly or through **Kibbutz Hotels Chain**, a central reservation service based in Tel Aviv (✉ 90 Ben Yehuda St., ☎ 03/524–6161, FAX 03/527–8088 ✆), although not all the kibbutzim are represented. **Moshav Beit Hillel** (✉ M.P. Upper Galilee 12255, ☎ 04/695–1806 or 04/693–5016, FAX 04/695–9861) also makes kibbutz and bed-and-breakfast reservations.

## Visitor Information

All hotels and kibbutz guest houses can provide tourist information, and many will arrange tours as well.

**Bet Ussishkin Museum** (✉ Kibbutz Dan, M.P. Upper Galilee 12245, ☎ 04/694–1704) has information about area nature reserves, natural history, and bird-watching. The **Golan Tourist Association** (✉ Box 171, Katzrin 12315, ☎ 04/686–2885 or 04/696–3583 ✆) has a wealth of information about the Golan. The **Rosh Pina Information Center** (✉ Rte. 90, at the Rosh Pina Junction, ☎ 04/693–6913 or 04/693–6603) provides tips on touring Zfat and Rosh Pina. The **Tiberias Tourist Information Office** (TIO; ✉ Habanim St., Tiberias, ☎ 04/672–5666) can furnish information on the entire region. The **Tourist Information Cen-**

**ter–Upper Galilee** is at the Mahanayim Junction, next to the gas station (⊠ Kibbutz Mahanayim, M.P. Hevel Korazim 12315, ☎ 04/693–6945). It's open weekends and holidays only. The **Zfat Municipal Tourist Information Office** (⊠ 50 Yerushalayim St., Box 227, Zfat 13010, ☎ 04/692–7411) is useful for regional information and has a list of licensed guides in the city.

# 7 EILAT AND THE NEGEV

In the sun-drenched city of Eilat, you can get to know the Red Sea by snorkeling through tropical reefs or just reclining on sandy beaches. To the north, in the Negev Desert—the biblical "southland"—you can explore the quiet vastness of the landscape and the civilizations that have made it bloom. And to the east, at Ein Bokek, on the Dead Sea, you can take the famed waters at one of the area's many spas.

THE NEGEV IS ISRAEL'S southernmost region, an upside-down triangle that constitutes about half the country's land mass, though
only about 6% of the population lives here. The Negev's north-
By Judy Stacey
Goldman
ern border, the base of the triangle, lies about 27 km (17 mi) north of
Beersheva, which is the capital of the Negev and the only large city
within its borders. The Jordanian and Egyptian borders mark its eastern and western limits, respectively, and Eilat, on the Gulf of Eilat at
the gateway to the Red Sea, is at its southernmost tip.

The Negev may well have changed more since the foundation of the
modern state of Israel than in the entire period since the end of the Roman
Empire. The region's first kibbutzim were established in the early
1940s, with new immigrants sent south after the War of Independence, in 1948. Two years later, people started trickling into Eilat, which
was nothing but a few rickety huts. Arad put down its roots in 1961.
The desert itself was pushed back, and the semi-arid areas between Tel
Aviv and Beersheva became fertile farmland. Today, agricultural settlements throughout the Negev make use of brackish water to raise tomatoes, melons, olives, and dates that are sent to winter markets in
Europe. The most recent desert crop is fish: St. Peter's, carp, and
shrimp meet local and foreign demand. (The desert's cultivation is most
evident when you fly over the Negev and see the patches of deep, rich
green below.)

The army has been deployed over a large part of the Negev since the
Sinai was handed over to Egypt in 1982. You'll feel a military presence at roadside diners, where soldiers stop to eat; at bus stations, where
they're in transit; and at tent-filled compounds here and there. Signs
declaring FIRING ZONES indicate areas that the public may not enter, and
checkpoints—where a smile and a wave-through are the order of the
day—are scattered throughout.

The area has a long and varied human history. The ancient Israelites
had fortifications here, as did the Nabateans and the Romans after them.
These early settlers developed irrigation techniques that were remarkably sophisticated, even by modern standards. Throughout these
periods of permanent settlement, the entire area was home to the
Bedouin, whose distinctive way of desert life developed thousands of
years ago and can still be seen today.

Despite its rapid development, the Negev remains Israel's Wild West.
It takes a certain kind of person to live and work here, someone who
relishes the challenge of turning the hot, bone-dry desert into a hospitable
place to live. The Negev draws those who have been seduced by the beauty
of great canyons and cliffs spilling over with color at dawn and dusk;
by the thousands of migrating birds who fill the skies twice a year; by
the endless expanses of still, rocky terrain where the only movement might
be a stone clattering down a hillside as an ibex makes a leap; by the sound
of the wind coming up at the end of a dusty day; and by the pleasure of
bright flowers carpeting the hills in winter.

The Negev contains some of Israel's most fascinating and dramatic
scenery, from gigantic *makhteshim* (erosion craters) and the Dead Sea,
the lowest point on earth, to carved-out *wadis* (ancient dry riverbeds),
the red granite mountains around Eilat, and long cliff faces along the
Arava Valley. You can visit the kibbutz home and grave of Israel's first
prime minister—David Ben-Gurion, the man who first dreamed of settling the desert—and the millennia-old ruins at Tel Beer Sheva, visited
by the biblical patriarch Abraham. The Hai Bar Nature Reserve, farther south, is home to animals described in the Bible, and the Timna

Valley Park is a wonderland of unusually colored rock formations. At the port city of Eilat you can snorkel past multicolored tropical fish and coral formations, and in both Eilat and Ein Bokek you can indulge in pampering spa treatments.

## Pleasures and Pastimes

### Adventure Tours

A thrilling way to see the Negev is by Jeep or camel, in the company of an expert guide who is not only familiar with every facet of desert life but who also knows how to prepare open-air meals and brew tea from desert plants (your guide might be a resident of a desert settlement). If you have time, take a several-day trek through the desert, an unforgettable experience; tour outfits provide the camping equipment. Certain desert expeditions combine hiking, camel riding, and rappelling. (For more details, *see* Guided Tours *in* Eilat and the Negev A to Z, *below*.) It's wise to reserve in advance; you can often do so through a travel agency or your hotel. Note that some tours don't operate in the summer, when it's very hot.

### Dining

If the word *dining* conjures up starched and draped tablecloths, gliding waiters, and gleaming silver, head for the upscale restaurants and luxury hotels of Eilat and Ein Bokek. Despite the fact that Eilat is at the southern tip of a desert, it has all the essentials—including Ben & Jerry's. Tastes range from Italian, Indian, and French to Argentinian, Yemenite, and Thai. Specialty fish restaurants abound—excellent sea fish, including delicacies such as *denise* (sea bream) and the Israeli specialty, *forel* (salmon-trout bred in the Dan River up north), make wonderful meals.

In the rest of the Negev, with the notable exception of the Mitzpe Ramon Inn, plan to dine in humble surroundings—typically a roadside diner—on meals that are apt to reflect the cook's ethnic background. You might find Tunisian carrot salad, Moroccan *cigarim* (flaky pastry with a meat or potato filling), or standard Middle Eastern fare: hummus, pita, grilled meat, french fries (known here as chips), chopped or shredded vegetable salads (*salatim*), strong coffee in small cups, and fruit or chocolate mousse for dessert. Keep in mind that outside Eilat restaurants close early on Friday, and since the main meal of the day is served at noon in the desert, lunch may be history if you arrive after 1:30.

If people are dressed up anywhere, it will be at the better restaurants (and nightclubs and discos) in Eilat and Ein Bokek, though ties are never required. Everywhere else, the finest attire you'll see is a clean T-shirt. Keep in mind, too, that it's always a good idea to make reservations at Eilat and Ein Bokek restaurants, especially on Friday and Saturday night.

| CATEGORY | COST* |
| --- | --- |
| $$$$ | over $35 |
| $$$ | $22–$35 |
| $$ | $12–$22 |
| $ | under $12 |

*per person for three-course meal, excluding drinks and service charge

### Hiking

Hiking the splendid scenery, rugged heights, and steep cliff faces of the Negev requires knowledge and skill. In summer the heat is extreme, and in winter the danger of floods is ever present. Hiking on your own is not recommended unless you're well versed in the art of reading topographical maps. The best way to hike the Negev is to join one of several excellent organizations (☞ Hiking *under* Guided Tours *in* Eilat and the Negev A to Z, *below*). If you do venture out without a guide, be sure to give the details to someone who is staying behind—where you're headed, the route you plan to follow, and when you expect to be back. Always follow the desert guidelines for water consumption (☞ Desert Precautions, *below*).

## Lodging

Hotels in sunny Eilat and Ein Bokek (Dead Sea) run from family-style to huge, lush, and luxurious. In Eilat, a few truly palatial hotels have opened in the last few years. Pleasure comes first: business facilities on a modest scale are available in larger hotels, whereas a beautiful and luxurious spa with a wide range of facilities is an important feature of each large hotel. Even many of the smaller hotels have installed spas in the last year. In Eilat, a few hotels operate on an all-inclusive basis.

Keep in mind that prices rise during high season and holidays. High season is Hanukkah/Christmas, Passover/Easter, and July and August, when Israelis take a break (and hotels are crowded with families). At Ein Bokek, high season is mid-March to mid-June and mid-September to the end of November. Eilat's hotels are crowded with Europeans from October until April. Be sure to reserve well in advance at any time of year.

| CATEGORY | EILAT AND EIN BOKEK* | OTHER AREAS* |
|---|---|---|
| **$$$$** | over $300 | over $99 |
| **$$$** | $250–$300 | $70–$99 |
| **$$** | $150–$250 | $40–$70 |
| **$** | under $150 | under $40 |

*All prices are for a standard double room, including breakfast for two but excluding 15% service charge.*

## Natural Wonders

The star of the Negev is the Makhtesh Ramon (Ramon Crater), one of a group of geological formations found only in Israel. But knock-out views abound throughout the area: the changing colors of the Wilderness of Zin as the day progresses; the sunsets that stain Eilat's waters a deep red; the snow-white blocks of salt clumped on the surface of the Dead Sea; and the erosion sculptures surrounded by brooding mountains in Timna Valley Park.

## Scuba Diving

Eilat is at the gateway to the Red Sea, one of the best dive sites in the world. After the Six-Day War, in 1967, Israeli divers opened facilities along the Sinai coast south of Eilat; although the Sinai Peninsula was returned to Egypt long ago, Eilat's dive centers still run regular dive safaris over the border. Amazing coral formations, underwater tropical plants, and a dazzling array of fish live in waters that stay warm year-round (22°C, or 72°F, in winter). The reefs are a mere 10 yards offshore, with an immediate deep drop, so a dive is just a walk away. Divers should bring their license, insurance certification, and appropriate footwear—the sea floor is rough, and so are the sea urchins. Top-level diving courses are widely available.

# Exploring Eilat and the Negev

Our peregrinations cover three basic areas in the inverted triangle of the Negev. The first is Negev's heart, with sites such as David Ben-Gurion's home and grave, the ancient Nabatean-Roman-Byzantine ruins at Tel Avdat, and the amazing Ramon Crater. The second includes the capital city of Beersheva, the spa-resort town of Ein Bokek at the Dead Sea, the ancient city of Tel Arad, and the modern city of Arad. The third, and southern, tip of the triangle encompasses carefree Eilat, the Underwater Observatory at Coral Beach, and Timna Valley Park. Eilat is also the jumping-off point for day or longer trips to Jordan (ancient Petra) or Egypt (the Sinai Peninsula); *see* Chapter 8 if these interest you.

As you travel through the Negev, you'll pass stretches of flat, uninhabited countryside under hot, blue skies, punctuated by the odd acacia tree, twisting wadi, or craggy mountain. In winter you'll see delicate desert flowers along the road. If you want to skip the desert-driving experience, you might limit your trip here to Eilat or Ein Bokek. In Eilat you can stay at a luxurious hotel, relax on the sunny shore, and dive or snorkel. In Ein Bokek you can settle into one of the numerous health and beauty spas that make use of the Dead Sea waters and medicinal mud.

## Great Itineraries

The following itineraries cover the major (and some off-the-beaten-path) Negev sights for travelers who are driving and have a limited amount of time. All assume that you're coming from Tel Aviv or Jerusalem. You can reach a few of these places by bus, but this is definitely not the most comfortable way to get around. You might consider combining one of our suggested itineraries with a short guided tour (☞ Guided Tours *in* Eilat and the Negev A to Z, *below*).

*Numbers in the text correspond to numbers in the margin and on the Eilat and the Negev map.*

IF YOU HAVE 1 OR 2 DAYS

You can cram a lot of Negev sights into a day or two; just get an early start from Jerusalem or Tel Aviv. You can either stop at the **Museum of Bedouin Culture** ① *or* drive straight to Beersheva on your way to see the reconstruction of a 1943 military desert outpost at **Mitzpe Revivim** ②. Next, visit renowned prime minister **David Ben-Gurion's desert home** ③ and **grave** ④, overlooking the Wilderness of Zin. Head down the twisting road near the grave site to get to **Ein Avdat** ⑤, a welcome respite of splashing waterfalls in the blazing summer and a green and picturesque sight in winter. It's a short drive from Ein Avdat to the 2,000-year-old Nabatean hilltop stronghold of **Avdat** ⑥, which you can explore on foot. If you have only one day, skip Ein Avdat and Avdat and drive straight to the visitor center at **Mitzpe Ramon** ⑦ to see the **Makhtesh Ramon** ⑦. If you have two days, spend the night in Mitzpe Ramon and explore the immense crater the next morning. (If you've brought children, they'll appreciate a visit to the **Alpaca Farm,** just outside town.) Your return trip brings you back to **Beersheva** ⑧, where you can choose between visiting **Tel Beer Sheva** ⑩ and the possible site of Abraham's Well and stopping at the **Israel Air Force Museum** ⑨, in Hatzerim, to see a field full of planes.

IF YOU HAVE 5 DAYS

Start at the **Museum of Bedouin Culture** ① for a look at the lifestyle of Israel's nomads. The sandy landscape along Route 31 takes you through ancient **Tel Arad** ⑪ and modern **Arad** ⑫. From Arad drive the dramatic 24-km (15-mi) descent on sharply curving Route 31 to the Dead Sea, the lowest point on earth. Stay overnight in 🏨 **Ein Bokek** ⑬. Devote the next morning to floating in the Dead Sea and enjoying your hotel's spa facilities. By afternoon you'll be well relaxed and ready to drive south to 🏨 **Eilat** ⑭ and spend two more days relaxing in an entirely different setting. Back on the road on the fourth day, going north, drive through the **Makhtesh Ramon** ⑦ to reach 🏨 **Mitzpe Ramon** ⑦, on the crater's edge; spend the night there. You might have time to go to the visitor center or at least enjoy the cliffside promenade before dark. On your last day head back to Tel Aviv or Jerusalem, stopping at either **Arad** ⑫, **Ben-Gurion's desert home** ③, **Ben-Gurion's grave** ④, **Mitzpe**

## Eilat and the Negev

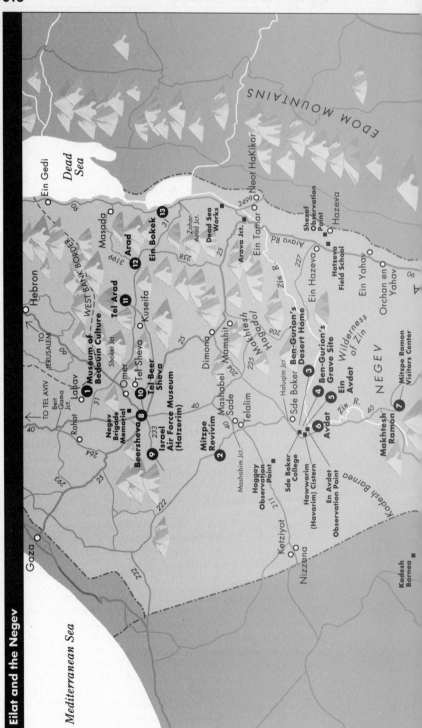

Mediterranean Sea

Dead Sea

EDOM MOUNTAINS

Ein Gedi

Masada

3199

Hebron

WEST BANK BORDER

TO JERUSALEM

TO TEL AVIV

Beit Qama Jct.

Rahat

Lahav

**1** Museum of Bedouin Culture

Shoket Jct.

Omer

Tel Arad **11**

Kuseifa

Arad **12**

Ein Bokek **13**

258

Zohar-Arad Jct.

Dead Sea Works

2499

Neot HaKikar

Ein Tamar

Arava Jct.

Shezaf Observation Point

Hazeva

Arava Rd

Hatzeva Field School

Ein Hazeva

227

Ein Yahav

Orchan en Yahav

90

**10** Tel Sheva
Tel Beer Sheva

Negev Brigade Memorial

Beersheva **8**

Israel Air Force Museum (Hatzerim)

**9**

233

40

284

25

222

293

232

211

Dimona

Mamshit

204

Mashabei Sade

Telalim

Mashabim Jct.

Haggay Observation Point

Sde Boker College

Hawwarim (Havarim) Cistern

En Avdat Observation Point

Kelziyot

Nizzana

Makhtesh Hagadol

225

Haluqim Jct.

Sde Boker

Ben-Gurion's Desert Home **3**

Ben-Gurion's Grave Site **4**

Ein Avdat **5**

Avdat **6**

205

Zin R.

Wilderness of Zin

NEGEV

Zin R.

40

Makhtesh Ramon

Mitzpe Ramon Visitors Center **7**

Kadesh Barnea

Kadesh Barnea

Mitzpe Revivim **2**

JORDAN

EGYPT

Har Harif

Makhtesh Ramon
(Ramon Crater)

Paran

Menucha Jct.

Arava Rd.

13

06

40

Isichor Jct.

Shizzafon Jct.

12

Ketura Jct.

Ketura

Grofit

**18** Hai Bar
Nature Reserve

**19** Timna Valley
Park

Biq'at 'Uvda

06

Netafim
Crossing

Mitzpe Har Hizkiyahu

Mt. Yaash

**21**

**20**

Schlomo R.

Ostrich Show Farm

Coral Reserve **15**

Dolphin Reef **16**

**17**

Coral World Underwater
Observatory and Aquarium

**14** Eilat

Airport

Aqaba

Gulf
of
Eilat

A R A V A

N

20 miles

30 km

0

**Revivim** ②, or the **Israel Air Force Museum** ⑨ (you won't have time to see them all).

IF YOU HAVE 9 DAYS

Follow the first three days of the itinerary above, spending the third and fourth nights in **Eilat** ⑭. On the fourth and fifth days, kick back, learn to dive, swim with dolphins, bird-watch, hike, or take a guided tour of the Eilat area. On Day 6 drive north to the **Makhtesh Ramon** ⑦. Stay overnight in ⛺ **Mitzpe Ramon** ⑦. On Day 7 you might take a Jeep tour, and perhaps visit the Alpaca Farm. Heading north on Route 40 on Day 8, visit ancient **Avdat** ⑥, **Ben-Gurion's home** ③, **Ben-Gurion's grave** ④, or **Ein Avdat** ⑤ on your way to ⛺ **Beersheva** ⑧ for the night. If your last day (spent in Beersheva) is a Thursday, you can get an early start at the **Bedouin market** or visit **Tel Beer Sheva** ⑩—or the **Israel Air Force Museum** ⑨ or **Mitzpe Revivim** ②—on your way to Tel Aviv or Jerusalem.

## When to Tour the Negev

October through May is the best time to explore the Negev. In the winter months of January and February it's dry and cold. Scorching-hot conditions prevail in the summer, from June through late September (though it's very dry), so your best bet then is to stay by the water, in Eilat. Ein Bokek, with its unique Dead Sea properties, attracts visitors even in the wildly hot summer. In early March, you'll be treated to the sight of scarlet, bright yellow, white, and hot pink desert flowers bursting out against the brown desert earth; March is also when Eilat's International Bird-watchers' Festival takes place.

Most Negev sites open at 8:30 AM and close by 4 PM in winter and 5 PM in summer. Restaurants (except for those in Ein Bokek and Eilat) serve their main meal of the day (hot food) at noon and often close by early evening. Most places close early on Friday; roadside diners close at around 1:30 PM.

Try to get an early start; plan to be inside or resting at midday in summer; and make every effort to reach your destination by nightfall. If you're traveling a long distance, stay alert and awake. Lock your car at all times, take your valuables when you leave it, and stash your bags where they're not visible from the outside. Women should not hitchhike.

DESERT PRECAUTIONS

To remain comfortable, happy, and *safe,* you must observe certain rules of the desert. You should drink two quarts of water a day in the winter, and, if you're active, one quart per hour in the summer; dehydration sets in quickly in the desert. Keep a jerrican (which holds five gallons) of water in your car, plus extra bottles. You'll find water fountains along the way, but they don't always function. Wear sunblock, sunglasses, protective lip balm, and a hat (a must year-round). (You'll forget personal vanity when you see *everyone* wearing hats, some that you thought you wouldn't be caught dead in.) Light hiking shoes and a small knapsack are indispensable for walks and hikes, as are bug spray and a flashlight.

Although it may seem incongruous in the desert, road flooding is a very real danger from September through March, especially the day after a rainfall farther north. In the spring, low-pressure systems from the Red Sea can bring torrential rains. If it's raining or has recently rained, call the **police** (☎ 100). You can also call the **Society for the Protection of Nature in Israel 24-hour Operations Center** (sometimes in Hebrew only; ☎ 02/622–2211) to ask if the road you intend to take is in passable condition. If you're already in the Negev, contact the local tourist office (☞ Visitor Information *in* Eilat and the Negev A to Z, *below*) for an update. If, while traveling, you see even a small amount of water flowing across the road in front of you, stop and wait, even if it takes a while for the water to subside. Water on the road is a warning of possible imminent flooding. When hiking, do not enter canyons or dry riverbeds on rainy days, or days when it has just rained farther north.

# THE HEART OF THE NEGEV

The area extending from the Negev Highlands to Eilat has a whole range of sights: the Museum of Bedouin Culture, Mitzpe Revivim, a reconstructed desert outpost; David Ben-Gurion's kibbutz home and grave site; an icy desert pool at Ein Avdat; the 2,000-year-old Nabatean hilltop stronghold of Avdat; and the immense Makhtesh Ramon (Ramon Crater). The first stop on this tour will give you an introduction to the Negev's indigenous people, the Bedouin.

## Museum of Bedouin Culture

★ ⑤ ❶ *95 km (57 mi) south of Tel Aviv, 24 km (14 mi) north of Beersheva. At the Lahavim Junction, turn east onto Rte. 31, turn in at the sign for Lahav (or Joe Alon Center).*

Once off the main road, you'll drive through a pine forest to reach this one-of-a-kind museum that focuses on the Bedouin people, who have long populated the Negev. The folklore center (marked with an orange sign), is named for the late Colonel Joe Alon, a pilot who took a great interest in this area and its people. Housed in a circular, tentlike building, the museum creates an authentic look at the Bedouin's rapidly changing lifestyle through various tableaux containing life-size mannequins. The tableaux are grouped by subject: wool spinning and carpet weaving, bread baking, the Bedouin coffee ceremony, wedding finery (including a camel elaborately decorated for the event and bearing nuptial gifts), donkeys and camels at work, and toys made from found objects such as pieces of wire and wood. The tools and artifacts—most handmade, and many already out of use in modern Bedouin life—form an outstanding collection. The film about Bedouin life in the Negev is worth watching. Admission includes a cup of thick coffee in a Bedouin tent, where the sheikh performs the coffee ceremony over an open fire. ⊠ *Rte. 325 off Rte. 31,* ☎ *08/991–8597 or 08/991–3322.* ⊠ *NIS 16 ($4).* ⊙ *Sun.–Thurs. 9–4, Fri. 9–2, Sat. 9–4.*

## Mitzpe Revivim

❷ *36 km (22¼ mi) southeast of Beersheva 9 km (6 mi) off Rd. 40, first left after the ostrich farm.*

Mitzpe Revivim is the site of an early desert outpost, and an interesting example of early Jewish settlement history. In 1943, in a desolate and empty Negev, three such outposts were set up to gauge the feasibility of Jewish settlement in the southernmost part of the country; one of these was Mitzpe Revivim (*mitzpe* means "lookout," *revivim* means "showers"). Revivim's very presence, along with a handful of other Negev settlements, influenced the U.N.'s decision to include the Negev as part of the State of Israel in the 1947 partition plan. During the War of Independence, isolated Mitzpe Revivim was besieged by Egyptian soldiers, and a hard battle was won by a small band of pioneers and Palmach soldiers. The defenders' fort and living quarters have been preserved: the radio room (the radio cackles original messages), ammunition room, and kitchen contain their original equipment. Outside are a cave—actually a Byzantine-period cistern—where a medical clinic was set up, and two airplanes, which were used to bring supplies and evac-

# BEDOUIN CULTURE

**F**OR ISRAELIS AND VISITORS alike, the Bedouin are a fascinating people. Dressed in flowing black embroidered dresses, their heads covered in white scarves, Bedouin women tending flocks of goats are the brightest touch of color in the treeless, waterless, and harsh Negev desert. Over the past 52 years of Israel's statehood, the Negev Bedouin men, most of whom are Israeli citizens, have served in the Israeli army, and some have lost their lives doing so. Ironically, however, they are at odds with government authorities, who would like the Bedouin to settle in specially-built towns near Beersheva, the capital of the Negev. Their simple, nomadic way of life becomes more difficult to maintain each year as they resist these policies. Currently, about 60,000 Bedouin have settled down in towns, while another 60,000 or so remain in the desert. There were 11,000 Bedouin in the area when Israel was established in 1948.

The present-day Bedouin of the Negev (and the Sinai) trace their origins to nomads of the Arabian peninsula who wandered west 400 to 600 years ago. The exceptions are members of the Jebeliya tribe, descendents of East European slaves sent by Emperor Justinian to serve Greek monks at St. Catherine's Monastery at Mt. Sinai. The slaves slowly adopted the Bedouin way of life, and they still serve the monks from their desert nearby.

The Bedouin's main livelihood is the raising of livestock, camels and black goats in particular. The animals supply hair for weaving, milk, meat, and dung for burning as fuel. The wanderings of the Bedouin are driven by the unending search for grazing land and water for their flocks. Marriages are arranged, taking family interests into account. It is not uncommon today for a man to have two wives, the first wife and a younger one to help her.

The family is structured as a business. Men make decisions about buying and selling livestock as well as finding new pastures. Women and children do the cooking, weaving, searching for firewood, and often caring for the flocks.

Bedouin are known for their warm hospitality. It is not only a pleasure to extend hospitality but the Bedouin sees it as a duty. A Bedouin host would never fail to invite a stranger into his tent. And refusing a Bedouin's invitation would be unthinkable because it would deny the host an opportunity to display his kindness. Having the honor of being invited by a Bedouin host to drink sweet tea or coffee, made over an open fire in his tent, is an unforgettable experience.

A rich heritage of poetry has been passed down through the generations by word of mouth. Only in the past few years have these words been recorded, written in their original Arabic, and preserved by scholars who recognize that the Bedouin way of life is rapidly slipping away.

uate the wounded. The one-page "self guide" brings the rooms to life, and a kiosk offers ice cream and drinks. ✉ *Rte. 222,* ☎ *08/656–2570.* 🎫 *NIS 10 ($2.50).* ☉ *Sun.–Thurs. 9–3, Fri. 9–1, Sat. 10–4, holidays and holiday eves 9–5.*

| | |
|---|---|
| OFF THE BEATEN PATH | **NEVE MIDBAR** – (☎ 08/657–9666), open Saturday–Thursday 9–6, Friday 9–4, is a new health spa (for daytime visits) that centers on a pool of natural thermo-mineral waters pumped up from deep underground, at a temperature of 39°C (around 102 °F). The spa also has two freshwater pools (one with a slide for those with disabilities) and a shallow pool for babies. A hot tub, sauna, various massages, and aromatherapy treatments make for an unusual desert experience. A gift shop, fish restaurant, and coffee shop share the premises. |

*En Route*   Proceed south along Route 40 and you'll come to the gas station at **Mashabim Junction,** which also serves as a roadside café (good for stocking up on bottled water). Continue on Route 40 for 2 km (1 mi) past the station and make a left at the sign for Mitzpe Ramon, at Telalim Junction. Heading southwest along this stretch of road, you'll pass through areas where signs announce FIRING ZONE. The signs indicate closed military areas, which you may not enter without proper authorization. It's perfectly safe to travel on the main roads; just don't wander off them.

Continuing along Route 40, you'll see a sign on the right for the **Haggay Observation Point.** The parking lot is on the opposite side of the highway at a curve in the road. After parking the car, carefully cross the road to the observation point for a glorious first view of the **Wilderness of Zin**—stark, flat, beige terrain—and **Kibbutz Sde Boker.** Except for the greenery of the kibbutz, the area looks just as it did to the wandering Children of Israel making their way from Egypt to the Land of Canaan more than 3,000 years ago, no doubt complaining all the while about the lack of figs, vines, and water.

## Ben-Gurion's Desert Home

**❸**  *24 km (15 mi) south of Mitzpe Revivim. Sign for Ben-Gurion's "hut" is just after Kibbutz Sde Boker.*

Thousands of people make their way to this pilgrimage site every year. Ben-Gurion himself hoped that tens of thousands would actually settle in the Negev, though his dream has not come true. He was passionate about the Negev, and the entrance path through the tree-filled grounds is lined with stones that bear his now-famous sentiments on the subject.

Amid the waving eucalyptus trees is Paula and David Ben-Gurion's simple dwelling. Ben-Gurion (1886–1973), Israel's first prime minister, was one of the 20th century's great statesmen, yet his small Negev home is commonly known as "the hut" because of its humble ambience. It's not actually a hut but a one-story wooden home with a small kitchen, an eating corner with a table and two chairs, and simple furniture throughout. Visitors such as Dag Hammarskjöld, secretary-general of the United Nations, drank tea with Ben-Gurion in the living room, with its miniature version of Michelangelo's *Moses* on a side table and a picture of Abraham Lincoln on the wall. Ben-Gurion's library shelves contain 5,000 books (there are 20,000 more in his Tel Aviv home)—in fact, most of the space in the "hut" is taken up by the Old Man's (as he was locally known) books. On Ben-Gurion's desk are the papers on which he copied out sentences from the Old Testament: "I will even make a way in the wilderness, and rivers in the desert . . . I give waters in the wilderness, and rivers in the desert, to give drink to my people, my chosen" (Isaiah 43). His bedroom, with its single picture of Mahatma Gandhi, holds the iron cot on which he slept (only three hours a night) and his slippers on the floor beside it. The house is exactly as Ben-Gurion left it.

Next door, in another painted-wood building, is an exhibition whose themes are the biography of Ben-Gurion's extraordinary life, original documents that show the leader's strong ties to the Negev, and the Negev today in light of Ben-Gurion's dream.

When Ben-Gurion resigned from government in 1953 (later to return), he and his wife moved to the isolated, brand-new **Kibbutz Sde Boker** to provide an example for others. "Neither money nor propaganda builds a country," he announced. "Only the man who lives and creates in the country can build it." This said, the George Washington of Israel—whose interests were history, philosophy, and politics, as the artifacts in his home indicate—took up his new role in the kibbutz sheepfold. In February 1955 he became prime minister once more and spent only holidays and weekends at the kibbutz; he returned here to live when he retired in 1970. (He returned to his Tel Aviv residence some months before his death, at the age of 87, in 1973.) ☎ 08/655–8444. 🎫 *Free.* ⊙ *Sun.–Thurs. 8:30–4, Fri. and holiday eves 8:30–2, Sat. and holidays 9–2:30. Arrive ½ hr before closing time.*

### Dining

$ ✕ **Sde Boker Inn.** At this cozy eatery under the trees, kibbutz members dish up homemade hot meals, plus salads and sandwiches, for breakfast and lunch. They'll also pack box lunches for the road. Bags of kibbutz-grown pistachio nuts are a delicious treat, and the shop next door sells kibbutz-made handicrafts, including jewelry. ⊠ *Next door to Ben-Gurion's home,* ☎ 08/656–0379. *AE, DC, MC, V. No dinner.*

## Ben-Gurion's Grave

**❹** *3 km (2 mi) southwest of Ben-Gurion's home, to the right of the main gate for Sde Boker College.*

Ben-Gurion's grave is not far from his former home. Walk through the beautiful garden until you reach the quiet, windswept plaza; in the center are the simple raised stone slabs marking the graves of David and Paula Ben-Gurion (she died five years before her husband). The couple's final resting place—selected by Ben-Gurion himself—overlooks Zin Valley's geological finery: a vast, undulating drape of velvety-looking stone in shades of cream, ivory, coffee, and soft brown that slowly changes hue as the day goes on. The cluster of greenery and palm trees to the right on the valley floor indicates Ein Avdat (Avdat Spring; ☞ *below*).

## Sde Boker College

*Enter through the gate with the traffic arm, next to Ben-Gurion's grave.*

Ben-Gurion envisioned a place of learning in the desert. This campus became part of Ben-Gurion University of the Negev, whose main campus is in Beersheva. Although there isn't much to see here, the **National Solar Energy Center,** where a research program investigates new ideas for the harnessing of solar energy, is interesting. For the traveler, the college is primarily a place to eat and possibly spend the night. The commercial center, in the middle of the campus, has a restaurant, a supermarket open until 8 PM, a post office, and the field school of the Society for the Protection of Nature in Israel (SPNI, ☎ 08/653–2016).

## Dining and Lodging

**$** ✕ **Zin Inn.** As hot a spot as you'll find in the middle of the desert, the modest Zin Inn is where everyone hangs out—desert researchers from overseas, soldiers from the nearby base, visiting schoolchildren from all over the country, and field-school guides. The menu is the usual desert-restaurant fare: soup, schnitzel (breaded and fried chicken cutlets), stuffed peppers, goulash, salad, ice cream, and coffee. Although it's not open for dinner, on Saturday it stays open until 6 PM. ⊠ *Sde Boker campus,* ☎ *08/653–2811. AE, MC, V. No dinner.*

**$$** 🏨 **Desert Research Institute Guest House.** A university-run facility for visiting scientists, the guest house sometimes has rooms available for travelers seeking the simple life. It's quiet and rather remote, situated on a winding path at the edge of a beautiful canyon, with the Wilderness of Zin as its backyard. Each room has two beds (you can add another two) and an alcove with a small refrigerator, a tea kettle, and a few dishes. Towels are provided. There is a small TV lounge, a communal kitchen for light cooking (you can stock up at the nearby supermarket), and a restaurant in the commercial center. There are no phones in the rooms, but there is a pay phone on the premises. ⊠ *Ben-Gurion University of the Negev, Sde Boker campus, 84990,* ☎ *08/659–6711 (8 AM–3 PM),* 🖷 *08/659–6704. 14 rooms. Lounge, air-conditioning. No credit cards.*

**$** 🏨 **SPNI Field School Hostel.** A short walk from the commercial center, this hostel is a cut above. Each of the octagonal units has a large room with a skylight, two bunk beds, two twin beds, a small desk, and a private bathroom (bring your own towel). You can use the large kitchen to prepare meals, and there's always hot water in the urn for coffee. ⊠ *Sde Boker campus, 84990,* ☎ *08/653–2016,* 🖷 *08/653–2721. 330 beds. No credit cards.*

# Ein Avdat

★ ☺ ➎ *3 km (2 mi) south of Ben-Gurion's grave and Sde Boker College.*

Ein Avdat (Avdat Spring) lies at the foot of the canyon that divides the plateau between the ancient Nabatean city of Avdat and Kibbutz Sde Boker, in **Ein Avdat National Park.** To get to the spring from Ben-Gurion's grave, head down the curving road to a clump of palm trees and the admission booth. Ask for the explanatory leaflet when you pay. Lock the car, taking valuables with you. Walk toward the thickets of rushes, and about five minutes later you'll see on the left, against the white-chalk cliff, a lone, ancient atlantica pistachio tree, the first of many reminders of a time when there was more water, and thus more vegetation, here. Look for ibex tracks on the ground, made with hoofs that enable these agile creatures to climb sheer rock faces. Try to spot the ibex, barely discernible against the cliff's rocks—they even have striped markings on their coats that resemble the rock's many strata. Rock pigeons, Egyptian vultures (black-and-white feathers, bright yellow beak, and long, pinkish legs), and sooty falcons nest in the natural holes in the soft rock and in cliff ledges.

The big surprise at Ein Avdat is the pool of ice-cold, spring-fed water, complete with splashing waterfall. To reach this cool oasis, shaded by the surrounding cliffs, walk carefully along the spring and across the dam toward the waterfall. Swimming and drinking the water are not allowed (you'll not be *sorely* tempted, though—the water is swarming with tadpoles), but relaxing and enjoying the sight and sound of water in the arid Negev certainly are. The trail continues up the cliffside (using ladders and stone steps), but you can't follow it unless your party has two cars and leaves one at the destination, the Observation

Point; the descent is considered too dangerous and is prohibited. ⊠
*Ein Avdat National Park,* ☎ *08/655–5684.* 🖾 *Parking NIS 12 ($3).*
🕐 *Apr.–Sept., Sun.–Thurs. 8–5, Fri. and holiday eves 8–4; Oct.–Mar.,*
*Sun.–Thurs. 8–4, Fri. and holiday eves 8–3.* ♺

*En Route*   For an eagle's-eye view of the waterfall and spring below, turn off Route
40 at the orange sign for Ein Avdat to get to the **Ein Avdat Observation Point.** Below you is the white canyon carved out by the Zin River,
with its waterfall (most of the year) tumbling into a pool, surrounded by
greenery. From the lookout, a path leads around the top of the cliff (be
very careful, especially with children), enabling you to see the rope marks
in the rock; these have been created over the years by Bedouin pulling up
water buckets. (For information on the hike from here to ancient Avdat,
consult the SPNI Field School at Sde Boker College, *above*.)

## Avdat

★ ❻   *About 20 km (12 mi) south of Ben-Gurion's desert home and grave.*

The Nabatean city of Avdat, a 12-acre acropolis, looms on a hilltop.
Here you can see the ancient stronghold and urban ruins of three peo-
ples who have left their mark all over the Negev: the Nabateans, the
Romans, and the Byzantines.

The Nabateans were seminomadic pagans who came here from northern Arabia in the 3rd century BC. Establishing prosperous caravan
routes connecting the desert hinterland with the port city of Gaza, on
the Mediterranean coast, they soon rose to glory with a vast kingdom
whose capital was Petra (in present-day Jordan), a city cut entirely out
of rock. Strongholds to protect the caravans, which carried gold, precious stones, and spices, were established along these routes, usually
a day's journey apart.

The name Avdat is the Hebrew version of Oboda (30 BC–9 BC), a deified king who may have been buried here. Another king of Avdat, Aretas, is mentioned in the New Testament. The prominent local dynasty
intermarried with the family of Herod the Great, and the Nabatean
kingdom was finally abolished by the Romans in AD 106, when it became a Roman province. Most of the remains on the acropolis date
from the 3rd, 4th, and 5th centuries—the Byzantine period, when the
Nabateans adopted Christianity. The city was sacked by the Persians
in AD 620 and was only rediscovered in the 20th century.

Start at the **visitor center** (the Avdat Data Shop), where you can learn
about the Nabateans in a 10-minute video, see examples of what these
ancient traders actually transported across the desert, and examine archaeological artifacts found in the excavations. The shop sells copies
of original Nabatean jewelry. Be sure to pick up the Nature and National Parks Authority's excellent explanatory brochure and map of
the site. Drive up the road (save your energy for walking around the
site itself), stopping first at the sign for the **Roman burial cave.** Park
and walk the 300 ft for a quick peek. The 20 burial niches cut into the
rock date from the 3rd century BC.

Back in your car, drive up a little farther to the lookout point at the
restored Roman building. The cultivated fields below were re-created
in 1959 by Professor M. Even-Ari of Hebrew University, who wanted
to see if the ancient Nabatean and Byzantine methods of conserving
the meager rainfall (measured in millimeters) for desert farming would
still work. The proof is in the cultivated crops and orchards before you.
Runoff water was collected and distributed using a clever system of
catchment areas, conduit walls, dams, and cisterns. Barren slopes

around Nabatean sites all over the Negev were put to use in this way. Groups (with a minimum of 10 people) may call ahead to arrange a tour of the farm (☎ 08/656–5741 or 08/655–8462) for a small fee.

With the help of the Nature and Parks Authority's map, you can trace the lifestyle of these former locals at sites that include a reconstructed three-story Roman tower (there are good views from the tower corner of the 4th-century AD fortress walls); a rare Nabatean pottery workshop, where you might just find some eggshell-thin shards; a winepress (indicating that grapes were grown here, a testament to the Nabatean genius for conserving water); cisterns; two Byzantine churches; and a large baptismal font (to accommodate the converted). Near the baptismal font you can walk down the steps on the eastern slope to see the 6th-century AD Byzantine dwellings, each consisting of a cave (possibly used as a wine cellar) with a stone house in front of it. At the bottom of the hill, north of the gas station, is a well-preserved Byzantine bathhouse. There is an eatery that serves light meals at the visitor center. ⊠ *Rte. 40,* ☎ *08/658–6391.* ⊠ *NIS 18 ($4.60) for all sights.* ⊙ *Apr.–Sept., Sat.–Thurs. 8–5, Fri. and holiday eves 8–4; Oct.–Mar., Sat.–Thurs. 8–4, Fri. and holiday eves 8–3.*

# Makhtesh Ramon and Mitzpe Ramon

★ ❼ *21 km (13 mi) south of Avdat, 80 km (50 mi) south of Beersheva.*

**Makhtesh Ramon** (the Ramon Crater) is Israel's most spectacular natural sight, an immense depression 40 km (25 mi) long, 10 km (6 mi) wide, and at its deepest it measures 2,400 ft. Because it's a phenomenon known only in this country (there are three others in the Negev), the Hebrew term *makhtesh*—meaning mortar, as in mortar and pestle—is now accepted usage. By definition, a makhtesh is an erosion valley walled with steep cliffs on all sides and drained by a single watercourse.

**Mitzpe Ramon** is a tiny town on the edge of the crater. The populace numbers 5,500 people, including recently arrived Russian immigrants. The town has one hotel, one small shopping area, and no theater except its own raison d'être, the greatest show in the whole Negev—the magnificent giant crater. The local main road runs through the crater (eventually arriving in Eilat), a promenade winds along its edge, and a huge sculpture park sits on its rim; outdoor enthusiasts will enjoy exploring the geology, nature (note the metal fences around the trees to keep the ibex from eating the leaves), and stunning scenery by foot or by Jeep (☞ Outdoor Activities and Sports, *below*).

Bear in mind that the Ramon Inn is the only hotel in town, though there is a hostel. If rooms are unavailable and you're continuing south to Eilat, you can still see the crater, as Route 40 goes right through it; just try to plan your day so that you won't be driving to Eilat after dark. There are no gas stations between Mitzpe Roman and Yotvata, a distance of more than 100 km (62 mi).

The impressive **visitor center,** at the very edge of the makhtesh, is built in the shape of an ammonite fossil (a spiral-shape sea creature that lived here when everything was under water, millions of years ago). The helpful staff are rangers with the Israel Nature and National Parks Protection Authority; these knowledgeable people will be happy to suggest various hikes in the Negev.

For a clear understanding of the makhtesh phenomenon, the center offers a huge, color, wraparound sound-and-screen presentation with a walk-around model of the makhtesh, which certainly outshines the 12-minute film shown in the auditorium. On the way to the top-floor lookout are informative, wall-size panels describing the makhtesh's geological makeup, ecology, vegetation, and settlement.

As you stand behind the glass, you peer out at a world formed millions of years ago. The crater's walls are made from layer upon layer of different-color rock beds containing fossils of shells, plants, and trees. The makhtesh floor is covered with nature's creations: heaps of black basalt formed by volcanic activity, the peaks of ancient volcanoes themselves, jagged chunks of quartzite, huge blocks of overturned rock, and beds of multicolor clays used by potters today.

Just outside the center's front door, and included in its admission, is **Bio Ramon,** a garden of desert vegetation and small desert animals, such as snakes, sand rats, beetles, turtles, and hedgehogs, who dwell in cages that imitate their natural surroundings.⌧ *On main road in Mitzpe Ramon,* ☎ *08/658–8691 or 08/658–8620.* ⌦ *NIS 15 ($3.75).* ☉ *Sun.–Thurs. 8–5, Fri. 8–4, Sat. 8–5.* ✎

You may be inspired to take a walk (about 1 km, or ½ mi) along the **Albert Promenade,** which winds east to west along the edge of the crater from the visitor center to the cantilevered observation platform. This is not the time to run out of film—the view is overwhelming. If it's late afternoon, you may see ibex along the cliffs and raptors wheeling overhead. The promenade is fashioned from local stone, as is the huge sculpture by Israel Hadani, the back of which faces town and represents the crater's geological layers.

With the crater as a magnificent backdrop, the **Desert Sculpture Park** exhibits a far-flung collection of huge stone sculptures. The park took shape in 1962 with the work of a group of Israeli and foreign sculptors under the direction of Negev artist Ezra Orion. Their idea was to add to the natural stone "sculptures" with geometrical rock formations of similar design. The sculptors, each allocated a space on the cliff's edge, brought their chosen rocks and formed their desert works of art with minimal hand shaping. ⌧ *Turn off near gas station on main road at sign marked MA'ALE NOAH.*

For a look at one of the crater's geological sub-phenomena, drive into the makhtesh to see the **Carpentry.** A path goes up to a wooden walkway, built to protect nature's artwork from travelers' feet. Long ago, the sandstone was probably hardened and slightly warmed by volcanic steam, and the rocks split into prisms, due either to cooling joints or to another unknown process. The formations look like wooden chips piled up in a carpentry shop and have a lustrous patina caused by a chemical reaction brought on by climatic conditions. ⌧ *Along Rte. 40, going south.*

Another of nature's works is the **Ammonite Wall,** which is on the right as you drive through the crater. A sign indicates a distance of 5 km (3 mi), which applies to the marked hike in the crater (for fit walkers only—take water). The rock face contains hundreds of ammonite fossils, which look like ram's horns and are indeed named for the Egyptian god Ammon, who had the head of a ram.

♻ Just outside town is the **Alpaca Farm,** with its large herd of 500 sweet-face alpacas and llamas. Young and old get a kick out of feeding the animals, even if they receive the occasional spit in the face from these long-eyelashed creatures. Children weighing less than about 50 pounds can take a llama ride; the camel rides are for one and all, and so is horse-back riding (☞ *below*). Everyone loves to watch the shearing at Passover.

⊠ *Turn off main road opposite gas station,* ☎ *08/658–8047 or 08/658–6067.* 🎫 *NIS 20 ($5).* ☉ *Daily 8:30–6:30 (9–4:30 in winter).*

*En Route*   It's a **scenic drive** through the Ramon Crater. The Negev's wadis increase in size from their source, in the Sinai, and cut through the Negev on their way to the Arava Valley, to the east. The sight of the Edom Mountains on the eastern horizon is beautiful, especially in the light of late afternoon. After the Tsichor Junction with Route 13 (which connects with the nearby north–south highway Route 90), you'll see limestone strata that have "folded" over the millennia. After the Ketura Junction (where Route 40 ends), there are breathtaking views of the Arava Valley (on your left), which marks the Israel-Jordan border and is part of the Great Syrian-African Rift, a fault line formed millions of years ago. From here, Route 90 leads straight to Eilat (52 km, or 33 mi). It's not advisable to take Route 12 to Eilat if you're finishing this tour after a long day's drive or toward dark; Route 90 is the better and safer road.

## Dining and Lodging

$$   ✕ **Tsukit.** If you're lucky enough to get a window table at Tsukit ("little cliff"), you'll be sitting right on the edge of the crater, and the scenery will outshine whatever's on your plate. Choose either self- or waiter service for standard fare including meatballs, chicken, schnitzel, pasta, hummus, and stuffed vegetables. You can raise a toast to the view with beer or wine. ⊠ *Beside Mitzpe Ramon Visitors Center,* ☎ *08/658–6076. Reservations not accepted. DC, MC, V. No dinner.*

$   ✕ **Misedet Hanna.** A cheerful roadside-diner atmosphere—dark-red ta-
★   bles and chairs and the enchanting spell cast by fluorescent lighting—prevails in this gas station–cum–restaurant opposite the Mitzpe Ramon Visitors Center. The owner, who seems to know everyone here and who talks warmly to all of them at the same time, says the food comes from "mother's kitchen." She does a fine job with both the food and the prices: a hearty breakfast of vegetable salad, *havita* (a crisp, plain omelet), cheese, bread, jam, and coffee costs only NIS 25 ($6.20). Breakfast starts at 7 AM. Lunch offerings include soups, salads (a round tray with six small, fresh vegetable dishes), schnitzel, chicken, fish, spaghetti, rice, and a tasty couscous with meatballs. ⊠ *Paz gas station,* ☎ *08/658–8158. Reservations not accepted. No credit cards. Closed Sat. No dinner Fri.*

$$   ✕🏨 **Ramon Inn.** There's nothing rugged about a stay at this desert hotel,
★   on the crater's cliff. The four-story building has no elevator, but the accommodations are entirely comfortable, and the staff is cheerfully helpful. Stay in a pastel-and-white studio apartment (for one or two) or a two- or three-room apartment (for four to six people); all are equipped with kitchenettes. The lobby has an open fireplace for chilly winter nights. The 20-yard, heated swimming pool, with terrace running along one side, would not be out of place at any luxury hotel; it's open all year. The front desk can arrange camel and Jeep trips, and bikes are available. The restaurant is worth a visit, even if you're not staying here; the hearty buffet meals are enlivened by jams, pickles, and other condiments made by local cooks. Lunch is not always served, so it's a good idea to call ahead. (The lobby lounge serves light meals in a pleasant atmosphere.) ⊠ *Mitzpe Ramon, Box 318, 80600,* ☎ *08/658–8822,* 🆖 *08/658–8151. 96 rooms. Restaurant, lobby lounge, kitchenettes, pool, massage, sauna, exercise room, coin laundry. AE, DC, MC, V.* ✍

$$$   🏨 **Sukkah in the Desert.** Deep in the Negev (but accessible by road) is an out-of-the-ordinary encampment of sukkahs, the portable dwellings used by the Children of Israel when they wandered in this very same

desert. You arrive in the middle of nowhere, and there on the rocky hillside are six small, isolated dwellings, each made of stone with a palm-frond roof. Guests get together and prepare their own meals in the central sukkah. It's an appealing combination: the starkness and purity of the desert and some modern amenities. Each sukkah has a carpet on its earthen floor and a mattress with cozy blankets; household essentials include a gas hot plate for cooking, a solar heater, and a clay water jar and copper bowls for ablutions. You use the great outdoors for anything else. ⊠ *On road to Alpaca Farm, 7 km (4½ mi) west of Mitzpe Ramon, Box 272, 80600,* ☎ *08/658–6280. 6 units that sleep 2, with shared bath. No credit cards.*

**$$** 🏠 **Youth Hostel.** Known in Israel for its high standards, and fairly luxurious as hostels go, this one has to be booked well in advance (June and September are busiest). Fine for families, the place is done in bright colors, with a plant-filled lobby and a cheerfully decorated dining room. Every room size is available, from those with three bunk beds and one cot to rooms with just one bunk bed (no rooms have double beds); each room has its own bathroom. Food is inexpensive and plentiful, and you can order box lunches; nonguests must reserve for dinner. ⊠ *Opposite Mitzpe Ramon Visitors Center, 80600,* ☎ *08/658–8443,* 𝖥𝖠𝖷 *08/658–8074. 276 beds. Dining room, snack bar, dance club. DC, MC, V.*

## Nightlife and the Arts

You have two options once night falls in Mitzpe Ramon: gaze at the starry skies above, or have a drink in the lobby of the **Ramon Inn** (☞ Dining and Lodging, *above*).

Distinctive paintings, sculptures, and crafts produced by members of the local Artists Guild are on display, and for sale, in the **Artists House** (⊠ opposite visitor center, ☎ 08/659–5145). It's open Sunday–Thursday 10–1, Saturday 10–noon, or by appointment.

## Outdoor Activities and Sports

### ADVENTURE TRIPS

If you want to include a **camel ride or Jeep trip** in your Negev experience, the well-established **Desert Eco Lodge,** operated by **Desert Shade** (☎ 800/222–211 or 08/658–6229), can fill the bill. Try to reserve well in advance (☞ Guided Tours *in* Eilat and the Negev A to Z, *below*). Desert Shade also rents **mountain bikes** for NIS 45 ($11.25) a day.

**Negevland Tours** (☎ 08/658–8125, 052/703–451, or 050/308–272), based near the Ramon Inn, leads **Jeep trips** and **hikes** and rents mountain bikes. Intensive **desert trips** are also offered by nature guide Peter Bugel (☎ 08/658–8958).

### HIKING

Desert hikes are ably led by individual guides at **Desert Eco Lodge** (☎ (800/222–211 or 08/658–6229). Experienced guides can also be found at **Hadar Desert Tours** (☎ 08/658–8125 or 052/703–451). The staff at the **visitor center** (☎ 08/658–8691) in Mitzpe Ramon will help you plan local hikes, though the explanatory maps are in Hebrew (☞ Desert Precautions, *above,* for planning information). The **Society for the Protection of Nature in Israel** (SPNI; ☎ 03/638–8673 or 03/638–8677) often includes the Negev heartland in its trips.

### SWIMMING

The only body of water in town (and for miles around) is the **municipal pool** (⊠ At entrance to town, near shopping center, opposite gas station, ☎ 08/995–7702). Call for hours and admission fees.

## Shopping

The **Amonit Gallery** (08/658–6166) at the visitor center has a varied and rather unusual selection: jewelry and batiks made by the owner, water pipes, Bedouin drums, Armenian pottery, place mats showing camels in the crater, T-shirts decorated with pictures of local animals, and small, framed sketches of the area. Both the Amonit Gallery and the **Alpaca Farm** (☎ 08/658–8047) sell skeins of alpaca wool—light as a feather, soft as down, and warm as toast. It comes in natural shades of white, gray, and brown.

# BEERSHEVA TO EIN BOKEK

This area stretches east from Beersheva, known as the capital of the Negev, to the resort town of Ein Bokek, on the Dead Sea. In between are ancient Tel Arad and modern Arad. Between Beersheva and Arad you'll encounter scenes that look strikingly biblical—black tents, Bedouin shepherds with robes flying, and sheep and goats bumbling around. And after several twists of the road from Arad, you'll arrive at the spa-resort area of Ein Bokek, at the southernmost part of the Dead Sea, the lowest point on earth.

## Beersheva

**❽** *24 km (14 mi) south of Museum of Bedouin Culture, 113 km (70 mi) southeast of Tel Aviv.*

Beersheva's emblem consists of a tamarisk tree, representing the biblical past, and a pipe through which water flows, symbolizing the city's modern revival. It was here that the patriarch Abraham constructed his well (*be'er* in Hebrew) and swore an oath (*shevua* in Hebrew) over seven (*sheva* in Hebrew) ewes with the king of Gerar, who vowed to prevent his men from seizing the well. And it was here that Abraham planted a grove of tamarisk trees. The Book of Genesis describes other patriarchal figures who lived in this area as well, wandering the hills with their flocks. It's easy to envision these scenes today thanks to the cloaked figures of Bedouin shepherds with their sheep and goats in the hillside surrounding the city.

Tel Beer Sheva (☞ *below*), just outside the city, is the site of the biblical Beersheva and could easily be the site of Abraham's well. An expression from the Book of Judges, "from Dan to Beersheva," once set the northern and southern boundaries of the Land of Israel; in biblical times, living farther south of the city meant living a true desert (nomadic) life.

Romans and Byzantines built garrisons in Beersheva, but the city was later abandoned. In 1900 the Ottoman Turks, who had ruled Palestine since 1517, rebuilt Beersheva as their Negev district center (the present Old City). They set aside an area for a Bedouin market, which still takes place every Thursday (☞ Shopping, *below*). During World War I, the British took Beersheva from the Turks after a difficult battle. During the War of Independence the town became an Egyptian base, and in 1948 it was conquered by the Israelis.

Beersheva is now the the fourth-largest city in Israel, with its own university—named after David Ben-Gurion, who envisioned a flourishing Negev—and a regional hospital that serves Bedouin shepherds, kibbutzniks, and other desert dwellers. Largely blue-collar, Beersheva is struggling to provide housing for thousands of recent immigrants, many from Ethiopia and the former Soviet Union.

Nowhere is the saying "Israel's national bird is the crane" more apt than in boomtown Beersheva. The city is blossoming: workers toil to construct the municipal buildings, all of which will be concentrated in the center of town, near the Paradise Hotel; entire new neighborhoods sit neatly under the sun. The Turkish-built Old City is being spruced up; there's already a wine shop and a charming wine bar with an exceedingly good list; and a tour bus with earphone explanations shows visitors the city sights.

The famed Bedouin Market, once a treasure trove of some of Israel's best ethnic handicrafts, has been hit by modern times (items from the Far East) and isn't what it used to be. But it finally has a permanent location, and it's interesting to visit with the hope that you'll find something authentic. Most intriguing are the Bedouin themselves, wearing desert clothing and sitting cross-legged with their goods spread out on the ground.

Considering the short distances from both Tel Aviv and Jerusalem, the city is more of a jumping-off point for Negev travel—main roads branch out from here, and buses and the train serving the Negev depart from here as well. For those travelers whose time schedule inclines them to stay overnight in Beersheva, the city provides a glimpse of a growing desert city with a visually interesting citizenry.

## Dining and Lodging

$$ ✕ **Bulgarit.** Bulgarit ("Bulgarian"), on the pedestrian mall in the Old City, has been in business for 50 years; the third generation is now at the helm. The owner sits with his cronies at a corner table under a fancy silver sconce and reels off the selections from his "international" and Bulgarian-style menu: roast lamb and grilled meats, oven-baked fish and meats (the lamb is very good), moussaka, vegetables stuffed with meat and rice, *gvetch* (an assortment of vegetables cooked together), and chocolate mousse for dessert. If you speak Bulgarian, your meal comes with stories of pioneer days; if not, you still get friendly, efficient service. ⊠ *K.K. le Israel St.,* ☎ *08/623–8504. Reservations not accepted. DC, MC, V. Closed Fri.*

$$ ✕ **Pitput.** The name means "gossip" in Hebrew, and it's probably flying around this restaurant, which attracts a young crowd. It's smartly redecorated with blond-wood chairs and washed blue-and-yellow walls. The staff here is congenial and the food beautifully served. Sitting outside on the busy street or inside listening to recorded jazz or blues, desert diners have a range of selections: salads, omelets, blintzes ranging from cheese to salmon, pasta, and grilled fish with grilled vegetables. Cheese sandwiches are made on seeded rolls called *begeles*. Half bottles of Yarden wine may be ordered. You can't go wrong with hot homemade pecan pie or cheesecake with fresh fruit. ⊠ *122 Herzl St.,* ☎ *08/623–7708. Reservations not accepted. AE, DC, MC, V.*

$$ ▥ **Paradise Negev.** This five-year-old hotel provides up-to-date lodgings in the desert's urban gateway. The building's soft beige-and-brown stone reflects its desert surroundings, and arched windows soften the city's square look. Guest rooms are comfortably outfitted with wicker chairs, and the curtains and bedspreads form a snappy color scheme of red, green, and butterscotch. Good reading lights are a welcome touch. Rooms on the business floor are equipped with hair dryers and minibars. The breezy outdoor patio, complete with bubbling fountains, is a lovely place to relax in the desert climate. ⊠ *Henrietta Szold St., near City Hall, 84100,* ☎ *08/640–5444,* ꤲ *08/640–5445. 257 rooms. Restaurant, lobby lounge, pool, sauna, steam room, health club. AE, DC, MC, V.*

## Nightlife and the Arts

The **Beersheva Sinfionetta** (☎ 08/623–1616) is well regarded. Once a year, in March or April, the **Light Opera Group of the Negev** presents two performances of Gilbert and Sullivan here, in English; contact the Tourist Office in Beersheva for details.

Beersheva's yuppies congregate for theater food and drink at the **Othello** (☎ 08/623–2230), in the Beersheva Theater Building.

Savor a long, leisurely evening of wine and tapas at the **Hatzer Hayain Wine Bar** (☎ 08/623–8135), in the Artists' Quarter. Proprietor, wine expert, and congenial host Michael will guide you through the intricacies of Israeli and other wines from 8:30 PM onward, except Saturday and Sunday nights.

## Shopping

The Negev is still the home of the Bedouin, but today's Bedouin women are less interested than yesterday's in staying home all day to weave and embroider. That's why you need an eagle's eye and a saint's patience to search through the bundles and stacks of rather ordinary stuff at the **Bedouin market** to find articles made by Bedouin grandmothers. The market, which starts at daybreak each Thursday and lasts until early afternoon, is on the eastern side of the huge outdoor market site near the bridge, at Derech Eilat and Derech Hebron streets. (Men conduct a goat and sheep market on the other side.) The best time to be there is 6 AM, an hour or so later in winter. For sale, if you can find them, are wonderful embroidered dresses, yokes, and side panels from dresses; woven camel bags; rugs; earrings, bracelets, amulets, and nose rings; decorative beads and beaded bags; coin headbands (used as dowry gifts); tassels; copperware; and *finjans* (Bedouin coffee utensils). An inexpensive necklace of simple beads and cloves, used to ward off evil spirits, also makes a pleasing purchase.

Right in the Hilton Hotel is the conveniently located **Dalia Schen's Gift Shop** (☎ 08/628–2785 or 050/622–363). An expert in Israeli handicrafts, Dalia seeks out the unusual and offers a small but careful selection of weavings, artifacts, Ethiopian crafts, modern Yemenite and Bedouin jewelry, locally made rugs, and other pieces by local artists. Ask to see her unusual T-shirts and blouses decorated with old Bedouin embroidery.

An elegant wine shop in the desert? You'll be impressed with the state-of-the-art design, large stock of imported and local wines, and well-informed staff at the **Wine Center** (✉ 117 Trumpeldor St., ☎ 08/628–9444).

*En Route*  On Route 40 northeast from Beersheva to Arad is the large and impressive **Negev Brigade Memorial**, designed and built by Israeli artist Danny Karavan. The monument's 15 symbolic parts and Hebrew text tell the story of the battle of the Palmach's Negev Brigade against the Egyptians after the birth of the State of Israel. The tower, representing a Negev settlement water tower, offers a great view of Beersheva and the surrounding desert.

**Kafriat Shoket** (☎ 08/646–9421), open Sunday–Thursday 6 AM–9 PM, Friday 6–6, and Saturday 8 AM–10 PM, is a kibbutz-run way station at the intersection of Routes 31 and 60. Its large cafeteria serves hot food, sandwiches, salads, cakes, and drinks; especially recommended are the apple turnovers and raisin Danish pastries. Snack inside at the long wooden tables or outside under the tamarisk trees. The on-site minimart sells bottled water.

Continuing east along Route 31 toward Arad, you can see Bedouin encampments along the way. The slow transition from a nomadic lifestyle to a more rooted one is demonstrated by the Bedouin village of **Kuseifa,** already more than 10 years old.

## Israel Air Force Museum

🕙 **9**   *7 km (4½ mi) west of Beersheva.*

For plane lovers, this is a field of dreams. The open-air Israel Air Force Museum (also known as Hatzerim, for the nearby kibbutz) is a gigantic concrete field with 90 airplanes parked in rows. The fighter, transport, and training (plus a few enemy) aircraft tell the story of Israel's aeronautic history, from the Messerschmitt—obtained in 1948 from Czechoslovakia, and one of four such planes to help halt the Egyptian advance in the War of Independence—to the *Kfir,* Israel's first fighter plane. The young air force personnel who staff the museum lead tours that take about 2½ hours and include a movie about this branch of the military. (The movie theater is an air-conditioned Boeing 707 that was used in the 1977 rescue of Israeli passengers held hostage in a hijacked Air France plane forced to fly to Entebbe, Uganda.) Another attention-getting display is a shiny, black Supermarine Spitfire with a red lightning bolt on its side. It was flown by Ezer Weizmann, the IAF's first pilot, who became defense minister and then president of Israel. Be sure to wear a hat to protect against the sun. ⊠ *Rte. 233,* ☎ *08/990–6855 or 08/990–6890.* 💷 *NIS 22 ($6.25).* ☉ *Sun.–Thurs. 8–5, Fri. 8–noon.*

## Tel Beer Sheva

★ **10**   *2 km (1¼ mi) east of Beersheva.*

Tel Beer Sheva, biblical Beersheva—traditionally associated with the patriarch Abraham—is an artificial *tel* (mound) created by nine successive settlements between 3500 BC and 600 BC. The tel is a recent addition to the Nature and National Parks Authority's roster, ask for the excellent explanatory leaflet.

At the top of the tel is the only planned Israelite city uncovered in its entirety. Most of the visible remains date from the 10th to 7th centuries BC. A fine example of a circular layout typical of the Iron Age, the city is believed to have been destroyed around 706 BC by Sennacherib of Assyria. In the northeast, outside the 3,000-year-old city gate, is a huge well more than 6 ft in diameter, which apparently once reached ground-water 90 ft below (it has not been completely excavated). This ancient well served the city from its earliest times, and scholars speculate that it could be the well that is documented in the Old Testament as Abraham's Well (Genesis 21:22–32). The observation tower is rather ugly, but it does afford beautiful views. ⊠ *Rte. 60,* ☎ *08/646–7286.* 💷 *NIS 8 ($2).* ☉ *Apr.–Sept., Sun.–Thurs. 8–5, Fri. and holiday eves 8–3; Oct.–Mar., Sun.–Thurs. 8–4, Fri. and holiday eves 8–2, Sat. 8–4.*

## Tel Arad

**11**   *38 km (23 mi) east of Beersheva, 8 km (5 mi) west of Arad.*

Approaching Tel Arad, the 25-acre site of the biblical city of Arad, from the west takes you through flat fields of the low shrub called *rotem* (white broom). At the information center, you can pick up the Nature and National Parks Authority's pamphlet, which explains the ongoing excavations, and purchase (for NIS 8, or $2) the plan of the early Canaanite city of Arad, with a map, recommended walking tour, and diagrams of the typical Arad house. (The center also has a souvenir shop and a snack bar.)

Arad was first settled during the Chalcolithic period (4000–3000 BC) by seminomadic pastoralists who lived and traveled together, herding and farming. It was they who first developed bronze. Arad was continually occupied until the end of the Early Bronze Age (3500–3200 BC), but the city you see most clearly here is from the Early Bronze Age II (2950–2650 BC). Here you can walk around a walled urban community and enter the carefully reconstructed one-room Arad houses.

After the Early Bronze Age II, Arad was abandoned and hidden beneath the light loessial soil for nearly 2,000 years, until the 10th century BC, when a fortress—one of many in the Negev (the first may have been built by Solomon)—was built on the site's highest point. It's worth the trek up the somewhat steep path. Take a moment to appreciate the view as you take your leave of the Early Bronze Age; at the top, you step into the Iron Age (10th–6th centuries BC). The small, square fortress served the area intermittently until Roman times; most of the visible remains date from the end of the First Temple period (935–586 BC). Note the small Israelite temple sanctuary, with its two standing stones (these are replicas—the originals are in the Israel Museum, in Jerusalem) and sacrificial altar of unhewn stone. In the 7th century BC, the southern part of the Israelite kingdom of Judah reached as far as today's Eilat. Artifacts found at the tel are on display at the visitor center in Arad (☞ *below*). ⊠ *Off Rte. 31,* ☎ *08/995–7690.* ⊡ *NIS 8 ($2).* ⊙ *Sun.–Thurs. 8–5 (until 4 in winter), Fri. and holiday eves 8–4 (until 3 in winter).*

## Arad

**⑫** *46 km (28½ mi) east of Beersheva, 8 km (5 mi) east of Tel Arad.*

The modern town of Arad was established as a planned community in 1961. Arad's population of nearly 25,000 now includes immigrants from Russia and Ethiopia; writer Amos Oz is its most famous resident. Breathe deeply: the town sits 2,000 ft above sea level and is famous for its dry, pollution-free air and mild climate. Arad has made a name for itself as a healthy home for asthma sufferers. Industrial waste and the planting of trees and bushes are government controlled to keep pollution and pollen at bay. Arad is a popular base for excursions to sites in the Dead Sea area, notably to Masada (☞ Guided Tours *under* Around Jerusalem A to Z *in* Chapter 2), and is the only approach (via Route 31) to Masada's sound-and-light show.

In the middle of town is the **Arad Museum and Visitor Center,** whose helpful staff dispenses maps, brochures, and hiking information. The 20-minute audiovisual presentation gives viewers a vivid sense of the desert; it explains the causes and effects of floods (complete with downpour), shows how animals adapt to a wilderness diet, and explores other Negev issues. The small museum displays the work of local artists as well as archaeological discoveries from nearby Tel Arad. You can see replicas of the so-called "Arad letters" (the originals are in the Israel Museum, in Jerusalem), 2,500-year-old inscribed potsherds in ancient Hebrew script, some written by the fortress commander Eliashiv, concerning provisions of flour and wine for the soldiers. One has the name Arad inscribed on it seven times. ⊠ *28 Ben Yair St.,* ☎ *08/995–4409.* ⊡ *NIS 18 ($4.60).* ⊙ *Sun.–Thurs. 9–5, Fri. and holiday eves 9–2, Sat. 9–5.*

### Dining

**$$** ✕ **Pundak Alon.** On Route 31 at the entrance to Arad, next to the gas station, this eatery has served as a roadside stop and provider of a square meal for decades. Mr. Steiner, the original owner, who had served local faithfuls and travelers since 1965, used to say that "people come to visit this restaurant as though it's a historical site." The cook is the same, but the bar is new, and the wood paneling lends a country air. You can order soup, grilled or baked meat with vegetables and french fries, plus fish and, newly added to the menu, pizza. The apple strudel is known far and wide. ⊠ *Rte. 31,* ☎ *08/995–3328. Reservations not accepted. No credit cards. Closed Sat.*

## The Road to the Dead Sea

*The steep, 24-km (15-mi) descent to the Dead Sea on Rte. 31 has one sharp curve after another. Watch for the sign on the right indicating that you've reached sea level.*

The drama of this drive is enhanced by the stunning canyons and clefts that unfold on every side. Two observation points soon appear on the left. You can't cross to the first—Metsad Zohar—from your side of the road. The second—Nahal Zohar—looks down on the light marl of the ancient, dry riverbed of Zohar, the last vestige of an eons-old body of water that once covered this area. The Dead Sea lies directly east, with the Edom Mountains of Jordan on the other side. To the right (south) is Mt. Sodom. You can walk back to the left to Metsad Zohar to see the Roman-built Zohar fort.

You'll soon see, from above, the southern end of the Dead Sea, sectioned off into the huge evaporation pools of the Dead Sea Works, where potash and salts such as bromine and magnesium are extracted. It's common to see row after row of plastic "tunnels," which act as hothouses for fruit (often tomatoes and melons) that is sold to Europe in winter.

Two roads lead from Route 90 to the Ein Bokek hotel area, and when you get there you're at *the bottom of the world*: 1,292 ft below sea level. Although the Dead Sea (☞ Dead Sea Region *in* Chapter 2) can be as deep as 1,320 ft, it's much shallower at this end—only about 6½ ft deep. This area is now an artificial basin that serves the resort area at Ein Bokek and provides an abundance of minerals for local use and for export.

### Dining

$$ ✕ **Grill Michel.** A prime example of the Negev's gas-station eateries, Grill Michel is a minimally decorated (just a few posters), *Baghdad Cafe*–style diner on the road to the Zohar–Arad junction. It's run by a desert-hardened but friendly proprietor who's usually surrounded by regular customers and friends. Truck drivers, Dead Sea Works employees, and other locals come as much for the conversation and laughter as for the grub, which features simple grilled meats, french fries, hummus, fresh chopped-vegetable salads, and good, strong coffee. ⊠ *At gas station north of Rte. 31, 10 km (6 mi) from observation points,* ☎ *08/658–4289. No credit cards.*

## Ein Bokek

🔞 *8 km (5 mi) north of Zohar–Arad Junction on Rte. 90.*

The rather startling sight, in this bare landscape, of multilevel, hot-white, ultramodern hotels surrounded by waving palm trees signals your arrival at the spa-resort area of Ein Bokek, which hugs the shore of the Dead Sea. According to the Bible, it was along these shores that the Lord rained fire and brimstone on the people of Sodom and Gomorrah (Genesis 19:24) and later turned Lot's wife into a pillar of salt (Genesis 26). Here, at the lowest point on earth, the hot, sulfur-pungent air hangs heavy, the odd cry of the indigenous grackle bird is heard, and there is often a haze over the Dead Sea itself. The temperature of the oily water, where you can float and cannot sink, is 30°C (88°F) from July through September; it's coldest in February, when the temperature gets as low as 19°C (66°F).

The legendary Dead Sea, whose rare physical properties attracted glitterati such as King Herod and Cleopatra in their day, retains its unusual attractions 2,000 years later. Its salt content (six times denser than that of the Mediterranean), high content of special minerals (bromine, for example, which has a calming effect on the nervous system), and thick, black mud, enriched with organic elements, are sought out for their curative and beautifying properties. They are found nowhere else in the world.

Ein Bokek, at the southern tip of the Dead Sea, is also the site of sulfur-rich hot springs with a temperature of 31°C (88°F). This water is used along with Dead Sea water and mud to treat rheumatic and arthritic problems—even tennis elbow or a sore back. The combination of sunshine (it's sunny 320 days a year), Dead Sea water, and mineral-rich mud seems to work wonders on psoriasis and other skin problems. (So positive are the results that German and Austrian health plans cover treatments here at Ein Bokek.) Harmful sun rays are filtered out by the haze that floats over the Dead Sea, so you can even tan more healthfully.

Once upon a time, Ein Bokek comprised a handful of hotels, each of which contained a "spa" of perhaps three or four treatment rooms, with a pebbly beach out front. Today, it's a collection of large and luxurious hotels with curvy pools and grassy, sprawling outdoor areas; each with a lavish, state-of-the-art spa full of beauty and health treatments, a private beach, and a rooftop solarium. Each hotel has one restaurant, if not two or three, where a rewarding dining experience may be found. There are no restaurants outside the hotels, though a few casual eating places are lined up along the beach. The cluster of hotels in the main area is linked by a palm-fringed promenade to the two hotels located at the very southern end of the area.

Ein Bokek is a 30-minute drive from Masada and a 45-minute drive from Ein Gedi. You can enjoy Jeep trips through the lunarlike landscape east of the hotel area and explore interesting local sights, such as the nearby white-marl **Flour Cave** (from which you emerge dusted with white powder) with a driver-guide arranged through your hotel concierge, or *see* Guided Tours *below.*

## Dining and Lodging

$$$–$$$$ ✕ **Cardo Culinarium.** If you'd care to eat a Roman-style feast, wearing a toga and a laurel wreath on your head while Roman "slaves" blow trumpets, juggle flaming torches, and duel (sometimes there's a belly dancer), the Cardo is the place to go. Though the restaurant does cater to groups, the staff welcomes individual guests; just call ahead to reserve. Seated at low tables, you'll be served fresh, large pita to be dipped in olive oil and wild hyssop spice, lentil soup, juicy roast chicken or breast of duck with vegetables and salad; fresh fruit for dessert, along with lemonade, red wine, and beer. Lunch is priced at the low end of this price range; dinner is slightly higher. ⊠ *Approach to Hyatt Hotel,* ☎ *08/652–0186. Reservations essential. AE, D, MC, V. No lunch Sat., no dinner Fri.*

$$$ ✕ **Kapulsky.** It's glass enclosed, with a view of the public beach outside, and it's always crowded. Best known for gooey cakes and good coffee, the light meals also appeal. Choose from fresh salads, blintzes, sandwiches, pizza, and St. Peter's fish, plus beer and wine (meat is not

served). Changing rooms and lockers are free to customers, and the place is open every day from 8 AM to 11 PM. ⊠ *Next to shopping center,* ☎ *08/658–4382. Reservations not accepted. AE, DC, MC.*

$$ ✕ **On the Beach.** Built in late 1999, On the Beach is a welcome newcomer to the casual dining scene, and it's open 24 hours a day. Music blares; there's beer and wine to accompany such fare as steak, grilled chicken, salmon (and other fish, depending on the catch up north), sandwiches, pizza, plus ice cream and milk shakes. Visitors and locals eat outside under umbrellas, at wooden picnic benches on staggered terraces overlooking the beach. ⊠ *Opposite the Carlton,* ☎ *08/652–0231. Reservations not accepted. AE, DC, MC, V.*

$$ ✕🏨 **Crowne Plaza.** Built in 1997 and at the high end of this price range, this 12-floor hotel is not quite as lavish as some of its neighbors, though its pool and beach facilities are top level. A distinct attraction is the Giraffe Restaurant, a noodle bar consistently praised by local food writers. Guest rooms, all of which face the Dead Sea (some have balconies), are decorated in bright blue and yellow, with wicker chairs. The pool has a central island reached by a bridge, and one section is specially marked off for laps. The Sansara Spa (guests pay a small entrance fee) is a luxurious assemblage containing a sulfur pool, two whirlpools, and an extended range of health and beauty treatments from massages to cosmetic treatments and pressure showers. ⊠ *M. P. Dead Sea, 86930,* ☎ *08/659–1919. 302 rooms. 2 restaurants, lobby lounge, pool, beauty salon, sauna, spa, exercise room, beach, children's programs. AE, DC, MC, V.*

$$$$ 🏨 **Caesar Premier.** Gleaming white both inside and out, the new terraced, nine-story Caesar Premier is across the road from the beach. Two 6-ft-high silver urns furnish the soaring lobby, and glass elevators add to the airy feel. Each room has a balcony; suites have balconies with whirlpool baths. The huge wooden wall at the entrance to the dining room is carved in a distinctive bas-relief with date palms, fish, flowers, and fruit. The gracious, ultra-equipped spa (small fee for guests) features a bath for two with an underwater aromatic-oil massage, and a sulfur pool. The Dead Sea–water pool starts inside the hotel and ends outside. A motorized trolley transports guests to the beach. ⊠ *M.P. Dead Sea, 86980,* ☎ *08/668–9666,* 🆔 *08/652–0301. 298 rooms. Restaurant, lobby lounge, 3 pools, spa, children's programs, playground. AE, DC, MC, V.*

$$$ 🏨 **Golden Tulip Privilege.** Many architectural elements are present in
★ the flamboyant, banana-colored, newly opened Golden Tulip: two terraced wings, arched windows here and there, a tower, public rooms in nonconformist shapes, plus an undulating front wall that swirls around a huge flower-shape pool. Mosaic designs on the golden marble floor wend their way from the reception area, past the open-cable elevator, and into the spacious lobby, where brightly colored sofa groupings look out on an airy terrace. The strong colors are also present in the well-appointed rooms, each of which has a sofa that opens into a double bed. There's a bowling alley, and the two-floor spa (guests pay a small entrance fee) features French Phytomer skin and beauty treatments, a sulfur pool, and a Turkish bath. The Castle Scottish Pub's decor includes suits of armor; and the French Metro restaurant is done in art nouveau blue glass. The Carousel dining room serves four styles of cuisine every evening. ⊠ *M.P Dead Sea, 86930,* ☎ *08/668–9999,* 🆔 *08/668–9900. 302 rooms. 2 restaurants, lobby lounge, pub, pool, beauty salon, 2 saunas, spa, tennis, basketball, bowling, exercise room, dance club, travel services. AE, D, MC, V.*

$$$ ★ ⌂ **Hyatt Regency Dead Sea Resort and Spa.** Opened in 1996, this lavish, white, 17-story hotel was the talk of the town because it contained the first luxury spa in the area; high standards are diligently retained. Twenty rooms are devoted to beauty, fitness, and recreation. Treatments include the use of therapeutic mud and a Dead Sea–water pool. The medical center offers various services including sports medicine, postsurgery recovery, and alternative medical treatments. Part of the grand outdoor pool is heated in winter. The comfortable rooms, all of which face the water, are decorated in calm, soft browns and beiges. Puffy white bed covers and pillows add a pleasant touch. An extensive collection of Israeli paintings and sculptures decorates the public spaces. A shuttle takes guests to the hotel's private beach. One restaurant serves Italian and fish specialties; the other mixes Caribbean, European, Far Eastern, and Middle Eastern fare. ⊠ *M.P. Dead Sea, 86980,* ☎ *08/ 659–1234,* FAX *08/659–1235. 600 rooms. 2 restaurants, bar, pool, mineral baths, spa, 2 tennis courts, exercise room, squash, dance club, travel services. AE, DC, MC, V.* ⬥

$$$ ⌂ **Sheraton Moriah Plaza Dead Sea.** A venerable beachside member of the Sheraton Moriah chain, built in 1975, this hotel keeps up with the times by constantly maintaining and refurbishing its modern and well-equipped spa, which contains a Dead Sea–water pool. Weeklong package options focus on beauty, relaxation, and rheumatic treatment. The always busy but cozy lobby overlooks the outdoor pool. Rooms are decorated in pastels, and their balconies have been thoughtfully walled for privacy and have lovely views of the pool or the Dead Sea. Rooms on the first and second floors have slatted-wood roofs. At press time, renovations are in progress on rooms on the fourth and fifth floors; the rest of the floors have been recently renovated. ⊠ *M.P. Dead Sea, 86910,* ☎ *08/659–1591,* FAX *08/658–4238. 215 rooms. 2 restaurants, piano bar, snack bar, pool, beauty salon, hot tub, massage, mineral baths, sauna, tennis court, exercise room, basketball, beach. AE, DC, MC, V.*

$$ ⌂ **Hod.** There's a lot of traffic in the lobby—Italian travelers consider this a home away from home—but the feeling at the Hod remains one of homey comfort in a cheerful, friendly atmosphere. At press time, the hotel was closed until December 2000 in order to upgrade the 13-year-old building. A beautiful spa (free entrance for guests) was opened recently; its contoured areas, lined with earth-tone tiles, curve around two sulfur pools, a Dead Sea–water pool, whirlpool bath, sauna, and treatment rooms where pampering includes underwater massage, and mud treatments for face, body, and hair. The dining room looks onto the water. A walkway leads to the hotel's private beach. ⊠ *M.P. Dead Sea, 86930,* ☎ *08/668–8222,* FAX *08/658–4606. 203 rooms. Restaurant, lobby lounge, pool, beauty salon, massage, sauna, spa, exercise room, Ping-Pong, dance club, playground. AE, DC, MC, V.*

## Nightlife and the Arts

You might like to try what's on offer in the way of lobby lounges and restaurants at one of the nearby hotels, followed by a stroll on the promenade under the stars. **Kapulsky** (⊠ Next to Kanionit shopping center, ☎ 08/658–4382) is open until 11 PM for cake and coffee, and **On the Beach** (⊠ Opposite the Carlton, ☎ 08/652–0231) is open 24 hours a day.

## Outdoor Activities

### BEACHES

The Tamar Local Council has beautified the beaches that lie between the Sheraton Moriah hotel and the cluster of hotels about 2 km (1 mi) north; they're free to the public and are usually fairly crowded. Facilities include changing rooms, rest rooms, and chair rental, and there's a lifeguard on duty from mid-March through November. There is ample parking alongside the promenade. If you're interested in water sports, keep in mind that the only water sport in the Dead Sea is floating.

Luxurious spas are an understood feature of Ein Bokek's hotels, but note that you must reserve treatments in advance and pay extra for them. Make arrangements with your hotel upon arrival. You can certainly sample the sybaritic delights if you're in Ein Bokek only for a day; again, make sure to reserve treatments in advance. Each spa is under medical supervision and has an indoor Dead Sea–water pool, a sauna, and a hot tub and offers a range of beauty and health treatments using substances from the Dead Sea. Sample prices for individual treatments are as follows: NIS 140 ($35) for a half-hour massage; NIS 24 ($6) for a sulfur bath; and NIS 200 ($50) for a mud treatment. Hotel guests pay lower fees. Other facilities and services often include fitness rooms, private solariums, and cosmeticians. Some hotels offer one- or two-week spa packages, and even a one-night luxury package.

## Shopping

Several companies manufacture excellent **Dead Sea bath and beauty products** made from mud, salts, and minerals; the actual mud is sold in squishy, leak-proof packages. Ahava, DSD, and Jericho are three popular brands whose products are sold at Kapulsky and most hotel shops.

**Danny's** (⊠ At shopping center, ☎ 08/658–4435) has a wide selection of gold, silver, diamond, and Eilat stone jewelry and a workshop on the premises. It's open Sunday–Thursday 10–10 and Friday 9–3.

**Miri** (⊠ Hyatt Hotel, ☎ 08/995–6543) creates unusual, handmade, soft-body dolls, about 2 ft high, as well as droll-face puppets.

# Arava Road

*North–south from Ein Bokek to Eilat.*

Arava Road (Route 90) traverses the Arava Valley from Ein Bokek to Eilat and parallels the Jordanian border, almost touching it at some points. To the east you'll see the spiky, red-brown mountains of Moab, in Jordan.

Arava Road follows an ancient route mentioned in biblical descriptions of the journeys of the Children of Israel. The Arava (meaning "valley") is part of the Syrian-African Rift, that great crack in the earth stretching from Turkey to East Africa, the result of an ancient shift of land masses. Along the road are several agricultural settlements, as the extremely hot climate is ideal for growing fruit, flowers, and vegetables year-round.

Just south of Ein Bokek, you'll pass signs for the settlements Neot HaKikar and Ein Tamar, whose date palms draw water from underground springs rather than irrigation. This area also has a number of commercial fishponds that breed gray mullet, St. Peter's, and other varieties plus fish to stock aquariums. Neot HaKikar's perimeter fence practically touches the border with Jordan.

With the Edom Mountains rising in the east (to your left), the road continues along the southern Dead Sea Valley. You'll cross one of the largest dry riverbeds in the Negev, Nahal Zin. It's hard to believe that the large valley to the right can fill with water during the winter months (mid-December to early April), causing flash floods dangerous to both hikers and drivers (☞ Desert Precautions, *above*). The landscape is dotted with acacia, the tree used by the wandering Children of Israel to build the Ark of the Covenant, which held the tablets given to Moses at Mt. Sinai; today the acacia is a source of food for grazing goats and camels. On your left at one point, you'll see an experimental farming station's greenhouses, used for research and development by local flower and vegetable growers.

An orange sign points to the **Shezaf Nature Reserve,** where the **Shezaf Observation Point** looks out over the reddish-orange sandstone hills, to the south, and the Edom Mountains and Arava Valley, to the east, roughly the Israel-Jordan border.

| | |
|---|---|
| NEED A BREAK? | About halfway between Ein Bokek and Eilat is **Kushi Rimon** (Km 101). Named for the eccentric Shimon Rimon (whose nickname is Kushi) and the legendary army unit in which he served, this is a particularly offbeat Negev road stop. The place is huge and is landscaped with lots of palm trees and large, metal-and-wire sculptures. Peacocks and ducks wander about, and cages house a monkey and a tiger (the latter with a quotation from Jeremiah affixed to its quarters). Inside is a cafeteria with all manner of hot food, a bar stocked with every liquor imaginable, and a minimart. You'll also find a game room with a billiards table, other games, and a TV. ✉ *Km 101 on Arava Rd.,* ☎ *08/658–1609.* ☉ *Daily 24 hrs except Yom Kippur.* |

# EILAT AND ENVIRONS

The Arava Plain comes to an abrupt end where it meets the Bay of Eilat, site of the country's southernmost town: the sun-drenched resort town of Eilat. The Gulf of Eilat gives way to the Red Sea, which lies between the Sinai Mountains, to the west, and Jordan's Edom Mountains, to the east. The Jordanian port of Aqaba is directly across the bay—Eilat residents will eagerly point out the Jordanian royals' yacht and vacation villa—and to the southeast is Saudi Arabia. The Sinai Desert is just over the Egyptian border.

Most travelers fly into or whiz down to Eilat to flop down on its beaches and snorkel or scuba dive among its tropical reefs. But if you have time, give yourself a chance to see the vast desert landscape to the north of Eilat. You'll find cliffs, canyons, and unique formations at the Timna Valley Park and indigenous animals at the Hai Bar Nature Reserve. Both make good side trips from Eilat; just leave time for a sunset stop at Mt. Yoash or Mitzpe Har Hizkiyahu.

## Eilat

**14** *307 km (190 mi) south of Jerusalem, 356 km (221 mi) south of Tel Aviv.*

Eilat's strategic location as a crossroads between Asia and Africa dictated its place in history. The Children of Israel stopped here as they fled from Egypt into the Promised Land, and it was long thought that King Solomon kept his fleet in the area between Aqaba and Eilat: "And King Solomon made a navy of ships in Ezion-geber, which is beside Eloth, on the shore of the Red Sea . . ." Later, because of its position on a main trade and travel route, Eilat was conquered by every major power: the Romans, Byzantines, Arabs, Crusaders, Mamluks, Ottoman Turks, and, most recently, the British, whose isolated police station (headquarters of their camel corps) was taken by the Israelis in March 1949. Called Umm Rash Rash, this was the first building in modern-day Eilat, a town founded in 1951 and developed as a port in 1956 after the Egyptian blockade of the Tiran Straits was lifted.

A legend says that after the Creation, the angels painted the earth. When they got tired, they spilled their paints: the blue became the waters of

Eilat, and the other colors became its fish and the corals. Add to this rainbow Eilat's year-round warm weather, its superb natural surroundings of sculptural red-orange mountains, and its situation on the sparkling Red Sea—whose coral reefs attract divers from all over the world—and you've got a first-rate resort. Fittingly or ironically, depending on your view, Eilat is the sister city of Los Angeles.

Most travelers decide that Eilat's natural assets more than make up for undistinguished architecture and overdevelopment. For wherever you are in Eilat, a glance eastward presents you with the dramatic sight of the granite mountain range of Edom, whose predominant shades of red intensify and fade with the light of day, culminating in a red-gold sunset blaze over the Red Sea. This incongruous name for a body of water that's brilliantly turquoise along the shore is the result of a 17th-century typographical error by an English printer: in setting the type for an English translation of a Latin version of the Bible, the printer left out an *e,* and thus "Reed Sea" became "Red Sea." The name was easily accepted because of the sea's red appearance at sunset.

With an average annual rainfall of about 7½ inches and an average winter temperature of 21°C (70°F), Eilat is a haven from the cold winter of Israel's north. Eilat's high season is mid-October to April, but the city is also crowded during Jewish and Christian holidays. It's hottest here in July and August (39°C or 102°F)—many travel agencies close their doors, and Jeep trips and hikes are curtailed. The burning summer brings a dry heat, though, without any mugginess. The wind picks up in late afternoon, and beaches, hotel terraces, and outdoor cafés fill up with loungers sitting, sipping, and watching the Edom Mountains turn red and the Saudi Arabian hills go purple. Summer walking in Eilat is pleasant in the early morning and the late afternoon; save indoor attractions, shopping, and siestas for midday, when the heat can be still and stifling.

Arava Road (Route 90) runs north–south through the town, bordered by the airport on the east side. The main intersection just south of the airport is Durban Road, site of the tourist office (behind the Burger Ranch). The section of Eilat called the North Beach includes the promenade south to the main marina and past the lagoon and contains many of the town's luxury hotels, restaurants, and boutiques. Eilat's residential area and the Central Bus Station are in the foothills of the Eilat Mountains, which rise west of Route 90.

South of Eilat, Route 90 (now called Eilat–Taba Road) continues past the port and navy base to Coral Beach; then passes Coral Reserve, Dolphin Reef, and the Coral World Underwater Observatory and Aquarium; and finally reaches the Taba border crossing to the Sinai, in Egypt. To reach sights south of Eilat, take Bus 15 (from the hotel area; the Central Bus Station, on HaTmarim Boulevard; or Arava Road) or grab a taxi. Although the sights are close enough together that you can walk from one to the next, the inexpensive taxis are a good alternative when the afternoon sun is searing.

Start exploring Eilat with a walk along the **promenade,** beginning at Herod's Hotel, near the Jordanian border. The 3-km (2-mi) promenade is also known as the Peace Walk, since it is hoped that one day it will continue to Aqaba, Jordan. Purple and pink bougainvillea pour down from the Royal Beach Hotel's terrace above; add to your enjoyment by stopping for an ice cream (say, mango) from one of the stands. If you're here at sunset, this is the place to sit and savor the show-stopping view of the Red Sea turning red, with the dark, reddish-gray shapes of the Edom Mountains to the east and the rugged Eilat Mountains to the west. On a clear day, you can see as far as Saudi Arabia and Egypt.

A stroll past swanky hotels and loads of shops, coffee bars, and restaurants, with palmy beaches on the other side, brings you to the Dutch Bridge, which opens for tall-masted vessels. On one side is the lagoon, or inner marina where yachts are anchored and various small craft are for hire; on the other is the marina, where cruise boats of all types wait to sally forth. The promenade winds along beside more beaches, covered with folks reddening in the sun. The scene includes sophisticated strollers, the backpack crowd, artists doing quick portraits, vendors selling earrings, tattoo artists, all accompanied by strolling street musicians. At the intersection of Durban and Arava streets (at the roundabout), you can continue along the waterfront, with the Sea Gate Mall on your right, until you reach a small palm-filled plaza with a tiny, cement block-shape building with a statue of four fighters boosting a comrade aloft while a flag "flies" above. This is Umm Rash Rash, where the Israelis first took control of the Gulf of Eilat in March 1949, as determined by the U.N.'s Partition Plan. The small building—the only one that existed then—is a far cry from today's Eilat, an internationally known resort packed with palace-size hotels.

NEED A BREAK?

At the western end of the promenade, at the Sea Gate Shopping Mall (identified by the seahorse over its entrance), is the outdoor **Mul HaYam** café, which feeds the crowd with ice cream, sweet drinks, and good coffee. Locals turn out in force here to sip, chat, and watch the tourists go by.

**⓯** Less than 1 km (½ mi) south of Eilat, the **Coral Reserve** is one of the finest such protected areas in the world. Close to the shoreline, its coral reef is 1¼ km (¾ mi) long and is zealously protected by the Nature Reserves Authority. Divers (☞ Outdoor Activities and Sports, *below*) will enjoy the especially beautiful Japanese Gardens, so named for the way in which the closely packed, multicolored corals overlap each other. You can rent masks, fins, and snorkels, and perhaps try *snuba,* a form of diving in which you breathe through tubes connected to tanks carried in a boat on the surface. Landlubbers can see the reef by crossing the beach into the shallow water; just be sure to wear water-resistant shoes to protect your feet from the rough seabed and spiny sea urchins. If you do have a brush with an urchin, don't pull out the stingers, as doing so may cause infection; they dissolve in a day or two. There are hot showers and a snack bar on the premises. ⊠ *Rte. 90 (Eilat–Taba Rd.),* ☎ *08/637–6829.* ☐ *NIS 15 ($3.75).* ☉ *Nov.–Mar., daily 9–5; Apr.–Oct., daily 9–6.*

**⓰** **Dolphin Reef,** 1 km (½ mi) south of Eilat, was developed for the study of marine mammals, specifically dolphins, in their natural habitat. (Only a flexible net separates them from the open sea.) Dolphin Reef allows you the novel experience of meeting bottle-nosed dolphins face-to-face: you can actually swim, snorkel, or scuba dive with them, or join in on their training. The guide who introduces you to these friendly creatures is there to protect them from people, not the other way around. Dolphins are trained daily at 10, noon, 2, and 4. Facilities include a dive center (☞ Outdoor Activities and Sports, *below*), snorkel rental, and a photo shop with on-the-spot film and video developing. After your frolic, unwind in a serious way under the palm-frond umbrellas on the pretty beach, or at the Reef Bar, a thatched-roof pub and restaurant serving tasty seafood. Eilatis come here on Friday afternoons to "welcome" Shabbat (☞ Nightlife and the Arts, *below*). Note that you must reserve a specific time to swim or dive with the dolphins; it's best to call in advance. ⊠ *Rte. 90 (Eilat–Taba Rd.)*, ☎ *08/637–1846.* ⊡ *NIS 32 ($8).* ⊙ *Daily 9–5.*

★ ℭ ⑰    The **Coral World Underwater Observatory and Aquarium,** one of Eilat's star attractions, is recognizable by the tall space-needle structure that floats offshore. A highlight of the complex is the onshore **Red Sea Reef** (the building with stones piled around it), a circular aquarium surrounded by a coral reef. The aquarium's 12 windows provide views of rare fish so magnificent and so Day-Glo colorful that it's hard to believe they're real. The **aquarium** offers a look at fish from other parts of the world— there's an unlighted room where phosphorescent fish and other sea creatures glow in the dark and, nearby, a stingray and sea-turtle pool (one turtle is 250 years old) and shark pools. The newest attraction is the **Oceanarium,** an audiovisual show in a simulated-motion theater where you sit on a moving chair and journey through the wonders of the sea.

The **Underwater Observatory** is reached by a 110-yard wooden bridge. You might notice a yellow submarine docked to the right; it submerges several times a day to show passengers the coral reefs. Once inside the circular building, you'll find yourself in an attractive bar and restaurant, with generous picture windows for drinking in the lovely view. Head down the spiral staircase and into the sea. You are now 15 ft underwater, in a round, glass-windowed room, looking at a coral reef. Swimming in and out of the reef are thousands of exotic tropical fish in colors and shapes you might have thought only Walt Disney could have created. The **Observatory Tower**—reached by elevator or stairs— is 70 ft above sea level, allowing certain views of Israel's neighboring countries. There's a café up here. ⊠ *Rte. 90 (Eilat–Taba Rd.)*, ☎ *08/ 636–4200.* ⊡ *NIS 80 ($20).* ⊙ *Sat.–Thurs. 8:30–4:30, Fri. and holiday eves 8:30–3.* ✍

## Dining

Eilat has so many restaurants that you can dine on a different cuisine each night over a long holiday. Savor the finest local seafood and fresh fish; charcoal-grilled meats of every kind; Chinese, Indian, Thai, and Italian cuisine and other ethnic meals, which reflect Israel's many waves of immigration. Dine at a simple, florescent-lit, fishing-shack look-alike or at an elegant, well-designed, worldly restaurant. You can even eat underwater in Eilat. Many restaurants have outdoor seating, often near the water or amid pots of pink bougainvillea. The luxury hotels serve lavish meals in their stylishly designed dining rooms and restaurants. On the other end, fast food, such as crunchy falafel, abounds on HaTmarim Boulevard between the Central Bus Station and Hativat HaNegev Street, and at the Pninat Eilat shopping area. Upgraded fast food, for example *shwarma* (juicy meat sliced from a rotating vertical spit), and pizza parlors sit side by side with upscale restaurants along the North Beach Promenade, in front of the huge, fancy hotels. Outdoor cafés are a way of life in Eilat—business deals are made over café *hafuch* (strong coffee with a frothy, hot-milk topping), and others come just to see and be seen—and several cafés face the water from the new Sea Gate Mall. They serve light food, such as cheese toast (grilled-cheese sandwiches) and salads, as well as rich cakes, ice cream, iced drinks, and various coffees.

$$$$    ✕ **Red Sea Star.** You can do lunch or dinner in this inside-out aquarium 20 ft under the sea, while Technicolor fish glide by, an eel gives you the eye, and spiny sea urchins float amidst the corals outside the window. The window frames are wavy, the red tables project inwards like continuations of the coral outside, and a watery light filters through from the water's surface above—all adding to the underwater feel. To reach the Star, diners walk about 85 yards along a wooden walkway

over the water. Start with a salad of lettuce and vegetables with shrimp, calamari, and tiny squid; then move on to main courses like sea bream in paprika cream; mussels in garlic, chili, and mustard; veal steak; or spareribs in melon and chili sauce. A dessert such as dates, figs, and melon in puff pastry, spiced with cinnamon, will nicely conclude the meal. Beer and Israeli wine are on offer, and other drinks are served at the bar. ⊠ *Arava Rd., near Reef hotel,* ☎ *08/634–7777. Reservations essential. AE, DC, MC, V.*

$$$$ ✕ **Salsa.** Dramatically designed by well-known Israeli decorator Adam
★ Tihani, Salsa serves an esoteric mélange of Californian–Mexican–New Orleans cuisine in a stylish setting. The doors open onto a huge, curved bar, while a series of colorful beams and arcs soar above the dining room. Start your meal with an innovative appetizer, like scallops served on a bed of polenta with saffron sauce, or layers of fresh sea bream with an orange, lime, and chili dressing. For the main course, tuck into beef fillet medallions served with mango and red wine sauce, or chicken breast marinated in Cajun spices with sweet potatoes and crème fraîche. Or choose from fajitas, tacos, sliced mallard with balsamic sauce, or Caribbean shrimps, fried and served with a pineapple and coconut milk sauce on a bed of rice. Save room for the forest fruit and pastry treat for dessert. The wine list is top grade. ⊠ *Dan Hotel Promenade,* ☎ *08/636–2295. Reservations essential. AE, D, MC, V. Closed Mon. No lunch.*

$$$ ✕ **Au Bistrot.** In this informal town, it's fun to sit at a white-napped table, with a small lamp gleaming on your gold-rimmed plate. This bistro only serves dinner, and it will not disappoint. The extensive menu—there's a separate one for dessert—includes Emperor fillet with goose liver and morel sauce (the house specialty); frogs' legs in butter and wine; fresh shrimp in Grand Marnier sauce; and lamb chops with tomato-and-basil sauce. The Moroccan chef studied in Belgium and returns yearly to hone his skills and collect new recipes. Top-of-the-line Israeli and French wines are available. ⊠ *3 Elot St.,* ☎ *08/637–4333. Reservations essential. AE, DC, MC, V. No lunch.*

$$$ ✕ **Eddie's Hideaway.** As the name implies, Eddie's is slightly hard to find. But the way affable Eddie prepares food makes it easy to understand why his place receives rave reviews, especially for the delicious steaks. Eddie's devotees also appreciate his shrimp and fish dishes. Starters such as Buffalo chicken wings and pâté *maison* can be followed by steak Eilat (with mushrooms, mustard, cream, and brandy) or Shanghai fish with hot soybean paste. For the grand finale, try lime divine or pecan pie. It pays to inquire if Eddie has prepared a "daily"—a dish he particularly likes to cook, "as the mood strikes him." ⊠ *68 Almogim St. (enter from Elot St.),* ☎ *08/637–1137. Reservations essential. AE, DC, MC, V. No lunch.*

$$$ ✕ **Last Refuge.** This fine seafood and fish restaurant beside a Coral
★ Beach marina is highly regarded by Eilatis, who take their guests from "up north" here as a real treat. The dining room, with dark wooden paneling and predictable nautical motifs, extends outside to a spacious balcony where diners eat beside the water, looking at Aqaba across the way in Jordan. Presented with a flourish are just-caught Red Sea fish, such as grouper and drumfish; calamari; creamed seafood served in a seashell; and fish, crab, or lobster soup. Also delicious are the charcoal-grilled lobster, jumbo shrimp, and salmon fillet. A Refuge specialty are stir-fried, spicy, small sea crabs, done in olive oil and garlic. Friday night is very busy, so it's smart to reserve two days ahead (ask for balcony seating). The staff is harried but professional and eager to please. ⊠ *Rte. 90 near overhead bridge, Coral Beach,* ☎ *08/637–3627. Reservations essential. DC, MC, V. Closed 4–6 daily.*

**$$$** ✕ **Mandy's.** The first Chinese restaurant in Eilat, Mandy's opened in 1976 with the late prime minister Yitzhak Rabin in attendance. It's in a quiet area 5 km (3 mi) south of Eilat and has a sea view. The steady stream of customers, many of whom ate their first local Chinese meal at Mandy's many years ago, still appreciates the original decor, which includes seven large Chinese-style paintings. Many also like the no-smoking room, a rarity in Israel. Try out your chopsticks on such tasty dishes as pork in oyster sauce, fish in hot garlic sauce, steamed fish with ginger, spareribs Szechuan style, crispy duck, dim sum, and the house special, Shrimp Kon Po. A business lunch costs NIS 50 ($12.50). Israeli, French, and some Chilean wines are available. ⊠ *Arava Rd., Coral Beach,* ☎ *08/637–2238. Reservations essential. AE, DC, MC, V.*

**$$$** ✕ **Tandoori.** Indian cuisine of the first order is graciously presented amid embroidered wall hangings, authentic Indian wood carvings, and brass table appointments. The food is prepared to order; while you wait, sip a *lassi* (a refreshing Indian drink of yogurt, fruit, and saffron) or one of the many cocktails on the menu. House specialties are various succulent meats cooked in a tandoor (a charcoal-fired clay oven), curries, and a selection of vegetarian dishes. Indian musicians and dancers perform at night. The moderately priced business lunch (from noon to 3:30), served in this pretty setting, is a welcome respite on a hot day. ⊠ *King's Wharf at the lagoon (below Lagoona Hotel),* ☎ *08/633–3879. Reservations essential. AE, DC, MC, V.*

**$$** ✕ **Lalo.** Here's a top-drawer example of ethnic cooking. Lalo's family has run this place since 1972 and his mother's Moroccan cooking is simply delicious. Upon your arrival, five different kinds of salads, made from eggplants or hot peppers, for example, are quickly placed upon the table; they're on the house. The menu may confront you with choices you've never eaten before, but this food is bound to reward your daring approach. Consider such delicacies as beef cooked with hummus (a house specialty), beef cooked with olives, brains served straight-up with Moroccan spices, couscous with vegetables and chicken, and fresh-caught fish cooked with hot spices. No fancy pita here—plain bread accompanies Lalo's food. Dessert is specially prepared fruit, such as oranges cooked until thick and soft, accompanied by tea with mint, or a local leaf called *sheba,* which has a mild, fruity taste. ⊠ *259 Horev, Shikun Alef,* ☎ *08/633–0578. Reservations essential. AE, D, MC, V. Closed Fri. and Sat.*

**$$** ✕ **Mai Tai.** This small and serene restaurant serves authentic Thai food, not the more common Israelized Asian cuisine. Thai cooking is popular in Eilat, and Mai Tai is often singled out by selective diners. The fixed menu of soup, egg roll, main course, rice, tea, and dessert comes to a moderate NIS 78 ($19.50), and there's an à la carte menu as well. The lamp shades made of Thai food baskets and rice-paper umbrellas are a nice touch. ⊠ *Yotam St.,* ☎ *08/637–2517. Reservations essential. AE, DC, MC, V. Closed 3:30–6:30.*

**$$** ✕ **Shauli and Guy.** Two brothers and their dad run this place, inviting you to feast on special Algerian-Tripolitan-style grilled meats such as veal chops, lamb chops, and skewers of lamb (there's fish, too). These guys know what they're about: three generations of butchers work in the family-run butcher shop next door. Start with a plate of hummus and mushrooms, and try to make room for the first-rate chips (french fries). The grilled goose liver here is sublime. The plain and simple setting is both spotless and homey—a Coke cooler looms large over the white-Formica tables and chairs, and the kitchen forms one end of the room. Wine and beer are available. It's in the middle of the Industrial Zone, so you can't walk here; but taxi drivers know this place well. ⊠ *"Azore Hatassia" (Industrial Zone),* ☎ *08/633–1930. Reservations not accepted. AE, DC, MC, V. No lunch Sat., no dinner Fri.*

$$ × **Spring Onion.** Vegetarians, front and center! Here's the place to get
★ garden-fresh salads dressed with interesting toppings, as well as deli-
cately cooked vegetable quiches, fresh fish, blintzes, and surprisingly au-
thentic pizzas. The noodles tossed with vegetables in ginger and soy sauce
is an appetizing dish. There's also a selection of what's known as cheese
toast in Israel: a grilled-cheese sandwich (with tuna, tomato, or egg). Por-
tions are large, but if you have room, try a layer cake or a cream cake.
Beer and wine are available. The two floors are always crowded (the top
floor is no-smoking), but there's plenty of outdoor seating. ⊠ *Bridge
House, near the bridge,* ☎ *08/637–7434. AE, D, MC, V.*

## Lodging

$$$$ 🏨 **Dan Eilat.** The 14-floor, U-shape Dan is on the North Beach Prom-
★ enade near the Jordanian border. The decor, designed by Israeli archi-
tect Adam Tihani, is nothing short of stunning, effectively combining
high style with comfort. The two connecting two-story lobbies feature
a winding glass stairway (as scary as it sounds), craggy rock walls with
a water cascade, floating ceiling sculptures, a huge aviary, a rock pool
with iguanas, and creative Italian furnishings. The spacious blue and
terra-cotta rooms have blond furnishings and lack for nothing—the
dresser mirror, for example, can be adjusted to reflect the sea. The large,
lush outdoor area features a 20-meter pool for serious swimmers, a
children's pool, a special pool with waterfalls and a slide, and a shaded
hot tub. One of the three restaurants serves Lebanese and Mediterranean
food, another French, and the third a meat buffet. As part of the local
Dan Hotel chain, this hotel is well managed. ⊠ *Promenade, North Beach,
88000,* ☎ *08/636–2222,* 𝔽𝔸𝕏 *08/636–2333. 374 rooms. 3 restaurants,
bar, 3 pools, hot tub, sauna, spa, Turkish bath, health club, squash,
video games, children's programs. AE, DC, MC, V.* 🍽

$$$$ 🏨 **Herod's.** Managed by Sheraton Moriah, this is the newest and most
★ extravagant hotel in Eilat. Set opposite the beach with Jordan's moun-
tains as a backdrop, Herod's—designed with legendary King Herod
as the theme—is all about over-the-top opulence. Luxury is found
throughout: from the minaret towers that greet you outside to the dra-
matic 12-story-high lobby, decorated with Italian wrought-iron chan-
deliers, carved marble planters, and mosaics. Romanesque domes,
arches, bridges, and niches are everywhere. Rooms are spacious and
comfortable, with warm, dark wood furniture; lush curtains; a CD player
complete with classical and jazz discs; and a coffee corner. The mar-
ble-and-gold bathrooms are equipped with shower massagers. A
Roman-style pool sits at the end of an avenue of palm trees and is de-
signed to look as though it flows straight into the sea. The Vitalis Spa
Hotel, affiliated with and next door to Herod's, is a boutique hotel
with 64 rooms, each with a hot tub and a private terrace. It was de-
signed as a health and lifestyle spa, and attention is paid to every de-
tail. The outdoor swimming pool leads gracefully into the indoor pool,
and the dining room, decorated in off-white, presents beautifully
served, healthy meals; menus changes daily. ⊠ *North Beach, Box
4201, 88000,* ☎ *08/638–0000. 300 rooms. 3 restaurants, lobby lounge,
piano bar, pool. AE, DC, MC, V.* 🍽

$$$$ 🏨 **Princess.** Geographically the last hotel in Israel (it's five minutes from
★ the Egyptian border), the Princess is also the last word in sophisticated
lodging. The light-filled reception area faces a two-story sheer rock cliff
through a glass wall. The public spaces are dazzlingly white with gold
trim, and six of the suites are decorated in themes, such as Chinese,
Moroccan, and Indian. The pool area is a country club in itself, with
squiggle-shape pools connected by bridges. Down at the beach, reached
by a tunnel under the road, two jetties lead to the water, and sun beds
beckon. The spa in this self-contained world is ultramodern; and other

amenities include shops, a drugstore, and a shuttle into town. The splendid Kings nightclub and disco is located on the premises. The Princess is at the low end of this price category. ⊠ *Rte. 90 (Eilat–Taba Rd.), Box 2323, 88000,* ☎ *08/636–5555,* FAX *08/637–6333. 418 rooms. 2 restaurants, pub, 2 pools, beauty salon, spa, 2 tennis courts, health club, dance club, children's programs. AE, DC, MC, V.* ✇

**$$$$** 🏨 **Queen of Sheba.** The imaginary palace that King Solomon built for the queen is what Hilton international set out to build, the first of its "theme" hotels. It certainly looks like a palace: an entrance capped with a pillared dome rises between two turrets, with a wing of more than 200 rooms on either side. The stunning interior was decorated by a designer who traveled to places like southern Africa and India for inspiration and authenticity. Khaki-color curtains cover the windows of the 40-ft-high lobby, and Italian mosaics of biblical animals cover the floor. The queen must have loved cats, because they're represented everywhere: on plant urns, on the backs of sofas; feline statues even stand guard over the pool. The elegant bedrooms have gold-framed mirrors, oversize beds covered with navy blue, beige-and-tobacco spreads, inlaid furniture, and marble bathrooms with hand-painted murals. Rooms on even-numbered floors have balconies facing the sea or the marina. Lotus flowers decorate the floor of the outdoor pool. The spa matches the hotel in luxury and comfort. ⊠ *North Beach, Box 2228, 88121,* ☎ *08/630–6666,* FAX *08/630–6677. 488 rooms. 2 restaurants, beauty salon, hot tub, massage, sauna, exercise room, children's programs. AE, DC, MC, V.* ✇

**$$$$** 🏨 **Royal Beach.** Isrotel's latest addition to its Eilat collection, Royal
★ Beach is the jewel in the company's crown. It's not glitzy (though there is a glass elevator), but the Royal holds its own in the glamour department. Opened in 1994, this beachfront property is well known for its interesting collection of paintings and sculptures by Israeli artists. The oversized terrace, filled with purple pansies, faces the Bay of Eilat, providing a stunning view at sundown. Rooms are decorated in warm blue and rose; all have comfortable sofas and chairs and a coffee corner, and the 22 suites come with whirlpool tubs. Two rooms are equipped for those with hearing impairments. There's a beautiful, fully equipped spa on the premises. ⊠ *North Beach,* ☎ *08/636–8888,* FAX *08/ 636–8811. 363 rooms. 5 restaurants, lobby lounge, bar, pub, 3 pools, hot tub, massage, sauna, children's programs. AE, DC, MC, V.* ✇

**$$$** 🏨 **Ambassador.** This spiffy hotel shares its grounds and facilities with the Manta Diving Club (☞ *below*), so you'll see lots of wet suits making their way through the splashily decorated lobby. (Ambassador guests get a discount at the Dive Center.) The hotel's entrance, facing the Eilat Mountains, is up a palm-lined lane; inside, the decor is ultramodern and lively. Rooms face the pool and the sea and have light-blue carpeting, wood furniture, and sea-green bedspreads. Every room has a coffee corner, with a small refrigerator, coffeemaker, and cups. The beach and seafood restaurant are just across the road. At press time, work was under way on a spa. ⊠ *Rte. 90 (Eilat–Taba Rd.), 88000,* ☎ *08/638–2222,* FAX *08/ 638–2200. 170 rooms. Restaurant, lobby lounge, 2 pools, sauna, dive shop, children's programs. AE, DC, MC, V.*

**$$$** 🏨 **Club-In Villa Resort.** This resort is a two-level arrangement of connected, self-contained "villas" set into the mountainside opposite the Coral Beach Reserve. Each unit has two bedrooms (which can accommodate up to six guests), a kitchenette with a microwave (there's a minimart on the premises), a balcony, and a living room with a TV. Picking up on the desert colors outside, rooms are beige with sky-blue ceilings and cacti painted on some walls. Front units face the pool; those in the rear have mountain views. If you don't want to prepare your own meals, just present yourself in the dining room. ⊠ *Rte. 90 (Eilat–*

*Taba Rd.), Box 1505, Coral Beach 88000, ☎ 08/638–5555, FAX 08/
638–5533. 168 villa units. Restaurant, bar, grocery, lobby lounge,
pool, tennis court, exercise room, dance club, children's programs. AE,
DC, MC, V*

$$$ 🏨 **Le Meridien.** Enter this elegant hotel and the first thing you'll see
★ through its glass walls is a breathtaking view of the shimmering sea
and Jordanian mountains beyond. This all-suite lodging will appeal to
the most refined taste. Junior suites are large enough to contain a
table for four and a good-size sofa. Parents can keep an eye on their
children in the Kids' Club via a closed-circuit system transmitted to
their television set. The acclaimed in-house Tricolore fish and sushi restau-
rant is supervised by one of Israel's top chefs. The spacious lobby lounge
has a bar and a dance floor (there's a quiet lobby as well). The spa of-
fers the last word in beauty and health treatments, and there's a beach
exclusively for hotel guests. ⊠ *Arava Rd., Box 2120, 88119, ☎ 08/
638–3333, FAX 08/638–3300. 245 suites. 2 restaurants, beauty salon,
hot tub, 2 saunas, spa, exercise room, children's programs. AE, DC,
MC, V.* 🛥

$$$ 🏨 **Sheraton Moriah Plaza.** Facing the beach from the promenade near
the marina, this pleasing, six-floor hotel could not have a better loca-
tion; everything is within walking distance. The eye-catching lobby has
a slanted glass roof, trees decorated with tiny white lights, and a cut-
glass wall that separates it from the dining room. Vanilla wicker chairs,
other furniture in blue and beige, with bedspreads in rose and soft
turquoise furnish the rooms, and balconies face the pool. The fourth-
floor business lounge has fax and e-mail facilities. Three pool areas ensure your rest and relaxation. The Moriah manages the beach out front.
⊠ *Promenade, Box 135, Eilat 88000, ☎ 08/636–1111, FAX 08/633–
4158. 306 rooms. 3 restaurants, lobby lounge, 2 pools, beauty salon,
hot tub, massage, sauna, exercise room, beach, business services. AE,
DC, MC, V.*

$$ 🏨 **Crowne Plaza.** You can count on competent service at this nine-floor
hotel, which faces the lagoon. The well-designed public areas are dec-
orated in cool white and beige; the entrance features a glass-domed ceil-
ing. Guest rooms have tasteful, light-wood furniture and bedspreads
of coral, pink, and blue. The entire fifth floor is no-smoking. ⊠ *La-
goon, North Beach, 88101, ☎ 08/636–7777, FAX 08/633–0821. 202
rooms. 2 restaurants, lobby lounge, pool, no-smoking floor, beauty salon,
hot tub, massage, sauna, health club, children's programs. AE, DC,
MC, V.*

$$ 🏨 **King Solomon's Palace.** Solomon's entire court could have been ac-
commodated at this hotel, one of the dignified senior members of the
Isrotel chain. It's huge and comfortably utilitarian, with an expansive
lobby furnished in beige wicker with gray upholstery. The staff attends
to your every need, and everything runs like clockwork. An excellent
new spa updates the venerable Solomon's, and there's a large games room
on the premises. The commodious dining room is divided into two small
restaurants serving Chinese and Italian food; the breakfast buffet is vast.
A palm-fringed pool overlooks the Lagoon. The garden-terrace suites
have their own hot tubs. Younger guests will love the children's building, with rooms for various activities. ⊠ *Promenade, North Beach,
88000, ☎ 08/633–3444, FAX 08/633–4189. 420 rooms. 3 restaurants,
piano bar, pool, hot tub, massage, 2 saunas, 2 tennis courts, health club,
dance club, playground, children's programs. AE, DC, MC, V.*

$$ 🏨 **Taba Hilton.** If you'd like to avoid the hubbub, you'll appreciate the
isolation of the Taba, which is just over the Egyptian border in the Sinai,
11 km (7 mi) south of Eilat. (A shuttle bus whisks you from border to
hotel.) The fine service and excellent cuisine (Italian and Middle East-
ern) put the Taba on a par with Israel's top hotels. Most rooms have

balconies overlooking the pool or the sea; and in case you don't feel like leaving the premises, there's a three-story gambling casino on-site. The two large pools (one seawater, one freshwater) have only one drawback: no lifeguard. The hotel's extensive beach (also unguarded) has a dive center and water-sports center, sunshades, a snack bar, and a playground. Nelson Village, an extension of the Taba Hilton, is an 84-room, three-level, stone-and-wood building on the beach; it's named after the late bohemian Rafi Nelson, a bearded local character and tourist attraction who set up his own "village" right here. ⊠ *Taba Beach, Egypt (mailing address: Box 892, Eilat 88107),* ☎ *062/530–140 in Egypt, 08/632–6222 in Israel;* FAX *02/578–7044 in Egypt, 08/632–6660 in Israel. 326 rooms. 5 restaurants, 3 bars, 2 pools, hot tub, massage, 5 tennis courts, beach, dive shop, boating, waterskiing, children's programs, playground, travel services, car rental. AE, DC, MC, V.* ⊛

$  🏠 **Eilat Youth Hostel & Guest House.** The word *hostel* takes on new meaning here: each room is air-conditioned and has its own bathroom. Rooms are simply furnished and sleep two to six. A mere 10-minute walk from the central bus station and right across the highway from the beach at the Red Rock Hotel, this hostel is a popular place with the backpack crowd, so make reservations well ahead of time. The dining room serves lunch and dinner if you order ahead. Bed linen and towels are provided in the Guest House section. ⊠ *Arava Rd., Box 152, 88101,* ☎ *08/637–0088,* FAX *08/637–5835. 80 rooms. Coin laundry. AE, DC, MC, V.*

$  🏠 **Reef.** This modest, stucco beachfront hotel occupies a quieter spot,
★  away from the clutch of hotels farther north. The corresponding perk—a notable plus—is your direct access to the beach from the Reef's wooden sundeck and pool area. Water-sports outfits, including a dive center, are but a splash away. The modern rooms are in soothing light green and mauve; all balconies face the sea. There are rooms around the pool on the ground level. The dining room is fresh and lively. Built in 1992, the Reef doesn't pretend to be luxurious; with its friendly staff it's good value for your money. ⊠ *Rte. 90 (Eilat–Taba Rd.), Box 3367, 88100,* ☎ *08/636–4444,* FAX *08/636–4488. 79 rooms. Piano bar, pool AE, DC, MC, V.*

$  🏠 **Topaz.** A tourist area has sprouted along the main road into Eilat, near the central bus station. It's surprisingly pleasant and set well back from the road. One of several hotels in this nicely landscaped area, the two-year-old Topaz attracts those who want good value for their money. It has 50 large studios and 30 four-person suites, decorated in blue and beige. Every unit has a refrigerator and space to eat, and the complex has a central, fresh-looking dining room, with a nice selection of artwork on the walls. ⊠ *Shfifon St., Box 609, 88103,* ☎ *08/ 636–2111,* FAX *08/636–2121. 50 rooms, 30 suites. Restaurant, lobby lounge, pool, children's programs. AE, DC, MC, V.*

## Nightlife and the Arts

For an overview of local events, pick up a copy of the detailed leaflet "Events and Places of Interest," available at the Tourist Information Office. For the coming week's arts and entertainment information, check out Friday's *Jerusalem Post* magazine, or the *Herald Tribune's HaAretz Guide,* both of which carry listings for the entire country.

### BARS AND CLUBS

Most hotels in Eilat have a piano bar (some with space for cutting loose), and many have dance clubs; all are open to the public. Pubs also abound; top bands perform at several, and at many you can even get a decent meal.

**Dolphin Reef** (✉ Eilat–Taba Rd. (Rte 90), ☎ 08/637–1846) is a good example of a bar-pub-restaurant. Eilatis have a soft spot for **Teddy's** (✉ Ophira Park, ☎ 08/637–3949), which has a long wooden bar (managed by a Welshman) and a restaurant. Very popular is **Three Monkeys** (✉ Royal Beach Promenade, ☎ 08/636–8888); good bands are the claim to fame here. For traditionalists, the nautically decorated **Yacht Pub** (✉ King's Wharf, ☎ 08/633–4111) is the real McCoy: it was transported from England.

**King's** (✉ Eilat–Taba Rd., ☎ 08/636–5555), at the Princess Hotel, tops the disco bill, with mirrored walls, fluted columns, and a checkered dance floor. **Platinum** (✉ Promenade, ☎ 08/633–4111), at the King Solomon Hotel, has laser light shows. **Yekev** (✉ Industrial Area, ☎ 08/633–4343), where the noise can't disturb anyone, hosts Israeli music and dancing on the tables; take a taxi there. Other dancing options are **beach parties,** where bronzed bodies groove to recorded music all night long; keep an eye out in town for English-language posters listing times and places. Admission is free.

For a taste of the nautical nightlife, consider dining and dancing under moonlit Red Sea skies while bobbing in a boat. **Eilat Cruises** (✉ At the marina, ☎ 08/633–3351) runs evening trips with live music for NIS 66 ($18.80). The **Red Sea Sports Club** (✉ King's Wharf, ☎ 08/637–9685) has night cruises.

Two of the country's most important music events have taken place in Eilat for the last several years, namely the **Red Sea Jazz Festival** (held in Eilat's cargo port during the last four days of August), and the chamber music concerts, called **Music by the Red Sea,** in December and January. At press time, the continuance of these two festivals was not certain; so check with the tourist office first. The **Philip Murray Cultural Center** (✉ HaTmarim Blvd., ☎ 08/637–2257) hosts classical music, art exhibits, and other cultural events year-round.

From October to mid-April, Saturday nights bring Israeli folk dance and entertainment to **Kibbutz Elot** (☎ 08/637–3565), or the Tourist Information Office (☎ 08/637–2111), 5 km (3 mi) north of Eilat. Tickets, which include transportation and a buffet dinner, are $48.

A pleasant way to spend an evening (or an afternoon) is to have coffee and a chat with an Israeli family at their home. For information and arrangements, call **Mrs. Morris** (☎ 08/637–2344).

For an early evening sampling of "Private Collection" Carmel wines (produced north of Tel Aviv in the Shomron area), drop in at **Ha Martef** (✉ 3 Haniyot Shva, ☎ 08/637–2787), Eilat's oldest wine shop. Owner and savant Itzik Ben Adiva will happily bring you up to date on Israel's burgeoning viniculture scene in his modest, jam-packed shop. It's in the Industrial Area close to Eddie's Hideaway and Au Bistrot restaurants; look for wall-size murals of women treading grapes with snowcapped Mt. Hermon in the background. Ha Martef is open Sunday through Thursday, 9 to 1 and 5 to 8, Friday 9 to 2, and closed Saturday.

## Outdoor Activities and Sports
Many of the activities outlined below can be arranged through your hotel or a travel agency. Several tour operators maintain desks in hotel lobbies and will take reservations there. For more information on guided activities, *see* Guided Tours *in* Eilat and the Negev A to Z, *below.*

### BEACHES

Eilat's beachfront—the North Beach and the South Beach—is unusual in that none of it is private; rather, the municipality grants licenses to individuals to run certain sections. In turn, the beach managers must ensure the cleanliness of their section and provide open-air showers and (for a fee) deck chairs. The Tourist Patrol makes sure that standards are maintained, and can also be called on for assistance. Most of the beaches are free and have a clublike atmosphere, with thatched-roof restaurants and pubs, contemporary music, and dancing day and night. The beach at the Plaza Neptune hotel is particularly pleasant. Although topless bathing is against the law, you'll often see European women indulging, mostly on the southern beaches.

Young people tend to hang out at the southernmost beaches, where the dive centers are, while families favor North Beach, which runs northeast from the intersection of Durban and Arava streets up to the marina and the bridge. North Beach is always full of action—you can go paragliding or rent paddle boats or a "banana" (a plastic boat towed by a motorboat), and dancing goes on into the wee hours, in the pubs and on the beach. Farther along, after the Bridge and opposite the Queen of Sheba, Royal Beach, Dan, and Herod's hotels, lies a beautifully landscaped series of beaches. The southern beaches (south of the port, along the Eilat–Taba Road) share the coast with the Underwater Observatory, Dolphin Reef, and the Coral Reserve.

### BIKING

Rent 18-gear mountain bikes from **Red Sea Sports** at the Ambassador hotel (☎ 08/638–2222), or at Bridge House near the marina (☎ 08/633–3666). Wheels cost $22, and riders must be over nine years old.

### BIRD-WATCHING

The **International Bird-watching Center** (✉ Entrance to Eilat, at Dor gas station, ☎ 08/633–5339) provides Thursday lectures at 6 PM at the Meridien Hotel (✉ North Beach) and also organizes Jeep bird-watching tours (☞ Guided Tours *in* Eilat and the Negev A to Z, *below*).

### BOATING

There are boat-rental and water-sports facilities at both Eilat's marina (near the Bridge) and Coral Beach, the area south of the port on the Eilat–Taba Road (Route 90). The **Red Sea Sports Club** (☎ 08/633–3666), at King's Wharf on the Lagoon, rents paddleboats, canoes, and minispeedboats. You can also charter a 150-horsepower speedboat piloted by a water-ski instructor for $120 per hour.

### HORSEBACK RIDING

**Texas Ranch** (✉ Rte. 90, ☎ 08/637–6663 or 08/637–9685), in Coral Beach, takes riders on trails through Wadi Shlomo (Solomon's Valley) and into the desert. The sunset rides are particularly popular. The cost is $35; call ahead to reserve a horse. Children over 12 who know how to ride are welcome on the trails, and younger children may ride in the ring for $17 for 30 minutes.

### PARASAILING

**Red Sea Sports Club** (✉ Bridge House, ☎ 08/633–3666) will give you a bird's-eye view of all those beach loafers for $35 per 10 minutes.

### RAPPELLING

It's actually called "snappelling" in Israel. **Jeep See** (✉ Bridge House, near the marina, Box 4188, ☎ 08/633–0133) runs trips for both novices and more experienced rappellers. Call in advance to reserve. Cost is NIS 160 ($40) per person, with a minimum of 10 participants.

## SCOOTERS

See the sights on a Piaggio scooter, available from **Doobie** (✉ North Beach, ☎ 08/633–4004 or 050/503–917), at the Dalia hotel. Depending on the type of scooter, the price for half a day ranges from NIS 70 ($17) to NIS 85 ($21). Double those amounts for a whole day.

## SCUBA DIVING AND SNORKELING

Divers have excellent facilities at the marina in North Beach and at Coral Beach, offering diving courses, introductory dives for the whole family, and night dives. Equipment is available for rental or purchase.

The **Aqua Sport International Red Sea Diving Center Ltd.** (✉ Coral Beach, ☎ 08/633–4404), where there's a beach and a bar, was the first diving center established in the Middle East. Aqua Sport offers one-day dive cruises with lunch NIS? ($77 per person) plus weekly diving safaris that run from one to five days. You'll take a Jeep to the most exotic dive locations, such as the famous Blue Hole and Ras-Nasrani at Sharm-el-Sheikh, in the Sinai. **Lucky Divers** (✉ Promenade, ☎ 08/633–5990), at the Galei Eilat Hotel, operates a top-quality, full-service dive center. **Manta Diving Club** (✉ Eilat–Taba Rd., Coral Beach, ☎ 08/637–6569), at the Ambassador hotel, is an excellent diving center.

The **Coral Reserve** (✉ Eilat–Taba Rd., Coral Beach, ☎ 08/637–6829), open daily 8–6 (8–5 in winter), is a great place to observe the fabulous fish and corals. Qualified divers, in limited numbers, can explore the unique coral formations of the so-called Japanese Gardens. Call ahead to reserve a time. You can't rent diving equipment here, but snorkeling equipment is available. Masks rent for NIS 6 ($1.50), snorkels for NIS 6 ($1.50), and fins for NIS 9 ($2.25). Admission to the Coral Reserve is NIS 15 ($3.75). Be sure to wear protective footgear. Facilities include hot showers, lockers, and a small restaurant.

Families (children must be over 10) will have fun "snuba"-diving at the **Caves Reef** (☎ 08/637–2722), south of the Underwater Observatory. In this snorkeling-diving hybrid, you breathe through tubes connected to tanks carried in a rubber boat. The price, NIS 120 ($30) per person, includes instruction, a practice session in shallow water, and a guided underwater tour that goes no deeper than 20 ft. Reserve in advance.

At **Dolphin Reef** (✉ Eilat–Taba Rd. [Rte 90], Coral Beach, ☎ 08/637–1846), you can "dive with dolphins" using snorkel equipment (NIS 150, or $38.75, for half an hour), and preserve the experience on video for posterity (for an extra charge). Call ahead for a reservation. Dolphin Reef also runs a professional dive center.

## SKI-DIVING

Fly high—from 11,000 ft—in a tandem jump where you free-fall for 40 seconds at more than 280 mph. Pull the cord and you slow to a six-minute ride with your instructor. Call **Sky Dive Eilat** (☎ 052/629–004 or 08/637–2745) for this big thrill, available on Fridays and Saturdays. The location is 72 km (45 mi) north of Eilat; the cost is a hefty NIS 880 ($222).

## SPAS

There isn't a hotel in Eilat that doesn't boast a spa, and those in the plush hotels are definitely the best. Many use Dead Sea mud and other products for health and beauty treatments. The new **Herod's** hotel (☎ 08/638–0000), has an exclusive, luxurious spa hotel attached to the main hotel, with state-of-the-art facilities.

SWIMMING

Most hotels have outdoor pools, but you can also go to the **public pool** (⌧ Hativat HaNegev St., ☎ 08/636–7233). Call for hours and admission fees.

TENNIS AND SQUASH

Many hotels have floodlit tennis courts. At the **Sport Hotel Country Club** (⌧ North Beach, ☎ 08/630–6338), tennis courts are available at the hourly rate of $10 in the morning and $12 in the evening; you can rent racket and balls. The luxurious **Dan Hotel** ☎ (08/636–2222) has two squash courts available to visitors for NIS 48 ($12) per 40 minutes.

WINDSURFING AND WATERSKIING

Windsurfing equipment and lessons are available at the **Aqua Sport International Red Sea Diving Center Ltd.** (⌧ Coral Beach, ☎ 08/633–4404); one hour on the board costs $24. **Mistral** (⌧ Coral Beach, ☎ 08/637–6416), near the Reef hotel, rents Windsurfers at the rate of $18 for 30 minutes and $70 for five hours. At the **Red Sea Sports Club** (⌧ Bridge House, ☎ 08/633–3666 or 08/637–9685), water-skiers can rent equipment and boats for $35 for 15 minutes.

## Shopping

Eilat is a tax-free zone, meaning that all items are exempt from VAT (Value-Added Tax) and/or purchase tax. Articles such as bathing suits and jewelry sold in chain stores are less expensive in Eilat branches. Items that are price controlled, such as gas, beer, cigarettes, and alcohol, are also cheaper.

The city has two shopping malls: **Sea Gate Mall** (at the western end of the promenade), where you'll find a plethora of clothing shops, gift shops, and fast-food restaurants, plus a postal agency, drugstore, bookstore, and coffeehouses outside facing the sea. **Kanion Adom and Shalom Plaza** (⌧ HaTmarim Blvd.), connected by a café-filled passage, has a variety of shops, though on a smaller scale, and a notable absence of souvenir and gift shops.

On the western side of the Marina Bridge, Eilat's four largest hotels sit tall and splendid. On the ground level of each hotel, along the beachside promenade, is one luxury shop after another, forming a continuous lineup of at least 40 stores, interspersed with restaurants, pubs, and coffee bars. There's an interesting variety of shops here. **Emporium** carries familiar designer names such as DKNY, Polo, and Calvin Klein. **Padani** (☎ 08/631–5038) has a good selection of diamond and gold jewelry. **Red Sea Sportswear** (☎ 08/633–0825) handles the latest in swim and surf wear. The **Royal Beach Rotunda** (☎ 08/636–8811) has everything from resort wear and cosmetics to T-shirts, jewelry, and toys. At Herod's hotel, the **Cardo** (☎ 08/638–0000 is an intriguing marketplace decorated with Bedouin embroidered dresses, where one finds rather unusual paintings, sculpture, Judaica, old-style objets d'art, Moroccan furnishings such as painted and inlaid mirrors, boxes and frames, gifts, and wall hangings. If you've been sunning during the day, you'll have time to shop at night—these shops are open until 9 PM and often later (except Friday night).

**Malkit** (⌧ HaDekel neighborhood, ☎ 08/637–3372) is a well-known store that houses a workshop where Eilat stones are cut, polished, and set in a whole line of jewelry designed in-house; it's open Sunday–Thursday 8–7, Friday 8–1.

**H. Stern** (☎ 08/637–2898), in the King Solomon, has an excellent reputation for high quality. It sells gold and diamond jewelry, pearls, and it also has a small selection of silver sculptures by well-known jewelry designer Frank Meisler. In case you forgot your watch, **Padani** (⊠ Royal Beach hotel, ☎ 08/636–8872) sells Breitling timepieces.

## Hai Bar Nature Reserve

**⑱** *35 km (21½ mi) north of Eilat on Rte. 90. Look for the sign for Hai Bar and Predator Center, opposite entrance to Kibbutz Samar. Drive 1½ km (1 mi) to entrance.*

The Hai Bar Nature Reserve makes a good day trip from Eilat and can be combined with a visit to the Timna Valley Park (☞ *below*) and a refreshing stop at the Ye'elim pool (☞ *below*). Try to see Hai Bar in the morning, when the animals are most active; excellent, one-hour guided tours leave the entrance daily between 10 and 3 (the last tour on Friday and Saturday is at 2).

Timna Valley Park is especially beguiling at sunset. In very hot weather, plan to see one of the two sights in the early morning and spend midday at the pool. If you're continuing north rather than returning to Eilat, you may want to visit Timna Valley Park first and then Hai Bar, with a stop at Ye'elim pool in between.

The Hai Bar Nature Reserve consists of a large natural habitat for biblical-era animals and birds and the Predator Center. The reserve was created not only as a refuge for animals that were almost extinct in the region but also as a breeding place; the animals are then set free to repopulate other parts of the Negev. Opened to the public in 1977, the 12-square-km (4½-square-mi) area re-creates the ancient savanna landscape, with lots of acacia trees; roaming around are the striped-legged wild ass, onagers (another species of wild ass), addaxes, gazelles and ibex, and white oryx. Ostriches come prancing over, ready to stick their heads into the van windows.

The 20-square-km (7¾-square-mi) **Predator Center** is where local birds and beasts of prey are raised and displayed. An audiovisual presentation introduces both history and wildlife. You can observe the animals without disturbing them because the glass you stand behind is one-way and soundproof. As you watch the hyena feed, notice that his front legs are stronger than his rear legs, enabling him to carry his heavy prey a long distance. (The meat fed to these animals comes from hit-and-run victims and sometimes animals that die of old age in local kibbutzim.) The birds of prey hang out in gigantic cages, where you'll see, among other species, the only lappet-face vultures left in Israel, with average wingspans of about 10 ft. ⊠ *Rte. 90, 35 km (21½ mi) north of Eilat,* ☎ *08/637–3057.* ⊠ *NIS 28 ($7), including tour; Predator Center only NIS 20 ($5).* ☉ *Sun.–Thurs. 8:30–5, Fri.–Sat. 8:30–3:30.*

---

NEED A
BREAK?

The **Ye'elim Restaurant, Swimming Pool, and Water Slide,** on Route 90, is a good place to stop to have lunch and cool off. The large, spic-and-span cafeteria-style restaurant serves hot meals (a variety of meats, rice, and vegetables), plus soup-and-salad plates. The pool area, lined with palm trees and equipped with changing rooms and showers (but no lockers), has children's play equipment and a water slide, and you can arrange poolside service for light meals. (Entrance to the pool is occasionally free if you order a full meal at the restaurant.) ⊠ *Rte. 90,* ☎ *08/637–3086.* ⊠ *Pool NIS 32 ($8).* ☉ *Restaurant daily 7 AM–9 AM, noon–4 PM, and 7 PM–8:30 PM; pool daily 10–7.*

# Timna Valley Park

★  *From Hai Bar Nature Reserve, return to Rte. 90 south toward Eilat. Turn right after 15 km (9 mi) at sign for Timna Park and Timna Lake. A 3-km (2-mi) access road (which passes Kibbutz Elifaz) leads to entrance booth.*

When you arrive, ask for the explanatory pamphlet, which shows the driving route in red. Because of the park's size (60 square km, or 23 square mi), we suggest driving from sight to sight, each of which can then be explored on foot (some of the sights are several miles apart). A small building just inside the entrance screens a video detailing humanity's 6,000-year-old relationship with the Timna area and its precious copper ore, mined well before Solomon's time by the Egyptians. Wall panels explain the valley's fascinating geological makeup.

Experienced hikers can pick up a map, or consult the wall map, which marks trails for good hikes. Trails have the self-explanatory names of the Geological Route, the Ancient Mines, and Ma'ale Milhan to Mt. Berech (along the cliffs) and are from three to seven hours long. They're best done in winter (the summer heat is scorching). Watch out for old mine shafts, take lots of water, and let the person at the gate know you are going and approximately when you'll be back.

The Timna Mountains (whose highest peak is 2,550 ft) surround a spectacular collection of cliffs, canyons, and rock formations. Millions of years of erosion have sculpted shapes of amazing beauty, such as the red-hued Solomon's Pillars (created by nature, *not* by the biblical king) and the 20-ft-high freestanding Mushroom.

People have also left their mark here. You'll soon come to an ancient smelting camp, with living quarters for the copper miners. Near the Pillars are the remains of a small **temple** built by Egyptians who worked the mines 3,400 years ago, during the Egyptian New Kingdom (the time of Moses); the temple was dedicated to the cow-eared goddess Hathor. Archaeologists discovered in the temple a snake made of copper (*nehushtan* in Hebrew)—according to Numbers 21:4–9, Moses made a serpent in the wilderness to heal people suffering from snake bites, and the snake remains a symbol of healing to this day (in, for example, the caduceus). The snake at Timna bears a resemblance to a votive copper snake made by the people who followed the Egyptians in this area, the Midianites (Moses's father, Jethro, was a Midianite), now in the collection of the Eretz Israel Museum, in Tel Aviv. Near the temple, a path and stairway lead up to the observation platform overlooking the valley. Above the platform is a rock-cut inscription whose hieroglyph you can see clearly with the aid of a sighting tube—it shows Ramses III offering a sacrifice to Hathor.

Timna Park is a lunarlike landscape of wide spaces interspersed with amazing geological shapes and ancient archaeological sites, surrounded by beautifully colored cliffs in a range of shades from sandy beige to rich red and dusky black. The late-afternoon hours provide unusual light for both spectators and photographers. ⊠ *Rte. 90,* ☎ *08/635-6215.* 🎫 *NIS 24 ($6).* ☉ *Daily 7:30–sunset, except Yom Kippur.* ✎

NEED A      Here's a surprise in the desert landscape, right in Timna Park: a lake
BREAK?      (man-made), and on its shore the roomy, air-conditioned **Timna Oasis Restaurant.** Built of local stone and decorated in desert colors, this self-service eatery serves hot dishes of chicken and beef, with sides of salads, rice, and vegetables; ice cream is the cooling dessert. Although swimming is not permitted, you can enjoy the lake from picnic tables in shaded areas on the shore. From January through March, a 20-minute demonstration of

ancient copper-mining and -smelting techniques is held on Sunday, Monday, and Thursday at 11 and 1; the staff will narrate in English upon request. ✉ *Timna Valley Park,* ☎ *08/635–6215.* ⊙ *Daily 11–5.*

## Mt. Yoash

**⑳** *Leave Eilat from junction of Rte. 90 (Arava Rd.) and Yotam Blvd., traveling west on Yotam (which becomes Rte. 12), with New Tourist Center on the left.*

This fine lookout along the border road with Egypt is an easy trip from Eilat. Notice the huge tanks as you drive along Route 12; they belong to the Eilat–Ashkelon oil pipeline. After you pass the tanks, you enter the Eilat Mountains Nature Reserve, with Nahal Shlomo, a dry riverbed, on your left. Drive in 12 km (7½ mi) and turn left at the orange sign for Mt. Yoash; then drive another 1 km (½ mi), bearing right up a rough, steep, and winding stone road. Park and prepare yourself for knockout views of the alternating light and dark ridges of the Eilat Mountains; Eilat and Aqaba; the mountains of Edom, behind Aqaba; the start of the Saudi Arabian coastline and the Nahal Geshron gorge, emptying into the Red Sea at Taba; and the plain of Moon Valley and the mountains of Sinai, in Egypt.

*En Route* From Mt. Yoash, take Route 12 and drive north; look for a green sign labeled NATAFIM CROSSING. The Israeli flag flies over the checkpoint at **Natafim Crossing,** where there are usually two soldiers. Nearby is a small base with two prefab buildings—one on either side of the fence. One flies the Egyptian flag; the other, the Israeli flag. The low fence is the border between the two countries. From this vantage point, looking toward Egypt, you can often see an Egyptian patrol, either walking or riding camels.

## Mitzpe Har Hizkiyahu

**㉑** *5 km (3 mi) from Natafim Crossing on Rte. 12; look for green sign for Mitzpe Har Hizkiyahu.*

As you drive along Route 12, you'll see an Israeli flag flying, and you'll be looking at Moon Valley, where the Wadi Nahal Paran starts. There are two lookouts here, each with an excellent etched plan. From one, you can see a base for the MFO (Multinational Force of Observers), a U.N.-sponsored international organization formed to supervise the Egypt-Israel peace accords of 1978; and an Egyptian military post that guards the border between the two countries. From the other, you can see Aqaba in Jordan, the salt ponds of Eilat, Aqaba's airport, and the Gulf of Eilat.

# EILAT AND THE NEGEV A TO Z

## Arriving and Departing

### By Bus

The national bus company, **Egged** (☎ 03/694–8888)—open Sunday–Thursday 6:30 AM–11 PM, Friday and holiday eves 6:30 AM–3 PM, and Saturday 4 PM–11 PM—provides frequent daily bus service (except Saturday) to Beersheva from Tel Aviv's Central Bus Station (✉ Levinsky St.) and Arlozoroff Station (✉ Arlozoroff St. and Haifa Rd.) and from Jerusalem's Central Bus Station (✉ Jaffa Rd.); the trip takes 1½ hours. From the Beersheva Central Bus Station (✉ Ben Zvi St., ☎ 08/629–4311) buses depart four times a day for Arad, Avdat, Ein Bokek, Mitzpe Ramon, and Sde Boker. For Ein Bokek, there's a daily 8:30 AM bus from Tel Aviv's Central Bus Station and several buses from Jerusalem's Central Bus Station. Most buses do not run on Saturday, though some routes do resume in the early evening.

At one time, *sherut* (shared) taxis ran between Jerusalem, Tel Aviv, and Eilat, but now that this service has stopped, the buses are more crowded than ever, especially on Friday and Sunday (return trips). You cannot buy tickets *or* reserve seats by phone; you have to go to the Central Bus Station. Once you've done that, it's wise to be at the bus station early. The bus to and from Eilat stops midway for refreshments.

Egged buses run from Tel Aviv to Eilat at least four times a day and twice at night. A round-trip ticket costs NIS 110 ($27.50). Buses from Jerusalem to Eilat leave during daylight hours from the Central Bus Station; the trip takes about 5½ hours and costs NIS 110 ($27.50) round-trip. It's important to buy tickets two days in advance at the Central Bus Station to ensure a seat. Be sure to reserve your seat for the return trip at Eilat's Central Bus Station.

## By Car

Beersheva is 113 km (70 mi) southeast of Tel Aviv and 83 km (52 mi) south of Jerusalem. The drive from either Tel Aviv or Jerusalem takes about 1½ hours. To Beersheva from Tel Aviv, take Route 2 (the Ayalon Highway) south until the turnoff marked BEERSHEVA–ASHDOD. After this you'll be on Route 41, which runs into Route 40 after 6 km (4 mi). Continue on Route 40 to Beersheva; there are clear signs all the way.

To reach Beersheva from Jerusalem, take Route 1 west to the Bet Shemesh turnoff (onto Route 38); traveling south, follow Route 38, then Route 32, which turns into Route 35, to Kiryat Gat. Here you'll pick up Route 40 south to Beersheva.

To drive to Ein Bokek from Tel Aviv, leave Tel Aviv via the Ayalon Highway (Route 2) south and join Route 1, following signs to AIRPORT–JERUSALEM. As you approach Jerusalem, stay left, on Route 1, which is marked JERICHO–DEAD SEA. Continue 30 km (18½ mi) to the unmarked Almog Junction (where Route 1 meets Route 90; there is a turnoff on the left, heading north, marked JERICHO). Stay on the same road, now Route 90, for 10 km (6 mi) to the Dead Sea. Bear right (due south) and follow Route 90 along the coast, passing Qumran, Ein Gedi, and Masada, until you reach Ein Bokek. To get to Eilat, continue south along Route 90 (Arava Road) for another 177 km (111 mi). The trip to Ein Bokek takes about an hour and a half.

The most direct way from Tel Aviv to Eilat is Route 40 south to Beersheva. Leave Beersheva via Route 25 (marked DIMONA–EILAT), driving 69 km (43 mi) to the Arava Junction. Turn right (south) onto Route 90 (Arava Road), and travel straight to Eilat. The trip takes about five hours.

## By Plane

Keep in mind that flights to the Negev are not always on schedule, so call ahead for the status of your flight and arrive at the airport early (a shuttle runs from Jerusalem to the airport). Regularly scheduled flights to and from Eilat use the **Eilat Airport,** which is actually in the middle of the city, and thus a five-minute cab ride from hotels and a two-minute walk to the center of town. Charter flights from Europe arrive at **Ovda Airport** (also known as Eilat West), 60 km (37 mi) north of Eilat; transportation to Eilat is arranged by the travel agents who book the flights.

**Arkia Israeli Airlines** (☎ 03/523–3285 main office, 08/638–4888 in Eilat) serves Eilat from the two Tel Aviv Airports: **Sde Dov Airport** (☎ 03/690–3333), in north Tel Aviv, and **Ben-Gurion International Airport** (☎ 03/690–3333); and from **Haifa Airport** (☎ 04/847–6165). At press time, flights from **Atarot Airport** in Jerusalem were being reconsidered, so check with the **main office** (☎ 03/523–3285). There are between four and eight return flights every day, including Saturday. Between Haifa and Eilat two or three flights exist, with one flight on Friday and one on Saturday nights.

**Israir Airlines** (☎ 03/795–5777, ☉ Sun.–Thurs. 7 AM–midnight; Fri. 7–4 and 10 PM–midnight) takes to the air from Tel Aviv's **Ben-Gurion Airport** to Eilat—and back to Ben-Gurion—three times a day. Flights go to and from Sde Dov Airport in north Tel Aviv to Eilat eight times a day.

### By Train

There is one train, and one train only, from the north to the Negev; it's from Tel Aviv's **Arlozoroff Station** (☎ 03/577–4000) to Beersheva. Trains depart three to five times a day, except Friday and Saturday; the fare is NIS 24 ($6).

## Getting Around

### By Bus

You *can* explore the Negev independently by bus, but you'll waste a lot of time waiting for connections, and the heat can make standing at a bus stop in the middle of nowhere very uncomfortable. Moreover, the buses don't go everywhere. However, Egged (☞ *above*) connects Beersheva (the transfer point for buses from Tel Aviv and Jerusalem) with all major Negev towns.

In Eilat, Buses 1 and 2 travel through the hotel area to town every 30 minutes. Bus 15 goes along Arava Road (Eilat–Taba Road) to the Egyptian border (Taba crossing), stopping at such attractions as the Underwater Observatory, Coral Beach, and the dive centers.

In Ein Bokek, a shuttle bus links all hotels to each other and the center of town.

### By Car

The only way to see the Negev Desert comfortably and efficiently is to drive (air-conditioning in summer is a must). All roads have two lanes. The conditions of secondary roads vary; only those in good condition are mentioned here. Roads marked in Hebrew only are not for public travel. To avoid dangerous wintertime floods, proceed with caution when there is any indication of rain (☞ Desert Precautions *in* Exploring Eilat and the Negev, *above*). Driving at night in the Negev is not recommended; plan to reach your destination by 5 PM in winter and by 8 PM in summer.

Apart from those in towns and cities, there are gas stations at Tel Avdat (near Sde Boker), Ketziyot (near Nizzana), Mashabei Sade Junction (40 km, or 25 mi, south of Beersheva), Zohar–Arad Junction (near Ein Bokek), Ramat Hovev, and Shoket Junction (on the way to Arad). You'll find gas stations on Route 90 (Arava Road) at Ein Hazeva, Ein Yahav, Ketura (tires fixed here), and Yotvata. There's a tire-repair shop in the industrial area just before the entrance to Mitzpe Ramon. Most gas stations share space with a roadside café, and a majority are open 24 hours a day.

The following are the main roads in the Negev: Route 40 goes through the Negev highlands to Eilat via Sde Boker, Mitzpe Ramon, and Makhtesh Ramon; Route 90 (called Arava Road in the Negev), which starts in Metulla near the Lebanese border, runs through Ein Bokek and along the Jordanian border and ends in Eilat; and Route 31 runs from Beersheva to the Shoket Junction, Arad, and Ein Bokek. Most of your driving will be along stretches of straight road; the exceptions are the winding (and in some parts rough and ill-maintained) road through

Makhtesh Ramon, and the steep road between Arad and Ein Bokek (one hairpin turn after another). Beersheva is 45 km (28 mi) from Arad, 80 km (50 mi) from Mitzpe Ramon, and 241 km (151 mi) from Eilat. Mitzpe Ramon is 148 km (93 mi) from Eilat. Ein Bokek is 177 km (111 mi) from Eilat.

### By Taxi

In Eilat, the preferred (and air-conditioned) way of hopping from one place to another is by taxi. Rides don't usually cost much more than NIS 25 ($6.20); you can hail a taxi on the street or order one from **Taba** (☎ 08/633–3339). In Beersheva, **Netz Taxis** (☎ 08/627–0808) operates seven days a week. Taxis are not necessary in Ein Bokek or Mitzpe Ramon.

## Contacts and Resources

### Car Rental
**Beersheva: Avis** (✉ 8 Henrietta Szold, ☎ 08/627–1777); **Eldan** (✉ 100 Tuviahu St., ☎ 08/643–0344); **Hertz** (✉ 5 Ben Zvi St., ☎ 08/627–3878); **Reliable** (✉ 1 HaAtzmaut St., ☎ 08/623–7123).

**Eilat: Avis** (✉ Tourist Information Office, ☎ 08/637–3164); **Budget** (✉ Shalom Center, ☎ 08/637–4125); **Eldan** (✉ 143 Shalom Center, ☎ 08/637–4027); **Hertz** (✉ Red Kanion Shopping Center, ☎ 08/637–6682); **Reliable** (✉ Hofit Center, Binyamin St., ☎ 08/637–4126).

**Ein Bokek: Hertz** (✉ Shopping center, ☎ 08/658–4433).

### Consulates
In Eilat, all English-speakers may contact the honorary consul of the United Kingdom, **Mrs. Almog** (☎ 08/634–0411 or 08/637–2344), for assistance.

### Emergencies
**Police** (☎ 100).

**Ambulance** (☎ 101, 911 for English-speaking operator).

**Hospitals:** in Beersheva, **Soroka Hospital** (✉ Hanessi'im St., ☎ 08/640–0111); in Eilat, **Yoseftal Hospital** (✉ Yotam St., ☎ 08/635–8011).

**Fire** (☎ 102).

PHARMACIES

Call the **Magen David Adom Medical Service** (☎ 100), the Red Cross of Israel, for assistance with emergency prescriptions. In Eilat, the **Michlin Pharmacy** (✉ Opposite Central Bus Station, ☎ 08/637–2434) is open Sunday–Thursday 8–2 and 4–8:30, Friday 8–3. Michlin will deliver to your hotel if necessary. In the Negev, there are pharmacies in Arad, Beersheva, Eilat, and Mitzpe Ramon.

### Guided Tours
AIRPLANE TOURS

From Sde Dov Airport in Tel Aviv, **Ayt Aviation & Tourism Ltd.** (☎ 03/699–0185) will take you for a two-hour flight over the Negev's *makhteshim* (canyonlike craters), the spring and waterfall of Ein Avdat, and the Dead Sea; the cost is $260 per person.

BEDOUIN LIFE

For a complete day in the desert (every Friday), **United Tours** (☎ 03/693–3412 in Tel Aviv, 02/625–2187 in Jerusalem) starts you off with a two-hour camel ride/walk in the Negev and includes a traditional meal hosted by Bedouin, winding up with a visit to the natural phenomenon of the Makhtesh Gadol (Big Crater). The cost is $74 per person.

Spend Wednesday evening in a **Bedouin tent** (☎ 08/637–3565 for hotel pickup and reservations), enjoying a Middle Eastern dinner, stories of the desert, and a dance show for $48.

### BIRD-WATCHING TOURS

Every spring and fall, millions of birds fly over **Eilat** on their long journey between winter grounds in Africa and summer breeding grounds in Eurasia. Migration takes place between mid-February and the end of May, and between the beginning of September to the end of November, although the **International Bird-watching Center** (⊠ Main highway, near Dor gas station, Box 774, ☎ 08/633–5339), just north of Eilat, is aflutter year-round; it's open Sunday–Thursday 8:30–5. The center conducts half- and full-day trips with intriguing names like "Morning Birder," "Desert Birding Trip," and "The Grouser"; you'll also see the Ringing Station. The center provides binoculars for better views of birds of prey, waterfowl, and songbirds, among others. Prices range from $3 to $50 per person per trip.

### BOAT TOURS

Take in the spectacular underwater phenomena near Eilat—unusual coral, tropical plant life, and colorful fish of all sizes and shapes—from one of the glass-bottom boats that depart from Eilat's marina. The *Jules Verne Explorer* (☎ 08/633–3666 or 08/637–9685; reservations suggested), a mobile underwater observatory with two upper decks and a glass-sided underwater section, takes a two-hour trip past the Coral Reserve three times daily (four in the summer). The cost is $18.

A novel way to see the fish and coral from down under is to take a ride on a **Yellow Submarine** (☎ 08/636–4222). The 72-ft-long *Jacqueline* departs four to five times daily (twice on Sunday) from Coral World Underwater Observatory, on the Eilat–Taba Road in Coral Beach. The sub—which really *is* yellow—dives deep beneath the surface to the renowned reefs of the Coral Reserve. A camera is mounted outside so that you can see the water closing around you as you descend. The 45-minute guided trip costs $67; it includes a tour of the Underwater Observatory. Reservations are required.

Take a daylong cruise in the Gulf of Eilat (Aqaba) on one of the many boats anchored in the marina. **Holiday Charter** (⊠ Marina, ☎ 08/633–1717, FAX 08/633–3351) offers a barbecue lunch cruise on an old world–style sailboat to Coral Island, 17 km (10 mi) south of Eilat, with time to explore its Crusader fortress—all for $55. There's also the *Orionia* (⊠ Red Sea Sports Club, ☎ 08/637–9685), a classic Spanish-built sailing yacht whose skipper explains what's to see at sea; it's wise to reserve ahead. Cost is $38 for a four-hour sail. In addition, there's a four-hour cruise on an all-wood, Cutty Sark–style schooner that anchors at the Lighthouse, near Taba, and costs $38. Service boats come along while you're out there, offering (for an additional fee) to take you parasailing or waterskiing or for an introductory scuba dive.

If you're itching for more active sailing, the operators of the 47-ft ketch *Shooneet* (☎ 050/286–334), in the marina, offer a day trip from 11 to 3 in which guests can take the helm and hoist the sails. Snorkels and masks are provided, while options include waterskiing, parasailing, and scuba diving. The trip costs $30 and includes a barbecue lunch, with wine.

### CAMEL TOURS

Based in the heart of the mountains near Eilat, **Camel Riders** (☎ 08/637–3218 or 053/700–899) runs adventure-filled desert crossings. The two-day "Smugglers' Route" trek sets out from the Shacharut Desert Adventure Center, 80 km (24 mi) north of Eilat. It crosses the Negev Highlands, through remote corners of the desert, on the hidden route taken by smugglers in centuries past. The trip departs twice a month (though it usually stops for the summer) and costs $165. The **Camel Ranch** (☎ 08/637–6663, 08/637–9685 evenings), at the Texas Ranch in Coral Beach, takes you into the desert mountains and canyons around Eilat; a half-day excursion (the sunset trip is fabulous) costs $50.

Once you're in Mitzpe Ramon, bite the bullet and wake up early for a breathtaking view of the awakening desert. The "Morning Tour" led by **Desert Shade Eco Tourism** (reserve through Tel Aviv, ☎ 03/575–6885) starts at 6:30, lasts an hour and a half, costs $30, and obligingly includes coffee; children must be over the age of five. There's also a two-day trip (weekly; minimum six people) following the ancient Spice Route, with a sleep-out under the stars.

### DIGS

If you fancy working all day in the dust under a blazing sun with the hope of finding Abraham's tent peg (and perhaps contributing to Holy Land archaeology and meeting interesting people), check out this Web site for the latest information on digs that need volunteers: www.is-rael-mfa.gov.il/archdigs. (It's so popular that they'll no longer give out their phone number!)

### GENERAL INTEREST

Several Tel Aviv– and Jerusalem-based tour companies, including **Egged Tours** (⊠ 59 Ben Yehuda St., Tel Aviv, ☎ 03/527–1212; ⊠ 8 Shlomzion Hamalka, Jerusalem, ☎ 02/622–1999 or 02/622–2929) and **United Tours** (⊠ 113 Hayarkon St., Tel Aviv, ☎ 03/522–2008 or 03/693–3412; ⊠ 9 Koresh St., Jerusalem, ☎ 02/625–2187 or 02/625–2188), offer one- and three-day air-conditioned bus tours to Eilat. Both companies will pick you up at your hotel, including those in Herzliya and Netanya. The one-day tour covers highlights such as Beersheva, Ben-Gurion's home at Sde Boker, Avdat, and the Ramon Crater; the three-day trip takes in the above attractions plus Eilat's Underwater Observatory and Timna Valley, among others. For an extra fee, you can arrange to make your return trip by air. The one-day trip costs $60, and the three-day tour is $360, with a small surcharge during peak season. Egged and United also organize half-day trips from Eilat to Timna Park, the Hai Bar Wildlife Reserve, and Kibbutz Yotvata.

**Yoel Tours** (⊠ Carlton Hotel, ☎ 08/658–4432 or 052–562563), in Ein Bokek, operates a half-day minibus tour to the Bedouin market in Beer-sheva followed by a cup of coffee with a Bedouin family in their tent. The trip costs $45 and runs every Thursday. Yoel also runs a one-day trip (on Tuesday, and priced at $62) to Eilat, which includes the Underwater Observatory and a swim in the Red Sea; a yacht trip and snorkeling are optional.

If you'd like to see the famed Mountain of Sodom, where Lot's wife looked back, **Yoel Tours** (in Ein Bokek) goes for half a day and includes a stop at the Flour Cave, for $30. Desert agriculture tours are also available.

**Amiel Tours** (⊠ Khan Center, ☎ 08/637–6308) takes travelers north from Eilat to explore Timna Park and visit a kibbutz; the trip lasts half a day and costs $39.

### HIKING TOURS

A safer—and probably more interesting—alternative to venturing out on your own is an off-the-beaten-track hike led by professional guides from the **SPNI** (Society for the Protection of Nature in Israel; ⊠ 13 Hash-fela St., Tel Aviv 66183, ☎ 03/638–8677; ⊠ 13 Helene Hamalka St., Jerusalem 96101, ☎ 02/624–4605). Although some one-day hikes are conducted in English, don't dismiss hikes conducted in Hebrew; English-speakers in the group are often glad to translate, and the outings are a good way to get to know nature-loving Israelis. SPNI day trips are planned only a short time in advance, so call to see what's happening.

The expert guides at **Hadar Desert Tours** (☎ 08/658–8125 or 052/703–451) take hikers down and around the phenomenal Ramon Crater.

The **Eilat Field School** (a branch of the SPNI) staff are helpful and friendly; they'll supply full details of various local hikes as well as maps in English. The office is opposite Coral Beach, and it's open Sunday through Thursday 8–10 PM, Friday until 8 PM, and Saturday until noon. Though not many of the myriad hikes are led in English, and most are designed for groups, you can call to see what's on the roster. (Consider joining a Hebrew-led trip; ☞ *above*.) Call ☎ 08/637–2021 for details.

JEEP TOURS

From Eilat, the well-established **Red Sea Sports Club** (✉ King Solomon Hotel, King's Wharf, ☎ 08/637–9685) leads Jeep trips through the Granite Mountains around Eilat to lookout points above Moon Valley. The cost is $35 per person for half a day, $49 per person, including picnic lunch, for a full day.

If you're over 23 and would like to try your hand at driving a Jeep, contact **Johnny Tours** (☎ 08/631–6215), in Eilat. Johnny also offers hardtop desert vehicles—not as romantic as Jeeps, which are open to the sky, but air-conditioning has its appeal. Routes include Amram's Pillars, Timna Park, and the desert oasis of Ein Evrona. The half-day trip costs $34; the full-day trip is $44–$55, including lunch.

**Avi Desert Tours** (✉ Moshav Givat Yeshayahu 16, Jerusalem 99825, ☎ 02/991–8855, 08/653–2004 in Eilat) leads carefully planned Jeep and four-wheel-drive expeditions from Beersheva, Eilat, and Ein Bokek. From Eilat, **Jeep See** (✉ Bridge House, near the marina, Box 4188, ☎ 08/633–0133) offers a half-day trip to the Red Canyon, which includes hiking, for $37, and, for the same price, a half-day trip to see Timna Park and the animals at Hai Bar Nature Reserve, with a desert snack of fresh-baked pita and herb tea. Jeep See also runs full-day Jeep tours.

From Mitzpe Ramon, **Desert Shade Eco Tourism** (✉ Box 238, Tel Aviv 80600, ☎ 03/575–6885) leads a tour of the Ramon Crater, including a desert-style lunch, a camel ride, and a visit to the Alpaca Farm. Tours run on Sunday from February to April; the cost is $88.

**Negevland Tours** (☎ 08/659–5106) creates personalized Jeep tours of Mitzpe Ramon, the Ramon Crater, and the Negev Highlands; they'll also take you to Mt. Karkom, thought by certain scholars to be the real Mt. Sinai.

SHOOTING

You don't need experience, or a license, to be a quick draw at **Red Sea Sports Club** advanced shooting range at the Ambassador hotel (☎ 08/638–2243), using live-fire video simulators. Qualified instructors are on hand for lessons.

## Hiking

Throughout Negev parklands and reserves, hiking trails have been marked by the SPNI, the Nature and National Parks Protection Authority. The **SPNI** publishes topographical maps (mostly in Hebrew but some are in English) on which the trails are color-coded to match the markings on the trails themselves. The trail markers have three short stripes: white/color/white, with the color either red, green, blue, or black.

Yellow indicates military areas. Maps are available at SPNI headquarters in Tel Aviv and Jerusalem and at its field study centers in Sde Boker (☎ 08/656–5016), Eilat (✉ Rte. 90, Coral Beach, ☎ 08/637–2021), Beersheva (✉ Meshachrerim St. at Tuviahu St., ☎ 08/623–8527 or 08/623–2156), and Har HaNegev (✉ Mitzpe Ramon, ☎ 08/658–8615). Keep in mind that at least 60% of the Negev is occupied by the military, and you are forbidden to enter these areas. Firing zones and mines are marked in yellow on SPNI maps.

The **Nature and National Parks Protection Authority** (✉ 3 Am ve Olamo, Jerusalem, ☎ 02/500–5444) is represented at the **Mitzpe Ramon Visitors Center** (☎ 08/658–8691) and at the **Coral Reserve** in Eilat (✉ Rte. 90, ☎ 08/637–3988). The rangers are experienced and knowledgeable and will help you get your hike off the ground.

## Travel Agencies

There is a host of travel offices in **Eilat** around the Central Bus Station, in the Khan Center, and at Bridge House, near the marina. Well-established Negev agencies include **Amiel Tours** in Ein Bokek (✉ Shopping center, ☎ 08/658–4433), **Galilee Tours** in Eilat (✉ Under the Howard Johnson Plaza Neptune, ☎ 08/633–5131), and **Lahish Tours** in Beersheva (✉ 79 Herzl St., ☎ 08/628–1057). Note that some agencies close in July and August.

## Visitor Information

There are **Tourist Information Offices** in Beersheva (✉ Hebron Rd. at corner of Kakal St., Beersheva 84104, ☎ 08/623–4613) and **Eilat** (✉ Arava Rd. at Yotam St., Box 14, Eilat 88100, ☎ 08/637–2111). Especially useful in Eilat is the detail-filled leaflet called "Events and Places of Interest," available at the TIO. Eilat's **Tourist Patrol** (✉ Tourist Information Office, ☞ *above*; ☎ 08/637–2111 or 08/636–7209), a sort of tourist police, is open from 8:30 to 4 daily. In **Ein Bokek**, Suzi Katz at Amiel Tours (✉ Shopping center, ☎ 08/658–4433) is knowledgeable and helpful. There are **visitor centers** in Arad (✉ 28 Ben Yair St., Box 824, ☎ 08/995–4409) and Mitzpe Ramon (✉ Top of the main street, Box 340, ☎ 08/658–8691 or 08/658–8620).

# 8 SIDE TRIPS TO THE SINAI AND PETRA

Egypt's Sinai Peninsula attracts adventurous travelers to trek in its granite mountains or dive in the magnificent coral reefs along its coast. The area also draws pilgrims with such sights as St. Catherine's Monastery and Mt. Sinai. Travelers to Jordan are flocking to Petra, the rose-red remains of an ancient Nabatean city carved into sandstone, whose gigantic monuments and royal tombs are treasures even in a region filled with antiquities.

F ROM ISRAEL, YOU CAN EASILY pop into Egypt or Jordan if you want to broaden your sense of the Middle Eastern region or pursue a particular passion. The Sinai Peninsula's location along the ancient trading route linking Africa and Asia has made it a meeting place of cultures since time immemorial. People from all over the world are still drawn to this pristinely beautiful part of Egypt, and the Sinai coast is a world-class diving attraction, with its year-round sunshine and dramatic granite mountains set against a teal-cobalt sea.

Petra, in Jordan, combines awesome scenery with another element: artifacts of the mysterious and ancient culture of the Nabatean people. The Nabateans controlled the famed spice route stretching from Arabia to the Mediterranean, and Petra became both their financial center and their royal necropolis. Hidden from Western eyes until they were first excavated in the early 19th century, Petra's tombs, carved out of the rust-hue sandstone cliffs of the biblical region of Edom, have gigantic proportions and intricately carved facades. Its Roman remains are a window to the culture that ruled the world 2,000 years ago. In a region studded with antiquities, Petra is still a crown jewel for students of ancient history.

# THE SINAI

Judy Stacey
Goldman

Updated by
Susan Lubell

Today the Sinai is nothing less than a paradise for adventurers. Its interior seems untouched and even forbidding, and its coast is famous for its marvelous coral reefs. Jeep and hiking trails beg to be explored, and at the end of every day the weary traveler is within a few hours of beautiful hotels and resorts.

The Sinai is a 61,000-square-km (37,820-square-mi) triangular peninsula, bounded on the east by the Gulf of Eilat (also called the Gulf of Aqaba) and on the west by the Gulf of Suez. The apex of the triangle, pointing down toward the Red Sea, was the main route to the East for the traders of antiquity. Many legends of ancient Egypt are set in the Sinai: the goddess Isis came here to search for the body of her murdered husband, and the goddess Hathor, patroness of the Sinai's copper mines and known to the pharaohs as "Our Lady of Sinai," also sanctified the area. Biblical references to the Sinai are numerous. Pilgrims have long been drawn to the scene of the wanderings of the ancient Israelites.

The Sinai's vastness can mislead the uninitiated into regarding it as one geographical unit. In fact, the peninsula can be divided into three major subsections, each very different from the other. The plains of the northern Sinai are bounded on their southern edge by Darb el-Haj, the Muslim pilgrim's route connecting Egypt to Aqaba and, finally, to Mecca. The immense limestone massif of the Tih Desert, whose western reaches are rich in water sources and dramatic canyons, dominates the central Sinai. The word "Tih," translated by some as "wanderers," has led some scholars to identify this wilderness with the wanderings of the Children of Israel. The southern Sinai is the most traveled part of the peninsula, as it's home to the traditional Mt. Sinai and, along the coast, some of the best diving in the world.

Most travelers to the southern Sinai, the area covered in this trip, follow a route leading from Eilat to St. Catherine's Monastery at the foot of Mt. Sinai. The simplest way to do this is by organized bus trip. This may not sound madly adventurous, but it allows you the freedom to do nothing but gaze at the wonderful scenery. A tour of the Sinai coast and St. Catherine's Monastery can be accomplished in one day. Longer tours allow for swimming or snorkeling stops and visits to additional sights.

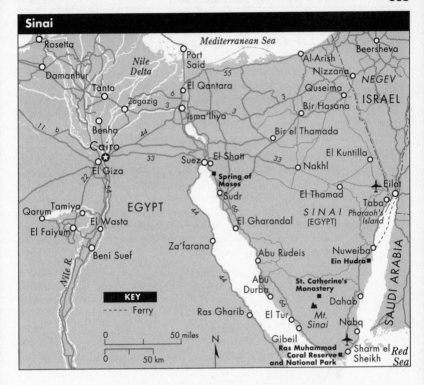

Independent travelers can see the region's highlights in a three-day driving trip. The road passes along the eastern coast, where the town of Nuweiba is both a crossroads to the interior and a vacation center. Nuweiba's beautiful beach has some of the best diving and snorkeling in the Sinai, and it can serve as a stopover on the road west to Sinai's interior and St. Catherine's Monastery, or on the way south to the coral reefs of Ras Muhammad (near the town of Sharm el Sheikh), at the peninsula's southernmost tip.

## Pleasures and Pastimes

### Dining
While the Sinai's location on the coast ensures a number of fish restaurants, proprietors come and go, and so does the level of hygiene. Keep an ear to the ground, gleaning information from fellow travelers about the latest gems. Otherwise, count on having your best meals in the resort hotels, and leave your exploring for the scenery. The most notable restaurants are in Sharm el Sheikh, where you can sample an array of good European and Eastern cuisines at reasonable prices.

| CATEGORY | COST* |
|---|---|
| $$$ | over $30 |
| $$ | $15–$30 |
| $ | under $15 |
| *per person for a three-course meal, excluding drinks and service charge | |

### Diving
The Gulf of Eilat is an extension of the Indian Ocean, linked to it by the straits of Tiran and Bab el Mandeb. The water temperature reaches about 25°C (77°F) in the summer and drops to 19°C (66°F) in the winter. This tropical sea is poor in plankton—a fact that accounts for the striking clarity of its waters—but rich in algae, which live in symbio-

sis with the coral around them. The result of this symbiosis is nature's most magnificent regional work of art: the Sinai coast coral reefs, home to some 1,000 species of fish and more than 137 species of coral. Diving safaris are organized at several points along the eastern Sinai coast, and nondivers can often rent snorkeling equipment there. Some well-known dive sites are Ras-a-Sitan, 54 km (33 mi) south of Taba, and Ras-Abu Gulum, an unspoiled reef about 50 km (31 mi) south of Nuweiba and accessible only by Jeep. From Dahab, the Canyon and Blue Hole are two favorite sites; from Sharm el Sheikh, the most popular spots are in the Ras Muhammad National Park and the straits of Tiran.

### Hiking and Trekking

The southern Sinai's landscape of gorges and valleys, towered over by multicolored granite mountains, provides virtually unlimited hiking opportunities. A few of the routes are well traveled, and you can enjoy them even if you only have a short time. The area around St. Catherine's Monastery has several trails besides the strenuous but not-to-be-missed hike up to the top of Mt. Sinai. Other widely available exploring options are Jeep and camel tours.

Experienced hikers can trek to remote parts of the Sinai, like the Tih Desert or Mt. Sirbal, though they should do so only with the leadership of experienced guides. Trails in the Sinai are largely unmarked, and attempting even the shortest ones without exact directions from experts can be risky.

### Lodging

Travelers can choose from luxury hotels and resorts and medium- and low-price hotels at Nuweiba, Dahab, and Sharm el Sheikh. Campsites also abound and are well advertised, although some may not be very clean.

| CATEGORY | COST* |
| --- | --- |
| $$$ | over $130 |
| $$ | $45–$130 |
| $ | under $45 |

*All prices are for a standard double room, including tax.*

## Gateway to Egypt

Once you leave Eilat and border formalities behind, you'll sense the freedom of the magnificent scenery that lies ahead. The turquoise waters of the Gulf of Eilat sparkle in the sunlight against the backdrop of the red and black mountains that nearly touch the water in many places. This is the landscape that will accompany you as you move down the eastern coast of the Sinai. The slopes are dotted with acacia trees, and wooden fishing boats bob offshore in the gulf waters.

## Pharaoh's Island

*17 km (11 mi) south of Eilat.*

With its ruined Crusader castle and Ottoman additions, Pharaoh's Island (also known as Coral Island) attracts many a roadside photographer. The island's recorded history begins during the reign of Pharaoh Ramses III, who reigned from 1198 to 1166 BC and was probably the source of the island's name—in Arabic, Jezirat Phar'un, or Pharaoh's Island. A document from this period relates that workers sent to mine copper from Timna, north of present-day Eilat, found shelter here. The island next served as a port for the region's rulers during the Byzantine period, when busy shipping lanes connected India with the Land of Israel via the Gulf of Suez and the Gulf of Eilat.

The best-known period in the island's occupation is marked by the dramatic remains visible from shore. These are the ruined walls of the Crusader outpost created here in 1115 by Baldwin I. For 55 years, the Crusaders controlled both the trade and pilgrimage routes that passed this way from the safety of the island. But in 1171, shortly after coming to power in Egypt, Salah El-Deen attacked the fortress by surprise, transporting his dismantled ships secretly through the Sinai on camelback. Despite repeated attempts, the Crusaders never again regained control of the island. Most of what now remains dates from the Mamluk period (14th century).

If you're intrigued enough by the ruins to make this a full-blown stop, you can cross the 250 yards from the shore to the island in a boat that leaves from the Salah El-Deen Hotel every 15 minutes from 9 to 5; a round-trip ticket costs L.E. 14 ($4) and entrance to the castle is L.E. 21 ($6).

Just a few miles south of the island, take the time to stop at the fjord, an impressively beautiful inlet, for another great photo op.

# Nuweiba

*48 km (30 mi) south of Pharaoh's Island, 125 km (78 mi) northeast of St. Catherine's Monastery.*

Nuweiba is one of the eastern Sinai's several growing resort towns. Its name means "bubbling springs," and Nuweiba has long been an important oasis for Muslim pilgrims en route to Mecca. Lovely, sandy beaches and colorful coral reefs accessible from the shore have earned it a reputation as the perfect place for a resort-style vacation, and it's an excellent starting point for tours to the Sinai's interior including the Colonial Canyon, the Tih Desert, or the El Makhrom mountain region.

Now a city of about 3,000, Nuweiba is the center for two tribes. Their members, once the outstanding fishermen of the Sinai coast, still inhabit the area in two villages: Nuweiba el Muzeina, south of Nuweiba city, and Nuweiba Tarabin, to the north. Nuweiba city also has a touristy center, with a Bedouin bazaar and several shops and restaurants. But you'll probably spend most of your time enjoying the beach, its coffeehouses, and the outstanding scenery.

One unusual attraction in Nuweiba el Muzeina is Holly, a solitary dolphin. Holly has been a dockside resident of Nuweiba el Muzeina since 1994 and will often allow visiting swimmers to approach her and engage her in play.

From Nuweiba a car-and-passenger ferry runs daily to Aqaba, Jordan. It's how the locals make the crossing, but it's slow going at 3½ hours' duration. A good alternative for travelers is the high-speed catamaran that makes the trip in 45 minutes, part of a package assembled by the Nuweiba Hilton Coral Resort (☞ Lodging, *below*), which makes a one-day round-trip to Petra, Jordan, every Friday at 6 AM.

## Lodging

$$$ 🏨 **Nuweiba Hilton Coral Resort.** This resort is a five-minute taxi ride away from Nuweiba's port and thus ideally situated for trips into the Sinai's interior as well as across the Gulf of Aqaba to Jordan. The hotel's public areas—restaurants, disco, and poolside—have a distinct shell motif. Rooms are plain, with basic white tiles, wooden furniture, underwater photography, and large balconies. With an eye toward ecological friendliness, the hotel asks that you limit your use of water to what's necessary and insert a power card to activate your room's electricity. Wheelchair-accessible and -equipped rooms are available upon request. ⊠ *Nuweiba port,* ☎ *069/520–320 or 069/520–321, 800/*

*445–8667 in the U.S.,* FAX *069/520–327. 200 rooms. 3 restaurants, 2 bars, 2 pools, tennis court, squash, dive shop, waterskiing, shops. AE, DC, MC, V. BP.* ✎

$  ✕🖼 **El-Badawy Camp and Restaurant.** Budget travelers will enjoy the friendly service and light atmosphere of El-Badawy Camp, the newest of the bungalow camps situated along the Nuweiba Tarabin coast. Bungalows with ceiling fans and rooms with private bath and air-conditioning are available. Just outside is the El-Badawy Restaurant, with Bedouin-style carpet and cushion seating and the Red Sea stretched out before you. The food is simple and tasty; the *sahlab* (orchid milk with nuts) is a must. ✉ *Nuweiba Tarabin,* ☎ *069/500–832. 10 rooms, 48 bungalows without bath. Restaurant, grocery. No credit cards.*

*En Route*   About 10 km (6 mi) past the junction of the Nuweiba–St. Catherine's road, you'll see a Bedouin hut by the roadside. Stop here to walk (about 20–30 minutes) to the point where you have a view of an emerald-green oasis, Ein Hudra, believed by some scholars to be the biblical site of Hatzeroth (Numbers 11:35). On the way, you can see a stone burial structure of the type known as *nawamis,* one of several in the vicinity; it dates from the Chalcolithic period. There are also rock inscriptions along the path, carved by shepherds and pilgrims over the ages in Greek, Armenian, and Hebrew. Make sure you get walking directions from the Bedouin, or, better yet, rent a camel here. As well known as these attractions are, they are not carefully signposted, and it's easy to get lost.

## St. Catherine's Monastery

★  *125 km (78 mi) southwest of Nuweiba.*

The sight of St. Catherine's Monastery, utterly isolated in a valley surrounded by great, craggy mountains, is extraordinary. One of the most sacred monasteries in the world, it was constructed by the emperor Justinian in AD 530. But one look at the looming, fortresslike complex is enough to realize that religious fervor was not the emperor's only incentive. Right on the main caravan route carrying goods across the Sinai from Africa to Asia, the monastery no doubt served the emperor's soldiers as a base of operations against the bandits who plagued this route. It is surrounded by sites immortalizing various biblical stories, including what is said to be the exact location where the Israelites worshiped the Golden Calf.

The monastery comprises several buildings, each built or expanded at different times over the centuries. Among them are a church, several chapels, and a library (closed to the public) containing thousands of rare books, including a copy of the Codex Sinaiticus (the 3rd-century AD Greek translation by Jewish scholars of the Hebrew Bible), one of 50 copies commissioned by Constantine the Great in 331. Within the complex are also the monks' living quarters, an ancient refectory, and a white mosque with a minaret built in 1106 (not in use). All of this is encircled by high stone walls. Originally named after Mary, the monastery was later named for St. Catherine, martyred in Alexandria in the 4th century (the round firework called a Catherine wheel is named for the form of torture to which she was submitted); the faithful believe that her bones were carried here by angels. About 12 Greek Orthodox monks currently live and work here; the archbishop, who resides in Cairo, visits at Easter and other important holidays. Outside and around the monastery live the Christian Bedouin of the Jabaliyeh tribe, who have long served the monks by working in the gardens and orchards.

Inside the **Church of the Transfiguration,** the apse is decorated with an ancient mosaic of the Transfiguration of Jesus, with Moses and Elijah. Oil lamps and decorated eggs hang from the ceiling, and some of the monastery's unique collection of icons adorn the walls. All around you are old and treasured works of art—inscriptions, wall coverings, inlaid metalwork, stone reliefs and other carvings, and chandeliers (some of which are lighted on religious holidays). The doors to the church itself date from the 6th century, and the outer doors were built in the 11th century; the bell tower, a gift from Czar Nicholas II of Russia, was built in 1897.

The **chapel** behind the church is the most sacred part of the monastery. Unfortunately, it's not always open to the public. Dating from the 4th century AD, the chapel is the oldest part of the church, and its walls are covered with icons, of which the monastery itself has 2,000. (You can see yet more icons in the hall next to the library; the rest are kept in secured rooms, closed to the public.) One icon, portraying the Sacrifice of Isaac, was painted in the 7th century. Outside the chapel, you can see the bush where, according to tradition, God spoke to Moses.

Many visitors are intrigued by the **Room of the Skulls,** a chamber to which the bones of deceased monks are transferred from the cemetery after five years of internment. (Their burial plot is very small.) The skulls number 1,500 and are lined up neatly in rows.

Above St. Catherine's Monastery looms the multipeaked summit of **Jabal Musa,** 6,855 ft above sea level. This, your local guide will tell you, is Mt. Sinai, where Moses received the Ten Commandments as the Israelites waited below. But how reliable is this designation? Scholars have wrestled with this question for years, with no solution in sight. Most sites mentioned in the Bible are "internal"—they were named for events that happened to the Israelites but are not noted in external sources. Other locations have been suggested for the biblical Mt. Sinai, but Jabal Musa has been the most enduring conjecture, probably because of its situation on the main trade route. Pilgrims' journals, the main guidebooks of earlier periods, passed the legend of Jabal Musa's holiness from one generation to the next.

If you can climb to the summit in time for sunrise, the sweeping view of the granite peaks from one end of the horizon to the other will probably convince you that no place could serve better as the site of Moses's epiphany. The climb to Jabal Musa takes 2½ to 3 hours, including 700 steps to the very top. There is a 3,000-step descent back down to the monastery. ☎ 069/470–346. 🎫 *Free.* ☉ *Monastery Mon.–Thurs. and Sat. 9–noon. Closed Greek Orthodox Christmas (Jan. 7) and Easter.*

### Lodging

**$$** 🏨 **Daniela Village.** This is a compound of double-bedded, air-conditioned bungalows. Spacious rooms with rustic wooden furniture and Bedouin rugs are a welcomed comfort after the trek up Mt. Sinai. Its restaurant, the Hala, serves Middle Eastern as well as international specialties. ⊠ *Near the Santa village square, c/o 18 Shehab St., Monahdessin, Cairo,* ☎ FAX *069/470–379. 74 rooms. No credit cards.*

**$–$$** 🏨 **Morganland Village.** Morganland recently completed a new extension including 168 more rooms, a pool, and a shopping center. Not far from the hotel is the Zeituna Camp, offering dorm-style accommodations, with up to 12 guests per room for $8 per person. ⊠ *3 km (2 mi) from the monastery, just east of St. Catherine Rd., near the Zeituna area,* ☎ *069/470–404,* FAX *069/470–331. 248 rooms. No credit cards.*

## Sharm el Sheikh

*240 km (150 mi) southeast of St. Catherine's Monastery.*

Fifteen years ago, Sharm el Sheikh, at the Sinai's southern tip, had one hotel, two dive centers, and a snack bar. Today this bustling little town has more than 40 hotels, with respective dive centers, malls, casinos, and restaurants—and more on the way. Sharm, as it's lovingly called, has inexhaustible activities for divers, loungers, and everyone in between, and plenty of nightlife, too—after a day of diving, snorkeling, or waterskiing you can knock back a pint of Guinness at the Pirate's Bar, go dancing at the Bus Stop, or just hang out on the outdoor patio at the Sanafir hotel (☞ Lodging, *below*).

Ras Muhammad National Park, at the southernmost tip of the Sinai Peninsula, is considered one of the best dive sites in the world. Most of the dives south of Sharm el Sheikh are wall dives—some reaching depths of more than 1,600 ft—rich in fan, fire, and plate coral, napoleon fish, puffer fish, barracudas, and not without the occasional shark (usually in slumber). With great beaches and more than 10 reefs, Ras Muhammad is a great place for both shore and boat diving. The yellow starkness of the desert contrasts wonderfully with the explosion of life and color under the water. The most popular boat dives include Shark's Reef and Yolanda Reef, where you'll see hordes of great fish, beautiful coral, and, surprisingly enough, some toilets and sinks. While Ras Mohammad is only 30 km (18 mi) south of Sharm, you will need an Egyptian visa coming from Israel (☞ Passports and Visas, *below*).

## Dining and Lodging

**$$    ✕ Kokai.** The kitschy decor (fake plants, red lanterns, and Stella beer bottles plastered onto the wall) is a bit much, but the food at this centrally located Asian restaurant is excellent. The menu is an array of Japanese, Chinese, and Thai cuisine, with everything from vegetable spring rolls to teppan-yaki. Dinner here is a good time: a Japanese chef smacks noodle dough against a table while an Egyptian chef chops fixings for omelets at supersonic speed. Come with an appetite—portions are generous. ✉ *Ghazala Hotel, Na'ama Bay,* ☎ *069/600–150. AE, MC, V.*

**$    ✕ TamTam.** Authentic Egyptian food is often hard to come by in a resort town, but TamTam fills the bill. Inside the furniture is basic, and outside there's typical Bedouin floor seating—a small price to pay for the live Egyptian music. Upstairs is an open-roof deck, perfect for keeping an eye on the boardwalk. Enjoy the falafel with a variety of traditional salads, or a *foul* (flavored fava beans) sandwich wrapped in pita bread. If you want carbohydrates, order *koshary,* a mixture of rice, macaroni, lentils, and tomato sauce sprinkled with browned onions. ✉ *Ghazala Hotel, Na'ama Bay,* ☎ *069/600–150. AE, MC, V.*

**$$$    ⊞ Ritz-Carlton.** Combining the sensuality of ancient Egypt and the breezy
**★** hush of a desert oasis, the Ritz offers its guests the definitive Red Sea resort experience. These people have thought of everything, from aromatherapy and massage treatments in a tent overlooking the sea to child-proofing rooms and bathrooms as part of the POLO (Protect Our Little Ones) service. A maze of freshwater streams allows guests to float through lush gardens and waterfalls. Explore underwater grottos and coral reefs during the day, and in the evening dine at one of five unique restaurants featuring Lebanese, Italian, and Asian cuisine. Finish your evening at the Cigar Divan, where tuxedo-clad waiters will serve you a perfect martini with your Cuban cigar. ✉ *Om El-Sid, Sharm el-Sheikh (Box 72, South Sinai),* ☎ *069/661–919 or 069/620–595,* 𝖥𝖠𝖷 *069/661–920. 259 rooms, 48 suites. 5 restaurants, 2 bars, lounge, in-room data ports, minibars, 2 pools, beauty salon, massage, sauna, spa, 3 tennis courts, health club, dive shop, snorkeling, nightclub, business services. AE, DC, MC, V.* ✧

**$$$    ⊞ Sofitel Sharm el Sheikh Coralia.** This fully equipped five-star hotel is perched on the northeastern tip of Sharm el Sheikh's famous cove, Na'ama Bay. The Arabesque theme gives it the desired Mediterranean effect—a stark, white Moorish exterior; brass chandeliers; and Arab tilework, all tastefully executed. Your private terrace looks onto the Red Sea and is perfect for watching the sun set. Four of the rooms are specially equipped for people with disabilities, including both bath and shower. ⊠ *Na'ama Bay,* ☎ *069/600–081,* FAX *069/600–085. 300 rooms, 4 suites. 3 restaurants, 2 bars, minibars, room service, pool, hot tub, massage, sauna, steam room, 2 tennis courts, exercise room, horseback riding, racquetball, squash, dive shop, waterskiing, children's programs, travel services. AE, MC, V. BP.*

$$ ⊡ **Sanafir Hotel.** Sanafir's prime location and relaxed atmosphere have made it a longtime hub and meeting place for those staying in Na'ama Bay. The rooms are basic and clean, with few accessories; two narrow beds, with a dome above the head of each; and a view of the pool at best. Sanafir is not about service or decor; it's about nocturnal activities. The nearby Bus Stop Disco and Pub, pseudo Bedouin Tent, and five on-site restaurants are the main draws. The new cyber café is open 24 hours. ⊠ *Na'ama Bay,* ☎ *062/600–197,* FAX *062/600–196. 50 rooms, 22 suites. 5 restaurants, 2 bars, pool, dance club. MC, V. BP. www.sanafir.com.*

# The Sinai A to Z

## Before You Go

### BORDERS

The border crossing at **Taba** (☎ 08/637–2104), just over the Egyptian border from Eilat, is open 24 hours a day, seven days a week, except for the Jewish holiday of Yom Kippur and the Muslim holiday of Id el Adkha. There is a tax of NIS 63 ($15.75) on the Israeli side and a tax of L.E. 17 ($6) on the Egyptian side. Crossing the border on either side can take anywhere from five minutes to five hours, so arrive with plenty of patience!

### CLOTHING

Although it's very hot during the day in the Sinai, temperatures dip at night. Even in summer it's wise to pack a jacket and socks. Winter days are generally warm and sunny, but the mountains around St. Catherine's are known for their freezing nights, including bouts of frost and snow. Modest dress is required in the monastery.

### CURRENCY

Egyptian currency is calculated in pounds (L.E.) and piasters. The exchange rate at press time was approximately L.E. 3.46 to the U.S. dollar, L.E. 2.35 to the Canadian dollar, and L.E. 5.18 to the British pound.

Visitors to Egypt must convert currency at authorized exchange points, such as those found in major hotels and banks. Convenient places to do this are the exchange office at the border and the bank in the Taba Hilton, which is usually open all day, every day.

### PASSPORTS AND VISAS

Both adults and children need valid passports to enter Egypt. If a child shares a parent's passport, the parent cannot enter Egypt *without* the child, even for a one-day visit. You can obtain visas at the border, or through Egyptian consulates in Israel. **Egyptian consulates** are in northern Tel Aviv (⊠ 54 Basel St., Tel Aviv, ☎ 03/546–4151 or 03/546–4152) and Eilat (⊠ 68 Avrony St., Eilat, ☎ 08/637–6882). U.S. citizens don't need visas to visit Nuweiba, St. Catherine's, or Sharm el Sheikh, although they're necessary for other destinations in Egypt including Ras Muhammad National Park, a popular dive site near Sharm el Sheikh.

## Arriving and Departing

### BY BUS

In Eilat, board Egged Bus 15 at the Central Bus Station. At Taba you'll switch to an Egyptian bus, which provides scheduled daily service to

Nuweiba, St. Catherine's, and Sharm el Sheikh. The East Delta Travel Bus Company's earliest departure is at 7:30 AM. Later buses depart around 3. Be patient; punctuality is optional here.

BY CAR

Only cars registered in their drivers' names may be driven into Egypt. For more information on driving into the Sinai from Israel, contact **MEMSI** (☎ 03/564–1122), the Israeli branch of the AAA, with an office in Tel Aviv.

BY FOOT

You may walk across the border from Eilat to the Taba Hilton Hotel in Egypt. A hotel representative has an office at the border crossing and will arrange transport to the hotel if you request it. If you're unencumbered by luggage, however, it's an easy walk.

BY PLANE

**Arkia Israeli Airlines** (✉ Red Canyon shopping center, Eilat, ☎ 08/638–4888; ✉ 11 Frishman St., Tel Aviv, ☎ 03/690–3333) and **Air Sinai** (✉ Migdalor Bldg., 1 Ben Yehuda St., 13th floor, Tel Aviv, ☎ 03/510–2481) have biweekly flights to Sharm el Sheikh on Sunday and Thursday mornings. They operate jointly on this route, so you can make reservations by calling either company. A one-way ticket costs about $125 (including tax).

## Getting Around

BY CAR

For information on entering Egypt by car, *see* Arriving and Departing, *above*. Unleaded fuel is not available in the Sinai. Drive with extreme caution on Sinai roads; there are an inordinate number of accidents, and emergency medical care is not always available.

BY TAXI

A popular means of transportation to Nuweiba and Sharm el Sheikh are Bedouin taxis, which you can pick up just across the Egyptian border or at the Taba Hilton. It's advisable to use the buddy system—at least two to a car—and negotiate the fare in advance, bargaining down if it sounds exorbitant (the taxis don't have meters). Typical fares from the Taba Hilton are Taba to Nuweiba, L.E. 130 ($38); Taba to Sharm el Sheikh, L.E. 350 ($101). Bedouin Jeep drivers are available for hire at the various tourist centers.

## Contacts and Resources

CAR RENTALS

**Europcar** rents cars at the Taba Hilton Hotel (☎ 069/530–333) and has offices in Nuweiba (☎ 069/520–321) and Sharm el Sheikh (☎ 069/600–136) hotels as well. The Taba Hilton office is open daily 8–1 and 5–8. You can also arrange to rent a car with a driver.

GUIDED TOURS

There are a couple of reliable tour operators with day trips to St. Catherine's Monastery.

**Mazada Tours** (in Tel Aviv: ✉ 141 Ibn Gvirol St., ☎ 03/544–4454 or ✉ 19 Jaffa St., ☎ 02/623–5777) has one-, two- and three-day trips to St. Catherine's, with cost between $68 and $150. **Neot Hakikar** (main office: ✉ 67 Ben Yehuda St., Tel Aviv, ☎ 03/520–5858; ✉ Khan Center, Eilat, ☎ 08/632–6281) offers two popular trips to St. Catherine's: a one-day trip costs $59; the two-day trip includes a visit to St. Catherine's, climbing Mt. Sinai, and a cruise to Coral Island. Cost for the two-day trip is $125 including an overnight camping stay and $165 with hotel accommodations.

The **JET Travel and Tours** (✉ 3 Ben Sira St., Jerusalem, ☎ 02/623–5535) offers a special five-day tour of the Sinai with specially equipped four-wheel-drive vehicles, at a cost of $445 per person. **Mazada Tours** (☞ *above*) has a four-day and a seven-day safari for $210 and $310, respectively. The **Red Sea Sports Club,** in Eilat (⊠ King's Wharf, ☎ 08/637–9685), has hiking and combination camel-hiking and Jeep-water sports trips. Choices include a two-day tour to St. Catherine's Monastery ($125–$165 per person, depending on accommodations), and a five-day Sinai dive safari ($600 per person, including accommodations).

The Sinai Department of the **Society for the Protection of Nature in Israel** (⊠ 3 Hashefela St., Tel Aviv, ☎ 03/638–8675; ⊠ 13 Helene Hamalka St., Jerusalem, ☎ 02/625–2357) has a well-earned reputation for expert, off-the-beaten-track nature tours; its four- and five-day trips cost $295 and $360 per person, respectively.

Information on diving in the Sinai, as well as diving safaris of varying durations and locations, is offered by several diving clubs in Eilat. **Aqua Sport** (⊠ Box 300, Coral Beach, ☎ 08/633–4404) offers several safari dive trips with prices ranging from $230 for two days and $580 for a five-day trip, all expenses included except border taxes. If you bring your own equipment, the prices drop by about 20%. The **Dolphin Reef Diving Center** (⊠ Box 104, Southern Beach, ☎ 08/637–5935) is most famous for its diving with dolphins packages in Eilat. They do offer a day cruise to Pharoah's Island near Taba for $68.25 with an additional cost of $40 for two guided dives. The **Red Sea Sports Club** is Israel's largest diving center and offers several multi-day trips to Sinai starting at $105 for one day (two dives plus equipment) and up to $525 for five days which includes a boat trip to the Straits of Tiran (⊠ King's Wharf, ☎ 08/637–9685).

In Egypt, **Abanoub Travel Agency** (☎ 069/520–201 in Nuweiba; ☎ 069/600–067 in Sharm El Sheikh), at the commercial center in Nuweiba, runs camel, Jeep, and trekking tours of varying durations to all parts of the Sinai. Their Sharm El Sheikh office at the Murgana Mall in Na'ama Bay offers overnight trips to Petra and Cairo for $320 and $260, respectively. **Divers' International,** with offices in Sharm El Sheikh, offers daily Jeep trips to nearby dive sites, including the popular Canyon and Blue Hole near Dahab (⊠ Ganet Sinai Hotel, ☎ 069/640–415) and Ras Muhammad and Tiran near Sharm (⊠ Novotel Coralia Hotel, Na'ama Bay, ☎ 069/600–276). A full day including two dives by jeep is approximately $40 and a full day with two dives by boat at either Ras Mohammad or Tiran is $60. **Fox of the Desert** (☎ 069/470–467) offers exceptional Bedouin guides for multi-day trips throughout the St. Catherine's Protectorate. Based in St. Catherine's Village, Fox guides can arrange trips all over Sinai. Ask for Faraj or Ahmed. If you want to enjoy the Red Sea without the hustle of Na'ama Bay, head 5 km (3 mi) north to **Umbarak Shark's Bay Dive Club** (⊠ Shark's Bay Bedouin Home and Dive Club, ☎ 069/600–942), offering Jeep safaris to remote dive sites inaccessible by boat. Opposite Tiran Island, Shark's Bay is known for its Bedouin hospitality and mellow atmosphere. And the prices can't be beat. The overnight desert dive is a two-day and two-night excursion including 5 dives, meals, and all diving and camping equipment for $125.

MEDICAL CARE

Medical care is available at Nuweiba, Sharm el Sheikh, and St. Catherine's Village. The new **Sharm el Sheikh Hospital** (⊠ Sharm El Sheikh, ☎ 069/660–425) has a decompression chamber for divers. The **Hyperbaric Medical Center** treats diving conditions (⊠ Sharm El Maya, opposite Travco Jetty, ☎ 069/660–922), open daily 10–6. There's a private pharmacy in Nuweiba and a hospital pharmacy at the new **St. Catherine's Medical Center** (⊠ St. Catherine's Village, ☎ 069/470–368). A doctor is in residence at the Nuweiba and Dahab Hilton hotels, available 24 hours a day. Many other hotels also have an on-site clinic with doctors on call.

When calling Sinai listings from Israel, add the prefix 002. The country code for Egypt is 20; the area code for the Sinai is 069.

In Israel, you can contact the Sinai Department of the **Society for the Protection of Nature in Israel** in Tel Aviv (☞ Guided Tours, *above*). In Egypt, the **Abanoub Travel Agency** (☞ Guided Tours, *above*) can be helpful. The official Web site for the Egyptian Ministry of Tourism (www. interoz.com) has some useful information about the Sinai Peninsula.

# PETRA

By Miriam Feinberg Vamosh

Poet Dean Burgon described Petra as the "rose-red city, half as old as time." Petra's boulevards, temples, theater, and splendid royal and noble tombs, secreted among the high cliffs, have an incomparable mystery and grandeur. Once inaccessible to all but an intrepid few, Petra's magnificent ruins were the epitome of romance. They're still romantic, but, fortunately, they're now easier to reach and overnight trips to Petra have been increasingly popular since the Israel-Jordan border was opened in 1994.

Petra lies in the biblical region of Edom, southeast of the Dead Sea in modern-day Jordan. According to the Book of Genesis, the Edomites were descendants of Esau, Jacob's brother and rival. When Moses led the Israelites into the Promised Land, he asked the Edomites' permission to pass through their land and was refused. The water sources and agriculture of this highland region were probably considered too precious to share with these newcomers from the wilderness (Numbers 20:14–21).

Edom's fertile land was a magnet that desert dwellers could not ignore, however, and the Israelites were not the last to appear there. By the 4th century BC, a new group had arrived from the wilderness to take advantage of the riches of the highlands of Edom: the Nabateans. It is their spectacular tombs and urban monuments that draw travelers to Petra today.

Little is certain about the origins of the Nabateans; historians assume they were nomads from Arabia. One rare source is an early 4th-century BC record kept by one of the officers of Alexander the Great, in which the writer describes the Nabateans as shepherds who wandered the wilderness. Later historical sources describe them as traders in frankincense and myrrh, the most valuable of biblical spices. They were also mentioned as highway robbers and even as pirates. When Alexander the Great died, his empire was divided between the Seleucids, in the north, and the Ptolomies, in the south. The Nabateans eventually won independence from the Seleucids, and historical and archaeological sources hint that they gradually abandoned their nomadic lifestyle and became the wealthy masters of the region's trade routes.

Aretas, who may have been the first Nabatean king, is mentioned briefly in the Book of Maccabees. According to the New Testament (I Corinthians 11:32), one of his descendants, also named Aretas, ruled in Damascus. In his book *The Jewish War,* the 1st-century AD Roman Jewish historian Josephus mentions "Petra, capital of Arabia," and writes of both a succession of Nabatean kings who ruled Petra and a Nabatean bowman who served with the Roman army in quelling the Jewish revolt of AD 66–70.

Most of Petra's famous tombs were carved during this period. Although the combination of a necropolis and a capital city may seem strange today, this custom was common among the ancients, who established cemeteries at the entrance to many of their capitals, including Rome itself. The presence of the tombs of Petra's rich and powerful near the city's major monuments seems to have been part of a cult of the dead. When traders and travelers came to visit the capital's marvels, they would leave offerings at the tombs to ensure the success of their journeys.

When the Nabateans emerged from the desert, they brought with them a faith in the deities who had protected them both as nomads and as traders. In the wetter, northern regions, they met people whose deities protected their crops and cities. The principal deity of the Nabateans had been Dusares, whose name means "Lord of Sarat"; near Petra, the Nabateans found an area called Shara, and Dusares easily changed his name to Dushara, "Lord of Shara." As Egyptian and Greek influences crept in, Dushara became associated with the chief male gods of those pantheons. The chief Nabatean goddess was al-Uzza, who reigned with her sisters Allat and Manat. She, too, took on Greek and Egyptian attributes, and her cult was eventually identified with Aphrodite, the Greek goddess of love; Tyche, goddess of fortune and protector of cities; and the Egyptian Isis. Almost all the shrines in Petra were dedicated to Dushara and al-Uzza.

In AD 106, during the reign of Trajan, the Romans annexed the Nabatean Kingdom into their new province of Arabia. Hadrian visited Petra in 130, after which it was renamed in his honor—Petra Hadriane. With the completion of the main north–south artery of the eastern Roman empire, the Via Nova Triana, Petra flourished as the region remained a prime trading conduit.

A unique combination of talents made the Nabateans the unchallenged masters of this route. Though they eventually abandoned their nomadic way of life, they did not forget its survival secrets. Into the rocky wilderness they carved cisterns, into which they channeled every drop of precious water that condensed on the desert floor or fell in rare rainstorms. Control over water enabled Nabatean caravans to cross vast expanses efficiently, and their cargo—frankincense, myrrh, and other spices—was worth its weight in gold.

The spices had their origin in what is now Yemen, and the caravan road stretched from Arabia to Petra before continuing across the Arava Valley to the Negev highlands of what is now Israel, and eventually reaching the Mediterranean port of Gaza. Another branch of the road continued north from Petra to Damascus and to the ports of Lebanon. According to Roman historian Pliny the Elder, the journey from Arabia to Gaza took 65 days. Each night the caravan would put in at a Nabatean trading post, where caravan masters would handsomely reward their hosts for their hospitality.

After the arrival of Christianity in the early 4th century, churches were built in Petra, and the new faith gradually replaced the old one. Bishops from Petra appear in ecclesiastical records as participants in the ecumenical councils that decided the early Church's doctrinal issues. By this time, Petra was far past its prime as a trade center; the ancient traders had learned that they could use the prevailing winds to hasten ships across the sea. Some Arabian goods thus began to come to Egypt and its Mediterranean ports via the Red Sea. The overland route that passed through Petra was still used, but to a lesser extent. Furthermore, a series of earthquakes left a ruinous mark on the city.

After Petra was captured by the Muslims in 633, both strategic alliances and crossroads changed course, and the world lost interest in the area. Capitalizing on the region's ancient strategic value, the Crusaders built fortifications among the old ruins in the 11th century, but in 1189 they surrendered to the Muslim warrior Saladin. After that, Petra sank into oblivion, and it remained there for more than 500 years, most knowledge of it confined to a few references in history books. It was not until 1812 that Swiss explorer Johann Ludwig Burckhardt (who had converted to Islam to facilitate his travels through the unknown area) penetrated Petra on the pretext of offering a sacrifice at the traditional tomb of Aaron. It was Burckhardt who provided the Western world with its first contemporary description of the marvels of the ancient city.

An overnight (two-day) trip to Petra will allow you to see many of the area's highlights. The closest border crossing is at Eilat. Cross the border early in the morning to be in Petra before noon. Petra is open daily from 6 AM to 7 PM; the city is gated and has an entrance fee of 20 JD (about $30) for a one-day visit, with a discount for multiple entries.

# Pleasures and Pastimes

## Dining

Dining in Petra represents both ends of the scale, from very simple, inexpensive fare to the very elegant and pricey. There is very little in between. Both dining experiences have one thing in common: courteous service and a warmly welcoming spirit. Don't be put off by the plainness of center-village eateries mentioned here. The locals enjoying their meal at the next table will remind you that the best fare is often to be had at such restaurants.

| CATEGORY | COST* |
|---|---|
| $$$$ | over $35 |
| $$$ | $20–$35 |
| $$ | $12–$20 |
| $ | under $12 |
| *per person for a three-course meal, excluding drinks and service charge | |

## Hiking

There are several hiking routes within Petra itself. One trail leads to the mysterious High Place of Sacrifice, and another to the mountaintop known as Jabal-al-Deir. These involve strenuous climbs, but the views and the antiquities at the top are well worth the effort for those in good physical condition. A third trek, for which you need to invest most of a day, ends at Jabal Haroun, the traditional burial place of Aaron, brother of Moses.

## Lodging

Petra offers numerous accommodation options. You can choose from luxurious to money-saving accommodations; both types can be found adjacent or near the site. The hotels closest to the site obviously provide the most convenient access to Petra and save you taxi money. A short car drive away in Wadi Musa are several good hotels, with some on the ridge above Wadi Musa. Taybet Zeman, in the village of Taybeh 9 km (5½ mi) from Petra, is the farthest from the site, but its uniquely authentic flavor is well worth the ride. All rooms have a private bath unless otherwise indicated.

| CATEGORY | COST* |
|---|---|
| $$$$ | over $160 |
| $$$ | $100–$160 |
| $$ | $50–$100 |
| $ | under $50 |
| *All prices are for two people in a standard double room, including taxes. | |

## Shopping

Petra's handicraft specialty is the work of its "sand artists"—artisans who fill bottles with sand in a variety of designs. They can customize your purchase by writing a name in sand. Those in the area known as the Open Siq will have you place your order in the morning and you'll pick up the finished work that afternoon. The most outstanding craftsman in the field is Adel Al-Amarat (dubbed "Picasso II"). Look for his shop, the Sand Castle, on the main street of Wadi Musa not far from the entrance to Petra.

# Exploring Petra

The walk that follows will take you through Petra's main sights. You can also hike to the High Place of Sacrifice, the Monastery (a-Deir), and make side trips to Little Petra or to Jabal Haroun.

*Numbers in the text correspond to numbers in the margin and on the Petra map.*

## A Good Walk

After paying your entrance fee, you'll see the **Horse Square** ①, with lean-tos where you can rent horses. After that, on the right of the path about 1,485 ft past the entrance, you'll come to the large **Djinn Blocks** ②. On the other side of the path is the **Snake Tomb** ③; step in and you'll see why it's so named. Back on the path, you'll see a large two-story tomb on your left. The lower story is called the Triclinium Tomb; the upper story is the **Obelisk Tomb** ④ and Bas-a-Siq Triclinium. From **Bab a-Siq** ⑤, a 1¼-km (¾-mi) walk brings you to the main ruins of Petra; from here you can see the remains of a Nabatean water tunnel.

Nineteenth-century travelers described a **triumphal arch** ⑥ that spanned the road at this point. As you traverse the narrow canyon of the **Siq** ⑦, nothing prepares you for the overwhelming first glimpse of the light at the end of the passage. The first burial monument is the magnificent **Khazneh** ⑧, or Treasury, adorned with figures from mythology. As you face the Khazneh, the Siq widens and soon makes a sharp turn to the right. It's here, in the area called the **Outer Siq** ⑨, that you'll meet the sand artists. On the right is **Uneishu's Tomb** ⑩. Across from the tomb, a flight of stairs leads to the path to the High Place of Sacrifice and the other tombs in the adjacent valley known as **Wadi Farasa** ⑪–⑰, south and west of the main street of antiquities (☞ Another Good Walk, *below*).

Continuing down this street brings you to Petra's **theater** ⑱, a sign of Roman influence. Continuing straight ahead, you'll see four elevated tombs on your right. The **Urn Tomb** ⑲ is the first in a series of some of the finest tombs in Petra, which also include the **Silk Tomb** ⑳, the **Corinthian Tomb** ㉑, and the **Palace Tomb** ㉒. No one really knows anything about those who were buried here, but the tombs' grandeur certainly suggests royal occupants. You can study them from the path or walk up and enter them. Northeast of the four tombs is a road leading toward the **Tomb of Sextius Florentinus** ㉓. The **House of Dorotheos** ㉔ is next, in an area where tombs were later reused for storage and habitation.

Returning to the main path in the city center, you'll come to the **Nymphaeum** ㉕, one of the most important monuments in Petra. The ancient main street, known as the **Colonnaded Street** ㉖, was built by the Romans; on the slope to its north are the poorly preserved remains of a **Byzantine church** ㉗. Nearby is one of the city's most elaborate temples, the **Temple of the Winged Lions** ㉘. At the western end of the Colonnaded Street stood a monumental gateway to Petra's *temenos,* or sacred precinct; here you can see the remains of statues of deities, in-

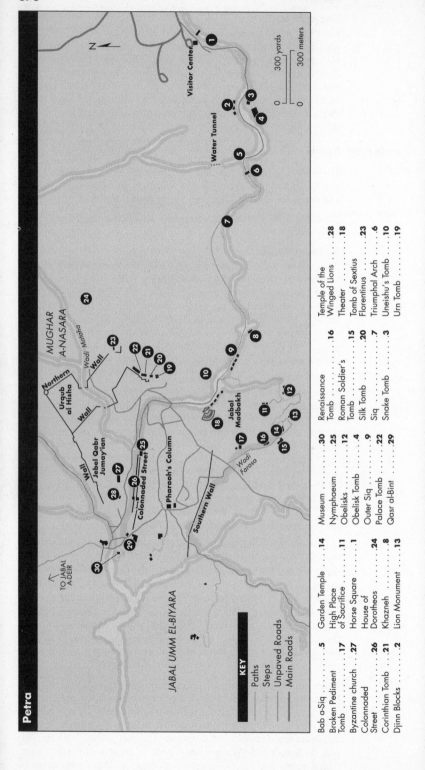

**Petra**

**KEY**
— Paths
— Steps
— Unpaved Roads
— Main Roads

Visitor Center
Water Tunnel
Northern Wall
Urqub al-Hisha
Wall
Wall
Jebel Qabr Jumay'ian
Colonnaded Street
Pharaoh's Column
Southern Wall
Wadi Faroso
Jabal Madbakh
Wadi Matoha
MUGHAR A-NASARA
JABAL UMM EL-BIYARA
TO JABAL A-DEIR

0  300 yards
0  300 meters

cluding Hermes and Tyche. The temenos leads you to a well-preserved temple, **Qasr al-Bint** ㉙. You can end your visit at Petra's **museum** ㉚.

TIMING

Plan to spend at least six hours rambling through the highlights of Petra; spend the first 40 minutes walking through the canyon (known as the Siq) to access the main sights. If you also want to climb to the Monastery (Jabal a-Deir), plan on spending the entire day. In summer, this area is very hot—wear a hat, and carry water.

## Sights to See

❺ **Bab a-Siq.** The Gate of the Cleft is near the Siq, the canyon-lined passageway leading to the main sights. From here you can spot the remains of a Nabatean water tunnel, built to divert flood waters from coursing through the narrow cleft and flooding the necropolis. A dam, constructed for the same purpose in the second half of the 1st century AD, was restored by the Jordanians after particularly serious flooding some years ago.

㉗ **Byzantine church.** Richly decorated with mosaics in the style of the period, this church appears to have been destroyed by fire soon after its construction, perhaps in a severe earthquake that took place in AD 551. Unfortunately the remains are now closed to visitors.

㉖ **Colonnaded Street.** The Romans built the main street of Petra over earlier remains in the early 1st century BC. In typical Roman style, it became the city's major thoroughfare, suitable for both commerce and grand ceremonial processions. After the Roman annexation of the Nabatean kingdom, the street was restored, as noted in an inscription dated AD 114 and dedicated to Emperor Trajan. In 363 an earthquake devastated Petra and the entire surrounding region, and the street never returned to its former glory.

㉑ **Corinthian Tomb.** Set among some of Petra's finest tombs is one named for the large number of Corinthian capitals, now badly deteriorated, that once decorated its facade.

❷ **Djinn Blocks.** The function of these large structures is unclear; they may have been connected to Nabatean worship, perhaps symbolizing one of their deities. In Arabic, *djinn* means "spirits," a common theme in Arab folklore.

❶ **Horse Square.** Horses used to be the conveyance of choice for the approximately 1-km (½-mi) trip to Petra's main antiquities. The growing number of visitors has made this mode impractical, but you can still hire horses for the first 800 yards, before the path narrows to become the Siq (☞ *below*). Carriages ply the route for those with difficulty walking. ☒ *Horse or carriage hire approximately 7 JD ($10), not including the expected tip of about 1 JD ($1).*

㉔ **House of Dorotheos.** The words THE HOUSE OF DOROTHEOS were found in this tomb in two Greek inscriptions. The area to the north of the tomb is called Mughar a-Nasara, meaning "caves of the Christians," and crosses carved on monuments here indicate their adaptation for Christian use.

★ ❽ **Khazneh.** Petra's most famous monument, this 130-ft-high structure has a splendid frontage graced by a number of mythological figures adopted by the Nabateans from Greek and Roman worship. Castor and Pollux (who after their death became the two brightest stars in the constellation Gemini), Amazons, Gorgons, eagles, and other creatures march across the Khazneh's rosy facade. Between the columns of the *tholos* (the rounded section above the tympanum) are the remains of a female deity holding a cornucopia; she is believed to be al-Uzza, the patroness of Petra and the Nabatean version of Aphrodite, goddess of love.

The Arabic name for this monument means "treasury"—its full name is Khaznet Fara'un, the Pharaoh's Treasury. It was assumed by archaeologists to be a tomb, but legends of treasures allegedly secreted within have led grave robbers here for centuries. The urn carved at the top of the tholos was thought to be the hiding place for the hoard. The Bedouin have been taking potshots at it for generations in the hopes of dislodging its contents, a practice whose results are still visible.

**㉚ Museum.** Petra's museum, and also rest rooms, is in the same building as the Petra Forum restaurant (☞ Dining and Lodging, *below*); another section of the museum is in a nearby tomb. Displays include a small number of Nabatean artifacts, such as jewelry and pottery.

OFF THE
BEATEN PATH

**JABAL A-DEIR –** Beginning near the museum, a strenuous, 45-minute climb up a steep path takes you to the summit of Jabal a-Deir, one of the most scenic points in Petra. The Mount of the Monastery takes its name from the crosses carved into the rock of the giant monument at its summit by monks who lived here in the 4th and 5th centuries. The monument's similarity to the Khazneh is remarkable, although this one is much larger; and its relatively remote location may suggest greater sanctity—the monument bears an inscription referring to the god Obodas. Nabatean king Obodas I is remembered for his triumph over both the Hasmonean ruler Alexander Jannaeus and the Seleucid king of Syria Antiochus XII. Obodas died in 86 BC and was deified shortly after; he's buried somewhere in the ruins of the Nabatean city of Avdat in the Negev. The site was probably a shrine constructed in his memory.

A clamber up the hill to the east of the monument affords a view of epic proportions: west of Petra, the highest peak in the region is the 4,455-ft-high sacred spot of Jabal Haroun, the traditional burial place of Aaron, brother of Moses. Beyond lies the wide expanse of the Arava Valley and, to the west, Israel's Negev Plateau.

OFF THE
BEATEN PATH

**JABAL HAROUN –** This seven- to eight-hour trek brings you to the tomb of Aaron, Moses's brother, and begins near the Pharaoh's Column within the site. You should hike this trail only with a guide, whose services can be obtained at the Petra Visitors Center. The ascent takes four hours on foot, but that time can be cut in half by doing most of it on camel-back, leaving a mere 20 minutes of (heart-hammering) climb at the end to the tomb itself. Reaching the tomb not only affords a sense of accomplishment and an amazing view but, for many, the added benefit of partaking of the sense of spirituality that pervades this place.

**㉕ Nymphaeum.** Dedicated to the water nymphs, this fountain was used for both refreshment and worship. The fountains of the two-story structure were fed by a water channel that continued along Petra's main street.

**❹ Obelisk Tomb.** This upper story of a two-story tomb is named for the four freestanding obelisks that decorate its facade. The lower story, the Triclinium Tomb, was so named because three walls of the empty room are lined with triclinia, a Latin word for this kind of bench. In other settings, diners would recline on these.

**❾ Outer Siq.** As you cross the area also known as Facade Street, you'll see several tombs with variations on Nabatean architectural themes, including repeated triangular step patterns and pilasters topped with Nabatean or more classical capitals. Water pipes set into channels along the facades of the last tombs on the right-hand side were the continuation of the system that brought water from the Siq to the city beyond.

**㉒ Palace Tomb.** This unfinished tomb is one of the few in Petra not carved entirely out of the rock. Many of the tomb's constructed segments have fallen away, so it's hard to ascertain its original dimensions. At the base of the Palace Tomb are the remains of the northern city wall, built after the 1st century BC.

**㉙ Qasr al-Bint.** This structure's full name, which translates as the "Palace of the Daughter of Pharaoh," stems from a legend that the pharaoh's daughter promised she would marry the man who could channel water to the city where she lived. When she had to choose between two winners, she asked each how he had managed his appointed task. The one whose answer she preferred won her hand. In fact, the structure is a temple, built in the early 1st century AD. As in the Temple of the Winged Lions, the identity of the deity worshiped here isn't known, but a statue depicting him or her—perhaps Dushara, the greatest deity of the Nabatean pantheon—certainly stood in the temple's inner sanctum.

**㉚ Silk Tomb.** The striations of natural color in the Silk Tomb's rock make it one of Petra's finest and certainly aid in identification. They flow across the facade like a multicolor silk scarf blowing gently in the wind.

**❼ Siq.** The Siq (meaning "cleft"), a rocky passage between towering walls of stone, leads visitors to the main ruins. The colors of the rock are astounding, varying in hues of red and purple. Nabatean paving is still visible in two locations along the way. Niches, some of which contain inscriptions dating from the 2nd and 3rd centuries AD, show that this road was as much a ceremonial path as a passageway. One niche is carved into a small outcropping of rock near one of the paved patches; it's unusual in that it faces away from the approach and may have been designed to bestow a blessing on those leaving the city. Film buffs may recall Harrison Ford riding through this area in some of the concluding scenes of *Indiana Jones and the Last Crusade.*

**❸ Snake Tomb.** No outward decoration marks this tomb, but 12 burial niches are carved into the floor inside. The name comes from a wall relief that shows two snakes attacking what may be a dog.

**㉘ Temple of the Winged Lions.** This impressive building takes its name from the sculptures that serve as capitals for its columns. The identity of the deity worshiped within is unknown, but figurines suggest that it may have been Isis, Egyptian goddess of the heavens and patroness of fertility. An inscription dates the construction of the temple to around AD 27.

**⑱ Theater.** This semicircular hallmark of Roman culture is a clear sign of the extent to which the Nabateans, like most other peoples of this region, had adopted the Roman way of life. The Nabateans apparently had no qualms about building a theater in a cemetery; their stone masons even cut into some of the existing tombs (the remains of which you can see at the back of the rock-cut theater) to do so. The capacity of the theater has been estimated at 10,000.

**㉓ Tomb of Sextius Florentinus.** The name of this Roman governor of Arabia appears in the tomb's inscription. Historical records indicate that he died in office in AD 128.

**❻ Triumphal arch.** Today, all that's left of this arch near the Siq are niches with the remains of statues that decorated the point where the arch's springers were built. The arch collapsed in 1895.

**⑩ Uneishu's Tomb.** This tomb in the Outer Siq got its name from an inscription discovered within that read UNEISHU, BROTHER OF SHAQILATH, QUEEN OF THE NABATEANS.

**⑲ Urn Tomb.** Named for the vaselike decoration at the top of its pediment, this tomb is supported by a series of vaults at its lower level, dubbed *al makhamah* (the law court) by the locals for some long-forgotten reason; the upper level was called *a-sijn* (the prison). According to an inscription within, Petra's Byzantine Christians turned the Urn Tomb into a church in AD 446.

## Another Good Walk

The path to the Nabatean shrine known as the **High Place of Sacrifice** ⑪ branches off from the main path through the city between the end of Facade Street and the theater. On a flat protrusion below the High Place are two **obelisks** ⑫ carved from the mountain. The curving path continues past the **Lion Monument** ⑬, a fountain. About 400 yards beyond, you'll see the tomb known as the **Garden Temple** ⑭. A short distance ahead lies the **Roman Soldier's Tomb** ⑮, an eclectic creation. Farther along are the **Renaissance Tomb** ⑯, named for its graceful facade, and the **Broken Pediment Tomb** ⑰. The relatively easy-to-follow path continues through Wadi Farasa and ends at the monument known as Pharaoh's Column, not far from the Colonnaded Street. From here you can continue on to the museum if you wish.

TIMING

The hike to the High Place of Sacrifice takes approximately three hours from the beginning of the ascent to the museum and its restaurant. To ascend to the High Place and then return to the main street of antiquities takes about 1½ hours.

## Sights to See

⑰ **Broken Pediment Tomb.** This tomb is characterized by the broken-off gable of its roof, supported by four pilasters topped with capitals in the unique Nabatean style.

⑭ **Garden Temple.** To the right, above this tomb (which also served as a temple), a wall closes off a cleft in the rock; it acted as a dam for water that flowed from a small spring south of the village of Wadi Musa. Two more channels also reached this point, bringing runoff from the area of the High Place of Sacrifice.

★ ⑪ **High Place of Sacrifice.** An ancient flight of stairs—restored in recent years by the Jordanian Department of Antiquities—leads to the top of Jabal Madhbah, the Mount of the Altar. At its peak is a rectangular court surrounded on three sides by benches in the triclinium style of the Roman dining room; in the center of the court is a raised block of stone, on which the priest may have stood. To the west are two altars accessed by steps, in front of which is a channel into which the blood of the sacrificial animal may have pooled.

⑬ **Lion Monument.** Surface runoff fed this fountain via a channel leading to the lion's mouth, from which water once streamed.

⑫ **Obelisks.** These two 20-ft-tall obelisks are examples of a common method of representing deities in the ancient Near East. Some scholars believe them to be representations of Dushara and al-Uzza; others believe they are simply the remains of quarrying activity.

⑯ **Renaissance Tomb.** This tomb bears a resemblance to the Tomb of Sextius Florentinus (☞ A Good Walk, *above*), in the main part of the city. It may have been created around the same time, the first third of the 1st century AD.

⑮ **Roman Soldier's Tomb.** The figure in the niche of this tomb's facade is dressed in typical Roman military garb, while the friezes and capitals appear more typical of Nabatean architecture before the Roman annexation. Directly opposite the Roman Soldier's Tomb is a triclinium; the rubble in between was probably once a courtyard connecting the two edifices.

## Side Trip to Little Petra

*3 km (2 mi) north of the village of Wadi Musa.*

Little Petra was the region's main commercial center in Nabatean times. To reach it, take the road through Wadi Musa that veers off before the visitor center marked "Al-Beida" and drive north. Continue along the narrow blacktop. You'll soon see a collection of ruins on a rocky outcropping on the left; this is all that remains of the **Crusader castle of al-Wu'eira**, built by Baldwin I in 1100. The first Crusader fortification east of the Jordan River, it was one of several strategic castles that protected the Crusader kingdom on its sensitive eastern flank, and in 1189 it was the last Crusader fortress east of Jordan to surrender to the Muslims.

Next you'll come to the village of Umm Saihun, whose residents are Bdhoul Bedouin, the main tribe of the Petra region. A 15-minute drive north will lead you to a T-junction. Turn left toward the area of **al Beida,** whose name—Arabic for "the white"—refers to the color of the sandstone formations along the way. (One of these formations, just beyond the village of Umm Saihun, looks exactly like an elephant. If you missed it going, look for it on the way back.) Excavations have uncovered the remains of an 11,000-year-old settlement from the Neolithic era, whose people were hunter-gatherers but also farmers and traders. Thousands of years after that culture became extinct, the Nabateans took over the same site and built agricultural terraces, some remains of which are still visible, about 200 yards south of the Siq al-Barid parking area.

After your left turn, you'll soon arrive at **Siq al-Barid,** a cleft in the rock that will remind you of the Siq at Petra except that it's much shorter and the sun does not penetrate it (hence the meaning of its Arabic name, "the cold cleft"). A walk through this passage brings you to Little Petra. This, rather than the city of Petra itself, was the staging area for the thousands of camels that would have arrived with each caravan. Merchants conducted business in Little Petra's rock-cut courtyard, but evidence shows that they made time for diversion as well. One room off the courtyard is a dining room, the ceiling of which was once richly painted; another is a theater.

## Dining and Lodging

$$ ✕ **Petra Forum.** This buffet restaurant is in Petra itself. It caters to groups, so it may not be the most imaginative meal you'll ever have, but it's spacious and the shady outdoor section is pleasant. It's definitely the best place to stop for a substantial lunch around the midpoint of your Petra tour day. ✉ *Petra Old City,* ☏ *03/215–6266. AE, MC, V.*

$ ✕ **Cleopatra.** No need to ask for a menu here; what you see cooking in the warmers is what you get. The specialty is chicken stewed in tomato sauce with chickpeas, potatoes, and other vegetables over rice. Locals and tourists gather at Cleopatra's for chicken barbecued over a wood fire in the evening. Like other local eateries, it's wide open to the street, so you can watch life go by as you dine. Dessert, here and everywhere in town, means a tiny cup of strong coffee spiced with *hel* (cardamom) and a dish of baklava or one of the many kindred versions of this honey-and-pistachio staple of Middle Eastern sweets. ✉ *Main street of Wadi Mousa. No credit cards.*

$ ✕ **El Mahbash.** Locals may automatically recommend this restaurant for lunch since it's geared to travelers, especially to groups. You'll recognize every dish on the buffet, which can be a comfort to some and a disappointment to those who like a culinary adventure. A full meal includes a limited array of salads and a main course of meat or fish. A light lunch of soup, salads, and fruit, might be just what you are in the mood for. ✉ *Main street of Wadi Mousa,* ☏ *03/215–7160. AE, MC, V.*

**$**   ✕ **Treasury.** After the garrulous owner–head chef invites you to squeeze yourself in at a table and has turned down the television (a fixture at all the local eateries), he'll proudly report that his was the first restaurant to open in Petra. This is the best place to try the Jordanian national dish, *mansaf*, lamb baked in yogurt sauce and served over rice. When cooked to perfection as it is here, the meat melts in your mouth. ⊠ *Main street of Wadi Musa,* ☎ *079/640–350. No credit cards.*

**$$$$**  ✕⊡ **Taybet Zeman.** Nine kilometers (5½ miles) from Petra, on the out-
★   skirts of the town of Taybeh, this unique lodging was once a Bedouin village. Abandoned for years, it was eventually revamped into a hotel that has every modern amenity but has been designed to steep its guests in aspects of Jordanian-Bedouin culture that have all but dis-appeared. Located high above Petra, Taybet Zeman has an incompa-rable view of the mountains of Edom, especially from the Diwan, its garden terrace. Rooms are very spacious and decorated in authentic Bedouin style with throw rugs and wall hangings—a colorful coun-terpoint to the natural stone walls. At the hotel's *souk* (market), you can watch unusual handcrafted items being made. The central court-yard has a spice garden, and its yields are served in the hotel's excel-lent restaurant, whose menu mixes Eastern and Western favorites. The buffet is worth a trip in itself. The hotel has one wheelchair-accessible room. ⊠ *Box 2, Wadi Musa,* ☎ *03/215–0111,* 📠 *03/215–0101. 105 rooms. Restaurant, sauna. AE, MC, V.*

**$$$**  ✕⊡ **Petra Movenpick.** This is Petra's finest hotel. Beyond its excellent
★   location, right by the city gates, the Movenpick has plenty of its own draws—first and foremost its staff, who are markedly cordial, helpful, and ac-commodating. Public spaces are beautifully decorated in an Arabic theme: the lobby has a Moroccan-tiled fountain and wooden furniture inlaid with mother-of-pearl. The hand-carved wooden screens in the Al'Maqa'ad Bar are intricately inlaid with turquoise and gold leaves, and the ceilings are exquisitely painted. Rooms are simply and elegantly decorated in soft col-ors and have exceptionally comfortable beds. There are two wheelchair-accessible rooms. The hotel's restaurant, Al Iwan, is excellent. Lobster from Dubai is the specialty of the house, and the buffet features a different and delightful variety every night. ⊠ *Box 214, Wadi Musa,* ☎ *03/215–7111, 800/344–6835 in the U.S.,* 📠 *03/215–7112. 155 rooms, 28 suites. 3 restaurants, bar, minibars, no-smoking rooms, pool, sauna, exercise room, library, car rental. AE, DC, MC, V.*

**$$$**  ⊡ **Petra Guest House.** The Guest House is conveniently located adjacent to Petra's entrance. Next door is the Petra Cave, the hotel's bar-dis-cotheque. They say the cave itself is ancient, but it's been decorated in such a way that the observer may find it, rather than reminding one of the surrounding Nabatean culture, more reminiscent of a set from the *Flint-stones* movie. Room decor is far less imaginative than the hotel's public areas, but the rooms are clean, if small. ⊠ *Box 30, Wadi Musa.* ☎ *03/ 215–6246,* 📠 *03/215–6724. 72 rooms. Restaurant, bar. MC, V.*

**$$**  ⊡ **Amra Palace.** The Amra is in the center of Wadi Musa. Rooms are airy and spacious. In front of the hotel is a rare and welcoming stretch of lawn where guests mingle in the evening. Although you won't be bowled over by luxury and over-the-top facilities, this is a very good option for those on a budget. ⊠ *Box 124, Wadi Musa,* ☎ *03/551–0001,* 📠 *03/551–0003. 48 rooms. No credit cards.*

**$$**  ⊡ **Edom Hotel.** The Edom is another good budget option, with the ad-vantage of very close proximity to Petra's entrance. Its dining room is built against a real cave; this is where people gather to enjoy an after-dinner drink and good cheer and to try out a water pipe (known here as a "hubbly-bubbly"). Rooms are rather unremarkable, though they do all have private balconies. ⊠ *Box 18, Wadi Musa,* ☎ *03/215–6995,* 📠 *03/215–6994. 135 rooms. Minibars. AE, MC, V.*

**$$**   🏨 **Kings Way Inn.** The Kings Way is in the village of Wadi Musa, 4 km (2½ mi) from Petra, across from the Ein Musa Spring, where a local tradition says Moses struck the rock to bring forth water. In the lobby you'll find the real warmth of Jordanian hospitality—guests sit informally on rugs around the musician-storyteller for an evening's entertainment. Rooms are spacious and clean and boast more attempts at a local accent in the decor than most other hotels in this category. ⊠ *Box 71, Wadi Musa,* ☎ *03/215–6799,* 𝔽𝔸𝕏 *03/215–6796. 81 rooms. Lobby lounge, pool. AE, D, MC, V.*

**$**   🏨 **Petra Inn.** As with the other budget hotels in this list, what the Petra Inn may lack in local color it makes up with other important advantages. Aside from the low price, rooms are clean, air-conditioned, and have beautiful views; and the staff is helpful and friendly. There is a doctor on-call around the clock, and no-smoking rooms are available. ⊠ *Box 155, Wadi Musa,* ☎ *03/215–6403,* 𝔽𝔸𝕏 *03/215–6401. 41 rooms. Restaurant, bar. AE, MC, V.*

## Nightlife and the Arts

A **candle-lit tour** of Petra is one of the city's new attractions. A stroll through the Siq as shadows play on the canyon walls is a dramatic way to discover aspects hidden by day. Music is played and stories told in front of the Khazneh at the end of the walk. The tour departs from the Petra Visitors Center on Monday and Thursday at 8:30 PM and returns around 10:30 PM. 🎫 *12 JD ($18).*

# Petra A to Z

## Before You Go

### BORDERS

The Arava border crossing, just north of Eilat in Israel, is open Sunday–Thursday 6:30 AM–10 PM, Friday–Saturday 8–8. The crossing is closed on the religious holidays Yom Kippur and Id el Fitr. There is a border tax of about NIS 180 ($45) on the Israeli side.

Two other border crossings might be convenient under certain circumstances. The Allenby Bridge crossing (four hours' drive from Petra) is about 45 minutes from Jerusalem. If you plan to enter Jordan here, you'll need to obtain your visa ahead of time at the Jordanian Embassy in Tel Aviv (☞ Passports and Visas, *below*) or in your country of origin. Bring passport photos. The Beit She'an border crossing (five hours' drive from Petra) is approximately 40 minutes from Tiberias.

### CURRENCY

The Jordanian unit of currency is the dinar, indicated by the suffix JD. The exchange rate at press time was approximately .71 JD to the U.S. dollar, .47 JD to the Canadian dollar, and 1.07 JD to the British pound.

### PASSPORTS AND VISAS

You need a valid passport to enter Jordan. Holders of non-Israeli passports can obtain visas on the spot after crossing into Jordan (except at the Allenby Bridge crossing; ☞ Borders, *above*) or through the **Jordanian Embassy** (⊠ 14 Abba Hillel St., Tel Aviv, ☎ 03/751–7722). A visa costs about $45, but a visa to cross at the Allenby Bridge costs about $100.

## Arriving and Departing

### BY BUS

There's only one bus per day to and from Petra from the Jordanian side of the Arava crossing at Aqaba: at 4 PM Aqaba–Petra and at 6 AM Petra–Aqaba. Even this bus service is somewhat unreliable.

### BY CAR

Only cars registered to their drivers can be driven into Jordan (☞ Car Rentals *in* Contacts and Resources, *below*). Note that unleaded fuel, not widely sold in Jordan, is available in Amman and Aqaba.

### BY PLANE

El Al and Royal Jordanian Airlines fly to Amman, Jordan's capital, from Tel Aviv's Ben-Gurion Airport. This option has limited appeal, as you must be at the airport two hours before flight time for the 15-minute flight, then drive three hours from Amman to Petra.

### BY TAXI

Shared taxis are available on the Jordanian side of the Arava border to take you into Aqaba, where you can rent a car. A shared taxi to Aqaba costs about 4 JD ($6) per person; a private taxi from the border to Petra or from Aqaba to Petra is about 35 JD ($50).

## Getting Around

### BY CAR

Driving the narrow, winding Aqaba–Petra Highway is an experience. Remember to stay well to the right, but bear in mind that the driver coming from the opposite direction may not be so inclined.

## Contacts and Resources

### CAR RENTALS

**Turath Travel and Tourism** (☞ Guided Tours, *below*) is a local agent for Hertz, Avis, and other companies and also rents four-by-four vehicles.

### GUIDED TOURS

A number of operators run tours to Petra that you can reserve in advance. These are a good option if you want to see the highlights without having to worry about logistics.

**JET Club Travel and Tours** (⊠ 3 Ben Sira St., Jerusalem, ☎ 02/623–5535) are experts at designing tours to Petra as well as to all other destinations in Jordan and other Middle East destinations. Tours can include hotel reservations, an English-speaking driver, local guides at the various sites, and visa arrangements.

**Neot Hakikar** (⊠ 67 Ben Yehuda St., Tel Aviv, ☎ 03/520–5858; ⊠ Tourist Information Center: 1 Yotam St., Eilat, ☎ 08/632–6281) has a two-day trip to Petra leaving from Eilat, including a Jeep tour of Wadi Rum.

**Turath Travel and Tourism** (⊠ Corner of Shamaissani and Abd-el Hameed Sharaf Sts., Amman, Jordan, ☎ 04/569–4067) arranges transfers from any border to Petra with an English-speaking driver, as well as hotel bookings, and expert guides who give tours of Petra. This tour is far more in-depth than the two-hour one sold at the site.

### MEDICAL CARE

There is a doctor at the **clinic** in the tourist compound near the Petra Forum Hotel, at the entrance to Petra. There is also a **public clinic** in Upper Wadi Musa next to the Acropolis Hotel, and a **private clinic** in central Wadi Musa next to the Arab Bank. The closest **hospital** (☎ 03/213–2222) is in Ma'an, about 40 km (25 mi) away.

### TELEPHONES

When dialing from Israel, dial 00–962 and the area code 3 before numbers in Petra; for Amman, use 00–962 and the area code 6. When dialing within Jordan, add a 0 before the area code. The international country code for Jordan is 962.

### VISITOR INFORMATION

Petra's **visitor center** (☎ 03/215–6020) has brochures and a computerized information service about Jordan, as well as a well-stocked souvenir shop. The friendly staff will answer all your questions. You can also arrange a local guide for a basic two-hour Petra tour here.

# 9 BACKGROUND & ESSENTIALS

Maps of Israel

Portrait of Israel

Books and Videos

Chronology

National and Religious Holidays

Smart Travel Tips A to Z

Hebrew and Palestinian Arabic Vocabularies

# Israel

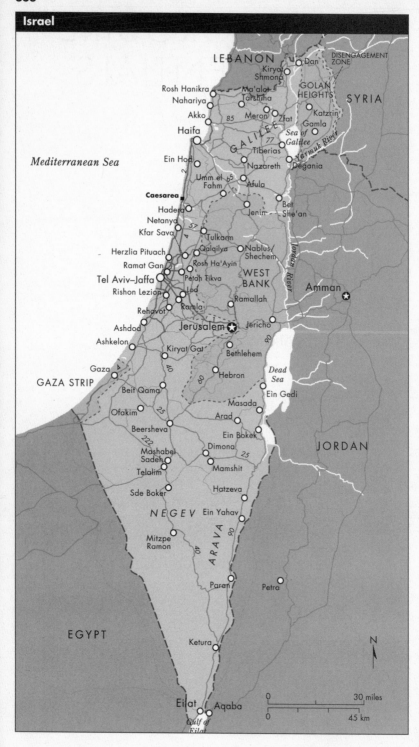

LEBANON

Rosh Hanikra
Nahariya
Akko
Haifa
Ein Hod

Kiryat
Shmona
Ma'alot
Tarshiha
Meron
Zfat

Dan

DISENGAGEMENT
ZONE

GOLAN
HEIGHTS

SYRIA

Katzrin
Gamla

Sea of
Galilee

Tiberias
Nazareth
Degania

Yarmuk River

*Mediterranean Sea*

Caesarea

Hadera
Netanya
Kfar Sava

Herzlia Pituach
Ramat Gan
Tel Aviv–Jaffa
Rishon Lezion
Rehovot
Ashdod
Ashkelon

Umm el
Fahm
Afula
Jenin

Bet
She'an

Tulkarm
Qalqilya
Rosh Ha'Ayin
Petah Tikva
Lod
Ramla

Nablus/
Shechem

WEST
BANK

Ramallah

Jordan River

Amman

Jerusalem
Jericho

Gaza

GAZA STRIP

Kiryat Gat

Bethlehem

Hebron

Beit Qama

Ofakim

Beersheva

Mashabei
Sadeh
Telalim
Sde Boker

Masada

Arad

Dimona

Mamshit

Hatzeva

*N E G E V*  Ein Yahav

Mitzpe
Ramon

*Dead
Sea*

Ein Gedi

Ein Bokek

JORDAN

A R A V A

Paran

Petra

EGYPT

Ketura

Eilat  Aqaba

*Gulf of
Eilat*

N

0        30 miles
0        45 km

# Geography of Israel

Mediterranean Sea

LEBANON

Kiryat Shmona

Mt. Hermon

DISENGAGEMENT ZONE

SYRIA

GOLAN HEIGHTS

Akko

Mt. Meron

GALILEE

Zfat

Hula Valley

Haifa

Tiberias

Sea of Galilee

Yarmuk R.

Nazareth

Afula

Mt. Tabor

Mt. Carmel

Jezreel Valley

Mt. Gilboa

Bet She'an

Jordan R.

Gilead Mts.

Jenin

Netanya

Tulkarm

Qalqilya

Nablus (Shechem)

WEST BANK

Amman

Tel Aviv-Jaffa

Rehovot

Ramla

Ramallah

Jericho

Ashdod

Jerusalem

SHEFELAH

Ashkelon

Hebron

JUDEAN DESERT

Dead Sea

Gaza

Arad

Ein Gedi

GAZA STRIP

Masada

Beersheba

Ein Bokek

JORDAN

Nahal Zin

Wilderness of Zin

NEGEV

Mitzpe Ramon

MAKHTESH RAMON

ARAVA

EDOM MOUNTAINS

EGYPT

N

EILAT MOUNTAINS

Eilat

Aqaba

Gulf of Eilat

| 0 | | 30 miles |
| 0 | | 45 km |

# SMALL COUNTRY, BIG HISTORY

Israel is a land of pastel landscapes and primary-color people; a land where the beauty of nature is subtle but the natives often are not. The sometimes rambunctious Israeli affability may envelop you as soon as you board your flight to Tel Aviv, especially if you're flying El Al, Israel's national carrier. Cries of recognition and the chatter of passengers exchanging stories about their trips and their duty-free bargains recall first days back at school after summer vacations. Some passengers greet El Al touchdowns on Holy Land soil with spontaneous applause, but these are the sentimental tourists; the red-blooded Israelis are already on their feet collecting their bags, despite pleas from the cabin staff.

The feistiness of Israelis can come across as assertive, intrusive, even aggressive; their fighter-pilot style of driving may be the best example. On the other hand, many claim that this attitude is what helped Israel survive in a hostile political and natural environment. The related lack of inhibition leads to fast and genuinely warm human contacts that come as a refreshing surprise to many visitors from more reserved cultures.

Hospitality has been a deeply ingrained tradition in this part of the world since the days of Abraham's tent. If an Israeli even casually invites you home for coffee or a meal, he or she probably expects that you'll accept the invitation. Do. There is no better way to dive into the culture, and you'll probably pick up instant expertise on local politics, ethnic differences, food, the cost of buying a house, and what your host earns. Be prepared for similar questions about *your* life; there are fewer conversational taboos in Israel than in most English-speaking countries. An oft-quoted example is that of the Is-

raeli company rep sent abroad, who was advised to avoid discussing politics, religion, and sex in social situations. "What *else* is there to talk about?" asked the astonished Israeli.

The key to understanding Israel is to understand that it was created to be a modern reincarnation of an ancient Jewish state. Israel was the "Promised Land" of Abraham and Moses, the Israelite kingdom of David and Solomon, and the home of Jesus of Nazareth and the Jewish Talmudic sages. Although the Jewish presence in the country has been unbroken for more than 3,000 years, several massive exiles—first by the Babylonians in 586 BC and then by the Romans in AD 70—created a diaspora, a dispersion of the Jewish people throughout the world.

The Jewish attachment to the ancient homeland weaves through the entire fabric of Jewish history and religious tradition. For the last 2,000 years, wherever they have lived, Jews have turned their faces toward Jerusalem daily in prayer. The Jewish liturgy is saturated with prayers for the restoration of "Zion and Jerusalem." Over the centuries, many Jews trickled back to Eretz Yisrael (the Land of Israel) while others looked forward to fulfilling their dream of return in some future—many felt imminent—messianic age. An 18th-century story tells of a certain Rabbi Yitzhak of Berdichev in Poland who sent out invitations to his daughter's wedding: "It will take place next Tuesday in the Holy City of Jerusalem. If, God forbid, the Messiah has not arrived by then, it will take place in the village square."

Not all were prepared to wait for divine intervention. In the late 19th century, a variety of Jewish nationalist movements began to emerge. Zionism was founded as a political movement to give structure and impetus to the idea of creating a home for the Jewish people in Israel. Some early Zionist leaders, like founding father Theodore Herzl, believed that the urgent priority was simply a Jewish haven safe from persecution, wherever that haven might be. Argentina was suggested, and Great Britain offered Uganda. In light of Jewish historical and emotional links to the land of Israel, Zionists rejected these "territorialist" suggestions. British statesman (later Earl) Arthur James Balfour was perplexed by this attitude and asked Zionist leader Chaim Weizmann to explain it. "Mr. Balfour," Dr. Weizmann responded, "if I were to offer you Paris instead of London, would you accept it?" "Of course not," Balfour replied, "London is our capital." "Precisely," said Weizmann, "and Jerusalem was *our* capital when London was still a marsh!"

The establishment of the state of Israel did not, of course, meet with universal rejoicing. To the Arab world, it was anathema, an alien implant in a Muslim Middle East. Palestinian Arabs today mark Israel's independence as the *Nakba,* the Catastrophe, when their own national aspirations were thwarted. To many ultra-Orthodox Jews, the founding of Israel was an arrogant preempting of God's divine plan; and to make matters worse, the new state was blatantly secular, despite its concessions to religious interests. This internal battle over the character of the Jewish state and the implacable hostility of Israel's neighbors—which has resulted in more than half a century of almost constant conflict—have been the two main issues engaging the country since its birth.

O F ISRAEL'S 6.5 MILLION citizens, 78% are Jewish. Some proudly trace their family roots back many generations on local soil; others are first-, second-, or third-generation *olim* (immigrants) from more than 100 countries. The first modern pioneers arrived from Russia in 1882, purchased land, and set about developing it with romantic zeal. A decade or two later, inspired by the socialist ideas then current in Eastern Europe, a much larger wave founded the first *kibbutzim*—collective villages or communes. In time, these fiercely idealistic farmers became something of a moral elite, having little financial power but providing a greatly disproportionate percentage of the country's political leadership, military officer cadre, and intelligentsia. "We are workers," they liked to say, "but not working-class!" The kibbutz movement still makes its voice heard and its economic presence felt, but it is not the dominant force it once was. A more ambitious younger generation has increasingly eschewed the communal lifestyle in favor of the lures of the big city.

Although most who immigrated before Israel's independence in 1948 were Ashkenazi Jews (those of Central or Eastern European descent), the biggest waves of immigration in the first decade of statehood were of Sephardic Jews, who came from the Arab lands of North Africa and the Middle East. Israel's Jewish population—600,000 at the time of its independence—doubled within 3½ years and tripled within 10. For a long time, the visible differences between the haves and have-nots broke down along the lines of the more established and better-educated Ashkenazim and the poorer, unskilled Sephardim. For a while it seemed that the distinction, the prejudices, and the resentment had somewhat subsided, but the rhetoric and success of a Sephardic religious party called Shas has proven this hope a bit premature.

The State of Israel was founded just three years after the end of World War II, in which the Nazis annihilated fully a third of the world's Jewish population. In light of the urgency of providing a haven for remnants of the shattered European Jewish communities, the Law of Return was passed in 1949 granting any Jew the automatic right to Israeli citizenship. Immigration and immigrant absorption became national priorities, warranting a full government ministry. Absorption centers were eventually established to give new immigrants an orientation and teach them Hebrew.

Although the system has been generally very successful, its resources and creativity have been sorely taxed in recent years. During the 1990s, Israel absorbed close to 1 million new immigrants, most from the former Soviet Union, increasing the population by more than 10%. Apart from the initial problems of housing and feeding such great numbers, the ongoing challenges were finding employment for the often overqualified Russian immigrants, and helping the small Ethiopian immigrant community bridge a centuries-wide cultural and technological gap and adjust to an industrialized society.

The vast majority of Israel's 1 million non-Jewish minority are Muslim Arabs, followed by about 80,000 Christian Arabs, 90,000 Druze, and a similar number of Bedouin (nominally Muslim Arabs, but a community apart). All are citizens, equal under the law, who vote for and may serve in the Knesset, the Israeli parliament. (Not included are the more than 2 million *Palestinian* Arabs of the partly autonomous West Bank and the autonomous Gaza Strip, who are not Israeli citizens.)

Social and economic gaps between the Arab and Jewish sectors continue to rankle, however, and have been the excuse for sometimes-violent demonstrations and other anti-establishment activity. Although the Muslims in Israel, mainstream Sunnis, are regarded as both politically and religiously moderate by the standards of the region, there has been considerable radicalization in recent years of the community's youth, who identify politically with the Palestinian liberation movement and/or religiously with the Islamic revival currently sweeping the Middle East.

Of the Christian Arabs, most belong to the Greek Catholic, Greek Orthodox, or Roman Catholic church; a handful of Eastern denominations and a few tiny Protestant groups account for the rest. The Western Christian community is minuscule, consisting mainly of clergy, and temporary sojourners such as diplomats and foreign professionals on assignment.

The Druze, though Arabic-speaking, follow a separate and secret religion that broke from Islam about 1,000 years ago. Larger kindred communities exist in long-hostile Syria and Lebanon, but Israeli Druze have solidly identified with Israel, and the community's young men are routinely drafted into the Israeli army. The Arab community itself is not liable for military service, in order to avoid the possibility of battlefield confrontations with kinsmen from neighboring countries.

There is no firm separation of religion and state in Israel. Matters of personal status—marriage, divorce, adoption, and burial—are the preserve of the religious authorities of the community concerned. For this reason there is no civil marriage; if one partner does not convert to the faith of the other, the couple must marry abroad. Within the Jewish community, such functions fall under the supervision of the Orthodox chief rabbinate, much to the dismay of members of the tiny but growing Conservative and Reform movements (many of whom are American expatriates) and of the large number of nonobservant Jews.

The confrontation between secular Israelis and the hard-line ultra-Orthodox has escalated over the years, as the religious community tries to impose on what it considers an apostate citizenry its vision of how a Jewish state should behave. Hot issues include the Orthodox definition of what a Jew is (either born of a Jewish mother or converted by strict Orthodox procedures) for the purpose of Israeli citizenship, and public observance of the Sabbath and of dietary laws. For many nonreligious Israelis, already irked by what they consider religious coercion, the fact that most ultra-Orthodox Jewish men avoid military service on the grounds of continuing religious studies just rubs salt in the wound.

Israel prides itself on being the only true democracy in the Middle East, and it sometimes seems bent on politically tearing itself apart in the democratic process. This is how the system works (or doesn't): once every four years, prior to national elections, every party publishes a list of its candidates for the 120-member Knesset. There are no constituencies or voting districts; each party that breaks the minimum threshold of 1.5% of the *national* vote gets in, winning the same percentage of Knesset seats as its *proportion* of nationwide votes (hence "proportional representation").

The good news is that the system is intensely democratic. A relatively small grouping of like-minded voters *countrywide* (currently about 50,000) can elect an M.K. (Member of the Knesset) to represent its views. The largest party able to gain a parliamentary majority through a coalition with other parties becomes the government. The bad news is that the system creates a proliferation of small parties, whose collective support the government needs in order to rule. Since no party has ever won enough seats to rule alone, Israeli governments have always been based on compromise, with small parties exerting a degree of political influence quite out of proportion to their actual size. Attempts to change the system have been doomed to failure, because the small parties, which stand to lose if the system is changed, are precisely those on whose support the *current* government depends.

Traditionally, the leader of the victorious large party became prime minister, but since 1996 the prime minister (PM) has been elected directly on a separate ballot. The move was designed to reduce the influence of the small parties by giving the PM a popular mandate, but the innovation has complicated the system rather than improved it. Voters can now split their vote, supporting one of the two big-party candidates as PM but casting their *party* vote in favor of the small party that most closely represents their views. The parliamentary strength of the big parties, Labor and Likud, has declined dramatically as a result, with a proportionate rise in the power of the small parties.

The country is small—just 470 km (under 300 mi) long, from Metulla, on the northern border with Lebanon, to Eilat, on the Red Sea; 110 km (69 mi) wide at its widest, across the Negev Desert; and as little as 50 km (31 mi) wide across the Galilee. In area Israel is exactly the size of Wales, or just larger than Massachusetts. The American writer Mark Twain was astonished by the smallness of the Holy Land when he visited in 1867. He had envisioned, he wrote, "a country as large as the United States . . . I suppose it was because I could not conceive of a small country having so large a history."

Mark Twain's astonishment is instructive: in Israel the past is more present than almost anywhere else on earth. There is something about the place that seeps into one's soul. For the Jewish visitor, it's a feeling of coming home, of returning to one's roots. For the Christian, it's the awe of retracing Jesus's footsteps in the Scripture's actual landscape, of seeing the Bible take on entirely new meaning. For the Muslim it's the opportunity to pray at the third holiest shrine in Islam.

Indeed, the country's biblical past has made names like Jerusalem, the Galilee, and the Jordan River household words for almost half the human race. Many a pilgrim has reached Israel expecting a Jerusalem preserved as an uncommercialized shrine, a Galilee of donkey traffic and tiny fishing boats, and a Jordan River "deep and wide." The reality hits as you find the ancient names shouted from store billboards and highway signs. You discover that Jerusalem is a modern metropolis of 600,000 people and Galilee is the name of a professional basketball team. To top it all off, the Jordan River is for the most part a little stream.

The past is far from forgotten, however. Archaeology is almost a national sport here (though less for today's video-game generation than for its parents), and any unusual find in one of the ongoing excavations is sure to make the prime-time news. There are prehistoric settlement sites more than a million years old; the world's oldest walled town, at Jericho; echoes of the biblical patriarchs; and evidence of the kings of Israel. You can stand on the Temple Mount steps that Jesus almost certainly climbed, or marvel at an ancient wooden boat by the Sea of Galilee. The word *ancient* has a particular currency here.

Despite its small size, Israel offers an astonishing diversity of climate and terrain. Drive east from Tel Aviv via Jerusalem to the Dead Sea, and in 1½ hours you pass from classic Mediterranean white beaches and orange groves through olive-draped hills and up rugged pine-wooded mountains, only to plunge almost 4,000 ft down the other side, through wild, barren desert, to the subtropical oasis of Jericho and the Dead Sea, the lowest point on the planet.

Half of Israel is desert, but don't picture endless sand dunes. Awesome canyons slice through the Judean Desert to the Dead Sea, a few with sweet waterfalls and brilliant shocks of greenery. The Negev highlands, south of Beersheva, are punctuated by three huge craters caused by eons of water erosion, the only such formations in the world. The resort city of Eilat sits on the coral-reef Red Sea against a backdrop of jagged granite peaks and desert moonscapes. And in the spring, after the meager winter rains, the deserts burst into startling bloom, the hard landscapes softened by a fuzz of grass and multicolored wildflowers. A desert excursion here—by foot, Jeep, or camel—is not quickly forgotten.

The northern and western parts of the country are a complete antidote to the desert. True, it's also hot in the summer and somewhat parched in the rainless season from May through October, but it's a land of good winter rains, some springs and streams, miles of Mediterranean beaches, extensive irrigated fields and orchards, mountainsides of evergreen forests, lush nature reserves, and the freshwater "Sea" of Galilee.

Despite its heritage and location—think of it as Eastern Mediterranean rather than Middle Eastern—Israel is as European as it is Levantine. Scientifically, the country is at the forefront of computer technology and software, lasers, medicine, biotechnology, aeronautics, electronics, and agriculture. Seven universities, some world-renowned, set exceptional standards. Although Israel's health system is groaning under the weight of financial deficits, and hospital conditions sometimes reflect this, the country's high medical standards do not seem to have been compromised. Doctors on call for your hotel will speak English and likely be on par with physicians back home.

Violent crime is relatively low in Israel. Periods of politically motivated violence occur sporadically, but the violence mostly occurs in areas at the center of Israel's conflict with the Palestinians (like the West Bank) that are not recommended tourist destinations. You *will* see automatic weapons on the street, obviously in the hands of uniformed security personnel, but also sometimes over the shoulder of a young off-duty soldier in civvies. The Israeli Defense Force is a people's army: almost all Jews serve, and a national serviceman or servicewoman, once issued a weapon, is *wedded* to it for the duration. The criminal misuse of army-issue firearms is very, very rare.

There are many large towns in Israel, but only three major cities. Jerusalem, the capital and spiritual center, lies 60 km (38 mi) inland, at an elevation of 2,500 ft, and is a limestone blend of the ancient and the modern. Tel Aviv, on the Mediterranean coast, is unlovely but lively—the country's commercial and entertainment center, the city that never sleeps. Two out of every five Israelis live within its metropolitan area. Haifa, 100 km (63 mi) north of Tel Aviv, sprawls up the slopes of Mt. Carmel, offering sweeping views and serving as one of the country's two main ports and industrial areas.

Urban life, at least in the metropolis, has changed dramatically over the years. Greater affluence and a sharp sense of international fashion and style have produced a consumerism not unlike that of North America or Western Europe. You can see it in the delis and supermarkets, the boutiques and home-furnishing stores. The growing popularity of dining out as an evening activity has created a clientele with sophisticated expectations, which are reflected in the large number of great restaurants and local fine wines. A good climate and fine beaches have spawned a burgeoning leisure industry as well. Add all of this to Israel's physical attractions, historical fascination, and profound religious impact, and you have one of the most intriguing destinations in the world.

–Mike Rogoff

# WHAT TO READ & WATCH BEFORE YOU GO

## History and Biography

If you haven't opened the Bible in a while, this is a good time to review biblical narratives; better yet, bring it along on your trip. For a modern look at the Bible, take a look at *Genesis and the Big Bang*, by Gerald Schroeder (Bantam). *Heritage, Civilization and the Jews*, by Abba Eban (Steimatzky), is a pictorial survey illustrating 5,000 years of Jewish civilization. *Jews, God and History*, by Max I. Dimont (Signet), is an old but very readable history of the Jewish people (and very portable for traveling). Karen Armstrong's *Jerusalem: One City, Three Faiths* (Alfred A. Knopf) traces the city's physical history and spiritual meaning from its beginning to the present day. *Understanding the Dead Sea Scrolls*, edited by Hershel Shanks (Random House), is a selection of essays by leading scholars. Last, but far from least, is Flavius Josephus's *The Jewish War*. The Jewish commander who defected to the Romans during the Great Revolt wrote a still-fascinating account of the Roman campaigns.

To better understand some of the leading players in Israel's modern history, try one of the following: *The Life of Moshe Dayan*, by Robert Slater (St. Martin's Press); *Ben-Gurion*, by Shabtai Teveth (Houghton Mifflin); *My Life*, by Golda Meir (Weidenfeld and Nicolson); and *The Revolt*, by Menachem Begin (Steimatzky), the former prime minister's account of the fighting unit he headed. *O Jerusalem*, by Larry Collins and Dominique Lapierre (Simon and Schuster), is a dramatic account of the establishment of the Israeli state.

*The Book of Our Heritage*, by Eliayahv Kitov (Feldheim), is a superb guide to Jewish holidays and traditions.

## Fiction and Poetry

*Exodus*, a novel by Leon Uris (Doubleday), deals with the founding of the State of Israel. *The Source*, by James Michener (Fawcett), is the novelist's vivid look at Israel's early history. *Closing the Sea*, by Yehudit Katzir (Harcourt, Brace, Jovanovich), is a book of short stories set in Israel. *The Black Box*, by Amos Oz (Flamingo), is a modern love story. *Saturday Morning Murder*, by Batya Gur (Harper Collins), is a psychological mystery. Among the works of the late poet Yehuda Amichai is *Poems of Jerusalem*. Other contemporary Israeli writers worth looking out for are A. B. Yehoshua, Meir Shalev, David Grossman, Irit Linor, Orly Castel-Bloom, Edna Mazya, and Michal Govrin.

## Modern Israel

*To Jerusalem and Back*, by Saul Bellow (Avon), conveys the flavor of modern Israeli life through the impressions of the Nobel Prize–winning author. *In the Land of Israel*, by Amos Oz (Chatto and Windus), is a series of articles depicting various settlements and towns and conversations with local people. In *Arab and Jew* (Times Books), David K. Shipler, a former *New York Times* correspondent, takes a contemporary look at the relationship. *Intifada*, by Zeev Schiff and Ehud Yaari (Touchstone), gives background and analysis of the Arab unrest in the late 1980s and early '90s. In *My Enemy, Myself* (Penguin), Yoram Binur, a journalist, imagines himself a Palestinian. Thomas Friedman looks at modern events and politics in the Middle East in *From Beirut to Jerusalem* (Farrar, Straus & Giroux). *Facing the Fires: Conversations with A. B. Yehoshua* (Judaic Traditions in Literature, Music, and

Art), by Bernard Horn and A. B. Yehoshua (Syracuse University Press), offers Yehoshua's highly analytical, and controversial, views on literature, politics, and philosophy. For a closer look at these cities, read *Jerusalem, City of Mirrors,* by Amos Elon (Fontana), and *Safed, the Mystical City,* by David Rossoff (Feldheim Publishers).

# ISRAEL AT A GLANCE

As the only land bridge between Africa and Asia, Israel has always been a thoroughfare, a distinction that has made it desirable to foreign powers and often turned it into a battleground. Moreover, the country's position between the desert and the Mediterranean Sea has determined its climate and economy and, by extension, the character of those who conquered the land and settled here.

Israel was once called Canaan, then the Land of Israel (Eretz Yisrael, in Hebrew), then Israel. Later, the name Israel came to represent only the northern Israelite kingdom, including Samaria and Galilee, while the southern kingdom was called Judah. Judah became the Greek "Judea," first applied only to a small part of the country centered on Jerusalem but later to a much larger territory. After the Bar Kochba Revolt (2nd century AD), the Roman emperor Hadrian changed the name Judea to Palaestina (after the long-gone Philistines) in order to dissociate the country from its Jewish identity. Palestine later became the name of this tiny district in the huge Muslim empires of the Middle Ages. To Christians it was always the Holy Land; to Jews, Eretz Yisrael. The use of the name Israel in the following chronology does not always imply any specific set of borders, past or present, but the country as a whole, the ancient Land of Israel.

## Prehistoric Israel

**ca. 1.2 million years ago**  Earliest known human habitation in Israel (Lower Paleolithic Period), at Ubeidiya, in Jordan Valley.

**ca. 7800 BC**  The establishment of Jericho (Neolithic Pre-Pottery Period), the oldest walled town ever found.

## Canaanite Period (Bronze Age) ca. 3200 BC–1250 BC

**ca. 3200– 2150**  Writing is developed in Mesopotamia; beginning of recorded history. Early Canaanite/Bronze Age in Israel. Major cities are built: Jerusalem, Megiddo, and Hatzor.

**ca. 2150– 1550**  Age of the Patriarchs: Abraham, Isaac, and Jacob. Middle Canaanite/Bronze Age.

**ca. 1550– 1250**  Time of Hebrews' enslavement in Egypt. Decline of Egyptian power. Moses believed to have led Hebrews in exodus from Egypt. Late Canaanite/Bronze Age: Israel divided into city-kingdoms.

**ca. 1290**  The Hebrews—the "Children of Israel"—receive the Torah (the Law) at Mt. Sinai. The nation of Israel is formed, the basis of its religion established, and its relationship with the one God defined. Forty years of desert wandering separate the nation from its Promised Land.

# First Temple—Old Testament Period
## (Iron Age) ca. 1250 BC–586 BC

**ca. 1250** Moses dies within sight of the Promised Land. Joshua leads the nation across the Jordan River and embarks on the conquest of Canaan, beginning with Jericho.

**ca. 1200–1025** Period of the Judges (e.g., Deborah, Gideon, Samson), charismatic regional leaders.

**ca. 1150** The Philistines invade from the west and establish a league of five city-states. Israelites appeal to the prophet Samuel for a king.

**1025** Saul, of humble origin, is the first King of Israel.

**1006** Saul and three sons, including Jonathan, are killed fighting the Philistines. David rules Judah.

**1000** David conquers Jerusalem, a Jebusite enclave, and makes it the national capital of unified Israel. Having brought the sacred Ark of the Covenant to Jerusalem, he establishes the city as the new religious center.

**968** Solomon becomes king, consolidates David's kingdom, and in 950 builds the First Temple to the Lord, in Jerusalem.

**928** Division of the monarchy after death of Solomon. The northern Tribes of Israel, under Jeroboam, break away to form the Kingdom of Israel. The southern Tribes, now known as the Kingdom of Judah, with its capital at Jerusalem, are ruled by Rehoboam, Solomon's weak son.

**ca. 865** Ahab rules as King of Israel (871–851) and Jehosophat as King of Judah (867–843). Peace between the two kingdoms. Ahab's wife, Jezebel, reintroduces pagan idol-worship.

**721** Kingdom of Israel destroyed by the Assyrians (now the region's superpower) and exile of its population (the "Ten Lost Tribes"). Kingdom of Judah comes under the Assyrian yoke.

**701** Hezekiah, King of Judah, revolts against Assyria. Assyrians lay siege to Jerusalem. With new fortifications, a superb water system, and the inspiration of the prophet Isaiah, the city withstands the siege.

**609** Josiah, last great king of Judah (640–609) and important religious reformer, is killed trying to block Egyptian advance. Jeremiah prophesies national catastrophe.

**586** Assyrians defeated by new power, the Babylonians, whose king, Nebuchadnezzar, conquers Judah and destroys Jerusalem and the First Temple. Of those who survive, large numbers are exiled to the "rivers of Babylon."

# Second Temple Period, 538 BC–AD 70

During this period the Babylonians are defeated, the Temple in Jerusalem is rebuilt, and the sacrificial rites are restored, but the Land of Israel must still share its preeminence with important Jewish centers in Babylon, Egypt, and elsewhere. Starting in the 3rd century BC, deep divisions appear within the Jewish nation over theological issues and the seductive Hellenistic culture, introduced to the region by Alexander the Great. The Sadducees, who draw their strength from the upper classes, take a literal, Bible-based view and are willing to accommodate elements of Hellenism. The Pharisees, a Jewish group of the common people, add the Oral Law (the unwritten rabbinic interpretation of the Torah) to the authority of the Scriptures; they reject accommodation of the pagan world and spin off groups like the ascetic Essenes and the militant Zealots.

**538** Cyrus, King of Persia, conquers Babylon and allows the Jewish exiles to return home. In Jerusalem, the returnees rebuild the Temple (completed circa 516). In Babylon, the synagogue, a communal place of assembly with an emphasis on the reading of the Bible and (eventually) on prayer, develops.

**445** Nehemiah, a Jewish nobleman, is sent by the Persian king with the authority to rebuild Jerusalem's walls and rule the district.

**333** Persian Empire is defeated by Alexander the Great, and the entire Near East comes under Hellenistic sway.

**323** Death of Alexander and struggle for control of his empire. Ptolemy rules in Egypt; Seleucus in Syria and Mesopotamia.

**301** Ptolemy establishes control over Judea (as Judah is now called) and Samaria and the Galilee (an area once known as Israel), to the north of it. Egypt's now Greek-speaking Jewish population burgeons. The Bible is translated into Greek and called the Septuagint.

**198** The Syrian Seleucids defeat the Egyptian Ptolemies at Banias, the headwaters of the Jordan, annex Judea, and establish good relations with the Jewish community.

**167** The Seleucid king Antiochus IV outlaws all Jewish religious practices. Beginning of the Maccabean Revolt.

**165** After four decisive victories over Hellenistic armies, Judah the Maccabee (Judas Maccabeus) enters the desecrated Temple in Jerusalem, purifying and rededicating it.

**142** Simon, brother of Judah the Maccabee, achieves independence for Judea and establishes the Hasmonean dynasty.

**63** Pompey, the Roman general, enters the country to settle a civil war between the last Hasmonean princes and annexes it as a Roman province.

**48** The influential royal counselor Antipater, a Jewish convert, appoints his sons, among them Herod, to key administrative positions.

**40** Mark Antony appoints Herod as king of the Jews.

**37** After fighting his way through the country, Herod claims his throne in Jerusalem. Hated by the Jews, he seeks to legitimize his reign by marrying a Hasmonean princess (whom he later murders).

**31** Antony is defeated by Octavian, now the emperor Caesar Augustus. Herod pays homage to Augustus in Rome and is confirmed in his titles and territories, then rebuilds the

Second Temple in Jerusalem on a grand scale, winning great esteem.

**AD 4** Death of Herod, called by history "the Great." His kingdom is divided among three sons: Archelaus rules in Jerusalem (and is exiled 10 years later, replaced by the direct Roman rule of Judea by procurators based in Caesarea); Herod Antipas rules the Galilee and Perea (east of the Jordan River); and Philip controls Golan, Bashan, and the sources of the Jordan River.

**ca. AD 5** Birth of Jesus in Bethlehem.

**ca. 27** Beginning of Jesus's Galilean ministry. He calls the disciples, heals and performs miracles, teaches, and preaches, mostly around the Sea of Galilee.

**ca. 29** Jesus and his disciples celebrate Passover in Jerusalem. Arrest, trial, and crucifixion of Jesus by the Romans on orders of the Roman governor, Pontius Pilate. For the Romans, the claim of Jesus as the Messiah (Hebrew for "the anointed one"), with its implication of kingship, is tantamount to high treason. The New Testament relates that Jesus's death and resurrection were divinely determined, an expiation for the sins of humanity. Identification with this event as the way to personal salvation becomes the basis for the community of faith that is Christianity.

**66** Start of Great Revolt against Roman oppression. Jews briefly reassert their political independence.

**67** Galilee falls to the Romans. The Jewish commander defects to the enemy. Romanizing his name to Josephus Flavius, he follows the Roman campaigns, eventually recording them in *The Jewish War*.

**69** Before the fall of Jerusalem, the sage Yochanan Ben Zakkai leaves the city, settling with his disciples in the town of Yavneh in the coastal plain, by grant of Roman general and Caesar-elect Vespasian.

**70** Jerusalem, torn by internal faction fighting, falls to the Roman general Titus after long siege. The Second Temple is destroyed. Slaughter and slavery of Jews follow. The revolt is officially at an end.

**73** The last Jewish stronghold, at Masada, falls. Its defenders take their own lives rather than surrender. With the destruction of Jerusalem and the Temple, Yavneh becomes the seat of the Sanhedrin, the Jewish High Court. Its sages find religious responses to the new reality of Judaism without the Temple, and the spiritual and legal authority of Yavneh is established.

## Late Roman and Byzantine Period, 73–640

**132** When the Roman emperor Hadrian threatens to rebuild Jerusalem as a pagan city, another Jewish revolt breaks out, led by Bar Kochba and supported by Rabbi Akiva. Secret preparations and a strong unified command lead to spectacular initial successes.

**135**    Death of Bar Kochba. The revolt is brutally suppressed, but only after severe Roman losses. Hadrian plows over Jerusalem and builds in its place Aelia Capitolina, a pagan city off-limits to Jews; the name of the country is changed to Palaestina, and Jewish religious practice is outlawed. The Sanhedrin relocates to the Lower Galilee.

**ca. 200**    At Zippori or Sepphoris, in the Galilee, Judah the Nasi (patriarch), spiritual and political head of the Jewish community, compiles the Mishnah, the summary of the Oral Law, which is the basis of Jewish jurisprudence. Period of peace and prosperity under the tolerant Severan emperors.

**325**    Emperor Constantine the Great makes Christianity the imperial religion and eventually converts to the faith. His mother, Helena, comes to the Holy Land in 326 and initiates the building of major churches—the Holy Sepulcher in Jerusalem and the Nativity in Bethlehem.

**330**    Constantine transfers his capital from Rome to Byzantium, now renamed Constantinople. Beginning of the Byzantine Period. Judaism is on the defensive.

**351**    Jewish revolt, primarily in the Galilee, against the Roman ruler Gallus is brutally suppressed.

**361**    Emperor Julian the Apostate (circa 361–363) tries to reintroduce pagan cults.

**ca. 400**    Final codification of the so-called Jerusalem Talmud, the result of years of rabbinic elaboration of the Mishnah. (The Babylonian Talmud, codified a century later, is regarded as more authoritative.)

**527–565**    Reign of Emperor Justinian. Many important churches built or rebuilt, among them the present Church of the Nativity in Bethlehem. Vibrant Jewish community despite persecution.

**614**    Persian invasion, with destruction of churches and monasteries.

**622**    Muhammad's *hejira* (flight) from Mecca to Medina in Arabia; beginnings of Islam.

**628**    Persians defeated and Byzantine rule restored in Israel.

**632**    Death of Muhammad. His followers, ruled by a series of caliphs, burst out of Arabia and create a Muslim empire that within a century would extend from India to Spain.

**636**    Arab invasion of the country and, in 638, the fall of Byzantine Jerusalem to the caliph Omar (circa 634–644).

## Medieval Period, 640–1516

**691**    Caliph Abd al-Malik builds the Dome of the Rock in Jerusalem.

**1099**    Sworn to wrest Christian holy places from Muslim control, the European armies of the First Crusade reach the Holy Land. Jerusalem is taken, and most of its population, Muslim and Jew alike, is massacred.

**1100**    Establishment of the Latin Kingdom of Jerusalem, with Baldwin I at its head. Chronic shortage of manpower puts the burden of defense on the monastic orders—the Hospitallers and Templars, for example—who build castles (among them Belvoir, in the Lower Galilee, and the underground quarter in Akko).

**1110** Most coastal cities in Crusader hands.

**1187** Crusader armies decimated by the Arab ruler Saladin. Crusaders expelled from the country.

**1191** The Third Crusade arrives, led by Richard the Lionheart of England and Philip II (Augustus) of France. The Latin Kingdom of Jerusalem never regains its former size and glory—nor, except for a very brief time, the holy city itself—and the Crusaders content themselves with the coast from Tyre to Jaffa and the Galilee. Acre (Akko) becomes the royal capital.

**1228** The Crusaders gain Jerusalem by treaty but lose the city again in 1244.

**1250** The militant Mamluk class seizes power in Egypt. The Crusade of King Louis IX (St-Louis) against Egypt fails. He is captured but comes to the Holy Land after his release.

**1260** The Mamluks check the Mongol invasion at Ayn Jalout (Ein Harod), in the Jezreel Valley.

**1265** Muslim reconquest of the land begins under the Mamluk sultan Baybars.

**1291** Fall of Akko and end of Crusader kingdom. Commerce and trade decline with destruction of coastal cities. Beginning of period of outstanding architecture, especially in Jerusalem's Temple Mount (Haram esh-Sharif) and Muslim Quarter and in the Cave of Machpelah in Hebron.

**1492** Expulsion of the Jewish community from Spain. Many of these Sephardic Jews later immigrate to Israel.

## The Modern Period, 1516–Present

**1516** Mamluk armies defeated in Syria by the Ottoman Turks, who extend control over the land of Israel (Palestine) as well. Jewish community throughout the country grows. Zfat is center of Kabbalah.

**1520–1566** Suleiman the Magnificent reigns. His many projects include rebuilding Jerusalem's walls.

**1700** Large numbers of Ashkenazi (Eastern European) Jews arrive.

**1799** Invasion by Napoléon Bonaparte founders at Akko.

**1832** Egyptian nationalists under Muhammad Ali and Ibrahim Pasha take control of Israel. They are expelled in 1840 with the help of European nations.

**1853** The Crimean War breaks out in Europe against the background of conflict between Catholic France and Orthodox Russia over the custody of holy places in Israel.

**1882** First Aliyah (wave of Jewish immigration), of mostly idealistic Eastern Europeans. Baron Edmond de Rothschild establishes new villages and wineries in the coastal plain and the Galilee.

**1897** First World Zionist Conference, organized by Theodore Herzl in Basel, Switzerland, gives great impetus to the idea of a "Jewish national home."

**1906** The Second Aliyah, or wave of immigration, of young Jewish idealists from Russia and Poland, including David Ben-Gurion, who would become Israel's first prime minister.

**1909** Tel Aviv founded. Degania, the first kibbutz, established on the southern shore of the Sea of Galilee.

**1917** British government issues Balfour Declaration expressing support for a "Jewish national home" in Palestine. General Edmund Allenby captures Jerusalem.

**1918** Ottoman Turkey, which had sided with Germany during World War I, abandons Palestine.

**1920–1939** As Arab nationalism rises in the post-Ottoman Middle East, tensions increase between Jews and Arabs in Palestine, peaking in the massacres of Jews in 1920, 1929, and 1936. Jewish militias form to counter the violence. Substantial immigration of European Jews, who come with growing urgency, as Nazis take power in Germany.

**1921** Transjordan is separated from Palestine.

**1922** The newly formed League of Nations confirms the Mandate entrusting the rule of Palestine to Great Britain and incorporating the text of the Balfour Declaration.

**1939** British Government issues white paper restricting Jewish immigration to Israel and Jewish purchase of land there in an attempt to secure Arab goodwill in the coming war. In World War II, Jews enlist on Allied side. "We shall fight the war as if there were no white paper," said Palestinian Jewish leader David Ben-Gurion, "but we shall fight the white paper as if there were no war."

**1945** End of World War II, in which one-third of Jewish people were annihilated by the Nazis. When British policy does not change, underground movements challenge British authority. Illegal immigrants, many of them Holocaust survivors, are brought in on ships; many don't get through British blockade. Clashes with Arabs increase.

**1947** United Nations Special Commission on Palestine recommends plan to partition the country into a Jewish state and an Arab state (three disconnected territorial segments in each) and to internationalize Jerusalem and Bethlehem. Jewish euphoria, Arab rejection. Beginning of Israel's War of Independence. Discovery of the first Dead Sea Scrolls at Qumran.

**1948** May 14: Last British forces depart, ending British Mandate. David Ben-Gurion declares Israel an independent state. The new state survives invasion by the armies of seven Arab countries.

**1949** End of fighting in January. U.N.-supervised cease-fire agreements signed. Transjordan annexes the West Bank (of the Jordan River) and East Jerusalem, which it captured in the war, and changes the country's name to the Hashemite Kingdom of Jordan. Egypt annexes the Gaza Strip along the southern Mediterranean coast. Palestinian Arabs who fled or were expelled during the conflict are housed in refugee camps in neighboring countries; those who remain behind become citizens of Israel. First elections to the Knesset, Israel's parliament. David Ben-Gurion is elected prime minister; Dr. Chaim Weizmann, first president.

**1949–1952** Israel absorbs great numbers of Jewish refugees, tripling its Jewish population by the end of the decade.

**1950** The Knesset enacts the Law of Return, giving any Jew the right to Israeli citizenship.

**1956** Sinai Campaign, in which British, French, and Israeli forces oppose Egyptian nationalization of the Suez Canal. Fedayeen terrorist attacks from Egyptian-controlled Gaza Strip become less frequent, but sporadic Syrian shelling of Israeli villages below the Golan Heights is a major security issue into the 1960s.

**1964** Formation of the Palestine Liberation Organization (PLO). Seeks independent state for Palestinians and refuses to recognize the legitimacy of the State of Israel.

**1967** June: Outbreak of Six-Day War. Egypt, Jordan, and Syria are routed; Israel occupies the Sinai Peninsula, Gaza Strip, West Bank, East Jerusalem, and the Golan Heights and finds itself in control of almost 1 million Palestinian Arabs. Some Jewish settlements are established in the West Bank and Golan Heights.

**1973** Egypt and Syria attack Israel on the holiest Jewish holiday, the Day of Atonement (hence, the name Yom Kippur War). Israel beats off the invasion but is sobered.

**1974–1975** Signing of Disengagement Agreement on the Golan with Syria and the Interim Agreement with Egypt.

**1976** Dramatic Israeli commando raid frees Air France passengers taken hostage in Entebbe, Uganda, by Palestinian hijackers.

**1977** Menachem Begin's Likud Party comes to power in May, ending almost four decades of Labor domination of Israeli politics. Egyptian president Anwar Sadat visits Israel.

**1978** Camp David Accords give direction to Egypt-Israel peace talks and produce guidelines for a solution to the Palestinian problem.

**1979** Israel-Egypt peace agreement signed.

**1980** Israeli prime minister Menachem Begin and Egyptian president Anwar Sadat share the Nobel Peace Prize.

**1982** Israeli forces cross into southern Lebanon in pursuit of Palestinians shelling civilian settlements in Israel. This escalates into the Lebanon War (1982–85), with unprecedented opposition from Israelis.

**1987** A road accident in the Gaza Strip triggers the beginning of the *intifada* (uprising), sustained Palestinian Arab street violence, demonstrations, strikes, and sporadic terrorist activity.

**1989–1992** Israel absorbs more than 500,000 Soviet Jewish immigrants.

**1991** Persian Gulf War; Israel under constant attack but restrained from retaliating. June: 14,500 Ethiopian Jews airlifted to Israel. December: Peace talks in Madrid between Israel and Jordan, Syria, Lebanon, and the Palestinians.

**1992** In June the Labor Party under Yitzhak Rabin, vowing to step up the peace process and halt Israeli "political" settlements in West Bank, is voted in after 15 years out of office.

**1993–1994** The Oslo Accords provide for mutual recognition of Israel and the PLO, as well as Palestinian autonomy in the Gaza Strip and Jericho. Nobel Peace Prize shared by Yitzhak Rabin, Shimon Peres, and Yasir Arafat.

**1995** Prime minister Yitzhak Rabin assassinated in November by an Israeli, a tragic climax to a year of rancorous national debate on the "territory for peace" concept. Six more Palestinian Arab West Bank cities are given autonomy.

**1996** New law for direct election of the prime minister brings Likud's Binyamin Netanyahu to power by a margin of less than 1%. Contrary to expectations, the major parties lose much strength, with the religious parties—now powerful partners in the new, far more conservative government—the big winners.

**1997** Israel and the Palestinians sign the Hebron Agreement.

**1998** Israel celebrates its 50th anniversary.

**1999** Ehud Barak, of One Israel (a Labor-led coalition), is elected prime minister by a landslide. Among his campaign promises is that Israel withdraw from Lebanon by July 2000. One of the biggest election surprises is the huge increase in Knesset seats won by the ultra-Orthodox Shas Party.

**2000** March: The first papal visit to Israel in over three decades, with Pope John Paul II visiting Jerusalem and the holy sites. May: Israel withdraws from Lebanon almost overnight—two months before Barak's pledge. July: Prime Minister Barak and Palestinian Authority Chairman Yasser Arafat meet with President Clinton at Camp David in the United States but fail to make headway on the peace talks. August: Likud's Moshe Katsav is sworn in as eighth President of Israel. September: Arab-Jewish violence breaks out in the West Bank and Gaza and briefly extends inside Israel's borders to some predominantly Arab towns. The violence continues through 2000, claiming hundreds of lives.

# NATIONAL AND RELIGIOUS HOLIDAYS

Time is figured in different ways in Israel. The Western Gregorian calendar—the solar year from January to December—is the basis of day-to-day life and commerce, but the school year, for example, which runs from September through June, follows the *Hebrew* lunar calendar (dated to when Creation is believed to have occurred). Thus fall 2001–fall 2002 is the Hebrew year 5762, reckoned from Rosh Hashanah, the Jewish New Year, which usually falls in September. Since the lunar year is 11 days shorter than the solar year, Jewish holidays are out of sync with the Gregorian calendar and fall on different dates (though within the same season) from one year to the next. Jewish religious festivals are observed as national public holidays, when businesses and some museums are closed (on Yom Kippur, the Day of Atonement, *all* sites are closed).

The Muslim calendar is also lunar, but without the compensatory leap-year mechanism of its Hebrew counterpart. Muslim holidays thus drift through the seasons and can fall at any time of the year.

Even the Christian calendar is not uniform: Christmas in Bethlehem is celebrated on different days by the Roman Catholic ("Latin") community, the Greek Orthodox Church, and the Armenian Orthodox Church.

## Jewish Holidays

Here is a calendar of holidays as they're observed in Israel. Remember that Jewish holidays begin at sundown the previous evening and end at nightfall; the dates listed for Jewish holidays in 2001 and 2002 are for the day itself, not for the beginning of the holiday on the previous evening. The phrase "Not religious" in the text indicates that the holiday might be part of the religious tradition, but

few or no public restrictions apply. On holy days, most of the Sabbath restrictions apply.

➤ SHABBAT (SABBATH): The Day of Rest in Israel is Saturday, the Jewish Sabbath, which begins at sundown Friday and ends at nightfall Saturday. By Friday afternoon, you can feel the country winding down, as most Jewish-owned businesses close until Saturday night or Sunday morning. Religious neighborhoods grow frantic as families do last-minute cooking and cleaning before the Sabbath begins. Devout Jews do not cook, travel, answer the telephone, or use money or writing materials during the Shabbat, hence the Sabbath ban on photography at Jewish holy sites like the Western Wall. In Jerusalem, where religious influence is strong, the downtown area dies on Friday afternoon, and some religious neighborhoods are even closed to traffic. In more secular and urbane Tel Aviv, Haifa, and Eilat, much of the populace spills onto the streets and into the nightspots.

Kosher restaurants close on the Sabbath, except for the main hotel restaurants, where some menu restrictions apply. In the Holy City itself, your dining choices are considerably reduced. Outside Jerusalem, however, you'll scarcely be affected; in fact, many restaurants do their best business of the week on the Sabbath because nonreligious Israelis take to the roads.

In Arab areas, such as East Jerusalem and Nazareth, Muslims take time off for the week's most important devotions at midday Friday, but the traveler will notice this much less than on Sunday, when most Christian shopkeepers in those towns close their doors. Saturday is market day, and these towns buzz with activity.

There is no public intercity transportation on the Sabbath, although the private *sherut* taxis drive between the main cities. Urban buses operate only in Nazareth and, on a reduced schedule, in Haifa. Shabbat is also the busiest day for nature reserves and national parks—indeed, anywhere the city folk can get away for a day. Keep this in mind if you fancy a long drive; the highways toward the main cities can be choked with returning weekend traffic on Saturday afternoon.

Sunday, then, is the first day of the regular work week (in Israel, says the old quip, the Monday-morning blues begin on Sunday). The country is moving rapidly toward a five-day work week, but, unlike in Western countries, the weekend will include Friday—already a half day and holy to the country's Muslim minority—and Saturday, the Jewish Sabbath. The public sector and most corporations work Sunday through Thursday only, and the schools may soon follow suit.

➤ ROSH HASHANAH (JEWISH NEW YEAR): Sept. 18–19, 2001, and Sept. 1–2, 2002. Yom Kippur and this two-day holiday are collectively known as the High Holy Days. Rosh Hashanah traditionally begins a 10-day period of introspection and repentance. Observant Jews attend relatively long synagogue services and eat festive meals, including apples and honey to symbolize the hoped-for sweetness of the new year. Nonobservant Jews often use this holiday to picnic and go to the beach.

➤ YOM KIPPUR (DAY OF ATONEMENT): Sept. 27, 2001, and Sept. 10, 2002. Yom Kippur is the most solemn day of the Jewish year. Observant Jews fast, wear white clothing, and avoid leather footwear. There are no radio and television broadcasts. All sites, entertainment venues, and most restaurants are closed. Much of the country comes to a halt, and in towns like Jerusalem the roads are almost completely empty aside from emergency vehicles. It is considered a privilege to be invited to someone's house to "break fast" as the holiday ends, at nightfall.

➤ SUKKOTH (FEAST OF TABERNACLES): Oct. 2–9, 2001, and Sept. 15–22, 2002. First and last days religious. Jews build open-roof "huts" or shelters called *sukkot* (singular *sukkah*) on porches and in backyards to remember the makeshift lodgings of the biblical Israelites as they wandered in the desert. The more observant will eat as many of their meals as possible in their sukkah, and even sleep there for the duration of the holiday.

Right before Sukkoth, colorful street markets sell special decorations and the four kinds of "species" used in the Sukkoth ceremonies—the *etrog* (citron, like a yellow lime) and the elements that make up the *lulav* (a palm frond and sprigs of willow and myrtle). The first day is observed like the Sabbath, except that food can be cooked. The intervening days are half holidays, and shopkeepers often take vacations. Many Israelis, and some tourists, join in the hugely colorful annual hike to Jerusalem through the surrounding hills. Many Evangelical Christians come to Israel to celebrate this festival as well, obeying the passage in the prophecy of Zechariah 14.

➤ SIMHAT TORAH: The last day of Sukkoth (☞ *above*), this holiday marks the end—and the immediate recommencement—of the annual cycle of the reading of the Torah, the Five Books of Moses. The evening and morning synagogue services are characterized by joyful singing and dancing as people carry the Torah scrolls.

➤ HANUKKAH: Dec. 10–17, 2001, and Nov. 25–Dec. 2, 2002. Not religious. A Jewish rebellion in the 2nd century BC renewed Jewish control of Jerusalem. In the recleansed and rededicated Temple, the tradition tells, a vessel was found with enough oil to burn for a day. It miraculously burned for eight days, hence the eight-day holiday marked by the lighting of an increasing number of candles (on a candelabrum called a *hanukkiah*) from night to night. Customary foods are potato pancakes (latkes or *levivot*) and a local version of the jelly doughnut called *sufganiah*. Schools take a winter break. Shops, businesses, and services all remain open.

Holidays

➤ TU B'SHEVAT: Feb. 8, 2001, and Jan. 29, 2002. Not religious. Israelis eat fruit and plant trees on the New Year of Trees, when the white- and pink-blossomed almond trees are in bloom.

➤ PURIM: Mar. 9, 2001, and Feb. 26, 2002 (one day later in Jerusalem). Not religious. Children dress up in costumes on the days leading up to Purim. In synagogues and on public television, devout Jews read the Scroll of Esther, the story of the valiant Jewish queen who prevented the massacre of her people in ancient Persia. Many towns hold street festivals.

➤ PESACH (PASSOVER): Apr. 8–14, 2001, and Feb. 26–Mar. 4, 2002. First and last days religious; dietary restrictions in force throughout. Passover is preceded by vigorous spring cleaning to remove all traces of leavened bread and related products from the household. During the seven-day holiday itself, no bread is sold in Jewish stores, and the crackerlike matzo replaces bread in most hotels and restaurants. On the first evening of the holiday, Jewish families gather to retell the ancient story of their people's exodus from Egyptian bondage and to eat a festive and highly symbolic meal called the seder (Hebrew for "order"). Hotels have communal seders, and the Ministry of Tourism can sometimes arrange for tourists to join Israeli families for Passover in their homes.

➤ YOM HASHO'AH (HOLOCAUST MEMORIAL DAY): Apr. 20, 2001, and April 9, 2002. Not religious. Special services take place at Jerusalem's Yad Vashem Holocaust Memorial and elsewhere in the country. Entertainment venues are closed, and at 11 AM all stand silent as a siren sounds in memory of the 6 million Jews who were annihilated by the Nazis in World War II.

➤ YOM HAZIKARON (MEMORIAL DAY): Apr. 27, 2001, and April 16, 2002. Not religious. This is a day of mourning for Israel's war dead. Commemorative ceremonies are held around the country, entertainment sites are closed, and at 11 AM a siren sounds in memory of the fallen.

➤ YOM HA'ATZMA'UT (INDEPENDENCE DAY): Apr. 28, 2001, and April 17, 2002. Not religious. Israel achieved independence in May 1948; the exact date of Yom Ha'atzma'ut follows the Hebrew calendar. Although there are gala events, fireworks displays, and military parades all over the country, most Israelis go picnicking or swimming. Stores and a few tourist sights are closed, but public transportation runs.

➤ LAG BA'OMER: May 11, 2001, and April 30, 2002. Not religious. The 33rd day between Passover and Shavuot marks both the end of the anniversaries of a string of historic tragedies, and the commemoration of the death of the great 2nd-century AD Rabbi Shimon Bar Yochai. Kids build bonfires, and the devout visit the rabbi's grave in Meron, near Zfat.

➤ SHAVUOT (FEAST OF WEEKS): May 28, 2001, and May 17, 2002. This holiday, seven weeks after Passover, marks the harvest of the first fruits and, according to tradition, the day on which Moses received the Torah ("the law") on Mt. Sinai. Many observant Jews stay up all night studying the Torah. It is customary to eat meatless meals with an emphasis on dairy products.

➤ TISHA B'AV (THE NINTH OF AV): July 29, 2001, and July 18, 2002. Not religious. Among the calamities believed to have occurred on this day was the destruction of both the First and Second Temples. Observant Jews fast and recite the biblical Book of Lamentations. Entertainment venues and many restaurants are closed.

## Christian Holidays

For up-to-date holiday information, contact the Israel Government Tourist Office (IGTO) in your country or region, or the **Christian Information Center** in Jerusalem (☎ 02/628–7647).

➤ EASTER: Apr. 15, 2001, and March 31, 2002. This major festival celebrates the resurrection of Jesus. The nature and timing of its ceremonies and services are colorfully different in each Christian tradition represented in the Holy Land—Roman Catholic, Protestant, Greek Orthodox, Armenian Orthodox, Ethiopian, and so on; check the dates for different groups.

➤ CHRISTMAS: Except in towns with a large indigenous Christian population, like Nazareth and Bethlehem, Christmas is not a high-visibility holiday in Israel. The Christmas of the Catholic and Protestant traditions is, of course, celebrated on December 25; but the Greek Orthodox calendar observes it on January 7, and the Armenian Orthodox wait until January 18. Shuttle buses from Jerusalem run to Bethlehem's Manger Square on Christmas Eve (December 24) for the annual international choir assembly and the Roman Catholic midnight mass. For more information, contact the **Palestinian Authority** in Bethlehem (☎ 02/674–1581 or 02/674–1582) or the Christian Information Center (☞ *above*) in Jerusalem.

## Muslim Holidays

Muslims observe Friday as their holy day, but it's accompanied by none of the restrictions and far less of the solemnity than those of the Jewish Shabbat and the Christian Sabbath (in their strictest forms). The noontime prayer on Friday is the most important of the week and is typically preceded by a sermon, often broadcast from the loudspeakers of the mosques.

The dates of Muslim holidays vary widely each year because of the lunar calendar.

➤ RAMADAN: Beginning Dec. 8, 2001, and Nov. 6, 2002. This monthlong fast commemorates the month in which the Koran was first revealed to Muhammad. Devout Muslims must abstain from food, drink, tobacco, and sex during daylight hours; the conclusion of the period is then marked by the three-day festival of Id el-Fitr. The dates are affected by the sighting of the new moon and can change slightly at the very last moment. The Muslim holy sites on Jerusalem's Temple Mount (Haram esh-Sharif) offer only short morning visiting hours during this time and are closed to tourists during Id el-Fitr.

# ESSENTIAL INFORMATION

## AIR TRAVEL

### BOOKING

When you book **look for nonstop flights** and **remember that "direct" flights stop at least once.** Try to avoid connecting flights, which require a change of plane.

### CARRIERS

The national flag carrier of Israel, **El Al Israel Airlines**, is known for maintaining the strictest security standards. It is not necessarily the cheapest way to fly. **British Airways, CSA/Czech Airlines,** and **Northwest/KLM** fly from the United States to Tel Aviv with stopovers in London, Prague, and Amsterdam respectively. Within Israel, **Arkia Israeli Airlines** has flights from Jerusalem and Tel Aviv (Sde Dov Airport) to Eilat and Rosh Pina, and from Tel Aviv to Haifa, Masada (Bar Yehuda), Mitzpe Ramon, Gush Katif, and the Dead Sea (Ein Yahav). There is also service from Haifa to Jerusalem, Eilat, and the Dead Sea. Children fly for half price. Tour packages sometimes offer better deals on these flights. **Isra-air Airlines** has service from Eilat to Tel Aviv and Haifa.

➤ MAJOR AIRLINES: From the U.S.: **British Airways** (☎ 800/247–9297). **CSA/Czech Airlines** (☎ 212/765–6545). **Continental** (☎ 800/231–0856). **El Al Israel Airlines** (☎ 212/768–9200 or 800/223–6700). **Northwest/KLM** (☎ 800/225–2525). **TWA** (☎ 800/892–4141). **World Airways** (☎ 800/967–5350). From Canada: **Air Canada** (☎ 800/776–3000 in the U.S.; 888/257–2262 in Canada). **El Al Israel Airlines** (☎ 212/768–9200; 800/223–6700; 514/875–8900 in Canada).

➤ FROM THE U.K.: **British Airways** (☎ 0207/434–4700; 0990/222–999; 0345/222–111 outside London). **El Al Israel Airlines** (☎ 0171/957–4100).

➤ DOMESTIC FLIGHTS: **Arkia Israeli Airlines** (✉ Sde Dov Airport, Box 39301, Tel Aviv 61392, ☎ 800/444–888, FAX 03/699–3134); in Jerusalem (✉ Clal Center, ☎ 02/625–5888, FAX 02/623–5758); in Eilat (✉ Shalom Center, ☎ 07/638–4888, FAX 07/637–3370); in Haifa (✉ 80 Ha'atzmaut Blvd., ☎ 04/861–1606, FAX 04/866–3097). **Isra-air Airlines** (03/795–5777 in Tel Aviv; 07/634–0666 in Eilat).

### CHECK-IN & BOARDING

**Security checks on airlines flying to Israel are stringent.** International passengers are asked to arrive at least two hours prior to flight time in order to allow time for security checks. Be prepared for what might sound like personal questions about your itinerary, packing habits, and desire to travel to Israel. Remember that the staff is concerned with protecting you, and be patient. Once you're in Israel, expect to have your handbags searched as a matter of course when you enter department stores, places of entertainment, museums, and public buildings. These checks are generally fast and courteous.

Assuming that not everyone with a ticket will show up, airlines routinely overbook planes. When everyone does, airlines ask for volunteers to give up their seats. In return, these volunteers usually get a certificate for a free flight and are rebooked on the next flight out. If there are not enough volunteers, the airline must choose who will be denied boarding. The first to get bumped are passengers who checked in late and those flying on discounted tickets, so **get to the gate and check in as early as possible,** especially during peak periods.

### CUTTING COSTS

The least expensive airfares to Israel must usually be purchased in advance and are nonrefundable. It's smart to **call a number of airlines, and when**

**you are quoted a good price, book it on the spot**—the same fare may not be available the next day. Always **check different routings** and look into using different airports. Travel agents, especially low-fare specialists (☞ Discounts & Deals, *below*), are helpful. Flights to Israel tend to be least expensive from November through March, except for the holiday season at the end of December. Prices are also higher during the Jewish New Year's holidays (usually in September) and during Passover (usually in April).

Consolidators are another good source. They buy tickets for scheduled international flights at reduced rates from the airlines, then sell them at prices that beat the best fare available directly from the airlines, usually without restrictions. Sometimes you can even get your money back if you need to return the ticket. Carefully read the fine print detailing penalties for changes and cancellations, and **confirm your consolidator reservation with the airline.**

When you **fly as a courier,** you trade your checked-luggage space for a ticket deeply subsidized by a courier service. There are restrictions on when you can book and how long you can stay.

**British Airways** offers a Europe Air Pass, good for travel on British Airways or GTAir to destinations in the Middle East, Europe, and Northern Africa.

➤ CONSOLIDATORS: **Cheap Tickets** (☎ 800/377–1000). **Discount Airline Ticket Service** (☎ 800/576–1600). **Unitravel** (☎ 800/325–2222). **Up & Away Travel** (☎ 212/889–2345). **World Travel Network** (☎ 800/409–6753).

➤ COURIERS: **Air Courier Association** (☎ 800/282–1202); **Courier Travel Service** (☎ 516/763–6898); **International Association of Air Couriers** (☎ 561/582–8320).

➤ DISCOUNT PASSES: **British Airways** (☎ 800/247–9297).

### ENJOYING THE FLIGHT

For more legroom, **request an emergency-aisle seat.** Don't sit in the row in front of the emergency aisle or in front of a bulkhead, where seats may not recline. If you have dietary concerns, **ask for special meals when booking.** These can be vegetarian, low-cholesterol, or kosher, for example. On long flights, try to maintain a normal routine, to help fight jet lag. At night, **get some sleep.** By day, **eat light meals, drink water** (not alcohol), and **move around the cabin** to stretch your legs.

### FLYING TIMES

It takes about 11 hours to fly from New York to Israel; from Los Angeles, it takes around 19 hours (including the usual stopover in Europe or New York).

Flights from London to Israel take about 5 hours and from Sydney 22 hours.

### HOW TO COMPLAIN

If your baggage goes astray or your flight goes awry, complain right away. Most carriers require that you **file a claim immediately.**

➤ AIRLINE COMPLAINTS: U.S. Department of Transportation **Aviation Consumer Protection Division** (✉ C-75, Room 4107, Washington, DC 20590, ☎ 202/366–2220, airconsumer@ost. dot.gov, www.dot.gov/airconsumer). **Federal Aviation Administration Consumer Hotline** (☎ 800/322–7873).

### RECONFIRMING

Reconfirmation obligations differ from airline to airline (and change from time to time); be certain to check with your carrier for all legs of your journey.

### AIRPORTS

The main airport is **Ben-Gurion International Airport,** which is about halfway between Jerusalem and Tel Aviv. Charter flights from Europe sometimes land at **Ovda Airport** or **Eilat Airport,** in southern Israel. **Sde Dov Airport** in north Tel Aviv handles internal flights.

➤ AIRPORT INFORMATION: **Ben-Gurion International Airport** (☎ 03/971–0111). **Eilat Airport** (☎ 07/636–3838 or 07/636–3813). **Ovda Airport** (☎ 07/637–5880); operates from late September through May. **Sde Dov Airport** (☎ 03/699–1058).

## BEACHES

Israel's Mediterranean coastline has many public beaches, most of which offer changing facilities and bathrooms for a modest fee. It's advisable to swim only in designated areas, where lifeguards are on duty. A flag system indicates how dangerous the waves and undertow are: a black flag means that conditions are rough, and swimming is not allowed; a red flag means moderate waves, swim with discretion; a white flag indicates a calm sea.

Women often sunbathe topless on the beaches in Eilat. At the other extreme, some beaches offer sections for women and men who prefer to bathe separately in the interest of modesty. Some Mediterranean beaches, and most beaches on the Dead Sea and the Sea of Galilee, are stony, so be sure to wear rubber beach shoes, especially amid the spiky coral reefs of the Red Sea.

## BIKE TRAVEL

With mountains, deserts, and rolling wooded hills—plus archaeological sites galore—all packed into a small country, Israel is ideal for bicycling. Off-road adventure tours take you places you'd only find on foot or bike. Keep in mind, though, that the riding can be difficult due to extreme heat much of the year, many winding and hilly roads, and aggressive drivers. Biking is best enjoyed from October to May. Trains don't accept bikes, but buses do. Mountain bikes are available for rental at **Red Sea Sports Club** in Eilat. Touring bikes are not available for rental, even in Tel Aviv.

### BIKE TOURS

The **Green Wheelers Mountain Biking Group** offers Friday and Saturday tours in the Carmel and Galilee areas. For Saturday tours in Tel Aviv and Jaffa, try the **Tel Aviv Bicycle Club**. **Walkways** runs country-wide 7-, 10-, and 14-day trips with professional guides. These tours combine cycling and hiking along biblical paths around the Carmel area, the coastal plain, the Galilee, the Red Sea, the Sinai Desert, as well as Petra in Jordan. Walkways handles all logistics, including round-trip transfer to the airport.

➤ BIKING GROUPS: **Green Wheelers Mountain Biking Group** (☎ 09/774–4524). **Tel Aviv Bicycle Club** (☎ 03/741–0386).**Walkways** (☎ 02/534–4452).

➤ BIKE RENTALS: **Red Sea Sports Club**(☎ 07/637–9685 or 07/637–6569).

### BIKES IN FLIGHT

Most airlines accommodate bikes as luggage, provided they are dismantled and boxed. For bike boxes, often free at bike shops, you'll pay about $5 from airlines (at least $100 for bike bags). International travelers can sometimes substitute a bike for a piece of checked luggage at no charge; otherwise, the cost is about $100. Domestic and Canadian airlines charge $25–$50.

## BOAT & FERRY TRAVEL

Israel can be reached by ship from Greece, Cyprus, and Italy. The chief port is in Haifa, with ships arriving from Venice, Athens, Rhodes, Crete, and Limassol, Cyprus. Any travel agent in Israel can easily arrange a booking on one of the two main lines: the **Stability Line** and **Sol Maritime Services**, Greek and Cypriot vessels, respectively. Ferry service goes to Rhodes and Cyprus, without stops. For boat and ferry travel from Haifa, there is a port tax of $25; bicycles and animals ride free, and cars are extra.

### FARES & SCHEDULES

Standard ship departures to Israel leave Athens on Thursday, stopping one day each in Rhodes and Cyprus, reaching Haifa on Sunday. The return trip leaves Sunday from Haifa and has the same stopovers. Prices are much higher June through September. Costs range from $100 for a deck chair to $270 for a cabin with a shower and three meals.

➤ BOAT & FERRY INFORMATION: **Port of Haifa Passengers Terminal** (☎ 04/851–8111).

➤ LOCAL AGENTS: **Caspi 76 Ha'atzmaut** (☎ 04/867–4444 in Haifa; 03/510–7423 in Tel Aviv; 02/624–4266 in Jerusalem). **Dolphin** (☎ 04/855–3278). **Mano Zpalmer** (☎ 04/866–7711).

## BUS TRAVEL

You can get almost anywhere in Israel by bus, and the Central Bus Station is a fixture in most towns: ask for the *tahana merkazit*. The **Egged** bus cooperative handles all of the country's bus routes except those in metropolitan Tel Aviv, where the **Dan** company also operates. Buses in Israel are modern and air-conditioned. Rates are relatively low, and timetables are accurate. You do not need exact change on city buses. If you get on a bus at a highway stop, you can pay the driver. Keep in mind that public transportation generally stops for Shabbat (the Jewish sabbath, which lasts from late Friday afternoon to Saturday evening), although some lines run minibuses in Tel Aviv. Haifa, with a large Arab population, also has some Shabbat service. It's a good idea to reserve seats in advance on buses from the major cities to Eilat and the Dead Sea.

Be aware that buses are often overcrowded on Saturday nights (after Shabbat) and during rush hours. **Be prepared to assert yourself** getting on or off the bus.

### CUTTING COSTS

For travel between major cities and within each city, **Egged** offers a multiride ticket, or *kartisia* (10% reduction of bulk tickets of 10 or 20 rides), and monthly tickets (unlimited service within the month) at nearly any city bus station or on the bus. These are particularly good for children and senior citizens, who get large discounts.

### FARES & SCHEDULES

➤ Bus Information: **Dan** (☎ 03/639–4444). **Egged** (☎ 02/530–4555 or 02/628–0382 in Jerusalem; 04/854–9555 in Haifa; 03/537–5555 in Tel Aviv; 06/681–8222 in Kiryat Shmona; 07/636–5120 in Eilat).

### PAYING

For both local and intercity travel, bus drivers accept payment for tickets, payable only in shekels. They won't make change for a bill over NIS 50 ($12). It's faster to buy tickets at the bus stations.

### RESERVATIONS

Reservations by phone are generally not accepted in Israel. It's best to buy tickets ahead at the bus stations if you plan to travel between cities on Thursday night or the weekend, including Saturday night and Sunday morning. The exception is for travelers going from either Tel Aviv or Jerusalem to Eilat: reservations can be made through the **Central Bus Station** in Tel Aviv. Reservations must be made on a credit card and should be done as early as possible to ensure a seat; last-minute travelers will still get on the bus but may have to ride in the aisle.

➤ Contacts: **Central Bus Station/ Tel Aviv** (☎ 03/639–4444).

## BUSINESS HOURS

For information on national and religious holidays in Israel and their effects on various businesses and services, *see* National and Religious Holidays *in* Chapter 9. The weekly observance of Shabbat (sabbath, from sundown Friday through sundown Saturday) has a different impact on different parts of the country: businesses in Jewish Israel close, but many nonkosher restaurants stay open.

Businesses are often open by 8:30 AM in Israel and shops a little later (9–10); neighborhood grocery stores usually open around 7. Some businesses still close for a two- or three-hour siesta between 1 and 4. Most stores do not close before 7 PM; supermarkets are often open later, and in large cities, there are all-night supermarkets. Arab-owned stores usually open at 8 and close in late afternoon. Most travel agencies are closed on Friday.

### BANKS & OFFICES

Although hours can differ among banks, almost all open by 8:30. Most close at 12:30 and then reopen on Monday and Thursday from 4–7 PM. Banks are closed on religious holidays and on Saturday except in Muslim areas, where they're closed Friday. In Christian areas they're open Saturday morning and closed Sunday.

### GAS STATIONS

City gas stations stay open into the evening, and quite a few are open around the clock. Many close for Shabbat and religious holidays, though many highway gas stations stay open through holidays and late into the night as well.

## MUSEUMS & SIGHTS

Museums don't have a fixed closing day, so although they're usually open 10–6, and often on Saturday mornings, **confirm the schedule** before you go.

## PHARMACIES

Most local pharmacies close at 7 PM. Large chain stores, such as Super-pharm and Newpharm, are usually open until 10 PM. In most cities a few drugstores are open all night, on a rotation basis. Daily listings can be found in English- and Hebrew-language newspapers.

## CAMERAS & PHOTOGRAPHY

There are camera stores everywhere in Israel, so purchasing and developing film should not be a problem. But you may want to bring lots of film with you, because it is expensive here, as well as extra batteries, which are not always available everywhere.

There are certain religious sites and neighborhoods where photography is forbidden, usually indicated by signs posted at the sites. Hasidic Jews and religious Muslims do not like having their picture taken, so try to show respect and resist the temptation. To really capture the local flavor, take snapshots of the spectacular Mediterranean sunsets, and within the Old City walls of Jerusalem.

➤ PHOTO HELP: **Kodak Information Center** (☎ 800/242–2424). *Kodak Guide to Shooting Great Travel Pictures,* available in bookstores or from Fodor's Travel Publications (☎ 800/533–6478; $18 plus $5.50 shipping).

## EQUIPMENT PRECAUTIONS

Always **keep your film and tape out of the sun.** Carry an extra supply of batteries, and **be prepared to turn on your camera or camcorder** to prove to security personnel that the device is real. Always **ask for hand inspection of film,** which becomes clouded after repeated exposure to airport X-ray machines, and **keep videotapes away from metal detectors.**

## FILM & DEVELOPING

One-hour film development is widely offered at the many photography stores in every city. For the best results, stick with the internationally known brands of film, such as Kodak and Agfa.

## VIDEOS

Video film, though expensive, is readily available at photography stores in all cities.

## CAR RENTAL

Rental rates in Israel start at around $68 a day and $450 a week for an economy car with unlimited mileage; some companies require a minimum of three weeks' rental in high season. There is no tax on car rentals in Israel.

➤ MAJOR AGENCIES: **Alamo** (☎ 800/522–9696; 020/8759–6200 in the U.K.). **Avis** (☎ 800/331–1084; 800/331–1084 in Canada; 02/9353–9000 in Australia; 09/525–1982 in New Zealand). **Budget** (☎ 800/527–0700; 0870/607–5000 in the U.K., through affiliate Europcar). **Dollar** (☎ 800/800–6000; 0124/622–0111 in the U.K., through affiliate Sixt Kenning; 02/9223–1444 in Australia). **Hertz** (☎ 800/654–3001; 800/263–0600 in Canada; 020/8897–2072 in the U.K.; 02/9669–2444 in Australia; 09/256–8690 in New Zealand). **National Car Rental** (☎ 800/227–7368; 020/8680–4800 in the U.K., where it is known as National Europe).

## CUTTING COSTS

If you book your car ahead of time, you may get a special package rate. Since car rental in Israel is expensive, your best bet is to travel on a weekly, unlimited kilometer basis. El Al passengers are offered special discounts on rental cars. Avis and Sixt/Reliable both specialize in car rental packages in Israel. To get the best deal, **book through a travel agent, who will shop around.**

Do **look into wholesalers,** companies that do not own fleets but rent in bulk from those that do and often offer better rates than traditional car-rental operations. Payment must be made before you leave home.

➤ LOCAL AGENCIES: **Avis** (☎ 800/ 638–4016) and **Sixt/Reliable** (☎ 877/ 4–SHALOM).

➤ WHOLESALERS: **Auto Europe** (☎ 207/842–2000 or 800/223–5555, FAX 800/235–6321, www.autoeurope. com). **Kemwel Holiday Autos** (☎ 800/678–0678, FAX 914/825–3160, www.kemwel.com).

### INSURANCE

When driving a rented car you are generally responsible for any damage to or loss of the vehicle as well as for any property damage or personal injury that you may cause. Insurance is generally not covered in the basic cost of renting a car. It is advisable to take the maximum coverage and verify exactly what this includes before signing a contract. Also, before you rent see what coverage your personal auto-insurance policy and credit cards already provide.

### REQUIREMENTS & RESTRICTIONS

Your own driver's license is acceptable in Israel, but an International Driver's Permit is still a good idea; it's available from the American or Canadian Automobile Association, and, in the United Kingdom, from the Automobile Association or Royal Automobile Club. This international permit is universally recognized, so having one in your wallet is extra insurance against problems with the local authorities.

### SURCHARGES

Before you pick up a car in one city and leave it in another, **ask about drop-off charges or one-way service fees,** which can be substantial. Note, too, that some rental agencies charge extra if you return the car before the time specified in your contract. To avoid a hefty refueling fee, **fill the tank just before you turn in the car,** but be aware that gas stations near the rental outlet may overcharge.

### CAR TRAVEL

The Hebrew word for a native-born Israeli is *sabra,* which literally refers to a prickly cactus with sweet fruit inside. You'll meet the sweet Israeli if you get lost or have automotive difficulties—helping hands are quick to arrive—but behind the wheel, Israelis are prickly, very aggressive, and honk their horns far more than their Western counterparts. Try not to take it personally.

### AUTO CLUBS

The local representative of AAA and of the British AA in Israel is **Memsi.**

➤ IN AUSTRALIA: **Australian Automobile Association** (☎ 02/6247– 7311).

➤ IN CANADA: **Canadian Automobile Association** (CAA; ☎ 613/247– 0117).

➤ IN ISRAEL: **Memsi** (☎ 03/564–1111 in Tel Aviv; 02/625–0661 in Jerusalem).

➤ IN NEW ZEALAND: **New Zealand Automobile Association** (☎ 09/377– 4660).

➤ IN THE U.K.: **Automobile Association** (AA; ☎ 0990/500–600). **Royal Automobile Club** (RAC; ☎ 0990/ 722–722 for membership; 0345/121– 345 for insurance).

➤ IN THE U.S.: **American Automobile Association** (AAA; ☎ 800/564– 6222).

### EMERGENCY SERVICES

Should anything happen to your rental car, call your rental company for roadside repair or replacement of the vehicle. In case of an accident or roadside emergency, call **Shagrir,** the national breakdown service.

➤ CONTACTS: **Shagrir** (☎ 02/625– 3530).

### GASOLINE

Service stations are generally full service. Many rental cars now take unleaded gas. At press time, a liter of high-octane gasoline cost about 4.30 NIS, which comes to 16.2 NIS ($4) per gallon. Gas stations are abundant in all areas of the country except in the Negev Desert. Most stations will accept international credit cards.

### ROAD CONDITIONS

Israeli highways are basically in good shape, except in some rural areas. Try to avoid entering and leaving the main cities at rush hours (7:30 AM– 8:30 AM and 4 PM–6 PM), when roads are absolutely jammed. Note that very few highways are lit at night, which can make for hazardous driving, especially on smaller roads.

It's a good idea to carry extra water—both for yourself and for your car—while driving at any time of year. Every winter there are several days of flash flooding in the desert; if it's raining, try to find a police officer or call the Israel Government Tourist Office (IGTO) to ask about road and weather conditions.

Israel is slowly assigning numbers to its roads and highways (north–south, even; east–west, odd), but most people still know them simply by the towns they connect: the Tiberias–Nazareth Road, for example. Intersections and turnoffs are similarly indicated, as in "the Eilat Junction." Orange arrow–shape signs indicate tourist sites; national parks signs are on brown wood.

### ROAD MAPS

Good maps in English are available at bookstores and through the Israel Government Tourist Office (IGTO).

### RULES OF THE ROAD

Unfortunately, there have been more Israelis killed by car accidents than in all of the nation's wars combined. It's advised to **use extra caution when driving a car** in Israel. By law, drivers and all passengers (front and back seats) must wear seat belts at all times. **Don't drink and drive.** Police recently began cracking down on drunk driving; the legal limit is .05% of alcohol in a liter of blood. It's against the law (and enforced) to use cell phones while driving. The speed limits vary little across Israel: motorways (represented with blue signs) have speed limits of either 90 or 100 kph (56 or 62 mph); highways (green signs), 80 or 90 kph (50 or 56 mph); urban roads, 50 or 60 kph (31 or 37 mph). If you're planning to cross the border into Egypt or Jordan, keep in mind that entering in a rental car is not usually allowed.

### CHILDREN IN ISRAEL

Israel welcomes young tourists, and baby supplies are readily available. Children travel at half price on domestic flights and on trains. Many museums and other tourist sites offer excellent educational programs that children will enjoy. If you are renting a car, don't forget to **arrange for a car seat** when you reserve—children four and under must use them by law.

### FLYING

If your children are two or older, **ask about children's airfares.** As a general rule, infants under two not occupying a seat fly at greatly reduced fares or even for free. When booking, **confirm carry-on allowances** if you're traveling with infants. In general, for babies charged 10% of the adult fare you are allowed one carry-on bag and a collapsible stroller; if the flight is full, the stroller may have to be checked or you may be limited to less.

Experts agree that it's a good idea to use safety seats aloft for children weighing less than 40 pounds. Airlines set their own policies: U.S. carriers usually require that the child be ticketed, even if he or she is young enough to ride free, since the seats must be strapped into regular seats. Do **check your airline's policy about using safety seats during takeoff and landing.** And since safety seats are not allowed just everywhere in the plane, get your seat assignments early.

When reserving, **request children's meals or a freestanding bassinet** if you need them. But note that bulkhead seats, where you must sit to use the bassinet, may lack an overhead bin or storage space on the floor.

### FOOD

For familiar food, many American fast-food chains can be found in Israel.

### LODGING

Most hotels in Israel allow children under a certain age to stay in their parents' room at no extra charge, but others charge for them as extra adults; be sure to **find out the cutoff age for children's discounts.**

Children's discounts are often less generous at kibbutz guest houses. Many hotels, especially in resorts such as Eilat, feature special entertainment that appeals to children and activities such as arts and crafts.

The **Hilton** hotels in Jerusalem and Tel Aviv offer a family plan, an organized youth camp during the summer months, and/or an all-day children's program. The **Dan** hotels offer the Family Advantage plan and usually have recreation programs during vacations. **Sheraton** hotels also offer a family plan.

➤ BEST CHOICES: **Dan** (☎ 212/752–6120 or 800/223–7773; 800/731–2789 in the U.K.). **Hilton** (☎ 800/445–8667; 0990/445–866 in the U.K.). **Sheraton Hotels** (☎ 800/325–3535).

## PRECAUTIONS

Remember that children dehydrate faster than adults, so bring along a canteen for each child when you head out. Sunscreen and sun hats are also essential.

## SIGHTS & ATTRACTIONS

Places that are especially appealing to children are indicated by a rubber duckie icon (☺ ) in the margin.

➤ CHILDREN'S ATTRACTIONS: JERUSALEM: **Biblical Zoo/Tisch Family Zoological Gardens** (✉ Gan Hakhayot St., Malkah, ☎ 02/675–0111). **Bloomfield Science Museum** (✉ Ruppin Blvd., ☎ 02/561–8128). **Ein Yael Living Museum** (✉ Nakhal Refaim, Malkah, ☎ 02/645–1866). **Liberty Bell Garden** (✉ Between Kind David and Jabotinsky Sts.).

➤ CHILDREN'S ATTRACTIONS: TEL AVIV AND ENVIRONS: **Kfar Daniel Monkey Park** (✉ At Kfar Daniel, right near the airport, ☎ 08/928–5888). **Lunar Park** (✉ Rokach Blvd., ☎ 03/642–7080).

➤ CHILDREN'S ATTRACTIONS: EILAT: **Texas Ranch** (✉ Opposite the Eilat port, ☎ 07/637–6663).

## SUPPLIES & EQUIPMENT

Major brands of baby foods, powdered formulas, and disposable diapers are available everywhere. Toys for older kids can be expensive, so parents might want to bring along a few from home.

## TOURS

If you'd rather have someone else do the planning, **Kids' Jerusalem Adventures** (☎ 972/2536–3449) specializes in tours and activities for families with kids of all ages; or if the folks want time alone, the company will plan a fun-filled day just for the children. Bar/Bat Mitzvah celebration packages are also available.

## TRANSPORTATION

Children under age five ride free on the buses; after that, it's full fare. There are, however, discounts on multiride bus tickets available to kids. Trains offer half-price tickets for children.

## COMPUTERS ON THE ROAD

Many hotels in Israel have data ports for your laptop. It is also possible to find Internet access at many cafés and money-changing booths.

## CONSUMER PROTECTION

Whenever shopping or buying travel services in Israel, **pay with a major credit card** so you can cancel payment or get reimbursed if there's a problem. If you're doing business with a particular company for the first time, **contact your local Better Business Bureau and the attorney general's offices** in your own state and the company's home state, as well. Have any complaints been filed? Finally, if you're buying a package or tour, always **consider travel insurance** that includes default coverage (☞ Insurance, *below*).

➤ BBBs: **Council of Better Business Bureaus** (✉ 4200 Wilson Blvd., Suite 800, Arlington, VA 22203, ☎ 703/276–0100, FAX 703/525–8277 www.bbb.org).

## CRUISE TRAVEL

Two types of cruises incorporate Israel into their itinerary, with Haifa and Ashdod as the major ports: "Around the World" cruises and Mediterranean cruises, which offer tours that may include the Greek Islands, Italy, Turkey, and Egypt in addition to Israel.

➤ AROUND THE WORLD CRUISES: **Royal Princess** (✉ 1320 Kalani St., Suite 304, Honolulu, Hawaii 96817, ☎ 877/835–1100). **SilverSea Cruises** (✉ 110 E. Broward Blvd., Fort Lauderdale, FL 33301, ☎ 800/722–9955).

Cruise Web Inc., for general cruise information (✉ 4455 Connecticut Ave. NW, Suite A-700, Washington, D.C. 20008, ☎ 202/362–2290 or 800/377–9383).

➤ MEDITERRANEAN CRUISES: **Costa Cruise Lines** (✉ 80 S.W. Eighth St., Miami, FL 33130, ☎ 305/358–7325). **Holland America Lines-Westours** (✉ 300 Elliott Ave., Seattle, WA 98119, ☎ 206/281–3535). **Royal Olympic Cruises** (✉ 805 3rd Ave., New York, NY 10022, ☎ 800/872–6400).

## CUSTOMS & DUTIES

When shopping, **keep receipts** for all purchases. Upon reentering the country, **be ready to show customs officials what you've bought.** If you feel a duty is incorrect or object to the way your clearance was handled, note the inspector's badge number and ask to see a supervisor. If the problem isn't resolved, write to the appropriate authorities, beginning with the port director at your point of entry.

### IN AUSTRALIA

Australian residents who are 18 or older may bring home $A400 worth of souvenirs and gifts (including jewelry), 250 cigarettes or 250 grams of tobacco, and 1,125 ml of alcohol (including wine, beer, and spirits). Residents under 18 may bring back $A200 worth of goods. Prohibited items include meat products. Seeds, plants, and fruits need to be declared upon arrival.

➤ INFORMATION: **Australian Customs Service** (Regional Director, ✉ Box 8, Sydney, NSW 2001, Australia, ☎ 02/9213–2000, FAX 02/9213–4000, www. customs.gov.au).

### IN CANADA

Canadian residents who have been out of Canada for at least 7 days may bring home C$500 worth of goods duty-free. If you've been away less than 7 days but more than 48 hours, the duty-free allowance drops to C$200; if your trip lasts 24–48 hours, the allowance is C$50. You may not pool allowances with family members. Goods claimed under the C$500 exemption may follow you by mail; those claimed under the lesser exemp-

tions must accompany you. Alcohol and tobacco products may be included in the 7-day and 48-hour exemptions but not in the 24-hour exemption. If you meet the age requirements of the province or territory through which you reenter Canada, you may bring in, duty-free, 1.14 liters (40 imperial ounces) of wine or liquor *or* 24 12-ounce cans or bottles of beer or ale. If you are 16 or older you may bring in, duty-free, 200 cigarettes and 50 cigars. Check ahead of time with Revenue Canada or the Department of Agriculture for policies regarding meat products, seeds, plants, and fruits.

You may send an unlimited number of gifts worth up to C$60 each duty-free to Canada. Label the package UNSOLICITED GIFT—VALUE UNDER $60. Alcohol and tobacco are excluded.

➤ INFORMATION: **Revenue Canada** (✉ 2265 St. Laurent Blvd. S, Ottawa, Ontario K1G 4K3, Canada, ☎ 613/993–0534; 800/461–9999 in Canada, FAX 613/991–4126, www.ccra-adrc. gc.ca).

### IN ISRAEL

Those over 17 may import into Israel duty-free: 250 cigarettes or 250 grams of tobacco products; 2 liters of wine and 1 liter of spirits; ¼ liter of eau de cologne or perfume; and gifts totaling no more than $200 in value. You may also import up to 1 kg of food products, but no fresh meats.

Israeli customs requires travelers, upon entry, to declare professional-quality video and computer equipment. This is to ensure that the equipment is not being imported for resale.

### IN NEW ZEALAND

Homeward-bound residents 17 or older may bring back $700 worth of souvenirs and gifts. Your duty-free allowance also includes 4.5 liters of wine or beer; one 1,125-ml bottle of spirits; and either 200 cigarettes, 250 grams of tobacco, 50 cigars, or a combination of the three up to 250 grams. Prohibited items include meat products, seeds, plants, and fruits.

➤ INFORMATION: **New Zealand Customs** (Custom House, ✉ 50 Anzac

Ave., Box 29, Auckland, New Zealand, ☎ 09/300–5399, FAX 09/359–6730), www.customs.govt.nz).

### IN THE U.K.

From countries outside the EU, including Israel, you may bring home, duty-free, 200 cigarettes or 50 cigars; 1 liter of spirits or 2 liters of fortified or sparkling wine or liqueurs; 2 liters of still table wine; 60 ml of perfume; 250 ml of toilet water; plus £136 worth of other goods, including gifts and souvenirs. If returning from outside the EU, prohibited items include meat products, seeds, plants, and fruits.

➤ INFORMATION: **HM Customs and Excise** (⊠ Dorset House, Stamford St., Bromley, Kent BR1 1XX, U.K., ☎ 020/7202–4227, www.hmce.gov.uk).

### IN THE U.S.

U.S. residents who have been out of the country for at least 48 hours (and who have not used the $400 allowance or any part of it in the past 30 days) may bring home $400 worth of foreign goods duty-free.

U.S. residents 21 and older may bring back 1 liter of alcohol duty-free. In addition, regardless of your age, you are allowed 200 cigarettes and 100 non-Cuban cigars. Antiques, which the U.S. Customs Service defines as objects more than 100 years old, enter duty-free, as do original works of art done entirely by hand, including paintings, drawings, and sculptures.

You may also mail or ship packages home duty-free: up to $200 worth of goods for personal use, with a limit of one parcel per addressee per day (except alcohol or tobacco products or perfume worth more than $5); label the package PERSONAL USE and attach a list of its contents and their retail value. Do not label the package UNSOLICITED GIFT or your duty-free exemption will drop to $100. Mailed items do not affect your duty-free allowance on your return.

➤ INFORMATION: **U.S. Customs Service** (⊠ 1300 Pennsylvania Ave. NW, Washington, DC 20229, www.customs.gov; inquiries ☎ 202/354–1000; complaints c/o ⊠ 1300 Pennsylvania Ave. NW, Room 5.4D, Washington, DC 20229; registration of equipment c/o ⊠ Resource Management, ☎ 202/354–1000).

### DINING

In the last few years Israel has earned itself a name in the gastronomic world, and the restaurants we list are the cream of the crop in each price category. Seafood is a specialty in many restaurants in Eilat, Haifa, and Tel Aviv. Mediterranean dishes such as grilled fish and plates of hummus and warmed pita bread are staples, but today you can also sample any national cuisine you want—Italian, Indian, Chinese, French, Indonesian, Japanese, even American. And whereas "kosher" once meant "uniform," kosher restaurants today have to compete with a growing number of nonkosher restaurants (which, among other differences, serve seafood, and milk and meat together), so the variety of kosher food is growing. Moreover, with street stalls and ice cream stores on every corner, you can be sure you won't go hungry in Israel.

### MEALS & SPECIALTIES

In hotels, the day begins with a huge, buffet-style breakfast comprising a variety of breads and rolls, eggs, oatmeal, excellent yogurt, cheeses, vegetable and fish salads, and American-style breakfast foods like pancakes and granola. Outdoor coffee shops serving salads, sandwiches, cakes, and delicious coffee abound. Every city and small town has modestly priced restaurants that open in mid-morning and serve soup, salad, and grilled meats.

Israelis do like Western-style fast food, such as hamburgers and pizza, but more traditional favorites are falafel served with salad and condiments in a pita pocket, *shwarma* (grilled meat), cheese, and *borekas* (phyllo turnovers filled with spinach, cheese, or potato). Many falafel stands have salad bars where you can fill the pita yourself. Supermarkets, particularly in the large cities, have long, eclectic counters of takeout food, with everything from fried eggplant to chocolate croissants. Familiar fast-food chains, like McDonald's, Pizza Hut, and Domino's

Pizza, are scattered throughout Israel, especially in the big cities.

## MEALTIMES

Israelis eat dinner fairly late, especially when dining out. It is not uncommon to wait in line at a restaurant for dinner at 10 PM; your best bet is to plan to eat around 8 PM.

Unless otherwise noted, the restaurants listed in this guide are open daily for lunch and dinner.

## PAYING

Many restaurants offer business lunch specials or fixed-price menus, but à la carte menus are most common. A service charge (*sherut* in Hebrew) of 10%–15% is sometimes levied and should be noted separately on your bill. Credit cards are widely accepted in restaurants, but always check first. If you are dining in a smaller town or village, it would be wise to have sufficient cash.

## RESERVATIONS & DRESS

Reservations are always a good idea: we mention them only when they're essential or not accepted. Book as far ahead as you can, and reconfirm as soon as you arrive. We mention dress only when men are required to wear a jacket or a jacket and tie. Dress in Israeli restaurants is generally casual.

## WINE, BEER & SPIRITS

The local brews in Israel are Maccabi (lager) and Goldstar (bitter), while Heineken and Tuborg are popular imports. Beer is most commonly available by the bottle, but some bars serve it on draught.

Wine has deep roots in Israeli tradition and ritual. It is common for Israelis to drink one or two glasses of wine; imbibing more is less common. Common table wines are not usually of the best quality in Israel; you're best off choosing a higher-end brand such as Dalton, Ben Ami, Golan, and Carmel's Rothschild Series. As for spirits, those with a taste for Greek *ouzo* will enjoy the comparable, local *arak*.

You can purchase liquor at nearly all of the numerous kiosks around; most are open until midnight. In the major cities, you'll find some stores open all night. The legal drinking age is 18 and is enforced.

## DISABILITIES & ACCESSIBILITY

Facilities for people with disabilities in Israel still lag behind those of many other Western countries. Crowded, hilly streets and steps can make it difficult to get around without a companion, and adapted minibuses and rental cars are hard to come by. However, new hotels are required to provide facilities for guests with disabilities, and several museums and other tourist sights are making improvements. There are several volunteer organizations that offer assistance to people with disabilities. From its 76 branches around the country, **Yad Sarah** provides free transportation for people who use wheelchairs and lends medical supplies and rehabilitation equipment at no charge. It's best to call at least two weeks ahead to book an airport pickup and to arrange for special needs.

To obtain a copy of "Access in Israel," a guide to accessible sights and accommodations in Israel, contact the **Pauline Hephaistos Survey Projects**. (⊠ 39 Bradley Gardens, West Ealing, London W13 8HE, England).

➤ LOCAL RESOURCES: **Roof Association of Organizations of Persons with Disabilities** (⊠ 6 Ibn Gvirol St., Tel Aviv 64952, ☎ 03/695–4236). **MILBAT—The Israeli Center for Technical Aids and Transportation** (⊠ Tel Hashomer, Tel Aviv 52621, ☎ 03/530–3739). **Pauline Hephaistos Survey Projects** (⊠ 39 Bradley Gardens, West Ealing, London W13 8HE, England). **ILAN—The Israeli Foundation for Handicapped Children** (⊠ 9 Gordon St., Tel Aviv 63458, ☎ 03/524–8141); ⊠ 4 Hagidem St., Jerusalem, ☎ 02/623–4091). **Yad Sarah** (⊠ 124 Herzl St., Jerusalem 96187, ☎ 02/644–4444, FAX 02/644–4423).

## LODGING

All new hotels in Israel are required to provide facilities for guests with disabilities. For a listing of accessible accommodations in Israel contact the **Pauline Hephaistos Survey Projects** (☞ *above*).

## RESERVATIONS

When discussing accessibility with an operator or reservations agent, **ask hard questions.** Are there any stairs, inside *or* out? Are there grab bars next to the toilet *and* in the shower/tub? How wide is the doorway to the room? To the bathroom? For the most extensive facilities meeting the latest legal specifications, **opt for newer accommodations.**

## SIGHTS & ATTRACTIONS

For a listing of accessible sights and attractions in Israel, contact the **Pauline Hephaistos Survey Projects** (☞ *above*).

## TRANSPORTATION

Before you arrive, notify your airline and hotel of any disability to ensure that proper accommodations will be arranged.

➤ COMPLAINTS: **Disability Rights Section** (✉ U.S. Department of Justice, Civil Rights Division, Box 66738, Washington, DC 20035-6738, ☎ 202/514–0301 or 800/514–0301; 202/514–0383 TTY; 800/514–0383 TTY, FAX 202/307–1198, www.usdoj.gov/crt/ada/adahom1.htm) for general complaints. **Aviation Consumer Protection Division** (☞ Air Travel, *above*) for airline-related problems. **Civil Rights Office** (✉ U.S. Department of Transportation, Departmental Office of Civil Rights, S-30, 400 7th St. SW, Room 10215, Washington, DC 20590, ☎ 202/366–4648, FAX 202/366–9371) for problems with surface transportation.

## TRAVEL AGENCIES

In the United States, the Americans with Disabilities Act requires that travel firms serve the needs of all travelers. Some agencies specialize in working with people with disabilities.

➤ TRAVELERS WITH MOBILITY PROBLEMS: **Access Adventures** (✉ 206 Chestnut Ridge Rd., Scottsville, NY 14624, ☎ 716/889–9096, dltravel@prodigy.net), run by a former physical-rehabilitation counselor. **CareVacations** (✉ 5-5110 50th Ave., Leduc, Alberta T9E 6V4, Canada, ☎ 780/986–6404 or 877/478–7827, FAX 780/986–8332, www.carevacations.com), for group tours and cruise vacations.

**Flying Wheels Travel** (✉ 143 W. Bridge St., Box 382, Owatonna, MN 55060, ☎ 507/451–5005 or 800/535–6790, FAX 507/451–1685, thq@ll.net, www.flyingwheels.com). **Hinsdale Travel Service** (✉ 201 E. Ogden Ave., Suite 100, Hinsdale, IL 60521, ☎ 630/325–1335, FAX 630/325–1342, hinsdaletravel@hinsdaletravel.com).

## DISCOUNTS & DEALS

Be a smart shopper and **compare all your options** before making decisions. A plane ticket bought with a promotional coupon from travel clubs, coupon books, and direct-mail offers may not be cheaper than the least expensive fare from a discount ticket agency. And always keep in mind that what you get is just as important as what you save.

## DISCOUNT RESERVATIONS

To save money, **look into discount reservations services** with toll-free numbers, which use their buying power to get a better price on hotels, airline tickets, even car rentals. When booking a room, always **call the hotel's local toll-free number** (if one is available) rather than the central reservations number—you'll often get a better price. Always ask about special packages or corporate rates.

When shopping for the best deal on hotels and car rentals, **look for guaranteed exchange rates,** which protect you against a falling dollar. With your rate locked in, you won't pay more, even if the price goes up in the local currency.

➤ HOTEL ROOMS: **Steigenberger Reservation Service** (☎ 800/223–5652, www.srs-worldhotels.com).

## PACKAGE DEALS

Don't confuse packages and guided tours. When you buy a package, you travel on your own, just as though you had planned the trip yourself. Fly-drive packages, which combine airfare and car rental, are often a good deal.

## ECOTOURISM

**Beerotayim Ecotourism Center** is a leading ecotourism company that offers adventure tours in the Negev Desert. Take its Camel Caravan and Donkey Tours, which range from a three-hour introduction to the ecology of the Negev Desert to an eight-day trek following ancient caravan trails. Or cruise along the sand dunes in a 4-by-4 vehicle and design your own tours. Whatever tour you take you're sure to enjoy the desert hospitality and splendid Bedouin meals against a desert backdrop.

**Carlson Wagonlit Travel USA** offer tours led by the **Society for the Protection of Nature in Israel (SPNI)** that combine religion and history with their tours in nature. Daily hikes and individual tours are available, ranging from one day to two weeks, incorporating climbing and hiking in all areas of the country.

The **Jerusalem Bird Observatory,** also in association with SPNI, highlights conservation and promotion of open spaces. The Observatory is located between the Supreme Court building and Knesset.

➤ ECOTOURISM INFORMATION: **Beerotayim Ecotourism Center** (✉ Beerotayim Tours, D.N. Haluza, Ezuz 85513, ☎ 07/655–5788, FAX 07/655–4369, tours@beerotayim.co.il). **Carlson Wagonlit Travel USA** (✉ 8404 W. Center Rd., Box 24149, Omaha, NE 68124, ☎ 877/895–4834). **Society for the Protection of Nature in Israel** (SPNI; ✉ 4 HaShfela St., Tel Aviv, ☎ 03/638–8677, FAX 03/688–3940). In the United States: **ASPNI** (✉ 28 Arrandale Ave., Great Neck, NY, ☎ 800/323–0035).

### ELECTRICITY

To use your U.S.-purchased electric-powered equipment, **bring a converter and adapter.** The electrical current in Israel is 220 volts, 50 cycles alternating current (AC); wall outlets take Continental-type plugs, with two round prongs.

If your appliances are dual voltage, you'll need only an adapter. Don't use 110-volt outlets marked FOR SHAVERS ONLY for high-wattage appliances such as hair dryers. Most laptops operate equally well on 110 and 220 volts and so require only an adapter.

### EMBASSIES

➤ AUSTRALIA: **Australian Embassy** (✉ Beit Europa, 37 Shaul Hamelech Blvd., Tel Aviv 64928, ☎ 03/695–0451, FAX 03/696–8404).

➤ CANADA: **Canadian Embassy** (✉ 3 Nirim Beit Hasapanut, Tel Aviv 67060, ☎ 03/636–3300).

➤ NEW ZEALAND: **New Zealand Honorary Consulate** (✉ 3 Daniel Frish St., Tel Aviv, 54731, ☎ 03/695–1869, FAX 03/695–0817); or **New Zealand Embassy in Turkey** (responsible for Israel; ✉ Level 4, Iran Caddefi 13, Kavaklidere, Ankara, Turkey 06700, ☎ 90/312/467–9054, FAX 90/312/467–9013).

➤ SOUTH AFRICA: **South Africa Embassy** (✉ Top Tower Floor 16, 50 Dizengoff St., Tel Aviv 64332, ☎ 03/525–2566, FAX 03/525–3230).

➤ U.K.: **U.K. Embassy** (✉ 192 Hayarkon St., Tel Aviv 63405, ☎ 03/524–9171, FAX 03/524–3313).

➤ U.S.: **U.S. Embassy** (✉ 71 Hayarkon St., Tel Aviv 63903, ☎ 03/519–7575, FAX 03/510–2444).

### EMERGENCIES

To obtain police assistance at any time, dial 100.

For emergency ambulance service, dial 101; 24-hour first aid and ambulance service are provided in nearly every town by the **Magen David Adom** (Red Shield of David). Clinics in major cities offer treatment on Shabbat or at other times when regular treatment is unattainable.

To report a fire, dial 102.

Emergency calls are free at public phones; no tokens or telecards are necessary.

➤ CONTACTS: **Magen David Adom** (✉ 2 Alkalai St., Tel Aviv, ☎ 03/546–0111).

### ENGLISH-LANGUAGE MEDIA

#### BOOKS

Many stores carry a wide range of English titles.

#### NEWSPAPERS & MAGAZINES

You can pick up a copy of the daily newspapers, *Ha'aretz* and the *Jerusalem Post,* or the semimonthly newsmagazine the *Jerusalem Report* at most newsstands. *Ha'aretz* consists of translations from Israel's Hebrew daily and is sold together with the *International Herald Tribune,* providing local and international news in one package.

## RADIO & TELEVISION

You can hear news in English on Reshet Alef, the "A" station of Kol Yisrael at 7 AM and 5 PM. There's an English news broadcast on TV Channel One (Ha'aretz Harishon) Sunday through Thursday at 6:15 PM, Friday at 4:30 PM, and Saturday at 5 PM. Movies are almost always shown in their original language, with Hebrew subtitles.

## ETIQUETTE & BEHAVIOR

"Etiquette" is not a key word in the Israeli vocabulary. In this highly informal society, there are many traditions but few rules. That said, both Jewish and Arabic cultures have their own social customs and strictures. Visitors (particularly women) to ultra-Orthodox Jewish quarters, such as B'nei Brak, near Tel Aviv, and the Jerusalem neighborhood Mea She'arim should wear modest dress. Local women keep their knees and elbows covered and do not wear pants; married women also keep their heads covered (keep a scarf handy). Tourists wandering the streets (especially in the Old City where the major sites holy to Christianity, Islam, and Judaism are located) will feel more comfortable if they observe this dress code, and it becomes essential when you enter a synagogue or other important religious institution (again, women in particular, though head covering for men will also be appreciated). Very religious Jews, who wear black garb, do not shake hands or mingle socially with members of the opposite sex.

Guests in Muslim households insult their hosts if they decline a drink (strong coffee or a soft drink is usually offered). Muslims do not drink alcohol, so a gift of wine is inappropriate. Like religious Jews, Muslims do not eat pork. Remove your shoes upon entering a mosque; women should cover their hair. Note that shaking hands or picking up food with the left hand is considered impolite.

## BUSINESS ETIQUETTE

English is the language of Israeli business culture. Business cards are very important and should be in English, although on the reverse side you can have it printed in Hebrew. Businesspeople on the international level tend to be secular. Israelis delight in debate (and may take a long time to arrive at a final decision). They have a tendency to come off as extremely opinionated: they are confrontational, emotional negotiators and their speech will often be peppered by broad hand gestures. Don't take offense—it's all part of the culture. In a business setting, dress should be modest and conservative. The standard greeting is to extend a *shalom* and a handshake. Orthodox Jewish men will not shake hands with women. Women may want to wait for a man to extend his hand before offering a handshake.

## GAY & LESBIAN TRAVEL

While gays and lesbians are still not widely accepted in Israel, Tel Aviv is a notable exception, with a large openly gay community and a thriving gay nightlife. Elsewhere, slow roads toward acceptance have been in the making since the 1988 abolishment of a law banning gay and lesbian relationships. It is commonplace for men to be affectionate in Middle Eastern culture, but this should not to be mistaken as approval for same-sex couples to be openly affectionate. No matter your sexual orientation, you should refrain from public affection in religious areas. The **Society for Protection of Personal Rights** has a gay and lesbian hot line.

➤ GAY- & LESBIAN-FRIENDLY TRAVEL AGENCIES: **Different Roads Travel** (✉ 8383 Wilshire Blvd., Suite 902, Beverly Hills, CA 90211, ☎ 323/651–5557 or 800/429–8747, FAX 323/651–3678, leigh@west.tzell.com). **Kennedy Travel** (✉ 314 Jericho Turnpike, Floral Park, NY 11001, ☎ 516/352–4888 or 800/237–7433, FAX 516/354–8849, kennedytravel1@yahoo.com, www.kennedytravel.com). **Now Voyager** (✉ 4406 18th St., San Francisco, CA 94114, ☎ 415/626–1169 or 800/255–6951, FAX 415/626–8626, www.nowvoyager.com). **Skylink Travel and Tour** (✉ 1006 Mendocino

Ave., Santa Rosa, CA 95401, ☎ 707/546–9888 or 800/225–5759, FAX 707/546–9891, skylinktvl@aol.com, www.skylinktravel.com), serving lesbian travelers.

➤ LOCAL RESOURCES: **Association for Gay Men, Lesbians and Bisexuals in Israel** (⊠ 28 Nahmani St., Tel Aviv 65794, ☎ 03/620–4327). **Community of Lesbian Feminists** (⊠ Box 22997, Tel Aviv 61228, ☎ 03/516–5606). **Jerusalem Open House for Gay Men and Lesbians** (⊠ 7 Ben Yehuda, 3rd floor, ☎ 02/625–319l or 3192). **The Society for Protection of Personal Rights** (⊠ Box 37604, Tel Aviv 61375, ☎ 03/629–3681).

## HEALTH

It is safe to drink tap water and eat fresh produce after it's been washed, but take care when buying cooked products from outdoor food stands; the food may have been sitting unrefrigerated for a long time.

Israel gets very hot: a sun hat and sunblock are musts, as is a canteen or bottled water (available even in the most remote places) to guard against dehydration.

No vaccinations are required; Israel has one of the world's most advanced health care systems.

### OVER-THE-COUNTER REMEDIES

It is very easy to find many of the same over-the-counter remedies as you would at home. Everyday pain relievers such as Tylenol and Advil are widely available. Medication can be obtained from pharmacies, which are plentiful. Fluent English is spoken in the majority of pharmacies. Locally produced medication is fairly inexpensive, but expect to pay more for drugs that are imported. In most cities a few drugstores are open all night, on a rotation basis. Daily listings can be found in English- and Hebrew-language newspapers.

## HOLIDAYS

*See* National and Religious Holidays *in* chapter 9.

## INSURANCE

The most useful travel-insurance plan is a comprehensive policy that includes coverage for trip cancellation and interruption, default, trip delay, and medical expenses (with a waiver for preexisting conditions).

Without insurance you will lose all or most of your money if you cancel your trip, regardless of the reason. Default insurance covers you if your tour operator, airline, or cruise line goes out of business. Trip-delay covers expenses that arise because of bad weather or mechanical delays. Study the fine print when comparing policies.

If you're traveling internationally, a key component of travel insurance is coverage for medical bills incurred if you get sick on the road. Such expenses are not generally covered by Medicare or private policies. U.K. residents can buy a travel-insurance policy valid for most vacations taken during the year in which it's purchased (but check preexisting-condition coverage). British and Australian citizens need extra medical coverage when traveling overseas.

Always **buy travel policies directly from the insurance company**; if you buy them from a cruise line, airline, or tour operator that goes out of business you probably will not be covered for the agency or operator's default, a major risk. Before making any purchase, **review your existing health and home-owner's policies** to find what they cover away from home.

➤ TRAVEL INSURERS: In the U.S.: **Access America** (⊠ 6600 W. Broad St., Richmond, VA 23230, ☎ 804/285–3300 or 800/284–8300, FAX 804/673–1586, www.previewtravel.com), **Travel Guard International** (⊠ 1145 Clark St., Stevens Point, WI 54481, ☎ 715/345–0505 or 800/826–1300, FAX 800/955–8785, www.noelgroup.com).

➤ INSURANCE INFORMATION: In the U.K.: **Association of British Insurers** (⊠ 51–55 Gresham St., London EC2V 7HQ, U.K., ☎ 020/7600–3333, FAX 020/7696–8999, info@abi.org.uk, www.abi.org.uk). In Canada: **Voyager Insurance** (⊠ 44 Peel Center Dr., Brampton, Ontario L6T 4M8, Canada, ☎ 905/791–8700; 800/668–4342 in Canada). In Australia: **Insurance Council of Australia** (☎ 03/9614–1077, FAX 03/9614–7924). In

New Zealand: **Insurance Council of New Zealand** (⌧ Box 474, Wellington, New Zealand, ☎ 04/472–5230, ⒻⒶⓍ 04/473–3011, www.icnz.org.nz).

## LANGUAGE

Hebrew is the national language of Israel, but travelers can get by speaking English only.

Hebrew has a unique history: the language of the Bible was long dormant as a spoken language, used only for reading the Holy Scriptures and prayers, writing religious works and poetry, and as the Jewish lingua franca for educated Jews to communicate with Jews in other regions of the world. The revival begun a century ago has given Hebrew a whole new life. If Abraham, Isaac, and Jacob came back today, they'd have to take *ulpan* classes just like other new immigrants. English has also had an impact on Hebrew, to the extent that you'll hear not only official words like *bank, telefon,* and *lefaksess* (to fax) but also slang such as *ledaskess* (to discuss) and *heppening* (happening, event). Arabic is Israel's other official language, spoken by Arabs as well as many Jews (especially those with origins in Arab lands). Because Israel is a nation of immigrants, mistakes and various accents are tolerated cheerfully, and polyglot Israelis speak so many different languages that you might be able to try out French, Spanish, Italian, Yiddish, or Russian. All Israeli schoolchildren study English and speak it to varying degrees of fluency.

Israelis use a lot of hand gestures when they talk. A common gesture is to turn the palm outward and press the thumb and forefinger together to mean "wait a minute"; rest assured that this has no negative connotations. Just as harmless is the Israeli who says "I don't believe you" to express that something is unbelievably wonderful. Few Israelis differentiate between "bus stop" and "bus station" (because one Hebrew word covers both), so if you want the Central Bus Station, make sure you ask for it (*tahana merkazit*). Different systems of transliteration have produced widely inconsistent spellings: so

is that Golan town Katzrin or Qazrin?

*See* the Hebrew and Arabic vocabularies below.

## LODGING

Nearly all hotel rooms in Israel have private bathrooms with a combined shower and tub. The best hotels have a swimming pool, a health club, and tennis courts; and with rare exceptions in major cities, most hotels have parking facilities.

Assume that hotels operate on the **European Plan** (EP, with no meals) unless we specify that they use the **Continental Plan** (CP, with a Continental breakfast), **Modified American Plan** (MAP, with breakfast and dinner), or the **Full American Plan** (FAP, with all meals).

The lodgings we list are the cream of the crop in each price category. We always list the facilities that are available—but we don't specify whether they cost extra: when pricing accommodations, always ask what's included and what costs extra.

In times of political unrest, it's best to call ahead to make sure that hotels are open.

### APARTMENT & VILLA RENTALS

If you want a home base that's roomy enough for a family and comes with cooking facilities, **consider a furnished rental.** These can save you money, especially if you're traveling with a group. Home-exchange directories sometimes list rentals as well as exchanges.

Short-term rentals are quite popular in Israel. Options range from basic studios to magnificent private homes. The cost of a studio is typically between $500 and $800 a month; one-bedroom apartments start at around $1,200. Agents can give you the biggest selection, but if you would rather do it yourself, it's possible to reserve a flat through the **Israel Tourism Center** and **Good Morning Jerusalem** (☞ B&Bs, *below*). Or, you pick up a copy of the *Jerusalem Post* for its comprehensive classified section of apartment rentals.

➤ INTERNATIONAL AGENTS: **Hometours International** (✉ Box 11503, Knoxville, TN 37939, ☎ 865/690–8484 or 800/367–4668, hometours@aol.com, http://thor.he.net/áhometour/).

➤ LOCAL AGENTS: **Rehavia Real Estate** (☎ 02/623–2604, FAX 02/625–2519).

## B&BS

Bed-and-breakfast lodgings have become increasingly popular in recent years, especially in northern Israel. They usually offer clean, pastoral accommodations and fresh country breakfasts. Many of Israel's *kibbutzim* (communal settlements) have opened B&Bs in which a visitor rents a simple room and takes meals in the kibbutz dining room. Most kibbutzim have large lawns, swimming pools (usually open only in summer), and athletic facilities and offer lectures and tours of the settlement. Private-home owners are also increasingly opening their doors to guests.

➤ RESERVATION SERVICES: **Israel Tourism Center** (☎ 888/669–5700). **Good Morning Jerusalem** (☎ 02/623–3459, FAX 02/625–9330). **Home Accommodation Association of Jerusalem** (☎ 02/645–2198). **Home Hospitality** (☎ 02/645–2198).

## CAMPING

Most Israeli campsites offer water, bathrooms, showers, first aid, telephones, and cabins for rent and often have mobile homes set on blocks. Some even have swimming pools or are near beaches. They are all guarded and lighted at night. Advance reservations are recommended for July, August, and Jewish holidays.

➤ INFORMATION: **Israel Government Tourist Office** (☞ Visitor Information, *below*).

## CHRISTIAN HOSPICES

Christian hospices (meaning hosteleries, not facilities for the ill) provide lodging and sometimes meals; these are mainly in Jerusalem and the Galilee. Some are real bargains, while others are merely reasonable; facilities range from spare to luxurious. They give preference to pilgrimage groups, but almost all will accept secular travelers when space is available. A full list of hospices is available from the Israel Government Tourist Office.

## HOLIDAY VILLAGES

Holiday villages can range from the near primitive to quite luxurious but tend to be relatively inexpensive. Commonly they offer simple facilities, usually sleeping from four to six persons in a unit, with basic cooking facilities in each unit. Some villages have full kitchens and even TVs, and most have a grocery store on the grounds. The rooms vary from huts and trailers to little houses.

## HOME EXCHANGES

If you would like to exchange your home for someone else's, **join a home-exchange organization,** which will send you its updated listings of available exchanges for a year and will include your own listing in at least one of them. It's up to you to make specific arrangements.

➤ EXCHANGE CLUBS: **Intervac U.S.** (✉ Box 590504, San Francisco, CA 94159, ☎ 800/756–4663, FAX 415/435–7440, intervacus@aol.com, www.intervacus.com; $93 per year includes two catalogs).

## HOSTELS

No matter what your age, you can **save on lodging costs by staying at hostels.** In some 5,000 locations in more than 70 countries around the world, Hostelling International (HI), the umbrella group for a number of national youth-hostel associations, offers single-sex, dorm-style beds and, at many hostels, rooms for couples and family accommodations. Membership in any HI national hostel association, open to travelers of all ages, allows you to stay in HI-affiliated hostels at member rates; one-year membership is about $25 for adults (C$26.75 in Canada, £9.30 in the U.K., $30 in Australia, and $30 in New Zealand); hostels run about $10–$25 per night. Members have priority if the hostel is full; they're also eligible for discounts around the world, even on rail and bus travel in some countries.

Youth hostels in Israel have improved in recent years and now compete with hotels and guest houses. Many of Israel's hostels provide family rooms with private baths; most are air-conditioned; some have communal cooking facilities; and all provide meals. It's worth coming equipped with a valid HI membership card—otherwise, the attractive, modern hostels charge guest-house prices. Even without a card, however, hostels are a good deal.

➤ BEST OPTIONS: The **Israel Youth Hostel Association** (✉ Binyenei Ha'Ooma, Congress Center, Box 1075, Jerusalem 91009, ☎ 02/655–8420, FAX 02/655–8430; ✉ 36 Bnei Dan, Tel Aviv 61021, ☎ 03/544–1748, FAX 03/544–1030).

➤ ORGANIZATIONS: **Hostelling International—American Youth Hostels** (✉ 733 15th St. NW, Suite 840, Washington, DC 20005, ☎ 202/783–6161, FAX 202/783–6171, hiayhserv@hiayh.org, www.hiayh.org). **Hostelling International—Canada** (✉ 400–205 Catherine St., Ottawa, Ontario K2P 1C3, Canada, ☎ 613/237–7884, FAX 613/237–7868, info@hostellingintl.ca, www.hostellingintl.ca). **Youth Hostel Association of England and Wales** (✉ Trevelyan House, 8 St. Stephen's Hill, St. Albans, Hertfordshire AL1 2DY, U.K., ☎ 0870/870–8808, FAX 01727/844–126, customerservices@yha. org.uk, www.yha.org.uk). **Australian Youth Hostel Association** (✉ 10 Mallett St., Camperdown, NSW 2050, Australia, ☎ 02/9565–1699, FAX 02/9565–1325, www.yha.com.au). **Youth Hostels Association of New Zealand** (✉ Box 436, Christchurch, New Zealand, ☎ 03/379–9970, FAX 03/365–4476, info@yha.org.nz, www. yha.org.nz).

## HOTELS

A buffet breakfast, often sumptuous, is almost always included in a hotel room rate (☞ Dining, *above*). Spas are an outstanding feature of hotels at the Dead Sea and most hotels in Eilat. Although the government's star ratings of hotels have officially been abolished, people still speak of "five-star hotels" in reference to the top category.

All hotels listed have private bath unless otherwise noted.

➤ TOLL-FREE NUMBERS: **Best Western** (☎ 800/528–1234, www.

bestwestern.com). **Choice** (☎ 800/221–2222, www.hotelchoice.com). **Hilton** (☎ 800/445–8667, www.hilton.com). **Holiday Inn** (☎ 800/465–4329, www.basshotels.com). **Hyatt Hotels & Resorts** (☎ 800/233–1234, www.hyatt.com). **Inter-Continental** (☎ 800/327–0200, www.interconti.com). **Marriott** (☎ 800/228–9290, www.marriott.com). **Le Meridien** (☎ 800/543–4300, www.forte-hotels.com). **Ramada** (☎ 800/228–2828, www.ramada.com). **Renaissance Hotels & Resorts** (☎ 800/468–3571, www.renaissancehotels.com/). **Sheraton** (☎ 800/325–3535, www.starwood.com).

## KIBBUTZ GUEST HOUSES

Kibbutz guest houses, popular in Israel for years, are similar to motels; guests are taken in as a source of extra income for the kibbutz and are not involved in its social life (with the possible exception of having meals in the communal dining room). Unlike motels, though, kibbutzes offer rustic, quiet settings and usually have pools and athletic activities.

➤ INFORMATION: **Kibbutz Hotels Chain** (✉ 90 Ben Yehuda St., Box 3193, Tel Aviv 61031, Israel, ☎ 03/527–8085, FAX 03/523–0527; ✉ Israel Tourism Center, 114 Essex St., Rochelle Park, NJ 07662, ☎ 201/556–9669).

## MAIL & SHIPPING

Israel's mail service has improved dramatically in recent years. The post office handles regular and express letters, sends and receives faxes, accepts bill payments, sells phone cards and parking cards, handles money transfers, and offers quick-delivery service. Nearly every neighborhood has a post office, identified by a racing deer on a red background, and English is almost always spoken. The main branches are usually open from 8 until 6 or 7, and small offices are usually open Sunday–Tuesday and Thursday 8–12:30 and 3:30–6, Wednesday 8–1:30, and Friday 8–noon. In Muslim cities and in Gaza the post office is closed Friday; in Christian towns it's closed Sunday; and in Jericho it's closed Saturday.

In most big cities, yellow mailboxes are for mail being sent within the same city; red boxes are for all other mail.

In mailing addresses, the abbreviation M.P. stands for Mobile Post (M.P. Gilboa, for example). You'll see this as part of the address in more rural areas.

## OVERNIGHT SERVICES

For overnight service within the country (or three-day express service internationally), use the main post office in any of the large cities.

## POSTAL RATES

A regular letter within Israel costs about 35¢. An air letter to the United States or Europe costs about 45¢. If you bring a letter to the post office before 10 AM, same-day delivery is guaranteed for about NIS 12 ($3) within the city, NIS 20 ($5) out of town. An airmail postcard to anywhere in the world requires an NIS 1.40 (40¢) stamp. Mail abroad takes 5 to 10 days. The first page of a fax costs about NIS 7 ($2) within Israel, NIS 11 ($3) to the United States.

## RECEIVING MAIL

Tourists who want to receive mail at a local post office should have it addressed to "Poste Restante" along with the name of the town. Such mail will be held for pickup free of charge for up to three months. American Express offices in the major cities also receive and hold mail free for card members; for a list of foreign American Express offices, call 800/528–4800.

## SHIPPING PARCELS

You must bring identification if you want to send packages.

## MONEY MATTERS

Israel is a moderately priced country compared to Western Europe, but it's more expensive than many of its Mediterranean neighbors. Tourist costs, calculated in dollars, are little affected by inflation. Prices are much the same throughout the country. To save money, try the excellent prepared food from supermarkets (buy local brands), take public transportation, eat your main meal at lunch, eat inexpensive local foods such as falafel once a day, and stay at hotels with kitchen facilities and guest houses. Airfares are lowest in winter.

Sample prices: cup of coffee, $1.50; falafel, $2; beer at a bar, $3; canned soft drink, $1–$2; hamburger at a fast-food restaurant, $4; 2-km (1-mi) taxi ride, about $4.50; movie, $8.

Prices throughout this guide are given for adults. Substantially reduced fees are almost always available for children, students, and senior citizens. For information on taxes, *see* Taxes, *below.*

## ATMS

Automated Teller Machines are quite widespread in the major cities in Israel and are known by the name of *kaspomat.* Look for machines that have stickers stating that they accept foreign credit cards or that have a PLUS, NYCE, or CIRRUS sign.

With a debit card, the ATM machine will give you the desired amount of shekels and your home account will be debited at the current exchange rate. Note that there may be a limit on how much money you are allowed to withdraw each day and that service charges are usually applied. Make sure you have enough cash in rural areas, villages, and small towns where ATM machines may be scarce.

The norm for Personal Identification Numbers (PINs) in Israel is four digits. If the PIN for your account has a different number of digits, you must change your number before you leave for Israel.

## CREDIT CARDS

Most hotels, restaurants, and shops accept major credit cards. They are also accepted at banks for cash advances, although some banks will accept one card but none of the others. For cash advances using a Visa card, go to the Israel Discount Bank or Bank Leumi; with a MasterCard go to Bank Hapoalim or the United Mizrahi Branch. All of the credit card companies give an exchange rate that can be up to 5% better than the rate commonly used by banks.

Before you leave home, you must have a Personal Identification Number (PIN) to withdraw cash while overseas. Even if you already have a PIN, check with your credit card company to make sure that it will work in Israel. Again, the norm for PINs in Israel is four digits. If the PIN for your account has a different number of digits, you must change your number before you leave for Israel. Most credit cards offer additional services, such as emergency assistance and insurance. Call and find out what additional coverage you have.

Throughout this guide, the following abbreviations are used: **AE,** American Express; **DC,** Diners Club; **MC,** MasterCard; and **V,** Visa.

➤ REPORTING LOST CARDS: To report lost or stolen credit cards, call the following toll-free numbers: **American Express** (☎ 800/327–2177); **Diners Club** (☎ 800/234–6377); **Discover Card** (☎ 800/347–2683); **MasterCard** (☎ 800/307–7309); and **Visa** (☎ 800/847–2911).

## CURRENCY

Israel's monetary unit is the New Israel Shekel, abbreviated NIS. There are 100 agorot to the shekel. The silver-color one-shekel coin is about the size of an American dime, but thicker. Smaller-value bronze coins are the half-shekel and the 10-agorot coin (both of which are larger than the shekel), and the less-used 5-agorot coin. There is also a 5-shekel coin (silver in color), about the size of an American quarter, and a similar-size 10-shekel coin (bronze center, silver-color rim). Paper bills come in 20-, 50-, 100-, and 200-shekel denominations.

Israeli currency fluctuates against the U.S. dollar, so exact rates vary daily. At press time, the exchange rate was about 4.1 shekels to the dollar. Because of the frequent fluctuations, prices quoted throughout this book are listed both in shekels and in their approximate equivalent in U.S. dollars. Because paying bills at hotels, car-rental firms, and special tourist shops in foreign currency eliminates the Value-Added Tax (VAT), price charts in the dining and lodging sections of the book are in U.S. dollars.

## CURRENCY EXCHANGE

For the most favorable rates, **change money through banks** (bring your passport). Although ATM transaction fees may be higher abroad than at home, ATM rates are excellent because they are based on wholesale rates offered only by major banks. You won't do as well at exchange booths in airports or rail and bus stations, in hotels, in restaurants, or in stores. To avoid lines at airport exchange booths, **get a bit of local currency before you leave home.**

➤ EXCHANGE SERVICES: **International Currency Express** (☎ 888/278–6628 for orders, www.foreignmoney.com). **Thomas Cook Currency Services** (☎ 800/287–7362 for telephone orders and retail locations, www.us.thomascook. com).

## TRAVELER'S CHECKS

Do you need traveler's checks? It depends on where you're headed. If you're going to rural areas and small towns, go with cash; traveler's checks are best used in cities. Lost or stolen checks can usually be replaced within 24 hours. To ensure a speedy refund, buy your own traveler's checks—don't let someone else pay for them: irregularities like this can cause delays. The person who bought the checks should make the call to request a refund.

## NATURE PARKS & RESERVES

For such a small, arid country, Israel has a good many parks and nature reserves. Obtain a full list of parks, including those with camping facilities, from the **Jewish National Fund,** which also runs summer camping programs for families. For information on nature reserves and national parks, contact the **Israel Nature and National Parks Protection Authority,** which also offers a pass for unlimited entry to all nature reserves and national parks around the country for one month.

➤ INFORMATION: **Jewish National Fund** (JNF; ✉ Corner of Keren Kayemet and Keren Hayesod Sts., Box 283, Jerusalem 91002, ☎ 02/670–7411). **Israel Nature and National Parks Protection Authority** (✉ 3 Am ve Olamo St., Givat Shaul,

Jerusalem 95463, ☎ 02/500–5444;
✉ 35 Jabotinsky St., Ramat Gan
52511, ☎ 03/751–2305).

## OUTDOORS & SPORTS

### GOLF

The **Caesarea Golf Club** (✉ Box
1010, Caesarea 38900, ☎ 06/636–
1172), an 18-hole golf course on the
northern coast, is open seven days a
week. Tourists can obtain special
memberships, and the club rents all
equipment. The new, 9-hole **Ga'ash
Golf Club** (✉ Kibbutz Ga'ash, ☎ 09/
951–5111) is 20 km (12 mi) north of
Tel Aviv.

### TENNIS

There are tennis centers throughout
the country, with nominal court fees;
reserve in advance. Ask for the **National Tennis Center** in your area
(Central office: ✉ Box 51, Ramat
Hasharon 47100, ☎ 03/645–6666).

### WATER SPORTS

Scuba diving and snorkeling are
popular in Eilat and at various
Mediterranean beaches. Dive trips to
the Red Sea, home to some of the best
diving sites in the world, leave from
Eilat. Information is available from
the **Israeli Diving Federation** (✉ Box
3404, 94 Hayarkon St., Tel Aviv
61033, ☎ 03/523–6436). Divers
must present an advanced open-water
license or a junior scuba license, or
take a course. Windsurfing and waterskiing are offered at various
beaches and hotels in Eilat.

## PACKING

Israel is a very casual country, where
comfort comes first. Rarely will you
need more than an afternoon dress or
sports jacket to feel adequately
dressed. Even posh restaurants do not
require a jacket and tie. For touring
in the hot summer months, wear cool,
easy-care clothing. If you're coming
between May and September, you
won't need a coat, but you should
bring a sun hat that completely
shades your face and neck. Take one
sweater for cool nights, particularly in
the hilly areas and the desert. Also
take long pants to protect your legs
and a spare pair of walking shoes for
adventure travel. A raincoat with a
zip-out lining is ideal for October to

April, when the weather can get cold
enough for snow (and is as likely to
be warm enough in the south for
outdoor swimming). Rain boots may
also be a useful accessory in winter.
Pack a bathing suit for all seasons.
Note that many religious sites forbid
shorts and sleeveless shirts for both
sexes; and women should bring
modest dress for general touring in
religious neighborhoods.

Along with the sun hat, take plenty of
sunscreen, insect repellent, a water
canteen, and sunglasses in summer.

In your carry-on luggage, **pack an
extra pair of eyeglasses or contact
lenses** and **enough of any medication
you take** to last the entire trip. You
may also ask your doctor to write a
spare prescription using the drug's
generic name, since brand names may
vary from country to country. In
luggage to be checked, **never pack
prescription drugs or valuables.** To
avoid customs delays, carry medica-
tions in their original packaging. And
don't forget to carry with you the
addresses of offices that handle re-
funds of lost traveler's checks.

### CHECKING LUGGAGE

How many carry-on bags you can
bring with you is up to the airline.
Most allow two, but not always, so
make sure that everything you carry
aboard will fit under your seat or in
the overhead bin, and get to the gate
early. Note that if you have a seat at
the back of the plane, you'll probably
board first, while the overhead bins
are still empty.

If you are flying internationally, note
that baggage allowances may be
determined not by piece but by
weight—generally 88 pounds (40
kilograms) in first class, 66 pounds
(30 kilograms) in business class,
and 44 pounds (20 kilograms) in
economy.

Airline liability for baggage is limited
to $1,250 per person on flights within
the United States. On international
flights it amounts to $9.07 per pound
or $20 per kilogram for checked
baggage (roughly $640 per 70-pound
bag) and $400 per passenger for
unchecked baggage. You can buy
additional coverage at check-in for

about $10 per $1,000 of coverage, but it excludes a rather extensive list of items, shown on your airline ticket.

Before departure, **itemize your bags' contents** and their worth, and label the bags with your name, address, and phone number. (If you use your home address, cover it so potential thieves can't see it readily.) Inside each bag, **pack a copy of your itinerary**. At check-in, **make sure that each bag is correctly tagged** with the destination airport's three-letter code. If your bags arrive damaged or fail to arrive at all, file a written report with the airline before leaving the airport.

## PASSPORTS & VISAS

When traveling internationally, **carry your passport** even if you don't need one (it's always the best form of ID) and **make two photocopies of the data page** (one for someone at home and another for you, carried separately from your passport). If you lose your passport, promptly call the nearest embassy or consulate and the local police.

### ENTERING ISRAEL

U.S., Canadian, and U.K. citizens, even infants, need only a valid passport to enter Israel for stays of up to 90 days.

Israel issues three-month tourist visas free of charge at the point of entry when a valid passport is presented. At press time, there were still some countries (particularly in the Middle East) that refused to admit travelers whose passports carried an Israeli visa entry stamp, so if you're concerned about regional mobility, you can ask the customs officer at your point of entry to issue a tourist visa on a separate piece of paper; or you can apply for a second passport and include a letter with the application explaining that you need the passport for travel to Israel. Be advised that it is not unheard of for Israeli customs officers to stamp passports despite requests not to do so; if you plan to travel repeatedly between Israel and those Arab states still hostile to Israel, a second passport is advisable.

### PASSPORT OFFICES

The best time to apply for a passport or to renew is in fall and winter.

Before any trip, check your passport's expiration date, and, if necessary, renew it as soon as possible.

➤ AUSTRALIAN CITIZENS: **Australian Passport Office** (☎ 131–232, www. dfat.gov.au/passports).

➤ CANADIAN CITIZENS: **Passport Office** (☎ 819/994–3500; 800/567–6868 in Canada, www.dfait-maeci. gc.ca/passport).

➤ NEW ZEALAND CITIZENS: **New Zealand Passport Office** (☎ 04/494–0700, www.passports.govt.nz).

➤ U.K. CITIZENS: **London Passport Office** (☎ 0870/521–0410, www. ukpa.gov.uk) for fees and documentation requirements and to request an emergency passport.

➤ U.S. CITIZENS: **National Passport Information Center** (☎ 900/225–5674; calls are 35¢ per minute for automated service, $1.05 per minute for operator service; www.travel. state.gov/npicinfo.html).

## POLITICS

For information about the political unrest and safety in Israel, *see* Safety, *below.*

## REST ROOMS

Public rest rooms are plentiful in Israel and most are well maintained, though it's a good idea to carry tissues just in case. You may be asked to pay one shekel at some facilities.

## SAFETY

Traveling throughout much of Israel is safe for the most part. You should, of course, use common sense when driving or walking in isolated areas at night. Still, you'll find that even the downtown areas of major cities are comfortable enough after dark, even if you're alone.

Israel has been the subject of such intense media attention over the years that, ironically, many would-be visitors are more rather than less confused about where to go and what regions to avoid. Despite the country's small size, trouble in one area does not necessarily influence travel in another. The Golan Heights, for example, are as safe as anywhere else in Israel. Ongoing disturbances at press time have discouraged visitors to Jerusalem, but generally the Old City is thronged during the day and relatively empty at night, when almost everything there is closed. Spend your evenings elsewhere. In times of particular political unrest, however, it is generally best to avoid shopping areas, public buses and bus stops, and other crowded areas. The Arab neighborhoods of East Jerusalem have become less hospitable of late, but, unless there are general security problems at the time, the daytime wanderer should not encounter any problems. In the Palestinian autonomous areas, Bethlehem and Jericho were not accessible to travelers at press time. If they are open when you visit, it's advised to see them on an organized tour or with a guide who knows the area well. The rest of the West Bank, including the city of Hebron, has been outside tourist itineraries for some years now. Do not drive your own car through these areas, and avoid the Gaza Strip entirely. There are standard security checks along the roads to the West Bank, but the routes are open except in periods of particular political tension.

For the latest governmental travel advisories regarding travel to and within Israel, check with your consulate (☞ Embassies, *above*) or with the U.S. State Department. The Israel Ministry of Tourism includes a section in its Web site with a non-alarmist perspective on visiting Israel during periods of unrest. For the latest local news, check the English-language papers *Ha'aretz* or the *Jerusalem Post,* available on-line.

➤ ISRAEL MINISTRY OF TOURISM: **Israel Ministry of Tourism** (www. goisrael.com).

➤ ON-LINE NEWS: *Ha'aretz* (www. haaretzdaily.com). *Jerusalem Post* (www.jpost.com).

➤ U.S. GOVERNMENT ADVISORIES: **U.S. Department of State** (✉ Overseas Citizens Services Office, Room 4811 N.S., 2201 C St. NW, Washington, DC 20520, ☎ 202/647–5225 for interactive hot line, 301/946–4400 for computer bulletin board, ℻ 202/647–3000 for interactive hot line, www.travel.state.gov/travel_warnings.html); enclose a self-addressed, stamped, business-size envelope.

**LOCAL SCAMS**

Watch your wallet in crowds, and keep valuables in the trunk of your (locked) car.

**WOMEN IN ISRAEL**

Women travelers feel at ease in Israel: dining alone is not uncomfortable, and even walking alone at night is safe (on the beaten paths). Men can be very forward, so if you're not interested, be very direct.

## SENIOR-CITIZEN TRAVEL

In most cities, travelers over age 60 get reduced admission to museums, theaters, and other attractions. It is important to carry a form of identification that verifies your birth date, like a driver's license.

To qualify for age-related discounts, **mention your senior-citizen status up front** when booking hotel reservations (not when checking out) and before you're seated in restaurants (not when paying the bill). When renting a car, ask about promotional car-rental discounts, which can be cheaper than senior-citizen rates.

➤ EDUCATIONAL PROGRAMS: **Elderhostel** (✉ 75 Federal St., 3rd floor, Boston, MA 02110, ☎ 877/426–8056, ℻ 877/426–2166, www. elderhostel.org). **ElderTreks** (✉ 597 Markham St., Toronto, Ontario, M6G2L7, Canada, ☎ 800/741–7956 or 416/588–5000). **The Mature Traveler** (✉ Box 50400, Reno, NV 89513, ☎ 800/460–6676).

➤ LOCAL PROGRAMS: **Association of Americans and Canadians in Israel** (✉ 6 Mane St., Jerusalem, ☎ 02/561–7151, ℻ 02/566–1186; ✉ 28 Shmuel HaNaziv St., Netanya, ☎ 09/833–0950).

## SHOPPING

The Ministry of Tourism publishes a guide to shopping in Israel, with frequent updates on special discounts for tourists; this is available at Israel Government Tourist Offices (☞ Visitor Information, *below*).

Israeli clothing is not cheap, but many travelers find its high-fashion designs appealing, particularly in bathing suits and leather goods. Tel Aviv is the fashion center.

### KEY DESTINATIONS

Jerusalem is a good place to look for antiques and Judaica (Jewish religious items). The downtown area known as Arts and Crafts Lane, the Cardo in the Jewish Quarter of the Old City, and the neighborhood called Mea She'arim have a large selection. Christian objects are also plentiful in Jerusalem, especially in the Old City. If you're shopping in an outdoor market (except a food market), stall owners will expect you to bargain.

### SMART SOUVENIRS

Jewelry, gems, and locally cut diamonds are considered good buys in Israel. The large cities have many reputable jewelry outlets. Ethnic items and crafts such as embroidered skullcaps (*kippot*, or yarmulkes), tie-dyed scarves, spice boxes, blown glass, Hanukkah lights, and the like are popular gifts.

### WATCH OUT

Antiquities trade is popular in Israel, but it is forbidden to export antiquities unless you are in possession of a written export permit. Such a permit can only be obtained through the Department of Antiquities and Museums of the Ministry of Education and Culture.

➤ CONSUMER COMPLAINTS: If you happen into any trouble while shopping in Israel, lodge consumer complaints to the **Ministry of Industry and Trade's Consumer Production Service** (✉ 76 Mazeh St., Tel Aviv, ☎ 03/560–4611).

### STUDENTS IN ISRAEL

The **Israel Student Travel Association** has 12 branches, in major cities and on university campuses throughout Israel. ISSTA offers discounted tours, car rentals, hotels, and flights. Students from abroad often take advantage of ISSTA's international travel programs.

➤ LOCAL RESOURCES: The **Israel Student Travel Association** (✉ 128 Ben Yehuda St., Tel Aviv 63401, ☎ 03/521–4444; ✉ 50 Dizengoff St., Tel Aviv 64332, ☎ 03/621–6100; ✉ 31 Hanevi'im St., Jerusalem 95103, ☎ 02/621–3600; ✉ 20 Herzl St., Haifa 33121, ☎ 04/868–2222).

➤ IDs & SERVICES: **Council Travel** (CIEE; ✉ 205 E. 42nd St., 14th floor, New York, NY 10017, ☎ 212/822–2700 or 888/268–6245, ℻ 212/822–2699, info@councilexchanges.org, www.councilexchanges.org) for mail orders only, in the United States. **Travel Cuts** (✉ 187 College St., Toronto, Ontario M5T 1P7, Canada, ☎ 416/979–2406 or 800/667–2887 in Canada, www.travelcuts.com).

### TAXES

The airport departure tax is $17.

### VALUE-ADDED TAX

A Value-Added Tax (17% at press time) is charged on all purchases and transactions except tourists' hotel bills and car rentals paid in foreign currency (cash, traveler's checks, or foreign credit cards). Upon departure, you are entitled to a refund of this tax on purchases made in foreign currency of more than $50 on one invoice; but the refund is not mandatory, and not all stores are organized with VAT return forms. Stores so organized display TAXVAT signs and give 5% discounts. If you charge meals and other services to your room at a hotel and pay with foreign currency, there is no VAT; the refund does not apply. Keep your receipts and ask for a cash refund at Ben-Gurion Airport or Haifa Port (Bank Leumi has a special desk for this purpose in the duty-free area); if you leave from another departure point, the VAT refund will be sent to your home address. You are expected to be able to produce the items on which you claim a VAT refund, so allow time and space for this procedure when you plan your departure. Tobacco, electrical, or photographic purchases are excluded from the refund. Eilat is a free trade zone; VAT is not charged on goods or services purchased there.

The Ministry of Tourism distributes a useful booklet, "Made in Israel," free of charge at Ben-Gurion International

Airport and at Israel Government Tourist Offices (☞ Visitor Information, *below*).

(☞ Visitor Information, *below*)

### TAXIS

Taxis are plentiful and relatively inexpensive, and they can be hailed on the street or reached by phone. On the whole, drivers are cheerful. According to law, taxi drivers must use the meter (you need to be firm when you request this) unless you hire them for the day or for a trip out of town, for which there are set rates. If you're pressed to take the cab at a set price, you can ask your hotel staff for an estimate of the cost of your journey. In such a case, agree on the price before you begin the journey and assume that the driver has built in a tip. In the event of a serious problem with the driver, report his cab number (on the illuminated plastic sign on the roof) or license-plate number to the Ministry of Tourism or the Ministry of Transport. Note that official rates are 25% higher after 9 PM and any time public transportation is not running (on Shabbat, for example). Tipping a taxi driver is not the norm, but your driver was extra helpful, a tip would be appreciated.

Certain shared taxis or minivans run fixed routes, such as from Tel Aviv to Haifa or from the airport to Jerusalem; such a taxi is called a *sherut* (as opposed to a "special," the term used for a private cab). These have fixed rates, which are generally slightly more expensive than bus rates; and they leave whenever they're full. Some sheruts can be booked in advance.

### GUIDE-DRIVEN LIMOUSINES

Modern, air-conditioned limousines and minibuses driven by expert, licensed guides are not only a good value for a family or a group of five to seven but also an outstanding way to see the country for anyone whose budget can bear it. At press time, the cost was $320 per day (nine hours) for up to 4 passengers, $365 for 5 to 7 passengers, and $415 for 8–11 passengers. Rates are based on 200 km (120 mi) of travel a day, averaged out over the entire tour, and nine hours a day of touring. An additional $60–$80 per night (depending on location) is charged for the driver's expenses if he or she sleeps away from home. Half-day tours are also available.

➤ LIMO COMPANIES: **Eshkolot Tours** (✉ 36 Keren Hayesod St., Jerusalem, ☎ 02/563–5555 or 02/566–5555, FAX 02/563–2101). **Superb Limousine Services**, Twelve Tribes' subsidiary at Ben-Gurion Airport (☎ 03/973–1780). **Twelve Tribes** (✉ 29 Hamered St., Tel Aviv, ☎ 03/510–1911, FAX 03/510–1943).

### TELEPHONES

Israel's phone company is called Bezek. It still has a monopoly on regular services within the country, but it now has competitors for international calls and cellular phone services, often with significantly cheaper prices. Israel's phone system is now digital, so all phone numbers have seven digits. Double-check the number if you don't get an answer.

Toll-free numbers in Israel begin with either 177 or 1–800 (the latter is becoming the norm). When calling an out-of-town number within Israel, be sure to dial the zero that begins every area code.

### AREA & COUNTRY CODES

When calling internationally direct from Israel, first dial the international access code and then the country code. The international access code for the United States is 001; for Australia, 0011; Ireland, New Zealand, and the United Kingdom, 00; South Africa, 09.

The country code is 1 for the United States, 61 for Australia, 1 for Canada, 353 for Ireland, 64 for New Zealand, 27 for South Africa, and 44 for the United Kingdom. The country code for Israel is 972. When dialing an Israeli number from abroad, drop the initial 0 from the local area code.

### DIRECTORY & OPERATOR ASSISTANCE

Dial 144 for directory or operator assistance. If the operator doesn't speak English or can't find your number, you can ask for a *mefakahat* (supervisor) to help you. Dial 188 for an international operator.

## INTERNATIONAL CALLS

You can make international calls using a telecard from a public phone. A call from Israel to most countries costs about 25¢ per minute. Large cities have central phone agencies—usually near or at main post offices—where you make your call and pay upon completion.

By dialing Israel's toll-free number (1–800 or 177) and the number of your long-distance service, you can link up directly to an operator in your home country. This service works from public phones without a telecard, and often from your hotel room (once you have an outside line).

### LONG-DISTANCE SERVICES

The area codes for dialing between cities within Israel are Jerusalem (02), Tel Aviv (03), Netanya and Hertzilia (09), Haifa and West Galilee (04), Tiberias, Zfat, Nazareth and East Galilee (04), Eilat and the Negev (08).

AT&T, MCI, and Sprint access codes make calling long distance relatively convenient, but you may find the local access number blocked in many hotel rooms. First ask the hotel operator to connect you. If the hotel operator balks, ask for an international operator, or dial the international operator yourself. One way to improve your odds of getting connected to your long-distance carrier is to travel with more than one company's calling card (a hotel may block Sprint, for example, but not MCI). If all else fails, call from a pay phone.

➤ ACCESS CODES: AT&T Direct (☎ 1–800/949–4949). MCI WorldPhone (☎ 177/150–1151). Sprint International Access (☎ 177/102–3412). Canada Direct (☎ 1–800/949–4105). British Telecom (☎ 1–800/943–2744).

### PUBLIC PHONES

Public phones operate with a magnetic telephone card (telecard), available in units of 20 (NIS 15, or $4) or 50 (NIS 35, or $9) and sold at post offices, many newsstands and kiosks, some hotel reception desks, and the occasional special vending machine. Competing phone companies also sell international phone cards. On public phones, the number you're dialing appears on a digital readout; to its right is the number of units remaining on your card.

## TIME

Israel is precisely 2 hours ahead of Greenwich Mean Time. Normally, New York and Montreal are 7 hours behind, California is 10 behind, London is 2 hours behind, and Sydney is 8 hours ahead. From late March until early September, Israel operates on Daylight Saving Time. When the Daylight Saving Times do not match, the time difference is reduced by one hour.

## TIPPING

There are no hard-and-fast rules for tipping in Israel. Taxi drivers do not expect tips, but a gratuity for good service is in order. If you have negotiated a price, assume the tip has been built in. If a restaurant bill does not include service, 10% is expected—round up if the service was particularly good, down if it was dismal. Hotel bellboys should be tipped a lump sum of NIS 8–NIS 15 ($2–$4), not per bag. Tipping is customary for tour guides, tour-bus drivers, and chauffeurs. Bus groups normally tip their guide NIS 20–NIS 25 ($5–$6) per person per day, and half that for the driver. Private guides normally get tipped NIS 82–102 ($20–$25) a day from the whole party. A small tip is expected by both the person who washes your hair and the stylist—except if one of them owns the salon. Leave NIS 4 ($1) per day for your hotel's housekeeping staff.

## TOURS & PACKAGES

Because everything is prearranged on a prepackaged tour or independent vacation, you'll spend less time planning—and often get it all at a good price.

### BOOKING WITH AN AGENT

Travel agents are excellent resources. But it's a good idea to collect brochures from several agencies as some agents' suggestions may be influenced by relationships with tour and package firms that reward them for volume sales. If you have a special interest, **find an agent with expertise in that area**; ASTA (☞ Travel Agen-

cies, *below*) has a database of specialists worldwide.

Make sure your travel agent knows
the accommodations and other services of the place they're recommend-
ing. Ask about the hotel's location,
room size, beds, and whether it has a
pool, room service, or programs for
children, if you care about these. Has
your agent been there in person or
sent others whom you can contact?

Do some homework on your own,
too: local tourism boards can provide
information about lesser-known and
small-niche operators, some of which
may sell only direct.

**BUYER BEWARE**

Each year consumers are stranded or
lose their money when tour operators—even large ones with excellent
reputations—go out of business. So
**check out the operator.** Ask several
travel agents about its reputation, and
try to **book with a company that has
a consumer-protection program.**
(Look for information in the company's brochure.) In the United
States, members of the National Tour
Association and the United States
Tour Operators Association are
required to set aside funds to cover
your payments and travel arrangements in the event that the company
defaults. It's also a good idea to
choose a company that participates in
the American Society of Travel
Agents' Tour Operator Program
(TOP); ASTA will act as mediator in
any disputes between you and your
tour operator.

Remember that the more your package or tour includes the better you
can predict the ultimate cost of your
vacation. Make sure you know exactly what is covered, and **beware of
hidden costs.** Are taxes, tips, and
transfers included? Entertainment and
excursions? These can add up.

➤ TOUR-OPERATOR RECOMMENDA-
TIONS: **American Society of Travel
Agents** (☞ Travel Agencies, *below*).
**National Tour Association** (NTA; ✉
546 E. Main St., Lexington, KY
40508, ☎ 859/226–4444 or 800/
682–8886, www.ntaonline.com).
**United States Tour Operators Associ-
ation** (USTOA; ✉ 342 Madison Ave.,
Suite 1522, New York, NY 10173, ☎
212/599–6599 or 800/468–7862, ℻
212/599–6744, ustoa@aol.com,
www.ustoa.com).

**TRAIN TRAVEL**

Train service from Tel Aviv to
Jerusalem recently went through a
complete overhaul and now runs with
repaired or replaced tracks and train
cars. Other train destinations include
Netanya, Haifa, Akko, and Nahariya.
Though more scenic, train travel in
Israel is slower, with less frequent
service, than bus travel.

**CLASSES**

There are no different classes of travel
aboard the trains.

**FARES & SCHEDULES**

Trains between Tel Aviv and Haifa
run almost hourly. Express trains take
an hour to make the trip, local trains,
about 1½ hours. The cost is NIS 21
($5). There are also trains from Tel
Aviv to Nahariya for NIS 32.50 ($8),
and to Beersheba (in the Negev) for
NIS 23.50 ($6). All train stations post
up-to-date schedules in English.

➤ TRAIN INFORMATION: **Central
Station** (also known as Arlosoroff) in
Tel Aviv (☎ 03/577–4000 or 03/542–
1515); in Haifa, **Bat Galim Station** (☎
04/856–4564); in Jerusalem, **Kikar
Remez Station** (☎ 02/673–3764).

**PAYING**

Purchase your train tickets at the
station ticketing booth before your
board.

**RESERVATIONS**

Reservations are not accepted for
train travel.

**TRANSPORTATION
AROUND ISRAEL**

Buses are the most common form of
transportation around Israel. They
tend to be reliable and inexpensive.
Trains are more scenic but less frequent. Another choice is the shared
taxi service, *sherut.* Sheruts travel
between most destinations and are up
to 20% more expensive than buses,
but still reasonable. For the quickest
travel you can fly the inland air
service, **Arkia.** There are daily flights
(with the exception of Shabbat)

connecting Eilat with Tel Aviv, Jerusalem and Haifa, and flights between Rosh Pina (near Tiberias), Jerusalem, and Tel Aviv.

## TRAVEL AGENCIES

A good travel agent puts your needs first. Look for an agency that has been in business at least five years, emphasizes customer service, and has someone on staff who specializes in your destination. In addition, **make sure the agency belongs to a professional trade organization.** The American Society of Travel Agents (ASTA), with 27,000 agents in some 170 countries, is the largest and most influential in the field. Operating under the motto "Integrity in Travel," it maintains and enforces a strict code of ethics and will step in to help mediate any agent-client disputes if necessary. ASTA also maintains a Web site that includes a directory of agents. (If a travel agency is also acting as your tour operator, ☞ Buyer Beware *in* Tours & Packages, *above*.)

➤ LOCAL AGENT REFERRALS: **American Society of Travel Agents (ASTA;** ☎ 800/965–2782 24-hr hot line, 🖷 703/684–8319, www.astanet.com). **Association of British Travel Agents** (✉ 68–71 Newman St., London W1P 4AH, U.K., ☎ 020/7637–2444, 🖷 020/7637–0713, information@abta. co.uk, www.abtanet.com). **Association of Canadian Travel Agents** (✉ 1729 Bank St., Suite 201, Ottawa, Ontario K1V 7Z5, Canada, ☎ 613/ 237–3657, 🖷 613/521–0805, acta. ntl@sympatico.ca). **Australian Federation of Travel Agents** (✉ Level 3, 309 Pitt St., Sydney 2000, Australia, ☎ 02/9264–3299, 🖷 02/9264–1085, www.afta.com.au). **Travel Agents' Association of New Zealand** (✉ Box 1888, Wellington 10033, New Zealand, ☎ 04/499–0104, 🖷 04/ 499–0827, taanz@tiasnet.co.nz).

## VISITOR INFORMATION

➤ ISRAEL GOVERNMENT TOURIST OFFICES: In the U.S.: ✉ 800 2nd Ave., 16th floor, New York, NY 10017, ☎ 212/499–5650, 🖷 212/499–5645; ✉ 5 S. Wabash Ave., Chicago, IL 60603, ☎ 312/782–4306, 🖷 312/782–1243;

✉ 5151 Belt Line Rd., Suite 1280, Dallas, TX 75240, ☎ 214/991–9097 or 800/472–6364, 🖷 214/392–3251; ✉ 6380 Wilshire Blvd., Suite 1700, Los Angeles, CA 90048, ☎ 213/658– 7462, ext. 03, 🖷 213/658–6543. In Canada: ✉ 180 Bloor St. W, Toronto, Ontario M5S 2V6, ☎ 416/964–3784, 🖷 416/964–2420. In the U.K.: ✉ 18 Great Marlborough St., London W1V 1AF, ☎ 0171/434–3651. The Israel Ministry of Tourism also staffs a toll-free information line at ☎ 888/774– 7723. For on-line information, try the IGTO Web site at www.infotour.co.il.

➤ U.S. GOVERNMENT ADVISORIES: **U.S. Department of State** (✉ Overseas Citizens Services Office, Room 4811 N.S., 2201 C St. NW, Washington, DC 20520, ☎ 202/647–5225 for interactive hot line, 301/946–4400 for computer bulletin board, 🖷 202/ 647–3000 for interactive hot line); enclose a self-addressed, stamped, business-size envelope.

## WEB SITES

Do check out the World Wide Web when you're planning your trip. You'll find everything from current weather forecasts to virtual tours of famous cities. Fodor's Web site, www.fodors.com, is a great place to start your on-line travels. When you see a 🕸 in this book, go to www. fodors.com/urls for an up-to-date link to that destination's site.

For more information specifically on Israel, visit:

**Association of Americans and Canadians in Israel** (www.aaci.org.il). **Beerotayim Ecotourism Center** (www. beerotayim.org.il). **Focus Multimedia Online Magazine** (www.focusmm.com. au/israel/is_anamn.htm). **Guide to Mideast Peace Process** (www.israel. org/peace/guide.html). **Home Accommodation Association of Jerusalem** (www.bnb-jerusalem.co.il). **Home Hospitality** (www.bnb.co.il). **Israel Embassy, London** (www.israel-embassy. org.uk). **Israel Tourism Guide** (www. index.co.il). **Knesset** (www.knesset. gov.il/knesset/engframe.htm). **Society for the Protection of Nature in Israel (SPNI)** (www.spni.org). **Yad Sarah** (www.yadsarah.org.il/engframe.html).

## WHEN TO GO

There is no bad time to visit Israel, in terms of weather. There are no rainy days at all from May through September, but some travelers prefer to risk rain and come in the cooler, less expensive season of November through March. In the winter months, snow falls occasionally in the northern and central hills. In April, May, September, and October, the weather is generally sunny but not uncomfortably hot. March and April have the added attraction of a lush countryside painted with vivid wildflowers.

During school holidays, particularly in July and August, Israelis themselves take vacations; accommodations and attractions get very crowded, and surcharges are often added to hotel rates. Hotel prices also jump during the Passover and Sukkoth holiday periods (early April and late September–early October, respectively), and services and commerce are sharply curtailed; many Israelis simply go away for Passover. Reservations for this busy week should be booked at least four months in advance, and plane reservations six months to a year in advance. Some hotels require full board for the week of Passover.

## CLIMATE

Temperatures along the Mediterranean coast are similar to those of Tel Aviv; hill cities and towns have climates more like that of Jerusalem. Temperatures at the Dead Sea and in Eilat can get very high and stay high through the night; in the Negev Desert, on the other hand, the higher altitudes cause nighttime temperatures to drop sharply. The following are average daily maximum and minimum temperatures for Tel Aviv, Jerusalem, and Eilat.

**EILAT**

| Jan. | 70F | 21C | May | 95F | 35C | Sept. | 97F | 36C |
|------|-----|-----|------|------|-----|-------|-----|-----|
|      | 49  | 9   |      | 70   | 76  |       |     | 24  |
| Feb. | 74F | 23C | June | 100F | 38C | Oct.  | 92F | 33C |
|      | 52  | 11  |      | 76   | 24  |       | 68  | 20  |
| Mar. | 79F | 26C | July | 102F | 39C | Nov.  | 81F | 27C |
|      | 58  | 14  |      | 77   | 25  |       | 61  | 16  |
| Apr. | 86F | 30C | Aug. | 102F | 39C | Dec.  | 72F | 22C |
|      | 65  | 18  |      | 77   | 25  |       | 52  | 11  |

**JERUSALEM**

| Jan. | 52F | 11C | May | 77F | 25C | Sept. | 81F | 27C |
|------|-----|-----|------|-----|-----|-------|-----|-----|
|      | 45  | 7   |      | 59  | 15  |       | 65  | 18  |
| Feb. | 58F | 14C | June | 81F | 27C | Oct.  | 77F | 25C |
|      | 45  | 7   |      | 65  | 18  |       | 61  | 16  |
| Mar. | 61F | 16C | July | 83F | 28C | Nov.  | 67F | 19C |
|      | 49  | 9   |      | 67  | 19  |       | 54  | 12  |
| Apr. | 68F | 20C | Aug. | 83F | 28C | Dec.  | 56F | 13C |
|      | 54  | 12  |      | 67  | 19  |       | 47  | 8   |

**TEL AVIV**

| Jan. | 63F | 17C | May | 70F | 21C | Sept. | 85F | 29C |
|------|-----|-----|------|-----|-----|-------|-----|-----|
|      | 49  | 9   |      | 61  | 16  |       | 70  | 21  |
| Feb. | 65F | 18C | June | 81F | 27C | Oct.  | 81F | 27C |
|      | 50  | 10  |      | 68  | 20  |       | 65  | 18  |
| Mar. | 68F | 20C | July | 85F | 29C | Nov.  | 74F | 23C |
|      | 52  | 11  |      | 72  | 22  |       | 58  | 14  |
| Apr. | 74F | 23C | Aug. | 85F | 29C | Dec.  | 67F | 19C |
|      | 58  | 14  |      | 72  | 22  |       | 52  | 11  |

➤ FORECASTS: **Weather Channel Connection** (☎ 900/932–8437), 95¢ per minute from a Touch-Tone phone.

## FESTIVALS AND SEASONAL EVENTS

New festivals appear on Israel's national calendar every year. Some, like the Israel Festival and the Red Sea Jazz Festival, are international in scope, with reliable dates. Some are permanent seasonal features, timed to coincide with the Jewish holidays in spring and fall. Still others are more local "occasionals," where scheduling is probable but not definite. Most dates were not available at press time; check with the Israel Government Tourist Office (☞ Visitor Information *in* Smart Travel Tips) or the nearest Israeli consulate for details. You can buy tickets for major events in advance at ticket agencies in the major cities.

➤ DEC.: A gala pre-Christmas performance of **Choirs from Around the World** takes place in Jerusalem. Choirs from around the world perform at the **International Christmas Choir Assembly** in Manger Square, Bethlehem, on Christmas Eve. International choirs also sing at Nazareth's **Christmas Parade** and songfest on December 26 and often give free performances as they tour the country.

➤ LATE DEC.–EARLY JAN.: The **Liturgical Festival of Choral Music,** sponsored by the Jerusalem Symphony Orchestra, runs from the end of December through the beginning of January. Also in Jerusalem is the **Classical Music Winter Festival.**

➤ JAN.: The **International Marathon** is run in Tiberias in early January. Eilat hosts renowned classical musicians at the **Red Sea International Music Festival** toward the end of the month.

➤ MAR.: The **Spring Migration Bird-watchers' Festival** is held in Eilat around the end of the third week. Mid-March brings the **Tel Aviv half-marathon.** The **Mt. Tabor Run,** in the Lower Galilee, is scheduled for the third week of the month. The **Artur Rubinstein Piano Master Competition** generates great interest among music lovers.

Many communities organize joyous street festivities to mark **Purim.**

➤ APR.: During **Passover,** when many Israelis go on vacation, the country hums with activities and events.

Inquire at the local tourist office and watch newspapers for details. The **Ein Gev Festival,** on the Sea of Galilee, features Israeli music of various kinds. **Days of Music and Blossoms,** in the Misgav region of the Western Galilee, is eclectic. The **International Festival of Sacred Music** comes to Nazareth. **Sounds of Spring,** a potpourri of musical events, in Zichron Ya'akov, is worth checking out. The **Haifa Festival of Children's Theater** appeals to families. The **National Parks Authority** in Tel Aviv (☎ 03/576–6834) can update you on the various performances and activities (many of them great for kids) scheduled for this period in parks throughout the country. **Stone in the Galilee** is a sculpture symposium in the Upper Galilee town of Ma'alot.

➤ LATE APR.–EARLY JUNE: The **International Book Fair** comes to Jerusalem, usually in May, alternating with the **International Judaica Fair** (books in 2001, Judaica in 2002). Jerusalem's **Independence Day Gala Concert** marks Israel's birthday, along with celebrations elsewhere in the country.

Israel's premier festival, the international **Israel Festival** of all the performing arts, takes place in Jerusalem every year in late May or early June. Get tickets to major events well in advance. The village of Abu Ghosh, west of Jerusalem, hosts a **Vocal Music Festival** during Shavuot. Eat yourself silly at the **International Ethnic Food Fair,** in Jaffa's port.

The popular **Food Trail,** in the Western Galilee, begins in late May and continues through early summer. Participating restaurants work up special menus, and guests work off the tasty food on guided nature walks between meals, accompanied by eclectic live music.

➤ LATE JUNE–EARLY JULY: The **International Folklore Festival,** much of which takes place in small villages, draws performers and artists from Israel and abroad. The **Israeli Folk-Dance Festival,** in Karmiel in early July, hosts ethnic-dance groups from around the world as well as community dancing. The **Jacob's Ladder Folk Festival** (mostly Anglo-American) takes place at Ha'on, on the Sea of

Galilee, the first weekend in July. The late-June **Cherry Festival** at Kibbutz Kiryat Anavim, west of Jerusalem, features musical events in natural surroundings, and a cafeteria devoted to cherry-based delicacies.

Jerusalem celebrates the **U.S. and Canadian Independence Days** the first week in July. Film buffs should watch for the **International Student Film Festival** in Tel Aviv in early June. Jerusalem's prestigious **International Film Festival** is held in early July.

➤ LATE JULY–AUG.: The **Voice of Music in the Upper Galilee,** on Kibbutz Kfar Blum, may be the high point of the year for chamber-music lovers. The **Klezmer Festival,** in Zfat (Safed), showcases Jewish "soul music." The Upper Galilee's **Jewish Music Festival** features a variety of music. The **Arts and Crafts Fair** outside Jerusalem's Jaffa Gate has a huge display of handmade items and nightly entertainment. Jerusalem hosts the **Zimriya,** the triennial World Assembly of Choirs, next happening from July 30 to August 8, 2001.

Eilat's fine **Red Sea Jazz Festival** has become an important date on the international jazz calendar. Israeli pop stars are in the limelight at the Negev's **Arad Festival. Nights of Love,** in Tzemach, at the southern end of the Sea of Galilee, brings in national pop stars. The **Jaffa Nights** festival offers music, theater, and general entertainment in the Old Jaffa square.

The one-day **Wine and Vintage Festival,** in Binyamina, features wine tasting and vocal and dance performances. The **Sea of Galilee Crossing** is a 4-km (2½-mi) swim from Kibbutz Ha'on to Tzemach.

➤ OCT.: The weeklong holiday **Sukkoth** brings almost as busy a calendar of events as Passover, in the spring.

The **Israel Fringe Theater Festival,** in Akko, features original Israeli plays, street theater, children's shows, and musicals. Rishon Lezion, south of Tel Aviv, and Zichron Ya'akov, on Mt. Carmel, both have festivals of **Wine and Song. Music in Tabgha,** on the Sea of Galilee, sponsors vocal and chamber music in the Church of the Loaves and Fishes. Haifa holds its **International Film Festival** in the fall. Yehiam, in the Western Galilee, is the site of the **Renaissance Festival.**

As in late spring, Abu Ghosh, west of Jerusalem, hosts the **Vocal Music Festival** during the week of Sukkoth. The **Christian Celebration of the Feast of Tabernacles** takes place in Jerusalem.

➤ NOV.: Tel Aviv hosts the **International Guitar Festival.**

The **Olive Festival** features crafts, food, and folklore in celebration of the olive harvest. It's held in villages throughout the central and Western Galilee over a series of weekends from late October through November.

# HEBREW

Many people in Israel speak at least one other language, in addition to Hebrew, and most can get by in English. So the chances of getting too lost for words are slim. At the same time, your traveling experience can be enriched by having at least a few words to share in conversation or to use while touring and shopping, even at the local grocery store. Here are some basic words and expressions that may be of use during your stay. Please note that the letters "kh" in this glossary are pronounced like the "ch" in *chanuka* or the Scottish *loch*.

## Greetings and Basics

| English | Hebrew Transliteration | Pronunciation |
| --- | --- | --- |
| Hello/good-bye/peace | Shalom | shah-**lohm** |
| Nice to meet you | Na'im me'od | nah-**eem** meh-**ohd** |
| Good morning | Boker tov | boh-ker **tohv** |
| Good evening | Erev tov | eh-rev **tohv** |
| Good night | Layla tov | lahy-lah tohv |
| How are you? (to a woman) | Ma shlomekh? | mah shloh-**maykh** |
| How are you? (to a man) | Ma shlomkha? | mah shlohm-**khah** |
| How are you? | Ma nishma? | mah-nee-**shmah** |
| Fine | Beseder | beh-**say-dehr** |
| Everything is fine | Hakol beseder | hah-kohl beh-**say-dehr** |
| Is everything okay? | Hakol beseder? | hah-kohl beh-**say-dehr** |
| Very well | Tov me'od | tohv-meh-**ohd** |
| Excellent/terrific | Metzuyan | meh-tzoo-**yahn** |
| Send regards! | Timsor dash! | teem-sohr **dahsh** |
| Thank you | Toda | toh-**dah** |
| Thank you very much | Toda raba | toh-dah rah-**bah** |
| See you again | Lehitra'ot | leh-heet-rah-**oht** |
| Yes | Ken | kehn |
| No | Lo | lo |
| Maybe | Oolai | **oo**-ligh |
| Excuse me/Sorry | Slicha | slee-**khah** |
| Again/Could you repeat that? | Od pa'am | ohd pah-**ahm** |

## Days

| Today | Hayom | hah-**yohm** |
| --- | --- | --- |
| Tomorrow | Machar | mah-**khahr** |
| Yesterday | Etmol | eht-**mohl** |

| Sunday | Yom Rishon | yohm ree-**shohn** |
|--------|------------|--------------------|
| Monday | Yom Sheni | yohm sheh-**nee** |
| Tuesday | Yom Shlishi | yohm sh-lee**shee** |
| Wednesday | Yom Revi'i | yohm reh-**vee** |
| Thursday | Yom Chamishi | yohm kha-mee-**shee** |
| Friday | Yom Shishi | yohm shee-**shee** |
| Saturday, Sabbath | Shabbat | yohm shah-**bat** |

## Numbers

| 1 | Echad | eh-**khad** |
|---|-------|-------------|
| 2 | Shtayim | shtah-**yeem** |
| 3 | Shalosh | shah-**lohsh** |
| 4 | Arba | ah-**rbah** |
| 5 | Chamesh | chah-**maysh** |
| 6 | Shesh | shehsh |
| 7 | Sheva | **sheh**-vah |
| 8 | Shmoneh | **shmoh**-neh |
| 9 | Teisha | **tay**-shah |
| 10 | Esser | **eh**-sehr |
| 11 | Achad esreh | ah-**chahd** eh-**sreh** |
| 12 | Shteim esreh | sht**aym** eh-**sreh** |
| 20 | Esrim | eh-**sreem** |
| 50 | Chamishim | khah-mee-**sheem** |
| 100 | Me'a | may-**ah** |
| 200 | Ma'tayim | mah-**tah**-yeem |

## Useful Phrases

| Do you speak English? | Ata medaber anglit? | ah-ta meh-dah-ber ahng-**leet** |
|-----------------------|---------------------|---------------------------------|
| I don't understand (man) | Ani lo mevin | a-**nee** loh meh-**veen** |
| I don't understand (woman) | Ani lo m'vina | a-**nee** m'veena |
| I don't know (man) | Ani lo yodea | a-nee loh yoh-**day**-ah |
| I don't know (woman) | Ani lo yodaat | a-nee loh yoh-**dah**-aht |
| I am lost (man) | Ani avud | a-nee ah-**vood** |
| I am lost (woman) | Ani avuda | a-nee ahvoo-**dah** |
| I am American | Ani Amerika'i | ah-nee ah-mer-ee-**kah**-ee |
| I am British | Ani Briti | ah-**nee** **bree**-tee |
| I am Canadian | Ani Canadi | ah-**nee** kah-**nah**-dee |

| What is the time? | Ma hasha'a? | mah hah-shah-**ah** |
| Just a minute | Rak rega | rahk **reh**-gah |
| Minute, moment | Rega | **reh**-gah |
| Now | Achshav | ahkh-**shahv** |
| Not yet | Od lo | ohd loh |
| Later | Achar kach | ah-**khahr** kahkh |
| I would like | Hayiti mevakesh | hah-**yee**-tee m-vah-**kehsh** |
| Where is..? | Eifo..? | **ay**foh |
| The central bus station | Hatachana hamerkazit | hah-tah-khah-**nah** hah-mehr-kah-**zeet** |
| The bus stop | Tachanat ha'autobus | tah-khah-**naht** hah-oh-toh-**boos** |
| The train station | Tachanat harakevet | tah-khah-**naht** hah-rah-**keh-veht** |
| The city center | Merkaz ha'ir | mehr kahz hah-**eer** |
| The post office | Hado'ar | hah-**doh**-ahr |
| A pharmacy | Beit mirkachat | bayt meer-**kah**-khaht |
| A public telephone | Telefon tziburi | teh-leh-**fohn** tzee-boo-**ree** |
| A good restaurant | Mis'ada tova | mee-sah-**dah toh-vah** |
| The rest rooms | Hasherutim | hah-shay-roo-**teem** |
| Right | Yemina | yeh-**mee**-nah |
| Left | Smola | s-**moh**-lah |
| Straight ahead | Yashar | yah-**shar** |
| Here | Kan | kahn |
| There | Sham | shahm |
| Do you have a (vacant) room? | Yesh lachem cheder (panui)? | yehsh lah-**chehm** **khed**-ehr (pah-**nooy**) |
| Is it possible to order a taxi? | Efshar lehazmin monit? | ehf-**shahr** leh-hahz-**meen** moh-**neet** |
| Taxi | Monit | moh-**neet** |
| A little | k'tzat | keh-**tzaht** |
| A lot | harbe | hahr-**beh** |
| Enough | maspik | mah-**speek** |
| I have a problem | Yesh li ba'aya | yehsh lee bah-**yah** |
| I don't feel well (man) | Ani lo margish tov | ah-**nee** loh mahr-**geesh** tohv |
| I don't feel well (woman) | Ani lo margisha tov | ah-**nee** loh mahr-**geeshah** tohv |
| I need a doctor (man) | Ani tzarich rofe | ah-**nee** tzah-**reech** roh-**feh** |
| I need a doctor (woman) | Ani tzricha rofe | ah-**nee** tzree-**khah** roh-**feh** |

| Help | Ezra | eh-**zrah** |
|---|---|---|
| Fire | Dleika | duh-leh-**kah** |

## Dining

| I would like | Hayiti mevakesh | hah-**yee**-tee m-vah-**kehsh** |
|---|---|---|
| Some water, please | Mayim, bevakasha | mah-**yeem** beh-vah-kah-**shah** |
| Bread | Lechem | **leh**-khehm |
| Soup | Marak | mah-**rahk** |
| Meat | Bassar | bah-**ssahr** |
| Chicken | Off | ohf |
| Vegetables | Yerakot | yeh-rah-**koht** |
| Dessert | Kinuach | kee-**noo**-ahkh |
| Cake | Ooga | **oo**-gah |
| Fruit | Perot | peh-**roht** |
| Coffee | Cafe | kah-**feh** |
| Tea | Te | teh |
| fork | Mazleg | mahz-**lehg** |
| spoon | Kapit | kah-**peet** |
| knife | Sakin | sah-**keen** |
| plate | Tzalachat | tzah-**lah**-chaht |
| Napkin | Mapit | mah-**peet** |
| Food | Ochel | **oh**-khehl |
| Meal | Arucha | ah-roo-**khah** |
| Breakfast | Aruchat boker | ah-roo-**khaht boh**-ker |
| Lunch | Aruchat tzaharayim | ah-roo-khaht tzah-hah-**rah**-yeem |
| Dinner | Aruchat erev | ahroo-**khaht eh**-rehv |
| Do you have a menu in English? | Yesh tafrit be'anglit? | yehsh tahf-**reet** beh-ahng-**leet** |
| A pita filled with felafel | Manat felafel | mah-naht feh-**lah**-fehl |
| Without hot sauce | Bli charif | blee khah-**reef** |
| It's tasty, delicious | Zeh ta'im | zeh tah-**eem** |
| I don't like the taste | Zeh lo ta'im li | zeh loh tah-**eem** lee |
| The check, please | Cheshbon, bevakasha | khehsh-bohn beh-vah-kah-**shah** |

## Shopping

| Do you have..? | Yesh lecha..? | yesh leh-khah |
|---|---|---|
| Milk | Chalav | khah-**lahv** |
| (Orange) Juice | Mitz (tapuzim) | meetz (tah-poo-**zeem**) |
| Butter | Chem'a | khem-**ah** |
| Cream cheese | Gevina levana | geh-vee-**nah** leh-vah-**nah** |

| | | |
|---|---|---|
| Hard cheese | Gevina tzehuba | gevee-**nah** tzeh-**hoo**-bah |
| Sausage | Naknik | nahk-**neek** |
| Jelly | Riba | **ree**-bah |
| Sugar | Sukar | **soo**-kahr |
| Ice cream | Glida | **glee**-da |
| Map | Mapa | **mah**-pa |
| Cigarettes | Sigariyot | see-gahr-ee-**yoht** |
| Telephone card (for public phones) | Telecart | teh-leh-**kahrt** |
| That one, please | Et zeh, bevakasha | eht zeh, beh-vah-kah-**shah** |
| May I see it? | Efshar lir'ot? | ehf-**shahr** leer-**oht** |
| How much does it cost? | Kama zeh oleh? | **kah**-ma zeh **ohleh** |
| That's expensive! | Yakar! | yah-**kahr** |
| No, it's too expensive | Lo, zeh yakar midai | loh, zeh yah-**kahr** meed-**igh** |
| Too big | Gadol midai | gah-dohl meed-**igh** |
| Too small | Katan midai | kah-tan meed-**igh** |
| Perhaps there is a discount ? | Yesh hanacha oolai? | yehsh hah-na-**khah** oo-**ligh** |
| I'll take it | Ani ekach et zeh | ah-nee eh-**kakh** eht zeh |

# PALESTINIAN ARABIC

Arabic is spoken by all Arab citizens of Israel, (about 20% of the Israeli population) and in the West Bank and Gaza. The areas where you're most likely to hear Arabic are East Jerusalem, Jaffa, and Nazareth, and in the popular sites of the West Bank, Bethlehem and Jericho (when these are open to travelers). Many people in these areas speak some English, but a little Arabic will come in handy with some vendors and taxi drivers or when you are in more rural areas and villages. It helps to have a written address for a taxi ride as well. You may run into small differences in dialect and accent between villages and cities, but for the most part Palestinians dialects are similar.

Some letters in Arabic do not have English equivalents. This glossary tries to approximate Arabic sounds. The letter 'r' is always rolled. When you see 'gh' at the start of a word, pronounce it like a French 'r', lightly gargled at the back of the throat. Any double letters should be extended: 'aa' is pronounced as an extended 'ah'; 'hh' is an extended 'h' sound; 'ss' is an extended hiss.

## Greetings and Basics

| English | Arabic Transliteration | Pronunciation |
|---|---|---|
| Hello/ peace be upon you | salamou alaikom | sah-**lah**-moo **aah**-lay-kom |
| (reply) Hello/ and peace be upon you | wa aalaikom essalaam | wah aah-**lay**-kom ehss-sah-**ahm** |

| Good-bye | maa issalameh | **maah** is-**ah-lah**-meh |
| Mr./ Sir | sayyed | **sigh**-yed |
| Mrs./ Madam | sayyida | **sigh**-yee-dah |
| Miss | anisseh | **ah**-niss-say |
| How are you? (man speaking) | keif hhalak | kayf **hah**-luck |
| How are you? (woman speaking) | keif hhalik | kayf **hah**-lik |
| Fine, thank you | bi kheir elhhamdilla | bee **khayr** el-**ham**-dihl-lah |
| Pleased to meet you | tsharrafna | tshahr-**ruhf**-nah |
| Please (man) | min fadlak | min **fahd**-lahk |
| Please (woman) | min fadlik | min **fahd**-lik |
| Thank you | shokran | shohk-rahn |
| God willing | Inshallah | ihn-**shahl-lah** |
| Yes | aah or naam | aah or naahm |
| No | la | lah |
| I'm Sorry (man) | mit assif | miht **ass**-sef |
| I'm Sorry (woman) | mit assfeh | miht **ass**-feh |

## Days

| Today | eliom | el-**yohm** |
| Tomorrow | bokra | bok-rah |
| Yesterday | embarehh | ehm-**bah**-rehh |
| Sunday | il ahhad | **il ah**-had |
| Monday | ittinein | it-tee-**nayn** |
| Tuesday | ittalata | it-tah-**lah**-tah |
| Wednesday | il 'arbaa | il **ahr**-bah-**aah** |
| Thursday | il khamees | il khah-**mees** |
| Friday | iljumaa | il zhum-**aah** |
| Saturday | issabet | **iss-sah**-bet |

## Numbers

| 1 | wahed | **wah**-hed |
| 2 | tinein | tee-**nayn** |
| 3 | talati | tah-**lah**-tee |
| 4 | arbaa | **ahr**-bah-aah |
| 5 | khamseh | **khahm**-seh |
| 6 | sitteh | **sit**-teh |
| 7 | sabaa | sub-**aah** |
| 8 | tamanyeh | tah-**mah**-nee-**yeh** |

Vocabulary

| 9 | tisaa | **tiss**-aah |
| 10 | aashara | **aah**-shah-rah |
| 11 | ihhdaaesh | ihh-**dah**-ehsh |
| 12 | itnaaesh | it-**nah**-ehsh |
| 20 | ishreen | iish-**reen** |
| 50 | khamseen | khahm-**seen** |
| 100 | meyyeh | **may**-yeh |
| 200 | mitein | **mee**-tain |

## Useful Phrases

| Do you speak English? | btihki inglizi? | btih-**kee** in-**glee**-zee? |
| I don't understand (man) | mish fahem | mish **fah**-him |
| I don't understand (woman) | mish fahmi | mish **fah**-meh |
| I don't know (man) | mish aarif | mish **aah**-ref |
| I don't know (woman) | mish aarfi | mish **aahr**-fee |
| I'm lost (man) | ana dayih | ah-nah **dah**-yeh |
| I'm lost (woman) | ana dayaa | ah-nah **dah**-ye-aah |
| I am American (man) | ana amriki | ah-nah ahm-**ree**-kee |
| I am American (woman) | ana amrikiyya | ah-nah ahm-**ree-key**-yah |
| I am British (man) | ana baritani | ah-nah bah-**ree-tah-nee** |
| I am British (woman) | ana baritaniya | ah-nah bah-**ree-tah-nay**-yah |
| What is this? | eish hada? | aysh **hah**-dah? |
| What time is it? | Addeish el wa'ed? | Ahd-**daysh** el **wah**-ed |
| Where is? | wein? | wayn? |
| The train station | mahattit iltrain | mah-huht-**tit il-train** |
| The bus station | mahattit el buss | mah-**huht**-tit el **buhss** |
| The intracity bus station | mahattit el bus eddakheli | mah-huht-**tit el** buhss ed-dah-**khe-lee** |
| The taxi station | mujammaa el takasi | moo-**jam**-maah el tah-**kah**-see |
| The airport | el matar | el mah-**tahr** |
| The hotel | el oteil | el **ooh**-tayl |
| The cafe | el ahwi | el ah-**weh** |
| The restaurant | el mataam | el **matt-aahm** |
| The telephone | el tiliphon | el tih-lih-**fohn** |
| The hospital | el mostashfa | el moos-**tash**-fah |
| The post office | el bareed | el bah-**reed** |
| The rest room | el hammam | el huhm-**mahm** |
| The pharmacy | el saydaleyyeh | el sigh-dah-**lay-yeh** |

| The bank | el bank | el bahnk |
|---|---|---|
| The embassy | el safara | el sah-fah-**rah** |
| Right | yameen | yah-meen |
| Left | shmal | shmahl |
| Straight ahead | doughri | doo-ghree |
| I would like a room | beddi ghorfi | bed-dee **ghor-fih** |
| A little | shway or aleel | shway or ah-leel |
| A lot | kteer | kteer |
| Enough | bikaffi | bee-kaf-fee |
| I have a problem | aandi moshkili | aahn-dee **moosh**-keh-lee |
| I am ill | ana mareed | ah-nah mah-reed |
| I need a doctor | beddi daktor | bed-**dee** dac-**tor** |
| Help | saadoonee | **saah-doo**-nee |
| Fire | naar or harika | naahr or hah-**ree**-kah |
| Caution/ look out | entebeh or owaa | in-teh-beh or ohw-**aah** |

## Dining

| I would like | beddi | behd-dee |
|---|---|---|
| Water | mayy | muhyy |
| Bread | khobez | kho-bihz |
| Vegetables | khodra | khod-rah |
| Meat | lahhmi | **lahh**-meh |
| Fruits | fawakeh | fah-**wah**-keh |
| Cakes/ Sweets | helou/ halaweyyat | **heh**-loo/ hah-lah-**way-yaht** |
| Tea | shay | shahy |
| Coffee | ahwi | ah-weh |
| A fork | shokeh | show-keh |
| A spoon | maala a | **maah**-lah ah |
| A knife | sikkeen | sick-**keen** |
| A plate | sahin | sah-hin |

## Shopping

| I would like to buy | beddi ashtri | bed-**dee** ahsh-tree |
|---|---|---|
| cigarettes | sagayer or dokhkhan | sah-**gah**-yer or dokh-**khahn** |
| a city map | khareeta lal madeeni | khah-**ree**-tah lahl mah-**dee**-nee |
| a road map | khareeta lal tareek | khah-**ree**-tah lahl tah-**reek** |
| How much is it? | addaish ha o | **ad**-daysh **ha** oh |
| It's expensive | ghali | **ghah**-lee |

# 450

# INDEX

# NOTES

# NOTES

# NOTES

# FODOR'S ISRAEL

**EDITOR:** Beatrice Aranow

**Contributors:** Taha Boutary, Karen Bressler, Judy Stacey Goldman, Robert Hoffmann, Susan Lubell, Lisa Perlman, Mike Rogoff, Muna Shikaki, Miriam Feinberg Vamosh, Linda Yachbes

**Editorial Production:** Stacey Kulig

**Maps:** David Lindroth, Inc., *cartographer*; Rebecca Baer and Bob Blake, *map editors*

**Design:** Fabrizio La Rocca, *creative director*; Guido Caroti, *art director*; Jolie Novak, *senior picture editor*; Melanie Marin, *photo editor*

**Cover Design:** Pentagram

**Production/Manufacturing:** Colleen Ziemba

## COPYRIGHT

Copyright © 2001 by Fodors LLC

Fodor's is a registered trademark of Random House, Inc. All rights reserved under International and Pan-American Copyright Conventions. Published in the United States by Fodor's Travel Publications, a unit of Fodors LLC, a subsidiary of Random House, Inc., New York, and simultaneously in Canada by Random House of Canada Limited, Toronto. Distributed by Random House, Inc., New York.

*No maps, illustrations, or other portions of this book may be reproduced in any form without written permission from the publisher.*

Fifth Edition

ISBN 0–679–00610–9

ISSN 0071–6588

## SPECIAL SALES

Fodor's Travel Publications are available at special discounts for bulk purchases for sales promotions or premiums. Special editions, including personalized covers, excerpts of existing guides, and corporate imprints, can be created in large quantities for special needs. For more information, contact your local bookseller or write to Special Markets, Fodor's Travel Publications, 280 Park Avenue, New York, NY 10017. Inquiries from Canada should be directed to your local Canadian bookseller or sent to Random House of Canada, Ltd., Marketing Dept., 2775 Matheson Boulevard East, Mississauga, Ontario L4W 4P7. Inquiries from the United Kingdom should be sent to Fodor's Travel Publications, 20 Vauxhall Bridge Road, London SW1V 2SA, England.

PRINTED IN THE UNITED STATES OF AMERICA
10 9 8 7 6 5 4 3 2 1

## IMPORTANT TIP

Although all prices, opening times, and other details in this book are based on information supplied to us a press time, changes occur all the time in the travel world, and Fodor's cannot accept responsibility for facts that become outdated or for inadvertent errors or omissions. So **always confirm information when it matters,** especially if you're making a detour to visit a specific place.

## PHOTOGRAPHY

Travel Stock: *Buddy Mays*, cover. (Masada)

Yosi Aloni, 30F.

Axiom: *Alex Misiewicz*, 25D.

Baha'i International Community, 30G.

Carmel Forest Spa Resort, 30A.

Corbis: *Neil Beer*, 4–5. *Dave G. Houser*, 18G. *Richard T. Nowitz*, 1, 16B, 16C, 20A. *Eldad Rafaeli*, 13 top left. *Jeffrey L. Rotman*, 24B. *David Rubinger*, 8E.

DIAF: *Guy Durand*, 10A, 15E. *Gerard Guittot*, 9J. *JM Leligny*, 23D. *Yvan Travert*, 13E.

Houserstock: *Dave G. Houser*, 12A, 13F.

Israel Ministry of Tourism, 8G.

Israel Nature and National Parks Protection Authority: *Hamar Eirinberg*, 3 top left.

Len Kaufman, 12C, 15D.

Garo Nalbandian, 30I.

Jolie Novak, 25E.

Richard T. Nowitz, 9H, 9I, 10C, 11E, 11F, 12B, 13D, 14A, 14B, 15C, 16A, 17 top, 17E, 18F, 18H, 19K, 20B, 21F, 22B, 24A, 25C, 28D.

PhotoDisc, 30D.

Picciotto, 30C.

PictureQuest: *Flat Earth*, 2 top right, 2 bottom left, 2 bottom center, 2 bottom right, 3 top right, 3 bottom left, 3 bottom right, 19J, 26A, 27B, 27C, 28 bottom right, 29E, 29F, 30B, 30E.

Red Sea Jazz Festival, 2 top left.

David Sanger Photography, 7D.

Sheraton Tel Aviv Hotel & Towers: *Jaime Ardiles-Arce*, 30H.

Stone: *George Mars Cassidy*, 32. *Paul Chesley*, 7B. *Kevin Cullimore*, 23E. *Richard Passmore*, 19I. *Hugh Sitton*, 11D. *Don Smetzer*, 7C. *Sarah Stone*, 6A, 8F. *Tom Till*, 10B, 23C.

Travel Stock: *Buddy Mays*, 20C, 30J.

Nik Wheeler, 17D, 21D, 22A.

Woodfin Camp & Associates: *Asap/Tably*, 21E.

464

# ABOUT OUR WRITERS

Our success in helping to make your trip the best of all possible vacations is a credit to the hard work of our extraordinary writers and editors.

**Karen W. Bressler** is based in New York and travels to Israel periodically to visit family and friends. She feels most at home in the bustling city of Tel Aviv. Karen has written for *Condé Nast Traveler* and *Bride's* magazines and is the Caribbean correspondent for the on-line *Condé Nast* publication www.concierge.com. She has authored and contributed to several Fodor's guides and co-revised the Tel Aviv chapter of this edition of *Fodor's Israel*.

**Judy Stacey Goldman** was born in Montréal and has lived in Israel, where she is now a professional tour guide, for 30 years. She has coauthored three books about Jerusalem and Tel Aviv and is currently preparing a new book on Jerusalem. Her Fodor's territories include the Northern Coast, Western Galilee, Eilat, and the Negev.

**Susan Lubell's** first trip to Sinai was in 1991. Seven woven bags, two carpets, a pair of Dahab pants, and a twilight camel ride later, she was hooked. Upon completing her degree in the States, she began a year of travels that would eventually lead her back to the Middle East. She's now settled for a spell in Beersheva where she writes project proposals for Ben-Gurion University of the Negev. This year she updated the Sinai, Egypt section of *Fodor's Israel*.

**Lisa Perlman,** a native of Australia, wrote her way through Japan and France before moving to Israel in 1986. She is a former editor of the *Jerusalem Post*'s Tel Aviv weekly, *Metro*. She contributed to the Hebrew glossary and several short features in this edition of *Fodor's Israel*.

**Mike Rogoff,** a professional tour guide and writer, has been exploring and studying the byways of Israel since he moved there from his native South Africa in 1970. His calling—to excite visitors of all persuasions about his new-old land—became a profession when he discovered that people would actually pay him for doing what he loved best. Mike lives in Jerusalem and is a recipient of the Israel government's Guide of the Year award. He has contributed to *Fodor's Israel* since 1985 and this year he created the new color section's Great Itineraries and updated the Jerusalem, Around Jerusalem, and Lower Galilee chapters.

**Miriam Feinberg Vamosh** hales from New Jersey and has lived in Israel since 1970. A tour guide since 1975, she enjoys interpreting the intricacies of Israel to both Jewish and Christian tour groups and has also written numerous articles and three books about Israel's history and lore. In addition to updating the chapter on her favorite areas of Israel, the Upper Galilee and Golan, Miriam is the writer and updater of our section on Petra, Jordan.

**Linda Yachbes,** who co-revised the Tel Aviv chapter of this edition of *Fodor's Israel,* is a native New Yorker who moved to Israel in 1989. She worked as a tour guide for visiting youth groups in Jerusalem for several years before moving to Tel Aviv, where she works in advertising and as a freelance travel writer. Her addiction to travel has led her in recent years to such varied destinations as Bali, Budapest, and Finnish Lapland.

## Don't Forget to Write

We love feedback—positive and negative—and follow up on all suggestions. So contact the Israel editor at editors@fodors.com or c/o Fodor's, 280 Park Avenue, New York, NY 10017. Have a wonderful trip!

*Karen Cure*

Karen Cure
*Editorial Director*